VOLUME ONE OF

Yale: College and University · 1871-1937

A PUBLICATION ISSUED ON THE OCCASION

OF YALE'S 250TH ANNIVERSARY

YALE COLLEGE

AN EDUCATIONAL HISTORY

1871 - 1921

BY GEORGE WILSON PIERSON

LUX ET VERITAS

NEW HAVEN

YALE UNIVERSITY PRESS

*This printing has been made possible
with assistance from the Norman Vaux
Donaldson Memorial Fund.*
© 1952 by Yale University Press.
Third printing, May 1970
*Printed in the United States of America by
Vail-Ballou Press, Inc., Binghamton, New York
and reprinted by The Murray Printing Company,
Forge Village, Massachusetts.*
Library of Congress catalog card number: 52-5356
ISBN: 0-300-829-5
*Distributed in Great Britain, Europe, and
Africa by Yale University Press, Ltd., London;
in Canada by McGill-Queen's University Press,
Montreal; in Mexico by Centro Interamericano de
Libros Académicos, Mexico City; in Australasia
by Australia and New Zealand Book Co., Pty.,
Ltd., Artarmon, New South Wales; in India by
UBS Publishers' Distributors Pvt., Ltd., Delhi;
in Japan by John Weatherhill, Inc., Tokyo.*

DEDICATED TO THE FACULTY OF YALE COLLEGE

PREFACE

Here begins a history of modern Yale. My hope is to describe the growth of the University from just after the end of the Civil War to the eve of World War II. It will be a comparative study written, so far as I am capable of it, without fear or favor. And the theme in the beginning will be the development of the College, the heart and for so long the strength of old Yale.

For the country, no less than for our graduates, this period has an arresting significance. In the early nineteenth century the United States was the land of small colleges. In the coming half century, if no disaster intervenes, we may become as famous for our universities as were the Romans for their roads and their laws. The years in between have been the critical time of transition. The generation after the Civil War saw the first organization of a thoroughgoing system of public schools, and the first encounter with all their advantages and unprecedented problems. With the turn into the twentieth century came the development of the great tax-supported universities, and the spread of the college-going idea.

Characteristically, we ignored the difficulties. The educational plant of the nation was expanded in haste and with great confidence. Colleges became ever more numerous, competitive, and unreflecting. The need for public support made it seem more important to be popular than to be right. With experiment making more noise than experience, the most magnificent gains were accompanied by a quite inadequate recognition of losses or mistakes. Today, with the demands of defense once again taking precedence over college-going, and with our colleges and universities themselves facing curtailment and reduction, men still have not reached agreement on the values which must at all costs be preserved.

The crisis that began with the last war did finally arouse the

vii

believers in a liberal and disinterested education. And this has given rise to a searching and most thoughtful debate. But too often the debaters have had only convictions and theories to offer. The reasoned histories, by which the achievements and the shortcomings of our universities might be measured, are only beginning to be attempted. On the evolution of college studies, since the breakdown of the time-honored classical-mathematical curriculum, all that we have had are a few tantalizing brief summaries for individual colleges—some statistical or topical studies—and one or two more substantial but partisan accounts so arranged as to buttress the doctrinaire assumptions of their authors.

In particular the celebrated and all-important elective system has never been fully understood. Beginning as a battle cry, it degenerated into a shibboleth, and today men damn it with the same enthusiasm and ignorance that they once brought to its worship. So innocent have we been that the same universities which tried to spread the elective idea to all our colleges and schools today can reverse themselves and champion the requirement of a "general education," without blushing and to solemn applause. Why elective freedom was at first so attractive, why it then proved so universally unsatisfactory, and by what multitudinous devices college faculties have been struggling for more than forty years to organize or replace it—all this should be better known.

In part for such reasons, in part for its central importance for the entire University, I have made my main theme in the beginning the *educational* development of Yale College. To maintain that an education is the most important thing a college has to offer is not to say that it must be acquired exclusively from books. The graduates of Yale will testify with gratitude and affection to the training they got here in friendship and strenuous living. Nor can it be emphasized enough that the old-fashioned college at its best, like the public school in England, was also a living society: a generator of loyalty and convictions. The power of such a college as Yale had to be experienced to be believed. Yet at the core were the college studies, without which the community and its spirit would have disintegrated. Fundamentally it was on Yale's teachers and on the

viii

content, quality, and proportion of what they taught that the continuing liberality of the education depended. By the same token it was upon the curriculum that the pressures of change sooner or later came to bear. The Course of Study became a battleground.

Yale's experience in this matter has been by no means simple to re-create. The Officers of the College were so little given to theorizing, and so much more prompt to act than to talk, that they have left only the most fragmentary memorials of their convictions in print. At the same time a thorough exploration of the Yale story helps explain developments in many of our most important colleges across the land. For here are encountered the subtle tensions in American society and the most perplexing problems that our higher education has had to face. Manhood suffrage and the great westward migration were spiritual movements of unexampled hopefulness, yet with implications of flight from learning and the past. So in the development of Yale's critical admissions problem may be glimpsed the repudiation of our classical heritage by the public high schools, and the expropriation of the B.A. degree to serve a wider, less discriminating clientele. Again the debates over Pass-Honors make vivid the conflict between quantity and quality in American life, and the dilemma of all our colleges which wished to be both intellectual and representative.

Thus we gain a case history which will help the lay reader to grasp why the modern curriculum has been so changeable and so hard to get right, at the same time that it helps the scholar to understand the forces with which he must still contend. In addition we shall have an analysis of Yale's noted conservatism and see how it operated in a critically important field. Perhaps this may enable outsiders to reason about that conservatism in a less prejudiced way, and insiders to manage it to better public effect.

This is also a study in university management. It is a well-known peculiarity of American colleges and universities that their property and legal authority have been confided to boards of Regents or Trustees, who are generally nonresident and inexpert. In practice the power of decision and appointment may be exercised by these Trustees, or with their approval by the President and his administrative assistants, or by the President in consultation with his senior professors—more rarely by the self-perpetuating Faculties themselves. In our democratic society it is an anomaly that so many of our universities are run like monarchies or dictatorships. By contrast Yale early developed republican practices, encouraged home rule, and under Porter, Dwight, and Hadley grew into a federalized University, with its professors treated as Officers and its Faculties as Governing Boards. For purposes of unanimity and quick action, this decentralization of sovereignty had marked defects—the same defects remarkable in self-governing societies generally, when in competition with dictatorships. I have treated this problem at some length because many of us still believe that in the long run republics call out more individual effort and self-sacrifice, and generate more power. Through times of unsettlement and adversity they have the vitality to endure.

Such are the thoughts and hopes which rise in one's mind as Yale reaches its two hundred and fiftieth anniversary, and moves on into the deepening crisis. From faith and knowledge united we may draw strength. If to graduate and layman, as well as to student and scholar, this book brings the security of a broadened understanding, my labors will be repaid. In the military emergencies still to come let us hold fast and remember that our universities and colleges have been not only the preservers of our European inheritance but the makers of much that we value most in American civilization.

GEORGE WILSON PIERSON

*Larned Professor of History
and Fellow of Davenport College
Yale University*

*New Haven
October 1951*

CONTENTS

CONTENTS

ILLUSTRATIONS

PART ONE: THE DAYS OF PORTER AND DWIGHT

CHAPTER 1 · YALE COLLEGE IN THE NINETIES

It is this marvelous esprit de corps, this habit of always pulling together. . . . Yale men are Yale men from the cradle to the grave.

—BUCHANAN WINTHROP, *Yale '62, 1892*

Harvard stands as the mother of movements, and Yale as the mother of men.

—CHARLES FRANKLIN THWING, *Harvard '76, 1897*

Yale, like New England, is serious and a little grim,—in fact it is one of the only characteristic New England institutions which has never suffered decay. . . . One feels the close energy and the solid logic of a rigorous Puritan stock. . . . The result is a competitive society of great ruthlessness and impressive achievement.

—EDMUND WILSON, *Princeton '16, 1923*

YALE WAS A NAME, a living legend. And Yale College was its center. To the older generation, to the graduates of the 1840's and 1850's and 1860's now scattered across the country, this name meant unforgettable things. It was their memory of youth. It was a shabby, dear familiar place: a row of battered buildings and great elms, an old fence in the twilight and perhaps a song, a band of friends.

Part schoolboy academy, they had found it, and part house of worship. An immemorial system of memorized lessons, chapel services, petty discipline, and marks. But these had been merely the bony structure of the institution. College life had offered a wider world with its own interests and laws, its heroes and inviolable tra-

3

ditions. As Freshmen they had been initiated by the fierce Class rushes. They had been hazed, or forbidden to sit on the Fence. They had been forced to pay for the Thanksgiving Jubilee, mocked at, and persecuted. So a fierce Class loyalty had been born, and soon they had tasted the long hours of idleness spiced with sudden mischief. They had drunk the wine of friendship and unconquerable joy. College meant carrying on the old customs, the torchlight parades and bonfires, the hilarious masquerades. Best of all, College meant independence and the chance to make your mark: societies—honors—and Class office. And never could one have asked for a fairer field and test for character. Never again would one encounter a society so open or a brotherhood so close. Euclid would be forgotten. The Greek and Latin, too. But the College trained you to work. It made you a man and fitted you for public trust. Yale was the mother of colleges and outstanding citizens. Yale made you succeed in life and in your success remained the best part of you. That was old Yale.

Strangely enough it was the new Yale, too. The graduates since the Civil War had been making their mark in life. And the young men of the nineties still gloried in their College. There were now more than twelve hundred undergraduates where in the 1850's the College had averaged a bare 450.* But through all the changes that time had brought the spell continued unbroken.

No question but that new interests had pushed in, so that worldly activities and ancient customs seemed strangely intermingled. Chapel still held—but discipline had relaxed. Freshmen still groaned in required recitations, but unheard-of subjects were now Junior privileges. The Burial of Euclid was no more. The unlicensed jubilees had been forbidden; and only the ceremony of Omega Lambda Chi now commemorated the old Freshman societies, long since abolished by Faculty edict. Yet Yale College with its publications and managerships and intercollegiate athletics—

---

* From 1850 to 1859 the enrollments in the Academical Department had ranged between 432 and 473 students, in the new Scientific School between 16 and 63, and in the University as a whole between 555 and 619. For 1898–99 the figures were: College 1,224, Sheff 567, University 2,511.

4

Yale College of the nineties—was still the full and testing life, the place where you measured yourself and learned to measure others, the experience that made you a man.

In their youthful exuberance they were sure there was no other college to match it.[1] Harvard might have its electives, its philosophers, and its professional schools. Johns Hopkins might be first in medicine. Cornell and Michigan might boast they were "universities." But Yale had the College and the winning teams. Yale could beat Harvard at any time—and Princeton, too. Yale's were the most famous and powerful secret societies, the Fence, the *Lit.*, and a score of colorful traditions. Yale was also national and democratic: the place where you met all kinds and any man had a chance to show what he was worth.

Another version of the legend—the version known to reformers or to some of Yale's rivals—stressed Yale's obdurate conservatism. Yale was obviously oligarchical and old-fashioned. Its government was clerical and its faculty had refused to experiment. The College always had resented new ideas. It had fought the elective system bitterly. It had pushed the sciences and social sciences over into its Scientific School and had strengthened the hand of the more backward, church-controlled colleges. Like them it preferred discipline to free thinking, organization to originality, athlete to scholar, customs to books. And always what Yale did seemed right to Yale.

The power of the place remained unmistakable. Yale was organized. Yale inspired a loyalty in its sons that was conspicuous and impressive. Yale men in afterlife made such records that the suspicion was that even there they were working for each other.[2] In short, Yale was exasperatingly and mysteriously successful. To rival institutions and to academic reformers there was something irritating and disquieting about old Yale College.

In 1892 a young Harvard instructor, George Santayana, was moved to investigate this disturbing Yale legend.[3] The athletic rivalry had become intense. Charges and insults—Yale "brawn" vs. Harvard "brains"—were circulating freely. In Cambridge it was

5

felt that Yale was at once the most similar and the most opposite to Harvard: in many respects the embodiment of what was most hostile to the Harvard spirit. But Santayana had a hunch that this hostility might not be justified. So, in a spirit of generous and disinterested scholarship, he paid a visit to the mysterious land of New Haven.

The Yale campus lay in the midst of the town, he reported, and was much more closely built upon than the Harvard Yard. In spite of the nearness of the streets and the well-trodden earth underfoot, it gave an effect of retirement. The paths were not restricted by new grass and stretched wire. The whole block suggested a "true college quadrangle." There was more noise and bustle than at Harvard. When the fire alarm sounded every student flung open his window, popped his head out, and yelled "Fire." * [4]

In the company of Yale's most ebullient instructor, William Lyon Phelps, the Harvard philosopher journeyed out to Yale Field where, on the broad-backed plateau above the river, the football players seemed locked in a prehistoric struggle. Standing about or walking behind the ropes, the undergraduates followed the play, absorbed and admiring, "commenting like the crowd in Homer upon the prowess of their chiefs." Here Santayana found the "most crying expression of that Yale Spirit" of which he had heard so much: a contagious energy and reckless love of success. Philosophers fond of "finding spirits in things should not fail to visit Yale."

But what made this spirit possible? Santayana's shrewd eye noticed first the students. The Yale undergraduates came from all over the country. This made them all strangers together, and de-

---

* Older graduates will remember the humorous custom of attributing the blaze of each campus bonfire to some unhappy scholar or immaculate deacon. "Who lit that fire?" a single voice would call out. And Durfee, Farnam, Lawrance and the old Brick Row would respond as one: "Highstand lit that fire." Presently there would come a slight pause, followed by a gentle "All over," started by some sentinel in a remote corner and passed along the line. Silence would follow in a minute.

A short generation later the same cry of "Fire!" would pack the windows with watching eyes as some lone girl picked her way across the campus.

6

pendent for their pleasures and success on their ability to make new friends and play a part in the undergraduate world. Hence the College ideals seemed the only ideals, the College traditions were accepted as sacred laws, the College activities all-absorbing pursuits. "The Yale man is not often such by halves or incidentally." There being no nearby Boston he was not divided in his allegiance. Snobbery of wealth or social position was in abeyance. The College heroes were more unreservedly admired—the coveted societies more open to achievement.

The relations of one Yale student to another are comparatively simple and direct. They are like passengers in a ship or fellow countrymen abroad; their sense of common interests and common emotions overwhelms all latent antipathies. They live in a sort of primitive brotherhood, with a ready enthusiasm for every good or bad project, and a contagious good-humor.

Yet another cause, Santayana thought, combined with isolation and internal homogeneity to give vigor to the Yale spirit. This influence was College discipline. Every morning at ten minutes past eight every student had to be at chapel. At half-past eight everybody had a recitation. All the work of Freshman and Sophomore years was prescribed. Doing the same tasks, Yale men sat together under the same teachers. There was a regular "tariff of black marks" for violations of this regularity. This compulsory system invited a mass reaction. "Common grievances are a greater bond than common privileges," and all the things they had to do and didn't want to do "are so many forces that make for union."

In fact, Yale is in many respects what Harvard used to be. It has maintained the traditions of a New England college more faithfully. Anyone visiting the two colleges would think Yale by far the older institution. The past of America makes itself felt there in many subtle ways: there is a kind of colonial self-reliance, and simplicity of aim, a touch of non-conformist separation from the great ideas and movements of the world.

7

However it was not only the past of America that was "enshrined at Yale"; the present was vividly portrayed there, too.

Nothing could be more American . . . Here is sound, healthy principle, but no overscrupulousness, love of life, trust in success, a ready jocoseness, a democratic amiability, and a radiant conviction that there is nothing better then one's self. It is a boyish type of character, earnest and quick in things practical, hasty and frivolous in things intellectual. But the boyish ideal is a healthy one, and in a young man, as in a young nation, it is perfection to have only the faults of youth. . . . No wonder that all America loves Yale, where American traditions are vigorous, American instincts are unchecked, and young men are trained and made eager for the keen struggles of American life.

Finally Santayana insisted on what seemed to him a vital and fundamental point. Yale believed. Yale had a religion. "The solution of the greatest problems is not sought, it is regarded as already discovered. The work of education is to instil these revealed principles and to form habits congruous with them. Everything is arranged to produce a certain type of man." Even the miscellaneous new electives were concessions to the foreign idea of being a university and of leaving nothing out. "The essential object of the institution is still to educate rather than instruct, to be a mother of men rather than a school of doctors. In this Yale has been true to the English tradition . . . a place where the tradition of national character is maintained, together with a traditional learning."

No doubt there was an undertone of crudeness and toughness about Yale, compared with the sweet mellowness of the English universities. But that was not Yale's fault. Yale would ripen with the country while maintaining its links to the past, its sympathy with American life. And its professors, whatever investigations they might take up, would remain primarily "masters of their pupils," teachers and transmitters of the treasures of experience to generations yet to come. Altogether, Santayana was surprised by Yale's "strength and agreeableness."

Of course he could not help asking himself what that left for

8

Harvard. Harvard might become a university—a collection of museums, laboratories, and special libraries; a group of specialist professors; a place where men went for professional training. But Santayana was afraid this would mean the surrender of moral leadership. And Harvard, he was sure, did not really mean to abandon the old Anglo-Saxon educational objective of forming character. Perhaps "some people" had momentarily lost sight of this ideal; but they would soon be reminded by public demand and their own sense of relative values. Perhaps Harvard had gone too fast in trusting such functions to the schools and to the students themselves. But Harvard had no protective tariff on ideas; her trust was in scholarship and in truth. Compared with Yale, Harvard had a vague but perhaps deeper religion: "the faith in enlightenment, the aspiration to be just, the sympathy with the multiform thoughts and labors of humanity." Harvard had the freedom, and the single eye for the truth, that would secure for her an incomparable future.

Yet Yale, meanwhile, had "more unity, more energy, and greater fitness to our present conditions."

Not every stranger was as perceiving as young Santayana or as sharply discriminating. But on most careful observers—whether foreign or American, whether from Harvard or the Middle West, whether in the 1880's or the 1890's or even considerably later—this old New England College made indelible impressions. In substance the judgment was that Yale was a thoroughly conservative institution: traditional in its habits, religious in its spirit, earnest and moral in its atmosphere, conforming in its opinions, old-fashioned in its education.

By an undeserved compensation as it seemed to some—or in natural consequence as it seemed to others—the Yale student body was an astonishingly manly and attractive lot. Representative in their origins, open in their manners, square in their judgments, fiercely competitive but wholeheartedly loyal: such were the qualities which recommended Yale undergraduates to friend and critic alike. But no mere catalogue can re-create so live a thing as a col-

9

lege. So, just as no entering Freshman has ever immediately understood, but has had to grow by experience into the strange ways of Yale, we must ourselves be humble and go slowly. And first we may inquire into certain much-remarked characteristics: characteristics so deliberate and so enduring that they could almost be called the hallmark of this place.

Yale was conservative beyond debate. And full of traditions. Observers kept saying so, and Yale men gladly accepted the charge. To the men of Yale its traditions had a special function and value in the College. But to strangers this traditionalism could be very disconcerting, and it sometimes seemed that Yale carried habit almost to absurdity. Witness the reaction of Edwin E. Slosson, a graduate of the Universities of Kansas and Chicago, who in 1908–09 would set himself to compare the most celebrated American universities:

. . . the past is not really past at Yale. It is a part of the present. . . . Ask a Yale man the reason for anything and he will give you the origin; and he thinks he has answered your question. . . .

"Why do all the dormitory windows have those big water bottles in them?"

"Because the city water was bad a few years ago."

"Isn't it all right now?"

"Oh, yes."

"Why do the college students have to attend chapel every morning?"

"They always have."

. . . .

"Don't you think that the *Lit.* would sell better if it had a new cover?"

"You don't understand. That is the original cover, and it has never been changed in the seventy-three years of its history."

Like one of those primitive African tribes whose quaint and unreasoned ways Professor Sumner lectured about, Yale had its accumulated oddities, its inescapable mores.* Coming from a part of the country where to accuse the students of a rival institution of maintaining traditions was to invite physical retaliation, Slosson would be puzzled, even a little irritated. But after trying in vain to justify his own prejudice by finding some really harmful Yale traditions, he felt compelled to admit that "they are on the whole good ones and undeniably useful, and that if a university has to have traditions . . . no other university in the country has a better lot than Yale." [5]

Again Yale had been, and would for some time continue to be, religious. In 1870 Timothy Dwight, professor in the Theological Department, had written: "Yale College is the largest and highest educational institution, under real and pronounced Christian influences, in the country." In 1887 the same Timothy Dwight, become President, had counseled reverence and neighborly love: "The cultivated infidel . . . is no true son of our University . . ." [6]

In 1892 Santayana had spoken of Yale as "believing" in truths already revealed. When William Lyon Phelps had gone to Harvard the one difference which surprised him most was that people didn't go to bed at night. At 1 A. M. all the dormitory lights would be on— whereas the Yale campus at midnight was like a Vermont churchyard. "Harvard men dress well and go abroad, Yale men play foot-

---

* In explaining the difference between Harvard and Yale, Slosson said: "This difference in spirit seems to me most clearly expressed by two books that appeared not long ago, 'Pragmatism,' by Professor James, of Harvard, and 'Folkways' by Professor Sumner, of Yale. 'Pragmatism' is the Harvard elective system applied to the universe. 'Folkways' makes the Yale system of social control the fundamental principle of all morals and manners. The former book preaches a defiant individualism that would free itself even from the bonds of its own past, that would shatter this sorry scheme of things and then remold it nearer to the heart's desire. The latter book shows how completely we are ruled by custom and tradition, and how righteousness and conformity come to mean the same thing. It would be hard to imagine 'Pragmatism' proceeding from New Haven or 'Folkways' being written in Cambridge."

ball and go to prayers," said a Radcliffe girl.[7] In 1897 the head of Western Reserve called Yale as Congregational as a college could be.[8] In 1899 one of Yale's most loyal sons would describe the place as if it were a great household of faith. To be a cynic "is to cease to be a Yale man." And in 1914 Secretary Anson Phelps Stokes '96 would echo these pronouncements: "The typical graduate has the believing attitude of mind. . . . A Yale atheist, or a Yale cynic, or a Yale pessimist, is rarely found." [9]

Yet Yale had lost all traces of monasticism at least as early as the Civil War. And its faith now had some rather special qualities. The chapel requirement, for example, had come into question. Despite an improved rotation of effective preachers, the Sunday services were not always inspiring; and it was noticed that the heartiest expression of religious feeling was apt to be the Doxology. As for daily chapel, that seemed hardly a religious service at all. A stranger would witness a gathering of some twelve or thirteen hundred students—the most massive congregation of young men in the country. But most of these worshipers shot into the aisle and rushed into their seats between eight and ten minutes past eight. Some kept their overcoats buttoned to conceal the fact that they were still only half dressed. Nearly all would have brought their books for their first recitation. And not a few, unless too near a faculty sentinel, would proceed to consult these texts, or the morning paper, during the service. As was whimsically recorded: "If a sociable dog is lingering about Chapel between 8.05 and 8.10, the chances are against his being outside after 8.10. Nobody in particular calls him in, but there is a general air of hospitality through all the stream of worshippers, and he will flow innocently along with them and into the centre aisle."

After the concluding prayer the President walked down the aisle, where the Seniors waited to bow him out. Like waves of grain before the reaper, pew after pew bent low as he passed by. That this ceremony derived perhaps from the English Puritan churches of the eighteenth century few knew or cared. What mattered was that it was an immemorial Yale custom and calculated to impress lower-classmen. In fact the Seniors so cherished their special privilege

12

that when the rumor had gone round, some years before, that the President might abolish the ritual by slipping out another door, it was reported that they had threatened to rush out and line the sidewalks to his house, to catch him on his way home.

> This bowing ceremony . . . as an impressive demonstration of respect of authority . . . fails in some points, when one notices the exquisite nicety of calculation by which those rows of heads go down, touching the nap but not the body of the cloth itself on the President's back, and the lack of any distance between the President and those who have fallen in line behind him.

Superstition had it that if you could manage to touch the hump on President Dwight's back as he walked down the aisle you would have good luck in your recitations all day. And the belief was strong enough to lead to cash transactions for preferred places. Thus bowing out had become something of a sporting event.

Now much of daily chapel could offend a sensitive stranger. Indeed there were men at Yale who argued strenuously against such an abuse of religion. But more still defended. Chapel brought the whole College together under the President. It emphasized man's dependence on God, and the idealistic purpose of the institution. It also got every undergraduate out of bed. And the strongest consideration of all was the fact that the Seniors, after having been through it all, always voted that the custom should be continued.[10]

In any case, the voluntary religious life of Yale College flourished and was plain to see. Nearly two-thirds of the undergraduates were members of some church. Each of the three upper Classes elected its Class deacons to the College Church, and some of the best men in College were regularly so chosen. Character counted as well as piety. Indeed a leader in Dwight Hall, the student Y.M.C.A., was almost as likely to be elected to a Senior society as an outstanding athlete. It was even charged that there was a "Dwight Hall ring"—with an underground tunnel into Skull and Bones. Taking up religious activities as a means of political advancement was unquestionably practiced. Yet these very facts made clear "the striking difference between Yale and most other universities in the student estimation of religious work." [11]

In Dwight Hall Yale's impulses toward piety and social preferment—with the political activity and practical altruism which they encouraged—had found happy communion. Every winter deputations of influential undergraduates went forth to the preparatory schools to talk about Yale and about the soldierly, Christian character that Yale stood for. Every summer the largest delegation at the Northfield conference was apt to be from Yale. Every fall the Yale Y.M.C.A. sent out a most catholic handbook to all incoming Freshmen. It gave the College cheer "in accurate Greek"; it listed the first textbooks and Freshman instructors; it described the Library and its rules, Peabody Museum and its wonders, and the Gymnasium with its equipment. It told how to get to Yale Field, how athletics and Glee Club and college papers were run, where the fire alarm stations were, and where to go when sick. The Freshman was carefully instructed what to do, when to do it, and *what not to do.* Finally the newcomer was invited to use Dwight Hall as headquarters, as a place to meet Yale's great men, and as a center for the social service that he would do afterward. There would be opportunities to conduct Bible classes, Sunday schools, and meetings for the Railroad Y.M.C.A. The Freshmen would run a Boys' Club; upperclassmen would help conduct the new Yale Mission.

On top of all this, Dwight Hall stood for clean living. And it was perhaps no accident that student sentiment was strong against the man of lax morals, and less and less tolerant of the excessive drinker. Dwight Hall made hypocrites? Perhaps, now and again. But hypocrites were not popular at Yale, and the intimacy of campus living almost surely betrayed them. In its religious activities the College stressed the activities quite as much as the religion. But this was the age of good works, and the undergraduates were neither philosophers nor mystics. So the humanitarian, even secular spirit of Dwight Hall seemed to meet the needs of the time exactly. It fitted the place and it worked.

What was much more impressive to the average observer, how-

14

ever, was the general atmosphere and activity of undergraduate life. Even allowing for occasional insobriety, Yale College seemed an unusually healthy community of immense good will and exuberant vitality. Individually and collectively Yale men were attractive. While they ran a little to a type, it was a good type. The typical Yale man was an upstanding fellow, full of boyish energy and idealism, earnest not cynical, simple rather than sophisticated. "Repression is supposed to be the mood of the Harvard, expression the mood of the Yale man." Sociable and enthusiastic, Yale men believed in friendship and in each other. Strolling the streets so jauntily, they were "as easily distinguishable among the town crowds as beings from another world. The town was only their background," and they picked each other out "as a dog sees only other dogs on a busy road." [12]

At first glance the impression was not always too favorable. The stranger might be disappointed by the dock weeds, dirt, and shabbiness of the campus, just as an old graduate might be troubled by the occasional slouch hats, or a chance encounter with golf knickers or a soiled sweater. Not that Yale students were deliberately careless in attire. On the contrary they took pride in being called "well dressed" and by later standards would seem models of an almost Chesterfieldian elegance. The traditional silk hats had gone out— except for the Washington's Birthday snowball fight, when the Sophomores tried to protect their stovepipes by tying them down with stockings knotted under the chin. For regular wear derby hats were the common headgear, even for informal games on the campus, which were played with coat jackets buttoned up. Starched shirts and straight stiff collars were also the fashion, though no longer the invariable custom. For in the quietest way a sartorial relaxation was indeed developing. Felt hats and straws and golf caps were appearing. In the late nineties the single choker collar gave way to the equally starched but more informal folded-over type. And the death knell of the starched shirt had been sounded a year or two earlier when a meticulously dressed young man was strangely thrown on his back by his friends on a summer evening and subjected to the first "fruiting" operation on the Yale campus. According to the best authority, no one knew just how it had happened.

There were a few minutes to do nothing in, so something unusual had to be done. This accurate young man probably troubled his excellent friends, simply by being too dignified, and so they decided that some indignity should be offered to him. How any one conceived of putting him on his back, undoing his coat, and cutting off the flap on the end of his shirt bosom, cannot be explained; but this was done. And it was no sooner done than the offending part of his costume was placed on the end of the knife which cut it off, and the illustrious youth in the group who had secured the trophy held it aloft, shouted "Fruit!" and rushed across the campus to a favorite elm in front of Durfee. The others followed, and in due order the shirt tab was tacked to the tree. And then this group continued the pastime fiercely that night, and fiercely for several days thereafter . . . until twenty-one of these curious trophies were pinned together on one elm-tree. And the game came to be called, first "Elm Fruit"; then "Fruit." [13]

College was the time for fun—the shortest, gladdest years of life—and theirs was "an arrogant and enchanting irresponsibility," a life of glad brotherhood and freedom where they could "let the whole being go." [14] When the mood was on them they would seize anything for their bonfires. In 1898 students took an Indian from a Chapel Street cigar store and laid it on the tracks of the Fair Haven and Westville Railroad to give the appearance of a man run over. In 1900 Jim Donnelly, the stout campus policeman, recorded that a certain undergraduate "would often test his strength by lifting and turning over some of the stone walks" and leave them to be put to rights by the superintendent of grounds. A few years earlier it had been a prank to fasten the Chapel Street gates of the campus, just to make everyone go round the block to get in.

In 1897 the heavyweight champion, James J. Corbett, paid a visit to the football field. When his title bout against Fitzsimmons came up, thirteen members of the Junior Class sent him a Yale flag and a message:

> Here at Yale we realize how much brain and science count in all athletic contests. We regard you as the highest exponent of the brainy boxer; hence our explicit faith and confidence in the outcome of the battle. . . .
>
> Now, Jim, we hope you will hang this Yale flag in your training quarters and in your corner at the ringside, and remember that it waves to you a message of Yale luck and pluck. Go in and win, and delight the hearts of all true Yale men.[15]

The year before some of the same undergraduates, inspired it may be by "Billy" Phelps, had formed the Kipling Club, for all those "who thirst for Kipling or tippling." The list included Julian S. Mason, John Munro Woolsey, Payne Whitney, James W. Wadsworth, and the football captain J. O. Rodgers. After many Indian tales and Mandalays and collations their President, Gouverneur Morris Jr., had a sublime idea—and they wrote inviting the genius to their first annual banquet. Alas, Rudyard Kipling could not come. Instead he sent a poem, still famous in Yale annals, which began:

> Attind ye lasses av Swate Parnasses
> An' wipe my burnin' tears away
> For I'm declinin' a chanst av dinin'
> Wid the bhoys at Yale on the foorteenth May.

"The bhoys at Yale" gave the whole poem to the *Lit.* and made the May 1896 issue worth its weight in gold.[16]

Parades on any or all occasions, but especially at election times, were a favorite diversion. In the 1892 election one boy marched with both the Cleveland Guards and the Phelps Brigade for Harrison, and so discovered that in a certain section of town the Republican Brigade was received with missiles, but when the Democratic Guards halted outside the same tavern they were greeted with seidels of beer.

In 1896 the students turned out en masse to hear William Jennings Bryan give a Bible-flavored speech which has been variously reported. Some remembered that he expressed his preference for one ewe lamb that returned to the fold, over the ninety and nine. Others heard him thunder, over the booing and applause, that "ninety-nine out of a hundred of the students in this university are spawn of the idle rich." In any case, he had given the magic numerals of the Sophomore Class. Suddenly everyone was shouting "Ninety-nine, ninety-nine." Someone called for a long cheer for '99. And the riot started.[17]

But college was also serious—the best preparation there was for the struggle of life. Like college men everywhere the undergraduates imitated the organizations and competitions of the outside world, and within this miniature market place each strove to establish his value. Only the men of Yale seemed unusually aggressive. Power was to be earned. Honor was coveted. Social recognition was necessary. And this recognition went to the fighter, to the man who made something of himself. Success also went to the unselfish worker, or to the man who knew how to handle men and make others work together. The instinct for organization was strong. And just as Yale had never been friendly to the sophisticated or to those who were merely clever, so now it was becoming less and less a place for the merely lazy or unambitious. Yale admitted no special students and tolerated no idlers. "Vacation," Timothy Dwight had once said, "is not the best part of living. The best part is the time of working." "When work is to do, the Yale spirit knows no hesitation"—so wrote Barrett Wendell in 1901.[18]

With all this Yale College—as Santayana and others observed—was primarily a united community. And whatever their competitions the undergraduates constituted an almost "primitive brotherhood." Their spirit was phenomenal. " 'Together' is the great word at Yale." Yale men could encourage each other. They were plucky, persistent fighters no less than constructive and efficient organizers. "Harvard seems to stand for the principle of individuality, Yale for the communistic or collective principle." [19] And Yale stood for team play. Thus by believing in each other and by bulldog tenacity

Yale almost always made up for any lack of individual brilliance. In athletics particularly Yale's success had become proverbial. Harvard men might win the one-man competitions, but the team contests went regularly and decisively to Yale. It had been so in football for almost twenty years, and it had come to be so in crew and in baseball. It could even be made so in debating—as had been demonstrated when a small group in the mid-nineties made this neglected activity a matter of civic pride.[20]

The Yale spirit, however, could not be called exclusive or even selfish. Yale men believed in their classmates and their teams, in each other and in their College, but also in the things that College stood for, and in their country. Campus life deliberately drew a man out of himself. And from time immemorial Yale had preached and practiced the ideal of public service. As Horace Bushnell had proclaimed at the commemorative service to honor Yale's Civil War dead, "Our young men are not . . . to be launched on the voyage of life as ships without wind, but they are to have great sentiments and mighty impulsions . . ." [21]

Hence two effects. Yale was patriotic and Yale conformed—two qualities which were so marked and would prove so enduring that a word about each is in order.

Yale conformed. There was no doubt about it. A true Yale man was not at Yale just for what he could get out of it. He was not even being educated to rely on himself or to pit his judgment against popular opinion. At some of the institutions of the newer West everything old was automatically suspect. At Cambridge, as a Harvard editor confessed, the Harvard man was apt to be such a law unto himself that team play and concerted effort were often impossible. But at Yale individualism was not encouraged. Campus sentiment was against it, and traditions stood in the way. A man's classmates valued his cooperation far more than his criticism. Originality of ideas was suspect and, outside of a tolerated range, eccentricity of dress or conduct was frowned on. To succeed at Yale one must avoid queerness, make friends, do something. And whatever the activity or however calculated the underlying motive, the assumption was always the same. To "go out" and do something was to work for the welfare of the College. Competition itself was patriotic.

The all-powerful Senior societies rewarded conformity and achievement. This was true in the 1890's, would be pointed out by Slosson in 1910, and would still seem an outstanding Yale characteristic in the 1920's. To quote the Princetonian, Edmund Wilson, Yale undergraduates were molded by the fear of this mysterious censorship. The most vigorous and alert minds were apt "to have their intellectual teeth drawn as the price of their local success." "At Yale the eccentric or non-competitive man, who might be happy at Princeton or Harvard, is likely to be juggernauted by the machine and acquire little but an extreme bitterness." [22] Did such taboos extend also to Yale's elders, so that it took the brutal weight and bullheadedness of a Sumner to be a rebel in the faculty? However that might be, it had to be observed that Yale taught men to work together. The joiner and the man of faith were beautifully at home.

In such a community loyalty flourished, and patriotism was its finest flower. The occasions for heroic self-sacrifice seemed to arise only seldom; but in the country's wars there was no holding back. Unquestioningly, enthusiastically, the men of Yale would enlist—and so it proved now in the war with Spain. The coming on of this conflict had not been viewed with entire approval. In fact William Graham Sumner persisted in outspoken disapproval. But once war had been declared, official Yale and undergraduate Yale closed ranks.[23] Student volunteers tried to organize a Yale Light Battery of 172 men; and when that was refused some sixty men went into training with the Connecticut Light Artillery at Niantic. Again when the government converted a liner into a cruiser and named it *Yale,* with spontaneous enthusiasm Yale men of all ages got together to buy a stand of colors and two guns for the cruiser—and in no time at all oversubscribed the necessary funds, the last gifts received being from Yale men in newly annexed Hawaii.* One evening the patriotic spirits of the students broke out; and for the bonfire they collected "bicycle crates, woodpiles from back yards,

* After the war the guns were returned and placed in the Trophy Hall of the Gymnasium. They were named Handsome Dan and Eli.

barrels and boxes from grocery stores, and even timbers from a nearby building. A six-foot teakettle sign was added." [24] Then there was called a great mass meeting to forward the guns and the fifty-one flags and a message from Yale. An old graduate cannot today read accounts of that gathering without a shiver of recognition traveling his spine.

> The night of May 20, 1898, is not one to be forgotten in Yale tradition or to be overlooked in Yale history. At twenty minutes after seven that evening at the College Street Hall, President Dwight opened a meeting without precedent. . . . All of Yale was there . . . by worthy delegates and by as many of them as could crowd into the old church, body, galleries, aisles, choir loft, and vestibule. The Yale undergraduate was there, full hearted and full toned; and those who had been Yale undergraduates, one or fifty years ago, perhaps; and the teachers of Yale were there . . .
>
> . . . To make it perfect, Yale was there from the camp as well . . . Just before the meeting opened, two young men in army blue were crowded unwillingly forward on the platform, and from the great crowd in College Street Hall rose a long roar of applause . . .
>
> The old church was all red and white and blue. . . . From the moment President Dwight announced "America" . . . the meeting was a success. . . . When it came to the "Star Spangled Banner," later in the evening, the spirit was all the more intense . . . For a closing song "Bright College Years" was sung. . . . The old church shook with it, and when the last line was reached the great audience took time and emphasis like a trained club and rolled it out in such a volume that people stopped on the streets blocks away to listen.
>
> "For God, for Country, and for Yale." This last line, sung with such an emphasis and impressiveness, was the text of the whole meeting. [25]

To outsiders the ability of Yale men to sing this last line without sense of anticlimax has ever since bordered on the marvelous or the ludicrous. Indeed a Yale man's loyalty could be so excessive

21

and his affection so unreasoning as to irritate the uninitiated and injure his institution. That was the reverse side of the bright shield of faith. Yale men could be—perhaps often were—so dazzled by their vision that they were blind to Yale's faults, incapable of studying their College objectively, reluctant to distinguish its good customs from its bad. As a result, Yale men tended to be complacent —or at least more content than Harvard men—and less ready for change.

Yet some of the strongest criticism of complacency now came from within the household.[26] And in any case Yale's standards had never been merely miscellaneous. Moral idealism was conspicuously high, and positive achievement, not simply negative conformity, was required. Yale believed in courage and character and taught all its sons that they were members one of another, with a duty to their God, their country, and their University. By which same faith they felt able to move mountains.

Fifty years later a Harvard graduate, speaking at a Yale Commencement, would still be moved to refer to "the old Homeric virtue of loyalty" which had always distinguished the place.[27] Loyalty was a part of the Yale legend—a part of the Yale that was and would be. *Lux et Veritas* was the ancient motto. We may conclude that the College had come to stand for *Virtus et Communitas,* too.

CHAPTER 2·THE YALE SYSTEM

. . . So much of it and the best of it is invisible. I felt on the campus as I do in the dynamo room of a great power house.
—E. E. SLOSSON, *Great American Universities, 1910*

THE THEORY of this College was . . .

But at once the shades of generations of Yale men cry in protest. Yale was not a theory. The College was a living thing, not a paper plan. It wasn't an intellectual construct. It wasn't even a deliberate system. It had just gradually grown—and not by a series of experiments so much as by wise adaptation. Experiments meant sacrificing proven values for newer but often ill-founded notions. Experiments were for other colleges. "The changes that mean much are the slow ones." Yale had grown by evolution, not revolution. Even the word "evolution" had an alien tang. "The progress of this College," as Timothy Dwight had once chosen to put it, "has been a steady and healthful development. Its guardians have carefully preserved whatever of good has been preserved from preceding generations, and have, at the same time, not lost sight of the teachings of their own age." [1]

So by virtue of throwing nothing useful away and adding only what was proven and what fitted, the guardians of the College had developed the peculiar Yale traditions: a system of assumptions, not theories, of time-honored practices, and of taboos. As the puzzled E. E. Slosson would report, "Yale not only had traditions, but was proud of them, advertised them, capitalized them as part of the productive funds, used them to draw students, made them do much of the educational and nearly all of the disciplinary work of the institution." [2] Even strangers had to admit that Yale's guardians had done more than merely accumulate some harmless and decorative customs. Yale's traditions had been harnessed. And their power

23

helped run what had become an exceedingly complex but massive College system.

The Yale system had the usual parts—but perhaps more than one distinctive emphasis. Just as in England and elsewhere in the United States, books were not everything. Instead, by long practice and consent, a college education had come to mean a many-sided education, playful as well as serious, social and physical as well as intellectual. Characteristically, the learning was to come by activity more than by contemplation. Perhaps we may even speak of so many interlocking circles of activity. For schoolboys were made into Yale men and responsible citizens through their experiences in: chapel, classroom and dormitory living—a wide range of competitions, athletic, extracurricular and social—a diversified training in discipline and command—finally also by being members of that all-important social organism called the Class.

About chapel and Dwight Hall—the religious observance and the religious activities of the College—enough has already been said to make plain, even to a more skeptical generation, how intimate was the connection with the moral idealism of the place and how close the association with its other fields of activity.

The intellectual element, or Course of Instruction, was the flywheel and governor of the whole machine. Yet to some minds the value of the classroom seemed dubious. Individuals wondered whether the curriculum belonged in the system, whether in fact it was not alien to the true purposes of College life. It was remarked, for example, that Yale students were enthusiastic about everything except their studies. As more than one old graduate was sure, "Yale College would be a very pleasant place, if its religious and literary exercises could be abolished." [3] No doubt such sentiments were either humorous exaggerations or rueful reflections on the methods of classroom instruction. In fact, not a few students were doing extra reading outside of class, and scores were browsing in the Linonian and Brothers Library. In 1895 the Junior Promenade Committee presented the Assistant Librarian with a check for $500

24

so that the Reference Library, too, could be kept open on Sunday. Meanwhile the discarding of textbooks in certain courses, in favor of broader readings arranged by the instructors on reserved shelves in "L. and B.," had won considerable approval.

But even a textbook could open unexpected vistas. And what student did not appreciate the personalities and idiosyncrasies of Yale's great teachers? Not even the most sophisticated could shrug off the disturbing power of W. G. Sumner—while athlete and scholar alike were charmed by "Limpy" Reynolds, stimulated by Billy Phelps, and enthralled watching Arthur T. Hadley gyrate through his course in economics. Yet about studies and studying in general College sentiment remained something less than enthusiastic. Perhaps it would be a fair observation that the average undergraduate pursued his extracurricular activities with such ardor that he made work of his fun. But he sometimes performed his classroom assignments in so perfunctory a fashion that he came close to making fun of his work.

This split, shrewd observers would think, struck deep into the mores of the place. A considerable element had come to College to learn not from books but from each other—not how to be scholars but how to succeed.[4] Success was really their goal, not Veritas. What they were surely preparing for in their competitions was the struggle of making a living. Henry Canby has given this anomaly its most telling treatment. And, as he has remarked, the explanation was that the main stream of American life was pouring through the College. So the undergraduates knew that, provided they first learned the rules of the game, they were destined for great prizes, sure to make fortunes, and bound for the managing posts in society.

This difference of objective could not but separate the students a little from the faculty—which would lead Canby to remark that New Haven itself was really divided not into two but into three distinct parts: "town, gown, and sweater." The point is worth noticing. Yet it is easy for a later generation to mistake the inherited formality of manners for real indifference—and we must guard against reading back into the nineties a divergence of standards and sympathies which even in the 1900's would be less marked in Yale College than in many a newer university. The fact was that the College faculty was still largely staffed by Yale graduates. In the years 1860–90 the percentage of Class leaders who had gone into teaching had been high; and the percentage of faculty members who had themselves been members of the Senior societies was infinitely greater than it is today. By attending society meetings President Dwight, Secretary Dexter, Dean Wright, and many of the more influential professors kept in sympathetic touch with undergraduate leadership. And it was quite usual for members of the faculty— even for those known as "stinkers"—to entertain their students at tea or at Sunday luncheons at their homes.

The most that can therefore be said is that non-Yale men were now for the first time beginning to hold chairs on the Faculty— while the clientele of the College was shifting its interest from the professions toward business. In this headlong rush to prosperity the older academic ideals would come to seem curiously out of place. Teaching might not be regarded as an occupation for a strong man. Society would notice that teachers were poorly paid and hankered after security. They belonged not to "the dominant party of action" but to what Canby describes as the "recessive opposition" who speculated on how life should be lived. So between the fundamental purposes of the College and the main stream of American industrial life a rift was beginning to open.[5]

But this rift or conflict will be one of the themes of our story. And the relation of the system of studies to the system of Yale training will be given full development. Suffice it to note here that there were elements of harmony as well as of conflict in the situation. Yale's Officers took a broad view of their College. Studies, also, were competitive and were deliberately kept strenuous. In the larger view not so much a conflict as a balance was contemplated. Book learning was a part, not the whole, of learning. As Timothy Dwight insisted, the truth could be "but dimly seen by the intellect alone." So we may turn at this point to Yale's other ways "of teaching young men and of letting them teach each other."[6]

Of these other ways the oldest, most fascinating, and most valued

26

was the common College life. On the face of things it almost seemed as if this life had been built up entirely by the students. But this would be to ignore the setting and a strong element of deliberate planning.

Traditionally a college had not been a college without collegiate living, i.e., unless its students lived together—slept, ate, and sported together—as well as studied. This English public school or college tradition Yale's governors had perpetuated for the widest variety of good reasons. It had been recognized very early that only on its own land could the College exercise the desirable authority. And only by proctoring its own dormitories could the College oversee the life of the students, discipline the disorderly, detect the wayward, and stimulate all. The College life should be a life removed somewhat from the distractions and temptations of the town. It was a life which had to be lived openly and in the sight of one's fellows. It encouraged straightforward conduct and made for reputable habits. As a social medium it multiplied the power of opinion and gave to established usages a cumulative effect. Its enforced intimacy generated Class loyalty, esprit de corps, and the careful evaluation of character. In a word the collegiate way of living had not only protected young men from influences which were undesirable but subjected them instead to those which would do them the most good.

Happily, campus life was also such fun that despite proctors and faculty supervision, schoolboy rules and petty discipline, none had believed in it more or taken a better advantage of it than the undergraduates. From time immemorial Yale students had roomed in the battered entries of the old Brick Row, eaten together, whiled away the hours in each other's company, talked and sung songs and got into mischief. To many an old grad the brightest spot on earth had been his College room. And one and all would think next of the College Fence.

The Fence was the palladium of College liberties. From almost prehistoric times, it seemed, this famous "seat of learning" had had the sanctity of an institution.[7] For it represented the most important clause in

> that unwritten constitution of democratic
> principles which is the creed of every Yale man.
> Night and day it receives innumerable rivulets
> of common leisure. . . . Thigh to thigh
> sit scholar, athlete and Bohemian, in a
> guild of fellowship far better than the
> dusty ruts of learning . . .

The Fence had always been divided into three parts: a generous stretch of rails each for the Seniors and Juniors facing Chapel Street, and a short stretch facing the Green for the Sophomores. Also a little tailpiece for the Freshmen if and when they overcame the Harvard Freshmen at baseball. In fighting days the Juniors had continually incited the Freshmen to break established law and seize the Sophomore Fence, "and then would the battle rage as over the ships at Troy, and many reputations be won." But the Sophomores had been too well organized. And after a time the Freshmen had declined any longer to provide amusement for the unscrupulous Juniors.

For the Sophomores the Fence had topped Olympus. There for the first time they could "rub elbows with upperclassmen and watch the grave and reverend Seniors at their games. . . . It is in Sophomore year that a man whittles his name upon it." By Junior year the more subtle delights of individual friendship replaced the explosive escapades, and madrigals and more elaborate glees the roaring songs of Sophomore year.

> The Seniors have a touch of sentiment at the thought of approaching dissolution and begin to feel its power as an institution even when they lay destructive and incendiary hands upon the seat of their affections. . . .
> . . . Here used Hannibal, student emeritus, to sell his wares of "saccharine sweetness." "Gentlemen," he would say, "I vow and assert that the confections which I now present for your consideration are worthy of that reputation which it has been my pride to create and my earnest ambition to uphold. Their perfection is most excellent and their sweetness unparalleled.

De gustibus." A favorite amusement of idleness was to provoke Hannibal and his ancient rival "Davy" to debate upon metaphysical subjects. The dead languages were revivified and quotation, aphorism, and, at the last, personal epithet hurtled in full shock until a sated audience would straggle down to Mory's and slake the fever of spring with cool ale.

In still older days the Fence had determined the battle line between town and gown. The Faculty had once tried to abolish the Fence but not succeeded. So there through the glorious generations the bonfire had blazed out the story of victory after victory. And to the old Fence all returning graduates instinctively bent their steps. Altogether the Fence had done more social work, it has been said, than any other campus institution.[8] In the Yale life of the nineteenth century, Brick Row and Fence alike had been indispensable.

But we must now notice that not even such tried and proven devices for "togetherness" had been perfectly maintained. Nor had they at any time yielded unmixed benefits. For one thing the College now maintained a Dining Hall where the poorer students could get meals at reasonable prices. But Commons had been abandoned. Despite repeated efforts in the earlier part of the century, the difficulties of obtaining good food and good order had proved insuperable. So Yale students were no longer required to eat together —but instead formed their own little social groups which followed the more enterprising and impecunious members from one eating house or landlady-cook to another. The Class of 1896 had four clubs which boasted football teams: the Vandals, Visigoths, Indians, and Underfeds. Other eating clubs which had their brief hour were the Epicureans, Lotus Eaters, and Three Bones; also the House of Lords (next to Commons) and the Consumer's Trust.[9]

Again the housing situation had fallen short of the ideal. For with the expansion of the undergraduate body in the eighties and nineties—and with the luxurious standards of living brought to New Haven by youths of comfortable backgrounds—the old Brick Row had come to seem not merely inadequate but antiquated and dilapidated. One consequence was that the wealthier students preferred to room off the campus, and a group of private dormitories had been built to cater to this demand. The College for its part had undertaken to replace the Brick Row buildings with fine stone dormitories of modern construction. And the authorities had recognized that, with the growth of town and College, some sort of barrier or shielding wall had become desirable as fast as money could be secured. So Timothy Dwight had bent his considerable energies to putting up a curtain of new dormitories and classroom buildings along College and Chapel Streets. And one by one the Brick Row buildings were torn down, thus clearing the interior of the ancient block and creating a great open quadrangle, protected from the encroaching city, for the perpetuation of campus life.

But such drastic rearrangements had necessarily offended many Yale men. In 1888, when Osborn Hall had been given and President Dwight had proposed to remove the old Fence from the corner of College and Chapel Streets, a strong petition had come up to the Corporation from a mass meeting of undergraduates and some 2,100 graduates in various parts of the world. [10] The Fence was the focus of College life, they protested. It was the opportunity and inspiration for community living; it symbolized Yale democracy— and the Yale past. Such traditions and associations could not be transplanted as easily as a tree. But in vain. The Fence had been transferred to a new position inside the quadrangle and in front of Durfee. There in the nineties the Class ceremonies had continued, perhaps with a diminishing spirit. Somehow the Fence no longer seemed the universal meeting ground—the place where all Yale could gather to look out upon the world.*

As for the old Brick Row, here too the forces of progress had had their way, yet not entirely. Again and again, responding to the plaints of disappointed graduates, Dwight had had to argue that

---

* The new Fence became an excellent grandstand from which to watch the spring pastime—Senior baseball. This sport was modeled on the great American game but with touches of improvement added, particularly football. At times the baserunner traveled behind perfect interference, and as many of the interferers were allowed to score as the umpire deemed best.

soon few would be left who remembered rooming in the old Brick Row. He also reasoned that the old buildings had been badly built, could not be repaired, and had no architectural beauty and no important historic beginnings. But coming at last to the most venerable of these monuments Dwight hesitated, and when he went out of office old South Middle still stood. Then in 1902–03, when demolition finally threatened, Lee Perrin of the Class of 1906, the red-headed son of Professor Bernadotte Perrin, organized a campaign of protest by alumni letters to the *News*. The Secretary of the Class of 1852 wrote a stirring plea for its survival: "When old South Middle falls every ancient graduate will cry, 'Ilium Fuit.' " And a group of impassioned Yale men, headed by Professors Simeon E. Baldwin and Henry W. Farnam, got together to rebuild and restore it, giving it the lines and the name that it had originally had. So alone in the newly cleared campus Connecticut Hall would still stand, a reminder of simpler days and a testimony to the strength of traditions. As a stranger remarked, it seemed as if a bit of the shell from which the chick had hatched still stuck to its back.* [11]

The compromise revealed much that was characteristic of the College in the late nineties. By necessity Yale's authorities were looking forward, but by sentiment Yale men could not help looking back. So in the end a great effort was made to preserve at least something of the old associations within a more spacious modern frame. Whether the compromise had been reached in time was a question. It would be a question for the next Administration, for example, whether enough new dormitories could be built to recapture the important segment of the student population which had taken to the private dormitories. It would be another question

* To not a few Yale men it was extraordinary that a man with Dwight's historical connections had so little sympathy with preserving the Brick Row. He told Secretary Stokes once, with much feeling, that his greatest regret was that he had not torn down South Middle "before Henry Farnam and you put your hands on it."

Another anomaly was the luxurious Vanderbilt dormitory which, instead of heeding Dwight's dictum that "the great quadrangle must look inward," faced outward on Chapel Street. Apparently it was the architect's desire for a sunny courtyard which led to this reversal in orientation.

31

whether the custom of Commons could be revived—if not for the whole College then at least for Freshmen. And it would be a still more important question by what means more adequate and appropriate than the Fence could the unity and freemasonry of campus living be cultivated and preserved.

The undergraduates were paying more and more attention to extracurricular activities. For the old casual intercourse, the long hours of loafing, and the devising of ingenious mischief, they had come to substitute a wide variety of activities: some literary, some musical or social, some chiefly managerial, some of a money-making sort. All were voluntary. In none did a student have to participate. But most were thoroughly organized, time-consuming, highly competitive; and to "heel" had become an honorable occupation. The *News,* the *Courant,* the *Record,* and the *Lit.* were now all flourishing and highly regarded. Each of them drew groups of candidates, and on the first day of the *News* competition anywhere from thirty to seventy students would turn out to heel for the half-dozen or so offices. Getting their instructions and their first assignments they would swarm out upon the campus, sleep never more than four hours a night, wear out bicycles in weeks; and the strongest and most persevering, after months of this self-punishment, would land themselves in editorial chairs, if by good luck they did not land in the infirmary instead. Perhaps this was why Yale's graduates in their maturity were so sure "that ability plus hard work can always win the game." [12] In any case every Freshman was urged to "go out" for something. And no man with social ambitions—unless he were already an athlete or unusually well connected—ignored this extra-curriculum, this second racecourse for the proving of ability.

Yale had no monopoly on such activities. In the twentieth century not a few public colleges or schools would quite outdo Yale and the other pioneer institutions in the multiplicity and exaggeration of their student enterprises. But what distinguished Yale life in the nineties was the extreme strenuousness of such activities, the solidity of the major organizations, the enthusiasm of the undergraduates as a whole and the participation of the ablest leaders. Nor was this a passing phase. In the twentieth century such activities would continue to grow in number and over-all importance.

Still more spectacular and absorbing were Yale's athletics. The champions of this form of activity never tired of insisting that there was a peculiar connection between Yale's teams and the virility and reputation of the College. If so the almost appalling record of Yale prowess in rowing, football, baseball, and track athletics spoke for itself. Walter Camp was sure that since the advent of organized sports not only had town and gown riots disappeared but gate-stealing and other, more dangerous trespasses had declined and discipline had immensely improved. ". . . best of all is the establishment of an all-around standard of clean morals and health, and an *esprit de corps* that carries the typical Yale man far towards the best goal in all his efforts." [13]

Yale's Officers stressed also the training in fair play. Older graduates will remember how unceasingly the English ideals of amateur sportsmanship were emphasized. Games were played to be won. Contests should be tests of resourcefulness and courage. "When you lose a match against a man in your own class," Walter Camp once said, "shake hands with him; do not excuse your defeat; do not forget it, and do not let it happen again." At student banquets Camp thought nothing of rising and quoting from Thackeray's "The End of the Play":

> Who misses or who wins the prize?
> Go, lose or conquer as you can;
> But if you fail or if you rise
> Be each, pray God, a gentleman. [14]

Camp taught Yale's athletes to keep faith with each other and deal squarely with opponents—and himself helped other institutions to get a start in the great game of football which he loved. With New England schools and Western colleges clamoring for Yale coaches, there poured out of New Haven a host of player-missionaries—to carry football and sportsmanship across the country as once Yale's mission bands had carried evangelical Christianity to Iowa and Illinois. The University of Pennsylvania and the Naval Academy knew Yale athletes. Michigan and Minnesota hired coaches from New Haven. In 1892 when Stanford and California began playing football, it was under the aegis of Camp and two old Yale captains, Lee McClung '92 and C. O. Gill '89, whose teachings would be remembered gratefully for many years. Parke H. Davis of Princeton, coaching at Wisconsin, would later remark that not less than 45 former Yale players, 35 from Princeton, and 24 from Harvard were actively teaching football in the nineties. Among all these perhaps the greatest apostle of muscular Christianity and clean sportsmanship was wiry and eager Amos Alonzo Stagg '88, who went with William Rainey Harper to Chicago to be Director of Physical Culture and Athletics on professorial tenure. Soon known as the "Old Man," Stagg brought Yale football and athletic traditions to the Middle West. With the result that many years afterward, in the days of the tremendous Notre Dame teams, when the celebrated Knute Rockne was asked whether a Yale coach might not go out to South Bend and learn something, Rockne is said to have replied: "Why I've learned everything I know about football from Yale. Lonny Stagg taught it to me." [15]

Athletics also made heroes for the underclassmen, excitement for the whole College, spectacles for the world. The annual contests against Harvard and Princeton had become epic battles, anticipated with anxiety, watched almost with agony, and celebrated as befitted Homeric victories. Meanwhile the team captains learned to command. The team managers organized the sinews of war and learned the lessons of effective cooperation. The players learned endurance. On field and river the never-say-die spirit of Yale was each day exemplified. And in the undergraduate body the fires of an undying loyalty were fed.

There were four major sports; but lately a series of minor athletic activities had been organized into official clubs, like the University Tennis Club in 1881, the Gymnastic Association and the Corinthian Yacht Club in 1893, Basketball and Hockey in 1895, Golf in 1896, and the Bicycle Association in 1898. There were also

34

Class contests in the major sports, and the Freshmen competed against Harvard and Princeton. So participation in athletics was far from confined to the gifted or the few.

In 1894 A. T. Hadley had noted that for a handful of positions of honor on the teams there were hundreds of men running their regular courses of exercise and filling the sidewalks of New Haven with costumes calculated to strike the stranger aghast. This athletic development had the advantages of helping to bring the Academic and Scientific students together. It counteracted the divisive tendencies of wealth and numbers. "What the critic claims to be preference for the body over the mind is in no small measure preference for collective aims over individual ones." Athletics, properly managed, trained young men to honor a success that was not commercial.[16]

There was also the magnificent new Gymnasium on Elm Street. Physical exercise had not been a College requirement; and physical examinations for upperclassmen were not compulsory. But almost all the Freshmen took such examinations and were advised as to diet, sleep, cleanliness, and corrective exercises. Altogether ten times as many men as in former days—so Walter Camp thought— now exercised to make their bodies sound and strong.[17]

In addition to athletics and extracurricular activities Yale College boasted a society system which, in its Senior societies of Skull and Bones (est. 1832), Scroll and Key (1842), and Wolf's Head (1883), came close to dominating undergraduate life.[18] Between 1832 and the Civil War there had developed a complete hierarchy of secret clubs divided along Class lines: fraternities for Freshmen, societies for Sophomores, fraternities for Juniors, and the two great Senior societies. These were not sleeping or eating clubs, but social organizations with secret and awe-inspiring ceremonials, competing for the outstanding leaders and honor men in each class. Theoretically there had been room for a pyramid of social preferment, with the Freshmen fraternities—Delta Kappa, Sigma Epsilon, and Gamma Nu—taking in almost the entire Class, with the Sophomore societies taking in somewhat fewer, and with the winnowing process continuing until on Tap Day, in the spring of Junior year, the elect of the elect were singled out for the final and greatest honors.

In 1864, 1875, and 1880, because of abuses, the Faculty had felt compelled to abolish both Sophomore and Freshman organizations. Then, under the guise of debating clubs, the Sophomores had formed two new secret societies, ἡ βουλή (1875) and Eta Phi (1879). Being small and banned and very shrewdly managed, these had achieved a coveted reputation and enviable connections with the Junior and Senior organizations. But they elected only 17 men each —so in 1895 a third Sophomore society, Kappa Psi, was formed. About the same time the Junior fraternities were reorganized, so that the three most powerful—Psi Upsilon, Delta Kappa Epsilon, Alpha Delta Phi—by mutual agreement divided up some 105 Juniors; while Zeta Psi independently pledged some 15 or 20 more.

From a numerical standpoint alone—with the Yale Classes now approaching 300, but the Senior societies electing 45, the Junior fraternities about 120, and the Sophomore societies only 51—there was something inadequate and even unjust about the existing arrangements. The Sophomore societies in particular seemed too exclusive. As to the proper remedy, some were for increasing the number of the societies and perhaps their memberships. But a good many others thought that all divisive social organizations before Junior year should be abolished.

Of the Senior societies some criticisms were still heard. Yet nothing to compare to the resentments of the early eighties, when their tombs had been disfigured and their members denied Class office and violently waylaid. Every Tap Day mistakes were made, some fine men overlooked, and some less worthy awarded the coveted honor. But by and large the judgment of the societies had won substantial approval. They looked for character rather than mere congeniality. They penalized immorality and other deviations from the mores. Juniors were often afraid to get drunk or run with low women lest they be "queered"—though some reformed characters were no better than whited sepulchers. Above all, the Senior societies rewarded achievement.

By 1899 so complex had Yale life become that a much fuller analysis would hardly do it justice. Already it is clear that four years at Yale offered no narrow experience but an education of soul, mind, heart, and body: all at once and in a sort of balance. The emphasis was on the whole man among his fellows. Yale men were educated—the word keeps returning—together. And this was true not merely because the students liked it, or because it had happened so, or because such an education was cheaper and easier to manage. Yale men were educated socially because some methods and theories of education were also involved. Perhaps the word theory is again too self-conscious and distinct. But certainly some rather positive beliefs can be identified.

The Yale system operated on the assumption, first of all, that the better part of a college education was a training in good habits: habits of worship and devotion; habits of industry and exact study; good moral and physical habits; habits of square and manly dealing. But habits come only by exercise and repetition. This meant that the undergraduates should be regularly practiced in hard and even unpleasant work, that their sense of duty to society and of obligation to each other should be cultivated on every occasion. Also that they should try out and develop their powers in constant action. Yet man by nature inclines to be lazy, perverse, and selfish. And college youth is mischievous and idly playful to boot. Hence, to assure attention to the progress of a college stimulators and stimulants are required.

Yale obviously relied on a mixture of incentives. Yale students could be induced to engage in the unending exercises that would give them good habits by example, discipline and punishments, competitions, and rewards. The example was part personal, part ceremonial. The discipline and punishments were the discipline of the classroom, the Laws and Rules for student conduct, the marks, penalties, and expulsions decreed by the Faculty, and, not least, the social ostracism or discipline of one's classmates. The competitions were the classroom rivalries on the assigned work, the prize speaking contests, and all the feverish competitions of undergraduate life—athletic, extracurricular, and social. Similarly not a part

37

of Yale operated without its elaborate system of recognitions and rewards—the Academic Appointments or Honors List, the DeForest and other prizes, the editorships and managerships, the captaincies and society elections. Moreover all the honors from the Commencement List to Tap Day were public; and most, for their appeal, relied in part on tradition and ceremony. Psychologically as well as physically the Yale system was a community system.

The College was also community governed. Its management was shared, graduates and undergraduates participating in supervising its manifold exercises. The partnership was informal and customary rather than constitutional; nevertheless the division of labor was well understood and had come to have behind it the authority of long acceptance. This division ran substantially along the following lines. The religious life, the public idealism, and the sense of community dedication were primarily the President's responsibility, with such aid as was furnished by visiting preachers, interested professors, and a graduate manager of the student Y.M.C.A. The curriculum and discipline and conduct of the students were in the strict charge of the Faculty, which to a degree felt and acted *in loco parentis*.

The extracurricular and athletic and social activities were run by the students themselves, with the advice and occasional help of interested graduates or graduate committees. This advice was unobtrusive but perhaps for that reason all the more effective. Thus faculty and other graduate members of the Senior societies maintained a lively interest in their welfare. Professor Eugene L. Richards and a group of alumni volunteers had secured the new gym. The Yale Field Corporation, composed of graduates, owned and maintained the Yale Field. A Boat Club, also incorporated, owned the boathouse, which had been erected by popular subscription. Walter Camp was not only the presiding genius of Yale football but supervised athletics generally, and committees of graduates existed for every major sport. Theoretically, and to a surprising degree in fact, the undergraduates ran their own show. They elected their own major sports presidents or managers, four of whom, together with Camp as graduate treasurer, composed the Financial

Union which received and disbursed the athletic moneys. Individually each manager was officially omnipotent in his own branch, responsible only to his captain and the University. The captain who had been elected by the players of the preceding team picked and coached the players under him. The captain of the year before might return to help out, and an occasional athletic hero from earlier years might come up for a week end or two to help whip the team into shape for the Harvard and Princeton games. But the captain ruled. Together with the manager he was responsible for the success of the season.

Strangers were often puzzled to know how Yale could be so phenomenally successful in athletics under so youthful and changeable a system of management. The answer had two parts: the captains and managers were generally very able men, and they almost always took advice. In fact, athletics had come to interest the graduates so intensely that in every major sport, more or less informally, there had come to be a group of men, or there was one man, whose word made unwritten law. Thus Robert J. Cook '76 had brought system and success to Yale rowing and made Yale crews pre-eminent from the mid-eighties. Walter Camp, who had done the same for football and who occupied the untitled position of ruler of the whole system, attributed Yale's success to what he boldly called "the czar principle" backed up by Yale loyalty.[19] I should point also to the talents and abilities enlisted, to the seriousness with which victory and defeat were taken, to the care with which the lore of the game was analyzed and handed down, and to the sense of shared responsibility and the tradition of cooperation between graduates and undergraduates for the name and welfare of Yale.

Reviewing the government of College affairs one is impressed by its informality and complexity. It was neither democratic nor purely monarchical, neither unified nor genuinely localized. The students had no student council but governed themselves by their own leaders, some elected in mass meeting, some chosen by specialized teams or boards, others inherited from their predecessors. The graduates had no graduate council. But local alumni associations had been organized. Through the six elected members of the Corporation they shared in the over-all control of the institution; and, through taking a private interest, individuals had a part also in the direction of important student activities. The Faculty, in turn, governed absolutely in some spheres but were prevented by custom and sentiment from interfering in others. In a word, Yale was run by a series of overlapping authorities who by usage knew what authority belonged to each.

Undergraduate life, however, was by no means as confused and confusing as its constitutional philosophy. For it had in the Class system a great principle of order and regularity. Almost all colleges accepted and promoted their students by Classes, and about these arbitrary age groups all sorts of functions had developed. But at Yale the Class unit was particularly sacred. It seemed doubtful that there was any other college where so many Class functions had been created or where all the great activities were run so generally along Class lines.

> Men study together for two years . . . before there is any appreciable break along the elective lines. For two hundred or more days in the year Yale College is gathered by classes in Battell Chapel . . . their prayer meetings and their Bible study meetings are by classes. Of course, they row and play football and baseball by classes. They loaf by classes, squatting together on the Fence rails. Again, in the College, and as a feature quite peculiar and most important, they break into secret societies by classes. They run their college journals by classes. They take up the various customs and privileges of college life, from the carrying of a cane and the wearing of a silk hat to the perfect liberties of top spinning and "nigger baby," by classes.[20]

Within Yale College intimate friendships across Class lines were perhaps less common than in other places. To a Yale man his Class was the first focus of his loyalty. Yet no Class could be a law unto itself for there was also a hierarchy of authority. Each of the four units had its own distinctive functions and recognized position, and each passed in turn through the time-honored progression of experiences.

The Freshmen were the neophytes, the learners, and the Sophomores to a degree the teachers. The custom of hazing had happily faded into the barbarian past. The Banger (Sophomore cane) Rush was no more. As for the shirt and push rushes between the two lower Classes, these had been reduced to a single affair at the Grammar School lot on the opening night of the year. In compensation Freshmen had to run the gantlet of the upper Classes on the night of Omega Lambda Chi. And as beginning Yale men they were still underprivileged. They were not allowed to smoke a pipe on the street or campus, to carry a cane before Washington's Birthday, or to dance at the Junior Promenade. They could not play ball, spin tops, or roll hoops on the campus—Senior pastimes. If an innocent newcomer so much as approached the Fence he was apt to find the atmosphere suddenly unhealthy. Obviously Freshman year was "intended by the inscrutable wisdom of tradition to take all the vainglory out of men." [21]

But as Sophomores they had arrived—and had a duty to the lowly Freshmen. Their sense of importance was even a little trying to their neighbors. Entering into the work of the community and participating in its delightful privileges, they now managed the Sophomore societies, plunged into the myriad competitions, ran the fierce race for honors—and before they knew it had become Juniors. By Junior year the Yale man was completely absorbed. His classmates were making places on the teams. His Class ran the greatest social event of the College year, the Junior Promenade. His friends and he now took over the College publications. In May came Tap Day.

Then there was running Yale as a Senior—going hatless if one pleased—putting a hand to many things—knowing all the great men and the faculty—judging men more by what they were than by what honors they had won—savoring life instead of devouring it. But to describe the paradise of Senior year would ask for a Yale Dante. What is more important here is the hierarchy and the progression. Yale students governed themselves. But they were first trained to govern by their division into Classes, each of which had its appointed times and tasks. And no Yale man was fully educated

41

who had not known what it was to go the whole way through. Four years of Yale was not just a stretch of time. It was a career—a concentrated lifetime of experiences.

One other way of organizing and energizing the College must now finally be mentioned again: its hierarchy of honors. The classroom honors were coveted by a few. The managers and editors were men of importance to the whole Class; and athletic heroes were the heroes of the whole College, for they fought for Yale's glory. But the distinction most coveted by the undergraduates and respected by their elders was conferred by the Senior societies.

In a way this was appropriate, yet it created a tension—perhaps even an uneasiness. Outsiders asked how so exclusive a system could be reconciled with Yale's democracy. The answer was not too hard. Yale stood for equality of opportunity, not equality of reward. Family connections counted for far less than at Harvard. And Yale had always been known as a place where poor boys did not suffer from discrimination. So every man had his chance—and a totally unknown high-school Freshman could make a Senior society if he had what it took.

The trouble with this defense was that there were too few Senior societies to reward all the men of merit or achievement. Also troublesome was the fact that the societies were secretive while Yale life was open. And the societies seemed to generate loyalty in small groups while the College taught loyalty to the best interests of the whole. Fortunately the societies had in the long run always stood for Yale values. In fact they acted as a powerful compressor, holding together the bursting energies of the place. So they were democratic also in enforcing a certain discipline on the whole College. But some good men always carried away scars. And the finality and exclusiveness of the choosing created and would continue to create a faint and enduring fault line in the Yale brotherhood.[22]

In the final analysis Yale College was not just a collection of students and professors, of laws and customs, of buildings and of books, but an organic society of enormous vitality and power. It was a generous and enthusiastic community with its own memories, discipline, and ambitions—perhaps in its peculiar way as effective and successful a society as was to be found anywhere on this earth.

For all its boyishness and spontaneity, the College was integrated. Not all the customs and manners and spirit and organization of the place were of a piece. Here youth ruled, there age. Here devotion governed, there pure sense of fun. Here physical prowess drew attention from the things of the mind. There loyalty to Bones or Keys perhaps narrowed men's thought of Yale. Yet by and large it was extraordinary how the parts of the institution knit together. The customs of the place were delightful rather than savage—and the very enthusiasm of the students helped perpetuate them. The religious tradition strengthened the classics, and the classicists would support the chapel requirement. The competitions, the athletic contests, the Class system all emphasized character. The code of loyalty and team play paid intercollegiate dividends and so perpetuated itself. The old traditions and the new experiences, remingled each passing year, strengthened the Yale spirit: unmistakable, enduring, alive.

CHAPTER 3 · COLLEGE OR UNIVERSITY

A university cannot thrive unless it is based upon a good collegiate system.

—D. C. GILMAN, 1880

It is to be hoped, however, that changes in this last direction may not be carried so far as to destroy, or partially destroy an excellent college . . . by crowding down upon its immature academic population the arrangements and methods of the Philosophical Faculty of a continental university.

—*Yale College in 1884*

IN THE DECADE following the close of the Civil War the need for wider instruction and more advanced scholarship led to the development of the first real universities in the United States. But how the old-style Protestant college was to be fitted into the new-style university was a question.

When the educational history of this period is written it will be recognized that more was at stake than has commonly been supposed. For thirty years the great public battles were over the so-called elective system. But what was fundamentally at issue was the character of our highest education. If *colleges* were no longer advanced or broad enough, what should the American *university* be? What shape should it take and who should govern it? What studies should it teach, to whom, and for what social purposes? Finally, what should become the place and role of the old undergraduate colleges?

In general four solutions were tried. Out West the State universities discarded the collegiate ideal and the traditional B.A. curriculum in favor of a series of undergraduate departments specializing in vocational subjects. In the East new foundations like Johns Hopkins and Clark subordinated the college or struggled to do without it in order to concentrate on graduate teaching and research. At Harvard Eliot tried to convert the college itself into a university by the elective system. At New Haven it was proposed to build the university above and around Yale College. Which of these solutions would give durable satisfaction the age of Ulysses S. Grant had few ways of telling. But plainly some answer would have to be found to the long-accumulating dissatisfactions.

Many criticized the old college curriculum because it was too narrow or elementary. The studies should be more universal, it was argued, or instruction should be carried to a more advanced level. Among such critics were increasing numbers who doubted the value of the classics, or who disliked the emphasis on grammar, or who begrudged so much time on Greek, or who wanted to substitute the modern languages, or who were protagonists of the new natural sciences and later also of the social sciences.

Again there were scholars who were conscious of how far our colleges fell below the best Continental universities. Especially the men who had trained in Germany wanted to introduce the German ideals of free teaching and free study, of lectures rather than recitations, and of specialized investigation and research.

The colleges had their social and economic critics, too. There were those who wanted the studies to be more technical or professional or practical. Many were in revolt against sectarianism or the domination of the clergy, or any private management. Others regarded the traditional liberal arts as class education and hence undemocratic.

Again there were theorists who rejected the old faculty psychology of learning—that all men had innate faculties to be disciplined and trained—in favor of the idea that if students could be interested rather than disciplined they would study with far greater effect. Such educators also tended to believe that students had individual natures and differing interests, hence should not all be appealed to in the same way but should be allowed to choose between studies. Finally, there were those who held to no particular

45

theory of education or view of society but simply reacted temperamentally against the old and in favor of the new.

On the other hand, the established system had a host of champions. And within the old, self-governing colleges these defenders were entrenched. So for every critic there was a satisfied faculty majority, for every idealistic reformer a swarm of believers in the old liberal arts, for every protagonist of the sciences or the new vocational interests a hard cluster of classicists with a vested interest in the traditional subjects and in the old disciplinary methods of instruction.

Such being the situation, it might have been advantageous if these centers of resistance could have been by-passed and if the new university-style subjects, methods, and faculties could have been *added* to the colleges, or made the basis for *separate* institutions. Indeed, as new universities were founded they showed a tendency toward a departmentalized form, with their college of arts and letters merely one among several equivalent schools or departments. But for the older Eastern institutions such a solution seemed out of the question.

For their whole history and reputation had been made as colleges. The strength of their faculties went to undergraduate teaching. Most of their students still were undergraduates, and all the alumni who really cared and counted had taken the undergraduate degree. It was to its own college-trained graduates that each institution had to look for endowment, for trustees and advice, and for more students. And it was the colleges—the generators of idealism and moral force—which still spoke loudest for the institution's public reputation. While the lay public might fancy the word university, it was the undergraduate college that boys and parents dreamed about. So in these venerable institutions the colleges became the battleground—and the elective system the great educational issue—of what might be called their Thirty Years' War.

The elective system became the issue because it was the instrument of transition. As such it became both a weapon and a symbol. Electives held out the promise of freedom: freedom for students to choose—for teachers to teach in new ways—for scholars in the natural and social sciences to advance their disciplines—for college administrators to experiment. Meanwhile, the elective principle could be used to breach the required curriculum by introducing a few new subjects into the old-fashioned college at a time when the reformers were not yet strong enough to abolish all requirements or eliminate the dead languages at one blow. If students could be lured into new elective courses, new departments of study could be built up, and some of the lifeblood could be drawn into the technical and professional schools.

Still more important was the tendency of the elective issue to unite the attackers of the established order but divide its defenders. The literary professor saw a chance to escape the grammarian, and the scholar glimpsed emancipation from the schoolteacher and the disciplinarian. On the other hand, critics and innovators of the most varied stripe could get together on the issue. For by the elective system, and in no other way, could the clashing philosophies and methods of such subjects as advanced physics and modern novels, appreciation of art and accounting, Sanskrit and physical education and blacksmithing gain acceptance together in a B.A. curriculum. Finally the elective system was secular and democratic. Without invidious distinctions it welcomed all the new knowledge, interests, and attitudes of industrial America. A shrewder, more necessary instrument for modernizing the old colleges would have been hard to imagine.

But the man who could wield this weapon had not yet been found. Then, within three years, the administrations at Princeton, Harvard, and Yale changed hands. In 1868 the Reverend James McCosh, Professor of Logic and Metaphysics, was brought over from Ireland to be Princeton's new President. In 1871 the Reverend Noah Porter, Professor of Moral Philosophy and Metaphysics, was elected to succeed Woolsey at Yale. Meanwhile in 1869 Charles W. Eliot, Professor of Analytical Chemistry at Massachusetts Institute of Technology, was made President of Harvard—and at once stepped forward as the champion of the elective movement.

47

Had Eliot chosen to back some other theory of education, or even no theory at all, his powerful personality, administrative ability, and gift for recognizing talent in others, supported by the prestige of his office, would by themselves have made him a notable figure at Harvard and in American education. The more so as Boston had long been a nursery of philanthropists, and Harvard was profiting earlier and more fully than any of its rivals from the newly rising tide of industrial prosperity. As it turned out, Eliot put these resources, human and material, into the building of Harvard University. By his championship of the elective system he drew to Harvard students in great numbers and new gifts and endowments in unprecedented amounts and for all sorts of purposes. With increased means he added scholars of vigor and original interests, strengthened the professional competence of his faculties, created a great graduate school, and built up the scientific departments and professional schools. So by 1900 it was generally conceded that he had made Harvard into America's strongest and most celebrated university.

About Harvard College opinions differed. In his own faculty and among the graduates there had been decided opposition. But Eliot had the money, the patience, and the assurance to wear down the conservatives, and by 1884 the elective system had conquered the required studies entirely. In the intellectual sphere Harvard College had been changed from a small college on the restricted, disciplinary model into a swarming university-style college, whose students could specialize in all sorts of new subjects or shift as they saw fit between departments and levels of study.

Thus the achievement of Harvard University had involved the transformation of Harvard College. Some New Haven observers insisted that Harvard was converting a good college into a bad university; [1] and though they were to be proved wrong on the quality of the result, they were approximately right about Eliot's intentions. He was not building a university by simply adding advanced schools to Harvard College. For he was convinced that it could only be made by changing Harvard College into a free Continental-style university.[2] All this challenged Yale, Princeton, and many another

48

institution in two ways. Should they, too, try to become great universities? If so, would it have to be at the expense of their own colleges and by following this extreme elective method?

YALE'S UNIVERSITY BEGINNINGS

In a way Yale College had long since ceased to be a simple College. As early as the American Revolution President Ezra Stiles (1778–95) had dreamed of professorships which would allow Yale College to "rise" into a University. His successor Timothy Dwight (1795–1817) had laid the foundations of the Medical Institution, the Law School, and the Department of Theology—thus providing for the three professional Schools of the traditional Continental university.

Under Jeremiah Day (1817–46), and with the particular assistance of Professors Benjamin Silliman and James Luce Kingsley, further enlargements had taken place. In 1832 the completion of the Trumbull Gallery had given Yale the first college-connected art museum in the country. In the early forties graduate instruction outside of the three professions had been organized. In 1842–46 the building later known as the Old Library had been erected—the library collections strengthened by purchase from Europe—and the first full-time Librarian appointed.

To these foundations the Administration of Theodore Dwight Woolsey (1846–71) made substantial additions. In the summer of 1846, just before Woolsey's inauguration, professorships of agricultural chemistry and applied chemistry were created "for the purpose of giving instruction to graduates and others not members of the undergraduate classes" by the laboratory method. The next year a Department of Philosophy and the Arts was established to embrace advanced work in the arts, together with the sciences not already being taught "and their application to the Arts." From its opening in 1847 the School of Applied Chemistry was included under Philosophy and the Arts, thus giving the new Department responsibility at two levels: for graduate instruction in the arts and sciences, and for undergraduate instruction primarily in the applied

49

sciences. At first this instruction was individual and unsystematic, without entrance requirements or final examinations. The fifties saw the organization of course programs—also the gradual differentiation of the overlapping functions and the establishment of distinct degrees. On the one hand the degree of Bachelor of Philosophy was authorized and a School of Engineering was added to the School of Applied Chemistry (1852); these proving successful at the undergraduate level, they were named the Yale Scientific School (1854), endowed by Joseph Earl Sheffield, and in 1861 renamed the Sheffield Scientific School. Meanwhile the informal graduate instruction in philosophy, history, language, and pure science had attracted only a handful of students; but in 1860, on appeal from the Scientific School Professors, the Yale Corporation took the pioneering step of authorizing the degree of Doctor of Philosophy so as "to retain in this country many young men, and especially students of Science who now resort to German Universities . . ."[3]

While the need of the nation was for both scholars and engineers, the public response had been so one-sided that what had started as a Department of graduate studies, with a chemical laboratory attached, had grown into a substantial undergraduate School of applied sciences, with only meager graduate extensions. Yet this undergraduate School itself had had to struggle for existence. In the forties science had been viewed with so much indifference that had the Silliman and Norton families not put their own money and talents into the venture the School might not have come into being. When the Corporation appointed John Pitkin Norton and Benjamin Silliman Jr. '37 Professors of Agricultural Chemistry and Applied Chemistry, it was on the understanding that no charge should be made against College revenues, and that they should support themselves by student fees and on the interest of a small donated fund. These two pioneers had to buy their own apparatus and at first pay rental to the Corporation for the old President's House in which their laboratory was installed. "The College indeed had no money to give, but even if it had it is more than doubtful if it would have given it. . . . The impression, indeed, seemed

50

generally to prevail that chemistry, like virtue, must be its own reward." [4]

When the Engineering School was established under Professor William Augustus Norton—and again when a chair in metallurgy was authorized (1855)—self-support was required and self-management expected. In 1854 the Corporation of the College did endow the two Schools with the Yale name; and in 1856 President Woolsey joined with Silliman and others in a public appeal for funds. But it was not until Joseph E. Sheffield stepped forward, bought the Medical Institution on Grove Street, enlarged and equipped it, and endowed the professorships that the Scientific School could feel any sense of security and could plan for the future.

Sheffield, a railroad builder, had an interest in engineering and an enthusiasm for the School which led him to make repeated gifts of buildings, books, funds, and fatherly attention. In 1863 the Sheffield School obtained a second external support when it was awarded the Land Grant Fund of the State of Connecticut—and Daniel Coit Gilman, B.A. '52, William H. Brewer, Ph.B. '52, Daniel C. Eaton, B.A. '57, and Addison E. Verrill, B.S. Harvard '62, were added to a faculty already distinguished by William Dwight Whitney, B.A. Williams '45, in modern languages, Samuel William Johnson in agricultural chemistry and George Jarvis Brush, Ph.B. '52, in metallurgy and mineralogy. On being appointed Professor of Physical and Political Geography, then also Secretary of the Sheffield Board, Gilman transferred his ambition and fertile imagination from the stagnant librarianship of the College to the teaching of modern subjects and the particular promotion of the Scientific School. In this endeavor Brush, Treasurer of the School, proved an invaluable partner. Gilman was quick, eloquent, and ingenious; Brush had slow judgment and great tenacity. The one started the nails, the other drove them home. By 1871 a fourth year preparatory to mining, and three-year undergraduate programs in agriculture, natural history, premedical studies, and a "Select Course in Scientific and Literary Studies" preparatory to business, etc., had been added to the applied chemistry and civil and mechanical engineering with which the School had started. Thomas R. Lounsbury, B.A. '59, had been made Professor of English. And it was widely acknowledged that the Sheffield Scientific School had achieved a success quite unmatched by the Lawrence Scientific School at Harvard.

Meanwhile Yale as a whole continued to expand. Its enrollment reached 700, then 800. Still going forward under Woolsey, it established or filled eight new professorships, including chairs in modern languages and history. This was one more than the total number of previous endowments. In 1861 Yale awarded the first Ph.D. in America and in 1863 conferred this degree on J. Willard Gibbs. The next year Benjamin Silliman, patriarch of Yale science, passed away. But headed by his son-in-law, James Dwight Dana '33, Yale's scientists in both College and Scientific School were adding to its international reputation. In 1866 Hubert A. Newton '50 made himself famous by predicting the return of a meteoric shower. The same year the endowment for the Peabody Museum of Natural History was received; and in 1870 Othniel C. Marsh '60, the second Professor of Paleontology in the world, led a Yale bone-digging expedition out to the West. In 1864–69, through the generosity of the Street family and the aid of men like Gilman, the first college Art School in the country was launched. In 1867 the Jarves Collection of Italian Primitives was received on deposit. The same year the reinvigorated Divinity School instituted the B.D. degree. And in 1871 a Board of Managers was appointed to administer the Winchester gift for the eventual development of a full-fledged Observatory in connection with the College. So in a variety of ways the elements for a many-sided modern University had been coming to hand.

Yale also felt the new ideas, and pressures toward the reshaping of the institution. Indeed it was widely sensed that a critical moment had been reached. The undergraduates debated whether the old College curriculum was any longer up to "an age in which men move by steam and their thoughts by lightning." [5] A "Young Yale" movement among the recent graduates argued strenuously for lay representation on the Corporation and for more progressive policies. Charles Phelps Taft '64 could not see why Yale should hesitate at German ideas; and he urged the creation of a real University, with a great library, scholars called from other institutions, and professors giving lectures and engaging in research and publication.[6] By far the most considered and substantial proposals, however, came from within the faculty.

In 1870 James Dwight Dana—who was Silliman Professor of Geology and Mineralogy in Yale College, Chairman of the Peabody Museum Board, and long champion of the rising Scientific School —asked the alumni and public to recognize the existence of what he called the "Yale University Scheme." The next year he enlarged on his ideas in a pamphlet on *The New Haven University: What It Is and What It Requires.* According to Dana, the friends of Yale were not aware that Yale College was fast becoming a subordinate member of a larger University. This New Haven University already had a pair of undergraduate colleges, each of which would soon have two years of required studies and two years of broader electives, for he thought that the Sheffield course would soon be lengthened to four years. The special studies of the Academical Department * would be the languages and literatures, mathematics and astronomy, history, philosophy and political economy—but it would also teach such elementary science as liberally educated amateurs should command. Vice versa, the Sheffield students would specialize in the sciences and engineering but would receive such instruction in English, the modern languages, philosophy and the social sciences as was needed for a well-rounded education. Each Department would teach the other's special subjects but in a different and more generalized way. A few men in the faculties and the more costly apparatus could be shared. Thus the varying interests of the students

---

* Academical Department was the official title of the College part of Yale from 1852 through 1914. Academic as an abbreviation for Academical apparently came in in the late nineties; President Dwight continued to use the older form, Dean Wright used both. Around 1910, to the dismay of the older College men, the Sheffield undergraduates shortened the name still further to Ac. As a nickname Sheff seems to have originated a good deal earlier.

53

would be subserved without attacking the classics and without introducing so many optionals as to break down Class unity or habits of thorough study.

But these two colleges, Dana insisted, were not the University. Rather they were the undergraduate parts of its great Philosophical Division and, as such, "tributary" to the postgraduate Schools which now offered two years' advanced instruction for the Ph.D. or C.E. degrees. Actually or potentially, the Department of Philosophy and the Arts contained five postgraduate Sections or Schools: the Philological School; the Section of Intellectual and Moral Philosophy, Political Science, and History; the Section of Mathematics, Physics, and Astronomy; the Sheffield Postgraduate Section; the Engineering Section. In addition to this grand Division, the University had four other self-governing Divisions or Departments—the Schools of Theology, Law, Medicine, and Fine Arts. Dana took a hopeful view of the prospects and asked recognition of their needs.

No less bold was the scheme proposed by the second Timothy Dwight. As Professor of Sacred Literature in the Theological Department, Dwight had just participated in a constructive campaign to raise funds to rebuild that School. Yale College, he suggested, had outgrown its old unpretending name; and in any case it was time to recognize that the University must be greater than the College. The wider studies of the University should be divided into separate Departments or coequal Schools, each giving its own instruction, each supported by the full loyalty of all Yale, the stronger helping the weaker, and all together sharing fairly in the total funds. The Scientific School should be accepted as a coordinate Department, not merged. The Academical Department should retain its Christian, classical, and disciplinary emphasis, but should encourage discussions in class and improve the teaching of the classics or its battle would be lost. It was also important that Yale should develop its informal postgraduate instruction into a regular Graduate School, with its own professorial chairs and with the function of training scholars or specialized instructors to replace the inefficient and impermanent corps of tutors in the College. The Art School should "bear on" students in all the Schools.

54

In addition Yale should have a central or supradepartmental organization. The President should not just sit and teach with the Academical Department; the several Faculties should meet together on general issues; and the University should have its separate University funds. Dwight recognized the importance of the alumni, as representatives of Yale in the world and as Corporation members giving advice and help in the larger planning. He also spoke for a Chapel, centrally located and with a chime of bells. And it was he who urged that the Brick Row be replaced with a quadrangle worthy of a University and built of stone. "The glory of architecture lies in stone." [7] Yet what he stressed most of all was Yale's need of funds—funds for every Department—funds for the central University.

Again in 1871 a strong committee of professors, acting on behalf of all the Faculties, submitted to the Corporation, graduates, and benefactors of the institution a statement of the Needs of the University. Re-emphasizing many of the points of Dana and Dwight, the Committee pointed out that the Corporation had the power to grant University degrees but that the corresponding Departments of instruction were inadequately developed. It emphasized the importance of the Library to a seat of learning. It defined the aim of the College as liberal culture by mental discipline, but insisted that the College must advance with the progress of science and letters. So new professorships in English, modern languages, physics, and history were needed, together with a building for the teaching of chemistry and physics and a new observatory tower for amateur instruction.

By contrast the Scientific School was a college for "the new education" which, while not dispensing with books or literary culture, took for its object the study of material nature and for its distinct method "instruction by object lessons" (the laboratory method). This School prepared for careers in pure and applied science, though not to the total neglect of English, French, and German, or other subjects of modern importance. Hence financial wants of a varied kind. In similar fashion the needs of the several professional Schools were analyzed.

55

What was really required to fill up the University scheme, it was argued, was advanced instruction in all the great branches. In graduate instruction almost everything was still to be done. Endowments for from six to twenty chairs were wanted. No hard and fast line should be drawn between the graduate and undergraduate Faculties. Rather a University Council should be created to bring the Schools into "more effective cooperation." And it should be recognized that certain administrative officers belonged to the University as a whole. First and last "a large increase of means must be had . . . before the conception of a true university can be realized."[8]

These proposals, in their range and detail, demonstrated how much had already been done toward the creation of a true University—how forward-looking were important elements in the Faculties—how critical was the need for funds and still more funds. The Faculties had apparently flinched at presenting anything like a definite total of the sums desired, but the scattered figures for various Schools, the Library, and the Museum could hardly have been less than two or three million. Dana had suggested as an over-all figure three and a half millions.

But such financial requirements were too staggering; Yale men as a whole were conservative. Many did not see the necessity of such radical changes and some were positively opposed. They wanted to continue the clerical tradition of the Corporation and to install a minister as President. What they believed in was the College. By comparison the needs of graduate instruction hardly seemed important. And not a few graduates, on the faculty and Corporation as well as in public life, were suspicious of the Scientific School. For the Scientific School was materialistic in spirit. It let down Yale's standards. It gave a Yale degree for only three years of study—and that study without either Greek or Latin. So the urgency of remaking Yale College into a coordinated University, with the "outside" departments brought "inside" and all made equal, hardly appealed to the majority.

It happened that these conservatives had found a spokesman who could state their views with eloquence and conviction. This was Noah Porter, Clark Professor of Moral Philosophy and Metaphysics in the College and Instructor in Didactic or Natural Theology in the Divinity School. In 1869 Porter had published a widely read defense of the traditional concept of education in *The American Colleges and the American Public*. One gathers that it was partly in warning against his collegiate emphasis that Dana and Dwight had made their pronouncements. But when, significantly on the day after the publication of the forward-looking address of the Faculties, the Corporation proceeded to elect Noah Porter President of Yale, the die was cast. As a tribute to Theodore Dwight Woolsey Yale did organize an endowment drive. But instead of three millions the goal was set at $500,000—and finally only $168,000 was raised.[9] Woolsey himself, like Jeremiah Day before him, was elected to the Corporation. But his collaborator and friend and successor in office, Noah Porter (1871–86), proved to have none of his innovating forcefulness.

THE CONSERVATISM OF NOAH PORTER

In the twentieth century so much has been said against Porter that it is not easy to return to the mood of his times and do justice to the man or his policies. To the world at large he was known as a philosopher with an international reputation, a scholarly writer, an editor of dictionaries, and a respected authority in the field of education. In person he was a most gentle and kindly man, shy and unassuming, and a believer in spiritual things—in many ways a sympathetic and winning product of old Yale.

To Porter the word University sounded pretentious. Instinctively he preferred the modest old name, Yale College.[10] With simple fervor he clung to the immemorial mission of educating young men to be citizens. Having offered graduate instruction himself, he questioned whether the American public was yet ready for real graduate schools. And he could not bring himself to a wholehearted belief in the Scientific School or the newer subjects of instruction.* The fact was, his whole faith was in the College. He believed in

* The story comes down that a visitor once found a sign posted on Noah Porter's door: "At 11:30 on Tuesday Professor Porter will reconcile science and religion."

its young men, its social life, its Class system, its moral purpose, its discipline, and in its traditional structure and method of instruction. So he found it hard to see how the sciences could be given a larger place without displacing what was really essential in the curriculum. And as for the elective system, that threatened the whole structure.

With the President this was not simply a matter of emotional prejudice but a rational and carefully worked-out theory of education.[11] To Porter—as to so many Yale men before and since—College meant something solid and shared: a communal experience that was organized and balanced. Such a system had several parts.

First came the moral and social training—the parental supervision and the lessons of collegiate living. What the members of a Class learned from each other was certainly as important as what they learned from their books. And the enforced intimacy of the whole College community was an educative force beyond imitation. Secondly the formal instruction should have a proper order. It should begin with exact studies and memory training in the languages and mathematics—the tool subjects. It should culminate in philosophy and a broad and generous introduction to culture—what we would call the sciences, social studies, and history. And every student should take the same studies; for these materials gave a foundation of inestimable value, alike to the men who would later study for the professions and to those who would make themselves leaders in practical affairs. In the third place, the discipline of having to do hard and unpleasant work was indispensable. "The student often most needs the discipline to which he is least inclined," President Porter would say.[12] This taught self-sacrifice and gave a man readiness and power.

Particularly was this so if the training were in Greek and Latin. For, like his colleague Thomas A. Thacher, Porter thought "no kind of intellectual athletics more useful . . . than the reflective analysis of classic sentences." "Language," said Porter, "is the chief instrument of intelligence," and "the study of language the most efficient instrument of discipline," i.e., of learning and memory. Among languages and literatures Greek and Latin were superior

58

NOAH PORTER
Eleventh President of Yale, 1871–86

in their structure and their content. The classical languages also gave the roots of modern languages and literatures, Christianity, and science. The ancients, so unlike Americans, opened a wider world through their still pregnant and unspoiled writings. The classics had been the immemorial staple of learning and gave the B.A. degree its abiding meaning. Porter added that modern knowledge could be got through modern living and that vocational studies were neither broad nor deep. Education should have a higher aim than professional preparation. "A hard and positive narrowness of mind is the besetting danger of the science and literature of the present day." [13]

Again, it was not for colleges to indulge the whims of youth or pander to the prejudices of the specialists. Studies that at first seemed remote might later prove the most valuable. Porter questioned the assumption that the elective system had the magic to make students eager and industrious, and thought even the most wearisome routine better than the superficiality and indolence which electives were likely to encourage.

But why could not the College teach both the classics and the modern sciences and add specialization to this old-fashioned discipline? One reason was cost. A second was that the students did not know what careers they were preparing for. Still a third reason was the backwardness of the American preparatory schools, which were incapable of taking over the full burden of a liberal education. But the chief reason was that a pint bottle could not be made to hold a quart. Yale's aim was still to provide the "general and generous" *foundations* of a liberal education. The Bachelor of Arts could not hope to be a finished product, but he would have the indispensable foundation for culture and effective work.

From all this it followed that Yale was something of a school, with a schoolteaching job. And if teachers were to be effective, said Porter, they should teach with authority, even though this was difficult in an age of skepticism. Teachers should take a personal interest in their students and should color the subject matter with their personality. Better the simplehearted teacher with strong convictions than the dispassionate skeptic or the rhetorical demagogue.

59

Porter approved a man like Professor Thacher—severe but loving, gentle but just. Both men believed that a teacher's vocation in a college or a great university was not primarily to advance science, or the reputation of the college or himself, or simply to examine pupils—but to become their thorough teacher and warmhearted guide. As a teacher President Porter himself was anything but exacting and severe. On the contrary, the Seniors found him sweet tempered and gentle to the point of indulgence. But he supported the conscientious drillmasters in their work. And he did not favor founding chairs for research. Teaching and research should go together; scholars benefited from having to present their theories to students in organized and convincing form. So were perpetuated traditions of scholarship and teaching that were destined to give shape to the College Faculty for generations and a direction to University policy which can be felt to this very day.[14]

With a like fatefulness, Porter's educational philosophy affected both the public position and the internal development of Yale.

To the public, the contrast with Eliot was dramatic. Instinctively Porter shrank from the contest. He was no trenchant die-hard but a sincere idealist, disposed to think well of the past. Yet Eliot's ideas and methods did such violence to his convictions that he could not but recoil. In his inaugural address he insisted that the highest education should be intellectual, disciplinary, ethical, religious; he protested also against the plan of elective studies as tending to narrow and shorten the liberal education while giving students a liberty they were not yet wise enough to use. In 1884 he would head the list of college presidents who begged the Overseers not to drop Greek from the Harvard admissions requirements. And the next year he was invited to participate in the debate in which the strong-willed President of Princeton attacked Eliot to his face and excoriated his policies. So in the public eye the gentle Noah Porter and the fiery McCosh came to be known as the great expositors and preservers of the conservative ideal of collegiate education.[15]

Meanwhile, within the portals at New Haven, Porter's Administration gave the larger Yale a delayed and rather one-sided development. As an emerging University Yale was affected in its government, in its funds, in its organization, and in its ruling ideas.

The first question was one of support. It stood to reason that a University would need a broader base than had the Congregational College. Exploring new interests, appealing to a wider clientele, and requiring great increases in resources, the University might also have to invite new partners into its management. There were those who felt that such growth was impossible under religious control. Ministers of the gospel were thought to be too narrow and dogmatic or no longer capable of raising the necessary funds. Said Eliot, "A University cannot be built upon a sect." [16]

By halting steps Yale moved toward lay government and a wider alumni participation. In 1869–70 the Young Yale movement had presented its case. In 1871 the Connecticut Legislature amended Yale's Charter to allow the substitution of six men to be chosen by the alumni for the six senior senators. But all suggestions that the ten Successor Trustees should themselves submit to election, or should at least choose for successors laymen as well as Connecticut clergymen, were resisted. In 1883–86, as the end of Porter's administration approached, a spirited debate was carried on in the public press which only hardened opinion on both sides. Meanwhile it was discovered that the clerical members of the Corporation continued to dominate. Also, the alumni representatives—presumably elected for six-year terms—liked to succeed themselves, and other graduates hesitated to run against them. Hence comparatively little new blood was brought into the Corporation. So as the close of the century approached silent pressures would again be felt toward electing laymen to the Successor Trustees, and Midwesterners among the laymen, to the end of giving Yale's graduate constituency a larger and fairer share in Yale's management.

The same division of feeling and the same slow drift were observable in the presidency. In 1871 not a few had been in favor of breaking the ministerial tradition and electing a layman—perhaps Daniel Coit Gilman—to Yale's highest office. But the Reverend Noah Porter had been chosen. And Gilman went as President to California—then to build America's first graduate university at Johns Hopkins. In 1886 again, though several lay names were put forward, once more a Reverend Professor from the Theological Faculty—Timothy Dwight—was selected. But this time Yale's graduates had the satisfaction of knowing that Dwight was a man of business capacity as well as a theologian. So half their point had been gained. Then in 1899, with the selection of Arthur Twining Hadley, Yale's first lay President would be chosen. It remained to be seen how soon secularization of the Corporation would follow —and how soon the spirit of the University would reflect these slow shifts in control.

The effect of these changes on Yale's finances also remained to be measured. The accession of the elected graduates to the Corporation had not increased the income of the University as much as had been hoped. In fact, while some graduates had grumbled about underrepresentation, the Faculties and Schools had had to complain of a constant undernourishment. The great cry of the planners of 1870–71 had been for more funds. And as time went on Yale's poverty, by comparison with Harvard's new wealth, became more and more marked and unfortunate. A number of welcome gifts for new buildings were received. But graduates seemed more eager to subscribe to boathouse and gymnasium than to the cause of teaching and investigation. In 1890, therefore, in an effort to organize the appeal for support on an annual basis the Alumni University Fund was started. No doubt Porter's reluctance to solicit, plus dissatisfaction with Yale's clerical conservatism, had delayed the coming of prosperity. And certainly when President Dwight showed himself more sympathetic to the business element he did distinctly better. But it was yet to be demonstrated that the loyalty of Yale's graduates could be brought to underwrite the full development of a many-sided University.* [17]

* In 1876 Gilman had estimated the property of Harvard College at more than five million dollars, that of Yale at about the same as the new Johns Hopkins University: three and a half million dollars. The income-yielding funds of Harvard were over three millions, those of Yale a million and a half. The annual revenues Gilman estimated at about $387,000 for Harvard, $200,000 for Johns Hopkins; while Yale's expenditures for its Academical Department were $126,000.

By 1900 Harvard's funds had grown to thirteen millions, but Yale's only to five. A few years later, when the University was seeking support from

A University organization and a University feeling were no less important—and difficult to realize. Yale by 1871, as we have seen, had many of the constituent elements of a University. People even spoke of it as such. But in law, in sentiment, and in administration Yale remained a College—a College with incidental appendages which made out the best they could. It was for this reason that Dana had asked recognition for the Sheffield college and the postgraduate Sections. This was why Dwight and the committee of professors had urged the establishment of an inter-Faculty council, and of a University Administration with responsibility for every School and with its own funds.

Porter and the conservatives were not persuaded. In 1872, on recommendation of the Academical Professors, the Corporation voted merely that "whereas Yale College has, by the successive establishment of the various departments of instruction . . . attained to the form of a University," thenceforward Yale College should be "recognized as comprising the four departments of which a University is commonly understood to consist, viz: the departments of Theology, of Law, of Medicine, of Philosophy and the Arts." [18] By this vote the Corporation recognized the existence of the University so far as to enlarge the Department of Philosophy and the Arts, which was now made to include the Academical Department and the Art School as well as the graduate courses and the Scientific School. Yet the several Faculties of Arts, Science, and Fine Arts were not merged. The Department of Philosophy and the Arts was given no inter-Faculty council, no head, and no funds. The graduate Faculty remained almost entirely a borrowed faculty, with only two graduate professorships, no full-time men, and no formal administration. The Art School was not used for the instruction of students generally and came to be attended almost exclusively by women. And the struggling Scientific School, for all its past achievements and theoretical inclusion, was not any more warmly embraced or supported.

Mr. John D. Rockefeller and was asked to account for this difference between Harvard and Yale, Secretary Stokes gave as the first and main cause: "Noah Porter writ large."

Porter did not favor a central council or Administration and, trained as he was, he could not bring himself to regard the other Schools as meriting comparison with Yale College. He even disregarded strong advice about giving them a fair share of his personal attention.* His was therefore a union of unequals in which nearly all the funds and prestige and students and attentions continued to go to the parent state—Yale College. In particular, Porter so neglected the Scientific School, and showed in so many ways his disregard for its purposes and welfare, that the remembered hardships of its beginnings were hardened into an enduring resentment and distrust. In 1871 a separate Board of Trustees was incorporated. In 1881–82, urged by Joseph Sheffield himself, the Scientific School Trustees obtained a new charter from the State, which would make secure and complete their control over their own funds. Full fifty years afterward it would be remembered that Porter had attended the meetings of the Governing Board just three times, and then merely to deal with the Washington's Birthday disorders or to ask that the Sheff students also should be made to attend chapel.[20]

In fairness it should be noted that a part of Porter's neglect of the Scientific School was due to overwork. In addition to the presidency he carried a full schedule of teaching and writing, editing and disciplinary duty. In fairness it should be added that the students and graduates of the College were no more broad-minded than their President. They made some friends among the students in Sheff or in the professional Schools. They encouraged such individuals, when they were good athletes, to come out for the College teams. But they looked down on the Scientific School because it was scientific and because it was easy, because it had no dormitories or adequate social system, and its men were sometimes of lesser ability or from more limited backgrounds. It should be recog-

* "We hold it to be even self-evident," Professor Dwight had warned, "that, if the governing body of any institution or of any country give their thought to one part of it alone, or if they manifestly place one part in their thoughts above the others, these other portions will . . . suffer in their life in consequence. Neglect, if it be only partial, always checks and dwarfs the thing neglected." [19]

nized, finally, that this stressing of inferiority tended to breed in Sheff's Officers a sensitive, almost aggressive pride. It strengthened their resolve to keep Sheff different, and a three-year college. Having had to depend on themselves, they made a stubborn virtue of independence.

It followed that when Timothy Dwight (1886–99) succeeded Porter in the presidency there were some things he just could not do. He could at once get the Connecticut Legislature to give Yale the legal title of University (1887). Like Hercules he might labor to provide Yale with a set of buildings worthy of a splendid University. He could work to improve Yale's organization, give the Graduate School its own management, put a Dean in charge of each School, and thus make himself the President of the institution as a whole. Again he could support Director Weir of the Art School and give his heartfelt friendship and cooperation to Director Brush of Sheff. The graduating exercises of the College would be transformed into a University ceremony of impressive dignity, with degrees awarded to the graduates of all the Schools. And in and out of season Dwight would urge the men of Yale to be loyal to all Yale.

But alone he could neither change the status of Sheff nor obliterate its suspicions. Nor could he make the College, which remained so much the strongest and most talented element in the University, pretend that the other Faculties or Schools were its equal. Only slowly could he build up University funds. Least of all could he hope, or even wish, to undermine the autonomy of the several Schools. For all his insistence on an even balance and loyalty, Yale remained a one-sided republic—a University in law, and with growing professional Schools, but in sentiment still a great College with university appurtenances.

Particularly was this true because of what had happened—or had not happened—to the College curriculum.

CHAPTER 4 · THE ELECTIVE STRUGGLE

In laying the foundation of a thorough education, it is neces-
sary that all the important mental faculties be brought into
exercise. . . . If the student exercises his reasoning powers
only, he will be deficient in imagination and taste, in fervid
and impressive eloquence. If he confines his attention to
demonstrative evidence, he will be unfitted to decide cor-
rectly, in cases of probability. If he relies principally on his
memory, his powers of invention will be impaired by disuse.
In the course of instruction in this college, it has been an
object to maintain such a proportion between the different
branches of literature and science, as to form in the student
a proper balance of character.

—Faculty Report of 1828

The notion that any body of men can now regulate the studies
of youth by what was good for themselves twenty, forty, or
sixty years ago is one which is calculated to ruin any institu-
tion which they control. . . . On the other hand, the system
of heterogeneous and nondescript electives . . . can never
command the confidence of sober teachers.

—William Graham Sumner, 1884

In the last quarter of the nineteenth century the elective movement laid siege to college campuses across the land. Where the institution was new or weak or under public control, or where the
resources were great and university ideas were in the ascendant, elective practices made rapid inroads. Where the college was small and
solid, or under strict denominational control, the challenge of new

and alien values was for a long time repelled. But where men wanted to have both a strong college and a great university, there fierce battles raged. For it was evident that to hasten the university by remaking its college might be to destroy incalculable values.

In its early stages the Officers of Yale College sought to by-pass this problem. Their intent was to meet the need for newer subjects and methods outside Yale College. In a federated university each school could stand for a different thing, and insist on its own required courses. Then students, in choosing between schools, would do their electing at the moment of entrance, not afterward. This meant that at the undergraduate level the Scientific School would become the safety valve. All those who wanted to concentrate on the new sciences, or to be trained as practical engineers, or to substitute the modern languages for the classics, would enter Sheff.

This ingenious federal solution promised in theory to be astonishingly effective. Yet as actually practiced it was a question whether Yale derived more good from it than harm. For one thing, the College proved unwilling to eschew modern subjects entirely, kept its great scientists, and increased its instruction in political science and history. In turn the Scientific School did not confine itself to the applied sciences or stick to the principle that linguistic study was primarily a tool. Its Select Course in science and literature not only omitted the engineering in favor of English literature, but stressed the social quite as much as the natural sciences. Thus competition rather than correlation resulted.

In another way this safety valve worked only too well. The presence of an alternative undergraduate School enabled the Academical Professors to postpone facing the problem of the classics and shrug off the demands for more emphasis on the newer subjects, thus continuing with a point of view and methods of teaching that were becoming outmoded. Misusing Sheff as a trash basket also had serious University disadvantages. Intellectually, it tainted whatever Sheff began; and it advertised to the outside world the inferior status at Yale of its Scientific School.

This last was where the federal scheme worked by no means well enough. For able students were reluctant to enter—and ambitious instructors perhaps reluctant to join—a second-rate institution. Dwight had warned that something of the sort might happen; yet Porter's whole policy and conduct only emphasized this discrimination. The result was that Porter defeated his own purposes.[1] The federal device failed to divert the modernizing pressures from the College: the safety valve failed to draw off enough steam. In due course, the teachers of the newer subjects became discontented with the minor roles assigned them in the Academic curriculum. More and more parents wanted their sons to have the social advantages of the College, but without the Greek. The students themselves were sure their College was best, but envied the Harvard freedoms.

Again, Yale had hoped to develop its research and scholarship through postgraduate work. But without its own funds and professorships, unable to arouse the enthusiasm of Yale's graduates and Administration, and not even being able at first to enlist the undergraduate faculties in much specialized investigation and instruction, the Graduate School proved slow to develop. After its head start of the 1860's it lost the lead to Johns Hopkins and Harvard. All in all, the Yale idea had been that for its highest studies the University ought to rise out of the College, not drop down into it like a bomb. And for the widening fields of knowledge the University ought to allow collateral undergraduate Schools, not burst open the B.A. curriculum. But the College was unable to escape so easily.

For a few years the Academical Department did succeed in defending its integrity against all disintegrating ideas. Yet its monopoly was too great, and the collateral and superior Schools remained too neglected and weak. So was launched what to a growing minority became a struggle for liberation. On the one hand Porter and the conservatives defended immemorial values. On the other the new science and the new social pressures proved too strong to be entirely resisted. Thus a compromise between the required and elective systems had to be worked out: a compromise which would itself bequeath to the twentieth century many unsolved questions.

68

THE OLD COURSE OF INSTRUCTION

Could we return to New Haven in the last winter of the required curriculum, 1875–76, we should find Noah Porter, with his lined face and deep-set, kindly eyes, serenely engaged in teaching. Sitting before Yale's President as he lectured on mental philosophy, moral philosophy, and the evidences of Christianity would be the Seniors —among them Arthur Twining Hadley, about to become valedictorian of '76. The oarsman Robert J. Cook, and the Iowan Otto T. Bannard, later to be a power on Hadley's Corporation, would also be there—unless they had cut: a thing one sometimes did with the gray-haired President, though seldom with young Professor Sumner. Listed as underclassmen would be four others destined for the twentieth-century Corporation, among them a large Midwesterner named William Howard Taft. And other young men of some future consequence would be rooming in the old Brick Row. All told, 582 students had enrolled in the Academical Department that year. As for the Faculty, it took but a single page to list all 26—the President, 11 Professors, 3 Assistant Professors, 10 Tutors, and a Registrar. The same slim catalogue required for a full outline of the Academic course of study—or "COURSE OF INSTRUCTION" as it was more appropriately called—exactly one page and a half.

In this curriculum of 1875 the academic year was organized on a three-session basis. First there was a fourteen-week term before Christmas, followed by a winter term of thirteen weeks, and a short spring term of ten weeks, each ending in examinations. This unsymmetrical calendar responded rather exactly, as primitive societies are said to do, to the seasonal peculiarities of the place. Since there were no elective opportunities and practically no alternative studies, the courses and the terms did not need to be of the same length. A subject could be studied for just as many weeks as it merited—or as could be found for it by a busy faculty in the crowded scheme of studies.

This Course of Instruction * began with classics and mathe-

* In order to visualize the old Course of Instruction, see Appendix, Table C, p. 706.

matics, proceeded to natural science, and came to a broad ending in philosophy and social studies. First a few ancient things were studied intensively under tutors; then many modern things were examined briefly and rather superficially under the professors. This was described by an undergraduate as "alternate exercise without food and food without exercise." [2] Freshmen, for example, recited in Homer and Herodotus; in Livy, Horace, and Arnold's Latin composition; in algebra, geometry, and beginning trigonometry. Moreover they recited in these subjects continuously throughout the year. It would appear from the catalogue that Freshmen were also required to read some Roman history, attend, *mirabile dictu*, a handful of lectures on hygiene, and undergo a few preliminary exercises in composition or rhetoric. But these were strictly marginal activities.[3] Sophomores continued to study Greek, Latin, mathematics, together each term with a little rhetoric—and nothing else. Juniors took four courses at a time, but the foundation disciplines tapered off, and the range broadened. Of the Junior courses, three went to Greek and Latin or Greek and calculus, two continued in rhetoric—of which a little was English literature—three were devoted to "Natural Philosophy" or what was beginning to be called physics, and one each was required in astronomy and in logic. For his final courses the Junior could choose either rather elementary French or German or both.

If this seems crowded, compare the program for Senior year—with no less than eighteen different subjects being taught, the majority by the lecture method and a number for only a few weeks at a time. Ten professors participated. To begin with, rhetoric was continued for two terms, astronomy (for which German could be taken) for one, and in place of physics the Seniors were briefly introduced to chemistry, geology, anatomy, and physiology. There was also a very brief course of lectures on linguistics with Professor William D. Whitney. The remaining two-thirds of Senior year went to mental philosophy, moral philosophy, history of philosophy, natural theology, and evidences of Christianity, all these with President Porter; to Guizot's *History of European Civilization*, Hallam's *Constitutional History of England*, and Tocqueville's *Democracy in America,* all with Professor Arthur M. Wheeler; finally to Professor Sumner's lectures on political and social science, with the following texts: Lieber's *Civil Liberty,* Woolsey's *International Law,* and Fawcett's *Political Economy.* Also in the last term Professor Simeon E. Baldwin gave some lectures on the elements of jurisprudence and American constitutional law.

But let us not be staggered. All this was really very simple and traditional. Encountering the materials for instruction, their distribution and sequence, a medieval schoolman would at once have known where he was. For what were the studies of the first two and one-half years but the old liberal arts, whose *Trivium* had been Latin grammar, rhetoric, and logic, and whose *Quadrivium* had been arithmetic, geometry, astronomy, and music? * And what could be more orthodox than to follow the seven arts with the Aristotelian philosophies: that is to say with natural philosophy or physics, with mental philosophy or logic and metaphysics, finally with moral philosophy or ethics and political economy?

On the score of method and purpose, this curricular system again had two easily identifiable parts. We have already noticed that it was dominated by what we today should call the school-and-tool subjects, to wit: mathematics and the languages, including practical English. These were studied in small divisions by means of daily textbook assignments and remorseless recitations. Evidently the main object was training in accurate observation, accurate memory, logical reasoning, and regular work—all that with a modicum of classical culture. The reasons for such emphasis and uniformity were clear. Habit had much to do with it. The moral and social advantages of a rigorous training were of decisive importance. Not least was the fact that the common curriculum made the students compete against each other in a stiff, fair race. Under such circum-

---

* To all appearances Yale's music was not in the curriculum but on the Fence. Remembering this, I find something delicious in the third word of the catalogue note:

"VOCAL MUSIC.—Gratuitous instruction in Vocal Music is given during a part of the year (the exercises being open to members of all the Departments of the College), subject, however, to a small charge for fire and lights." [4]

stances victory amounted to something. The valedictorian was a marked man and generally became a distinguished one. As for the grammatical studies, the powers that they developed were believed to be timeless and transferable in their value: the indispensable foundation for competence in anything. Under the guise of discipline they had been emphasized by Jeremiah Day and James Luce Kingsley in the celebrated Faculty Report of 1828.* In fact they had formed the core of Yale studies from the beginning.

The Yale curriculum recognized also a second time-honored purpose: that of introducing young men to their own modern world, and to themselves. This was effected through lectures on the natural sciences by James D. Dana, Elias Loomis, and Arthur W. Wright; through Porter's encyclopedia on *The Human Intellect;* through Sumner's economic and social sciences; and finally, through the European, English, and American histories of Professor Wheeler. The coverage is so impressive that one questions whether Yale students today would be able in their whole program to cover what the Seniors of 1876 tasted—the reason being that with the advancement of learning courses now spend more time on relatively smaller segments of knowledge. Yet still the College was not satisfied. So the Seniors were required to attend lectures on law, on anatomy and physiology, and on linguistics, as well as on the evidences of Christianity. "What every educated man should know about the professions" might have been an apt description.

Yet we need to remind ourselves that this system was moribund. For it attempted the impossible—that is, to embrace all knowledge —while failing to develop a specialization that might have been quite profitable, at least to the faculty and to the more ambitious students. In consequence, everything was elementary and much too cut and dried. "As far as we can understand, in our studies, discipline stands in an inverse ratio to the interest"; so remarked the

* "The two great points to be gained in intellectual culture, are the *discipline* and the *furniture* of the mind; expanding its powers, and storing it with knowledge. The former of these is, perhaps, the more important of the two. A commanding object, therefore, in a collegiate course, should be, to call into daily and vigorous exercise the faculties of the student." *Reports on the Course of Instruction in Yale College,* 7.

Seniors of '76. "The more disagreeable and abstruse studies are, the more they conduce to that grand aim of our curriculum—discipline." [5]

Discipline and exact knowledge being the objectives, there was no room for the aesthetic. Yale cultivated the emotions, not the imagination. Recitations on texts or examinations on lectures being the method, inquiry was not in order: [6] the College valued character above intellectual curiosity. Only in its oratorical competitions, if there, did this system offer incentives to original work. And only in the classics or mathematics, and then under stultifying handicaps, could any advanced work or genuine mastery be achieved by the undergraduates. The College Officers, too, were imprisoned in the grind. Repetition from year to year being the formula for teaching, untrained graduates recruited from the high stand men were still being employed for the tutor's tasks—and constituted almost half the whole faculty.

The cohesion of the College was impressive. In its curriculum the authorities had a formula which had weathered the centuries. They had even managed to force into it the beginnings of an astonishing number of modern studies. Unfortunately, the beginnings only. Meanwhile, the demand for the modern languages, which were the keys to the learning of the Continent, was growing stronger. At the same time the natural sciences were clamoring for development. And political science was expanding with great vigor in the direction of economics and sociology. Yet the barn was already bursting. Into the hayloft of Junior and Senior years it was impossible to stuff another straw. Under these circumstances there was something inevitable in the appointment by the Faculty of a committee to bring in suggestions for optionals. [7] With that, in the fall of 1876, the College started on a road that has since had many turns but even yet no ending.

THE OPTIONALS BEGIN: 1876–83

The invasion began very modestly. First, the College year was consolidated into two terms. Next, it was provided that both Juniors and Seniors should be allowed a four-hour-a-week optional—the

73

noxious word "elective" was avoided—and a list of optional studies was announced. Finally, the classics-mathematics requirements were eliminated from Junior year, and some courses in history and social science from Senior year were made optionals in favor of the modern languages and the natural sciences. Thus German and French were increased, chemistry and zoology were moved down into the Junior requirements, new lectures by the elder Dana on evolution and cosmogony were required of Seniors, and a new group of studies in mineralogy, meteorology, paleontology, and advanced physics were listed as Senior optionals.*

President Porter and the Faculty, however, had not lost their grip. For in the main the optionals were in addition to, rather than in place of, any element of the old curriculum. They were placed in the afternoons, so as not to disturb the morning calendar of required studies. Mark also that more optionals were offered in the ancient languages than in any other discipline, even in Senior year —a year from which the classics had long since disappeared. This leads to the discovery that the new freedom of Junior year had been so safeguarded that the only optionals available until the very end of the year were Greek, Latin, mathematics, and French: that is, precisely those studies which were no longer supposed to be required. Yet instead of spending a fraction of the year on each of three disciplinary subjects, a Junior *might* now study a single one throughout the year. And in certain fields he could carry his chosen subject still further in Senior year. By twentieth-century standards this would scarcely qualify as specialization. Yet for the first time it was possible to hope that it wouldn't be long before instructors could become pioneers and students begin to concentrate in really modern studies.

So to these provisions for slightly greater freedom, slightly greater variety, and slightly greater attention to science was added the whispered suggestion that the College should not rest content with elementary work. In such limited and indirect ways began the disintegration of the old Course of Instruction, the promise of a better day.[8]

* In order to visualize the Course of Instruction with Optionals, 1876–77, see Appendix, Table D, p. 707.

The word "promise" is advisable, because for eight long years almost no progress was made. In political science objections were raised against Herbert Spencer's *Study of Sociology* as an irreligious textbook, and Sumner had to survive his battle for freedom of inquiry before the subject could grow.[9] Zoology was added as a Junior optional; and in 1881 there appeared certain courses in vector analysis and thermodynamics by a shy and quiet man named J. Willard Gibbs. The natural sciences as a whole, however, remained frozen in the status of 1876.[10] In those years American history did follow chemistry down into the Junior requirements. And new courses in English literature, Spanish, Italian, and painting swam over the horizon into the optional world. But a student could still take only one four-hour optional—or, with luck, two two-hour optionals—at a time. What could be the use of further optionals, since they only competed with each other—to say nothing of requiring more professors than the College could afford?

As a test let us examine the courses pursued by (or administered to) the young New Havener Leonard Daggett '84, who would become one of the Proprietors of the New Haven Green and live to smile as this chapter was read aloud. In order to educate himself for life and prepare for the law, Daggett took French for his Junior optional and the Senior German optional with Tutor Ripley. Also, just at the end, a little more economics with the hard-hitting Sumner, and seven weeks in international law with the urbane and stimulating Kent Professor of Law, Hon. E. J. Phelps. Otherwise he studied:

Freshman year:	Greek, Latin, and mathematics
Sophomore year:	Greek, Latin, and mathematics
Junior year:	chemistry, physics, astronomy; English and German; American history and logic
Senior year:	psychology–ethics–philosophy with Porter and Ladd; political economy and political science with Sumner; geology with Dana, history with Wheeler, law with Phelps.

With insignificant exceptions Gustav F. Gruener, future Professor of German, took the same studies. So did Yung Kwai from China, Frederick Scheetz Jones from Missouri, Allison V. Armour from Chicago, and Henry Raup Wagner from Philadelphia—all of 1884. Henry deForest Baldwin, Wilbur Lucius Cross, George E. Vincent, and their classmates in 1885 were pretty well along in the same program. Charlton M. Lewis, John Christopher Schwab, William Adams Brown, and the men of '86—W. L. Phelps, Robert Nelson Corwin, and all the young hopefuls of '87—were setting out on the same journey, step by step. In other words, these men who would later become professors of English or economics or theology, librarians or book collectors, deans or college presidents, engineers, patrons of science, lawyers, governors, or statesmen, all prepared for their variant careers with almost identical studies. The simple reason was: they had to.[11]

Most took the situation for granted and sawed wood like Wilbur Cross. Some acquired permanent "sours" on particular subjects or instructors. W. L. Phelps could not master—or stomach—the mathematics. A few men became outspokenly critical. Yale was not keeping pace with Harvard in wealth or enrollment. Yale was not taking enough account of what the schools were beginning to teach. Yale's curriculum was a place "where Virgil and Homer change from poets to grammarians." When Lord Coleridge in chapel complimented the College on maintaining the classical education and testified to the rewards from a reading knowledge of the classics, his words fell like satire on undergraduate ears. For how few there were who could with any ease read either Latin or Greek.[12]

Another point of criticism was the authoritarian attitude. The elementary instruction, the emphasis on memorizing and repeating, made automatons of the tutors and disciplinarians of the professors. There was small cheer and sparkle. The only joy in some classrooms came in sudden outbursts when, after almost an hour of rigid repression, some comical mistranslation by a student or some ridiculous slip by a tutor would touch off an explosion of merriment as violent as the repression had been austere. Students could resent the sarcasm with which the experienced professors controlled and stung their classes. A few regretted the lack of opportunity for discussion. Many more protested the system of marks, which made it seem like currying favor if one so much as approached a member of the faculty. The professors themselves, in their uncompromising dignity, seemed like the high priests of an iron faith.[13]

Not that Yale's Officers were all alike or forbidding. As Freshmen discovered, the tutors could be surprisingly individual. One would seem bent on showing up the students' ignorance. Another, perhaps teaching a subject he had not chosen, might begin with an acknowledgment of his own inexperience and the remark: "It is my business to get as much ——— into you fellows as possible." [14] Still a third type was the nervous and unhappy theologue, quite at a loss to handle the barbarians. Yet with good luck there would be at least one firm and understanding young graduate, filled with the love of the place and of his fellow man.

So also with the professors: each seemed to have developed a personality and idiosyncrasies unmistakable and never to be forgotten. Thus the senior professors of astronomy and of Latin were alike disciplinarians and conservative in temper—but no one who had ever clambered after the lank-haired and literal Elias Loomis up the observatory tower ("turn to the right, turn to the left, let go of my leg." *) would for one moment confuse him with the benign and great-hearted "Tommy" Thacher.

Of the two Wrights on the faculty—Arthur W. and Henry P.— one was Professor of Molecular Physics and Chemistry and taught by textbook and desk demonstrations, while the other was the junior Professor of the Latin Language and Literature and heard recitations in the immemorial way. But what set them apart was the fact that the first had a bushy black beard and was called "Buffalo"; while the second, gaining a new friend for every hair that fell from his head, would for more than thirty years to come be affectionately known as "Baldy." Again in sarcasm and the use of devastating irony Yale's instructors had much in common. Yet none quite matched the

---

* This is a modern translation. By all accounts what he really said was "Release the limb." Legend also has it that when a student, reciting on Loomis' text in geometry, tried to give a theorem in his own language, he was cut short with: "Not a superfluous word in the book."

brutal factualism of "Billy" Sumner, who would read from Henry George or the newspaper, or put an innocent bank statement on the board, and then tear both statement and gullible student into shreds. Another master of the art—but one who used sarcasm and irony for comic theater instead—was the rotund and ingratiating Cyrus Northrop, who was called "Gutsy" and who had a worldly air, for he acted as Collector of the Port of New Haven as well as teaching rhetoric and composition to all four Classes.

Northrop would begin by asking a division to write a composition so he could get a line on their talents. Some recitations later, as faces were lifted to him in lovely expectation, he would take the compositions one by one from the pile and, to the confusion of the author but delight of his classmates, damn each with pithy comments. In quizzing on rhetoric he used a Socratic method, setting traps in which the unwary were certain to be caught with direct self-contradictions. Governor Cross has recalled how, amid the stillness that fell upon the class after one such trap was sprung, Northrop called out his name.

"Mr. Cross, what was Macaulay's method of composition?" "According to the book, he wrote rapidly, paying little attention to details, and afterwards put everything into shape." "Is that the correct way?" "It was Macaulay's way." "Yes, but is it the correct way? Is it *your* way?" "I have never written anything except a few high school compositions. I can't write fast—without thinking. I have to think out in advance what I want to say and then try to say it."

All through the colloquy the class laughed and Northrop, beginning with a smile, laughed too. His final comment was: "There is no one way to write. Much may be said for the Macaulay way. Much may be said for the Cross way. It all depends on the kind of mind one has. Certainly you should think out ahead of time what you intend to say." [15]

In Yale College the methods might seem antiquated, but the personalities were pungent. Some of these instructors the students loved, some they feared, some they positively despised. No question but that the preoccupation with discipline cost young and old many pleasures. Every fall before the opening of College Henry A. Beers would say to his family: "Well, to-morrow the old c'rric. begins to grind again." Yet graduates would carry away memories that were indelible.* And out of these same classrooms would come careers so notable that it is hard not to believe in the power of the teaching.

One argument in defense of the system at the time carried special appeal. A *Lit.* editor might call the Yale curriculum and the Yale student life "a curious marriage of disappointment with satisfaction, mated but not matched." But his elders felt that these two halves of the Yale system were deeply related. Class loyalties were breaking down at Harvard, whereas the stiff drill in common kept all Yale together. In the mid-eighties the opinion would be that it also gave Yale's athletes an invaluable hardiness and self-discipline. So the undergraduates were by no means persuaded that the

* Recollections ranged from the warm to the icy. Many years later, in his *Autobiography,* W. L. Phelps would record this judgment: "Many professors were merely hearers of prepared recitations; they never showed any living interest, either in the studies or in the students. I remember we had Homer three hours a week during the entire year. The instructor never changed the monotonous routine, never made a remark, but simply called on individuals to recite or to scan, said 'That will do,' put down a mark; so that in the last recitation in June after a whole college year of this intolerable classroom drudgery, I was surprised to hear him say, and again without any emphasis, 'The poems of Homer are the greatest that have ever proceeded from the mind of man, class is dismissed,' and we went out into the sunshine." (William Lyon Phelps, *Autobiography with Letters* [New York, Oxford University Press, 1939], pp. 136–37. By permission of Mrs. Celeste Phelps Osgood.)

In contrast, W. L. Cross would protest against the opinion that the faculty "in those days kept aloof from their students. Nothing could be further from the truth. It is true that we did not live together in colleges. Nor was there any organized system of counselors. But every member of the faculty was available for consultation in his office. Dean Wright, whom I saw as often as once a fortnight, kept in touch with my general studies; Professor Seymour with my Greek; Professor Wheeler with my history; Northrop and Beers in turn with my English; and so on along the line. They all advised me in talk as familiar as that between father and son. My last word to their memory is that they were a delightful and noble race of men." [16]

gain of Harvard's advantages in the classroom would compensate for the loss of Yale's advantages outside.[17]

Of course this was to shift the defense of intellectual principles to nonintellectual (even anti-intellectual) grounds. And what this could mean was beginning to be noticed. In 1881 the Annual Statement to the graduates insisted that the prize winners in the scholastic and literary competitions were the only aristocracy in this very democratic community. "There is no other passport so valid." But such statements could no longer be repeated. The next year athletics were mentioned as a "flourishing department of College discipline." In the eighties crew and baseball and football heroes were the big men on the campus. The heroic age of Yale football had already begun. And not a few Freshmen arrived in New Haven, their hearts overflowing with a worship that had as much to do with pigskin as with books.[18]

Such was the posture of affairs at the moment that Harvard acknowledged the complete mastery of President Eliot and opened all but a small fraction of Freshman studies to student election.

THE BATTLE OF 1884: UPPER-CLASS ELECTIVES

In this same winter of 1883–84 the decisive Yale battle was fought. The pressures having become too insistent, a series of committees was appointed to liberalize the curriculum of each year. Considerable argument and compromise culminated in agreement at the Faculty level, and four of the strongest-minded professors—Sumner, Dana, Ladd, and Peck—were called upon to draft a memorial to the Corporation.[19]

William Graham Sumner, the protagonist of modern and advanced studies, saw eye to eye with his young colleague E. S. Dana, the champion of the sciences. But between Sumner and the Reverend George Trumbull Ladd, Professor of Mental and Moral Philosophy, there was distinct lack of esteem. Having no use for philosophy Sumner would gladly have abolished the subject, but Ladd's mental and moral philosophy still enjoyed "a consideration second only to that of revealed religion." Moreover Ladd himself, while willing to transfer other disciplines to the optional list, clung stubbornly to his own subject as a required Senior course.

With respect to the classics, Sumner was of two minds. Having studied and taught them, he still considered them a valuable prerequisite to literary or academic careers. Yet they had mischievous limitations. They seemed to him to cultivate facility rather than clarity, to teach reverence for what was written rather than a thirst for what was true, to exalt authority over new ideas. Hence to require the classics of everyone in College seemed to Sumner ridiculous. Yet once again the power of the old subjects with the conservative majority was too great.

So the reformers experimented at their own risks. Increased time for electives was obtained chiefly by removing some of the natural and social sciences from the upper-class required list. In gist the memorial they drafted came to this: French and German were to be moved down and added to the requirements of Freshman and Sophomore years. In Junior year the sciences alone, and in Senior year only the philosophy group were to be required. Finally, eight Junior and twelve Senior hours were to become elective.*

On 14 May 1884 the Faculty approved the memorial to the Corporation. Just at this juncture President Noah Porter announced "his non-concurrence in the entire scheme" and stated that "as a member of the Corporation he would oppose it." He declined to give his reasons. In his biography of Sumner, Starr records that the Faculty had consulted the President on every detail and met his every objection. Now the whole future seemed jeopardized. The Corporation appointed a conference committee. Sumner's committee thereupon reminded the Corporation's representatives that arranging the curriculum was by tradition and law vested in the Faculty; they also pointed out that, contrary to the Corporation's instructions, Porter was refusing to confer. Then one day they went to the President's office, resolved not to leave until they secured his consent. After two or three hours' bombardment Porter finally capitulated. " 'It was a brutal procedure,' said Professor

* In order to visualize the Course of Instruction with Electives, 1885–86, see Appendix, Table E, p. 708.

Dana, 'but it was effective.' " [20] For a year the scheme was on trial. Then in 1885, after insisting on the retention of Porter's evidences of Christianity, the Corporation gave final approval.[21] So the way to the complete conquest of the curriculum by the elective principle had finally been opened.

Just how these new elective opportunities should be used was still undetermined. Apparently no one had been in favor of unrestricted student freedom. Sumner himself regarded the Harvard policy as the elective system gone wild. The amateur public might see no difference between electing courses and electing programs: between the haphazard grazing encouraged under Eliot and the divided-pasture systems at Johns Hopkins and Cornell. Sumner knew better. What he favored was upper-class concentration. He would have liked to create "Schools" in different fields, with the alternate programs of study carefully planned in advance. "A university . . . ought to give complete liberty in the choice of a *line* or *department* of study, but it ought to prescribe rigidly what studies must be pursued." [22]

Sumner's Schools, however, had been blocked by the insistence on keeping general upper-class requirements. Indeed, had this not happened the idea would still have been almost impossible to put into practice because of the want of appropriate courses, of experts to teach them, of money to finance them, and of students to support them. The fact was that if Sumner had rejected the possibility of a common introduction to knowledge, others still clung to the ideal of a balanced education. And if he had embraced scholarly concentration and professional preparation, neither undergraduates nor parents were anxious for specialization. Accordingly, all the reformers succeeded in getting was the admission that to try to teach the rudiments of everything an educated man should know would result in studies so fragmentary as to produce "mental dissipation rather than mental discipline." To this was added the hope that these expanded optional opportunities would lead the students, with the personal advice of the instructor, to pursue coherent programs of study.[23]

To help the students make intelligent plans, the College now took several steps. First the elective courses were increased in numbers, reduced in hours per course so as to encourage multiple choices, and carefully located in the College calendar in order to open up progressive sequences. Already Sumner, Beers, and others had begun offering long and short courses in their subjects to meet the need of the Senior specialist as well as that of the amateur explorer. In French a two-year upper-class program was offered to carry forward from the required Freshman-Sophomore work. Old French and Old Spanish appeared. Medieval and renaissance and American colonial history began to be offered.

The most marked assistance to intelligent planning came with President Dwight's Administration which, in 1886, completely reorganized and revised the University catalogue and prefaced the Yale College section with a characteristically firm statement: [24]

> In the Freshman and Sophomore years all the work is *prescribed*. The kind and amount of study in these two years are believed to be such as are essential for laying the foundation of a liberal education, whatever the department or profession that may be pursued in after-life; and no more than is needed to give the student a proper basis of knowledge and discipline for the study of the *elective* courses which follow, and that knowledge of himself, and of the subjects before him which is needed for a judicious choice.

To promote the rational choice of elective courses "SPECIAL HONORS" in the various groups of studies were offered—rewards, in other words, as well as opportunities for a reasonable amount of coordinated elective study, pursued presumably along the lines of a student's needs or professional interests. "Distinction" in this work and the presentation of a "meritorious thesis" were expected.

But the drift was all toward exploration rather than concentration. The students preferred browsing to specialization, and fine lectures to minute mastery. Given their liberty of choice, the Juniors and Seniors of the mid-eighties elected Sumner, and then Hadley in political science, Wheeler in history, and the Senior course in law—with smaller groups finding excitement with "Balls" Tarbell in logic,* or perhaps with Seymour or Reynolds in the classics. But for the rest of their twenty hours the students began to shop around for subjects that sounded intriguing, instructors reported to be friendly or spectacular, and courses rumored to be soft. Whereas from electives which threatened hard and unrewarding work they industriously stayed away. So, as word got around, the average student used his new freedom for a conventional variety of elementary studies rather than an organized concentration or mastery. Nor could the managers of Yale College find it in their hearts to condemn a tendency which promised rewards to able young teachers and at the same time kept the undergraduates sitting under some of the best of the older men.

Thus the elective victory really brought more freedom than system into the upper-class curriculum; and the total effect was to broaden the students' responsibilities in their first two years, their liberties in the last.[26]

* Frank Bigelow Tarbell '73, Assistant Professor of Greek and Instructor in Logic, was so tall and thin he was described as "a mathematical straight line having neither width nor thickness." But he had such sincerity and a mind so close to pure reason that the '85 Seniors in his optional course in logic petitioned him to continue the course into extra hours without credit. Which he did on late Saturday afternoons. "Whereupon the utterly unheard-of scene was enacted on many a spring afternoon of men voluntarily coming from tennis courts and filling a room to standing for the sake of discussing Mill's famous chapter on Liberty and Necessity." [25]

From another one of Tarbell's classes derives the Yale College cheer. The Class of 1886 studied the *Frogs* and *Clouds* of Aristophanes with him as Sophomores. One evening in the spring of 1884 an eating group calling themselves the Thirteen Club, after celebrating the prizes won by two members, turned the chorus of the *Frogs* into a Class cheer, and gave the cheer (slowly) under the windows of Durfee where Tarbell lived:

> Brék, ek, ek, éx.
> Koáx, koáx.
> Brék, ek, ek, éx.
> Koáx, koáx.
> O-óp, o-óp.
> Parabalóu.

By a strange irony, hardly had this menacing cry risen on the air than Harvard abolished its Freshman requirement in Greek.

84

For two years no slightest shift disturbed the equilibrium of this ideological compromise. Then the plays of William Shakespeare insinuated themselves into Sophomore English, and in 1887 the half-term Junior requirement in geology was dropped. In 1888 this was followed by telescoping Junior logic and psychology into a single-term course, thus reducing the required hours from seven to six. And after President Dwight had taught the Senior course in evidences of Christianity to Juniors for a year, that, too, in practice was omitted. However inconsiderable such expediencies, they signaled the coming on again of the elective tide.

Thereafter the expanding variety of electives proved hard to contain. With the increase of courses there seemed to come an increased enrollment, more funds, a slow enlargement of the faculty, and then a still further expansion of course offerings. These had to compete with each other for a limited number of hours in each student's schedule and, just as with the optionals of 1876, the point of diminishing returns was soon reached. Hence renewed pressures to reduce the amount of compulsory study.

In 1890 the requirement of ethics, theism, and evidences of Christianity was taken out of Senior year and joined to Junior logic and psychology. And Seniors were released from all requirements except that they had to elect one of the two-hour courses in philosophy, which was interpreted to include psychology, ethics, and the history of philosophy. In other words, the ex-President's department, now under the command of Professor Ladd, could still count on five hours of compulsory study in its sphere of learning, in the last two of which students might even advance a trifle beyond the elementary level. But this consolation, if consolation it was, could not have been great. For there was no blinking the fact that philosophy no longer crowned the Yale curriculum. Once the core of Senior studies, these Aristotelian and Noachic disciplines had bowed their heads and were taking the downward path. It can have been no accident that all trace of "Evidences of Christianity" disappeared from the catalogue in 1892 immediately after the death of the aged Porter.

In these same years, 1890–93, the Freshman and Sophomore

85

programs were enlarged to make room for more rhetoric—and then English literature swallowed the rhetoric. Thus in 1892 a survey of English literature and Shakespeare's plays were taught for the first time to Freshmen by Instructor W. L. Phelps. Meanwhile astronomy, which had been removed from the Junior year to give room for ethics, managed to escape being dropped entirely by getting included in Sophomore mathematics. But this refuge was good for only three years—after which it took the same trail as geology in 1887, chemistry and zoology and evolution and cosmogony in 1884. So of the old cluster of required Junior-year sciences only physics was left. And in 1893 physics itself dropped down into Sophomore year. Since Sophomores were already required to study five full courses (Greek, Latin, mathematics, French or German, English), physics was made an alternative course. Now for the first time since 1710 it could be avoided. And so could any single Sophomore subject, Greek or Latin included. In a word, Sophomore year was no longer an inviolable whole.* [27]

Mathematically, the changes of 1893 merely added one Junior elective and one Sophomore alternative to the student's freedom.† But the implications were enormous. For by this shift the elective principle had gained entry into lower-class work. Having shouldered its way through the upper-class studies for breadth, it was now pushing into the foundation disciplines. Only too clearly the elective principle was self-expanding, and within a closed space it consumed all competitors. Immemorial usefulness was no protection to a study, for the sanction of the ages had become almost a public liability. The Faculty had tried to save the most valued requirements by placing them earlier in the course. But the Freshman and Sophomore years had finally become so crowded with refugee subjects that when physics came along there was room for

* As a necessary corollary, all the courses of Sophomore year were made three-hour courses and given an equal credit value. So was extended downward into Sophomore year the necessity of measuring course values in hour units.

† In order to visualize the Course of Instruction under Dwight, 1894–99, see Appendix, Table F, p. 709.

it only on an alternative status. At this instant the camel's nose was in under the tent.

By 1893 it had come to this. So long as a single required study remained, there was no logical stopping point. Financially one could not go too fast. Logically one could not stop going.

After 1893, nevertheless, there came a pause. Probably it was the human element which was responsible. The leaders of the Faculty were men of slow-moving conviction, not logicians. The undergraduates were afraid of what the opening up of Freshman and Sophomore years would do. And the influence of Timothy Dwight must not be underestimated.

Dwight liked variety. He welcomed English literature into lower-class studies. And he was so interested in the new learning generally that he wished he could attend the new upper-class lectures as an auditor. But the Class system, he warned, was "one of the great educating forces of college life." Like his predecessors he believed that it was an advantage for men to measure themselves against their fellows in a common set of tasks. And in the matter of electives Dwight thought the College had gone far enough. "The ordinary youth, when he enters college, is unsettled as to his future work in life. If he is not, in almost all cases, he ought to be. . . . The years between seventeen and twenty have much to tell him concerning himself. . . . Linguistic studies and mathematics are in a peculiar degree the disciplinary studies for this period of life." [28]

So Dwight elected to stand on a compulsive-elective system, the first two years of College studies being required and the second two almost entirely free. And the Faculty, having thus divided the curriculum roughly into halves, proceeded to ignore the logic of further concessions. In 1894 a resolution to open chemistry to certain Sophomores failed. And in 1895 "the Faculty entered into a very full discussion of the question of making the studies in Philosophy optional in Junior and Senior years, but . . . the general sentiment was against a change 9–12." Thus by three votes philosophy was saved; and the changes which would have delivered over Sophomore, Junior, and Senior years lock, stock, and barrel to the

87

elective system were arrested for the remainder of Dwight's term in òffice.[29]

Thus far the military strategy of the retreat has been described but not the changes of tactic and command. We have seen which subjects survived as requirements, but not which ones benefited by electives or were injured or displaced. This story is as yet imperfectly explored. But enough can be gathered from the catalogues to correct some long-standing misapprehensions and trace the outline of an interesting transition.

First it must be recognized that the reason for breaking down the required curriculum was not so much to gain admission for new subjects as it was to get them more liberty. For however elementary and fragmentary was the presentation under the old order, the various scientific and social subjects were more widely included in the programs required of all the undergraduates in 1876 than they ever were in any but the exceptional elective combinations afterward. The charge that the traditional colleges had ignored the modern subjects was therefore not true at the elementary level. What the closed system had done was to prevent a more advanced development.

If we ask which subjects were responsible for breaking this log jam, the answer is: the modern languages and the natural sciences. The subjects which first exploited the elective opportunities by the offer of additional courses were the same, plus the ancient languages and mathematics. But these traditional disciplines were rather slimly elected. So were the sciences. And German became something less than popular because it seemed too hard and impractical. So, to a degree, did French when the instruction was stiffened and the levels were raised. In fact if the modern languages had not been insisted upon in the preparatory schools and in lower-class work, it seems possible that they might have dropped to a relatively minor role in the liberal arts.

With the opening of the second phase of the elective movement in the 1880's, the political and social science courses and history completed their passage from the shelter of requirement into competitive enterprise with entire success, and the new courses in English literature flourished—whereas the natural sciences died on the vine. After the sciences were dropped out of the Junior requirements they were still offered as electives; but they were not elected. Why these subjects should have been so unpopular with Yale undergraduates—though so popular later in the State universities—is a teasing question. By all accounts the teaching was uninspired. Yet even a driving personality like O. C. Marsh,* or an enthusiastic explorer like the eagle-headed elder Dana had trouble arousing more than a momentary interest. Parental indifference and the attitudes of the classical and church-controlled preparatory schools must have been inhibiting. No doubt the inferior social prestige of Sheff had something to do with it, too. In any case, the Academical undergraduates conspicuously failed to take advantage of their opportunities in the sciences. So it was proved that English and the social studies would be taken, whether required or not; but the sciences, modern languages, and philosophy courses would apparently be taken only *if* they were required.[30]

This demonstrated that some of the arguments of the reformers, as far as the student body went, were unrealistic. Left to themselves Yale's Academical undergraduates would not elect a genuinely rounded program of subjects. Instead, what the majority found attractive were studies in their own language, nearer to their social interests, and easier to understand. What Hadley had to say about railroads seemed to the men of the nineties both entertaining and important. The fact that E. J. Phelps had been Minister to England and was counsel for the Government in the Bering Sea Arbitration naturally heightened the fascination of his classes in international law. In history such was the teaching ability of George Burton Adams that he was making his solid course on the Middle Ages a popular staple with the undergraduates. But the way they thronged

---

* The preference for Tennysons over pterodactyls in the 1880's is commemorated by the popularity of the lines:

> Break, break, break,
> At thy cold gray stones, O.C.!

89

to Wheeler's magnificent, sweeping lectures on modern Europe—
then elected American history because it was easy—was no less
characteristic. Meanwhile, alone among the languages, English
flourished. For here was not only the future enrichment of life
that Dwight praised, but more immediate rewards from the *Lit.*,
the *Courant,* and the *Record* competitions, with instructors alive to
what the students wanted. From this last point of view the ups and
downs of English in the course of its emancipation from rhetoric
are particularly revealing.

Taking advantage of the new elective opportunities, at first
Henry A. Beers and two keen young instructors, E. T. McLaughlin
and J. E. Whitney, worked out a series of courses covering the full
sweep of English literature with a touch of American authors—and
found themselves increasingly rewarded. Then ill health removed
Whitney; "Yellow-belly" McLaughlin's main energies were transferred to reading Sophomore compositions; and the distinguished
philologist A. S. Cook was brought in. Too demanding or too
scholarly for the average undergraduate, Cook emphasized the
critical analysis of literature—also dialects, Old English, and the
theories of poetry—and the elections in English dwindled. Then
in 1893, just after his appointment as Professor of Rhetoric and
English Literature, the popular McLaughlin died. And Beers
looked in vain for a man of eminence in English scholarship and
literature to fill the Sanford professorship. So it was not until young.
William Lyon Phelps carried the torch of his enthusiasm from
Freshman English (1892) to Sophomore literature (1893) to the
Elizabethan drama (1894) and the revolutionary "Modern Novels"
(1895), finally also to Cook's old course in Tennyson and Browning
(1898) *—indeed it was not until the department in the last years

* It was one of those happy accidents that Phelps began and for four years
continued his teaching with the exceptional Class of 1896. Eventually a record
number of '96 men themselves went into teaching: a few in his own subject
and many of them at Yale. One thinks of J. M. Berdan and G. H. Nettleton,
who became Professors of English in the College; and of J. C. Adams who became Director of Undergraduate Literary Activities. Among thirteen others
who made names for themselves in the University were H. E. Hawkes in
mathematics, A. G. Keller in the science of society, H. A. ("Tute") Farr in

of the century added Charlton M. Lewis, Edward Bliss Reed, C. G. Osgood, and R. K. Root that English recovered its rank of third in popularity and gradually forged ahead.[31]

This earmarks the role of accident and of teachers in elective developments. Unquestionably the factor of personality was important. As a Senior in '90 remarked: "Some men will invariably take it straight; others take it with a good deal of the Professor in it." [32] The students would elect certain professors religiously, even though their courses were by no means easy, just as they would shun other teachers who were merely pedestrian or hard. Year after year the Seniors tended to vote Hadley and W. L. Phelps their "brightest" instructors; Adams, Wheeler, and Perrin the "best teachers"; and Hadley, Adams, E. J. Phelps, W. L. Phelps, Dean Wright, and Lewis their "favorites." While Sumner's and Hadley's political economy was consistently voted the "most valuable," Sumner after the eighties did not receive a high vote as "best teacher." Probably the rise of Hadley and Sumner's transference of attention from economics to the science of society had something to do with it. Perhaps also the Sumnerian impact had become a little too brutal and pessimistic for the mood of the nineties. As one of his hearers recorded, there was in his teaching

> Something disturbing and unkind
> That left its aftermath behind.[33]

This was rather different from the generous warmth or crackling sparkle of a Phelps or a Hadley. Yet it would be a mistake to suppose that the electives were distributed entirely on a personality basis. For the upperclassmen also showed a decided preference for content and for method: for the sweeping lectures or the dramatic exposition, for the histories of the great nations or for the unheard-of novelty of a course in modern fiction.

German, E. L. ("Tubby") Durfee in history, H. E. Gregory in geology, and A. P. Stokes. At least nine '96 men became professors in other institutions. The Class also graduated Edwin Oviatt who became editor of the *Alumni Weekly*, Alexander S. Cochran who later endowed the Elizabethan Club, and the inimitable author of *Life with Father*, Clarence Day.

91

Such choices made it plain that faculty and student purposes under the new dispensation were not wholly the same. The faculty were becoming professionalized, and the more professional elements were trying to develop their subjects beyond the elementary levels. This meant adding inquiry to exposition—giving advanced seminars and courses "for those intending to teach"—trying somehow to lure the undergraduates on toward mastery.[34] As a research tool German was obviously more important than French; and the faculty were coming to be almost as much interested in Old German, Old French, and Old Spanish as in the modern literatures of those subjects—the students just the reverse. In the early nineties Sumner again tried to develop a School of Political Economy with readings in French or German in one of the advanced courses, but the students elected chiefly his introductory courses in the field.

Thus year after year the catalogue presented the spectacle of a general course or two in each of the more popular subjects, rather heavily elected. Also a whole series of specialized, semiprofessional courses in all fields which—though open to graduates and undergraduates alike—were hardly elected at all.* On the one side the more scholarly elements in the growing faculty, afire with the new German standards of scientific study and athirst to find out the roots of things, explored languages, archaeology, and the medieval foundations of the modern world. On the other the Yale undergraduates stuck to large, generous, easy courses of contemporary bearing and to the men they trusted.

The relations between students and faculty, nevertheless, were improving. In part at least the reason was that discipline as an ideal of upper-class teaching was giving way to enthusiasm. Today this hopeful improvement is generally credited to Billy Phelps. But it had begun earlier. In the eighties the lean Tarbell had shown what could be done with so unpromising a subject as logic. And Tutor Ambrose Tighe had almost made the Romans come alive. Then Hadley and Yellow-belly McLaughlin and Reynolds—who was lame and was called "Step-and-a-half" or "Steppy," later "Limpy"— had awakened the admiration or affection of their pupils. When

* See Appendix, Table G: Increase of Upper-class Elective Offerings, p. 710.

92

Billy Phelps came along with his irrepressible zest and his enormous gift for teaching, he roused not merely devotion among the students but imitation among his contemporaries. Dwight approved of this and, in his quiet and cautious fashion, helped Phelps to stand by when his rather cocky venture into modern fiction aroused the antagonism of his elders and delayed his promotion. For a year or two the Novels course had to be given up. But in due time Phelps was allowed his freedom in English even as Sumner had once survived the threatened censorship of the social sciences.[35] So all the ambitious young instructors could look forward to developing their own fields in the directions where curiosity led and where enthusiasm would bring rich rewards.

This development made the disciplinary ideal of Freshman or Sophomore teaching seem outmoded. And it emphasized as well one sobering fact: that the College as a whole had not as yet reached an understanding as to how the upper-class years should be organized or the elective opportunities best employed. The old education had been mainly by compulsion. The new education was largely by seduction. To link the two in sequence had both advantages and disadvantages.

In Freshman and Sophomore years, while the zeal and interest of the teaching were growing, the pupil was still driven, not led. He had to do tasks chosen for him by others, and he was held rigidly to almost daily tests of faithfulness. At its best "this rude process," as Professor Perrin observed, "fostered in the pupil a confidence in his own powers, an expectation of conquest and a delight in it . . ." On the other hand, he observed,

> Where three or four hundred men are forced through the same course of study, regardless of their individual preferences or tastes, there results a kind of collective or mass individuality. . . . And so this lower undergraduate life at Yale fosters mass movements of every kind; keeps alive the old 'class-spirit,' with all its objectionable rivalries and petty collisions; brings out crowds of noisy boys to fires, processions, celebrations, and open air functions of every kind . . .[36]

93

Presumably the upper-class electives cultivated individualism and maturity. It was claimed also that the modern education by seduction gave larger and more varied acquisitions. But the mental fiber of his pupils seemed to Perrin to lack "the aggressive vigor of the older days." Evidently the Juniors and Seniors also lacked a plan and purpose in their studies. After twenty-five years of experiments and compromises these two incompatible theories of higher education were still pulling in opposite directions.

CHAPTER 5 · TIMOTHY DWIGHT

> *"I judge, gentlemen . . . you have come to inform me*
> *of my election to a Senior society. I am greatly obliged to you*
> *for the invitation. I am of that society and it becomes you to*
> *go around to the Junior man."*
> *"We have."*
> *"Did he accept?"*
> *"Yes."*
> *"If he did, all I have to do, as a Senior, is to make a*
> *speech to him, recommending him to follow his illustrious*
> *predecessor—in the coming year."*
> *—Speech of* TIMOTHY DWIGHT *to a parade of under-*
> *graduates upon the occasion of the election of his*
> *successor—Arthur Twining Hadley—on Tap Day in*
> *the month of May, 1899.*

TIMOTHY DWIGHT looked forward as well as back. Meeting him
for the first time, one could be deceived. The bushy side-whiskers,
and shaggy eyebrows over a scholar's bespectacled eyes, the manner
so quietly courteous and the old-fashioned, slow-winding turn of
speech seemed to betoken in Yale's retiring President more the
teacher and clergyman than the man of affairs. Evidently he had
been born a conservative. It stood out all over him that he had been
bred in the Yale traditions. And always in his mind and speech there
echoed the thought of his descent from the great Timothy Dwight.
Yet this second Dwight, too, had the strong instincts of a builder
and ruler of men. Gently persistent where his ancestor had been
magnetically persuasive, quietly firm where the first Timothy had
magnificently commanded, without question Dwight proved himself an able and constructive executive. He was prudently pro-

95

gressive. Stoop-shouldered and humorous—was it not he who had described himself and ex-President Woolsey as "the two stoopedest looking men in the city"? [1]—he had an eye for things to come. Old Yale he labored to perpetuate, but in a nobler frame.

Even as a professor of theology he had been busied with Yale's material concerns; and in the first two years of his presidency he had acted as Treasurer, too. Hadley would remember that when he had called upon President Porter he had usually found him reading Kant; but when he called upon President Dwight he found him reading a balance sheet.[2] These balance sheets grew steadily more substantial. Between July 1886 and July 1899, according to Dwight's confident reckoning, Yale's income had increased from $263,000 to $720,000, its permanent funds from just over two millions to four and a half. When Jeremiah Day had gone out of office in 1846 Yale had owned and occupied fourteen buildings. Under Woolsey eight had been added; under Porter nine, with two torn down. Dwight had then seen that six more were torn down, leaving twenty-three old buildings—and to these he had added seventeen new. In the same period the student enrollment had grown from 1,076 to 2,684; and the Sheffield enrollment now equaled the Academic of 1886. In citing such figures he would give them emphasis by his observation that nearly one-third of all the graduates had received their degrees within the thirteen-year span of his administration.

With his faculty increasing in like proportion the total Board of Instruction, which in 1870–71 had numbered 64, now included 120 persons holding professorships, assistant professorships, or similar positions and 140 instructors on term appointments. What gratified Dwight particularly was that these gains had been confined to no single School or Department but had been shared happily by all. Relations with the Art School had been improved and a Music School had been founded. The Law and Medical Schools had lengthened their courses of training. The Department of Theology had added optional courses taught by the new seminar methods of instruction. Finally the Graduate School, by the use of electives and the organization of clubs and libraries in the various arts and sciences, had strengthened the scholarly life of the whole University.[3]

In all this Dwight had not entirely escaped criticism. Loyal graduates regretted losing the Fence and Brick Row. On the other side, some of his faculty questioned whether he was really a good judge of scholars, or whether in choosing scholars he did not accord too much weight to character and religious orthodoxy. There were those who remembered a sort of purge at the beginning of his administration, when such excellent men as Tarbell, Ripley, and Tighe had been let go, ostensibly for innocent reasons but perhaps also because Dwight was not satisfied with their religious views. There were even a few impatient research men who felt that the University was being held back for the College, and who referred with some disdain to "Dwight's School for Little Boys." [4]

Yet Dwight had insisted on being excused from teaching and handling disciplinary matters in the College. He had approved the substitution of teachers for texts. He had given each School encouragement to develop new branches of learning under its own Deans. And if he had kept referring to the first Dwight it was because he was determined to complete the university-building work which his illustrious predecessor had inaugurated.[5] "The past in its ordering has reason in itself." [6] There still spoke the conservative. But times were changing and Yale must heed "the demands of the time." So reasoned the effective administrator. Despite years of administrative care Dwight remained fascinated by the future and eager for its opportunities.

To him progress and happiness were foreordained. He could see the Departments becoming increasingly specialized and skillful and the College now needing a varied faculty. On his colleagues he urged a more intelligent distribution of labor and the further delegation of function. Men of research would be increasingly desired. But teachers should be appointed as well as scholars, and real administrators promoted along with inspiring instructors. Petty discipline should be taken from the whole Faculty and confided to men who had the "gift of prevention." Especially the College should have men of "effective character," to cultivate personal re-

97

lations with the undergraduates and stimulate their enthusiasm. At the same time the Graduate School should be more broadly developed, the professional training strengthened. In eloquent plea to Yale's graduates he urged that the coming Bicentennial be celebrated by raising funds for every one of Yale's Schools. And four or five million dollars—a mere redoubling of Yale's endowments—seemed to this conservative and clerical President by no means too much to ask, or greater than Yale's needs.[7]

The work that he had meant to do, Dwight said, was now about completed: the century of the two Dwights was rounded out. But the work of the twentieth century would be greater still. So in 1899, having brought his University to the border of the Promised Land, Yale's Moses took an almost puckish pleasure in stopping resolutely on the threshold. Not merely because he had reached the age of seventy, but because he thought the new Administration should have a little time—a two-year spell—in which to prepare plans for the magnificent age that would open in 1901, he told the Corporation that he was resigning and made them accept it. Then another thought struck him. The local newspaper had its office on Crown Street, at the head of two long, steep flights of stairs. It was noon, and the cub reporter was just about to go and collect announcements on the Corporation meeting when Timothy Dwight came up the stairs and asked to see the manager.

"I came down to give you a little piece of news. I have just resigned as President of Yale University. Thought you might like to put it in the paper." Then he went downstairs. A moment or two later he came all the way up again, put his face in the office: "If there is anything to pay for this service, please let me know."[8]

To judge by the President and his leave-taking, Yale faced no really serious problems. Dwight had such faith in the divine plan that he seemed invariably serene. By temperament, also, he was too self-possessed to advertise difficulties and too loyal to give airing to other men's doubts or undignified disputes. Indeed his devotion to Yale was so boundless and implicit that when an instructor re-

TIMOTHY DWIGHT
Twelfth President of Yale, 1886–99

ceived, and ventured to consider seriously, an offer from some other institution, Dwight could not help thinking him both disloyal and unwise. It was noticeable, too, that the President never seemed to recognize any superiority in the experiments or new solutions adopted elsewhere. So it remained a question whether he fully appreciated how much the world was changing or how serious were certain public developments—serious for all colleges and some of them particularly serious for Yale.

There was, first of all, the sheer speed of change. Industrial society was being completely transformed—and how could the College escape? After only fifty years of steam the age of oil and electricity had already begun. To the discomfiture of nocturnal miscreants, electric lights had been installed on the campus. Streetcars were now running in College and Chapel Streets—the automobile was coming—and the practice of spending week ends in New York had got a start. So also with ideas: convictions were being discarded, values made over, with revolutionary haste. Less than forty years after the *Origin of Species* the Spencerian evolutionism to which it had given birth was already out of fashion. Sumner was lecturing pessimistically about the mores. The boys were drifting into business rather than the professions, and Greek and philosophy had come to seem irrelevant disciplines. The inevitable question, accordingly, was whether colleges could keep pace with the advance of science and technology and the widening vocational ambitions. And for Yale the special, additional problem was whether its gradualism was any longer adequate or its traditionalism safe.

Again there were new political developments with unfathomed implications. In 1899 the United States had just fought the Spanish-American War, and in its optimistic and well-meaning but unplanned and disturbingly casual way was embarking on imperialism. At home the high-school idea had finally been generalized; the tax-supported State and city universities were beginning to grow hand over fist; and in an equally hopeful but unthought-out fashion American society was moving toward the provision of higher education for everyone. Yet how the private colleges were to be related to America's new foreign responsibilities or to the broadened do-

99

mestic program was far from clear. It was by no means inconceivable that, by reason of developments entirely beyond their control, the nation's most venerable institutions of learning would find their functions restricted and their leadership repudiated.

Most far reaching, however, was the drift in popular interest away from spiritual values and in favor of pragmatic results. In 1897, when President Thwing of Western Reserve felt called upon to enumerate the dangers confronting American colleges—and no one was better qualified to judge—no danger seemed greater than this growing materialism. The new attitude expressed itself in many forms, some open, some insidious. In college government, for example, the boards of trustees were coming into the hands of businessmen. While the scholarship of the faculties was growing richer, that of the superintending bodies was therefore declining. Thwing made no allusion to the restless desire of Yale's lay graduates to have a larger voice in Yale's clerically dominated Corporation. But he did point to another telltale occurrence. "Soon after the death of that pre-eminent scholar, W. D. Whitney, was held a Yale Dinner in New York at which no allusion was made to the great man." And in New Haven the signs were the same. H. S. Canby recalls some words over Whitney at a reception in one of the great town houses of Hillhouse Avenue.[9]

> There was our famous Chaucerian scholar, Lounsbury, his sparse white beard wagging under his rapid tongue, his eyes a little bleary, an epigram worth quoting with every glass of champagne. 'Why do they want to inscribe old Whitney's name on the Court House Wall? All he knew was Sanskrit. What did he ever do for New Haven?' says a banker. 'Do!' Lounsbury shoots back. 'By gorry! It's enough that he lived here!'

Again materialism showed in the new luxury and here, unfortunately, the colleges seemed to be leading. Once scholars had been so poor that in the Middle Ages the laws on begging had been suspended in their behalf. Once by definition American colleges had been "many, small, poor, sectarian, and rural." Happily not all colleges yet had such luxury as could be observed in New Haven or in Cambridge. The great British universities, Thwing suggested, would have had more influence if they had kept to plain living. "Our peril is that increasing luxury shall result in decreasing intellectuality." [10] To not a few Yale men, mindful of simpler days, it seemed that Yale's social democracy was also being threatened. Again materialism betrayed itself in the athletics craze which had begun to infect both the colleges and the public.

As for religion, Thwing had called Yale as Congregational as an undenominational college could be. But the day of denominationalism of any sort was now clearly past, and the problem of just keeping a college Christian was going to prove difficult enough. Again this sympathetic observer was concerned because training for character and leadership had recently been neglected; and he asked how colleges were going to inspire the country with the culture it so badly needed. But we need hardly complete Thwing's catalogue. For here and there, and in their own terms, Yale men were asking the same questions and saying the same things—not always publicly, of course, nor with entire agreement.

In the matter of intercollegiate athletics, for example, the enthusiastic students and alumni were in control, the Faculty divided in mind, and President Dwight said nothing officially.[11] So the problem of overemphasis—if overemphasis there was—would be one for the next Administration. About luxury Dwight was positive, even a little astonished and scornful. That the new buildings and greater comforts might endanger Yale's democratic spirit seemed to him an unwarranted apprehension.

> The democratic spirit of this institution has never had its vitality dependent on the fact that every individual in the university brotherhood was spending, or could spend, only the same amount of money . . . or that each student must have the same accommodations, or the same number of books, or the possibility of the same personal privileges in every respect, which were open to the college life of all his fellow students. The democracy of the institution would never have existed; it would never have been possible, if such a condition of things had been essential to its existence. It would have been unworthy of educated and

intelligent men . . . The true and genuine democratic spirit—
that which our University has always claimed for itself—is the
spirit which estimates a man according to what he is, and not
according to what he has.[12]

The growing materialism and loss of religious fervor Dwight
could not help but notice. But he preferred to speak of the former
as externalism: "we are in the outward age now." And he professed
to think that the newer philanthropy had advantages over the
older introvertive sense of sin. Practical Christianity generated
more useful energy than strict theology. The Christian life was now
"happier for thoughtful men." [13] He also approved of the Y.M.C.A.
and its activities. Personally he was a devout and unwavering believer. In his own career he could see the hand of Providence, helping at every stage. And as a young professor he had subscribed wholeheartedly to the theory that, while man might have made the presidents of a rival institution, God made the presidents of Yale.[14] In
fact he still believed in the tradition of minister presidents so wholeheartedly that it was at first almost impossible for him to conceal his
shock and disappointment when the Corporation now proceeded
to heed the voices of the alumni and of the times and to elect a layman rather than a clergyman as his own successor.[15] Yet he rose to
this occasion magnificently, as the whimsical speech quoted at the
head of this chapter bears evidence.*

Meanwhile others were more concerned because prosperity
and the increase of enrollment were beginning to threaten Class
unity and Yale's vital community of spirit. Efforts had to be made
to improve the poor students' opportunities to meet the growing
expenses. And already undergraduates were beginning to boast of
knowing all their classmates—as if Classes had grown so large that
such knowledge had become almost impossible.[16]

* President Angell once told me that at his own inaugural it began to rain
as they moved out for the procession, and Mr. Hadley was reminded of a
similar occasion twenty years before. It seemed that on going outside and
finding the rain, Hadley had moved to open his umbrella. President Dwight
had stopped him, however, with the admonition, "Don't forget, Mr. Hadley,
this is still my reign."

Thus socially, politically, and spiritually Yale was feeling strains of an increasingly awkward kind. Publicly the Yale legend might be as strong as ever. Santayana, glimpsing the exuberant competitiveness of undergraduate life, might insist that the College showed an admirable "fitness to our present conditions." And Hadley might remark that in the past Yale had succeeded because it had gone neither too fast nor too slow for the American people.[17] Yet under the surface, and even behind the assured statements of President Dwight, an uneasiness lurked. Between the expanding secularism of the age and the peculiar usages and spirit of the Yale system the tensions were growing. For all the youthful vigor of Yale College it remained to be proved how far the theory and custom of the nineteenth-century institution could be projected into the years to come.

At bottom the greatest challenge, however, was not monetary or athletic, not religious or even broadly social. It was intellectual, and it concerned the Course of Study. Such an assertion may surprise some students today, even as it would certainly have outraged the average undergraduate or young alumnus of the nineties. Nevertheless for Yale College the most important problem for many years to come would be the problem of what and how it should teach. The enthusiasm for athletics would continue, and the practice would spread. Competitive extracurricular activity would change more in volume than in character. In the twentieth century the Senior societies would continue to dominate, still criticized but still unchallenged. And in the face of secularism and disillusionment the chapel requirement would survive until 1926. Yet in these same years the formal education of Yale's undergraduates would have to be almost made over to meet the exigencies of change.

As Dwight and the older graduates well realized, it was the despised curriculum which had given the college much of its discipline, its unity, and democratic equality. No small part of its public reputation derived from the same source. By its choice of subjects and of teaching methods and by many a persuasive statement of its educational philosophy, in particular by the famous Faculty Report of 1828, Yale had exercised a commanding influence on other colleges and had helped form the character of the country's educated class. Again, by modifying that traditional curriculum only slowly and in its own way, the College had deliberately been setting itself off from Harvard and other elective universities. By what it would accept or refuse for admission it would soon either connect with or cut itself off from the high schools of the country. By what subjects it allowed to be taught, and in what way, the College would help or hinder Yale's professional and technical Schools and so give shape to the entire University. In fine, through the government of its curriculum Yale College had the power to welcome or to oppose the new public trends. In however disguised a fashion, it was on this great cogwheel of instruction that all the frictions of change were coming to bear.

By the same token the curriculum had become Yale's most vulnerable feature. For it was here that the Faculty had been most obstinate—here that innovation seemed to some to have left Yale furthest behind—and on this point that Timothy Dwight now permitted himself to express his most open anxieties.[18]

Timothy Dwight was anxious about the curriculum—but on no narrow grounds. He saw it with the eye of a statesman as well as of a scholar. In his view the Course of Study gave not only shape to the Faculty but character to the Yale system.

The President's second avowed concern was with the relations of the College to the surrounding University, and of the University to its several Schools. In the years to come, Dwight was confident, Yale would grow mightily. But he could sense that not all of the Officers and graduates of the College either understood the changes that had been taking place in Yale's structure or sympathized with his own vision of Yale's broader destiny. There was a real danger that Yale's growth might be one-sided, or in a wrong direction. The other Schools, so long overshadowed by the mighty College, might get less than their share of attention and support. Yale College itself might take on improper responsibilities.

So as Yale faced "the opening of the new century" Dwight publicly urged upon his successor, upon the Corporation, and upon all who had a living interest in the place "one all-important thought." Yale, he insisted, if it was to be worthy of its best ideas and the grandeur of its past, "must have its future development *as a University,* and not simply, *as a College.*" No Department or School must be slighted or subordinated. Instead *"the University idea"* must govern.

> The University means all interests, all studies, all departments. It means comprehensiveness, large-mindedness, generosity in providing for every need, a wide outlook, and a far outlook. . . . Yale will have in the coming years a distorted growth, or an imperfect growth; it will fail of the promise that offers itself with richness and fulness, if its officers and its graduates do not have magnanimous loyalty to it in all its interests.[19]

To make all of Yale's Schools equal, however, was not to give them identical or exchangeable functions. So Dwight's third piece of advice was that Yale's Departments should be kept separate. Since they prepared their students for different educational ends, it would not do to mingle them with each other or confuse them with the larger University. This applied in particular to Yale College. The College was preparatory, not all embracing. It gave a general and well-rounded foundation. It aimed to produce not educated lawyers or doctors but educated men. Accordingly, the College ought to retain an organized, four-year curriculum. It should neither admit electives too far nor permit its students to specialize too early. It should instruct its own students and appoint its own faculty. And precisely because the aim was not professional training or the highest specialization, the College should continue to appoint for teaching ability and talent in handling young men as well as for promise in research.

Elsewhere it might be accepted that "college" and "university" were incompatible. At particular institutions men might be laboring to make the university by remaking the undergraduate curriculum. But Yale's growth and development had been "in the line of distinct and separate departments," each concentrating on its own problems, each generating its own esprit de corps, and all doing the better for it. In his Report for 1898, and again in his *Memories* after retirement, the retiring President hoped and urged that these great "life principles" of a Yale education might still be maintained.

Noah Porter had conducted a rear-guard action, and in the eyes of the world Yale had lost. Timothy Dwight, leaving to Harvard its experiment, had insisted on a more progressive conservatism, and in his firm and confident hands Yale had prospered and grown. Without question both University and curriculum had achieved a new solidity and definition. In thirteen short years Yale seemed to have accepted change and to have tamed it.

Yet underneath was the feeling of restlessness—as if some suspected that change could not be controlled indefinitely—as if others realized that the modernization of Yale was still but half completed.

Somehow the University had not quite been realized. Somehow Yale was more nearly a University in its talents than in its organization, and in its organization than in the spirit of its students or alumni. New studies had been accepted, not welcomed. The "outside" Schools had been strengthened but not admitted to equality. The sciences had not prospered; and, whosesoever the fault, the Scientific School had grown into a rival rather than a partner. The professional Schools were now beginning to desire a closer integration with the studies of Senior and Junior year, but Dwight and many others were reluctant.

In the curriculum the College Officers had worked out a fair and even compromise between discipline and specialization, between the Freshman who was still a boy and the Senior who was very much a man, between the teacher who wanted to teach and the professor whose calling lured him to research. But this compromise had been achieved at the cost of the old unity. The College was now divided between two different philosophies and practices of education. And neither the champions of the new nor the defenders of the old system were fully content. So as the last of Yale's nineteenth-century administrations drew to a close, it was not Dwight alone who looked wonderingly forward.

PART TWO:
THE CONSULSHIP
OF HADLEY

CHAPTER 6 · THE FIRST LAY PRESIDENT

> *We listened chiefly because Hadley more than anyone else had caught the poetry and the romance of Yale; because he could express what we felt but could not express. With all his brilliance, with all his fame, we thought of him always simply as the truest Yale man of all.*
>
> —Charles Seymour

On the afternoon of 25 May 1899, when the news got about that the Corporation had chosen Professor Arthur Twining Hadley to be the new President, it was as if all New Haven cheered. Long years afterward Charles Seymour would recall as one of his sharpest boyhood memories the spring-day spectacle of "the entire undergraduate body, swelled by enthusiastic townsfolk, rushing *en masse* to Hadley's house. . . . It was a tremendous and entirely spontaneous confession of admiration and tribute to quality." In October came the great inauguration. Then in Battell one saw

> a man of unimpressive face and figure, surrounded by a group of men in academic costume of varicolored hoods, addressing with strident voice and with graceless gesture an assemblage such as is seldom gathered in this country. In the fading light of the afternoon the thirteenth President of Yale was speaking his hopes for the new day. Those who knew the spirit of this unimposing figure were blind to his awkward gesture and found his voice pleasant to their ears; for the soul of this man has surmounted all physical obstacles, and made all Yale his friend.

That evening every room about the campus was lighted, every porch had its lantern, and every tree and tower its colored lights for an unprecedented carnival. Twenty-four hundred students marched in the great procession, each Class and School headed by a symbolic device. In tribute to the President's hobby and his world-wide reputation for railroad economics, the Academic Department had got up an engine and a train of cars, one for each Class, marked HADLEY TRANSPORTATION CO. Singing and cheering and waving their torches, the entire student body followed on, parading the streets until near midnight, winding up with a monster bonfire on the old gymnasium lot.[1]

The man they were cheering was not only Yale's first lay president. Arthur Twining Hadley was an education in himself. Intellectually, physically, and socially, at forty-three Yale's new leader was still boyishly exuberant, still New Haven's prodigy and favorite spectacle. His manner of speaking and his manner of thinking, each for its own reason, were unforgettable. His omnivorous curiosity, the incredible memory from which at a moment's notice he seemed able to call up the smallest detail of everything that he had ever seen or read or heard or tasted: these, like the extraordinary range and sparkle of his learning, had become proverbial. So had his wit and his absent-mindedness.

They would tell some of Mr. Hadley's stories. They would tell some stories about Mr. Hadley. There seemed to be no end to admiration and to laughter. Sometimes the anecdotes about the President were apocryphal—like the one about his shaking the streetcar conductor's hand and giving his friend the nickel.* Almost always there was a touch, some bit of the Hadley flavor—unmistakably incredible, humorous, and beguiling.

Strangers were startled that a man intellectually so deft could be so awkward and so homely. One writer described his face as "a narrow New England oval," with full forehead, strong nose, "chin reticent, not to say retiring," eyes full of sparkle. His mouth was

* Hadley denied the truth but admitted the probability of this story. At all events it is still being handed down. One version insists that it was a young instructor, not an old friend, to whom Mr. Hadley absent-mindedly gave his five cents. When teased about it, the President is quoted as saying it wasn't such a bad mistake, for he had given social recognition—where it would be most appreciated—and financial aid—where it would do most good.

"almost overstocked with teeth," which gleamed constantly as he talked. Excessively nervous, "he vibrates, rotates, gyrates," all the time striking off ideas. In fact he seemed to think with his hands, his arms, his feet, and even his clothes. In the best description of his earlier lecturing style his fists were

> tightly clenched in pugilistic fashion. One arm—this was the famous Hadley pump-handle motion—was constantly pounding an imaginary object in front of the speaker; the other was shooting obliquely up in the air or describing revolutions about his head. Occasionally Mr. Hadley would address the young men looking at them; at other times he would turn sidewise; there were periods when he would lecture with his back actually turned flatly to the class, his hands meanwhile agitating his coat tails.[2]

Unconsciously he would teeter for minutes on the very edge of the platform. In one of the lecture halls there was an iron column about which he would get himself entwined. In his office his habit was to walk round and round, dictating and not looking where he was going, and his penchant for getting his feet caught in scrap-baskets was proverbial. But all these eccentricities were apt to be forgotten in the interest of what he had to say. A classic epigram gave him "the mind of St. Paul and the manners of St. Vitus." In one of his classes Hadley instituted a question box, to let his students put in questions which he would answer at sight. Once, so legend has it, he took out a paper that a joker had put in.

> "It says on this paper," read Hadley, "Is
> the man who makes his money in a good way
> but spends it badly better than the man
> who makes his money in a bad way but spends
> it well?"
> "The answer is—Yes—a-and No."[3]

As President, Hadley still addressed the undergraduates in chapel and on great College occasions. And they, out of a mixture of astonishment and delight, took to imitating the graceless manner-

111

isms of their President: his agitated jerks and bobs, the pump-handle gesture, not least the Hadley voice: now drawl, now sing-song, like as not a high and wobbly middle passage—a pause—then the sudden spatter of rifle fire for an ending. According to some impersonations the shouts of laughter would then be acknowledged by a series of quick bows and a most idiotic grin. Each Class soon developed its own favorite Hadley mimics, who would later be fixtures at the Class reunions. And Hadley would enjoy these performances as much as anyone. He was a modest man, liked men, and was at home with them.

With zest he would recall his one appearance, in his early days, as an amateur actor. "They didn't give me any words to speak; all I had to do was to walk across the stage, but it brought down the house." "I suppose the reason you asked me to speak before you," he told some student debaters, "was that you wanted the best illustration you could get of how a man ought not to behave himself upon the platform." To his classmates he gave away a secret: "By never going into tennis matches, but making valuable suggestions to those who do, I have acquired wide reputation as an expert player." [4] So also in higher matters. Hadley was witty rather than boastful. He could see through a proposition but remain considerate of the proposer. He had a gentle way of deflating people but a cheerful way of carrying his own burdens. His door was open to everyone. A professor with a problem would be received in his office with all courtesy and friendliness. Kindling to the subject in hand the President might almost at once launch into a story—his stories were always apt. After some time, on a reminder of other engagements, the presidential arms would stop waving, the feet would come down, and the professor would find himself being propelled out the door by a series of profound and cordial bows. Only later would the visitor realize that the complaints that he had come to make had somehow got mislaid. Or perhaps the problem now seemed a little simpler and easier of solution.

As a member of his faculty so justly states, Mr. Hadley had a "genius for putting familiar facts and ideas in a new light." Especially he knew how to analyze, to set things apart. One of his most telling devices was contrast. "The trouble," he would say, "was not that men played too much, but that they studied too little." "In introducing competition among the instructors we have lost the benefit of competition among students." And to two hundred Yale men at Philadelphia he told a story:

A German professor in explaining to a friend the difference between European and American methods in theological training, said, "In Germany the schools are not centered in one particular part of the city as in America, but the theologians are dissipated all over the city." Our aim at Yale is not to have either our energies or our students dissipated.[5]

The enthusiasm of the graduates for their witty, gesticulating, and transparently hopeful new President was phenomenal. Indeed by public account it was Professor Hadley's popularity with the undergraduates and his standing with the alumni that had carried his election. Yet the faculties generally had favored the choice, and influential professors had made sure that the Corporation received a private memorial of their feeling that no one was better qualified to lead the University into the expansive new age.[6] In this expression of confidence liberals, moderates, and conservatives had all joined.

Hadley's whole record breathed of practical scholarship, eagerness to experiment, concern for contemporary society. Was he not a man of the world—a friend of bankers and railroad presidents? And of what more sober academic learning, ancient or modern, was he not master? In a characteristically eccentric and independent career he had in brilliant succession tutored in Greek, Latin, Roman law, logic, and German, studied statistics and economic history in Berlin, gone in for financial journalism in New York, made himself the leading authority on railroad transportation, served as Labor Commissioner in Connecticut, lectured on socialism and political economy under Sumner, coached the student debaters to intercollegiate victory, and become Dean and first real organizer of the Graduate School. It was under him that women for the first time had been admitted to graduate study.

113

Evidently he was open-minded. Certainly the younger men, the champions of elective freedom and the social sciences, were full of plans and of hope. Not Hadley's master, apparently; not Sumner who "had taught him all he knew." The story is that the gruff and skeptical Sumner did not join in the huzzaing—instead wrote his pupil he ought not to accept. Yet if the old war horse thought the post too difficult, or the man perhaps not downright or decisive enough, he was soon admitting himself pleasantly surprised.[7]

Meanwhile Sumner's opponents in the faculty, the defenders of the ancient studies, had grounds of their own for pride and congratulations. For if Hadley was neither a clergyman nor a classicist, his father had been Professor of Greek in the College,[8] and he himself was a man of the broadest culture and literary sympathies. When queried by a member of the Corporation as to his Christian faith and standing, and as to his inclination "to *revolutionize* or 'rip up,' " classical studies and "to act the part of a *radical reformer*," the candidate had replied that he was a member of the Church of Christ in Yale College, believed in the preservation of its Christian character, and was a conservative on the classics.[9] Having been brought up on the campus he understood its ways; having come up through the ranks he was familiar with the Faculty system. Loyalty to all that was best in the Yale traditions would keep him from unwise changes. And, as spokesmen for both the Corporation and the Faculties at the induction ceremonies emphasized, Hadley had the sense of public obligation and concern for the country's honor that made him the fit head for "an *American*" university.

So it was as a patriot and a Christian as well as a scholar—and as a Yale teacher alive to the new yet instructed in the practical wisdom of the old—that the new President was inducted into office. In the same spirit and with a characteristic eagerness, almost impetuosity, Hadley invited his constituency to consider the problems ahead. How could the University serve the public within the forms fixed by its own character and development, he asked. Especially

114

how could Yale meet the demands for intellectual progress without endangering the moral side?

This inaugural address [10] was Hadley's first major effort—and as such more of an exploration than a statement of fixed policy. It touched on many things: on athletics for honor unmixed with the love of gain, on reconciling Departmental home rule with University needs, on preserving Yale's economic democracy without pauperizing students through free scholarships, on compensating for the diversity of student interests by esprit de corps. On all questions of policy Hadley urged not compromise of interests but reconciliation through intelligent understanding. The College should require of the secondary schools only those things which the schools could do well. Otherwise Yale would be in danger of receiving students "who have been crammed for their examinations rather than trained for their work." As for the problem of College expenses "it is all very well to talk of returning to the Spartan simplicity of ancient times, but . . . we cannot, for the sake of saving the cost of a bathroom, return to the time when people took no baths." Past usage should make its peace with present need—yet unifying customs like the religious observances should not be changed unless it should clearly appear that Yale was but modifying the letter of a tradition the better to preserve its spirit. Like Edmund Burke's England, Yale was a strange combination of liberty and prescription; like Burke himself, Hadley would "hesitate to cast away the coat of prejudice and leave nothing but the naked reason."

As for the studies of the College—and to this Hadley gave much attention—the elective system, however convenient, seemed attended with serious dangers and evils. For one thing it promoted methods of instruction which were bad for the ordinary students. Daily oral examination was not possible. The choice in many lines of study lay between having recitations with fourth-rate men or lectures from first-rate ones. "I never met a good teacher who really approved of the lecture system, or who did not prefer small classes to large ones." Another evil connected with the elective system was the loss of esprit de corps.

115

As soon as the inaugural was over, Hadley took to the road to emphasize his ideas and show himself to his constituency. To the Pittsburgh alumni he explained about the elective system. "Now the word elective is all right enough, but the word system does not apply to it at all. It has been arranged . . . very much the way they arrange the River and Harbor Bills in Congress." Yale must therefore discuss what methods and what courses would give the various students a means of meeting their several needs, "and arrange the courses." This would require, he told his Cleveland hearers, a better system of intellectual training in College plus better connections with the preparatory schools and with professional training. The trouble with Yale's professional connections was that in making gentlemen Yale had perhaps neglected the making of breadwinners. The College was not to train merely for the organized professions; on the contrary, the most important of its duties was to the average man. The curriculum should mean something to every student. The fundamental reason why the Academic course should be remodeled was to prove that it had a right to exist as a means of training for citizenship. "It has always been the Yale idea that a man should be a citizen first and a specialist afterward," was his epigrammatic phrasing. Again, a little later: since the elective system had to a degree run mad, Yale's problem was to advise a man what he was fitted for. "Then the ideal system in my mind is to teach a man the facts and details which he is *not* going to use by the method which he *is* going to use." [11] Hadley dispensed *Lux et Veritas* and —forked lightning.

Also moral idealism.[12] For Hadley's cultivation and brilliance were governed by a character of shining enthusiasm and faith. He believed unaffectedly that men are of good will and that the truth needed but to be presented to gain public support. No theologian and no stickler for forms, his beliefs were confidently Christian, constructive, and humane. To him Christianity had this superiority over other faiths: that it rejected neither man's passions nor his powers of reason but turned them both to public account. God revealed himself through Christ—but through men also. "Faith in man, or faith in the truth, or faith in God; they are but different names for the same thing." A man learned to love God by loving his fellow men and to believe in God by believing in his fellow men. From which followed man's duty to serve God by serving his fellow men.

The role of a Christian gentlemen was therefore to see not what he could get out of but what he could put into society. Life was "not a cup to be drained but a measure to be filled." The role of Yale College was to prepare its students for this test of successful living. And the role of the President was to awaken and instruct. Hadley believed in the lessons of history and in the eternal moralities, but also in homely illustrations. So he preached Christ and St. Paul, the failures of Napoleon and the patience of Frederick the Great, the brilliance of McClellan but the greatness of Lincoln and Lee. Character could be learned from military history or undergraduate competitions as well as from *Pilgrim's Progress*. Selfishness could be identified in current economic practices no less than in parables. So in his addresses at the opening of the College year, in his "Sunday Morning Talks to Students and Graduates," finally in the fervent Baccalaureate sermons, he would invite the young men of Yale to examine the things they knew, then go on to manhood and the highest leadership by sharing in the burdens of society.

Hadley's system of Christian manhood had four great points: a man should be active, he should be loyal, he should keep his own code and character, and he should be intelligent.

First: "Men are saved by what they *do;* not by what they profess." Yale men least of all needed persuasion on this point. Signal achievement appealed to the imagination. Nansen's efforts to reach the North Pole, though unsuccessful, were far more admirable than his later explanations. Hero worship was what made progress possible. People would not hazard their comfort for a philosophic idea but would follow a leader to the ends of the earth.

Again, a man should be loyal. He must strengthen his friends and be strengthened by them. The experience and tradition of the campus taught no stronger lesson. The early commanders of the Army of the Potomac had eventually to be replaced by generals from the Western theater. Why? Because they had not learned to sink personal ambitions and suspicions in a larger devotion. "A man who is alone stops in seasons of discouragement." But a team would carry the faltering along. Isolation was dangerous, and monastic withdrawal seemed to Hadley not really Christian. Better to live and struggle in the world and make some mistakes than to nurse an unspotted but fragile reputation in seclusion.

An even more important corollary was this: competition was consonant with Christianity—but competition could be abused. Liberty and power were not for personal benefit, and selfishness could not be the basis of morality. Even enlightened self-interest would eventually, as a policy, lead a nation to ruin. Fundamentally, the future would have to accept the ethical principle that "private business is a public trust wherever the public welfare is affected by it." Hadley also proposed social ostracism for malefactors of great wealth—and drew cheers and jeers from coast to coast. As a practical idealist he taught that the principles of politics were those of morality enlarged.[13]

Hence a man must have the character to cling to his ideals with patience, endurance, and faith. He must not flinch or cheat no matter how important the stakes. The man who cheated at football would find a similar excuse for cheating in business. The man who cribbed on an examination and so sold his honor for a piece of parchment was preparing for himself a life of distrust—a sentence to jail if found out.

> Character has been defined as the habit
> of doing the same thing under different
> circumstances. There is no higher praise
> that can be given to a good man than to
> say that you know where to find him.

> *Vir tenax propositi* . . . was the Roman
> idea of a true man, and by virtue of that
> idea the Romans conquered the world.

Hadley had a touch. His was the telling phrase, the swift shaft of light. It was not simply a warm human morality that he preached

118

but morality guided by intelligence. He was no admirer of Bunyan's pilgrim, a man named Honest who came from the town of Stupidity. At bottom he favored neither church nor secular schools but schools that educated *both* heart and head. Accuracy and ideals, rather than information plus doctrine, were his counsel. A man must learn judgment and discard prejudice. The study of science should reveal the enduring value of truth and the lesser values of personal ambition. History should teach that it was character rather than money or office which moved the world. And literature should inspire idealism and devotion. "We must interest ourselves in the things that are really large . . . to give us a sense of the size of things as they come before us."

Energy, loyalty, character, intelligence: all were essential and all were taught at Yale. Yet Yale itself needed to be measured against greater things, needed to learn its faults. Energy and loyalty the College had in particular abundance. But, Hadley warned, in these very qualities lay peculiar dangers. The temptation was to act thoughtlessly and to follow the crowd. "Yale is an intensely democratic community, and therefore peculiarly liable to this mistake." The temptation of popularity must be resisted. Loyalty ought not to be interpreted as always going along with the majority. Friendship must not be carried to the extremes exemplified by Grant after the Civil War. "The sleep of convention is of all slumbers the most fatal." "I have no respect for any one who says that he has to do as the crowd does; and least of all do I respect such a man when he is in a college that gives him so large a chance to make the crowd do as he does."

Such lay sermons as these gave the President his great opportunity. "We have had time," he would say, "to think of the things that make nations great."

Gentlemen of the graduating class: The life of a strong man has two sides: the effort to find his place in society in keen competition with his fellow men; and the whole-hearted acceptance of his place, when he has found it, as a trust to be used unselfishly. In the aristocracies of the Old World exclusive stress

119

was laid on the second of these elements. We were exhorted to be content to fill the station to which God had appointed us. In the American democracy the emphasis is all on the other side. We are told to find the best place we can. We are encouraged to compete until we sometimes forget that there is any end outside the competition, and lose sight of the unselfish purpose which must animate every professional man and every business man and every politician who would call himself either a gentleman or a Christian.

No one else could make idealism so understandable to the undergraduate. He never spoke long. The story got around that one day a visiting clergyman had asked how long he was expected to preach to the students.

"Of course, we put no limit upon you," replied President Hadley, with his usual pump-handle gesture, "but we have a feeling here at Yale—that no souls—are saved— after the first twenty minutes." [14]

Hadley also had a private list of qualifications for a college preacher, which deserves to be better known. First, "he must talk to his audience, and be free of all suspicion of listening to himself"; second, he "must proceed straight to the predicate"; third, he must be clear and concrete; fourth, and especially important if there is a defect in the others, "he should have the divine gift of brevity." Hadley had all those gifts—with worldly wisdom and a radiant friendliness added.

How could young Seniors do other than respond? In service after service in Battell Chapel they had been filled by his winged words—and afterward had bowed him down the aisle. They knew him lovable and very human. Obviously he took an equal pleasure in the bowing out. Head up, eyes sparkling, he would hustle down the aisle, about to be engulfed by the following wave of Seniors, yet always mysteriously just keeping out of reach. Small wonder that by the time they graduated "the very gestures of his hands and the in-

ARTHUR TWINING HADLEY
Thirteenth President of Yale, 1899–1921

flections of his voice" had become somehow symbolic of the spirit of the place.

Hadley touched and inspired his College by what he was, but he shaped it by his policies. In particular his theories of administration—and his ideas of what a university should stand for—affected the development of the place.

Yale had grown too large, he thought, to be run entirely from the top. The various parts of its work were too different and peculiar for any single individual to control. By tradition Yale men were a band of brothers. And the Departments or Schools were, or ought to be, partners in the enterprise, members of the same University team. Hence trust and delegation of authority were in order.

His subordinates Hadley picked with great care. "No man can do a really large work who does not believe in his friends." But "if you are going to trust men you must take the trouble to judge them. The extreme of indiscriminate trust without judgment is about as bad as the extreme of indiscriminate criticism without faith." * [15] Having picked his men—his Secretary Anson Phelps Stokes, his athletic adviser Walter Camp, his Librarian John C. Schwab—Hadley gave them full confidence and power. "The more things you can decide without my ever hearing about them, the better I will like it," he often assured Stokes. And Stokes repaid the consideration and generosity that accompanied this trust with a loyalty and energetic devotion such as a president and his university cannot always hope to find: "Mr. Hadley was a good person to work under." [16]

Another mainstay of the Administration was Helen Morris Hadley, the ideal president's wife.[17] Interested in people, the daughter, sister, wife, and mother of Yale men, the hostess for the Uni-

* "Believe in people's good intentions, even when you cannot approve their actions or concur in their judgment; but beware of concurring in their judgment or approving their actions merely because you believe in their good intentions." So runs a note of 1903 quoted by Morris Hadley.

121

versity and its distinguished guests, a friend of those in trouble and sympathetic alike to town and gown—such was the partner who helped Hadley speak for Yale and deal with the complex problems of his office. When students needed mothering, she had them to dinner. When newcomers on the faculty brought their families to New Haven, she helped them get a start. In every storm that agitated her gifted husband she remained serene, a miracle of quiet efficiency and tact. Theodore Roosevelt paid tribute to "Mrs. Hadley, still radiating calm." Indeed she was so beloved that one never heard an unkind word about her. The President's house became the center of the University; and on her quiet judgment the whole Administration relied. When Hadley had hesitated about the presidency, because he did not want to give up his writing and lecturing on ethics and political economy, she had helped persuade him, observing that his matriculation sermons and addresses would give him not only scope but an audience. When he then took the presidency, she helped moderate his extreme eccentricities but wisely did not try to make him over. When Stokes and he found themselves in disagreement Hadley was likely to say, "Let's talk it over with Helen." And with her decision both Officers would rest content. Mrs. Hadley steadied her brilliant husband in his orbit.

With such helpers and esprit de corps, the secret of good administration seemed intelligent decentralization. Also the realization by the many that many shared in this trust. The Schools were expected to discover their own problems, and afterward to take the initiative. Hadley had no panacea for the social ills of undergraduate life. At most he could remind the students of Yale ideals—and leave it to them to work out their own salvation. A constantly improving moral tone would bear witness to the effectiveness of the method. The pride of the College Faculty, and its increasing activities on behalf of better studies, would testify in their own ways to the health and vigor that may be born of a feeling of responsibility. In the President's view the Yale commonwealth extended far beyond the bounds of New Haven, and the graduates were a part of the spirit and government of the institution. So in turn many prominent and able graduates would be drawn back into the burgeoning alumni organizations, to help, to advise, finally even to interfere.

Hadley's theory of university government had the further advantage of matching his own interests and capacities. For he was not interested in details. Nor was he anxious to direct the research or policies of others. By nature he was an idealist, no dictator. Live and let live, teach and let teach was his rule. Anything but a cold-blooded executive, he disliked to make unpleasant decisions. He even hesitated to intrude his own policies into a Departmental situation. As Mr. Stokes testifies, Mr. Hadley "was the most humble man for a person with a brilliant mind I have ever known." [18]

In part by instinct, in part by deliberate choice, his own role became therefore that of moderator or spokesman. Mediator rather than master, as a journalist would later put it, he was "a kind of intellectual clearing-house, sitting with open mind toward the policies of the different colleges and professional schools, dispensing appropriations, granting or withholding concurrence, influencing opinion, giving impulse and direction to the tendency of the whole . . ." [19]

In time it came to be suggested that his mind was too open. He could see so many facets of a new problem, and so many possibilities of a solution, that it was difficult for him to focus on the decisive factors. More than once those close to him "heard him add, after expressing an opinion on some question under consideration, that he might quite easily have reached a contrary conclusion if he had approached it from a different angle." Hence, once again, a disinclination to be authoritative or dictatorial. Yet this imparted to the affairs of the University a touch of uncertainty. Unable to get divergent Departments to agree, and unwilling to cut through Gordian knots, he would find himself more than once forced to witness internal struggles, change his own decisions, and then put the best public face he could on reversal of policies. It was not that he himself lacked aims or policies, but in his role of influence and persuasion he had to await rather than create his opportunities.

The "University idea"—the discovery of what a university could and should be—presented a fascinating challenge. To Hadley existing universities seemed hopeful but complicated affairs of unsettled organization and disputed purposes, managed differently in different lands, yet perhaps nowhere perfectly accommodated to men's needs. Certainly American universities were still in a mixed and unsatisfactory condition.

The ideal university, Hadley thought, should have one spirit but many obligations—and he found himself exploring these obligations. It should be an institution for hard work and general culture. Again it should be a place where men from widely separated backgrounds, and with differing destinations, came together for the competitions of youth, the cementing of friendships, and the apprenticeship to learning. At the same time it should foster the discovery, preservation, and teaching of truth—and maintain the highest standards:

> A university has two distinct objects in view. Its primary object is to establish and maintain high standards of scientific investigation, general culture, and professional training. Its secondary object is to teach as many students as possible in the different lines with which it concerns itself.
>
> The two things cannot well be separated. Unless the matter of standards is held in the foreground, a place does not deserve the name of a university . . . But no university can let its zeal for standards interfere with its efficiency as a teaching force. The presence of a great body of pupils, engaged in common tasks and imbued with common aspirations, is by far the most important means which an institution has at its command of making its standards effective throughout the community.[20]

But how were students to be obtained if standards were kept high? Like Solomon, Hadley called for a sword to cut the baby in two. The public should have the say as to *what things* should be taught, but the university should retain the right to say *how well* they should be taught.

However, even high standards and popular programs, clusters of schools and numbers of the students, were insufficient. For the university had such broad obligations to the public that it would be doing its full duty only if, in addition to training students and sending graduates out into lives of usefulness, it made direct contributions to society. This public service should be rendered through its museums, through public lectures and concerts, through assistance to teachers, and by publication.[21]

Again, a university was not a university if it consisted solely of a college, or of a college with negligible appendages, or of a college with respectable but disconnected schools. Hadley was therefore convinced that Yale's graduate and professional Schools and various outlying Departments should be both strengthened and integrated. As we have noted, he thought of the student and faculty bodies, with their traditions and separate examinations, as virtually autonomous affairs. But he favored exchange of students between Schools, and he thought of the higher faculties as eventually uniting in a single body of University scholars. In due course, his Administration was to reach the conclusion that all the teachers of a given subject should be organized into a single "Department of Study," rather than divided into rival groups, each associated with a particular School. So all the historians—whether in the College, the Scientific School or the Graduate School—should be joined into a single Department of History. And the same should be true of apparatus and facilities. The Library should be a common resource. It was wrong for the College and Scientific School to have separate chemistry laboratories. Instead there should be University laboratories—available to all the Schools—in each of the great fields of science. All this meant a considerable emphasis on University ideals as distinguished from School loyalties: an emphasis that showed in budgets, building policies, and professional appointments.

Yet it cannot be said that Hadley went the whole way. He did believe in research, particularly in well-chosen and socially useful projects of investigation. He approved the raising of standards for professorships to the extent of leaving a chair vacant if no man of sufficient caliber were available. He agreed that it was not enough for the Medical School to train practicing doctors; it must inculcate the scientific spirit and so supply the discoverers and the teachers of the future. He persuaded the Corporation to subsidize the long-range project of Professor Ernest W. Brown on the Tables of the Moon. But in general he was more interested in teaching and in public usefulness than in the University as pioneer investigator.

"Research may be either good or bad. Bad research—the mere gathering together of worthless facts with a muck rake—is about the poorest occupation that a man can take up and still maintain his position as a respectable member of society. It is an unfortunate fact that we have too many men of this kind in the teaching profession." [22] On the other hand, good research—the advancement of knowledge of things worth while—was the most valuable quality a College professor could possess. The reason was that it helped him to grow. A man who was a good teacher at thirty but not an investigator or constructive writer was apt to be a less good teacher at fifty. Yale experience showed that with few exceptions the great investigators did better and better teaching as they grew older.

Professors who did research were also valuable because their writings gave authority and public influence to the University. By comparison with Noah Porter, or even with Timothy Dwight, Hadley's views of the professorial function were elevated and broad. Yet between the professor as discoverer and the professor as teacher or public figure his sympathies were at first not evenly divided. He insisted on the magnetic teacher. He hoped for some figures of worldly standing and influence. But pure research was exceedingly expensive and belonged perhaps in research institutes.* Given insufficient funds, the University must foster teaching first, then, if possible, encourage research. It has been well said of Hadley that "even as an economist he was never so much interested in new discoveries or theories as in relating the facts of a modern world to the age-old problem of human conduct and human happiness." [24]

* "The studies which are to be essentially the privilege of the few seem to me to belong in the research laboratory rather than in the university. That provision is being made for specialized work by munificent gifts of capital, I rejoice to see; but I should deem it a misfortune if the size of these endowments and the distinction of those who were entrusted with their use led our professors to believe that such research was a function superior in dignity or public importance to the plain everyday work of teaching men to do their work as men." [23]

When the great Willard Gibbs died in 1903, Hadley quoted the judgment of European observers that Gibbs was the greatest scientific discoverer that America had produced. Then he added his own encomium: Gibbs was "emphatically a teacher of teachers." [25]

So also with his concept of Yale University. Just as it was more important for the College to train citizens than to develop experts, and for the graduate Schools to train teachers than to foster pure research, so it was supremely important for the undergraduate Departments to keep doing their job. For they most intimately touched the public. Theirs were the strongest loyalties: the sentiments and ceremonies and customs that gave vigor and life to the place. In particular the College was still the heart and soul of the University. Instinctively, to Hadley Yale meant Yale College. In his inaugural he had come close to ignoring the collateral elements in the University.* And again and again as President, after using the word University, Hadley would go on to talk about the College. In his view, without its amateur, undergraduate College in which was perpetuated the living spirit of Yale, the University would cease to exist.

Whatever a later generation might think of such an emphasis, in the early 1900's it matched the conditions of the times. In fact Yale was still an undeveloped University. It had more teachers than investigators, more undergraduates than technical or professional students, more resources, force, and devotion in the Academic Department than in all the other parts of the University put together. This would not last forever. Hadley was right in building for better balance in the future. But he was equally right in recognizing where Yale's strength still lay—and right in cultivating that strength. He knew that Yale's secret lay as much in spirit and custom

* When as President-elect he had sent an advance copy of his address to the young divinity student and graduate of '96 who was to be his administrative Secretary, Anson Phelps Stokes returned three criticisms. He thought the President should put even greater emphasis on Yale's Christian tradition and training for public service. And the address gave entirely too much attention to the College, too little to the University. Hadley should emphasize the University ideal. "President Hadley frankly wrote me that he had spent most of the night revising his address and bringing out these emphases." [26]

as in books. He cherished the customs, idealized its aspirations, and rededicated it to the welfare of the nation. Most of all, Hadley believed in men of character, living and working as friends. His system of government—or of lack of government, as it has sometimes been described—appealed to the democratic genius of the place.

CHAPTER 7 · THE GOVERNMENT
OF THE FACULTY

A visitor from Europe is struck by the prominence of the president in an American university or college, and the almost monarchical position which he sometimes occupies towards the professors as well as the students. . . . No persons in the country, hardly even the greatest railway magnates, are better known, and certainly none are more respected.

—JAMES BRYCE, *The American Commonwealth*

It is undesirable, as I think, that the President of a college should have in his hands too much power.

—TIMOTHY DWIGHT

THE YALE COLLEGE FACULTY was—and it still is—so different from most other college faculties that in American higher education the Yale example has become either famous or notorious: the envy of professors and the horror of college presidents in many an institution across the land. Few undergraduate faculties anywhere, and none in so large a university, have known such independence and such power.

To the Yale Faculty belonged the dominant share in management. They truly were the College Officers. They exercised at least as much autonomy as the faculties of the small New England colleges which had not turned into universities. They were probably freer from presidential direction or trustee interference than the faculties of the older denominational colleges of the Middle West which owed so much to Eastern examples and personnel. As for the newer institutions across the mountains, and especially the State-

129

supported universities, there was no comparison. Most significant of all, the Professors handled distinctly more power than their colleagues at either Princeton or Harvard. There would be a saying at Cambridge to the effect that the trustees ruled at Princeton, the president at Harvard, but at Yale it was the faculty.[1]

When George Lincoln Hendrickson arrived from Chicago to succeed Tracy Peck as Professor of the Latin Language and Literature in 1908, he was struck not only by the relative importance of the College but by the seriousness and dignity with which the College Officers undertook their responsibilities. First of all, nearly every professor called on him. They all seemed to know each other intimately. There was a feeling of vitality and coherence. And at the sessions of the Professors there was decision as well as discussion. Having served at Wisconsin and Chicago—places where the presidents or trustees seemed to run everything and the faculties had had to struggle for a little recognition—Hendrickson was impressed and gladdened. His colleague in Latin, E. P. Morris, described the New Haven posture of authority with pith and clarity:

> In the government of Yale College,
> the Faculty legislates,
> the President concurs,
> and the Corporation ratifies.[2]

Morris repeated this aphorism half humorously. Yet also seriously. For there was substantial truth in what he said. And Hadley, who had been born into the system, and who by force of circumstance was learning to play in it two different roles, in effect agreed with Morris. In the public definition that he would give of the Yale manner of government, he had this to say about the "Powers and Duties of Professors": [3]

First, Yale's teachers were not "hired servants." Instead they were responsible partners in the enterprise. As organized in the United States there were, it seemed to Hadley, two theories and practices of college government—the modern corporation and the old-fashioned craft guild. The Western university was modeled on the modern corporation: its methods were autocratic and its teach-

130

ers were employees. "The Eastern university, on the contrary, is organized like the guilds and associations of an earlier time, and is essentially republican in its methods of government."

As partners Yale's teachers were organized into two groups. The professors, assistant professors, and such instructors as they chose to associate with them formed the general Faculty, with wide statutory powers. Theirs it was to initiate and determine the courses of study leading to degrees. The general Faculty also regulated attendance and conduct. But, as Hadley observed,

> . . . this jurisdiction . . . wide as it is, does not constitute the distinctive feature of Yale University organization. This is to be found in the "Governing Boards," made up of the relatively small group of full professors or "permanent officers" within each faculty. The statute on the subject is as follows:

> > In the decision of all questions which concern the permanent policy of the institution in respect to either instruction or government, and in the nomination to the Corporation of candidates for permanent positions in the faculty, the permanent officers may hold sessions by themselves as a governing board at the discretion and call of the President; and their conclusions shall be final when sustained by a majority of said officers, including the President, unless reversed by the Corporation.
> >
> > —(*Yale Corporation,* p. 27.)

> And it is further provided by statute that nominations for positions in the faculties of the several departments shall come originally from the permanent officers or governing board of the department concerned.

> The power enjoyed by the professors under these statutes is limited in two ways: by the reserved right of the Corporation to approve or disapprove, and by the necessity of securing the concurrence of the President.

> The right of the Corporation to reverse a decision of the faculty has, so far as I know, never been exercised. The with-

131

holding of approval is used but rarely, and only for one of two reasons: either as a suspensory veto, in order that there may be fuller discussion of points not sufficiently considered at the outset; or on grounds of finance, when a project as elaborated by the faculty will involve an amount of expenditure which can not be safely undertaken. The real check upon the actions of the faculties lies in the necessity of securing the concurrence of the President. Under the letter of the Corporation statute just quoted, and of one or two others, couched in similar terms, no faculty vote and no vote of a governing board is valid without such concurrence; so that the President appears to have an absolute veto power. Actually, no wise president would make use of such a veto power when he could help it; because his own power in initiating new measures with success is so largely dependent upon the cooperation and the vote of the professors that an attitude of defiance or of antagonism on his part would be suicidal.

What practically happens is this. The professors, knowing that such a veto power exists, abstain from putting their proposals into forms obnoxious to the President. The President, knowing that the initiative in matters of policy and in the nomination of candidates rests with the faculty, will not only take pains on his part to abstain from vexatious opposition to the will of the majority, but will frequently give his assent to measures of secondary importance which he does not quite approve, in order to concentrate his attention on measures which he regards as of more fundamental importance.

No doubt, added Hadley, the Yale system had "its disadvantages —the disadvantages which are incident to a republican form of government everywhere." The need for discussion and compromise prevented rapid forward movement. Independent professors made mistakes which a wise President could avoid, particularly mistakes of duplication. Worst of all, the system allowed professors of narrow views to stand in the way of younger men with larger ideas than their own.

In spite of these difficulties and dangers, I believe that the good of the republican system of university government outweighs the evil. It gives greater dignity and independence to the position of a professor. It stimulates the majority of the members of the faculty to work harder than they otherwise would. It avoids quarrels. It increases their public spirit and their loyalty to the institution as a whole. Of the various elements that enter into the idea of academic freedom, this position of professorial independence seems to me the most important.

Whence came such independence and authority? Hadley hinted at European guild practices. Most of his colleagues would have referred it, along with so much else distinctive of Yale, to local traditions of long standing. There was nothing in the constitution to account for "the government of the faculty." Legally the Fellows of the Corporation had always exercised absolute and uncontested authority within the limits of their Charter. In fact the absentee and nonprofessorial personnel of Yale's Board of Fellows and the apparent exclusiveness of its control have been made a text for warning sermons by a writer on college government.[4] Yet from the earliest times custom had acted to correct the dangers. And in the nineteenth century positive theory first and then Corporation legislation had reinforced Yale's teachers in their share of management.

In the beginnings various colonial experiences and conditions— the early failure of nonresident management, the personalities of Rector Williams and President Clap, the difficulties of communication and the necessities of schoolboy supervision—had put into the hands of the President considerable responsibility and had established habits of association between the President and his handful of tutors. Under the first Timothy Dwight this practice of sharing in the responsibilities had deliberately been broadened to include the new professors whom he nominated and in whom he trusted. The Corporation had approved, and its members thenceforward practiced a conscientious consultation with the College Officers. Thus arose a twofold trust: between Fellows and President on the one hand, and between President and Professors on the other. When Jeremiah Day became President, he continued this academic partnership which he, under Dwight, had enjoyed with Silliman and Kingsley, extending it to the widening circle of their colleagues and passing it on to President Woolsey. And such was the character of these men and their satisfaction in the partnership that by the time of his retirement in 1871 President Woolsey was able to give the Yale tradition of the government of the Faculty a most positive public recommendation. In general, he said, college teachers should be free in matters of belief and conduct. Except in extreme cases, trustees should not interfere with a faculty's management of either curriculum or teaching or discipline. And no new laws and no new appointments should be made by the Corporation without consultation with those affected. As for the attitudes and practices of Yale's Corporation, whose member and spokesman he had now become, at President Porter's inauguration Woolsey had this to say:

> The Board, in whose hands the ultimate and highest decision rests, have ever felt that their interference, without the request of the officers of instruction, in the study and order of the institution, would be uncalled for and unwise; that independent, unsolicited action on their part would amount to a censure of the faculties, and would lead to discord and confusion. With scarcely an exception, no law has been passed, no officer appointed, unless after full consultation and exchange of views between the boards of control and of instruction. And hence, if there are defects in our system, the faculties are, as they ought to be, mainly responsible; if an inefficient or unfaithful officer comes into a chair of instruction, the faculties, who know him best, and not the corporation, are to bear whatever censure is justly due. I hope that this may always continue.[5]

So to long practice had finally been added an official declaration of policy. Thus strengthened, the tradition of professorial statesmanship proved strong enough to carry the institution through the Sumner-Porter crisis, the first elective battles, and more than a decade of hesitant presidential leadership.

Then, after Porter's retirement, two divergent trends had set in. On the one hand the Corporation had proceeded to formalize into by-laws, and thus legislate into rights, the controls over discipline, curriculum, and appointments long practiced by the various governing boards. On the other hand the second Timothy Dwight, facing an expanding College and University, had quietly begun to exercise a more positive presidential guidance and control, particularly over finances. As other colleges wrestled with the same problems of expansion and diversification, they developed an even stronger centralizing tendency. At Harvard, by the mid-eighties, Eliot had already captured authority. A stranger might have been forgiven for supposing that Yale would soon follow. But the addresses at Hadley's inauguration and his classic definition as set forth in 1911 all showed that Yale was not so inclined.[6]

Given this preference, what happened to the Corporation? The Corporation still had to approve. It was the only legal entity and the final authority. In personnel that body remained nonacademic and nonresident. Members of the Faculty had never been elected to its Board, and this was not now proposed. Thus in 1913, when ex-President Taft was appointed to the Kent Professorship of Law in Yale College, he tendered his resignation as one of the Alumni Fellows, with the statement that "I do not deem it in the interest of the University that a member of the Corporation should at the same time be a Professor under its appointment and in its employment. I understand the theory of the government of the College to be that the only relation between the Corporation and the Faculty shall be through the President."[7]

In everyday practice, of course, the estrangement was by no means so complete as Taft implied. Members of the Corporation had classmates or friends on the Faculty. Alfred L. Ripley, who had once been a tutor of German himself, took a particular interest in the German department and in the Library. In fact he was coming to be regarded as the one Fellow with firsthand experience and knowledge of faculty problems. Occasionally an aggrieved professor would take a plaint directly to one of the Fellows. Hadley was unwilling to discourage this. If the professor presented a one-sided view the bias would soon betray itself, he thought. The Administration adopted the policy of having Deans and Directors and groups of faculty members lunch with the Corporation after the monthly meetings. And whenever serious differences of opinion arose a practice was made of inviting the Dean and perhaps one or two other professors to appear before the Prudential Committee. Even the most irreconcilable differences "shrink into quite small size when discussed with a group of able business men who know what our finances do or do not permit us to undertake." [8]

What functions were left for the President? First, for the regular business of the Schools, he was the spokesman of their Faculties before the Corporation. Second, his functions as coordinator between Schools or Departments were considerable. Third, he was the mouthpiece of University policy before alumni and public. Fourth, his financial responsibilities required not only a general oversight but constant consultation with the Treasurer on the one hand, and with Deans, Directors, or senior professors on the other. Every new appointment, apparatus, teaching or laboratory method had to be fitted into the next year's plans. Customarily these estimates were made up in February; and so great was the need for consultation that the President found it unwise to absent himself for two days at a time during the midwinter season. The President also took much part in the call of new professors, consulting locally and corresponding with other universities. Finally, the President was authorized to approve any acts not by custom or statute referred to the Corporation.[9] In addition to these manifold functions, did Hadley have no powers of origination? He did. But these were to be exercised outside of the regular Schools, in the margins and interstices, in the small but hopeful area of University rather than Yale College funds. In a private letter he wrote:

The power of initiating new action on the part of the President, independent of the members of his faculty, is not with us very great. There are, however, a good many parts of the University organization—for instance, the Library, the Museums, the Athletic Field, or the so-called University professorships and lectureships—over which no faculty has any control; and these, I think, would provide any right-minded President a sufficient field for his initiative without straining the question of faculty jurisdiction.[10]

All this added up to a custom of the constitution which did not at all correspond to the constitution under the Charter. The law vested all power in the Corporation but practice placed most of it elsewhere. While the Corporation retained a strong financial veto, and some powers of initiative in the new University areas, large parts of its powers were divided between the Administrative Officers and the various Faculties in a most republican distribution.

Yet there remained one important power in the President: the power of participation in Yale College meetings. Timothy Dwight had presided over those meetings, with a gloved grasp. Hadley got Dean Wright to preside over the general Faculty and occasionally over the Academical Professors as well. Later Deans would preside over both. Yet Hadley sat regularly with these Permanent Officers, participated in debate, voted on resolutions, and retained what he called his "suspensory veto." Apparently the professors took it naturally and were enlightened rather than intimidated. He did not talk them down. They knew he knew the need of cooperation and the unwisdom of using his veto.

"In the actual working of the machine," Professor Morris later repeated, "the veto was negligible; a sensible president would not use it." Or rather he would use it only for delay when the Faculty was itself divided; and his refusal to concur would thus represent not his own will but that of the Faculty. The crucial point was that Hadley would not veto a voted measure merely because he had himself opposed it in open meeting. As Hadley himself would confess to an altogether different sort of President—M. Carey Thomas of Bryn Mawr—in seventeen years he had had only two occasions to use the veto—and then only to delay and modify rather than block.[11] Yale's President knew the force of custom and the rules

137

of tact. He was personally unaggressive. He found himself too busy with University affairs to know any longer everything that was going on in Yale College. And finally he could see too many sides to each problem. To his colleagues he even betrayed a disconcerting vacillation, arising out of intellectual indecision. I quote from Governor Cross's *Connecticut Yankee:*

> When any question came up for discussion in the faculty of Yale College, it was said, he would canvass it from various points of view and stop there, just short of recommending a course of action. This habit was called by the younger men of the faculty merely boxing the compass without using the instrument to steer the ship. There was a degree of truth in this. . . . in his prime he could see any subject from five or six points of view. This often led him to change his mind and sometimes resulted in no action at all.* [12]

As someone put it, "Hadley didn't believe in having a policy." He relied on his lieutenants and his Faculties for initiative, believing that his own work was to illuminate rather than decide. If the debate started to go the wrong way, it would make the President quite uncomfortable. He would squirm, make gestures, finally arise and say he must absent himself and go out. On one occasion this left the Faculty "pretty mad," but a moment later the door reopened and Hadley appeared to announce with a grin that he found he had picked up someone else's hat and coat. He did not nurse a grudge. Once a decision had been made, he accepted it.

The only trouble was that to vote was not to act and, once a decision had been reached, Hadley sometimes seemed to assume it had already been carried through. This is not for a moment to suggest that he gave up his broad governing ideals. As he said, he liked

---

* Sumner once said to Keller: "When an idea comes to Hadley, it comes in a fuzzy condition . . . *and whirling.*" I am told that Sumner used to sit on Hadley in public. Among the awful things he once said before Hadley was: "Well, gentlemen, we must realize that they have a President at Harvard." Afterward Sumner would apologize and ask Hadley, "Why did you let me talk that way?"

to let his mind "work around" a problem. His confidence and trust in others represented an intelligent default. Later he would describe himself as inclined in educational matters to be an opportunist "which means a man who does the best he can under the circumstances." [13]

All of which invited the Academic Officers to be opportunists and policy makers on their own account. The President would take a considerable part in the calling of a new man. Yet for most purposes they were still the initiators, the first judges, the most active partners in the old three-cornered enterprise. And they built to perpetuate the system. Under Hadley was the republic. Now, after two hundred years, the democratic custom of the constitution had again come to bloom. Between 1899 and 1914 Yale's habits of autonomy were rationalized, organized, and made solid. While other old colleges were centralizing and newer universities starting as autocracies, the Officers of Yale College stood on their own feet: self-governing, self-disciplining, self-perpetuating, and even virtually self-paying. For good or ill over this stretch of years were strengthened and made durable that spirit of independence, those habits of responsibility, that jealousy of outside rivals or superior authority, which were destined to keep peculiar character in the College and to give shape and twist to so much of the future University.

"We—elect—each—other; *that's the reason*," *he pronounced slowly and impressively. He warned against executive encroachment upon this privilege:* "*We professors own the College.*"

—WILLIAM GRAHAM SUMNER *quoted by Albert Galloway Keller*

THE COLLEGE FACULTY was growing in weight of duties no less than in sense of authority. But the Faculty was primarily a teaching organization, whose scholarly functions were steadily being refined. So the problem had been: how handle the increasing responsibilities with a diversified personnel but no specialized administrative staff? The solution was a unique administrative system, staffed and directed by men whose essential function it still was to teach.

Strictly speaking, Yale College had always had a multipurpose Faculty, with duties that were moral and custodial as well as pedagogical. But over the course of two centuries the emphasis had been shifting from the lower discipline toward the higher scholarship. By the time of the second Dwight some specialization of function had also set in. Certain professors still acted as curators. But librarians had taken over the most important book collections. Records of attendance and the enforcement of discipline, etc., were falling into the hands of designated Officers. In 1888–92 the angular and accurate Franklin B. Dexter, who had been not only Secretary to the Corporation and Assistant Librarian but Larned Professor of American History and also Registrar of the College, was released from the latter two jobs.* In 1892–93 the College elected its own

* It is said that Dexter could look at you forbiddingly and write simultaneously with both hands. But had he returned in 1950 he would have found his functions requiring the services of five professors of American history, a

Secretary, Professor Andrew W. Phillips, and a young, nonteaching Registrar, Alfred K. ("Flash") Merritt. President Dwight as we have seen—teaching only a little New Testament after Porter's death— had carried the Treasurer's duties for his first two years, and thereafter continued to occupy himself with buildings and material management. By 1897 he had become convinced that further delegation was in order—and the College appointed its own Bursar. Hadley himself was too busy to teach at all and was the first Yale President to become wholly an administrative officer—likewise, it is said, the first to employ a full-time secretary.

There was also the Dean of Yale College. But neither the officer nor his office corresponded to what they have since become. Actually Baldy Wright still taught part time, administered the regulations of the College, kept its records, and regarded himself as its servant rather than director. He neither desired nor exercised any such influence over the Permanent Officers as Director Chittenden did with regard to the Governing Board of Sheff. The natural business of the office, as Wright explained, was to have, "under the direction of the Faculty, a general oversight of the attendance, scholarship, order, and discipline of the College, and to form a means of communication between the Faculty and the students." [1] By general consent the office had grown into a clerical convenience rather than an authority in its own right. The Dean relieved the President chiefly by presiding, and the Faculty by the handling of routine discipline.

In any case, neither Hadley nor the professors felt free to relinquish their inherited moral obligations. Hadley not only preached occasionally but took his place in daily chapel, and some volunteer professors conducted the daily services. A minor crisis occurred when someone walked off with the typed file of prayers

---

whole Registrar's Office, two associate librarians and a dozen department heads —to say nothing of the staffs for reference, circulation, and cataloguing— and finally the University Secretary with his office staff, Clerical Bureau, News Bureau, Alumni Records Office, and assorted stenographic services. From these calculations I have deliberately omitted the fact that Dexter found time for his invaluable books on early Yale history—on the side.

Professor Perrin had started. The general Faculty disciplined cases of drunkenness, suspended cheaters, regulated Glee Club and Dramat. So the larger disciplinary and social obligations also remained. Thus, in spite of the tremendous growth of the student body since the Civil War, and an even greater growth in the complexity of College teaching, only a few of the most obviously clerical, technical, or University-wide responsibilities had successfully been sloughed off.

Meanwhile the whole structure of the Faculty had changed. In less than two generations the regular teaching staff had increased more than fivefold. In 1860 that staff had consisted of the President plus eight other professors and eight tutors—a total of seventeen. By 1908 the total was ninety-three, and it included thirty-six professors, twenty-seven assistant professors, and thirty instructors. Like the withdrawal of the President from teaching, the increase of numbers, the introduction of assistant professors, and the substitution of instructors for tutors had been of both moral and administrative significance.

In pre-Civil War days the structure of the Faculty had been oligarchical and had consisted simply of two small bodies of men, divided by an almost impassable gulf: on top, a respected, stable, and homogeneous body of scholar-managers called professors—below, a mixed, changing, and harried handful of graduate-disciplinarians called tutors. Though often personally respected, in function the tutors had been inferior indeed. They were experts on nothing and teachers of everything, who were hired to keep order and forced to live in. After 1830 tutors had finally been allowed to specialize, or at least to teach one subject to many divisions instead of all subjects to one division. But which subject depended as much on the chance needs of the College as on the wishes of the tutor. The custom had been to hire a tutor for two or three years and perhaps reappoint him once. Rarely would he be lifted into a professorship. Under Porter the qualities still sought had been character and the ability to handle and sympathize with young men. Thus A. T.

Hadley '76, after studying history and economics, had been made a tutor first in Greek, then in Latin and German. So likewise Horace D. Taft '83 was invited to tutor Latin despite the fact he knew next to nothing about the subject—"I guess he can learn the Latin," said Dean Wright—and after three years Taft went off to found his own school.* [2]

For quite a few years processes had been working to transform these transitory tutors into scholars, or eliminate them in favor of instructors with professional ambitions. Also the rank of assistant professor, which originally had been used to designate merely the junior professor of a given subject, had developed into a useful rank of intermediate status. In 1890 the whole University had known but nine assistant professors; but by 1908 Yale College alone would have twenty-seven and in that year the last surviving tutor, appointed in 1906, was converted into an instructor. The old dichotomy had been converted into a hierarchy.

Now a likely assistant, upon getting his Ph.D., might be named instructor for one year and be reappointed for one, two, or three years. After three years of exceptional promise or five of good service, this instructor could hope for promotion to assistant professor "on first appointment" for three years. If all went well, but no chair fell vacant, he would be elected assistant professor "on second appointment" for five years. Thereafter he was either promoted to a permanent professorship or encouraged and helped to find a place elsewhere. Yet one or two men who did not seem to possess all the talents for original scholarship that were now asked of the full professor were showing themselves so valuable in administrative work that still a third grade of assistant professor was beginning to be recognized, the assistant professor on indefinite tenure; and in a few years this would lead to the question of establishing still another intermediate rank, that of associate pro-

* Albert Galloway Keller '96 records that Sumner advised him to get a foothold by teaching Greek or anything that offered. When he accepted an assistantship in social science, teaching economics, Sumner remarked: "Now you've got a foothold; hang on!" and added: "Just strictly between us, you don't know much economics."

fessor.[3] So the vast gap in security, learning, and public usefulness between the ruling oligarchy and the apprentice tutor had been filled in. The College Faculty was now a pyramidal structure, up whose successive steps were climbing trained groups of younger scholars, many with experience in the ways of Yale.

These younger men were beginning to be divided into groups, dealing with the various areas of learning, called departments of study. But the organization of these departments of study within the general Faculty was informal. The departments had no official chairmen: instead merely "senior professors" or "heads," who exercised a greater or lesser influence over the teaching field and appointment of the younger men.[4] There was no department devoted to academic administration, nor were there administrative posts within the scholarly departments of study. No ladder of promotion for administrators—no hierarchy of offices—no recognizable career in academic administration, and hence no formal administrative training existed. Instead the ideal was general training and broad participation. In scholarship the College Faculty had become professional, but in administration its duties were still general and its standards amateur.

Irrespective of their town-meeting traditions and whatever their preoccupations with scholarship, the Officers of Yale College had to exercise the autonomy they claimed. Not merely were they legislators. They were judges and executives and had to carry out the policy they made. So this teacher-parliament had gradually evolved within itself a congeries of organizations, half formal and half informal, with overlapping memberships and varying degrees of power. At the top sat the Academical Professors—themselves irremovable and with the sole power of nominating their successors—a busy, care-laden Faculty full of secrets and authority. This small but powerful board was the fountain of policy and the arbiter of personnel.*

* In 1910, as part of a general revision in nomenclature, on recommendation of these professors the Corporation allowed them the formal title of Permanent Officers of Yale College, instead of Academical Professors or Professors of the Academic Department.[5]

By adding to this executive nucleus the growing group of assistant professors and such instructors as had served two years or otherwise commended themselves—and by letting Dean Wright take the chair in place of the President—the general Faculty was formed. This larger legislature had powers more general but somewhat inferior and duties more miscellaneous. By statute it regulated the curriculum, recommended for degrees. In those particulars it seemed a board of instructors rather than a true governing board. For convenience, however, it sometimes acted as the court of last resort for students delinquent in their work or in their conduct. And by general consent it was handling most of the miscellaneous business of the College, the things that could not finally be disposed of by individual Officers or committees. In the nature of the case it knew no business in which the Permanent Officers did not share. Yet it was becoming a body possessed of its own weight and moral influence.

One reason for this was the system of committees without which the College could not have run. Final authority, indeed, rested with the Faculty, but it was the committees who pulled the laboring oars. There were committees for every purpose of government, inherited or new.

For example, the College had inherited a group of Freshman instructors, some of whom were also Division Officers, organized under their own chairman as a Freshman Faculty. These Division Officers each had charge of a fraction of the Freshman Class. Week after week they met together, compared notes, submitted attendance and other records to the Dean's Office, recommended promotions, suspensions, make-ups, or the regulation of Class ceremonies. In 1905 the Sophomore Tutorial Board became a second such junior Faculty, though without the title. Meanwhile, for upperclassmen Dean Wright administered the same questions of attendance, standing, and public order. If we may regard the Dean's Office as a committee itself—and in fact it was the most highly developed of the College committees—we may say that the Faculty had developed three standing committees to handle its disciplinary duties.

Again there were the standing committees on academic matters:

i.e., on Admissions, on Course of Study, on Honors, on the B.A. degree, on the Semi-Annual Examinations, and on Changes in Electives—to say nothing of a special Committee on Advanced Standing for the year 1901–02. There was a Committee on Public Entertainments and another on College Choir. By the third year of Hadley's administration the College boasted no fewer than eleven standing committees—twelve if we count the Dean's Office, the busiest and most useful of them all. At that the College felt the need to set up still further standing committees and a series of ad hoc committees, some handling the gravest issues. In 1905 a powerful Committee on Ways and Means was created. And by 1908 the grand total of standing committees reached seventeen, for a teaching force whose full professors still numbered but thirty-six.

It will be noted that these committees were of all degrees of importance and promise. The Admissions Committee, after merger with its Sheff counterpart, would in 1920 be lifted to the status of an independent University office. The Freshman Faculty of Division Officers would be replaced in the same reorganization by the self-governing Faculty of the common Freshman Year, with its own counselor system. Theoretically each of the other committees was headed toward independent administrative status, or toward absorption in a greater Dean's Office. In 1901, however, all these committees were still private agencies of Yale College rather than administrative organs of the University. They were appointed by the Faculty or its presiding Officer and their work was subject to direction, approval, or review.

How was the work distributed? Apparently the professors headed most of the committees and staffed some of them completely. But for the full performance of so many administrative tasks they needed assistance.[6] In six crowded years they would undertake to remake the curriculum, revise entrance requirements, raise undergraduate standards, and reform Faculty practices—all of these in addition to their regular duties of teaching and publication, of student discipline and supervision, of appointment and promotion—and all under volunteer leaders. Small wonder that the professors delegated lower-class discipline and allowed younger members of the Faculty to help with important investigations. In fact, had it not been for the development of a competent junior personnel it is difficult to see how so much constructive work could even have been attempted.

Yet the full professors still considered themselves apart, kept hold on their prerogatives, treated the younger men distantly or even stiffly, and acted on occasion as if a little discipline and hardship were good for instructors. Each professor was still a free agent, the master of his own teaching domain, and without effective superior. In groups they ran the departments of study. In other small groups they dominated the important committees. All told they constituted a chamber of peers of enormous power and no little dignity and pride. Despite the filling of the middle ranks and the emergence of departments of study, the professors still ruled. The first decade under Hadley was the age of the barons in Yale College.

The professors ruled for three reasons. First, as Sumner rightly emphasized, they chose their own colleagues. Collectively, their control over income and expenditures made them very nearly independent. And in the years 1907–09 they chose their own Dean. All these were unusual powers, and the manner of their exercise was no less extraordinary.

In consultation with the President the Academical Professors had long been accustomed to exercise an almost untrammeled power of appointment. Yet full professorships did not often fall vacant; and the professors in each growing subject had obtained a dominating influence over beginning appointments. With the enlargement of the University, either centralization in the President or a further decentralization toward the departments of study might have been looked for. Instead the Board of Professors asserted its own prerogatives and set up authoritative procedures.

The critical occasion was supplied by the philosophy department. Philosophy and psychology, which were still tied together, had fallen on evil days. Too long dominated by George Trumbull

Ladd, these disciplines had failed to develop a personnel of scholarly distinction to compensate for their loss of place in the undergraduate firmament. With Ladd transferred to a University professorship, quarrels as to control of courses, research facilities, and assistants had broken out. The situation became trying and all the authorities began losing patience.

In 1903 the Corporation voted to give Edward W. Scripture, Assistant Professor of Psychology, leave for a year but not to renew his appointment. This put the interests of psychology, and presumably control of its laboratory, into the hands of Instructor Charles H. Judd. The quarreling continued. In 1904 the Corporation instructed President Hadley to advise Professors Ladd and George M. Duncan that after July 1905 their services would be no longer desired. Professor E. Hershey Sneath was transferred to a professorship in the Theory and Practice of Education and it appeared that the whole staff in philosophy was to be cleaned out.

This created an issue both constitutional and intellectual. On the constitutional question of security of tenure no formal protest was voted by the Professors. But the dismissals evidently shocked even the unsympathetic. After tense private negotiations Ladd was allowed to resign, the Corporation expunged its notification to Duncan, and the title of his professorship in the College was changed to Logic and Metaphysics. He thus caught on, it was said, "by his fingernails." [7]

When Duncan proceeded to make recommendations for the professorship of psychology, however, his colleagues in the other fields hesitated. Having lost most of their faith in philosophers, the Permanent Officers first asked themselves whether or in what ways philosophy should be continued. Sumner was for abolishing the study outright. With his customary bluntness he said that philosophy was "as bad as astrology . . . a complete fake. Yale has a great opportunity now to announce that she will take the lead and banish the study of philosophy from the curriculum on the ground that it is unworthy of serious consideration. It is an anachronism. We might as well have professors of alchemy or fortune-telling or palmistry." [8]

More moderate counsels prevailed. The Professors appointed

their own committee to take charge of the affairs of the philosophy department. This committee explored the field, considered John Dewey among others, and finally recommended Charles M. Bakewell from California. The Permanent Officers, with one dissenting voice, so voted and in 1905 Bakewell took charge. In 1907 he brought in young W. E. Hocking from California; and Judd, originally from Wesleyan, was promoted from Assistant Professor to Professor of Psychology. A promising new nucleus was thus formed.

As a significant part of this philosophy settlement, the Professors made up their minds to regularize the procedure on appointments generally:

> Resolved: That during the coming year if any Professorship in Yale College is to be filled, whether in the first instance or by way of promotion, a Committee of five persons—two from the department directly concerned, and named by that department, and three from other departments—be appointed by the permanent officers of the Academical Faculty to investigate the whole situation and report to them.

Then in October 1905, for jurisdictional convenience, a special committee of Wheeler, Dana, and Seymour divided the professors into departmental sections.* The Corporation's new retirement

---

* Their tabulation is interesting not only as giving the membership of the governing board but as showing how the Division of Languages and Literature, with eighteen representatives, dominated the Division of Philosophy, History, and Political Science with ten, and the Division of Mathematics and Science with only eight:

    I. Greek—Professors Perrin, Seymour, Goodell, Reynolds.

    II. Latin—Professors Peck, H. P. Wright, Morris.

    III. Semitic Languages and Biblical Literature—Professors Torrey, Kent.

    IV. English—Professors Beers, Cook, Lewis, Phelps.

    V. Germanic Languages other than English—Professors Palmer, Gruener, Oertel.

    VI. Romance Languages—Professors Lang, Warren.

    VII. Mathematics—Professors Richards, Phillips, Beebe, Pierpont.

    VIII. Natural and Physical Sciences—Professors A. W. Wright, Dana, Gooch, Gregory.

    IX. Philosophy—Professors Bakewell, Duncan, Sneath.

    X. Political and Social Sciences—Professors Sumner, Fisher, Emery.

    XI. History—Professors Wheeler, Smith, Adams, Bourne.

rule opportunely cleared the oldest of the incumbents out of their professorial chairs. Separate committees on vacancies in physics, economics, political science, and mathematics were appointed. Three professors were elected and two successfully inducted. It became the practice to entrust such problems to two representatives of the department concerned, one from an allied department, and two from distinctly separate departments. And in 1909 the jurisdiction of the standing Committee on Appointments was extended to assistant professorships of the second and permanent grades.[9]

The particular advantage of the system was that it reminded all parties of their common responsibilities. What made this general scrutiny all the more solemn and impressive was the custom of inviting each professor individually to give his oral opinion on the nomination before balloting. It came likewise to be understood that no name would be forwarded to the Corporation unless there was a pretty high degree of unanimity. If they pleased, the Academical Professors could also refuse to accept into their board a Graduate School professor, or a Scientific School professor, or an emergency summer appointee. Thus they exercised a veto as well as the initiative, yet not without the gravest consideration. Indeed it was less easy for an insider to get promoted than was commonly assumed. Thomas Day Seymour, imported from Western Reserve, had made that discovery years earlier; and E. G. Bourne noted in his diary

> N.B. Remark of Prof. Seymour's. First
> wondered how a non-Yale graduate ever got
> elected to a professorship. After two or
> three years there, wondered how Yale graduate
> ever got elected. Always someone remembered
> something.[10]

At one time the Professors had handled finances with almost the same freedom as appointments. More lately they had had to consult with President Dwight in all matters involving expenditures. Under Hadley this became at first a three-cornered consultation between Academic spokesmen, President, and University Treasurer. In the strict sense, there was still no fixed and known budget. In practice the College's own Bursar collected student tuitions and room rents. Since the College did its own admitting of Freshmen and firing of upperclassmen the most substantial items of income were known to the Academical authorities in advance; and the income from endowment and gifts could be guessed. Hence the Professors had a very shrewd idea what they could afford. They went to the Administration only when there was some special emergency—or the hope that University funds could be drawn on for College account —or the conviction that College funds were being unfairly divided.

The University, by contrast, was in an awkward position. Whatever its constitutional authority, financially it had to humor the Academic Department. For most of the professorships, scholarships, and other endowments had originally been given to Yale College, or intended for the Academical Department, and had been so continued on the books. The University had only the slenderest of funds, and the Bicentennial buildings. Yet it faced costs that grew annually more staggering. The expenditures of the Medical School would soar from $28,000 in 1905–06 to $298,000 in 1921. There was the desire to build up a distinguished Graduate faculty, and the obligation to maintain such institutions as the Peabody Museum; yet for none of these Departments was an adequate income in prospect. Hence the absolute necessity of raising a University endowment—and meanwhile the need of getting the College to sustain many marginal enterprises. Hence a natural desire to hold down Academic expenditures and an almost irresistible temptation to borrow Academic or Sheff surpluses in times of University deficit. In 1904 this was exactly what the Prudential Committee proceeded to do. Apparently the expropriation was greeted by the Professors with some protest. For Hadley rehearsed the obligations of the Academic Department before them—and various ways of increasing income were discussed. Then the Permanent Officers resolved to set up a standing committee to advise on finances. The Corporation approved.[11] And in April 1905, after Faculty consultation, Dean Wright appointed Professors Wheeler, Dana, Warren, and Fisher to serve with him on a Ways and Means Committee which should economize expenditures, increase income, organize building projects, and in general centralize and plan Academical finances.

In allowing this innovation the Corporation no doubt had efficiency and a reasonable accommodation in mind. But in effect the Ways and Means Committee gave the Professors an informal and representative planning authority, and under the persistent and skillful leadership of E. S. Dana it became an organ of increasing power, even able to defend the budget against executive retrenchment. In 1909, for example, Dana took the floor in opposition to certain presidential suggestions and saved from elimination the equivalent of three full professors' salaries.

The most decisive exercise of power came in 1907–08 when the Permanent Officers of Yale College chose their own Dean. With Baldy Wright due to retire in 1908, his colleagues had been disturbed at the prospect of finding a successor. They felt great admiration and affection for the old Dean, and gratitude for the manly and sympathetic way in which for almost twenty-four years he had dealt with individual students and the problem of student morale.[12] No doubt there were younger men, trained in the Dean's school, who could be counted on for effective student leadership. What troubled the Professors was another difficulty: that of finding a man who would also be a leader and director of the Faculty. As Officers they felt that they had individually been carrying too much executive work. Also that the College had not been strongly enough represented in its dealings with Woodbridge Hall.* Perhaps the other Schools were justified in criticizing the College for its lack of unity and stable policy in interdepartmental dealings. They wanted a man who would combine the qualities of Prime Minister, Ambassador Plenipotentiary, and Chief of Police. How to find such a man, especially while Hadley was away lecturing at the Uni-

* Woodbridge Hall is Yale shorthand for the Administration. It had been erected as one of the Bicentennial buildings in 1901 to house the offices of the President, the Secretary, and the Treasurer, and to be the meeting place of the Corporation, thus giving the University a center both visible and symbolic.

versity of Berlin? The best thing, no doubt, would be to invite Dean Wright to continue one more year, so as to give them time to explore.

The President was not disturbed—even at the prospect of the choice being made in his absence. He was quite prepared to have the Permanent Officers choose their own Dean. In 1883, when the Sheff Professors had wanted to appoint a Director, the Corporation had given the Governing Board of the Scientific School the authority to elect for a definite period, subject only to its confirmation. Hadley regarded this precedent as having established a tradition for such appointments by governing boards, and for indefinite periods, too. For Deans and Directors were hard to displace and they never, in practice, resigned.[13] Indeed he felt that whoever was chosen would get the best support if it was perfectly clear that the choice had been governed by the initiative of the Professors themselves. He insisted only that the Professors get at the problem. And at their official request and private suggestion on 4 October 1907 he appointed a nominating committee of five: Professors Seymour (chairman), Dana, Beebe, Warren, and Clive Day.[14]

The committee hardly hoped to find all the desired abilities in one man. So they put first the search for a man of vision and power, a "president" of Yale College who could set the standard of college education not only in New Haven but for the country. Young Clive Day drew up and discreetly circulated a statement of the functions the new Dean was to discharge. He was to lead the Faculty on educational policy, in planning appointments, and in administration; to represent the interests of the College in the University; to speak for the College before alumni, schools, and public; and to act as the symbol and agent of its authority with the undergraduates. Morally he should be devoted to the work, of sound character, courage, reliability, and fairness. Intellectually the Dean should have vigor, breadth of interests, constructive imagination, experience as an educator, power as an advocate, and talent as a speaker. Socially he should be of sympathetic and inviting intercourse, and capable of inspiring devotion. In short the functions exercised by Dean Wright could now take a distinctly subordinate place, and might perhaps be farmed out to a sub-dean. Even the capacity to "rope in" students or beg for money was secondary to educational leadership.

The committee's first choice fell upon George E. Vincent '85, Dean of the Faculties of Arts, Literature, and Science at the University of Chicago. When, as they feared, he declined, the search was extended to graduates in law and in business. Neither Charles W. Pierson '86 of New York nor John Crosby '90 of Minneapolis would consent to let their names be brought forward. Instead Crosby and others suggested the name of the Dean of the Engineering College at the University of Minnesota—Frederick Scheetz Jones of the Yale College Class of 1884. And in May 1908, on unanimous recommendation by the Permanent Officers of Yale College, the Corporation elected Jones to be Dean of Yale College for an indefinite period at a salary of $5,000. The Professors had picked their own head, in the absence of the President, yet with his approval. And in this unilateral fashion was determined the future of Yale College for almost twenty years.

CHAPTER 9 · TYRANNOSAURUS SUPERBUS

Here's to the town of New Haven,
The home of the Truth and the Light,
Where God talks to Jones
In the very same tones,
That he uses with Hadley and Dwight.

Academic freedom is the privilege which professors assume
of saying what they think without thinking what they say.
—FREDERICK SCHEETZ JONES

WHEN DEAN JONES arrived from the West, he is said to have boasted that he could typewrite the fastest and spit the farthest of any man on the Yale faculty. He was a man's man, with a gruff manner, a warm heart, and a great liking for boys.

Also he had a voice—a bull of Bashan voice—a deep and rumbling monster of a voice. Pinned to the wall by the thundering Niagara of sound, thoughtless rowdies soon discovered what they had done wrong, artful dodgers could hardly credit their own excuses, even obdurate rebels threw in the sponge. By sheer weight of personality and of sound the Dean swept them all bodily along to their appointed destinations. At first you were scared stiff. Then you recognized the essential warmth of the man. The bark was much worse than the bite. He would scare you first, then punish you, then help you. Perhaps even remit the punishment, if you were trying.

Inheriting a tradition of paternalism, Jones made the most of it. Dean Wright had been the kindly agent of the Faculty, not author of student ills. Perhaps his intellectual range had been somewhat limited; but he had been an effective teacher of Latin, and his

155

human sympathies were broad. Steadfast, reliable, kindly, he was "the kind of man who would reform a boy, not by talking, but by being what he was," and graduates would carry with them the memory of "his quiet, inscrutable, self-contained face." The story is told of how a graduate, back in New Haven to celebrate his Class reunion, called on Dean Wright at his house. "You don't remember me." After leaning forward to peer at him the Dean replied, "The name escapes me but the breath is familiar." He had a strong will and no hesitation in putting on the screws. But he was fair, and personally concerned for the welfare of each man of Yale.[1]

The new Dean took to this inheritance like a duck to water. Perhaps he was at first more uncompromising and severe: Dana had told him discipline needed to be jacked up. One of his first acts was to banish the bottles of spring water from the dormitories. The students who hoarded traditions—and used some of them for throwing purposes—were properly indignant. When, some days later, Jones forgot the Lord's Prayer at morning chapel, a student exclaimed in hushed but most audible tones: "Good God, the dean has abolished the Lord's Prayer."[2] It is said of Dean Wright that when his young men in class were somewhat less appreciative than usual, he used to end the session with the quiet remark: "Ingratitude is the fault of young men. That is all for today." By contrast Jones shouted and blustered. He conducted no classes, but in the imaginary seclusion of his office he would browbeat, cajole, persuade, and organize the healthiest of the young animals entrusted to his charge, and win their admiring cooperation.

Stephen Vincent Benét '19 has left a description of how he suffered the universal fate. He had stood in line in the Registrar's Office anywhere from five minutes to an hour and a half at various times, "to be finally pushed up in front of a desk where a large man with the sleepy kindness of a tired brown seal had once advised him into a cubbyhole of a room in Pierson, with roommate attached, and on other occasions informed him as to his scant remaining chapel-cuts or the fact that so far he did not even seem to be trying to pass Physics."

156

From the deadly little chamber on the opposite side of the hall he had sometimes heard, as men hear thunder in sleep, the shouts and sudden trumpetings of the Dean—and had once been sent himself into that dreadful presence, to find merely a healthy old gentleman with the frosty hair, red face and gusty manners of a hunting squire, who, the moment Philip appeared shrinkingly within the door, began to rate him . . . and left him with the general feeling of having been out in a cloudburst without an umbrella and the vague impression that he would have to stand up straighter when he talked and specialize in Advanced Chemistry and Business Economics if he ever expected to leave with an A.B. Let it here be said, however, to the credit of Tyrannosaurus Superbus (as Dick Sheldon bitterly rechristened him after being made to sweat his way through Elementary Geology when he wished to specialize in the Metaphysical Poets) that his yearning for forcing square pegs into the roundest possible holes did not apply to offenders of Philip's stripe alone, as the five wretched shot-putters and wrestlers forced to flunk three hours a week of the History of Music because he thought they needed broadening, attested in their own inarticulate but sad-eyed way.[3]

Dean Jones loved to threaten unmentioned terrors. But an experience of his own Senior year had taught him not to rely on circumstantial evidence and never to lay a serious charge against a man unless he had the facts. So he would bluff men into confession if he could—and, if he couldn't, let them off with a grumble and a warning. He had a shrewd eye, and loved the game of trading.

He made a special rule of confidence. Boys could confess, or even tell on friends. But it wouldn't be used against either party except for their own good. He once paid a $600 gambling debt of a rich man's son who was afraid to tell his father, and when after two years the boy paid him back, in installments out of his allowance, Jones made the boy tell his father—who was then almost abjectly grateful. Another boy he kept from marrying a State Street

dancer, finally sending him home and getting the boy's friends to
put him on the train. To still a third he loaned money so that he
could take his girl to the Prom—and was repaid in every possible
way. The Dean made no claim to knowing them all. He liked to
pick his groups and through such leaders work on the whole Class.
He got to know them; they gradually got to know him. They admired him, loved him, sometimes imposed on him. But he ruled
them for their own and the College's good.

The stories about the Dean are legion and full of a characteristic
flavor. In the Class of 1914 a gang got together to try to pin their
room applications so they could all live in the same entry. They
went in to see the Dean and he wouldn't let them do it. "No, they
couldn't do it. Absolutely not." Then, when the draw came out,
by some freak of luck they found themselves in consecutive rooms.
One of them even crowed a little to the Dean and pointed out how
the lottery had given them what he had refused. "Aw, give the devil
his due, won't you? I drew them, didn't I?"

Years later the Chairman of the *News,* finding himself short of
cuts just when a special girl was coming down from Smith to spend
a week at Madison, figured out that even if he got zero on a certain
exam he could still pass the course. He went to the Dean and explained that he had been working very hard and was badly in need
of a rest; he could pass the courses. Anyhow, disregarding all that,
he wanted to see this girl. The Dean drew back. "That is the most
outrageous request," he bellowed, that had come to him in many
years. "Go ahead."

The Vicennial Record of the Class of 1920, Yale College, con-
tains, in "An Open Letter" from Dean Jones:

> And what of the protracted poker game, the ill-gotten gains
> of which you were forced to disgorge? You gave up the cash
> with some reluctance, but voted that I might use it as I saw fit
> so long as none of it went back to the 'squealer' who lodged a
> complaint against his classmates and demanded the money back
> out of which he claimed to be fleeced. He never got it. The sum
> of three hundred and fifty dollars went into the War Chest of

the Red Cross as a contribution from certain 'anonymous undergraduates of Yale College.' [4]

The squealer ultimately "withdrew" from college, on grounds distinct from the poker game. The other players were suspended indefinitely, but the suspension was held in abeyance during good behavior—and was never enforced.

A Southerner by birth, a poor boy who had worked a part of his own way through Yale and been elected to Skull and Bones, a Westerner by practical experience, Dean Jones had many advantages for his office and touched the life of the campus in many ways. Though as a physicist he had been commanding engineers, he believed in a wide and varied education: moral, athletic, and social as well as intellectual. He completely loved the place. Furthermore, he had been brought in to make the most of the College. So with brusque cheerfulness and vigor he pitched in. The hope was that he would guide the Faculty educationally, and no sooner had he been elected than he was reminded of this by Hadley himself.

We must organize in such a way as to substitute definite aims for indefinite ones. . . . the professors here, as a body, feel strongly the necessity for some such movement, and will follow enthusiastically any man who can lead them; and . . . if we can organize such a movement here at Yale the effects will be felt not only all over the East, but if I am competent to judge the situation, all over the country and to a certain extent in England. If I had not so many things to do in half a dozen different directions I should have taken up the matter myself. [5]

Again Hadley was anxious that Jones should take responsibility for the Academic budget. Others stressed the need for efficiency in the office and a better administration of affairs. Indeed when Jones walked into the Dean's Office he found an empty desk in an empty room. Apparently Baldy Wright had had no filing system and no regular secretary—and had written most of his letters longhand.

Fred Jones promptly hired a secretary and started a filing system. He also brought the Dean's and other College offices from inconvenient quarters in Lampson Hall to the ground floor of old Connecticut Hall: "he wanted to get to the center of his college and went to it first physically. There on the old campus he has spun his web where most of the flies are flitting. By pressing a buzzer he attracts them into his sanctum and eats them alive." [6]

From the first Jones presided over the Permanent Officers. When Clive Day became secretary to the Faculty its records were put into better shape. Order was brought into the annual budgetary grab bag by Day's careful preliminary surveys of expiring appointments, so that everyone could know in advance what the needs and opportunities were. One of Jones' first efforts as presiding officer was to define the duties of the standing committees and regularize their relations to the general Faculty. In due course this Faculty voted to "observe the simpler rules of parliamentary procedure," and had its organization and jurisdiction overhauled by the Permanent Officers. After 1913 no one was to be ranked as an instructor unless he had completed his work for his second degree—and instructors of two years' standing could be invited by the Dean to sit with the general Faculty. Some delegation of administrative or supervisory duties was also practiced. In 1914 John Chester Adams, Assistant Professor of English, was given for an indefinite period the additional post of Faculty Adviser in Literary Competitions with professorial rank. Hollon A. Farr, Assistant Professor of German, was confirmed on a permanent basis as Chairman of the Freshman Faculty. Tute Farr also helped to modernize procedures in the Registrar's Office. [7]

Meanwhile the Dean had to deal also with the more serious issues of power and policy. Even while his acceptance was under negotiation it had been hinted that the College was being menaced by the Scientific School; and during the year before he took office the issues of the scientific laboratories on the Hillhouse property were brought to battle. No sooner did he reach New Haven, therefore, than he was plunged into the inter-School rivalries and became the College's spokesman and champion. The College was supplying heat to the Divinity School. Free heat, at that. Jones was called in to help settle the dispute. The College had admissions problems. Jones traveled out to address the alumni.

He was the servant of the Permanent Officers. Yet not subservient. After the Faculty turned down his proposal for a second science requirement he pounded the table and told Samuel B. Hemingway, who was editing the Course of Study pamphlet, "Put it in, the Faculty will never notice and the students will think they have to take it."

He could horse-trade with the Faculty as well as with the boys. Wright had advised him privately not to ask too much advice, but make his own decisions—if necessary getting the Faculty to ratify afterward. At first the Professors voted to appoint a committee to nominate to all the committees. Jones acquiesced but then suggested some names. These were accepted and in no time at all he was consulting and appointing without hindrance from above or below. Since he also organized and marshaled the Professors for their work of making promotions and filling vacancies, he necessarily exercised some intellectual responsibility and influence.*

Next to the undergraduates, however, his greatest interest was administrative. Fred Jones became the head of Yale College—its manager, conservator, and team captain.

He was told to put its finances into efficient shape and did so. He had been called to help organize and plan its management. Construing this mandate broadly, he poured energy and devotion into

---

* In the fall of 1938 "the old Dean"—retired, half blind, living in Berkeley College and his memories—recalled to me some of his early experiences and ambitions. He had known Lowell; they had come into office together. Lowell, he said, used to ask him whether he really presided over the general Faculty and the Permanent Officers. Yes, at their invitation. Did Jones appoint the Faculty committees? Well—and Jones explained what had happened. What about salaries? Well, Jones would be called in by the Administration to go over salaries and make recommendations. He then talked with the Professors and recommended; and his recommendations were accepted. Did Hadley really sit under Jones? Yes. The budget? The Faculty made it up; he merely recommended. Appointments? Same idea.

"Jones, I wouldn't have you at Harvard for ten minutes." 8

161

the task. He found Yale College apparently owning its own land, buildings, endowments, and income and still exercising an almost untrammeled power over salaries and appointments. Yale College was the only School that was wealthy and, with the occasional exception of Sheff, the only one that was making money. The others of necessity had to look to the College, or to the University, for survival. The trouble was the arrangements had been too informal and too casually handled. Moreover the College's own funds had not been properly nursed. All this was taken in hand. Under Jones and Dana the Ways and Means Committee flourished. For more than a decade it was, next to the Permanent Officers themselves, the most powerful group in Yale College, restraining expenditures, cautioning on appointments, planning improvements, bargaining with the University and the other Schools.

The University authorities did not give up their wider efforts. In 1909 Treasurer McClung secured a ruling that the Deans had to submit their budgets by 15 June and could incur no extra charges thereafter. The College was presumably indebted to the University for various facilities and services. Year after year Hadley approached Dana, or the Prudential Committee reasoned with Dean Jones, for a more generous College participation in the University deficit or in building up the other Schools. Little by little the University was beginning to get the lion's share of new endowments, and its income was growing faster than the receipts of most of the Schools. But not everyone realized the implications. Meanwhile Dean Jones found it hard to persuade himself that Yale College should pay for University administrative expenses as well as for its own. In 1916 Secretary Stokes and Corporation Fellow Kelsey would put on a determined drive to sequestrate any School surpluses for repayment to the University of advances alleged to have been made over the preceding decade. But the most they could secure was the allocation of future School surpluses to individual School contingency funds against future School deficits.[9] So it would not be until the loss of tuitions in World War I, and the Reorganization following, that the financial power of Yale College would be broken.

When Dean Jones took office the campus boasted some fine old trees and a great waste of bare ground: a desert arena for the games and battles of undergraduate life. No grass was to be seen, no ivy on the eastern battlements, and a dirt road ran round in front of the buildings. Jones proposed to use $1,500 of Yale College funds to improve the campus. "Eddie" Dana snorted. What was the matter with the old campus? he wanted to know—and overrode the proposal. But Dean Jones persisted, and Hendrickson helped him beat down Dana. They got $1,500 voted and Jones went to work. He had wanted to abolish the road entirely, but as a concession had it paved in brick. Then the Dean put in hedges, planted grass, set out ivy against the walls, and enforced the rules against ballplaying in the early autumn and spring. Year after year he put a little College money into the campus, until it seemed a greener, fairer place. The campus became in a sense his personal memorial.[10]

Dean Wright had pleaded for more College dormitories, and on his retirement the devoted sons of the College subscribed to the building of Wright Hall in his honor.[11] This helped considerably. But it was Jones and the University authorities who forged ahead to realize the dream of housing all undergraduates in College buildings. Having known Charles W. Harkness as a member of the Class of 1883, the Dean helped interest the Harkness family. Could a site for more dormitories be found? Perhaps Peabody Museum could be induced to surrender its building and move. Though it seemed possible that the College already owned at least part of the land, Jones offered to transfer $750,000 of College moneys to the general funds of the University in payment for the site. The Corporation accepted, the Museum Trustees consented, and Mrs. Stephen V. Harkness came forward with an offer to erect the desired buildings, in memory of Charles W. Harkness.[12] So with a new Memorial Quadrangle in prospect it seemed that they would soon have all the dormitories that would ever be needed for a student body of 1,400. This meant that Yale College would have its land, buildings, endowment, income, Faculty—and cash to spare. Such was the golden dream.

As the Dean later said, he and the Professors had done all this together. They had been "Partners in a Great Enterprise."

PART THREE: REBUILDING THE COURSE OF STUDY

CHAPTER 10 · A NEW AND PROMISING LINE

The reform in the course of study . . . as far as it affects the last three years, has been carried to its logical conclusion. The principle of a fixed curriculum has been entirely abandoned. . . .

. . . not . . . that the system as thus arranged now allows a mere haphazard choice of the studies which may prove easiest or most agreeable. On the contrary, the new rule requires a certain range of choice and a certain quality of advanced work . . . there is no question that the system adopted represents a serious attempt to solve a difficult problem on a new and promising line.

—Arthur Twining Hadley, *1901*

At the outset of his administration Hadley had made clear to his constituency that the curriculum needed remodeling, both to improve Yale's public relations and to introduce some order into the elective grab bag. But there had to be a meeting of minds and neither dictation nor reluctant compromise. For the best results Yale could afford to go slowly.

In most American universities—which were run, as Bryce said, in an almost monarchical fashion—reform could be initiated from the top. "Prexy" Dwight, on the other hand, had thought presidents generally too powerful. And now Hadley was moving toward a state-rights federalism, trying to make his Deans take responsibility for their several Departments, urging Baldy Wright to preside at the College Faculty meetings, and inviting the judgment of his professor peers. Control over the curriculum, in particular, belonged to the Officers of the College. So it was not in the President's office but at the meetings of the Academical Professors that the great remodeling would take place.

The inside story of this remodeling has never been adequately studied or presented. The pertinent records, official and private, are either disappointingly cryptic or overwhelmingly detailed. Yet with patience the most exasperating minutes may be made to yield much that is of interest to the student of collegiate government and reform. By following the parliamentary maneuvers one learns how this self-governing Faculty operated. Buried under the mass of details one finds fundamental perplexities. And in the slow-motion gestures of debate can be seen an important twentieth-century compromise being painfully hammered into shape.

A month after his inaugural the President "brought up the question of the Course of Study, and it was voted that the next meeting be devoted to an expression of opinion by the Professors, on

1. What evils in the present course they regard as most needing reform, and

2. What lines, if any, they suggest for dealing with them." [1]

Who used the word "evils"? Surely it could not have been Hadley, who on occasion would quote a saying of President Dwight's: that you do have to tell the truth, but you don't have to put it butt end foremost. Yet one suspects that it *was* Hadley—and that in this homely slip he betrayed much of his own feeling about Dwight's half-and-half curriculum. Evidently the Faculty were of like mind, for they voted to discuss not whether evils existed but what evils *most* needed reform.

Accordingly the Professors "individually expressed their opinions on the evils in the present course of study." And there seemed to be so many evils that the Faculty hardly knew where to begin. This gave Hadley the opportunity to make a strategic suggestion:

that we should start with some motion which (a) deals with a generally recognized evil, (b) in a line whose general direction is approved by as large a number of persons as possible, and (c) which involves principles whose discussion will naturally lead to the subsequent discussion of the other evils noted and other measures proposed . . .

The evil most universally recognized would seem to be the haphazard grouping of studies, often somewhat elementary, near the close of the college course. The line of treatment which commanded the most general approval was that suggested by Mr. Smith and Mr. Schwab: a classification of the elective studies into grades . . . and a requirement as to the proportions of elementary and advanced work allowed in each year of study.

This proposal seemed to Hadley not only valuable in itself but certain to lead into all the other major problems. In his memorandum, therefore, he suggested beginning with a motion requiring for each year not only a certain quantity of work but a certain quality of work, measured by its degree of advancement. Others could name the exact standards more wisely than he.[2]

Accordingly, with Dean Wright presiding, the Professors prepared to discuss procedure. Yet while means were being debated, ends were already being proposed. Buoyed up by the President's trust and approval, at least one member of the Faculty had been furiously at work. This was Hadley's junior officer and personal friend, John C. Schwab. Schwab had a number of ideas and had gone around consulting members of the Faculty, with the result that he had some far-reaching proposals drawn up. The Professors welcomed this leadership and voted to make his "scheme" the special order of the next meeting.

By such easy stages the Faculty took up a program of reform that with amendments, additions, subtractions, and unforeseen extension was to be the main business of Yale College for the first four years of the new presidency. Small wonder time would be needed. For here was no inconsiderable milestone in American collegiate history. Under a disarmingly modest title a revolution was being projected. It was a revolution in seven acts and I give the document entire.[3]

169

A PROPOSED COLLEGE CURRICULUM

I. A candidate for the degree of A.B. must successfully complete courses aggregating 60 hours per week through a year, but under the following conditions:

II. Freshmen shall take 15 hours per week, Sophomores and Juniors from 15 to 18 hours; Seniors, at least 12 hours.

III. The sequence of courses shall be indicated by grades: First, Second, Third, Fourth. First Grade courses must precede Second Grade Courses, etc., or the equivalent of the lower grade course must be offered and passed.

IV. Each student must complete or anticipate at least one Third Grade course in one, and two Second Grade courses in two, of the following divisions of study: (a) Languages and Literature; (b) Mathematics and Natural Science; (c) Mental, Historical and Political Science.

V. Each student must complete (or offer the equivalent of) First Grade courses in three languages (either in two ancient and one modern, or in one ancient and two modern languages), and one First Grade course each in English, Mathematics, and Natural Science, aggregating $3 \times 6 = 18$ hours of required work.

VI. The remaining 42 hours (60 − 18) each student may devote to the higher grade courses in the above required subjects, or to the first and following grade courses in other subjects.

VII. Languages, First, and Mathematics, First, must be taken not later than Freshman year.

Natural Science, First and English, First, not later than Sophomore year.

History, First, not later than Junior nor earlier than Sophomore years.

Philosophy, First, and Political Science, First, not earlier than Junior year.

With Professor Schwab's program before them the Academical Professors set to work methodically, and apparently with a fair degree of unanimity. Taking up its first two provisions they voted them through. By this act it was made plainer than ever that a degree would be awarded at Yale not for specific studies—not even for four years in New Haven—but for a certain number of tickets or credit hours, all studies presumably to be of equal weight. A 60-hour practice (or its equivalent) having been in effect for a number of years, the novelty and importance lay in the word "successfully" in the first section, and in the permission of extra hours in the second. Hadley had mentioned quality as well as quantity and the College was deciding that no longer would it be enough for students to have a passing *average* for all their courses lumped together. Henceforth each course—or at least 60 credit-hours' worth of courses—would *individually* have to be passed. In other words, viewing the activities and distractions of undergraduate life, the prevailing scorn of study and the low estate of scholarship in the College, the Professors were girding their loins to stiffen the requirements and ask for better work.

In any case the yearly standards should also be made definite so that an orderly progress could be required. For if lower-class opportunities were to be enlarged, and 60 hours remained the sole requirement, in theory there would be nothing to prevent a man taking 20 hours a year and graduating in three years—or 12 hours a year, to graduate more comfortably in five. More realistically, what was to prevent a man from adding to his load in the early years so that during Senior year he had practically no work left to do and could enjoy a delightful loaf?

This problem becomes clearer when posed from a different angle. From sections III, IV, and VII of the Schwab program it may fairly be deduced that the reformers were trying to find some substitute for the old and now almost abandoned upper-class requirements—the required series in the sciences, the social sciences, and philosophy which formerly had given warrant and structure to Junior and Senior years. They wanted a reason for hard work and a logic to support the old four-year norm or new 60-hour

171

requirement. A way would have to be opened so that a new sequence of intellectual disciplines could be introduced. Evidently the Faculty had a feeling that it already knew what the two purposes of the upper-class curriculum ought to be. First it should get beyond the superficial and aim at mastery as well as at breadth. Second, it ought to make possible for interested students an organized preparation for their life work. How far such preparation should be general and preprofessional, or on the other hand how many hours should be allowed for straight technical study, would have to be carefully worked out. At the moment it seemed reasonable to provide at least a small opening for professional courses. So it was voted that Sophomores and Juniors in good standing could get up to three hours each ahead on their B.A. work, with a corresponding latitude for noncredit professional or practical studies during Senior year.

With this opening made, the Faculty ought to have been ready to take up the grading of courses. Or perhaps discuss the strict philosophy of requiring sequences of increasing intensity. Or on the other hand approve the safeguarding provisions for breadth. But no. These proposals of Professor Schwab, as set forth in his sections III, IV, and V, were not so simple as they looked. However innocently and logically they were phrased, the Professors discovered in them revolutionary implications. Nearly all of Yale's famous requirements were to be abandoned; for one after the other these proposals attacked philosophy, classics, and the Freshman curriculum—the last strongholds of the old system. As a result, every department in the College would be affected, and one or two might be threatened with extinction.

Section V, for example, could be interpreted to abolish the required curriculum of Freshman year. It was true that mathematics, English, and three language courses would still be required. But English could be postponed to Sophomore year. By implication a science, or some other subject perhaps, could be elected by Freshmen in its stead. In any case, either Greek or Latin could be omitted if the students were willing to study both French and German. No longer would both classics be insisted on. And all this implied additional elective opportunities for Sophomores. Section VII, for instance, suggested that history would be opened to Sophomores and that chemistry and geology, in the guise of "Natural Science," were also to be brought down into lower-class studies. Again, this program called for a *new* requirement: one in natural science. But did everyone realize that the old Senior philosophy requirement and the logic-ethics-psychology course of Junior year were omitted? The professors of philosophy needed no magnifying glass to discover what this threatened for themselves as well as for their discipline. In turn other departments could see that more than curricular principles were at stake. The debate would obviously be political, with the opponents of reform seizing on every omission or technical difficulty.

Listening to the pragmatic questions, sensing the genuine doubts of the meeting, it must have become apparent to the proponents of the new curriculum that no quick ratification could be hoped for. In fact it was doubtful whether the thing could be discussed and passed in anything short of another winter. Yet the Professors were not overwhelmingly hostile. So it was agreed not to try to hurry through the whole program but to continue discussing it, as occasion offered, until some agreement could be reached. Meanwhile it was voted to consider what, if any, changes of a more limited nature should be introduced into the curriculum for the coming year.

At the opening of this next session the Secretary, reading the call for the meeting, concluded with the statement that "The following have been suggested as possible changes:

(1) Abolition of the requirement of Philosophy in the Senior year.

(2) Introduction of History, Chemistry and a second Modern Language as possible choices in Sophomore year.

(3) Introduction of uniform three-hour courses in Freshman Year." [4]

So it had been decided by Professor Schwab and his allies to try for a limited set of reforms specifically destroying the old as a preliminary to introducing the new. And the reforms were really limited. Instead of throwing out all upper-class requirements, only the Senior alternative in philosophy was to be eliminated, while the Junior logic-ethics-psychology requirement would continue. On Freshman year the reformers also retreated. Instead of explicitly introducing alternatives to classics and English into the Freshman curriculum, they now proposed a far more modest step—the equalization of the courses. This meant the enlargement of the twelve weeks of English for the first time into a full-year study, on a par with the rest. This could be done if Greek, Latin, and mathematics, which had been getting an average of four hours each, consented to a reduction to the same three hours that the modern languages had had and that English was now to enjoy. Would the entrenched departments consent? In any case, would they not see in this proposed equalization only the disguised preliminary to the later introduction of the elective principle into Freshman year?

This inference was the more inevitable because the elective system was now to gain full entrance into Sophomore year. Since 1893 a physics option had been allowed to Sophomores. But now three alternative upper-class subjects were to be added. Thus a Sophomore, instead of choosing five out of six, could now elect five or six out of nine. And instead of being forced to study two out of the ancient triad—Latin, Greek, mathematics—he could now avoid all three in favor of the modern languages and sciences. Thus would begin the elimination of the ancient disciplines from Sophomore year.

There was, of course, a more hopeful way of understanding the same proposals. Subjects were once more migrating downward. History, chemistry, and a second modern language would now join physics in Sophomore year, while English, a recent arrival in Freshman year, expanded to normal dimensions. This meant progress in the raising of subject standards and year standards. Likewise it meant that, by beginning his history and his science earlier, a student could carry these studies farther, and that instructors could make the advanced teaching in these subjects "far more systematic and extensive." Hadley said later that this increase in thoroughness had been necessary if the graduate of Yale College was to be as well prepared to begin his professional studies as were graduates of other first-rate colleges of the day. Yet it meant trusting Sophomores to make intelligent choices. And there was no dodging the fact that in both Sophomore and Freshman years the proposed changes could only be at the expense of the old disciplinary and foundation studies.

Despite the calculated modesty of their new suggestions the reformers must have felt uneasy, for they elected to open the argument on the most favorable and constructive ground possible: the improvement of Sophomore year by the admission of additional subjects into that year. Possibly Schwab hoped to cement the alliance with the modern language men and the scientists before having to meet the open attack of the classicists?

The approach was successful. Apparently the majority liked the new subjects and the new opportunities, for the Professors soon voted in favor of history, of chemistry, and of making French and German "independent subjects." With true academic caution, however, each of these votes had been carefully prefaced with the safeguarding formula: "in case the studies of Sophomore year are increased." So the vital decision as to Sophomore year had not yet been taken. In an effort to placate the old guard, before the matter was brought to final vote, the reformers suggested that Greek, Latin, and mathematics might also offer extra courses in Sophomore year.

Then the debate began and it became a battle. Writing in his diary, Professor Bourne recorded: "strong opposition fr[om] Classical men, espec[ially] Goodell & Morris." The classicists could see that despite the opportunity to elect extra courses in their subjects the Sophomores would be able to omit the classics entirely—or all further languages. The true implication therefore was to reduce the importance of linguistic studies in the foundation work. A principle and a power were at stake, and on this the classicists were obdurate. Perrin reported afterward that one of the professors of

Latin was "in a very inflamed state of mind about it." And both the Greek and Latin men declined in the end to enlarge their Sophomore offerings. On the other hand the mathematicians, perhaps because they saw technical advantages in being able to offer another Sophomore course, accepted the olive branch.

This ended the debate.[5] In short order the Professors approved a nine-subject Sophomore program and accepted the equalization of hours in the courses of Freshman year. Professor George Martin Duncan of the philosophy department himself moved the abolition of the Senior philosophy requirement. And it was so voted. The interim Schwab compromise had gone through, and the Course of Study for 1900–01 would give 42 hours out of 60 to electives.

In connection with this 60-hour credit rule certain loose ends remained to be tied in: the problem of students falling behind, the problem of students wishing to forge ahead, and the possibility of applying the time thus gained to professional training. As to failures and conditions the Professors voted that a man who fell more than three hours behind would not be promoted but that a repeating Freshman might recoup by taking three extra hours of Sophomore work. The possibility of men in good standing anticipating further courses was twice debated and postponed; and a grudging permission would not be accorded until the following December. Meanwhile, showing a lesser hesitation, the Professors were induced to authorize for Seniors five hours of elementary instruction in law, and a course, outlines of forestry, to be offered by Professor Graves.

That was all for the first winter of President Hadley's Administration. But it was already a great deal. The general principle of required studies, and the particular subjects of classics, mathematics, and philosophy, had suffered damaging losses while the elective system had made good its strategic advance into Sophomore year. And it looked as if the new freedoms might be applied not merely to more thorough study of liberal subjects but to professional preparation as well.

The next winter was to be one of achievement in which Yale College could pass from the destruction of outworn requirements to agreement on positive and constructive legislation. In December 1900, at their last meeting of the old century, the Academical Professors took up sections III, IV, and V of Schwab's original revolutionary program.[6]

These sections dealt first of all with the question of what basic courses should be required. For the future there was suggested a still further revision in the doctrine of what was indispensable in a Yale College education—this revision to be in favor of the modern languages and science. Next the "Proposed College Curriculum" provided for the grading of all courses into levels of progressive difficulty, and required students to do advanced or intensive work in at least some of their elective subjects. In the eighties the Faculty had hoped that the institution of Special Honors would lead a few upperclassmen toward an intelligent specialization. Now concentration, whether of Honors grade or not, was to be required of everyone. In the third place, to forestall a lopsided concentration, the subjects of instruction were to be grouped into "natural" families or Divisions, and some spread of effort enforced.

Philosophically this Schwab program came close to the assertion that a good curriculum is composed of three parts: foundation, breadth, and concentration. Pragmatically, it questioned the adequacy of the traditional foundation disciplines. And just as realistically it suggested that an ungoverned elective system did not with enough regularity produce either the breadth or the concentration. So at the very moment that the reform attacked the old required studies through an extension of the elective system, it attacked the elective system itself by a reduction in its freedom. In the twentieth century the aimlessness and frivolity fostered by entire liberty would have to be brought under control. That is, into the elective *principle* there should now for the first time be introduced some *system*.

But instead of drawing up a declaration of faith or voting the grand principle of distribution and concentration the Professors at once proceeded—as is so often the case with our impractical profession—to the most practical details. In section V Schwab had introduced three novelties: the abolition of all mental science requirements, the substitution of a requirement in natural science, and the satisfaction of the foreign language requirements either by the traditional rule of two ancient languages and one modern or by a new dispensation of two modern and one ancient.

At once three amendments were moved. The first proposed "to insert Philosophy including Logic, Ethics, and Psychology" in the list of required subjects. The second proposed to drop natural science from that list. And the third proposed to strike out the language alternative that favored the modern languages. With all three issues thus squarely joined, the Professors debated for two full meetings without reaching a vote.

The struggle to save the philosophy requirement was so protracted in part because it was symbolic of old Yale. Yet there must have been impatience with the professors of the subject and strong drive to reach some decision after a year and more of argument. In the end the amendment to require philosophy was overwhelmingly defeated "by a vote of 6 for it to 20 against it." In 1895 a comparable effort had resulted in a 12 to 9 vote to keep philosophy. But now the group of disciplines that President Porter had held most dear could muster only six supporters.

Yet the Faculty were far from rushing madly after new gods. The amendment to "strike out Natural Science" was adopted; and it was voted after discussion to strike out the words "or in one ancient and two modern languages." Thus the friends of science and of modern languages were too few, and of the classics too strong, to permit such liberties with the established Freshman curriculum. There followed in due course a vote refusing to allow the first course in English to be deferred to Sophomore year, and another affirming the five existing requirements for Freshmen. Thus the elective idea was barred from the stronghold of Freshman year. The Officers of Yale College were still differentiating between foundation discipline and upper-class kinds of work.

With these decisions made, the Professors next took up the

report of their committee on the grouping and grading of courses and voted to classify all the courses offered by the College into three levels of progressive difficulty and maturity: A, B, C. The Freshman or elementary or first-year courses in each department were lettered A; the Sophomore or second year or intermediate courses were lettered B; and these in turn were arranged to lead into the advanced C courses for upperclassmen. To give these new sequences meaning, it was also voted to establish what was coming to be known as a major and minor system:

> Each student must complete, or offer the equivalent of, connected courses of Grades A, B and C, aggregating at least 8 hours, in one of the three following departments of study: and connected courses of Grades A, and B, aggregating at least 5 hours, in each of the two other departments:
>
> 1. Languages and Literature
> 2. Mathematics and Natural Science
> 3. Mental, Historical, and Political Science

The eight hours of progressive study in the major were to make certain of advanced and concentrated study, while the five-hour minors in the other two grand Divisions of knowledge would guard against one-sided programs. In the final moment, early in 1901, the time requirement in the major was reduced from eight hours to seven, and promotion standards were made a trifle easier. Then at long last a unanimous vote called for the reference of the amended Course of Study to the Corporation for adoption.*

The Corporation accepted the new curriculum with exemplary promptitude—suggesting only that it might be wise to give the Freshmen some guidance in their unaccustomed responsibility of choosing Sophomore courses and upper-class majors. And so the Professors passed to a consideration of improvements made possible by anticipation and by these new Sophomore opportunities.

How great a flood may be released by pulling a single brick from the academic dike, few laymen appreciate. Thus the placing of

* See Appendix, Table H: "Classified" Electives, 1901–03, p. 711.

inorganic chemistry in Sophomore year made it easy for a student to elect qualitative analysis in Junior year and quantitative analysis in Senior, thereby supplementing the study of geology or mineralogy. A substitution of organic chemistry in Junior year would look toward biology and medicine instead. Again if a man wished to concentrate in applied chemistry, and perhaps on graduation enter a technical school with advanced standing, he could take all three and add certain courses still more specialized and advanced. Yet once the impediments to chemical study in Yale College were removed there were those who saw the possibility and advantage of going still farther.

Accordingly, the Academical Professors inserted among the Senior electives a new premedical course in histology and embryology. Anatomy, which had been made a one-hour Senior elective in 1893, was enlarged to three hours. Taken with Sophomore and Junior chemistry, Junior physiology, and the combination course for Seniors in anatomy, biology, and physiological chemistry, these new offerings made possible a logical sequence of more than fourteen hours of premedical science. In short, an ambitious Yale student was now to be allowed to complete the whole first year of his Medical School curriculum while still an undergraduate working for his four-year B.A.

The Professors also voted to allow two hours of credit for practical music and to continue the five-hour Senior program in law. The addition of a second mathematics course in Sophomore year made it possible to regularize a special six-hour sequence of courses in descriptive geometry and machine designing, preparatory to graduate work in mechanical engineering. In the fine arts elective opportunities to a total of eight hours continued automatically. Finally an incoming Senior was permitted to count for credit five hours of work in the Divinity School. As a natural consequence of this increase in advanced courses and degree of specialization, the standards for Special Honors were also raised.

So by four allied methods—by the A–B–C grading of courses, by the major-minor requirements, by the enlargement of professional instruction, and by the reorganization of Special Honors—

Yale College was moving toward higher, harder, more specialized, and more "useful" instruction. Simultaneously, by the grouping of subjects and by the new distribution requirements, the peculiar values of different kinds of studies were recognized and a reasonable breadth introduced into each undergraduate's experience. And all this was gained without sacrificing the foundation disciplines— the school-and-tool languages of the still-required Freshman curriculum.

In effect what the Academical Department was proposing was that the aims of a college education should be a solid foundation, plus cultivation, plus hard work, plus mastery. The college opportunity was too important to tolerate any dissipation of energies. Efficiency required that there be sequence of effort and progressive levels of instruction, with promotion depending upon the student himself and with the best prepared allowed to go a little faster. Not all undergraduates would be aiming at the same careers; hence choice should be allowed. But these should be connected and intelligent choices, guided by the experience of the faculty. In fine, after two years of consideration and argument the College had not accepted the Schwab program entire. But some long strides had been taken on the road toward an effective twentieth-century curriculum. Yale could enter its Bicentennial year with this hope and satisfaction: *A way to reform the elective system had perhaps been found.* The evils that its champions and the lay public had refused to recognize could at last be curbed, and the full benefits of variety and freedom realized.

"A new and promising line," Hadley had called it. The phrase was appealing and within reason just. But how clear was the line and how far was Yale prepared to go along it? The first public misunderstanding had been over the year-and-hour provisions. "In some of the announcements of this change . . . it was represented as being a step toward a three years' course. This is an error," the President rather flatly declared.[7] True, one of the purposes of the reform was to enable a few well-prepared and mature students to complete the course in three years. But it was not expected that many would avail themselves of the opportunity, for the entering student would have to be exceptionally well prepared and maintain a very high rank in Freshman year. Even then, a special vote of the Faculty would be required.

Were the authorities now taking back with one hand what they had offered with the other? Not entirely. What they had in mind was to keep the advanced student in College, while letting him put his saved time into professional preparation. That is, Yale would eliminate a year, not in College but afterward. There were some, Hadley confessed,

> who object to this movement on principle, holding that a man is better off if he pursues his professional training in the school which is steeped with an atmosphere of its own. But it has always been the Yale idea that a man should be a citizen first and a specialist afterward. Any reform in the course of study which prolongs the time during which a man remains under broadening influences is from this standpoint a thing to be desired.

Very good. But it was still far from clear how much technical instruction Yale College was prepared to absorb in order to keep its four years. The Professors had just legislated in favor of a full year of premedical science. But a Senior could take only five hours of law. And the intending musician could get credit for only two hours of practical music. As a matter of fact the Law Faculty, which had succeeded in drawing seventy Seniors into its special program during the first winter, felt quite disgruntled at the refusal of the College to enlarge its permission into a full year of law. On the other hand there were already signs that the College had doubts about this end of its new and promising line. Dean Wright stressed the effort to prevent undue concentration on any single subject. And in his annual Report President Hadley quite artlessly betrayed his own doubts when he said: "For those who are anxious to enter into professional life as soon as possible, and who can obtain in their professional studies the stimulus which preparation for such life gives, the Sheffield Scientific School furnishes an admirable choice of courses."

Perhaps it was the undergraduates themselves who made clearest the distinction between concentrated work and professional preparation. For when the choices for 1901–02 were in it developed that the incoming Juniors had chosen to major overwhelmingly in history and English, while taking their elective courses predominantly in history, English, philosophy, and the social sciences.* Only too plainly the popularity of the technical subjects in Yale College was limited. Yet the undergraduates were quite capable of taking advantage of new opportunities, as was indicated by the incoming Sophomores' choices, now that the Sophomore electives had expanded to ten. Dean Wright tried to put a good face on the matter, but the showing of the traditional subjects was nonetheless ignominious. In such elective choices there was a warning. Yale College undergraduates would perceive little charm in either the old disciplines or the preprofessional studies. And as between speed or professional study or more free election, it was only the third that evoked any widespread enthusiasm among these beneficiaries. In short what they wanted, if anything, was more of the same "evils" the Hadley-Schwab program had been designed to correct.

Still a further matter for note was that the Freshman program had been kept compulsory—which, all things considered, seemed a little illogical. But Hadley justified this conservatism on two grounds. The first was the desirability of common studies and collective ideals. The second was the fact that any change in the Freshman curriculum would mean for all practical purposes the abolition of Greek. "While there is a considerable group of boys who at present desire to be rid of Greek for good and wise reasons, the real reason for most of the dislike is that it is hard . . . the college that resists this change will gain in quality more than it loses in numbers."

So where did Yale stand? The first conjecture had been that the College might be going toward a three-year degree—or toward pro-

* See Appendix, Table J: Elections under the New System, 1901–02, p. 712.

fessional specialization—but the authorities promptly pulled back. Next an extension of elective opportunities had been offset by arguments for an old-fashioned disciplinary Freshman year. No one knew whether the new upper-class regulations would work, and it was becoming noticeable that the Academical Faculty were themselves showing signs of uncertainty.

In his inaugural Hadley had warned against resting "content with a compromise between conflicting interests rather than a reconciliation of conflicting views." But did not the new scheme partake more of compromise than of reconciliation? The classicists were angry. Professor George Trumbull Ladd, head of the philosophy group, had insisted on being transferred to a University professorship so that he would no longer be an Officer in Yale College. So far from being enthusiastic about the new line, or even willing to go along, he now proceeded aggressively to publish, in some *Forum* articles that attracted national attention, a series of excoriating attacks on the elective idea and other devices of the new education.[8]

This publicity was unfortunate, for however obviously irritable, dogmatic, and reactionary some of the Ladd pronouncements, they were ably stated, contained a great deal of truth, and were not publicly answered. They advertised a rift—and the continuance of a thorough conservatism on the part of some members of the University. Soon Professor Perrin would be assuring the alumni:

> If, in the strenuous competition between colleges and universities which marks these latter days, Yale also feels obliged to change somewhat the content of her education in response to popular demands, we must insist that the spirit, the method, and the product of her education remain essentially the same as heretofore. . . . We cannot have Yale's intellectual training-table converted into an intellectual pastry-shop. We cannot see her arena for strenuous intellectual conquests . . . turned into a sanitarium for victims of the kindergarten habit.[9]

While Perrin was not Hadley, some of this phrasing had a familiar ring. Yale's epigrammatic President himself seemed somewhat less than confident about solutions. In private correspondence and public addresses he made it plain that in his opinion neither the encyclopedic and eclectic system at Harvard nor the return to classical prescription of Professor Ladd was the answer. What Hadley really believed in was "an ordered and organized elective system." [10] But after two years of planning and a year of trial and explanation neither he nor anyone else had succeeded in defining Yale's proposed reorganization in such a way as to be either clear or persuasive to the educational world.

What the College had actually done was free Seniors and Juniors entirely from course requirements and give to the Sophomores for the first time a considerable range of choice. But instead of abandoning the three upper years to the whimsey of students under complete elective freedom, Yale's Professors had organized their courses into levels of progressive difficulty—the A, B, C sequences—grouped them into types of knowledge or discipline, and required of every student both concentration and distribution, i.e., a planned and reasonably systematic use of his opportunities. Unfortunately this had involved a fight within the Faculty. Some of the concessions to conservatism had been psychologically damaging. The publicity had been badly handled. Finally, neither graduates nor undergraduates seemed too sure that Yale had really reformed and some of them were saying so out loud. [11] Small wonder this new and promising line looked to outsiders suspiciously like one more grudging retreat to positions not too tenable or well prepared. Even to devoted friends of Yale, the line seemed a trifle blurred.

CHAPTER 11 · FAREWELL TO GREEK

*The instinct for beauty is set in human nature . . . we may
trust to the instinct of self-preservation in humanity for keeping Greek as a part of our culture. We may trust to it for
even making the study of Greek more prevalent than it is
now.*
    —MATTHEW ARNOLD, *lecture on "Literature and Science,"
    delivered in New Haven, 21 November 1883*

*You will lie awake at night and say to yourself: "I can't read
Greek."*
    —KARL YOUNG *to Yale graduate students in English, 1934*

GREEK WAS THE NUB of the problem. With philosophy out of the
way, Greek, Latin, and mathematics stood as the last survivors of
the ancient disciplines. And of these Greek had been singled out
as the crucial, symbolic study—the most irritating, the most vulnerable, the next victim of the elective movement. It was difficult,
"useless," and aristocratic. It represented the private schools and
the well-to-do classes, the old order of privilege in the professions.
To the swelling high-school systems Greek was the club held over
their head by the exclusive colleges: it prevented new studies and
stood for interference in their concerns. To more and more parents, who had made their way in business and who sought for their
sons a social rather than an intellectual training, Greek seemed
old-fashioned and quite impractical.

Of course the problem of Yale's public and school relations was
larger than a single language requirement. But if the College
really believed in substituting "organized" election for the old
oil-and-vinegar combination of absolute requirements and free

186

electives, and if the plan was to begin the social sciences and other studies for breadth earlier, that meant enlarging the Freshman curriculum. At once quite a number of first-year men would substitute some more inviting study for Greek. Whatever the strict logic of the matter, Yale would then find it politically impossible to require for entrance what was no longer being asked of all its Freshmen. And finally the schools would no longer have time to teach what was not required for college. In short, to reduce Greek would lead to its being abandoned.

This dilemma was hardly new. For a long generation the din about Greek had swelled and diminished, only to rise more stridently than before. Most of the church schools and the smaller denominational colleges were still not prepared to abandon the language of Protestantism and the Renaissance—this study that for three hundred years had been used to turn plowboys and townsmen into a responsible American leadership. Yet with the rise of the newer studies and the modern multipurpose universities, the pressures from within as well as from below had become almost intolerable.

Under the advanced ideas of President Eliot, Harvard had ceased to require Greek either in college (1884) or for entrance (1887)—and had been called a traitor to the cause. Now, under its first lay President, Yale's turn had come. If so, there were two important problems to be worked out: on the one hand the revision of the Freshman curriculum, on the other the question of what substitutes for Greek Yale College would be willing to accept from the schools. A study of the unpublished documents shows that the struggle over Greek proceeded through four distinct phases.

The issue had first been brought squarely before the professorial Faculty in 1899 by Professor Schwab's modest proposals for opening up Freshman year. His suggestion had been that Freshmen be allowed to substitute a modern language for either Greek or Latin. But the whole problem of Freshman electives seemed too explosive. As Hadley pointed out, such a change would threaten not only Freshman standards of hard work but their social unity and morale. As he did not say, it threatened the property interests of the classicists, the scholarly foundations of the ministry, and perhaps the cultural interests of society too. The stand that Yale took would be almost certain to influence other colleges and schools. Yet despite and perhaps because of these immense implications, domestic repercussions were uppermost in the minds of the Professors; and so by general consent the revision of Freshman studies had been shelved until a systematic program for the three upper years could be put through.

Meanwhile exploration was started on the precollege aspects of the problem. In January 1901 the Academical Professors consented to the appointment of a committee, headed by George Burton Adams and composed of leading professors, whose delicate responsibility it would be to come up with a substitute for the entrance requirement in Greek. The record of their deliberations traces a difficult investigation, tactfully and effectively conducted by Professor Adams. At first the committee examined school catalogues and college entrance requirements, finding an almost hopeless variety and confusion. Then they explored their own strong convictions, but with sufficient good temper so that out of a variety of plans a single recommendation was ultimately fashioned.[1]

This final suggestion was that four years of German be accepted as a substitute for the three years of required Greek. The proposed alternative was certainly as hard as Hadley could have desired. Presumably German was better taught in schools than French or history. It had the further advantage of being the language of modern scholarship. But "after a full expression of opinion" the committee was discharged and its report went over to the fall. So the entrance requirement issue was likewise postponed.

The third round in this crucial debate opened in October 1901 —but not by any vote on a four-year German substitute. Professor Adams had been growing anxious lest Yale take a halfway position that would be thought grudging and be without influence on the national movement. He therefore revived his own more generous plan of allowing candidates to substitute, for one or three years of

Greek, the same number of years of *any* subject which students were then allowed to anticipate. This idea of not increasing the difficulty of getting into College found support. But the extension of elective freedom down into the school system was apparently pushing things further than a majority thought proper. So instead Professor Adams regretfully offered a resolution to the effect that in case Greek was dropped both French and German should be required.

At the next meeting Professor Dana secured the Professors' attention to still a different scheme—for the benefit of the sciences. He proposed that if one year of Greek was to be replaced, it should be by the anticipation of Freshman (fourth year) mathematics. In Freshman year these students would then continue with Sophomore mathematics or with physics. On the other hand, if no Greek at all were offered, then the students should present either the fourth year of mathematics and one extra year of both French and German or three extra years divided between the modern languages. This proposed "choice of courses" was adopted.[2]

The rest of the story for that winter is curious. After considering and rejecting a series of additional "equivalents," the Faculty also adopted Professor Dana's proposal for the continuation of the substituted studies through Sophomore year. Thus a set of Greek substitutes, in the shape of mathematics and modern languages, had apparently been approved for College as well as for school. But after the holiday President Hadley read to the Professors several letters from preparatory-school principals in reference to a substitute for Greek in the entrance examination. Thereupon the Faculty adjourned—and took no action on Greek all the rest of the winter. So this third round, like the preceding two years, passed without decision. Why? The President gave an official explanation. It was that investigation among teachers in secondary schools had revealed

> . . . a strong and rather surprising trend of opinion that men taking a long course of secondary education were better off with Greek than without it. Generally, it may be added that the men who have sent the best boys to college were the ones that most

deprecated the change. Under these circumstances, it seems likely that the efforts at reform in the immediate future within the Academic faculty will be directed toward improving the quality of the teaching and the character of the examination methods, rather than changing the scope of studies prescribed —especially as the courses in the Sheffield Scientific School furnish such an admirable opportunity for those who wish to save time by the omission of Greek before going into their active professional work. For the present at any rate, the Academic faculty does not see its way clear to advising a secondary course which spends the time and omits the Greek.[3]

While this explanation located an important obstacle in the secondary schools, it presented but a single facet. For example, the student who goes through Hadley's letter files will discover that it was not the secondary-school teachers whom Hadley had consulted but the heads of leading private preparatory schools: Hill, Taft, Exeter, Groton, and Hotchkiss. He did in the end write also to the principals of some large high schools in Connecticut and the Middle West—but not until after he had personally arrested Faculty action by reading the replies from the Eastern preparatory schools. Perhaps the change of heart was as much Hadley's as the Professors'. In private conversation he allowed that there was uncertainty or opposition in other quarters—in the Corporation and among the alumni. He had been listening to men of big business as well, with their preference for "drill on the old-fashioned lines." [4] He quoted a leading employer of railroad labor:

When I want a college man, I want a man who knows that it is hard work to use books that are worth anything; and as a preparation for railroad service I would rather have a man who has learned to use one hard book without liking it—a Greek dictionary if you please—than a man who thinks he knows all the experimental science and all the shop work which any school can give him and has enjoyed it because it is easy.[5]

The fourth winter in the Greek war opened with a minor engagement, but this time the result was anything but inconclusive.

190

Before this engagement was broken off not merely Greek but Latin, mathematics, and the whole course of study were brought into the question—and not merely the Faculty and President but the Corporation, the alumni, and the whole theory of College government.

It began on a fringe issue. The Departments had arranged their offerings into A–B–C levels of progressive difficulty and maturity. Under the new major and minor rule, with its requirement of so many hours in intermediate or advanced work (B and C courses), a department of study found itself at a handicap in its competition for students if its introductory work did not begin before Junior year. Thus there was pressure to add to the electives of Sophomore year. In January 1903 notice was given that the departments of Biblical literature and political economy wished to introduce their subjects into Sophomore year. This provided the head of the Kent Chemical Laboratory, Frank Austin Gooch, Harvard '72, with a chance to open up the Freshman year, too. The scheme he proposed went promptly to the Course of Study Committee, and there followed a swift series of meetings marked by intense discussion.[6]

It was proposed to open practically all the A courses to Freshmen. This would make available the same number of subjects as at Harvard, but taught in two-fifths as many courses. It would give Freshmen the Harvard advantage of a wider range without undermining the Yale principle of required sequence. Since practically all the needed instructors were on the ground, no real financial burden was involved. On the contrary, a prompt adoption might attract boys to the incoming Class and improve the financial outlook. This last thought was beginning to sway President Hadley. For it was a sobering fact that since 1896 the Yale College enrollment had not grown at all, while Harvard had doubled its lead. Greek was costing the College tuitions as well as prestige. Perhaps it was also driving away the boys of moderate means and threatening Yale's social democracy.

The proposed additions to Sophomore year were accepted, but the Freshman proposals underwent a grueling analysis. Finally, after four meetings, the Faculty voted that in Freshman year a student might take any five of the following A courses: Latin,

Greek, French, German, English, and mathematics. They also voted to include in the list beginning courses in history and in chemistry.

And so the Faculty finally discovered its willingness to abandon compulsory Greek. And not Greek alone. For the permission to take history, chemistry, English, French, *and* German meant that thenceforward undergraduates would be able to drop Latin and mathematics as well as Greek on entering College, and so get their B.A. degree without any work in these time-honored subjects. By the same token Yale College would also be abolishing the last of its required studies. The decisive action came on 28 February 1903, on the question of recommending the Freshman and Sophomore changes to the Corporation. The matter was considered of such importance that a yea and nay vote was taken, which showed fifteen in favor, ten opposed, one abstaining, and eleven absent.[7]

This was uncomfortably close, especially as Hadley had warned them that the Corporation was disturbed and might be reluctant to sanction so great a revolution. But a vote was a vote. So a strong committee was appointed to present the subject, when properly formulated, to the Corporation in connection with other improvements in the A–B–C system. The ratification of this formulation was also by formal vote and this time the vote was decisive—22 to 8, with only 7 members absent. Only two mathematicians—the great Willard Gibbs and Andrew W. Phillips—remained stoutly with the six professors of classics, trying to hold the narrow pass into Freshman year: their modern Thermopylae. And Dean Wright was added to the precedent-shattering committee to wait on the Corporation.

Two days later the Corporation gave answer. Its votes were unanimous.[8] The revised Course of Study was approved as recommended. Then came the stunning blow:

> Voted, to request the Academical Professors to consider earnestly the advisability of passing such regulations as will prevent the possible simultaneous abandonment in Freshman year of the three disciplinary studies presented for entrance examinations, namely Greek, Latin, and Mathematics.

In short, now that the Academical Professors were ready to cut loose from the ancient disciplines, it was discovered that the Corporation still was unwilling to give them up entirely, and was even taking a hand in curriculum-making. The Faculty reacted with considerable firmness and no little dignity:

Gentlemen:

The Professors of the Academical Department have taken the proposition of the Corporation into serious consideration and, in view of the following facts, would respectfully ask the Corporation to reconsider its request:

1. In the opinion of the Dean and of representative officers of the Departments concerned, it would be detrimental to the interests of those Departments to adopt the suggestion of requiring every Freshman to take Latin, or Greek, or Mathematics.

2. The recommendation interferes with the prospective changes in entrance requirements, to which the Faculty proposes to give early attention.

3. The recommendation runs counter to the leading principle involved in the scheme already adopted by the Faculty and sanctioned by the Corporation.[9]

The Faculty's committee offered to wait upon that influential executive arm of the Corporation—the Prudential Committee. But there was no action. Hadley went on tour to the Western alumni. The *Alumni Weekly* editorialized and the letter writers had their say in its columns. After a month's canvass the Corporation's fears of relaxing old standards were in no way lessened. So the Faculty, however unenthusiastically, had to find a compromise.

The Professors' minutes recite that several plans were submitted to meet the Corporation's wishes. There was a proposal that thirty out of sixty credit hours should be required in courses above grade A, and that Freshmen should be encouraged rather than required to take one of the old disciplines by classifying Latin, Greek, and mathematics in grade B. Apparently this was not strong enough.

A proposal to make one of these disciplines inescapable by reducing the number of Freshman subjects to seven was decisively defeated. Then by the narrow margin of 14 to 11 the Professors accepted Professor Goodell's proposal that Freshmen would have to continue in College three out of the five subjects which they had offered for entrance—English, French or German, Greek, Latin, and mathematics. And finally—after a show of hands reaffirming their preference on its merits for their original proposition—it was voted to submit the Goodell compromise to the Corporation: "22 in favor; none voting against." [10]

So the Professors caved in. After four years of dogged defense, and without ever mustering more than seven or eight votes on the merits, the champions of Greek, Latin, and mathematics had succeeded in putting a picket fence around their favored disciplines. And no one had stood out against the will of the Corporation. A handful had finally abstained from voting at all and more still had not attended. But the capitulation of the Academical Professors was nonetheless striking. In effect, twenty-two men on behalf of some thirty-seven had said "Yes, sir." They then proceeded formally to abolish the requirement of Greek for entrance. In its place a student might offer mathematics and modern languages, as had been agreed to the year before.*

So came to a pause the great campaign against the classics and the old foundation disciplines. Greek was no longer to be required for entrance. Neither Greek, Latin, nor mathematics would any longer be absolute requirements for Freshmen. In fact no longer would all the Yale B.A.'s have had any single study or course together in College.†

* This scheme of equivalents was to go into effect for the Class of 1908, entering in 1904. See Appendix, Table K: Regulated Electives: The Second Phase, 1903–08, p. 713.

† It was true that most Freshmen would elect English, most Juniors would continue to take elementary economics, and the great bulk of the Seniors would still be sitting under Sumner and listening to Wheeler's lectures on European

President Hadley, who had never presumed to predict when Greek might go, but who must have been somewhat embarrassed by the abandonment of the position that he had announced only the year before, adopted the following argument: Nearly every university on both sides of the Atlantic had abandoned Greek as an entrance requirement. Yale had found it could get the same "consecutiveness and difficulty" in the newer subjects. Modern languages might prove at least as hard. Meanwhile, relations with the schools would be improved. And as for "the loss of that coherence and public spirit for which Yale College has been distinguished," were not these things "grounded in the social system of the college rather than in its class room organization"? Besides, Latin and mathematics were required for entrance. Greek would continue to be studied by the great majority of applicants for admission, and would be "extensively pursued" in the College course itself.[11]

While post-mortem rationalizations do not always make edifying reading, on these last points Hadley was not far from the fact. For, however revolutionary the public abandonment of Greek might seem, at least two legacies of the past would still be found imbedded in Yale's future system. The first was the principle of the continuity of study from school into college—the refusal to abandon the disciplinary, school-and-tool type of training in Freshman year. And the second was the substantial quantity of Latin, of mathematics, even of Greek saved for the twentieth-century undergraduates. Under the pressure of the elective idea, professional ambitions, competition for students, and a school system that was getting increasingly out of control, Yale had modified its definition of the content of a liberal education. It had not, like Harvard, abandoned subject requirements entirely.

Perhaps Yale had reached the proper solution. But the announcement made a poor public impression. The reaction of the modernists was particularly critical. Just as Professor Adams had feared, the liberalization had taken too long and had been drawn

---

history. In 1906 Wheeler was continued as a lecturer so that he would not be compelled to retire.

on too narrow lines to appeal to the liberal view. The New York *Evening Post* described the extension of electives into Yale's Freshman year as "a capitulation to educational progress of more than passing interest"—but not likely to call forth any echoes comparable to the controversy over Harvard's original action. The *Nation* also spoke of "the final surrender to the elective system," and rather rubbed in Yale's repudiation of Professor Ladd and of President Dwight's system of Freshman-Sophomore requirements. Nor did the *Nation* take notice of the principle of connected study put forward by Yale, preferring to cite a report of the Harvard Class of 1893, and a study of the Harvard Class of 1901, showing leanings toward related or grouped studies.

"Slowly and deliberately Yale is coming into line with Harvard," sadly conceded a conservative writer in the New York *Sun*. "Yale will follow Harvard's baneful example, too, in allowing options in the requirements for admission. . . . It begins with the experiment that failed completely at Harvard, the substitution of advanced mathematics for Greek." All the same, perhaps Greek and Latin would be safer at Yale than at most other places. The *New Haven Register* thought so, too, and emphasized "the fact that Yale is still to hold aloft, higher than any other institution, the conservative banner." Too bad it had gone so far, and especially at such a time. "For just now the so-called new education is being more criticized than ever before in its history. . . . Has Yale yielded to the new influence just when that influence is beginning to wane?" [12]

The alumni were likewise divided, but with the vocal element distinctly regretful. Having gone through with Greek themselves, they thought it a good thing for the young—just as Seniors always voted for the chapel requirement. There had been "a great many strong differences of opinion," the editor of the *Alumni Weekly* stated; not all could be changed by Corporation vote or a large majority on the Faculty. The new system would have to do exceedingly well to match the achievements of the old. If it did not, then a frank withdrawal was in order. A hopeful sign was that good men were behind the venture. In any case

196

loyalty demands not only cheerful acquiescence . . . but the heartiest support of the administration in applying the new system. . . . And the graduates and friends and allies of this good old Yale will also sustain and cooperate according to their opportunity . . . A great deal will depend upon the attitude of this body of men, who according to President Hadley, 'are Yale.' It may occur to some of them that they have not been consulted much about these radical changes—and there's a subject for further consideration—but it is certainly true that an honest effort has been made to sound their views.[13]

As for the undergraduates, surprisingly they were apathetic. The upperclassmen, like the loyal graduates of 1896 and 1898, were inclined to think that the literature and discipline of Greek had been good for them. The Class of 1906, for whom the liberation came just too late, were understandably divided. The editors of *News* and *Lit.* wrote as if they might have just been talking with President Hadley. In 1908 George Soule Jr. of the first Class to go through under the new arrangements, exhorted his public: [14] "By all means, while we are here, let us find out as much as we can about Greek, Latin, Philosophy, and the more fundamental sciences." The special train, he added, could be taken later.

When put into practice the new regulation produced but a modest change at the start. In the first year only a small number of applicants—mostly men who had prepared for or had entered other colleges—offered the equivalents for Greek. Only seven were finally admitted. In 1904 the first real application of the new rules brought but thirty-eight non-Greek students into the Class of 1908. Meanwhile only English had exceeded Latin, mathematics, and Greek in popularity as a Freshman elective.

Evidently the abandonment of required Greek had not caused a great upsurge in Yale's applications—or a complete boycott of Greek by those already entered. And quite obviously the modern language and mathematics alternatives were hard. Or at least the schoolboys proved badly prepared. Dean Wright pointed to an abnormal proportion of conditions in French and German and commented on the poor school training in grammar. Better teachers and more severe instruction were needed. The next year President Hadley observed that there were a few French teachers who could train as well as the average teacher of Greek, but not enough. Probably this situation would improve, and more and more schoolboys would offer modern languages instead of Greek. "But this will not prove that we have changed our standard. It will prove that the schools have changed theirs. By adapting our choice of subjects to the needs of the schools we can make the schools adapt their method of teaching to our needs." [15]

This was putting a tolerable face on the matter. But would the schools adapt their methods of teaching? In mathematics and German the examinations showed signs of improving; but in French the candidates continued to do poorly. They seemed to show more fluency than grammar, as indeed did the Greek students trained by the newer methods. Yet, according to the Yale theory, forms and syntax should come first. In the old days, observed Dean Wright, the average student had read Latin and Greek more accurately if less fluently. "He had also acquired the power to take up other difficult subjects in the same thorough way." Now the boys were being hurried over the elements. And even so the schools complained of want of time. After careful inquiry the College learned that the preparatory-school teachers thought they needed more time for the equivalents for Greek than they had formerly devoted to drill in Greek, and the majority of them believed it was easier to enter Yale with Greek than without. So strong was this feeling that Yale found it necessary to reduce the mathematical substitute for Homer, and to parry accusations about the narrowness of its list of equivalents.

These latter complaints about the equivalents were disturbing. They indicated that the elective fashion was making further inroads in the schools and thus the retreat from a common standard of secondary education had not been arrested by Yale's concessions. The contingent of applicants for admission without Greek grew inexorably larger. In point of quality these non-Greek candidates seemed to divide rather sharply into the better-than-average and the poorer-than-average student. All of them, however, tended as Freshmen to prefer English and history to the older disciplines.*

The authorities drew back at the suggestion that history be accepted for entrance, too. As Greek and Latin declined, the classicists had been keen to get more ancient history taught; but neither they nor the historians had been willing to accept modern European history as an equivalent. Nor was Hadley, modernist though in many ways he was, at all favorable to the idea of encouraging prep-school American history. What the student needed instead was to get perspective—an outside point of view such as ancient history might provide. Political science, also, had better be reserved for college, or until a boy knew what hard bookwork and "daily exercise in close reasoning" meant. Otherwise there was the risk that school courses in history or economics would attempt "to teach a boy what to think, instead of teaching him how to think." [16]

Finally there was the growing unpopularity of Latin. The amount of Latin was complained of by individual schoolmasters; and an attempt to substitute for Ovid a more thorough paper in grammar and syntax was not welcomed.[17] Apparently the public was becoming less and less inclined to put up with an insistence on thorough grammatical work, no matter in what language it might be required. In Latin composition the answers on Yale's entrance examinations grew poorer. Then the alumni began to complain. A "Friend of the Classics" wanted to know why Latin could not be taught as literature and culture rather than as language and philology. A heretical suggestion to study the classics through translations started a heated debate in the *Alumni Weekly*. This settled nothing, but it hinted how uncertain the public support for Latin, too, might become. Finally the *Alumni Weekly* announced its conversion. In 1903 it had resisted radicalism but in December 1908 its new editor, Edwin Oviatt '96, published the opinion that the day would soon come when the remaining dead language would go.[18]

Notwithstanding these defections, and despite the disappoint-

* See Appendix, Table L: Presentation of Greek for Entrance, p. 714, and Table M: Subject Choices by Freshmen, 1903–19, p. 715.

ing public response to all Yale's efforts to maintain the old studies
—or at least an equivalent standard of preliminary training—the
authorities were reluctant to give up. Hadley thought it infinitely
harder to manage a college where the students did not want to
study Greek: harder to organize intellectual competitions, harder
to enforce regular habits, harder to test ability. To Yale's President
mental discipline, rather than literary quality, historic value, or
practical information, still seemed of first importance. The beauty
of Greek was not the beauty in Greek but the fact that

> Greek is an intellectual game where the umpires know the rules
> better than they know the rules in the game of French, for in-
> stance, or history or botany. . . .
> Unfortunately, a large number of the strongest men . . .
> have decided that this game takes more time than it is worth.
> Personally, I believe that this change of mind is in many re-
> spects a misfortune, that in trying to get more practical knowl-
> edge or culture a great many college boys have lost the training
> which Greek would have given them and gained nothing of
> equal value in its place. But colleges cannot teach a thing to a
> public which does not want to study it.

Thus Hadley gave up Greek, and even came to doubt whether
any equivalent for Greek which took the same amount of time
would ever satisfy the majority. Yale had first tried to ignore the
drift, then to direct it. By 1909 he was conceding that the College
had failed either to stem or to channel the tide. It was necessary
to face the facts. "We cannot decline solving the problem of today
because we like the problem of yesterday better." [19] And the facts
were that Harvard had been growing faster than Yale; the Scientific School itself had grown faster than the Academic Department.
And now the schoolmen were predicting that the movement away
from Greek would accelerate rather than stop.

CHAPTER 12 · CLAIMANTS TO
THE CURRICULUM

Our object is not to teach that which is peculiar to any one
of the professions; but to lay the foundation which is common
to them all.

—*Faculty Report, 1828*

We must apparently experiment with a policy which should
allow the introduction in larger and larger measure of
courses which are really professional within the framework
of the undergraduate electives. We should not only encour-
age a man to experiment as to what he is good for—which is
the principle underlying the elective system as administered
at present—but we should also permit him, when he has
found out what he is good for, to begin seriously the work of
professional study.

—ARTHUR TWINING HADLEY, *1907*

IN MANY an American college and university, as the elective fashion swept the old fixed requirements out of the courses of study,
new interests stole in and sought to appropriate the vacant ground.
In the first years of the twentieth century the Presidents of Harvard, Columbia, and Chicago went so far as to reopen the question
of the four-year B.A. and to canvass publicly the introduction of
professional instruction into the liberal arts curriculum.

At Yale, such questions of speed and practicality had been hesitated over rather than settled. For even had the Schwab-Hadley
program of 1899–1901 proved more decisive, the subsequent abandonment of Greek and the diminution of Yale's school-and-tool

requirements would have invited reconsideration. So now, alike for public and private reasons, Yale, too, had to wrestle with this conundrum of the elective principle: what was to replace the old required values and the old theory of a liberal education?

The departures from the older system were unmistakable. Whatever the shortcomings of the former Course of Instruction, it had been characterized by both order and purpose. The stages in a liberal education had been marked by progression from a solid foundation in the traditional languages and mathematics to a superstructure composed of philosophy, psychology, history, political economy, and the earth sciences. By long-standing practice the classical-mathematical studies had been used to cultivate accuracy, thoroughness, and discipline—the mental, moral, social, and natural sciences to widen and refine the understanding. The whole had constituted an unfinished but balanced preparation, with general ability rather than specialized competence the end product. Thus training for citizenship, ability for social relations, cultural literacy, and a solid basis for professional training had all been assured. *Consule Planco.*

By 1903, with the abandonment of Greek, the Academical Professors no longer felt able to insist that there were any fundamental, indispensable college disciplines—or any necessary sequences between subjects. For that matter, the authorities were no longer sure for what careers the undergraduates might be or ought to be preparing—or even who should or should not come to college. All that had apparently been agreed on was the requirement of sixty credit coupons, to be spread across three somewhat amorphous divisions of knowledge under a mild A–B–C system of progression. Each student could choose his own major and his minors. And a whole quarter of his studytime, being freely elective, could be given to courses broad or narrow, easy or hard, pertinent to a career or utterly erratic.

Thus the theory of a liberal education had become so neutral as no longer to dictate any specific content. Yet once its content had been called into question, inevitably there was precipitated a controversy over its duration; and rival interests sought to appropriate portions of this undirected studytime for other legitimate purposes. This struggle took three different forms—all facets of the same underlying competition. First there was agitation to telescope the traditional four years into a three-year B.A., to the end that all hands could get on sooner to their careers. Second, there was canvassed the possibility of letting the abler students achieve this end by taking extra courses and by anticipating the requirements of others. Finally came an organized drive to amalgamate general instruction with professional training in "Combined Courses"— what for clarity may be called Combined Programs—so that those particular students who were seeking entry to the professions might save a year or more on the road.

As we look back from the vantage point of a later generation, it begins to be clear that immediately following the introduction of the new liberties the authorities of the College heard the competitors, considered, experimented, and finally decided. And their decision fixed for Yale—and quite possibly for other colleges too— the duration and purpose of the B.A. curriculum right down to the second World War.

THE PROPOSED THREE-YEAR B.A.

The proposal to reduce the standard B.A. course from four years to three had behind it much logic, considerable European precedent, and from the later nineteenth century some powerful American support.

Originally, the four-year curriculum for the Bachelor of Arts degree had been an inheritance from the medieval universities, transmitted to America through the great English universities. At the time of colonial settlement and college founding Cambridge and Oxford still maintained the requirement of four years' residence; and President Dunster, after the trying early years of Harvard's establishment, impressed the quadrennium upon his college so firmly—making it stick in spite of student strikes and Overseers' complaints—that it held there and throughout the country for centuries.[1] But already, at the time of his action, the customs abroad had been changing. On the Continent the arts curriculum had largely been pushed down into the secondary schools (later *gymnasium* or *lycée*)—the college was squeezed out between these preparatory schools and the higher or professional university—and the B.A. degree dropped out of use. In Scotland the four-year course remained, but using the M.A. as the first degree in arts. Then Cambridge and Oxford, with the passage of time, reduced their course to three years.

By English precedent alone, then, a general and liberal education could be acquired in three years, if the lower schools were doing their job. Or to be frank, even if they were not. For in the United States the B.A. had not recently represented a fixed value. In the absence of national certificating authorities, and with each college setting its own tasks, holding its own examinations, and making its own awards, inevitably standards had varied. Neither the quantity nor the quality of studies made the four-year curriculum immutable.

Since 1850 the three-year practice had also acquired American precedents, and no little educational authority. For example, the Sheffield Scientific School had modeled its course after the École Centrale des Arts et Manufactures in France, and had succeeded so well with its three-year programs for engineers, scientists, and non-classical students as to win the admiration of President Eliot. For a long time Eliot had been urging the same goal at Cambridge—with the result that no small number of Harvard students were going through in three years, and obtaining degrees *cum laude* into the bargain.[2]

Again there was the argument that students needed the full four years less than formerly. The number and competence of the private preparatory schools had greatly increased in the preceding decades. The public-high-school movement was filling a big vacuum with more or less systematic instruction. Entrance standards had been rising steadily and Freshmen came better prepared. The desire to draw advantage from this improved schooling had the more force because of the growing specialization of modern life.

The sciences and the semitechnical callings were becoming so complex that more and more occupations were beginning to need a formal schooling in addition to the usual shop training. Likewise the older "learned professions" were having to lengthen their courses from two to three years or from three to four.

Inexorably the road into practice was lengthening and its cost was increasing. This consideration weighed heavily with President Eliot. The period devoted to strict professional training had, he said, more than doubled in the past forty years. And now the additional requirement of an A.B. for entrance, as recently instituted by the Harvard professional schools, was having the happiest effect, and other universities should imitate it. Yet the interests of society required that men should begin to practice no later than twenty-five. This meant that preprofessional training should end at twenty-one. Since boys entered college at eighteen, this left just three years for college. Thus the Harvard policy was to encourage the secondary schools, and consent to a three-year college program, under a higher standard of expectation.

In 1903 the issue boiled up into a public debate [3] which showed that neither Andrew F. West at Princeton, nor William Rainey Harper of Chicago, nor Nicholas Murray Butler of Columbia quite liked the Eliot solution. Dean West argued that time counted as well as the studies taken. In any case, the three-year program would result in confusing the foundation and exploratory halves of the curriculum, and would make impossible any community of culture based on our intellectual inheritance. President Harper pointed out that the high schools could not, like the Eastern preparatory schools, be expected to take on any more college work. If anything were to be done for the professions it ought to be in college, by giving professional instruction in Senior year. President Butler decried the confusion of professional with college needs. The colleges should agree in demanding a ten-year preliminary schooling, after which the four-year elective course was not too long for the future scholar, teacher, or man of affairs. On the other hand the university colleges ought to set up a separate two-year B.A. curriculum, purely liberal but carefully planned, for the preprofessional student. And on this basis the university professional Schools ought to require two years, not four, of college work for entrance.*

A final argument for shortening the B.A. was that there seemed so much waste motion in college. Here and there faculty committees were just discovering how little of his four years the average undergraduate actually spent in studying. This slack could be taken in. In three years the student could be provided with such languages and sciences as were needed, such concentration and distribution as would train and broaden him. Then the random electives which were so hard to justify on any pragmatic grounds could be omitted. The more so as this intellectual dissipation tended to encourage other forms of dissipation.

All these considerations made Hadley genuinely uncomfortable. The immense prestige of Eliot and of Harvard, in particular, and the tendency of professional schools to build up to postgraduate status, had seemed to threaten the University with isolation and the loss of some promising men. In his Report for 1900–01 he hinted to the alumni that it would be harder for Yale to shorten its degree than for Harvard, because Yale required sixty hours of classroom work and regular classroom attendance as compared to a much smaller load (48 to 51 hours) and much freer cutting at Harvard. He would later point out privately that Yale also required progression, i.e., some work of an advanced character.

The moment President Butler of Columbia came out for his two-year B.A. and it became evident that the other universities were not rushing after Eliot, Hadley breathed a sigh of relief. If all the leading universities had turned to a three-year course, Yale could not have stood out. But if it was merely a scramble for brevity and a meaningless symbol, Yale could stick by its guns with advantage.[4]

* Thus were foreshadowed the high-school problem, the idea of junior or community colleges, and the concern for general education which—fifty years later—would still be of first importance. In 1903 the representatives of Columbia, Princeton, and Chicago agreed that a three-year B.A. for all students would be a makeshift, not a defensible educational principle. But only West stood out for the complete integrity of the liberal arts course.

206

While the President worried, the rest of Yale remained utterly calm. Neither professors nor students bothered to argue the issue. On the part of the faculty, no doubt the difficulty of even beginning—let alone finishing—a liberal education in four years may have seemed reason sufficient. But intellectual deprivation can hardly have moved the more casual students to a like unanimity in favor of the four-year course. One's guess about these students is that genuine educational conviction had less to do with keeping them content than habit and the competitions and social delights of College life. Moreover the proportion of those going on into professional study was if anything decreasing; and even these seemed to feel no compelling drive toward haste.

Yale did contain some undergraduates who were in a hurry, or who disliked the language requirements of the College, and so took a three-year course. But these men were either engineers or scientists or the Select Course men in the Sheffield Scientific School. Thus an avenue already existed at Yale whereby it was possible to enter into business or professional life one year sooner. As Hadley observed: "Having a good three-years course for the men who want a three-years course, there is no particular reason why we should compete with ourselves in order to shorten the four-years course for the men who want a four-years course." [5]

In their hearts the Academical Professors could see still less reason why they should reduce the College requirements to imitate Harvard. In any case, despite the example of England and considerable public support for the idea in this country, the Officers of Yale College never seriously debated the three-year B.A. With Hadley making up his own mind in the spring of 1903, the die was cast. Yale University would keep its double standard and Yale College its regular four-year course.

THE ANTICIPATION OF COURSES

Despite Eliot's urgings, the country's oldest college would itself never quite go so far as to reduce the curriculum to a three-year program for everyone. But the anticipation of courses by individual students had long been a favored practice. At Harvard the better prepared and more ambitious had for years been encouraged to achieve advanced standing—to the point of entering as Sophomores or of taking all the required hours in three years. Thus for the able or the professional-minded or the impatient an authentic three-year degree had been made practicable and even somewhat fashionable.

At New Haven the authorities no more believed in individual haste than in general haste. And neither faculty nor undergraduates had been keen on premature specialization. Hence the anticipation of studies had been guarded with jealousy, and in the main had been employed for breadth rather than for technical acceleration. In such matters the focus of attention governed, and at Yale it was the College that dominated.

Historically the use of the anticipation device had been linked to the progress of elective practices. From the introduction of upper-class optionals in 1876–77, Juniors and Seniors had been allowed to anticipate one or more of the remaining requirements, in favor of further optionals, by passing examinations *in the required work* in advance. After 1886 this opportunity was extended to all four Classes, though for lowerclassmen necessarily in a very limited way. In 1894 it was for the first time specifically stated that *any* Freshman or Sophomore course could be anticipated by examination, and a course of an equivalent number of hours from the elective list be substituted, provided the student was qualified for the latter course. Experimental inorganic chemistry was indicated as particularly available. And the same year a Junior could for the first time officially elect eighteen hours of studies—leaving him with only twelve hours to take for credit toward his B.A., and freeing the rest of his Senior time for social activities or straight professional study. Thus if a man anticipated one Freshman course, took one chemistry course early, followed this with other chemistry and anatomy courses, passed off eighteen hours in Junior year, and took some noncredit professional courses in Senior year, he would find himself considerably advanced toward his medical degree.

By this means there was added to anticipation in the interest of breadth a disguised acceleration in the direction of professional study. For it was inherent in the situation that if any required studies were transferred to the elective list, by that much would speed have to replace general culture as the object of anticipation. For why anticipate an *elective*, if not to get nearer to the degree? Yet until the end of President Dwight's administration the dike held, and the Yale undergraduate hardly touched the possibility of a B.A. in three years.

Then came the release. In 1900 and 1901 the Senior-Junior requirements in Philosophy and in Logic-Ethics-Psychology were canceled, and the Sophomore electives expanded to nine; in 1903 the Freshman curriculum itself was converted into a choice among eight subjects. This meant the end of anticipation for breadth. Instead, all undergraduates were now allowed to accumulate advance credits by examination. Sophomores as well as Juniors were allowed to take eighteen hours of courses. And in Senior year five hours of strictly professional courses could be counted for the B.A. degree. All this added up to the fact that if a student managed to get ten credit hours ahead by the fall of his Senior year he could give the whole of this last year to professional study, counting five hours for credit toward both degrees and the remaining eight to ten hours for extra credit toward his second degree.

Momentarily Dean Wright even encouraged serious students to think of a B.A. in three years. But the Professors generally continued antipathetic. They hedged the new opportunities about with many restrictions. To anticipate a course a candidate had to make special application, pay a special fee, and pass a special examination in September. The anticipated course might count toward the sixty hours for the B.A. only by the explicit consent of the Faculty, and even a student coming with substantial advanced preparation was still to be rated as a Freshman. Thus was it made plain as day that Yale did not mean to follow Eliot all the way on anticipation any more than it would go all the way to complete elective freedom. There would be few fast elevators through the Yale House of Knowledge, and each individual trip would have to be freshly authorized.

The results were meager. In 1903 only about twenty men managed to anticipate any of the studies of the Freshman year. By 1906 only three or four candidates in all had had their applications for a three-year program before the Faculty. As if this were not limited enough, in 1905 Dean Wright acted to discourage too much anticipation *within* the College. The next year the general privilege was restricted to those with at least a good (C) average; and the course anticipated could be counted toward the degree only if a grade of C or higher were obtained. In 1915 the Faculty would approve Dean Jones' practice of excluding the courses in a student's major or minor from anticipation; and in 1918–20 the qualifying average would be raised to the mark of B, while a mark of C would be required to count the course for the degree.[6]

Any accounting for a Faculty policy so hostile to anticipation must refer again to the example of Harvard and to conservatism. Also to a genuine faith in a broad cultural experience rather than a narrow specialization. As we shall see, Yale's experience with preprofessional instruction had something to do with the matter. And so did the Yale social system.

Although anticipation by a few scattered individuals would not —like the three-year B.A.—uproot all the accumulated customs, activities, and social honors of Yale's Senior year, it would unquestionably deprive some of the abler boys of the benefits of Class friendships, team loyalties, and social recognition. In turn the withdrawal of such leaders would diminish the integrity of the Class system, upset competitive activities, and perhaps even undermine the authority of the Senior societies. Book learning and the quick degree were hardly so important that the authorities could afford to jeopardize Yale's cherished undergraduate life. Yale College believed in a democracy of character more than in an aristocracy of brains. Specific programs of study might vary; a man might omit whole areas of knowledge if he so elected. He might also, if he were poor, earn his way rather than "heel" a magazine or join a fraternity. But he might not elect to hurry—to omit his Senior year. Not if he wanted the respect of the Yale community.

On behalf of this point of view there was, and there still is, a great deal to be said. The Yale decision corresponded to the American attitude. It made sense to the country. Other colleges felt, and acted, in the same way. Actually, within a year or two of Yale's refusal to carry anticipation to the point of a three-year B.A., Harvard itself would visibly begin to waver. As the movement against the quick degree gathered force, Harvard would soon be trying to revive rather than abbreviate its college.* After some years of debate, the Sheffield Scientific School would have its own three-year programs forcibly made over into a standard four. Nor would the preparatory schools protest. In short the stand of Yale and of other colleges at the beginning of this century would help rivet the four-year college into the framework for American education.

True, this system delayed the entry of a few men into professional life. Since it tended to define a liberal education less in terms of knowledge and power than as a four-year social life in an intellectual community, it also may have tended to diminish self-criticism and soul-searching on the part of the colleges as to their educational methods. On the other hand, this decision to reserve the habitual number of years for college education rendered one service to society that deserves to be remembered.

It bolstered that education, perhaps even saved it from partition and disintegration, just at the moment when the victory of the elective theory and practices had robbed the old curriculum of much of its character and meaning. By refusing to allow the preparatory schools to take over Freshman and possibly Sophomore years, and by refusing to transfer Senior and possibly Junior years to the complete control of the professional or technical schools—in a word by keeping the four-year college intact and self-controlled—Yale and the other institutions gave themselves time to explore for a new system and order of studies to replace what had been lost. They refused to let the liberal arts college disappear as in Europe. All things considered, this was a decision and a stand for which we should be very grateful.

* President Eliot, who in 1903 had found it "comical" that the President of Chicago could still argue for the dead four-year course, in 1909 heard his own successor declare: "the most vital measure for saving the college is not to shorten its duration, but to ensure that it shall be worth saving." This has been called the only major reform on which Eliot met defeat.[7]

THE PROFESSIONS INVADE THE CURRICULUM

The advantages and the penalties of a university have not always been understood in the United States. One of the marks of the American university, distinguishing it from a college, is the close proximity of professional and graduate schools to the undergraduate teaching institution. This makes possible a profitable exchange of students and of faculty, even a pooling of buildings and resources. One uses the word possible for melancholy reasons. The exchange is far from automatic and the obstacles, human and technical, can be enormous. In fact a stranger to the academic world would perhaps be startled to discover what physical and legal barriers may exist between the separate parts, and what lack of sympathy and understanding. So the rise of the Scientific School in the shadow of Yale College had by no means been followed by a flourishing exchange of students. In 1887 the assumption of the legal title of University had not bridged the gap between the College and the half-private little Law School in its offices in the Court House at the bottom of the Green. No more had it pumped the seething vigor of undergraduate life into the remote little Medical Institution far to the west on York Street. Such gains had been possible but they had not been automatic: in fact they had been slow to materialize.

With the advent of elective practices in Yale College, doors began to open. With the encouragement of specialization, and the ever widening acceptance of new subject matter into a once closed curriculum, specialized instruction became needed and Academic courses began to offer social or scientific materials of interest to professional students. Hence almost from the start there had set in little trickles of students between the professional Schools and the Academical Department, between the College and Sheff, and between the several professional Schools and the Courses of Graduate Instruction.

By 1887 Academical Seniors could take a two-hour nontechnical course in law; [8] Law School students might attend Graduate Department courses under Sumner, Hadley, and the two Wheelers; the Graduate Department listed among its "other instructors" a whole group of professors from the Law School as well as G. P. Fisher from the Divinity School; the Divinity School carried W. R. Harper, Professor in the Graduate Department, as Instructor in Hebrew; while the Medical School admitted graduate and special students to all but the "practical" courses. By the early nineties opportunities had widened still further. Finally, in 1896 it was ruled that a Bachelor of Arts might complete, if he were able, the new three-year Yale Law School course in the old two years. Or a Yale student could take advantage of the provision that graduates in arts, philosophy, or science, who had pursued studies in chemistry, physiology, anatomy, and histology, might be admitted to the second-year class in the Medical School "with conditions." Again he might find himself with some of his theological training already completed.

Thus over a twenty-year period the barriers had slowly eroded. Department by Department, a few students and a course or two at a time, resources had been loaned about in a mutually promising exchange until by 1899 the various Schools in Yale were hesitating on the verge of translating these casual exchanges into a series of deliberate and purposeful combinations. This hesitation was finally overcome by Professor Schwab and his allies when in the first two years of the new Hadley Administration they put through Yale College the decisive legislation permitting undergraduates to elect a full year of medical science and five hours of professional training in the law without losing credit toward their B.A.

This Bachelor of Arts degree was the crucial point. Everyone wanted it and no one was ready to do without it. But who should control it and what it should stand for were matters of increasing argument. It had become the key, perhaps, to the future of the professional Schools. Yet it was still an arts and not a professional degree. It symbolized the old College dominance, and a power of College loyalties that would inevitably give character to the particular compromise adopted at Yale. Four parties had a stake in this issue: Yale College, the Yale professional Schools, the world of

213

competing colleges and universities, and the consuming public. Hadley was umpire.

The Academical Professors had the easiest decision. They were concerned for liberal education, and they were determined to run their own show. Theoretically, they could be interested in more effective upper-class specialization. But when it came down to cases, they could not help preferring the amateur's cultural course in law to the narrow topical beginnings of strict legal training. In science what was theoretical and preliminary seemed better than what was technical or clinical. So also what was learned and literary had a place; mere artistic appreciation or instrumental practice perhaps did not.

On the part of Yale's Law and Medical Schools the desire for improvement was plain; but their situation was complicated, if not positively uncomfortable. All university schools faced the necessity of longer training, greater specialization, and higher costs. But the Yale Schools confronted an unusually powerful College. Except for the Divinity and Forestry Schools, they had quite inadequate funds and had to subsist on tuitions. The Law School had originated as a proprietary enterprise, and had long been carried on with one hand by practicing lawyers and judges. Simeon E. Baldwin and Judge Wayland had taken in boys of miscellaneous ages and backgrounds, most of whom still came without college degrees. For years the great majority of Yale's own undergraduates, on the other hand, had preferred to take their professional training outside of New Haven: in particular at the Columbia and Johns Hopkins medical schools, or at the New York, Harvard, and Columbia law schools.*

An intercollegiate movement was afoot to raise university professional schools to postgraduate level. But if the Yale Schools were suddenly to insist upon the degree for entrance, they risked driving away their New Haven and Connecticut students—the bulk of

* See Appendix, Tables N-1 to N-6: Prior Education of Yale Law, Medical, Divinity School Students; Where Yale Undergraduates Took Their Law, Medical Degrees; and Advanced Degrees Taken by Yale B.A.'s, pp. 716–721.

their clientele—without any certainty of capturing the Yale Seniors. On depleted income the necessary study programs and facilities could not be built up without perhaps bankrupting the Schools. Hence the sensible thing would be to work out a scheme whereby more high-school students could be lured into Yale College, and more Yale College men persuaded to take their M.D.'s and LL.B.'s in New Haven.

From the consumers—the alumni, the students, the law offices, and the general public—came confused demands. Aside from the vocal protests against the lengthening professional course, it is enough to recall that this was the period of the expansion of public education from high school to State or city university—and of the struggle of many a craft or semiprofession like journalism, banking, or government service to reach the status of profession, with organized academic preparation. John Dewey was in the ascendant. Vocationalism was on the rise.

Sitting in the middle of this welter of contentions, President Hadley was fascinated by the problem, albeit less happy over the implications. To his mind the professional school problem involved the whole strategy of university organization—and with that the whole question of intellectual and moral values. There he felt at home. The problem appealed to his powers of logical analysis. He had such brilliant and irresistible insights, and it was his chance to lead. Yet not a little would depend on which end of the stick he picked up—which question he asked first.[9]

As an economist, he approved the introduction of practical training into Senior year, and welcomed the extension of professional instruction from the premedical sciences to law, divinity, engineering, art, and music. But he was also a moralist, and an old College man. It struck him that specialization encouraged selfishness, and professional studies tended to separate a man from his fellows.[10] It followed that the professional Schools should not be given power over Yale's Senior year. Weighing the pros and cons, the umpire's decision was apparently that a moderate overlapping of technical with academic instruction was worth promoting—but

215

that Yale's obligations as a nursery of good citizens, and the judgment of the College Faculty, should govern.

As President, he had also to consider the future of Yale's professional Schools. In the third winter of his administration he took hold of the situation from their end, and posed this important question: Should Yale's Schools of Law and Medicine require a collegiate degree for entrance?

Many thought they should. The President acknowledged that at the time of his election he himself had been so disposed. But the more he studied the subject in its "less obvious bearings" the more he was persuaded that such an answer would be to the injury of both the public and the universities. This for the reason that professional education was coming to take too long and cost too much. The requirement of a bachelor's degree would force the professions to recruit only from the wealthy, and would deprive them of new blood. They would become privileged orders just at the moment when other vocations and occupations were achieving a democratic recognition as equals of the professions. Such exclusiveness, he insisted, would have barred John Marshall and Abraham Lincoln from the law.

But if Yale's professional Schools did not require the degree, a friend had remonstrated, would they not lose the most advanced students and teachers and methods; and would not Yale fall behind the other great universities and lose caste? This word "caste" gave Hadley the cue he was looking for. No. He was not afraid of losing caste. If the Eastern universities insisted on standards that the Western universities could not match, then Yale and its neighbors would be cutting themselves off from the rest of the country. There was something private and exclusive about the ambition to have the best students only. The University should exist for the public and for the professions, not the other way around. The proper policy for the professional Schools was therefore to admit both those who could afford to go to college and those who could not, asking only that the candidates should have a "necessary basis of knowledge." It would be better for Yale to resist the current which would raise professional schools to postgraduate level, and instead lead the way toward a more Germanic system in which arts and professional education would have coordinate status.*

As for Yale College, having rehearsed the whole matter Hadley was confirmed in his doubts about professional claims on academic time. "I believe we should arrange the college course to suit the needs of the men who really want it, rather than for those who . . . take it as a preliminary to something else." At most Yale College might allow some undergraduates by a combination of studies official and private to get a year ahead toward their professional degrees. Logically it might have seemed that the College ought to refuse to concede even five hours of professional study for credit. But such a refusal might drive the intending physicians and lawyers to other colleges. So Hadley's conclusion was that the part-way compromise, tentatively organized in 1899–1901, would continue to be the Yale solution. It was less dramatic than the three-year B.A. It was less simple than a Senior year in straight professional study.

* Here Hadley came face to face with the great dilemma of American education: the choice between quantity and quality. But his assumption that all professional schools could and should follow the identical policy prejudiced his reaction. And the thought of Abraham Lincoln was to stick in his mind and make him hesitate for many years. Apparently he did not recognize that in the twentieth century Lincoln could go to a law school in Illinois—or might even be stimulated to earn his way through Yale College. Nor did he seem to realize that if the standards were such as to make sure that all unrecognized Lincolns could get into the Yale professional Schools, the better prepared students would soon be going elsewhere; while the training which these Lincolns, and their less able friends, would find waiting for them would be of inferior quality.

Again the "caste" business seems a straw dummy. The logical deduction from Hadley's reference to the State universities would have been the proposition that Yale College, too, would really serve the public best if it took all kinds and all qualities of students, even down into the grammar-school level.

To do justice to Hadley, one should read his Report of 1901–02, or the generous excerpts from it in his son's biography. It is full of acute observations and striking antitheses. It breathes sincerity and self-sacrificing idealism. What prevents our assent today, and what must have troubled Yale men at the time, are the inconsistencies, the occasional loaded words and bogus issues, the reluctant recognition that, though Hadley had given the matter much thought, he had apparently not thought his own argument through.

217

But the scheme seemed to meet Yale's special circumstances—and it might even commend itself elsewhere.

THE COMBINED PROGRAMS

The President had miscalculated. The professional Schools differed so greatly in their intellectual requirements that no single undergraduate formula could meet their needs. They also differed in power. Not all were any longer so weak as to feel compelled to accept the half-and-half concessions of Hadley and the Academical Professors. Thus he discovered that the medical and legal groups, though both looking for ability, were not really looking for the same kinds of ability or the same kinds of preparation. Moreover, they had influence.

The medical men wanted their candidates well grounded in specific subjects—biology, physics, chemistry, etc.—and they wanted them young. The law crowd, by contrast, were insisting less on specific grounding—in history, politics, or economics—than on wide human knowledge and maturity of mind. In other words, the preprofessional training now desired for a doctor was specific, scientific, and intensive; whereas for a lawyer it ought to be varied, cultural, and extensive—or not so very different from what would benefit the future businessman.

By the same token, the transition from preprofessional to strictly professional studies, which for the doctors was beginning earlier, would for the lawyers necessarily remain late and abrupt. And any increase of anticipation would only sharpen this contrast. It would also involve the College authorities in a further difficulty—the necessity of borrowing instructors. In science this might mean competing with the Scientific School, to say nothing of paying for the instruction of the Medical School staff. For more law they would have to allow the Law School men to teach within Yale College. Neither expedient appealed to the Academical Professors. For them the temptation to stick to the compromise of 1899–1901 remained very strong.

But the disappointment and restlessness of the professional groups proved stronger still. Protest after protest came from the

218

influential Law Professors. In 1902 the Law School had hoped for ten credit hours in the College instead of five. In 1903, under pressure, the Academical Professors accepted the addition of a sixth hour in international law by Professor T. S. Woolsey, and were willing to allow candidates to take in addition three other law courses for credit only toward the LL.B. But they disapproved any transfer of funds from the Academical Department to pay for such excess instruction.

Impatient and determined, Dean Henry Wade Rogers and Judge Simeon E. Baldwin took their case for a full year of law to the Prudential Committee of the Corporation—which proceeded to upset the rationalizations of their President and the careful compromise of the College authorities by expressing a desire for more undergraduate work in law. Under such compulsion the Academical Professors worked out a scheme for fitting a full year of law training into the A–B–C system. They approved a three-hour course in elementary law, available to both Juniors and Seniors, and five Senior B-level courses totaling eleven hours in contracts, torts, evidence, constitutional and international law. At the same time Professor G. B. Adams, spokesman for the College, made it perfectly plain to Dean Rogers that the College still regarded the law program as Academic courses, temporarily on loan to the Law School Faculty, and to be taught as nearly as possible in harmony with the College ideal.[11]

As for President Hadley, he fell back on the consoling consideration that the same amount of law taught in successive years, at graded levels, and under broadening influences would be quite another thing from a straight year of technical instruction within a professional School.[12] And in 1907 he gave ground still further. Provided the undergraduates were kept under the influence of the College, he announced himself as willing, even anxious, to have professional specialization begin at any time after Sophomore year. Hard work was more important than breadth of culture.* Yale

---

* In rationalizing Yale's change of policy, Hadley came close to squeezing the liberal out of the liberal arts. In 1903 a graduate of '53 had raised the danger signal: "fifty years ago a liberal education was conceived . . . as an ideal whole, to refine the texture of the intellect and give harmonious and general

feared intellectual dissipation more than too early technical study. In any case he could see no equally practicable alternative. Thus was reached a landmark, but far from the last landmark, on the road toward the Combined Programs.

One reason for continued agitation was that the Law School had set its sights on postgraduate status. First, in 1904 the School completed the long process of conversion from the old semipro-prietary status and became a regular budgetary Department of the University: its professors were put on annual University salary and for the most part on full- rather than part-time work. Then two years later a sympathetic Corporation voted that, beginning in 1909, candidates for admission to the Law School would have to present either a diploma from some approved college or scientific school or evidence that they had performed the equivalent of at least two full years of collegiate work. In 1911 a rule requiring four years of college work was adopted, with authority to the Dean to admit students prepared under the old rules "in special cases." Before the adjustment to the new rule was made war conditions caused a postponement, but by November 1920 a full college course would be required of all but the Combined Program men in Yale College.[14]

Meanwhile, albeit the Senior year anticipation courses had not proved entirely satisfactory to either party,[15] the encroachment proceeded inexorably. In 1905 Seniors were allowed to take extra courses for credit toward the LL.B. beyond the fourteen-hour program. In 1911 a straight technical eight-hour law major was sub-stituted to count for both degrees, with minors in either philos-ophy, history, anthropology, or economics, and with extra hours of law available to count for the LL.B. The record shows that in 1916 this eight-hour major was enlarged to ten hours, and in 1922 to thirteen hours. But now the full first year of the regular Law School

development." Under the new theory Yale should seize on what a student could do and make the most of his special abilities. The distortion of his nature might be disregarded. Under the older theory Yale should supply his defects as well as realize his aptitudes. The efficient workman vs. the perfect man.[13]

curriculum had to be taken, rather than a fraction of it plus equivalents. The minor courses were prescribed. And the Dean of the Law School controlled substitutions. In 1927 undergraduates were required to have an average of 75 to qualify. In 1928 this was raised to 80. Then in 1930 the Combined Course privilege was canceled altogether.

So what the College had been reluctant to start, the Law School first took over and then scrapped. The explanation for this reversal is not far to seek. During the first seventeen years of Hadley's presidency the Law School concentrated on raising entrance requirements, modernizing the curriculum, and improving the caliber and seriousness of the student body. Under Dean Swan (1916–27) spectacularly successful drives were then launched to attract to the faculty professors of national reputation, and to strengthen the School's connection with the big law firms. The result was that applications from graduates of other colleges went up astonishingly in number and quality. Meanwhile the annual crop of Yale Seniors remained too attractive a clientele to lose. With the further raising of standards, and the decision to limit the enrollment to one hundred new men a year, the Yale Seniors were again privileged by being allowed to qualify outside of this limitation. But sooner or later they had to come up against the competition of the exceedingly able college graduates from elsewhere, and this competition they were no longer meeting so well. Being undergraduates they didn't work so hard as the regular first-year graduates. The diversions were too many, the distractions too alluring. So where once it had been insisted that the professional Schools lacked the atmosphere and qualities of College Life, now the Law School complained that Yale College lacked serious atmosphere and stimulus. By the mid-twenties the School stood at the top. It could require the full B.A. for entrance yet be overapplied for by the best student talent in the country.

And so the combined College-Law program was given up. At best it had been a compromise that kept some able students flowing in while the Law School made the tremendous leap from a Freshman entrance standard to the requirement of a B.A. degree and from a local semiproprietary School at the collegiate level to a national School of consistent University standards. The transition had taken thirty years,[16] but it had been negotiated with success and increasing reputation. Once achieved, University standards demanded a full seven years for the two degrees. And whether the School would ever wish or be able to invade Yale College territory again would seem doubtful.

With the Medical School, the Divinity School, the Art and Music Schools, cooperative arrangements were also worked out. In each case the patterns of development bore a marked resemblance to the College-Law School experience, allowance being made for the peculiarities of the different disciplines and for the markedly differing reputations of those professions with the American public.

For example, the Medical School had started earlier and was destined to go further in the direction of combined courses than the Law School. Yet in the end it did not succeed in making so clean a break. For these variations the reasons were several.

The combining began earlier at Yale, one surmises, because of the extraordinary success of the premedical training in physiology and physiological chemistry under Director Chittenden of the Sheffield Scientific School. Also because the premedical sciences were easier to recognize and more essential than the prelegal studies in politics, economics, or history. In due course the interpenetration of the two curricula went further because medical knowledge was growing at a frightening pace. This forced on the better Schools a lengthening and constantly intensified period of training. The law degree remained a bachelor's degree and took only three years, whereas the medical students needed four years of professional schooling to become doctors, and even then they had two years of hospital internship ahead of them. It was also an uncomfortable fact that not enough Yale men were going into medicine. So Yale gave its students a choice between two combined programs: one to save one year on the regular eight (1903–22), the other to save two (1907–18).[17]

The requirement of at least two years of college work for admission to the Yale Medical School (1909), the limitations on enrollment, and the ultimate insistence on at least three years of college education (1920 and after), paralleled the rising standards of the Law School. Finally, the Medical School failed to withdraw entirely from the academic level because of the overwhelming pressure for more science. There were also a number of other factors, not all admirable. The competition for first-class medical students was too stiff. The medical schools failed to get together on entrance requirements and developed no adequate code to govern recruiting. And, in the matter of Yale College at least, there were powerful doctor fathers, anxious for their sons to enjoy both the Senior societies and a privileged entrance to the best medical schools. So the logical transfer of medical studies from the College to the Scientific School was never completely effected. Instead, a few men would continue to prepare for medicine, yet remain enrolled in the College, right down through World War II.

While the Academic-Theological arrangements followed the pattern laid out by medicine and law, there were variations induced by a certain nebulousness within the theological situation. In the decades before the combination plan developed, the Divinity School had been losing its grip on conviction, and its purpose in the modern industrial world was being reinterpreted. Should its education be orthodox, historical, and theological—should it be philosophical—or should it be more in the line of good works and social welfare? Being unable to choose, or to eliminate, the School took advantage of the elective idea and set up three different curricula for the B.D. By 1910 these had developed into four departments—Pastoral Service, Missions, Religious Education, and Practical Philanthropy. In the process arose a need for economics, government, psychology, and organic evolution, and an interest in a considerable range of College courses on the part of the intending theologian. In the wide-open period of 1907–18 intending divinity students were not merely allowed to credit first eight, then ten hours of professional study toward the B.A.; they found majors in philosophy and psychology as well as in Biblical literature available, and an unusual range of minors from which to select. And between 1915 and 1928 they were given the additional option of thirteen-hour Honors programs in philosophy, or Biblical literature, or Asiatic history.[18]

Meanwhile the recession was setting in. Qualitative standards began to be imposed. In 1928 Honors candidates were no longer allowed to combine courses. Then in 1935 the arrangements for overlapping curricula were terminated. Thereafter the Divinity School required a college degree for entrance from Yale men as well as from others, and seven years of general and professional education once again became the norm. The odd thing about this experiment in religious training was that it served so few. Over the thirty-five years but a handful of students took advantage of the unusually generous opportunities. To most Yale undergraduates divinity seemed the profession of the past.

Perhaps the fine arts were the profession of the future. Unquestionably more students were beginning to dabble in painting and music than were electing the Combined Programs in medicine or divinity. By 1909–13 there was noticeable enthusiasm for dramatic and artistic activities and for wider instruction in such subjects.* But admission of music and the fine arts to equality in the College curriculum came grudgingly. And the Combined Programs developed so late that they were but midway through the standard cycle of development when interrupted by the catastrophe of World War II.

For this tardiness three things were primarily responsible. The first was an adverse, even scornful public opinion. Music and the

* In 1902–03 Academical students were enrolled in other Schools of the University as follows: Law 87, Graduate 59, Music 57, Scientific 54, Art 32, Medicine 10, Divinity 3, Forestry 2. By 1909 complaint was being made that the College offered 106 courses in language, literature, classical archaeology; 51 in mathematics and the sciences; 72 in philosophy, education, history, and the social sciences; but in the fine arts and music only 8.[19]

224

fine arts were just not taken seriously in America. The second impediment was that the fine arts were technical or in part unintellectual disciplines. Their training was to a degree manual and seemed to have little in common with a linguistic-scientific education based on books. The combining of programs was the more difficult because these Schools admitted high-school graduates of both sexes. The Schools also awarded certificates and were slow to develop effective programs for bachelor's degrees.

Administrative prejudice was the third obstacle. Hadley doubted, and many an old-line professor doubted, that art for undergraduates could be made disciplinary or could be thoroughly taught. At Harvard all the lazy men had elected courses in the fine arts, which were proverbial "snaps." Director John F. Weir wrote letters of great charm and appeal to the President, and he applied again and again to the College Officers for permission to offer more courses or to bring art instruction down into Sophomore year. But the President kept putting him off, and the Professors kept refusing to countenance any real expansion. In 1909 Hadley argued courteously but publicly that subjects in which you could not create competition or test power by examinations did not belong in the formal curriculum.[26]

But this turned out to be another theoretical position impossible to maintain against the rising tide of interest and demand. The defenders first found their flank turned by courses which married the arts to such established and respectable pursuits as history and classical archaeology. The theory and literature of the arts were next developed and sequences of progressive difficulty were organized by the Schools. So from occasional electives the artistic disciplines struggled painfully upward to achieve acceptance as majors or minors—then full-fledged status as Combined Programs.

Inevitably it was architecture, the most learned and literary and scientific of the arts, which in 1913–14 first broke through the barriers of habit and prejudice.* In 1922–23 music consolidated

* Architecture had a further advantage in the fact that it depended upon, and gave credit for, instruction in *both* undergraduate Schools. By the Scientific School it was supplied with mechanical drawing, mathematics, and engi-

its rather casual arrangements into an intensive College major and a five-year Combined Program for the B.A.—Mus.B. In 1929 painting and sculpture were dignified by Combined Programs. In 1938–39 distinct majors in the history of art and in drama were set up in Yale College—but as yet without formal recognition as Combined Programs.

Meanwhile one other handicap continued to hold the fine arts back in their rise toward postgraduate status. This was the problem of their entrance standards. Unlike the Law and Divinity Schools, the several departments in art and music either did not wish or did not succeed in requiring a college degree for admission. Like some men in the medical profession, they desired to catch and train their apprentices young. In turn the art and music students were too impecunious, or too uninterested in book learning. It was true that the proportion of college graduates proved high in the new Drama School,[22] and constituted a majority of the architectural enrollment in the years 1930–32. But even the architecture courses admitted three different classes of students. To Yale graduates, who had taken the Combined Program, the B.F.A. (later B.Arch.) was awarded after three years. Other college graduates, or those who had at least two years of college work, were allowed to go through in four years. High-school graduates were required to take five years and to include some "cultural" studies from Yale College in their program. In 1937 the prospects were still against the other departments of art reaching the point of requiring a bachelor's degree for entrance.

This great swing toward making upper-class work professional did not pass without influence on graduate studies and on a number of marginal disciplines. For a short time it was thought that Yale College undergraduates might get ahead on their work for

---

neering: i.e., technical training. From the College it obtained archaeology, classical civilization, and joint courses in the history of the arts: i.e., background. Reciprocally, the improvement of professional instruction was to a degree paced by undergraduate developments. And Dean Meeks later felt that the university art schools had been bent toward an unnatural and perhaps damaging worship of what was classical and forever past.[21]

the M.A. or the Ph.D. By 1903 a substantial exchange of students and instruction was already taking place and in 1905 the inauguration of a summer session suggested possibilities of anticipation. But the Summer School failed. In 1908 the College Faculty voted not to award both M.A. and B.A. the same year. Next the Graduate School, under Deans Oertel and Cross, entered upon a vigorous program of expansion, self-government, and standard raising. Then the control of the M.A. passed to the new Graduate Faculty, and the standard for this degree was raised to two years of postgraduate study. Hence by the 1920's the most that a Yale College man could hope to do was to complete his full B.A. requirements, and at the same time take so many hours of specialized instruction that he would be given credit for his first year of residence toward the M.A. No doubt a genuine conviction on the part of both Faculties—that future teachers and scholars needed all the College education they could get—helped keep Yale's College and Graduate School curricula from fusing.*

Meanwhile a series of novelties on behalf of the unorganized professions and branches of the public service had been suggested. For some of these Hadley was enthusiastic, for some distinctly not. He favored public objectives. Only in national service was the University doing its full duty. The founding of the Forestry School met the new conservation movement halfway and would bring

---

* Possibly the fear of reviving the old M.A. in absentia had something to do with the University's reluctance. In any case, it is a point worth noting that whereas Harvard organized its instruction in the arts and sciences at three levels and mingled graduate students with upperclassmen in the intermediate level courses, Yale soon receded from its parallel experiment with the C and D courses and insisted on separate graduate instruction for its graduate students.

From one point of view, this decision invited a certain amount of wasteful duplication, while at the same time repelling outside candidates for the M.A. From the prevailing Yale point of view it helped to emphasize and preserve the peculiar character of each kind of instruction: the College was kept more liberal, the Graduate School was enabled to concentrate on the Ph.D. and on a higher level of professional instruction. The optimum standards for each School had not been jeopardized by a weak effort to lure a few College men into teaching.

Yale into active connection with the country's business. So might instruction in sanitary engineering, or the projected School of Irrigation for which he could never get endowment.

Most promising of all, he thought, was the opportunity to train men for the nation's new colonial responsibilities, consequent on the Spanish-American War. In his first Report he hoped for endowment for a School in Colonial Administration, and while waiting he set to work to build up a strong staff in the geography, anthropology, languages, and histories of non-European areas. In 1905–06, pursuant to a suggestion of Dr. Franz Boas of Columbia, a joint program in preparation for consular or commercial service in the Far East was organized and announced—with Columbia offering more on the linguistic side and Yale more on the economic and political. Students completing the required and elective courses were to be awarded certificates, and if they were college graduates they would have the right to submit their records for the M.A. or the Ph.D. at the university where they had done the bulk of their work.[23]

In such enterprises, to the President's mind, there could be no conflict between the cultural and the utilitarian. He would have had every Yale man go out with "a passion for public service." Unfortunately such idealism was far ahead of the times. The undergraduates displayed little interest in forestry or sanitary engineering. The alumni failed to endow the study of foreign affairs. And as for consular training, the trouble was that there seemed to be no place in the government for trained consuls. The public was still unaware of the need for experts. In the area of public service American society was not yet ready to meet our universities halfway.

It is possible that the public might have greeted more warmly a few semiprofessional programs in business, manufacturing, or journalism. But to these suggestions Hadley was distinctly cold. It was not the function of a university to serve money-making or private ends.[24] Nor to organize programs of study, no matter how popular, if they were really inappropriate. Economics courses were chiefly valuable, he thought, "for the light which they throw on public questions. . . . A man does not learn to do business by hearing it talked about, but by seeing it done and actually doing a part of it himself." As for journalism, "if a man can keep his eyes open, distinguish facts from inferences, and write good English, a very little knowledge of history and economics and elementary law will go a great way."

A review of the Combined Programs against the background of their circumstances and times precipitates certain conclusions. First of all, they were made possible by the victory of the elective principle. Had the fixed curriculum not been destroyed—even more important, had the fixed ideas of Yale and other colleges not been unsettled by a quarter century of retreat into relativism and doubt —it is difficult to see how this invasion into the sacred enclosure of the four-year liberal arts curriculum could ever have been effected.

Again, the decision to locate the Combined Programs in the College rather than in the professional Schools was not due merely to the dominance of the College in University affairs, or to its hold on alumni affections, or simply to Hadley's prejudices against a three-year B.A. and in favor of "broadening influences"—though all these local factors were of major importance. It was due as well to the aforementioned doctrinal weakness of the College. While the professional Faculties knew what they wanted, the College authorities for a while did not, or at least were not in agreement. Under the simultaneous pressures for the lengthening of professional training and the shortening of the total educational process, it was small wonder that the old liberal arts curriculum was infiltrated. Of course these pressures did not go unresisted. Wherever, as in the Divinity School, the professional Faculties were undecided about their own objectives or unable to fix entrance standards, then some at least of the overtime electives and some of the telescoping came to be located in the professional programs.

In any case, from modest beginnings, restrained as to number and character by College traditions, the Combined Programs for a long while grew in size and technicality, and fell more and more completely under the control of the respective professional Deans. Then, slowly, as the College stiffened—and as professional expectations went up and student preparation improved—the invaders withdrew into their own enlarged and renovated postgraduate spheres. And ultimately the College found itself once again full master of its methods and its four years of time.

The retreat was uneven; and this leads us to speak again of certain distinctions between the Schools. For most, if not all of them, the Combined Programs may be regarded as having been a transitional device, a stepladder from collegiate to graduate status. The first step was achieved when the professional School succeeded in requiring entrance examinations, or imposing conditions on high-school graduates. The second step was gained when the School demanded at least two years of college for entrance. The third step came with Senior credits and the Combined Programs. The final triumphant step was the insistence on a college degree.

We have noticed that some subjects did not succeed on the stepladder. And that those which did nevertheless began and ended their climbs at different moments. First came the older Schools, expanding and intensifying their traditional disciplines under the invigorating stimulus of the late nineteenth-century scientific movement. Next, but separated from medicine, law, and divinity by a lag of fifteen to thirty years, came the Departments whose disciplines were of more recent origin and whose place was less secure in popular esteem. The learned professions had their day in the Yale College curriculum in the first and second decades of the twentieth century, the aesthetic and artistic callings theirs in the third and fourth decades, when Medicine, Law, and Divinity were already withdrawing. Curiously enough, the technical sciences and engineering studies hardly considered the journey to graduate status at all. Was this to be a permanent refusal? Or were not the engineering sciences destined rather to form a third corps, whose migration would be the story of the sixth and seventh decades?

We return to the idea that the Combined Programs were essentially a temporary accommodation between the different parts of the University to meet some private discomforts and a public need.

Granted that the temporary nature of the arrangement may not have been clear to all parties—and that the transition period did in fact last thirty to forty years—it was transitory nonetheless, and almost from the first experiments was labeled for eventual discard. For the professional Schools employing the device at any given moment were too few, the proportion of their clientele secured in this way too small, and the gains to School and student too dubious. Somehow the incentive and industriousness of professional study never quite made the passage into Yale's glorious Senior year. Moreover no professional School with national ambitions could long extend special privileges to its own Yale men and refuse them to able graduates of other first-rate colleges. Thus even from the point of view of the party with the most to gain, a Combined Course was at best a temporary expedient.

The same reasons explain why Yale College was not to become the slave of the system or the tool of any graduate School or group of professional Schools. The vast number of undergraduates simply were not looking for a quick professional degree. What they wanted —if anything—was academic credit for a modicum of practical training. The College Officers, in turn, never ceased to prefer law for amateurs; and they learned to like music and architecture as a part of a cultural education. In other words, there was a reason sufficient in itself to expel these professional majors from the College sooner or later. This was the difficulty of mixing two different kinds and spirits of education. Somehow the professional and the liberal were never comfortably blended. And the liberal, general, broad, and disinterested philosophy survived in the College because the Faculty, the students, the Administration, and Yale's public constituency all refused to give it up.

CHAPTER 13 · DISCONTENT, INVESTIGATION, AND REFORM

We toil not, neither do we agitate, but we play football.
—CLASS OF 1901

Scholarship has apparently declined throughout the country; certainly at Yale. . . . In fact, in late years the scholar has become almost taboo at Yale.
—COMMITTEE ON NUMBERS AND SCHOLARSHIP, 1903

We should, therefore, in public and in private, lay more weight on the intellectual life of the College, and on study as the . . . primary justification for membership in the student body.
—COMMITTEE ON IMPROVING INSTRUCTION, 1904

IN THE YEARS 1899–1902 the College Faculty came to the rueful realization that the most careful replanning of the Course of Study was not going to be enough if the students themselves did not respond. No professional courses and no major-minor system would produce the desired improvement unless there was a change also in undergraduate attitudes and performance.

At first this worry had been a minor thing. After all, if the young men were anything like their fathers, they would not exactly be eager for study. The authorities were not so foolish as to expect an "awakening." In fact this august College Faculty was about the last body of men on earth to insist on perfection, or to go suddenly off on some utopian crusade.

There was said to be a good deal of drinking. But the Faculty

232

was not to be jostled into hasty action just because some temperance periodical had intemperately accused Yale students of tavern haunting and football week-end debauchery.[1] Nor were football victories the same thing as professionalism—or muckerism either —whatever some of Yale's less successful opponents might hint. If the schoolmen were protesting about the caliber of Freshman instruction, or parents wailing over sons who had been allowed to fail in their studies, such plaints were hardly new. As for students helping each other through, no one could remember when such things had not been a recognized part of undergraduate Yale.* With the growth of lecture-type courses, some increase in the use of "digests" had likewise to be expected. And a few boys, always, would step over the line into straight cheating. Inevitably there would also recur moments when the whole College suddenly gave vent to high spirits in boisterous parades and rowdy society initiations. To a captious critic President Hadley replied that the testimony as to intellectual standards fifty years earlier was "entirely and absolutely conflicting." And Baldy Wright would remain convinced that despite a growth from 600 to 3,000-odd students, the University did not have one-tenth the lawlessness and public disorder that had been known about the time of the Civil War.[3]

So Faculty uneasiness and impatience derived perhaps from raising their own standards of expectation too fast. Yet experience did seem to show that the disorders, infractions, and petty irritations had been getting rather frequent and unnecessary. Such an unending stream of individuals had to be disciplined for cheating, or for drunken disorder, or for throwing bottles out of windows,

---

* There was an engaging flavor of good fellowship and ingenuity about some of these practices. For example, in 1902–03 there was formed a large Lucian Club composed of football players and dullards who took a course with Limpy Reynolds on Lucian. "Clare" Mendell '04 used to translate the whole assignment for the Club the night before class. When Clare had another engagement, he would put a notice in the News saying that the Lucian Club would meet at such and such a time. One day Limpy Reynolds saw the notice. He said he was very interested and pleased that there was such a club and would like to attend one of its meetings. They stopped putting notices in the News.[2]

or even for going sailing with low women. Whatever could be said for or against football—and no little was being muttered—the emphasis on athletics was clearly out of proportion. Concern for Yale's reputation was felt, and irritation also that teams and crews should always be coming back for cuts or special favors. In turn the Glee Club had to be cautioned about its stock of beer and "other liquids" in the dining car on its trip to the Pacific coast, and forbidden to take along anyone whom the managers would not vouch for as sober and reliable. In the spring of 1902, at the very moment that Professor Bourne was inviting the Faculty's attention to the problem of cheating, the questions on Professor Wheeler's history examination somehow got out, and so many upperclassmen took advantage of the knowledge that the papers had to be thrown out entirely. Already the Faculty had been forced to vote that it regarded the publication of digests or the delivery of lectures in preparation for examinations as "so serious an evil" that they could not recommend for a scholarship or a fellowship any student who helped others in this manner.[4]

All the same, nothing unusual might have come of these undergraduate misdemeanors had it not been for the larger problem of College morale. The underlying trouble was that the whole student body was too tolerant and lax in its standards—in fact too interested in the wrong things. And what finally drove the Faculty from petty interference toward wholesale legislation was public disorder combined with an unhealthy "society" situation.

In a sense social regulation was not the Faculty's business. By tradition Yale undergraduates were proudly self-governing: ran their own teams and competitions, maintained their own customs, passed down their own values and taboos. And over all still loomed the Senior societies, defining success, setting the moral tone. Unfortunately the multiplication of Senior societies had not kept pace with the expansion of the College under Dwight; they were now too few to give recognition to all the deserving. Their standards had also become too unintellectual. The situation was aggravated by the fact that the Sophomore societies by their cabals and in-

234

trigues against each other—their initiations and flamboyant disorders—had lately brought themselves to the verge of abolition. A particularly unfortunate by-product of these lower-class societies was the fact that, to get elected, the rich and the socially ambitious all congregated in a private dormitory on Crown Street known as "The Hutch." Poor boys couldn't afford the Hutchinson. Hence a growing distinction between the well-to-do prep-school men and the rest, to say nothing of a rift in each Class that was now being carried through to the Class elections of Senior year. The social democracy of the College was being threatened.

On May Day 1900 occurred an unusually irritating brawl. First there was a violent rush between Freshmen and Sophomores, then a big parade through the streets to celebrate the second anniversary of the Battle of Manila. The battle ground for the rush was the Sophomore Fence in front of Durfee Hall. Following Dewey's example the Freshmen used strategy. Half of the Class was stationed on Elm Street, near Battell, while the other half went around by Vanderbilt. At a given signal the two flanks swooped down, taking the Sophomores from both front and rear. The struggle was long and fierce. After one Freshman had been knocked out and two other contestants injured, the Freshmen won. Parts of the Fence were torn away.

The parade, with "red-fire and cannon crackers," collected members of the College band and hired two open hacks. Individuals dressed up as Oom Paul Kruger, Governor Roosevelt, Admiral Dewey, and others. With the two hacks in the van, and four hundred undergraduates in the ranks, the parade swarmed out Prospect Street to Sachem Street and then to Hillhouse Avenue. Halting at the house of Judge W. K. Townsend, it heard the Judge speak well of the crew and optimistically about the races soon coming up. The procession also stopped at the homes of President Hadley and ex-President Dwight, who were at a reception at the Art School. Then the mob roared back to College Street and ransacked a partly torn down building on the future site of "new Yale." With boards, etc., from this building they made a great bonfire on the campus and danced and sang around it. In complete disregard of possible public repercussions, "Governor Roosevelt," "Dewey," and others made humorous speeches.

Aware of accumulated frustrations, the President was apprehensive. He was not unmindful of the fact that one of the first acts of the Freshman Officers under his presidency had been to threaten cancellation of Freshman football because the numerals of the Class had been painted on the Sophomore Fence. So now he worked hard to moderate the Faculty irritation. Class athletics, he pointed out, were not connected with this disturbance in the student mind. On the other hand, the occasion might well be used as a warning. The abolition of Thermopylae, for example, would be welcomed; also Bottle Night. But Omega Lambda Chi and the election customs were less objectionable and more picturesque.* And abolishing the Fence would only drive disorder to other places. Reflecting on the presidential advice, the Faculty acted. They abolished the old rush of Thermopylae and the new custom of Dewey Day. Fence orations were discontinued for the year. And after a full discussion of the Sophomore societies these troublesome organizations were merely forbidden to take in new members "until further notice." [6]

President Hadley was pleased that, in the face of strong pressure generally and an almost unanimous petition from the nonsociety Seniors, the Faculty had had the courage to be moderate. For aboli-

---

* Though the water supply was now approved, spring water was still kept in the dormitories. Bottle Night was the occasion, usually a warm May evening, when all these containers—and any others that would smash and crash—were hurled out the windows in a wild orgy of destruction. Tute Farr, whom generations of chastised Freshmen will remember with affection, confesses to having started either the first Bottle Night or the first Bottle Night of 1893 his own Freshman year. Being awakened by two drunks arguing beneath his window, he dropped a bottle of ink between them. The response from all sides was beyond expectations.

Omega Lambda Chi was a late spring parade around the campus, each Class under its marshals, to cheer the College buildings. The Pass of Thermopylae was a newer custom, which forced the Freshmen to run a gantlet of upperclassmen from Phelps Hall out into the campus, the object being to maul and to escape mauling. This had produced no serious injuries hitherto, and it was a good deal of fun—for the upperclassmen. [5]

tion might merely drive the secret societies underground. And he was particularly eager to establish the point that the real evil could only be reached by persuasion and voluntary action. His argument was: "The democratic spirit of Yale is to be maintained primarily by the students; secondarily by the public sentiment of the alumni behind the students; thirdly, and in relatively slight degree only, by the legislation of the faculty." [7]

Voluntary action was tried, through a joint committee representing both the Sophomore societies and the hostile majority of the Senior Class. A scheme was drawn up for creating a pyramidal structure by converting the Junior fraternities into Sophomore fraternities, electing more men, and letting the Sophomore societies remain small but operate in Junior year. The Sophomore societies had balked at this, but understood that they would have to produce a scheme as good. Accordingly, in the fall they were allowed once again to elect members. But they then failed to bring forward any scheme for self-reform—and staged a joint dance in New York in flagrant disregard of a ban on society germans. So in December 1900, on motion of the President himself, the Sophomore societies were required to disband. And President Hadley in person broke the news to their astonished representatives.* [8]

With this act of authority behind them, the Academic Officers continued uneasy. They were puzzled that Yale College was not attracting more students, and troubled that those who did come made intellectual improvement so exceedingly difficult. It was disquieting that Yale was not growing as fast as certain rivals. And it

---

* For some reason it was supposed that a certain Professor of Mathematics, personally kindly but of a disciplinary disposition, had been chiefly responsible for all the Faculty ukases. Which inspired Brian Hooker to bitter song:

He'll abolish the *Lit.*, he'll abolish the *News*,—
Bee-be, Bee-be—
He'll abolish the fence where the snowballs fly,
He'll abolish the Omega Lambda Chi,
And the first thing you know he'll abolish the JO—
Bee-be, Bee-be—

was hard not to notice that the Freshmen were making a poorer scholarship record than ever before. The same thing might be true of upperclassmen, too. After fumbling with one minor expedient after another, in December 1902 the Faculty appointed a Committee on Numbers and Scholarship to ascertain the facts.[9]

Under the chairmanship of Irving Fisher, another of Sumner's pupils and Hadley's colleagues, a mixed handful of College Officers —Seymour, Keller, Bancroft, Perrin, and Registrar Merritt— buckled to their unusual task. It happened that a committee of the Harvard Faculty, with Professor A. Lawrence Lowell as a member and LeBaron R. Briggs as Chairman, had already started an investigation of low standards of scholarship in Harvard College. It happened also that this Harvard committee in time made a public report which, because it was based in part on a spectacular questionnaire to the students, attracted much favorable attention. The Yale men, by contrast, proceeded more privately, consulted the students personally, and altogether investigated a considerable educational horizon. Perhaps because they compared colleges, and because many of their findings reflected unfavorably on Yale, their Report was never published and never became known. Yet this investigation was so thorough, and became the basis of so much University legislation, that no student of our academic progress at the beginning of the century should overlook it.[10]

The facts it turned up were sobering, even shocking. As to enrollment, Yale's plight was easily documented. Between 1888 and 1896 the size of the Freshman Classes had grown encouragingly, and faster than the corresponding Classes at either Princeton or Harvard. But since 1896 Yale College had hardly grown at all, whereas Harvard had kept right on growing and in 1902 had reached the point of admitting more Freshmen than Yale College and the Scientific School, or Yale College and Princeton, combined.* Harvard had also been catching up to Yale in the competition for students from outside New England. Across ten geographical divisions Yale had decreased in all but two, Harvard had increased in all but one. Harvard seemed more of a city man's college,

* See Appendix, Tables O-1 to O-4: Freshman Enrollments, pp. 722–723.

especially in the South. Yale's decrease was both urban and rural and was especially noticeable in New York City and the Middle West. Yale's enrollment from the high schools had increased, but the increment was not keeping pace with the increase of available high-school material. And circulars returned from other colleges confirmed statistical indications that Yale College had been losing ground to all of its chief rivals in its own feeder schools.

The returns from other circulars sent out to 284 schools made it plain that Yale's entrance requirements, its rather rigid curriculum, and its refusal to satisfy the public demand for a faster and more practical education all had something to do with the schoolboy drift. So did the failure of Yale Faculty members to visit or lecture at the schools. By contrast Harvard and other universities seemed to be making a regular practice of such visits. Harvard also manufactured supporters by its Summer School course for teachers. The education of Cuban teachers at Cambridge was an excellent advertisement. A concerted effort was made to place Harvard men in Western colleges, in the preparatory schools, and in the summer camps. Harvard also made use of the newspapers to answer criticism and to advertise.

Moreover Yale's Senior societies and general social system operated to drive away some students. Up to 1902 the number of men taken into Senior societies had remained stationary at forty-five per year. Some fathers would refuse to send their sons where they were so likely to be disappointed on Tap Day. Even with the establishment of a fourth organization, the Elihu Club, boys would hesitate to enter a college where there was only one chance in six of getting into the social "swim." The University would also for some time to come feel the unfavorable influence of the Sophomore societies, with the segregation of the socially ambitious in private dormitories. The conclusion of the committee was that the chief causes operating to decrease Yale's numbers were conservatism and expense. The conservatism showed in society system and studies, and in the lack of summer work, school relations, or advertising. The increase of expense was caused by the destruction of the Brick Row and the abolition of student waiters in Commons.

Scholarship, the Report stated, had been declining since 1896–97. Analysis and check of the yearly grades of the last eight Classes showed unmistakably that this decline had been regular, consistent, and due neither to chance nor to changing marking standards. All the Classes tended to get better grades in Junior and especially in Senior year. But that was due to the easier course materials and easier marking as well as to increase of elective interest and student maturity. In any case the later Classes reflected less Senior year improvement than the earlier. And this decline was greatest among the high-stand men. In point of scholarship the almost invariable order of the Classes had been: 1900 (highest), 1899, 1901, 1902, 1906, 1903, 1904, 1905 (lowest).

The causes of this decline appeared to be in part general, in part peculiar to Yale. Generally speaking, the spirit of study in the whole nation seemed less than formerly. There were too many competing activities. The committee quoted a letter from Abraham Flexner to the effect that the continued exaltation of the social, fraternal, and athletic interests would make the American college an important agent in the demoralization of the well-to-do. They thought perhaps scholarship had declined also because of "the abuse of kindergarten methods of instruction through which all severe discipline had been abandoned."

We give next causes peculiar to Yale. The fact that Yale is a college where public opinion has great force is very significant. It means that any opinion which once invades the college has, added to it, the force of *custom*. . . . An impression is very strong and very prevalent that the athlete is working for Yale, the student for himself. To be a high-stand man is now a disadvantage rather than otherwise. . . . In fact, hard study has become *unfashionable* at Yale.

Concrete evidence for all this was the fact that scholarship was no longer being rewarded by social honors. And Irving Fisher's committee came up with some staggering statistics. Once the high-stand man had had a superior chance of election to the societies, now his chance was not even as good as that of the ordinary man.

Of nine valedictorians since 1893 only three had been elected to a Junior fraternity and not a single one to a Senior society. Whereas in the period 1861–94 out of thirty-four valedictorians only three had failed of fraternity election and only eight of being tapped. "In general, the man who attends strictly to study (the 'grind') is regarded as peculiar or even contemptible. It is believed that a man should 'know men' at Yale; that 'study is a mistake.' " * The committee felt that the society system was in part responsible for such fantastic standards. At least it was noticeable that better and more cheerful studying was done after Tap Day. The Faculty's attention was also called to the exceptional records made by men who transferred to Yale late in their course and so were free from society distractions.

Having faced this series of unpleasant truths, Chairman Fisher and his colleagues proceeded to some pretty blunt recommendations. Yale conservatism should be moderated to the extent of adopting a more attractive curriculum and limiting the entrance requirements to the minimum necessary for College work. Schools should be visited and consulted. A College press agent should be appointed whose function it would be to give out news, to note

* In 1906 the Yale *Courant* would publish a table which showed that in the years 1882–1905 24% of the nonsociety men had achieved an Oration stand or better, as against only 13.6% of the society men. But perhaps the annual Senior Class Books embalm the prevailing undergraduate attitudes in the most telling language:

1900 Class Book

—— [most popular] would never have gotten through Yale had he not been so fortunate as to sit next to —— in all of his studies.
—— [came to Yale] "just for fun." He got what he came for.
Have you ever used a trot? [Yes, 246. No, 15.]

1901 Class Book

We have studied well as a class, as is attested . . . by the fact that only 47 men have voted their main regret to be that they have not studied enough. This vote usually passes the 100 mark.

1905 Class Book

Never since the Heavenly Hosts with all the Titans fought
Saw they a class whose scholarship approached so close to naught.[11]

and answer public misrepresentations, and to prepare articles that would arouse interest in Yale. The expense problem should be met by providing cheaper rooms, cheaper board, a dormitory for Sophomores, opportunities for paid employment, scholarships, prizes. Distractions from studies should be limited and counterattractions provided.

In view of the unpopularity of scholarship, the University should try to bring about a different student sentiment by selecting good and inspiring teachers and not impairing their efficiency with overwork, by competitive prizes and scholarships, by putting successful scholars into prominence, especially before Freshmen, and by reviving the social rewards for scholarship. To all of which were added two specific proposals of some importance. Yale ought to establish a Summer School, and the College ought to appoint a committee to consider improving instruction.

The Faculty, recognizing the melancholy accuracy of these findings, took their educational calomel manfully and set to work. Their concern over undergraduate study attitudes and their search for remedies were intensified. Without question the Fisher investigation helped correct Hadley's picture of secondary-school opinion and so contributed to the decision to drop Greek. No College press agent was at once hired, but Anson Stokes was already undertaking the improvement of the University's public relations, sending pictures of Yale to schools and colleges, giving out announcements, building up a staff, collecting data, answering criticisms. It strengthened the Secretary's hand that the Professors should vote to cooperate in supplying useful information, and that the general Faculty should request him to arrange for College Officers to visit the schools. It was probably no mere coincidence that in May 1903 the Prudential Committee of the Corporation decided to set up a permanent Bureau of University Publications and explore the possibility of a University printer and publisher.[12]

Similarly it cannot be assumed that the Fisher committee alone forced Yale to try a Summer School. Yet it was certainly responsible for the appointment of a committee to consider the question. And within a year a Department of the Theory and Practice of Education had been recommended. This was to create the Summer School of 1905 and 1906, and thereafter to carry on as a Department of Education in the University.[13]

But the most important consequence of the Fisher Report was Faculty willingness to look into their own performance and recognize that it was not public opinion or student practices alone that needed reform. Immediately a second committee was appointed * which did another thorough job of statistical investigation and opinion research. But this time the questions asked were about large classes and small, snap courses and hard ones, marking standards and lecturing habits, teaching loads and study loads, digests and cheating, length and sequence of courses. Even instructors' salaries came in for consideration.

The first line of investigation showed that some of the largest and most popular courses—Phelps, Sumner, Wheeler, Smith—had a low percentage of idlers and poor students. But it was unmistakable that the courses with few elections had the reputation of being hard. Also the loafers tended to congregate in certain courses rather easy to identify. The committee was not so innocent as to publish its list of snaps in the *News*. But the Faculty were induced to rule that the figures on low-stand men should be sent to each department head and to each instructor. More important, it was voted to revise or discontinue all A and B courses in which no definite work was required for each exercise, with tests at brief intervals—also all

* The membership was Professor Duncan, Chairman; Professors Emery, Goodell, Gregory, and Warren, Assistant Professor Reed and Instructor Hawkes. Directed to consider improving the instruction and marking of different instructors with the object of eliminating snap and too difficult courses, the committee began sitting in May 1903. It interviewed students, colleagues, and alumni, had the counsel of Dean Wright, used his records, and examined the somewhat similar findings of the Harvard committee of 1902–03. Hawkes was the man who dug up statistics that put dynamite into the hands of the committee; the enthusiastic and liberal E. B. Reed acted as secretary and stimulator; and in February–March 1904 it was Duncan, Reed, and Hawkes who drafted the committee's Report.[14]

those advanced or C courses in which preparation could be long postponed.[15]

Having looked a bit farther, the Duncan committee concluded that the Faculty were often as anxious to give large courses as the students were to elect them. Instructors had the notion that the popularity of their course had much to do with whether or not they were promoted, and the departments themselves competed for student favor. Easy marking was not the most important attraction, yet students did ask "Is he a good marker?" and marks as high as 4.50 and 5.00 had been given in one class (4.00 = 100%). There was a general feeling that students ought not to be told their marks, unless below 2.25. And the Committee got the Faculty to vote that the Registrar should not give out for publication the student elections each spring. Dean Wright had reminded the committee that there were Officers who kept their classes but half an hour, and other instructors who dismissed their classes anywhere from five to twenty minutes early.* The Committee thought this custom demoralizing: the fifty-minute period was "none too long for effective instruction." Officers should either include more matter in their courses or reduce the hours per week.

The younger faculty came in for extended discussion. Apparently Freshmen transferred their dislike of the required work to their instructors. No question, also, but that some of these younger men were unsympathetic, or inexperienced, or unequal to the best preparatory-school standards. It was therefore voted that every elementary course should have the cooperation of at least one professor or assistant professor. A pamphlet of "Suggestions to Instructors" was drawn up. The committee, however, thought the fault did not lie wholly with the younger men. The Permanent Officers should take more care to see that these younger men were not loaded down with too many hours or subjects of instruction. And the Administration itself was put on warning that in the judgment

* The Dean, however, was not disposed to stiffen up the Seniors. When C. W. Mendell '04 took his schedule of electives for his last year to the Dean, Wright crossed out two courses in Greek and insisted he take easier work. "Senior year should be a year of gentlemanly leisure," he said.[16]

of the committee the younger Officers were "inadequately, and most unequally, remunerated."

Standards of instruction came next. It was agreed that make-up and anticipatory examinations should be stiffened and conducted more systematically. Lecturing should not be overdone. "The recitation system has been, and still is, the fundamental method of instruction at Yale, and the Committee does not believe that the Faculty is willing to see it replaced, in the first two years of the college course, by the lecture system." Accordingly it was recommended and voted that divisions for recitation or quizzing be small enough to enable the instructor to hold the attention of all and to know intimately the work of each.

In the conviction that the subdivision and multiplication of small courses for undergraduates had gone far enough, the committee recommended that a number of these courses should be consolidated, or simplified and made more general. What disturbed them no less was that some C courses had proved easier than Freshman courses, while others were actually too difficult for undergraduates. They called the attention of the Faculty to its own failure to conform its offerings to the three-level idea of the A–B–C program, asked for cooperation, and suggested that a grade of at least 2.25 be required in an A course for admission to a B course in the same subject.

Then the committee turned to examine the performance of the students. And what they had to report must have made even the case-hardened drillmasters blink. For it appeared that the writing of themes for sale had become a regular profession,* catering to large numbers and not condemned even by members of Dwight

* The committee reported that "a member of the Class of 1901, now a Senior in the Law School, is said to have earned $1,100 between Easter and June of one year, from the sale . . . of his written abstracts and essays. The use of purchased themes has become so common that the price per theme is said to have fallen from $5 to $2. The Committee is informed that on three floors of a large student dormitory, not a single man wrote his own theme. In one large course where digests or summaries are required, the venders of such wares have been known to stand on the walk and hand them out to their patrons as the latter came to the class room from Chapel."

245

Hall. This meant that many students were handing in work not their own. But were they doing any studying at all? Patient inquiry had revealed a considerable diversity in undergraduate estimates of how much time most men gave to the preparation of their lessons. In some courses some men apparently did not work at all except to cram for exams. Others spent from fifteen minutes to half an hour per class. One committee member, who had inquired of eighty Seniors, Juniors, and Sophomores, reported that the average of preparation per day seemed to be: Freshmen 2½–3 hours, Sophomores 2½ hours or less, Juniors less than 2 hours, Seniors 1½ hours, 1 hour, or less. And this declining pattern held for the high-stand men as well as for the rest.

Worst of all was the open practice of cheating. One Senior, a candidate for the Christian ministry, had given it as his deliberate judgment that more than 10 per cent of the students cheated. A prominent undergraduate, caught in the act, felt no compunction because so many were doing it. The situation was so general that the younger instructors rather felt it "undesirable for them to report cases of cheating to this Faculty." What could be done? The committee recommended that in A and B courses all required writing of themes be done in the classroom. They also considered advising smaller divisions and mechanical safeguards against cheating like alternate questions. Finally, feeling unprepared to deal comprehensively with so grave a matter, they preferred to lay it before the Faculty.

Turning to the unpopularity of scholarship, the committee underlined the fact that only the athletic or social honors were well known to entering Freshmen. One man, who had become a fellow in the Graduate School, confessed that he had not even known of the existence of Phi Beta Kappa until his Sophomore year. Such being the possibility, the Faculty were induced to take under consideration Professor Reed's recommendation that a time should be set aside each year for the conferring of prizes and scholarships. On this occasion an invited guest of reputation and distinction should deliver an address and the President himself confer the prizes.

Never in its history had the College offered such opportunities for a liberal education. And never had its Officers had a greater responsibility to counter the tendencies which would make the College, in the practice of its instructors, "a sort of Chautauqua" and in the eyes of students "a mere Social and Athletic Club, with superficial literary appendages." With feeling and eloquence the Committee on Improving Instruction urged a restoration of the "disturbed balance of Yale life."

Invigorated rather than abashed by these uncomfortable revelations, the general Faculty voted a large proportion of the measures recommended by the Fisher and Duncan committees. From this start the work of improvement spread in many directions. The winters from 1903 to 1905 constituted a period of concentrated activity, followed in the years 1905 to 1908 by the working out of what had by then become a many-sided and decidedly substantial reform.

The Faculty did not hurry, or get excited, or try to do everything at once. Recognizing that loafers were not to be converted into reasonable scholars without some pains and delay—and that professors themselves were more easily enlightened than changed —they allowed a cautious gradualism to govern legislation. The College trusted to men as much as to measures and, like an army in training, looked first to disciplining in small units. Thoroughness rather than popularity or public appeal was the effect aimed at. And alongside of this quiet workmanship the most marked characteristic of the movement was balance. The results can be described under three heads: more solid instruction—more thorough study —and a better distribution of elective choices.

The movement to make instruction more solid was resourcefully conducted. To begin with, the Faculty labored to increase its instructor staff and to appoint men of character as well as scholarly curiosity. It reinvigorated the recitation system, increased the number of recitation rooms by occupying the new Lampson Hall, saw to it that lowerclassmen were taught by experienced men in small divisions, gave more regular assignments and make-ups, checked up on tests and examinations, and even established special scholarship divisions in Greek and in a modified way in Latin and German.

Next the proliferation of course offerings was checked, in favor of greater solidity at the advanced levels and a better balance through the four years. Thus the Faculty allowed a guarded enlargement of Sophomore-Freshman opportunities but authorized repeated scrutinies, consolidations, and eliminations at the Junior-Senior level. In 1903 history and chemistry had been added to the Freshman subjects—and economics, physical geography, and Biblical literature to the courses open to Sophomores. In the next four years Sophomore opportunities were further enlarged by extra courses in history and chemistry (1904), elementary Spanish (1905), biology (1907). At both levels a modest increase in variety was achieved by the establishment of alternate courses within the accepted subjects of study. Before 1900 all Freshmen had had to take the same five subjects and all Sophomores five out of six, but by 1908 eight subjects were being taught in thirteen different courses for Freshmen, and sixteen subjects in thirty-two different courses for Sophomores.*

At the Junior-Senior level, by contrast, the periodic discovery that the multiplication of offerings had run foul of the law of diminishing attendance operated with almost seasonal regularity to check or to eliminate unnecessary courses. First the total number of courses was reduced, then allowed a guarded expansion, then reduced once again. The net result was that, for the first time since the original sprouting of elective offerings, the ceaseless, perennial enlargement of the Course of Study pamphlet was virtually arrested. President Hadley put his stamp of approval on this pause.[17]

There was a sort of feeling that a college course ought to provide everything which any student might want to study—a feeling that it was a school in which the student ought to learn the

---

* See Appendix, Table K: Regulated Electives: The Second Phase, 1903–08, p. 713.

theoretical elements of anything that he intended to study or thought of intending to study afterward. This had been the policy of Harvard; and the great and well-deserved success of Harvard in many other lines where she was right led our American colleges to follow her blindly in this one where she appears to have been wrong. But we are coming to recognize that a smaller number of studies well taught will give a student a far better idea of the direction in which his powers really lie, and will lead him to conserve those powers instead of dissipating them.

Still another set of assumptions gave bounds and flavor to the curriculum. These were the assumptions as to what kinds of learning were appropriate to an undergraduate education. Courses seeking admission into the Course of Study were narrowly examined; the claims of accepted subjects to fuller presentation were carefully reviewed. As a result, the recently developed but marginal offerings in physical education were entirely disestablished. The ancient but unsatisfactory discipline of rhetoric was separated from English literature, discussed, wrestled with, and improved until finally restored to such satisfactory shape that it would be accepted as an effective part of the English offerings.[18] Such subjects as botany and forestry were subordinated to biology. Japanese and Russian were admitted, and classified in the Division of Language and Literature. But neither of these languages, nor music and the fine arts which also were classified in this Division, could be taken as a major or a minor. Education and anthropology gained independent status but only a limited development. Some particular courses were returned to the Graduate catalogue. By contrast English and history flourished. And economics, after admission to Sophomore year, built up into the most popular major in the College.

Such choices came close to redefining the liberal arts. The Faculty never formally codified its new standards. But in 1915, in Yale's most important official restatement of the liberal arts since 1886, President Hadley would summarize his own criteria for a B.A. subject in terms that were to open and close doors in a number of directions:

249

1. It must contribute to the intellectual training of the student. Rightly or wrongly, we exclude those studies which involve manual or physical ability alone. We do not count the ability to play an instrument . . . unless it is accompanied by a knowledge of musical theory and musical composition. . . .

2. The subject should be one where it is possible to test the attainments of the students. . . . How are we to test the appreciation of pictures? . . .

3. The subject must be one in which we can obtain proper teachers . . .

4. . . . the course should be such as to invite a certain degree of emulation . . . If a study is of such a nature that each man works in isolation and does not derive help and stimulus from others about him engaged in the same pursuit, his place is in the graduate school or in the research laboratory. . . .

5. . . . It must make him a profounder thinker and a better citizen. A public motive rather than a private one must constitute the dominant note in its appeal. . . .[19]

To get the maximum effect with the courses that survived such tests and scrutinies was naturally a Faculty concern. Worth-while small courses were aided by a reorganization of the weekly time-table which deprived the big lecture courses and the popular departments of their monopoly of the best classroom hours. Other small courses were encouraged to add more subject matter of general interest. A distinct effort was made to get away from fragmentary instruction. As far as possible all Freshman and Sophomore courses were required to meet three hours a week. Two-hour courses had been much preferred for upper-class instruction, but the three-hour courses were now gaining; and one-hour courses were frowned on except at the most advanced levels. Single-term courses came into disfavor, it being found that they were patronized mainly by the poorer scholars.

With the consolidation of their materials, the instructors began to chafe at the uneven length of the terms. By a custom inherited from the days of required studies, the College year was divided into a fall term which ran only until Christmas, and a second term which lasted from January clear through to Commencement. It was like an old-fashioned high-wheel bicycle. For instructors and students alike the short football season spun by incredibly fast; and then, once mounted atop the big wheel of the winter term, you pedaled, it seemed, forever. Finally in 1912, after one unsuccessful agitation, the College would decide to trade in its outdated cycle for an academic calendar of more efficient construction. Starting in 1913–14 the terms would be made of even length, with term examinations and Junior Prom alike set for the end of January or early February.[20]

The second major stroke of policy was the effort to achieve a better distribution of studies by perfecting Yale's system of "classified electives." In 1903 an extra major and an extra minor were added to the concentration-distribution requirements. This was a logical precaution, in view of the relaxation of Freshman requirements, and it seemed a reasonable development as well. For the 1901 rule of one major and two minors had guaranteed, at the most, seventeen hours of planned and connected study out of sixty—and of these seventeen hours but two had to be in C courses, and only six at the intermediate B-course level. About a third of the undergraduates had promptly elected more C courses than required, but another third were taking advantage of the opportunity to avoid advanced work almost entirely. This indulgence in A-level, elementary work seemed excessive. So now, with two majors of seven hours each, and three minors of five hours each, twenty-nine out of the normal sixty hours were secured for distributive studies, of which fourteen were to be in nonelementary work. Thus just over half of a student's program could still be chosen almost without restriction, but all the rest of a man's courses would have to be planned practically from the start.

For five years—1903–08—Yale College gave this half-and-half system a trial, adjusting details here, ironing out difficulties there, seeking to bring the course of study into still better balance. Theoretically, the B.A. curriculum was now a mixture of freedom and responsibility. Actually, the responsibilities like the liberties were still weighted on the side of breadth and curiosity. This was an in-

251

herited Yale preference that was decidedly agreeable to student tastes. Hence the new distribution arrangements imposed no hardships on the undergraduates and proved eminently easy to administer. They would have proved almost satisfactory but for one unforeseen difficulty.

This difficulty concerned science. The theory was that the major-minor system was impartial as to subject matter and broad in coverage. In the interests of a balanced education it laid as much stress on the sciences as on the languages or on philosophy and history. Actually, the average student wanted very little of the sciences, and the exceptional man wanted just such premedical opportunities as would advance him faster toward his two degrees. The result was that the necessity of taking a minor in the second Division of knowledge—that of mathematics and the sciences—at once turned out to be the single most binding requirement of the whole classified elective system. And the Faculty had to allow a combination of Freshman mathematics with elementary physics, or of elementary physics and chemistry with each other, or with geology, or of geography with geology, to satisfy their minor requirement.

This time it was not any scornful linguists, or the impecunious state of the treasury, or the famous Yale College conservatism that placed impediments in the way of the study of the sciences as a part of a liberal education. On the contrary, President Hadley advertised the fact that a man who wished to devote his time to pure science could find more opportunity in the Academic Department than he could in Sheff.[21] Here was the morning of the greatest scientific age that the world had ever seen. In a year or two the College was going to elect a physicist its Dean and at Hadley's retirement a psychologist was destined to become its President. But the undergraduates were not interested in studying science.

The third major emphasis of College policy in this period was the insistence on study: regular and exacting study. On the subject of hard work the College authorities spoke with a single and emphatic voice. They were for it. And with Hadley it was a positive fetish. He conceded that earlier generations had been too exclusively bent upon enforcing hard work. But to him culture without

252

work was "an even more demoralizing ideal than work without culture."

Being full of idiosyncrasies and independence, the individual Officers sometimes found the application personally a little inappropriate. Sarcasm and human understanding had been the mixture that made a recitation go. Not every old war horse had earned his place in the heart of Yale by being tough. Nor did every aspiring assistant professor, competing for students and recognition, feel free to make his classes as hard as G. B. Adams' Medieval History. Besides, there were some subjects that just did not lend themselves to disciplinary instruction. By cultivating the art of lecturing, enthusiastic and engaging instructors could make unheard-of subjects "interesting." As Hadley was fond of pointing out, anyone who had actually taught the culture subjects "knows how easy it is to let his courses degenerate into pleasure resorts." [22]

Nevertheless, a direct charge against the Eliot system had been that it lowered the minimum standards. While only the most conservative professors would subscribe unreservedly to Ladd's charges about "the baleful influence of the 'elective' temper of mind and habit of conduct," the Faculty as a whole were deeply persuaded that unless work standards were vigorously maintained, the increase of elective opportunities would indeed come to mean that more and more boys would "cram, cram to get into college, and sham, sham to get through." Hence the systematic efforts to reform student abuses, improve course standards, raise the requirements for make-ups and anticipations, and stiffen the challenge all along the line. Attendance at classes was more rigorously required, and in January 1904 it was voted that an instructor might, with the approval of the Dean, exclude from his class a student whose conduct or attendance or scholarship was unsatisfactory.

In the matter of regulating the undergraduates' social life and activities, the Faculty played a much less successful yet not altogether passive role. Absenteeism came in for attention. The week-end problem was getting serious. Students were overcutting Sunday chapel and their Saturday or Monday classes, too. Nor were such absences being adequately reported. Under the downright chairmanship of Professor Albert Galloway Keller, a special committee called for an exercise of authority: "To leave these things entirely or mainly to 'student sentiment' we regard as foolish and invertebrate. We regard subjection to discipline as part of the education needed by students, who in these days seem to get little enough of it at home and in the lower schools." The Faculty took action. In the spring of 1908, the number of out-of-town games having been reduced, it was decided to restrict chapel cuts, appeal to the parents for cooperation, hold all possible courses to the Monday-Wednesday-Friday or Tuesday-Thursday-Saturday cycles, put some of the popular courses on Saturdays or in the afternoon, and in general encourage a more even distribution of work throughout the week.[23]

After the disappearance of the Sophomore societies, the Junior fraternities tended to expand into the void; and of course the private dormitories remained. It had become too expensive to build new, fire-proof dormitories out of the College funds. Fortunately the immediate shortage of good College rooms was alleviated by the contributions of the Corporation, the alumni, and even the undergraduates toward the renovation of old South Middle and of Durfee Hall. Dean Wright quietly commissioned certain influential lowerclassmen, among them the son of "Goat" Seymour, to pack an entry or two in Durfee and Welch with outstanding Sophomores. When these groups were overwhelmingly successful in the Junior fraternity elections, the fashionable element started to flow back to the campus. At the same time the unfavorable influence of the off-campus dormitories on both scholarship and social democracy was given such repeated publicity that the traditional Yale policy of having all students live in College buildings was effectively revived.[24]

Cheating it was impossible to stamp out overnight. By 1904 some of the best Juniors had become concerned—and in friendly alliance with the authorities were doing what they could. But a year later the Faculty felt forced to make plain their determination by firing a Senior who was rowing on the crew. This was the first penalty of dismissal for such an offense in many years. In view of the prominence of the individual—and of the fact that previous offenders had almost all escaped with suspension for the short fall term, or even with merely the loss of a course—this action seemed to many discriminatory and unjust.[25]

On another front the Faculty encountered what seemed to be insuperable difficulties. It was possible occasionally to suggest that no man should serve on the board of more than one undergraduate magazine—but the general problem of excessive activities eluded restraints. Most difficult and prickly of all was the problem of athletic overemphasis, and particularly of football. For Hadley's sympathies were with the undergraduates, and he saw through the eyes of his "dean of football," Walter Camp. He was indeed worried by the increasing roughness and got together with Camp, President Eliot, and Percy Haughton to open up the game by introducing the onside kick and the forward pass. But with the other abuses he did not seem disposed to interfere or to brook interference. It made no difference that the gate receipts were getting too large, the charges about professional athletes and the abuse of funds ever harder to overlook. Athletics were not the Faculty's business. They could rule on scholastic eligibility, not on whether gate receipts or intercollegiate football should be abolished. After some stormy and frustrating sessions in 1905–06, the reforming element recognized their defeat and subsided. Yet they had succeeded in forcing the reluctant authorities to recognize that intercollegiate athletics could not go virtually unregulated very much longer.[26]

In addition to setting minimum standards of performance and conduct, much constructive work was done to improve student attitudes—particularly in the matter of high scholarship. The Phi Beta Kappa society was reinvigorated, publicized, and officially supported.* Freshmen were instructed in the use of the Library; and the history instructors made a deliberate effort to require research

---

* Dean Wright in 1904–05 praised Phi Beta Kappa as "the only Society at Yale which offers all men an equal chance, and elects all members on a basis of merit alone and according to a standard which no one can criticize." By

reading there as a part of the preparation for the regular essays. Efforts were made to moderate personal eccentricities of marking, or departmental standards that seemed out of line. In 1901–02, at the time of the renovation of the Board of Freshman Class Officers, a decided effort had been made to create more sympathetic and helpful relations. In 1905, at the suggestion of Professor Goodell, a Sophomore Tutorial Board was constituted, with friendly, advisory functions rather than disciplinary supervision in view.[28] Necessarily these Sophomore Officers found that most of their work was with delinquent students—and, as such, not always pleasant. But it is worth remarking that the charges of paternalism and interference, which had been leveled by the unreconstructed Classes of 1902 and 1903, were not now swelled into a chorus.

Instead, scholarship began to go up. As Freshmen the Class of 1906 had improved on their immediate predecessors. The Class of 1907 did better. In the Class of 1908 the percentage of first-division men was more than double what it had been in the Class of 1905 and a decline in warnings and failures was telling the same story at the other end of the scale. To be a "gentleman scholar" became the thing; and the number of Phi Beta Kappa men who exercised real influence as Seniors became notable. Of the fifteen Bones men in 1910, six were Phi Beta Kappa. Already in 1905 Dean Wright had permitted himself to report: "It is believed that the class-room work [i.e., teaching] in Yale College was never better done than it is to-day." [29]

How much the great investigations of 1902–04 had really accomplished was a question. The public had not heard of them. And it would be some time before the quiet improvements in teaching, conduct, studies, and general undergraduate attitudes would show to unmistakable effect. Later there would be debate as to when the change had taken place. To this day, for example, there persists a friendly rivalry between the Class of 1904 and the Class of 1905 for the honor of really having hit the scholastic bottom.[30] And it

---

1906 membership in the society would seem important enough for objection to be raised to the methods of election.[27]

will be insisted that not until the next decade did literature and learning really come back into their own. Yet somewhere in the first years of the century the College rounded a corner. By 1906, though the academic millennium still seemed on the misty horizon, at least the undergraduates no longer had their backs so obstinately turned.

CHAPTER 14 · RETROSPECT: A NEW SYSTEM ON OLD PRINCIPLES

Yale compromised. The Yale system is halting, piecemeal, a grudging attempt to make an old-fashioned curriculum melt imperceptibly into the elective scheme. But the difference between the two is not a difference of principle.

—Abraham Flexner, *1908*

It was recently remarked to me by the president of a leading New England college, himself a graduate of Harvard, that the new group system of Yale was the best solution of the elective problem that had been made, and constituted the most important contribution to educational methods in the last fifteen years.

—H. C. Emery, *1906*

The progress of Yale College in the first nine years of Hadley's presidency has not been a simple page to interpret. Evidently there was a continuation of earlier trends—and also a turning. In retrospect the great problem concerns Yale's position on the elective issue. Did Yale capitulate to the elective system—or reform it?

Whether or not Yale ever adopted the elective system has been a fighting question, and one to be answered according to the rooted prejudices of the speaker. Champions of vocational studies have chorused: No! In fact to Progressive schoolmen, to the disciples of Teachers College, and other professional educators brought up on the tradition of Yale's ultra-conservatism, the mere suggestion will bring a scornful smile. Of course Yale was beaten by the forward-looking universities. In the nineteenth century it had been "old Yale, that stronghold of everything conservative in education." In the eighties and nineties Yale and Princeton had stood together as "the archtypes of the conservative position." By the turn of the century Yale had indeed been forced to admit some electives. But it never really reformed, or accepted the consequences of its defeat.

The adherents of Harvard, on the other hand, have thought or have found it more comfortable to believe that Yale finally did capitulate to the great Eliot system. In his beguiling *Three Centuries of Harvard,* the distinguished historian S. E. Morison has said:

> By the dawn of the twentieth century the 'pure' elective system seemed to be as firmly established as the trivium and quadrivium in the middle ages. Every large college or university in the country had adopted it except Yale (which did so in 1904) . . .

This is a suggestion that has been somewhat deprecated in New Haven.

Then there were those who held to a still less flattering view, which was that Yale had delayed a long time but had gained no wisdom in so doing. Surveying the college scene in 1908, Abraham Flexner was more impressed by the way Yale had dragged its feet than by the regulations it had devised to bring system into elective chaos. Fundamentally he could see no differences of theory or practice between Yale and Harvard: just differences of speed and enthusiasm on the same road to destruction. Harvard, at least, had had the joy of pioneering.

> When the Yale system gets into full swing, it is practically just as unorganized, just as innocent of controlling educational purpose as the Harvard system, even though it lacks the Harvard abandon at the start; it is not, in a word, redeemed by its tardiness or its few external checks.

But, replied the *Alumni Weekly,* Yale's controls did amount to something. Yale had never accepted snap courses as inevitable. "In the Yale elective apparatus the brakes are on all the wheels some of the time and on some of them all the time, they are never off all of them at once. Yale has never surrendered discipline . . . In a word Yale is not for *laissez faire.*" And Yale, at least, had bowed to no dictator. As to whether this was a proof of genuine educational originality or just a sort of democratic obstinacy, spokesmen for the College betrayed divided minds. Some publicly admitted that the elective system had come to stay: as indispensable as structural steel. On one occasion the *Alumni Weekly* would allow itself to speak of Yale's "brief but thrilling experience" with the elective system. On others President Hadley would insist that the College had never made some of the worst mistakes—or would refer to Yale's classified electives.[1]

Thus the question as to whether Yale's long retreat had ended in unconditional or only partial surrender was handled in various not too flattering ways. For the truth was that by the elective system different men understood different things. Too often they made it simple: a mere matter of student choice. Too often men also thought of the pre-Eliot system as just a classical-mathematical course: essentially a monolithic affair, to be maintained by compulsion and shattered as soon as freedom and new subjects entered in. So perhaps it will make for a clearer judgment if not only rules and practices are taken into consideration but attitudes and convictions, too: the unwritten constitution and spirit of the place.

Philosophically, Yale College never abandoned certain century-old convictions. This may be asserted without reference to Porter or Ladd, to the Corporation or the embattled classicists. For the famous required curriculum handed down by Kingsley and Jeremiah Day had stressed "discipline" or exactness—"the furniture of the mind" or solid information—and "emulation" or competition between students. It had assumed that men were much alike, all of one spiritual and intellectual inheritance, and all members of one body politic. The duty of College instructors was therefore to teach, discipline, and guide. And the duty of students was to College and country sooner than to themselves. In the most natural way it had been insisted that some studies were better than others, the best foundation studies being exact, hard, and without immediate utility or application. The classics by choice. In Senior year, to crown their experience, these future citizens should then all be given ethics and philosophy—plus a brief but comprehensive introduction to the contemporary world.

By contrast the elective revolution had stressed man's freedom and individuality: freedom to teach, freedom to study and investigate, freedom to discover and improve one's personal aptitudes. Compulsion was poor psychology. Students if encouraged to follow their bents would be more interested, would work harder, and go farther. Society would prosper in proportion as new knowledge was discovered, individual talents were specialized, and nature exploited. Literature and the fine arts were interesting; the natural and social sciences were the studies for power; and professional training was a conspicuous goal.

Measured against such contrasting standards, Yale at the start of the twentieth century was obviously a far freer and more secular place. To a striking degree the scientific revolution and the elective idea had transformed the faculty's role. They were all now expected to search as well as to teach, and in teaching to enlighten far more than to drill. If the sciences had never really flourished, informative studies had now achieved pre-eminence, with emphasis on the social and the "cultural." The classics were on their way out, the school-and-tool languages generally were pushed down. With studies for breadth no longer the crown but the body of the curriculum, a vacancy was beginning to appear in upper-class studies that would invite the specialization so much aimed at by elective reformers. The students themselves were more independent. At least, by 1903 each individual was assembling his own program from a wide list of subjects, no one of which was any longer entirely privileged or forbidden, and all of which now had an equal standing in the sight of the world. Reviewing such gains of freedom and maturity one would be tempted to conclude that the old system with the old sanctions was gone or going fast.

Yet it will not do to confuse form with spirit, or to exaggerate the impact of elective ideas. Whatever its concessions or expediencies, Academic Yale obviously still believed in the hard task, in competition, in fundamental disciplines and in a general rather than a technical education. The students had not taken full advantage of their opportunities in the direction of either speed or specialization. Moreover, freedom to teach and freedom to study were still limited, especially at the Sophomore and Freshman and entrance levels. The College could no longer require Greek. But not all forms of knowledge or methods of instruction or kinds of instructor or ways of study were considered valuable to Freshmen or of equal value for Seniors. Nor were the students yet recognized as the only or best judges of such worth. Instead it was the duty of the College to set minimum objectives, offer experienced advice, and positively prevent too eccentric a selection.

In organization, a liberal education should be a balanced rather than a specialized education, to be pursued consecutively and progressively rather than at random: from the foundation disciplines, through the studies for breadth, and toward just a modicum of concentration. The purpose of this liberal education was information and broad culture, with power for work more important still, and character most important of all. The good was still more important than the new, and society higher than the individual. Ultimately College should prepare for public service not private advancement, for citizenship rather than special skills. And this it should do in part by plain hard work, in part by athletics and the social competitions, in part by the handing down of traditions and the colorful undergraduate ceremonies, in part by the example of teachers and scholars who were fresh in imagination and possessed of the human touch.

Admittedly these aspirations were by no means fully realized in practice. Yet the more all the detailed actions of 1899–1908 are studied—the more one observes how new standards of breadth were being substituted for old, new requirements in science for compulsory Greek, new continuities and sequences of difficulty for the order that was passing away—the more convincing is the conclusion that not even in its practices did the College really embrace the elective system. It was true that first the Sophomore year, then the Freshman year, had been opened to elective practices: so what in 1899 had been a 2:2 ratio between elective and required studies by 1901 stood virtually at 3:1 and in 1903 was made almost 4:0. It was also true that in this same peak year of elective dissolution the pressures of competition and of public animosity against Greek led the Faculty to suggest relaxing Yale's foundation requirements faster than the Corporation was willing to approve.

Yet it should be noted that the College authorities never surrendered their responsibilities or lost their grip. Mistrusting the materialism of vocational studies, the secularism of the new scholarship, the selfish, asocial individualism of the elective principle—fearing also its financial costs and academic indiscipline in practice—the College could be seen laboring to admit freedom of teaching and freedom of study *only so far and only so fast as safeguards could be provided:* safeguards in the shape of a new ordering of studies and a reinvigorated idealism of College purpose.

In the years 1899–1908, therefore, there was both a survival and a revival of ideas; there was overlap of practice and method. At the level of theory the ideals of wider freedom and a higher mastery had been added to rather than substituted for the old beliefs in industry, discipline, and quality of subject matter. In the field of practice Yale had never given more than a part of its energies and talents either to faculty specialization, to student individualism, or to a carefree eclecticism. Old requirements had been kept in force until a new system of distribution could be given a start.

From this review emerge the following conclusions. First, elective theories and elective practices invaded Yale slowly, painfully, extensively, and without entirely coming to a halt in 1903. Second, no victory of the elective practices was ever complete. Third, by 1908 the elective theories had not really conquered the older convictions at all. And finally for nine years it had been Yale's preoccupation to harmonize what was indispensable or unavoidable in the new with what had been invaluable in the old.

If it be conceded that Yale College compromised rather than surrendered, we may ask how significant was its compromise. Before estimating the importance of what Yale did with and to the elective system, a glance elsewhere is in order. Without question, by 1901 the expansion of electives had gone further in American colleges than in the colleges or gymnasia of any other land. Moreover that use was still growing and spreading. However, what had never been clearly appreciated in all the hullabaloo was the fact that only a handful of our important university colleges had ever gone practically the whole way to unregulated studies—notably Harvard, Cornell, Stanford.* And these were now quietly surveying and reconstructing their positions.

Johns Hopkins still refused to allow more than an election between required groups, and in 1905–06 established the four-year in place of a three-year degree. At Columbia not only did the faculty vote down Butler's two-year degree, but a committee of 1904–05, carrying on the work of its predecessor, moved against too many elementary and unrelated courses by a revision of the prescribed courses and the introduction of a concentration requirement, with a system of quality credits. At Stanford in 1906 the faculty managed to resist the request of the trustees for greater prescription and President Jordan's suggestion of fixed groups of optionals. But Cornell, which in 1896 had entered on a scheme of practically free election, decided in 1905 on regulations for eight half-years of work, distribution among four groups, and later concentration in one.

Finally at Harvard itself the joy and satisfaction of pioneering were giving way to something very like dismay: a dismay that betrayed itself in the reports of faculty committees, the dissatisfaction of Overseers, and an open recantation by no less a figure than Charles Francis Adams, Overseer and former excoriator of the classics. This "Harvard Iconoclast" now found that the elective system, however good its fundamental idea, had become an educational fad, "crude, ill-considered, thoroughly unscientific, and ex-

---

* An intercollegiate survey, published in June 1901, asserted that in some ten colleges (Columbia, Cornell, Cincinnati, Harvard, Missouri, Stanford, Virginia, Washington State, West Virginia, and William and Mary) all or practically all of the work was elective. Thirty-four institutions reported 70% or more of their work as elective; 12 reported 50%–70%; while 51 (many of them in the South, but including Princeton and Brown) reported that more than half of their courses were still required. This may be compared with Morison's statement about the adoption of the "pure" elective system.[2]

264

tremely mischievous," based on a false notion of the average youth's competence to recognize his needs and choose wisely. He saw a re-action impending and proposed that it take the form, for Harvard at least, of a group of small colleges, giving a partly prescribed and disciplinary preparation under close faculty supervision. The *Yale Alumni Weekly* received these remarks with glee.[3] And in short order President Lowell, too, would be praising the "wise turning" of our colleges to more severe requirements.

So also at many another college and university could be de-tected a mood of thoughtful hesitation. Their presidents described the elective system as a fixture—"we will never go back"—but their faculties were tinkering and experimenting. Majors here, majors and minors there, group systems and distribution requirements of assorted varieties were quietly being tried. In a few years the con-viction would seep out to the general public that perhaps the elec-tive freedom had been carried too far. There would be no question of going back to Greek. The new subject matter should, of course, be kept. And freedom of choice, however abused, still seemed more appealing than its old-fashioned opposite. Nevertheless, some limi-tation on unlicensed electives, some regulation of frivolous eclec-ticism, some rules for order, breadth, and solidity in the new pro-gram would have to be worked out, if collegiate education was to meet the challenge of the new age.

It was still too soon for a new order of authority to rise: too soon for people to feel the need for survey or orientation courses, and much too soon for any drive to set up a new "core" curriculum in place of the classics. In fact it was even too early for the colleges to understand the dimensions of their problem or come together in recognition of the more promising solutions. No doubt it would have been foolish also for Yale to expect its own reputation for unconstructive conservatism to evaporate overnight.

So while a well-informed observer might have guessed that the tide was beginning to turn, it happened that Yale's contributions toward a revised and balanced system made little impression. In comparison with Wilson's spectacular Preceptorial Plan at Prince-ton, Yale's drive for better teaching seemed colorless and unin-spired. Professor H. C. Emery of the economics department might assert that, having studied at a country college and two larger universities, he believed the method of instruction at Yale to "possess, to an unusual degree, the advantages of both, and to be equal to the methods of any institution in the country." But if other college educators felt the same way, they said little about it in public.[4] So not only had Yale's equivalents for Greek been interpreted as illiberal and its limitation on Freshman-Sophomore studies as narrowly conservative, but its stand for a four-year degree was taken for granted, and its revision of the materials and methods of undergraduate instruction was apparently unheard of. Even its insistence on consecutiveness and balance went largely unrecognized. And whether its doctrine of hard work won any following it would be difficult to say.

The fact remained that in the period 1899–1908 Yale College had been working to enlarge the opportunities of undergraduate education without sacrifice of culture or solidity. In effect it had taken hold of the fundamental problem facing the twentieth-century American university: how gain the new university opportunities without losing the older collegiate values. And to this question Yale College had returned its answer: by a new system based on the old ideals. The modern college, in taking advantage of elective devices, should so limit and regulate their application that foundation, distribution, and concentration could be obtained without sacrifice of discipline, duty, or community interest.

But Yale worked toward its solution in piecemeal fashion, understood or assumed its cardinal elements rather than formulated them for public consumption, practiced rather than publicized. The Yale answers, too, foreshadowed a solution rather than achieved it. To rebuild old Rome out of contemporary materials was not going to prove easy. Everywhere some sort of reconstruction was going to have to be made; and nowhere would the first solutions prove stable. Perhaps it may be concluded that the Yale tendency to develop a new order and content of studies, on principles that had been time tested and approved, was among the earlier and more interesting experiments—a substantial and not unpromising beginning.

PART FOUR:
THE COLLEGE, THE
UNIVERSITY, AND
THE PUBLIC

CHAPTER 15 · TEACHERS AND TEACHING

. . . the college of my day was a combination of sporting resort, beer garden, political convention, laboratory, factory of research, and nurse of the liberal arts. And it was trying to be a public school of the English type, a college, and a university, all at the same time. I doubt whether values were ever more completely mixed, muddled, and concealed than in the battle (if you can call it that) between our perfunctory and our preferred education.

—HENRY SEIDEL CANBY

THE TEACHERS at Yale ruled a realm larger than that known to other educators. Each man felt free to teach and study nearly as he chose. Collectively they were masters of their own destiny, self-governing and self-perpetuating. And here under their hands were the sons and heirs of the American ruling class.

Under their hands but by no means all in their power. For it was fundamental that the College offered also another kind of education—by campus as well as by classroom—and of these two the academic was not always the preferred. Next to their formal classroom exercises Yale's future captains of industry and finance found the informal, romantic, competitive College life incomparably exciting and important—the perfect training for success in our confident acquisitive society. Of course their instructors could go into class swinging, could teach ideas and dangle before the eyes of the able undergraduate the vision of the great things men had done:

> Climb high yourself. There's little satisfaction
> In summing life up by a bank account.[1]

But the life of the campus was so dynamic and vital that even professors and pedagogues believed in it, and thus at heart half accepted the fact that ideas, the search for truth, and scholarship, must be among the lesser products of their show. Their campus was no ivory-towered cloister. Living under quasi-siege, jostled even in this refuge, young scholars found it hard not to notice the indifference of parents and old classmates, harder still to avoid realizing that their exploring existed only because the graduates were tolerant and generous. From this could come a certain loneliness and sense of expatriation. Hence also the desperate craving for security, which the enterprising classes in our society have held in such low regard.

It followed that an exuberant Senior, confident that he had the world by the tail, had only to keep on in New Haven and enter the faculty to discover that he had crossed the threshold into a shadowland. By day one joined the teachers and disciplinarians, straining in the harness of their stubborn tasks. But the night could be filled with self-questionings. Indeed it is not easy to describe the agonies of this calling. Happily for our comprehension one young Sheff English instructor had the observant eye, the reflective mind, and the understanding skill to set it all down. And no more brilliant diagnostic report can be found than has been drawn by H. S. Canby in his *Alma Mater* of the campus "where two philosophies of living saluted in passing and sometimes stopped for a chat."

For most, I am told, the campus remained a sunny and cheerful place. No doubt the shadows in Canby's canvas and his own disappointment have deepened a little across the years. At all events what is explicit in his account, and what should be emphasized, is the fact that the members of this beleaguered community neither abdicated nor surrendered. "Our embattled teaching was quite as American in tradition and spirit as the get-rich-quick ideas of our students. We kept hammering away in spite of discouragement and frustration." No amount of public indifference could deflect some of Yale's older scholars from the quiet, "unprofitable" pursuit of truth. And no precedent of failure could prevent fresh and idealistic instructors from challenging the success cult of the younger generation. "Admiring the undergraduate, while hating his ideas," the younger faculty knew instinctively that they "must fight the materialism spilling over into the campus from this American energy on the loose, or be downed by it." [2]

Hence a recurrent concern for the curriculum and its reform. New subjects and new methods of teaching were weapons in this battle. When Canby and his friends had been undergraduates the old curriculum had been "tottering like a rotted house about to fall and in parts already fallen." When they became instructors new subjects by the score had come in—yet still taught for the old ends and by methods that had failed. The curriculum "was no longer a summary of the intellectual past of the race. It became unhappily a digest of examinable subjects about which concrete questions could be asked after due memorizing, and to which other subjects could be added . . . as soon as they could be made examinable." Edward Bliss Reed and other young idealists might despair of the slowness of change. Yet over and over again the entire faculty would return to curriculum planning. They would experiment with new teaching devices, new incentives. And they betrayed a passion for teaching so absorbing as to make even subject matter secondary, a conviction so profound as to lead some of the scholars themselves to challenge the research fetish. Such concerns, such constant revisions in their own practices, proved that they had not given up. However superficial the public's devotion to formal education, at least the Yale faculty still believed.

Another hopeful sign was that the students were more courteous and considerate of their instructors than formerly. Roughnecks and rowdies were still noticeable in the classroom—and hordes of the indifferent. Seniors could read newspapers in their seats with Sumner himself waiting to begin. But hazing the instructor, making his life miserable, driving him to despair and resignation—such barbarian practices were finally disappearing.*

* When Dean Jones arrived he found that hazing of the incompetent instructors still went on—but confined to the worst instructors. If the students felt the man had some brilliance or importance, they treated him more decently. There was one man who just could not control his class. Students set fire once to the notes that he held over his behind as he wrote something on the blackboard. They blew spitballs at the map, the board, and him. They

271

Whether this change was related to improved classroom methods may be debated. But it is observable that the younger faculty no longer as in the seventies thought it *infra dig* to show a personal interest in their students. So likewise for a Junior to stop and speak with his instructor was not necessarily to be labeled a grind. No doubt such intimacies were still a little restrained and tentative. Yet more than one assistant professor was moving in his own way down the trail of enthusiasm and friendliness and popularity that William Lyon Phelps had blazed. The old rule by discipline and marks, the old defiance by crib and bluff, the old taboos against having anything to do with each other outside of class were yielding to intimations of a mutual appreciation. Tute Farr made himself into the counselor and friend of each new Freshman Class. Herbert Hawkes was studying student choices. With eager instructors searching their classes for the responsive minds, with Albert Galloway Keller delighting both Sheff and College with his pungent observations, with the sympathetic Reed dreaming of the enthusiasm that an Honors plan might evoke, with Tinker already challenging the admiration of the campus by the brilliance of his teaching, it could hardly be long before these inherited antipathies would be forgotten and even the vast sea of good-natured indifference start to evaporate.[4]

Whatever its public helplessness, the College remained a sanctuary which attracted not only the seekers after knowledge but some dreamers, some born disciplinarians, and some lovers of culture or missionaries of the printed word. By the 1900's it sheltered a wider range of talent than in days gone by. Above all it offered to teachers a way of life that could be profoundly satisfying. In the classroom, reports Canby, "there were five schools of the theory of teaching in my day: the hard-boiled, the indifferent, the idealistic, the factual, and the enthusiastic." [5]

---

would also pretend an unquenchable thirst for outside reading, then stack the books he brought behind the door. Dean Jones tried to stop them forcing the poor man to carry so many books back and forth from the Library. But it was such wonderful fun—and a "gut." The culprits used to plead not to be deprived of it.[3]

The hard-boiled thought students worth bothering about only if they were interested. They refused to coddle the incompetent. But this theory ran counter to Yale instincts:

> With us, education was what religion had been to our ancestors, something to be spread abroad to all who had minds that could be saved. Which meant that those who felt as I did worked harder over a weary football player, or a perfectly cynical broker's son, than with the fine minds already lit with enthusiasm for learning . . . our energies were exhausted in trying to educate the almost uneducatable.

The indifferent in the faculty were those who had given up trying to inspire the undergraduates or change the system. They busied themselves with committees and rose in administration, making themselves useful and respected. More difficult to describe was the idealistic group. Some, "having hitched their wagons to an earlier century," taught by the praise of other days. Others used their literature for romantic moralism. All struggled to make the students think. Daily they went forth to battle, and daily they were defeated. The factualists were the competent men who methodically and contentedly taught every detail of their subjects; while the enthusiasts were the revivalists, who "triumphed even when their voices went sharp or flat of the truth." "One could be enthusiastic about Shakespeare when it had already become a little vulgar to be enthusiastic about being saved."

One gathers that the factual approach was still somewhat practiced by the faculty. But what the students looked for and rewarded were qualities more human and beguiling—personal color, idiosyncrasies of manner, peculiarities of conduct or address. Accordingly, the trend was to breed great personalities rather than great thinkers.

Great thinkers were destined somewhat for neglect. Willard Gibbs had been an insubstantial figure. Admired by his colleagues and revered by scientists abroad, to the students and alumni he had been hardly even a name—an almost unnoticed figure crossing the campus. Yale College had given him place, in fact just the shelter

273

he needed for his remote and quiet thinking. But his mathematical courses were too advanced for the undergraduates or the alumni. They had not been trained to seek out intellectual eminence. In any case, scholarship so abstract and theoretical was not popularly understood.[6] And even a recognized originality of mind would have counted for less than character.

Witness William Graham Sumner. Sumner did have stature on the campus. His words carried weight. But for all the legendary challenge of the man, and the still surviving cult of Sumnerology, one has the uneasy feeling that his teachings would have seemed like the rantings of a crank had they not been backed by his massive personality—and spiced by the excitement of political controversy.* Ironically, some of the excitement departed when he shifted from Spencerian economics to his genuinely original folkways and mores.[7] He could still be truculent and filled with the power of brutal speech. The realism of his marriage statistics made sensational headlines, and when he pointed out that dress was the mother of decency, not decency of dress, he shocked the younger generation almost as much as his attacks on the protective tariff had shocked their brothers of the 1880's. In the early 1900's the Seniors elected his Science of Society and cheered him at the end of the year—just as always. But some of the enthusiasm and appreciation had seeped away. He even had trouble with one or two classes. The story of how members of the Class of 1904 decided to present "Billy" Sumner with a loving cup has been variously told. As Starr relates the incident,

> The captain of the baseball team was delegated to make the presentation. Accordingly, just before the written test always held at the beginning of the hour, he stepped up to the desk and made his speech, while Sumner sat there with an expression on his face which, as the young man expressed it, "made me feel as

---

* As Phelps, introducing Sumner for his honorary degree in 1909, put it: "No Yale man, on hearing Professor Sumner's name, thinks primarily of his books. Men are more important than books, and it is the virility of this great teacher that has impressed so many generations."

if I would like to poke it over to him with a stick." Sumner, evidently disconcerted, took the cup awkwardly, and realizing that some response was necessary, remarked: "I don't often make valedictories, but one seems called for this time." Then a pause. "I've been counting the hours till I got rid of you," he continued. "You seem to want to do the right thing. All I can say is that I will try to think as kindly of you as I can the rest of my life."

Toward the end his health troubled him, and in 1907 he suffered the first slight stroke. Thereafter the massive power and bite were gone from his lectures, though in the evenings at his home one might still strike fire from the flint. Ever cold and autocratic, there was something "a little ghostly" about him in his last years. Van Wyck Brooks has called him "the preacher of force in a world of fate." Was it this fatalism or its popular repudiation—the hardness of his doctrine or the obvious survival of the unfit—that helped darken his later days? Rugged individualism, he knew, was going. Wars and socialism were surely coming. But what dent did that conviction make on the world or on the blithe student body, "so self-absorbed in their hour, so easy to capture for an idea, so sure to escape its implications?" Canby notes "the defeatism of a first-rate mind in the face of this impregnable youth."

With Gibbs and Sumner other giants were passing. In this first decade of the century a whole cluster of well-known professors, eccentric campus figures with familiar nicknames, reached their appointed time and died or were retired. The first losses to teaching had been those of Jules Luquiens in Romance languages and of Hadley in economics, followed in March 1900 by the death of E. J. Phelps, the much admired and stimulating Kent Professor of Law.* In 1901 the defeat of religious and philosophical instruction

* For the 1899–1921 list of retirements, resignations, and deaths of professors in or closely connected with the College, see Appendix, Table P: Permanent Officers of Yale College: Losses, New Appointments, and Promotions, p. 724.

in the College was symbolized by the transfer of Professors Ladd and Sanders out of the College Faculty, and the retirement of George Park Fisher, elder statesman and Professor of Ecclesiastical History in the Divinity School. In 1903 and 1904 came the turn of the sciences, with the death of Gibbs and resignation of H. Shaler Williams, geologist. In 1906 "Dicky" Richards, Buffalo Wright, and Waterloo Wheeler all had to be retired from their professorships, albeit Wheeler was kept on as a lecturer. But it was 1908 and 1909 that saw the devastating losses. With the deaths of T. D. Seymour and E. G. Bourne, the resignation of C. H. Judd, and the retirement of Sumner, Tracy Peck, Dean Wright, and Bernadotte Perrin, not only had history and the social sciences lost key men, but the classics had been almost wiped out. Within four years upward of one-third of the entire body of professors had addressed their classes for the last time—and stepped quietly down.

There was Eugene Lamb Richards '60,[8] Professor of Mathematics, who had challenged small handfuls of students to walk with him between dawn and dark clear across the State of Connecticut from the Massachusetts border to New Haven harbor. Richards had come down from the first glad morning of the athletic age at Yale. As an undergraduate he had rowed on the '60 crew and, but for an accident, might have been valedictorian of his Class. Instead, stretched flat on his back by a wrestling injury, he had been helped by Professor Newton who sent him boys to tutor in mathematics. This determined his occupation. With a gift for clear and factual instruction, in 1871 he had been appointed one of two Assistant Professors in the College, and in 1891 Professor of Mathematics. But all through the 70's and 80's he had shown himself more interested in teaching than in Faculty meetings, and more interested in boys and in games than in either. It was his theory that to make a man not merely knowledge from books and experience from companionship were needed but health and exercise. Man should be both scholar and athlete. Thus "Dicky-bird" Richards encouraged athletics, organized Yale Field, helped build the gym and served as its director. In 1884–85 he had had the exquisite pleasure of seeing Eugene L. Richards Jr. become captain of football, chairman of the *Lit.*, and Phi Beta Kappa with a Philosophical Oration stand. On the walls of our gym at this moment hangs a plaque:

> *Docebat, discebat, discessit*
> *Multis ille bonis flebilis*
> *Si monumentum requiris, circumspice.**

A second sympathetic and regretted figure was Thomas Day Seymour—classicist, scholar, and representative of much that was best in the old Yale faculty.[9] A graduate of Western Reserve—the Yale of the West—whither his father had gone to be professor after graduating and tutoring in New Haven, Seymour had been given an *ad eundem* degree in 1870 and in 1880 brought from Western Reserve to be Professor of Greek. It was said that he had looked old almost from the start. He dressed his hair like Homer's bust and in fact there was something Olympian about him. "Digamma" had been his original nickname, but Goat Seymour was what the students had called him ever since the day when he had remarked that the pass at Thermopylae was very narrow, so narrow that a goat could just about get through. "I—ah—have—ah—been—ah —through," he said. This hesitation was another idiosyncrasy: "Aris—a—totle" was the way he pronounced it.

Seymour was the scholar of the Greek department, with a fondness for allusion and a poetic touch. Music he loved, and Plato and the Bible. But Homer most of all. And like his Greek heroes he labored prodigiously. The manager and leading supporter of the American School at Athens, he was perhaps the best Homeric scholar America had produced, and his book on *Life in the Homeric Age* (1907) would long be a classic. His colleagues knew him

---

* Always of frail health himself, though through constant exercise with dumbbells tremendously strong in the arms, he had lived in what is now Mory's, then built himself a house on a hill in Woodbridge from which he walked four miles to the car line. A sensitive upright figure, blue-eyed, white-bearded—a fisherman in his youth, an amateur naturalist in his age—he had not been able to teach for some years. It is said that he read Greek every day. Though deeply religious, he no longer went to church. When his family went he would stay on the lawn and, as he said, "open the windows of the soul."

as a cheerful, indefatigable worker on innumerable Faculty enterprises. Indeed it was in private conversations between Seymour and one or two fellow statesmen that the most important questions were apt to be decided. Others might propose, but it was Sumner, Wheeler, and Seymour—or Perrin, Seymour, and Dana—who disposed. With the years, it is said, his teaching had become a little old-fashioned, but graduate students of all kinds liked to read Homer under him. Coming in exactly on the hour from his office across the hall, he would ask someone to start translating while still walking into the room.

One year he taught twenty-four hours each week, and the hours for one of the courses were from ten o'clock until midnight. The five sturdy graduate students in this course eventually succumbed and he reluctantly changed the time to eight o'clock. When the students withdrew at ten, he cheerily bade them good-night and turned to other occupations.

With his undergraduates he would alternate his courses from year to year—now exploring the Sicily of the ancients, now reading their orators and tragedians, now traveling their Mediterranean world, but ever and again returning to Homer. Always busy, he seemed, and always kindly. As Leonard Bacon recalls in *Semi-Centennial,*

In queer old sham-Gothic Alumni Hall at the end of a soft June afternoon, I laid my blue examination book on a pile before an old gentleman who had the beard and air of Capitolian Jupiter. He glanced at my name on the book and turning with a godlike smile said to me: "It's good to see them coming back." What kinder word could have been said to a timid sub-Freshman?

Then there was Waterloo Wheeler. As Tom Beer records in *The Mauve Decade,*

little Arthur Wheeler . . . faced the football players of the Iron Age at Yale and lectured on European history, puncturing legends with a succession of groaning sniffs. . . . "Lord Nelson now arrived at Naples, where Lady Hamilton greeted him. Her

experience of men was great and Nelson's intelligence was that"
—sniff—"of a sailor. . . . The Duke of Wellington, being"—
sniff—"an Englishman, believed in letting his allies have a fair
share of trouble in any undertaking. . . . If Napoleon's ambition to spread French culture in the Orient was reprehensible,
that of the English to enlighten India has somehow escaped the
attention of English"—sniff—"historians." [10]

Wheeler had been a faculty manager and Dwight's right-hand man
in dealing with John Sterling and other graduates. He had also
been one of Yale's earliest and most successful lecturers. But it was
as the champion of Napoleon that he was celebrated. Year after
year he had given his famous lecture on the Battle of Waterloo.
This had become a College occasion which faculty and students
alike attended, whatever their engagements. No doubt Wheeler's
facts about Napoleon were a little romantic and out of date. Nevertheless some students heard the lecture every year they were in College, and most Seniors elected his Europe Since 1789 as a matter of
course. In harness ever since 1865, he had become an institution—
a common possession and memory of all Yale's graduates since the
end of the Civil War. It was not until 1911, five years after the
formal retiring age, that the Corporation finally decided this tradition had to end.

Another loss came with the retirement of the Public Orator of
the University, the red-haired and red-bearded Professor of Greek
Literature and History, Bernadotte Perrin. Impulsive and mag-
nanimous, with a zest for society yet a strong sense of decorum, Perrin had been an impressive and respected campus figure. The
alumni recognized in him an even-handed commentator on Yale
affairs. His colleagues knew him as elder statesman and mediator
among the classicists. It is reported that he was the second member
of the faculty seriously considered for the presidency in 1899.

Out of an interest in heroic character Perrin had undertaken
the translation of Plutarch's *Lives*, bringing to the task a blend of
scholarly curiosity, enthusiasm, self-discipline, and craftsmanship
peculiarly his own. Meanwhile to generations of Sophomores he
had been the evangelist of Greek culture. Toward the end of each

hour's session it was his custom to gather up the results in his own translation. In the words of Henry B. Wright,

> First there would come a reverent dignified pause, and then, as we sat enraptured, the lines of the *Prometheus Bound* would fall upon our ears with a pathos in their majestic beauty and a manliness in their scornful defiance which only he could have interpreted to us who was himself warrior and poet of the truth.[11]

Perrin had a quick temper. Once when he was conducting chapel a collie got into the gallery, wandered down to the balcony rail, and raising itself on its forepaws looked gravely down at him. As the undergraduates tilted their heads to watch the dog—"Ye men of Galilee," read Perrin, "why stand ye gazing into heaven?" Laughter swept Battell. Outraged, Perrin shut the Bible with a slam and walked out. A Senior who was delegated to call and apologize on behalf of the College found him still furious. But when he finally understood what had happened, up went his red beard in Homeric laughter.

Cut off before his time was a quite different and modern type of historian—the lame and sympathetic Edward Gaylord Bourne: scholar-investigator, critic of legends, and protagonist of the truth. He it was who exploded the Marcus Whitman legend, and reassessed the Spanish conquest in the Americas. Bourne was the friend of those who wanted to know—and would be the model upon whom the next generation of historians would pattern their scholarship.[12] One must notice again the departure of Dean Wright. And Sumner gruff and indomitable. So stepped off the stage the earth-shaker of Yale College—and with him a group of scholars, lecturers, orator-disciplinarians—on the whole a fatherly and schoolmasterly type: respected by the students and remembered with an odd affection by the graduates of simpler days.

Yet much that they stood for remained, and not least the tradition of Yale teaching. "Indian" Smith—old "One-Lung" Smith, with his stage whisper and methodical instruction—retired in 1910. But G. B. Adams, the real master of historical scholarship and an intellectual organizer of dignity and power, carried on with his courses in English constitutional history and English political history. The "Visigoth" they called him—and smiling inwardly he would give his whiskers an extra flourish. Together with E. S. Dana and Dean Jones, Adams and E. P. Morris were the men whose opinions carried weight in College and administrative circles in the years 1909–17. E. P. Morris, in Latin, was of New England character: independent, straightforward, and the soul of honor. His specialty was syntax but his pride was in the College and his real love was sailing. He came to know so much about the history of the fore-and-aft rig that he published a book on it—and much of his spare time went into designing and building his own boats. In what he would write about his friends, or the early history of the curriculum, delicacy of feeling and simplicity were beautifully blended. It is a pity that he never came to a history of Yale College, which his hand would have ennobled.[13]

Less of a scholar than Seymour or Adams, less concerned with the usages of Yale government than Morris, but himself the type of perfect, complete gentleman was Horatio M. Reynolds '80—Limpy as he was affectionately known. His was a special appeal. For more than twenty years he had been charming his students into reading outside of class. In the eighties he had got Billy Phelps to read Grote's *History of Greece* every night from ten to eleven. In the early 1900's athletes were known to read Greek on the train. When Reynolds found a student floundering, he wouldn't take advantage. "Perhaps I can handle that for you," he would say—and from that moment he might do all the translating to the end of the hour. The College allowed half-cuts or "dry-cuts" for those confessing unpreparedness in advance. But when Reynolds had planned to do all the translating himself, he would say to an applicant like Emerson Tuttle '14, "I don't believe I should take a cut today, Mr. Tuttle, not today, Mr. Tuttle." He also had his favorite stories, which he would tell year after year at the same textual passages—including a famous anecdote out of Yale annals, to illustrate a passage where the Greeks had got drunk. On the occasion of his marriage, when Reynolds entered the last session on the Iliad with the men of 1903 and 1904, he found two magnums of fine old wine on his desk, with a huge bow of blue ribbon fastened about and between them. Not many professors were better loved by the bashful barbarians of the College.[14]

These same young men were wont to dismiss the senior Professor of English as ineffectual and dull: a kindly old man who with nearsighted eyes and toneless voice read patiently from yellowed, crumbling notes—sometimes holding the note up and turning it round so that he could read what was written on the margin. Henry Augustin Beers would let them smile. "Athletes and dumb-bells slumbered unrebuked in his classes." But those who had a spark of poetry sat up front, where they could hear what he said, and catch the quick shafts of light flashing out so suddenly and so quietly from the rich and imaginative storehouse of his mind.* There was no gush or rhetoric in his speech, but a fine Gallic economy, penetrating and wonderfully illuminating. Though he never talked of "scholarship"—was in fact considered defeated and outdated by the newer schools of scientific research—he seemed to know all the writers and all their books, as if they were living companions and friends. He could tell stories of Emerson, whom he had known, and of Willis about whom he had written a book. He discoursed on the Connecticut Wits and other still remembered figures from our past. But also of the great books of the ages, in all the languages of the great tradition. Milton he would quote by the hour.

Inevitably the young writers sought him out—and graduate students who had learned his value. He would press on them one of the Pittsburgh stogies of which he was inordinately fond. Then he would talk. In a moment Emerson or Hawthorne would be in the room. Before the evening was out Dante and Goethe had spoken in shining and deathless song. He made you see the beauty you had

* When Beers taught in the short-lived Summer School, he was filled with astonishment. "What an experience to teach . . . people who are anxious to learn!"

missed. For he was so saturated with it himself that he could hardly speak without evoking images.

There was something pathetic about his personal history. As a young graduate he had come back from his law books in New York to this peaceful college town "where in the tree-tops hide belfry and bell." Dressed rather loudly "like a city feller" he had come, but full of a poet's longing for the haunts of his boyhood, where through the slow-paced hours he could give himself to teaching the books he loved and to writing:

> See, I am going back
> Where the Quinnipiac
>   Winds to the bay,
> Down its long meadow track,
> Piled with the myriad stack,
> Where in wide bivouac
>   Camps the salt hay.[15]

There had followed a little singing of songs so sweet and clear they are still treasured by all who have ever known the place. His *Ways of Yale in the Consulship of Plancus* made live again the youth of bygone days. He also wrote the book of essays, *A Suburban Pastoral,* and two fine scholar's books on the Romantic Movement. But the drudgery of the teaching, the cares of maintaining not only his own but a classmate's family on his slender College salary, above all the demands of an age that was making after goals less delicate and insubstantial than literature, in time took their toll. All too clearly the bustling world had passed him by. His clothes became old fashioned and shabby. Yet he could still smile, and tell stories about himself:

> One day as he was standing in front of
> the window of the Illuminating Company,
> looking at a display of lamps, deciding
> which he wanted to buy, a hobo stopped
> beside him and said:
>   "Not for us, Mister, not for us."

Was he really defeated? Outwardly he put up no struggle. But more and more he was sought out—quietly, persistently, by those who had some touch of the poet's longing. And within himself there shone a light, a love for what he had always loved. In a powerful and competent faculty he remained a figure of infinite and quiet charm, the poet and true humanist.[16]

An altogether different inheritance from the era of Timothy Dwight was the school of scholars who had been trained in the German methodology: scientific and detailed in their work, and painsgivingly exact. In the eighties and nineties they had come back from Europe convinced that the facts were what mattered and that scientific methods could be applied to the humanities as effectively as to the phenomena of nature. In their hands literature and language turned into the exploration of origins, into linguistics and a kind of literary archaeology. The Yale language departments were dominated by this school, insisting on their brand of discipline and learning, for Juniors and Seniors hardly less than for graduate students. Riding the wave of scientific scholarship they had made themselves into the authorities with outside reputations. Henry Roseman Lang in Romance languages, Thomas Dwight Goodell in Greek, and Arthur Hubbell Palmer in Middle and Old High German were outstanding representatives. But the most formidable philologist, the man regarded by many as the champion of the whole movement in America, was Beers' colleague in English, Albert Stanburrough Cook.

Cook was a challenge to his students, his colleagues, and his College—and a contradiction to himself.[17] Educated to be a scientist, self-taught in Greek, the favorite pupil and translator of Sievers at Jena, he had been brought to Yale in 1889: the year of catastrophe, so his opponents later declared. Yet Cook taught a philology that was far broader than linguistics. Knowing more about Old English than anyone else in the country, he was also an Aristotelian, a student of Chaucer, a writer on Petrarch and Boccaccio, and a lover of Dante, Shakespeare, and Milton. With an erudition at once minute and encyclopedic, his three-hundred-odd publications would range from the Greek and Latin authors—and the King

James version of the Bible, on which he was an authority—to Tennyson, Arnold, and Ruskin. He was before his time in emphasizing the continuing tradition of the classics in medieval literature and the continuing tradition of medieval ideas in modern times. Supposed to be a relentless German methodologist, by conviction he was really a Christian humanist and taught that the study of literature should serve the cause of human conduct. Invariably his students were expected to know the great masterpieces and to memorize short passages as "touchstones" after the manner of Arnold. "Winsome" was a favorite word, and one of his most famous essays bore the revealing title: *The Artistic Ordering of Life.* As Cook insisted, "We must never forget that the philologist is a lover." Loving poetry, he not only founded the first poetry prize in the history of Yale (1896) but edited most of the classic treatises on poetics and through his pupils became a leading progenitor of courses in the theory of poetry in this country. By his own definition "the ideal philologist is at once antiquary, philosopher, grammarian, lexicologist, expounder, critic, historian of literatures and, above all, lover of humanity." Perhaps that line speaks for itself. At all events he was a medievalist who believed in what was great, but who often seemed to deal with what was insignificant and to allow his students to do likewise.

What made it the more difficult for Cook to attract or persuade was a pedantic dogmatism and a willingness to correct his colleagues. Also his teaching was to the last degree exacting and remorseless. He did not lecture, but conducted his classes by Socratic questioning, never if he could help it divulging a fact himself but forcing each student to expose his ignorance, and then invariably examining him the next time to see if he had corrected it. "There were no rules of fair play in his quest of truth." He even tried to correct faults of character.

If you could stand such exposure, and struggled ahead, then he would give you unlimited time and excellent practical advice, and would exult in your victories as if they had been his own. The dreamers and appreciators of literature, however, together with the mediocre and the lazy would find themselves tormented with questions they could not answer, and when they tried he would say: "That's two thirds of the truth." In retaliation they whispered: "What are Professor Cook's initials? A–S–C. That's two thirds of the truth." As "Two Thirds True Cook" he became a marked figure. The undergraduates had a limerick:

> There was a professor named Cook
> Who thought he knew more than the book;
> He shot off his mouth
> From Durfee to South
> To show what a great man was Cook.

To many graduate students and to a few hardy undergraduates —one thinks of Osgood and Root of Princeton, Lane Cooper at Cornell, and men of the stature of C. B. Tinker, Frederick A. Pottle, and Robert J. Menner at Yale—Cook was either one of the greatest teachers or the very greatest of their entire experience. He made their ignorance so painful, and so filled them with the desire to know, that when his graduate classes broke up, "the members ran (they didn't walk) to the Library stacks." But at least a third of every class hated this man who always hurt them, never praised them, and never allowed them to shine.

Whatever the reaction, Cook remained serene, never doubting he was right. His case is worth study, for it demonstrates how some of Yale's more vulnerable philologists, no less than the original thinkers or the shy humanists, could be disappointed men. For science in literature had brought neither serenity nor local regard nor enough rewarding discoveries. Their researches forced them to deal with smaller and smaller matters, mere fragments of subjects that yielded no universal laws. President Hadley was obviously unimpressed by their kind of publication. And public opinion, on which as pioneers and discoverers they had counted, was turning against them.

Yale College was insisting as never before on scholarship, and thorough training for its instructors—but not at the expense of the life of undergraduate teaching. The advanced courses offered by these philologists were complained of. In fact they now found themselves being removed more and more from College work. "Tommy" Goodell was interested in the best students, but temperamentally and intellectually he had become isolated from his colleagues, who were moving, however belatedly, toward the revival of the classics as humane learning. Lang was a pioneer authority on early Portuguese and Spanish literature; but he had the reputation of not caring for anything that had happened since 1350 A.D. Palmer seemed rather German to the undergraduates, and his offerings in the Scandinavian languages were virtually ignored. As for the powerful Cook, even he felt the pressures, or decided that the undergraduates were not serious, and so got himself transferred to graduate teaching. There he became the progenitor of distinguished pupils, founded the Yale Studies in English, almost single-handed supervising some 75 volumes in this series, and saw the Yale English department achieve an outstanding reputation in the profession. Bacon records: "In his later years, with visible reluctance, he grew kind to the point of gentleness."

For men less assured, all this came close to personal tragedy. It was grievous to have the bright dream of science-applied-to-learning producing such meager returns—still more bitter to face the realization that for all their work and learning the American colleges and the American public were still unappreciative. But the facts could not much longer be blinked. The years 1900–17 witnessed the beginning of the retreat for Yale's philologists. For the College, on the other hand, this was one more sign that a liberal education must not be made too professional or too hard.

As the old masters departed, their successors were coming through the mills of promotion and appointment. With regard to both persons and fields of scholarship this process of choosing would produce substantial changes in the character of the College faculty. At the top more eminence was demanded than ever before. Long service still counted, and character; but the faculty now thought of professors primarily in terms of scholarly distinction. The President thought also of national reputation and was particularly keen to get men of influence and recognized practical capacity. Boys would admire and work for men who had made their mark in the world. To Hadley a chief difference between a college and a university was the fact that a university's work was known and respected everywhere. A university, therefore, must have among its teachers men who can *do* things and the getting of real leaders into the teaching profession was "more important than everything else put together." [18]

To secure men of such caliber and interests, he realized, was bound to prove exceedingly difficult. Men of reputation were expensive and, if they then engaged in productive scholarship, they would be even more expensive to maintain. Often such leaders were too absorbed to be willing to give up everything for teaching and academic administration. Hadley proposed to meet this difficulty by employing a group of lively young assistants to relieve outstanding professors of the drudgery of committee work and lower-class instruction.[19] Again he was at great pains to accommodate the outside interests of distinguished candidates by allowing them to serve at Yale only part time. In this way he succeeded in attaching to Yale such men of accomplishment as John Hays Hammond in mining engineering (1902) and Gifford Pinchot in forestry (1903). But his most spectacular catch—or, as Hadley half-humorously put it, "our greatest acquisition"—was William Howard Taft, who in the winter of 1912–13 accepted appointment as Kent Professor of Law, with membership in both College and Law School faculties.[20]

On most occasions distinction had to be sought directly in full-time scholarship—and so through the cooperation of the departmental professors and of one or more of the governing boards. In consultation with E. S. Dana, Hadley tried repeatedly but in vain to lure the great physicist Rutherford. Again there is evidence that John Dewey, James Rowland Angell, and G. Lowes Dickinson were approached, the last two with direct aid from the President's Office. Unsuccessful efforts were likewise made to secure Davis R. Dewey in economics and among others John R. Mott and George Adam Smith for the Divinity School, Harvey Cushing for the Medical School, and J. H. Wigmore for the Law School.

THE THREE PRESIDENTS
Dwight, Taft, and Hadley. Commencement 1911

Still shooting high, and generally but not always in cooperation, the University and the College did succeed in bringing in Ernest William Brown from Cambridge by way of Haverford in mathematics, Ross Granville Harrison from Johns Hopkins in zoology, George Lincoln Hendrickson from Chicago in the classics, Charles Cutler Torrey from Andover Theological Seminary in Semitics, Ernest Carroll Moore from the West coast in education, Charles McLean Andrews from Johns Hopkins in history, and Julius Petersen from the University of Munich in German. Of these all but Andrews and Petersen were given functions in the College as well as in the Graduate or Scientific Schools. The unquestioned distinction of this group added luster to the University and scholarly reputation to the College faculty: a reputation confirmed when the College promoted from within the junior ranks men of such scientific promise in their respective fields as Hanns Oertel in linguistics, Henry Andrews Bumstead (from Sheff) in physics, and Joseph Barrell in geology—while Bertram Borden Boltwood, Assistant Professor in the College, was promoted to Professor of Radiochemistry in the Graduate School.*

A study of the Table of Losses, New Appointments, and Promotions † under Hadley reveals also the acquisition by the College for its Board of Permanent Officers of men of two other kinds. There was the group of scholar-teachers or teacher-administrators —professors of varied capacities and general University usefulness

---

* Characteristically, Hadley took pains to judge these men personally and give them individual treatment. When Corporation Fellow Ripley undertook to remonstrate with a certain slow-moving, old-time language teacher in the College, the President approved. "What he needs is a dose of bumble bees," was his comment. So also when the University Physics Laboratory had to be staffed, Hadley intended that the two new appointees should complement each other. "Boltwood is a man of great mechanical ingenuity, and an untiring experimenter. His vivacity will counteract the effects of Bumstead's seriousness, and Bumstead's concentration will prevent Boltwood from scattering his brains loose around the table. . . . I predict great things for them." [21]

† See Appendix, Table P: Permanent Officers of Yale College: Losses, New Appointments, and Promotions, p. 724.

289

—men like Charlton M. Lewis and C. B. Tinker in English, Henry Crosby Emery and Clive Day in political economy, Max Farrand and Allen Johnson in history, Herbert Ernest Gregory and Lorande Loss Woodruff in the sciences. Finally there were those who were appointed to professorships primarily on the ground that they were superb teachers—and who needed no other justification. One thinks of Phelps and Keller, of Tinker again, and of Sydney Knox Mitchell later on.

All these varied motives for appointment resulted in a professorial body that was lively and resourceful. If none of them exceeded the classroom style and celebrity of Waterloo Wheeler, this new senior faculty nevertheless boasted half a dozen superb lecturers where the old had known but one. Were the giants gone? Certainly there was no second Sumner to dominate his colleagues or shake the student world to its foundations. And no one with the remote and quiet genius of Willard Gibbs. But such men are the gift of the gods, and not always to be had for the seeking. Meanwhile great personalities were still being found, and Yale's classrooms were beginning to know an increasing number of teachers impressive alike for scholarship and personality.

This last was not achieved without pain. As we have noted, the system emphasized research. Faithful schoolmastering was no longer enough even for beginning instructors. Nor was keeping track of the phenomenal expansion of knowledge in one's field— now a task to stagger the most resolute—quite sufficient proof of scholarship. No doubt character remained an important consideration; and if a man could make himself useful—show promise of executive talents—some promotion was likely to come his way. Just the same, the tendency was to arrest such men, like the teachers who did not publish, at permanent assistant professorships. High salary and security might compensate for lack of title—but Hadley was chary of this expedient and as time passed he became more and more persuaded of the necessity of "constructive scholarship." Only the exceptional man could be promoted for teaching alone. General abilities fitted a man "better for other positions than full professorships." [22]

All this changed the objectives of the younger staff, added to their burdens, and introduced into the intensifying competition a fresh note of uncertainty. For the insistence on publication gave outsiders a much better chance at the available professorships. Thus the young instructors and assistant professors on the inside, having had to bear the heat and burden of the day, felt a little exploited. Anxious and insecure, as Canby shows, they criticized the system, though not the place:

> They might grind our faces for years on insufficient salaries, exploiting our belief that our duty was to toil for *alma mater*. They might encourage us to think that we would be happy nowhere but on the home campus, then drop us with a sickening crash because we were inbred. They might overwork us in teaching and then break us because we had accomplished too little in scholarship. All this we bitterly resented, without shaking our love and loyalty for the college . . .[23]

Was Yale inbred? The charge had often been made, and now the elders were sensitive on the subject. In 1908 the *Alumni Weekly* printed a statistical summary which revealed that from 1801 to 1877 Yale College had appointed only one non-Yale man to a professorship. From 1877 to 1900 a broader policy had introduced a nucleus of outside talent, without sensibly threatening the established order. And since 1900 more than half the professorial appointments and more than one-third of the junior appointments had gone to graduates of colleges other than Yale. For all ranks in the arts and sciences (College, Sheff, and Graduate School) the percentages of new blood had been: appointed before 1900, 25%; since 1900, 41%.

Actually the new ratios were not so very different from those in the eighties and nineties, but the appointments under Hadley had been so much more numerous as to have an important cumulative effect. In the total active faculty the proportion of men who had taken their undergraduate work in other colleges was now 37%, "as compared with a little over 33% at Harvard among the same classes of instructors."[24] On the other hand, the overwhelming preponderance of the younger men, wherever graduated, had now begun to take their postgraduate training at Yale. In short, a non-Yale man entered the College faculty most easily either via graduate study or at the very top. But in the middle ranks particularly—to a lesser extent in the faculty as a whole—the Yale College graduate still dominated.

This domination had always been warranted by the outstanding ability of the men who came up through the College. The preference for home talent was based, too, on the instinctive conviction that a self-governing faculty ought to retain a strong nucleus of those who had been brought up in Yale's spirit and traditions. The newer balance of personnel in turn represented the rapid development of the Graduate School and of graduate scholarship. Perhaps also a shade of feeling can be detected that the College needed outside blood to keep up with the new ideas or trends in education and scholarship.

While a national service was implicit in this choice, so was a local pain. Internal promotion became less than ever automatic. The ranks were expanding, but by no means fast enough. So much depended on the perceptions of the senior professors. The old-fashioned disciplinarian—or the narrow-gauge philological scholar —was having to submit his judgment of instructors to a broader College tribunal; yet he could still block promotions.

Hence occurred a fair number of departures—and among them some much-regretted losses. Woodrow Wilson took young Robert K. Root and Charles G. Osgood, both protagonists of Cook, to be Preceptors in English at Princeton. History lost Guy Stanton Ford to a professorship at the University of Illinois and R. L. Schuyler to Columbia. Emerging from his graduate studies, the sparkling Wallace Notestein found no place open, and accepted a post at Minnesota. Mathematics not only let Edwin Bidwell Wilson— Gibbs' pupil—slip away, but in 1910 failed to promote Assistant Professor Herbert E. Hawkes and so lost him to a professorship at Columbia and a notable career as Dean of Columbia College. Apparently one of Hawkes' elders, a brilliant mathematician, did not feel that he was enough of a research man and scholar: told him in fact he would do better teaching in some small college. The Permanent Officers did not fully appreciate the effectiveness and promise of Hawkes' long service on the Freshman Faculty and Entrance Committee, and Hawkes himself did not foresee a career in administration. There would come a time later when he would be considered for most of the high offices within the power of the College or Corporation to confer. But in 1910 the only thing clear was that Yale had let him go. And some of his colleagues among the younger men were mightily discouraged. On them the economies of the period bore hard.[25]

If the central authorities had their own complaint, it was that the College was too narrow rather than too economical.* The Administration needed help if new fields and graduate levels of instruction were to be established and manned. It sometimes seemed as if the College Officers paid too much attention to the probable effectiveness of the lower-class instruction by the nominee and not enough to his general University usefulness. Yet the College in turn discovered that the undergraduate public was not easily to be won for unfamiliar subjects, no matter how significant. The special provincialisms of the student world were not lightly to be disregarded.

Out of all these factors came a very uneven departmental development. I select for illustration the broad division of the social sciences, and first the particular fields of geography and Oriental studies.

Some day it will be hard to believe that in 1900–14 Americans

---

* Secretary Stokes worked hard and successfully to establish fair and even rates of remuneration (i.e., the normal salary scale). But at a time when salaries generally were having to be raised and new levels established at the top, both Secretary and President approved the policy of advancing popular and effective professors to the higher levels while giving only the minimum advance to those professors who taught so minutely or so stiffly as to attract few students. As Hadley explained many times, only outstanding publication or instruction of an adequate share of students would justify additional drafts on income from tuition.[26]

were so little interested in the outside world. With the nation having built up to industrial supremacy as early as 1890, and having plunged into the competition for colonies and power in the war with Spain, one might have expected that more than a handful of political leaders, exporters, and intellectuals would be concerned, and that in our colleges the fields of international relations and what we today call foreign area studies would have come into favor. But no alumnus had endowed Hadley's project for a School of Colonial Administration. And how the public and government failed to support the Yale-Columbia venture in training for the consular service has been reported. Yet here and there scholars were beginning to be concerned with such matters—and Hadley refused to give up entirely.

One promising study was geography, which took the whole earth for its province and treated it in many ways. Politically, geography was international. Intellectually, many kinds of knowledge could be fostered and drawn on. Physical geography would organize information that was geologic, topographic, climatic, oceanographic. Commercial geography would draw on materials that were agricultural, industrial, financial, and political as well. Social geography would lead from anthropology into archaeology or sociology. And presumably no foreign countries could be studied effectively without their languages and histories. Hence a particular need for Asiatic tongues and learning—and the desire to strengthen Yale in the fields of Far Eastern and Latin American studies.[27]

To build up a staff in fields so unusual and for secular needs so unrecognized was hazardous. Yet there were some promising young scholar-graduates in the offing. And in due course there was attached to Yale an impressive list of specialists and courses. One notes the name of Hiram Bingham '98, whose Yale forebears had pioneered in the mission movements to Hawaii and the Gilbert Islands, and who was to uncover Machu Picchu, lost city of the Incas, and to make in the Yale Library a great deposit of Latin American books. Herbert E. Gregory '96 and Isaiah Bowman (Harvard B.S. '05) would work with Bingham in Peru and then make outstanding reputations for themselves: Gregory in the vast area of the Pacific, Bowman in the cultural geography of South America, as an organizer of geographic scholarship, and as President of Johns Hopkins University. Still a fourth explorer, with a global range and an interest in the long-buried past, was Ellsworth Huntington (Beloit '97), whose revolutionary ideas about climate were destined to challenge the accepted theories of civilization. Then there was Kan-Ichi Asakawa (Waseda '95, Dartmouth '99), shy young scholar-gentleman, who through years of indifference would bury himself in the historical wilderness of old Japan and emerge as the authority on Japanese feudalism. With a number of colleagues from the established disciplines, these five began offering courses in Yale College.

The promising Sophomore course in physical and commercial geography flourished and disappeared. While Ellsworth Huntington's desert experiences were fantastic, and his theories about climate and the pulse of progress little short of epoch-making, he lacked the will or the art to present such materials dramatically— and few of the students exercised enough imagination to grasp the spectacular possibilities.* Gregory, though a more successful teacher, found that Yale College was a "particularly unfavorable field for the development of geography, for the departments of history and economics seem to be organized on the theory that there is no such thing as Nature, and that Man is the whole show. Sometimes I feel very much discouraged." [29] Hiram Bingham by necessity and choice was absent a considerable part of the time, and in 1915 Isaiah Bowman left to direct the American Geographical Society. So the teaching of geography came to depend on one instructor, and when in 1918 he went into the service the subject died. Meanwhile Huntington had resigned from the College, and joined Assistant Professor Asakawa and Professor Bingham on precarious ten-

* Leonard Bacon '09 was one of the exceptions: "It was something to a boy who had never been ten miles from a highway, to visit Asia in thought, with a man who sat down in the middle of the Gobi Desert to write up his diary, after the stampede of camels, whose more than probable failure to return would make the continuation of that diary wholly impossible." [28]

ure in the Graduate School; then in 1919 Gregory began spending half his time in Hawaii to organize and direct the Bishop Museum.

As for the other specialists and specialties, "Oriental Bill"— Frederick Wells Williams '79—was the inheritor of a distinguished missionary name, a man of much breadth of culture who over the years had opened more than one undergraduate's eyes to the mysterious world of the East. But because he had never mastered Chinese, Sumner and others stood in the way of his promotion to a professorship, while the undergraduates for the most part elected his course as an inviting gut. Few of them wanted to study Japanese history, or the Japanese or Russian languages, or the archaeology or history of Latin America. Other than Andrews' graduate work on colonial America, courses on colonial history disappeared entirely. Bourne's work on the Spanish Empire in the New World and the Philippines was not continued, and College or Graduate School courses in international law and Spanish law lapsed.[30]

On the surface the whole movement had been a mistake: just a flight of scholarly curiosity and an academic failure. Yet only twenty years later, in World War II, knowledge of Oriental languages, the Far East, Russia, Southeast Asia, and colonial history and administration would suddenly become of such vital importance that the Armed Services would subsidize a series of foreign area studies in our universities. So the stone that had been rejected of our builders would become one of the cornerstones of American security. This epitaph to our scholars is ironic, but sufficient.

A second field worthy of notice was government—but this Hadley declined to back. He believed in instruction that took account of political developments, contemporary as well as past, yet doubted apparently that there was or could be such a thing as a science of government or of politics. He and others used the example of Sumner to justify their aversion. Everyone who had sat under Sumner would testify to the "fascination and grip that his teaching derived from his constant reference to current political and economic events." Other instructors in semipolitical branches were free to seize the same opportunities. As Hadley wrote to Professor Allen Johnson, "I incline to make constitutional law a branch of law, municipal administration a branch of economics, and politics a branch of history." [31]

About the social sciences generally Hadley had many doubts. He regarded the true social sciences as equivalent to what he called the philosophical sciences: i.e., law, ethics, and political economy. To those varieties of sociology or political science which involved "mere descriptions of social phenomena" he attached small educational value. Professor Allen Johnson was brought into the history department in part because of his strong interest in politics and government. When Johnson pointed out the inadequacy of Yale's staff in political economy and urged the creation of a new department of political science, Hadley demurred: "Where you get an organizing head like Lawrence Lowell you unquestionably gain much by organizing a department of political science and grouping a number of subjects around it." But in the absence of an exceptional man, he did not feel that such a step "conduced to good teaching." No doubt his clear perception of the difficulty of giving to the study of politics any scientific independence or exactitude contributed to his reluctance.

The net results were that political science never got a start; the historians carried a heavy responsibility for political history, constitutional history, comparative politics, and government; and finally the so-called department of the social sciences, instead of dividing into autonomous departments of economics, politics, anthropology, sociology, and perhaps geography, remained an amorphous federation of professorial teams in economics, anthropology, and law, dominated by the most numerous element, the economists. So the group of disciplines which Sumner had done so much to advance and differentiate remained for more than a decade almost in statu quo.

By contrast history, with all its responsibilities for politics and government, grew steadily stronger. Adams and Bourne, then Andrews, had given the historians a considerable professional reputation; and the department had been even more successful as an undergraduate teaching organization. In 1908 Max Farrand and in 1910 Allen Johnson were brought in to professorships from the outside. Meanwhile in the lower ranks first O. H. Richardson '89 (1897–1909) and G. S. Ford from Wisconsin (1901–06), next a group led by Edward L. (Tubby) Durfee '96 (1903–16) did yeoman service. Then Stewart L. Mims '04 (1911–19), Charles Seymour '08 (1911–37), John M. S. Allison from Princeton (1914–44), and Ralph H. Gabriel '13 (1915–   ) joined Sydney K. Mitchell '98 (1907–43) and George E. Woodbine '03 (1906–44) to give the instruction a verve and distinction that surpassed anything yet known.

And English flourished like the green bay tree. Bred almost entirely from Yale stock, the English faculty provided the greatest excitement and the most characteristic demonstration of how the faculty was now growing. In 1898 at the head had been Beers and Cook, Beers the living embodiment of the older New England literature, Cook the embattled champion of masterpieces and thorough scholarship. Then in 1899 Lewis had been promoted to the Emily Sanford Professorship and in 1901 Phelps to the Lampson Professorship: the first endowed chairs of English in the history of the College.

Lewis had the touch of a poet, a distinguished style, and a natural twist of anecdote and humor—yet still he held his lecturing in a shy and severe restraint. It was said he would delete from his lectures the passage which had suddenly made the class laugh. Many students who took Sophomore English under Lewis because they had to then took his English Poets of the Nineteenth Century because they wanted to. They would later remember him "seated on a platform in a swinging chair with his head turned a little to one side, and a mildly distant expression on his face, while from his lips issued words of enchantment." [32]

Where Lewis combined the dignity of the old with the art of the new—scholarship and literature in a union that the undergraduates themselves could appreciate—Phelps was youth, novelty, enthusiasm, and personality personified. He taught almost unheard-of subjects—novels, drama, American literature—in equally unheard-of ways. Prodigious energy, astonishing teaching talent, and a vast and somewhat undiscriminating enthusiasm for things, places, writers, athletes, cats, dogs, and undergraduates had given him an extraordinary hold on the students. Twenty years after his debut he was going stronger than ever, smuggling "an interest in reading into many a recalcitrant and oafish breast." [33] And now a small army of disciples, from his first electrified listeners in the Class of 1896 and from other Classes following, were joining the ranks of the younger faculty—and not in English alone—to help make over the style and matter of undergraduate teaching. By 1915 the English department itself boasted the following additions: Professor Tinker '99—disciple of Cook and Lewis and Beers—Assistant Professors E. B. Reed '94, J. C. Adams '96, John M. Berdan '96, C. F. Tucker Brooke (West Virginia '01, Oxon. '06), and Samuel B. Hemingway '04; while among the instructors were "Larry" Mason '04, Robert D. French '10, and Stanley T. Williams '11.

In this period English replaced the classics as the backbone of the humanities at Yale. No sooner did it achieve equal status with the traditional Freshman studies than it was elected by almost every entering Freshman. The rise of its popularity must be traced in part to a general popular drift, but probably in no college of the day was literature more successfully taught.[34] One sign was a faculty enthusiasm, another was the flowering of personalities, and a third was the variety of method employed. The younger men, and the instructors in the lower-class courses, believed in small divisions and an intimate personal instruction. As the upper-class courses grew into popular lectures, different arts came into play. As John M. Berdan described the situation,

> in the old-time class of fifteen men, one could be delicate and subtle, in the modern class of one hundred and fifty a joke must be clever indeed to be bellowed at full lungs, and subtlety is apt to evaporate before it reaches the back benches. . . . Thus are we conditioned by our audience that our work, profound or not, must be popular, and our truths masquerade in epigrams.[35]

Throughout the middle years of the Hadley administration teachers and teaching were in a course of transformation hardly less significant than the modernization of the Course of Study. One phase was a process of self-examination and solidification. What seemed extraneous to College purposes was being cut off—at the top, at the bottom, and on the sides. Inappropriate courses, unadaptable instructors, subjects of study not elected by the students or unsusceptible to satisfactory development were being eliminated. This was achieved by elevation to the Graduate School,* transfer to other Schools, or refusal to recommend promotion.

Another phase was the diversification and specialization of scholarship at the College level and within the recognized College subjects. With this came invigoration of teaching methods and a renovation of the teaching personnel. Gone was the amateur tutor, and on his way too was the semiprofessional professor. Specialization was now indispensable. Scholars of universal knowledge were no longer being bred. In Sheff, Brewer had been the last of the universal scientists. In the College no one after Sumner would be able to make original contributions to knowledge in so many areas of the social sciences, and polymaths like Hadley would have few successors.

The disciplinarian and the grammarian were also retiring. Enthusiasm and an emphasis on ideas were beginning to replace factual quizzing and drill. And a generation of instructors of unusual vigor and dramatic talent were coming up. In English this period saw the rise of a star of the first magnitude in Tinker, to say nothing of the appealing and fanciful characters decorating the younger ranks. In history, after crippling losses, a growing nucleus of talented scholar-instructors helped recapture student elections and— under Adams, Farrand, and Johnson—made this the second department in all-round capacity and distinction. Economics promoted first Clive Day, then Fred R. Fairchild (Doane '98), and en-

---

* It was in 1911 that Oertel was made Dean of the Graduate School, in 1912 that the College surrendered jurisdiction over the M.A., in 1913 that the budgets were reorganized, and in 1916 that the Graduate School was allowed to set up its own governing board. As a result, really advanced or professional study of the arts and sciences now for the first time achieved a government, a faculty, courses of study, and standards of its own.[36]

joyed an increasing undergraduate vogue. Next to English more men majored in economics than in any other subject; and in 1913 Ray Bert Westerfield, in 1916 E. S. Furniss began working up through the ranks.

Even the sciences and less popular departments made their own contributions to this hopeful movement. In physics there was David Albert Kreider (B.A. Lebanon Valley '92), who snapped questions and pieces of chalk with unerring aim around the room, terrifying the most sophisticated and somnolent into wakeful attention. As Leonard Bacon recalls:

> A gang of seniors with hangovers and otherwise not prepared for intellectual debate, grew wild with excitement as that blond Mephistopheles, with a mixture of irony and enthusiasm, drew from unwilling lips, faltering admissions that with dramatic suddenness elucidated the hitherto wholly boring behavior of the atom. I never knew a man who came so near to the Platonic ideal of the Socratic method.[37]

Out of the materials of the life sciences L. L. Woodruff (B.A. Columbia '01) was soon to create the first exciting and popular course in general biology that the College had known. From the great bone house of Peabody Museum emerged the courtly Lull, to charm vast audiences with his drama of organic evolution. In the old discipline, philosophy, a sad-eyed young Irishman, C. A. A. Bennett (B.A. Oxon, '08), was beginning to mix humor and mysticism with such searching eloquence as to tease wooden Indians into astonished thought. Latin had gained Clare Mendell, full of fire and understanding. But it was losing "Slugger Bill" (J. W. D.) Ingersoll '92 who had fought his battle against disease with a kindness and humble courage to move the most careless, carefree young animal. From Steve Benét's *The Beginning of Wisdom* [38] I borrow one final sparkling portrait—that of Sydney K. Mitchell:

> The other, a great, burly, bearish man with the face of a Visigoth king and a sandy beard that never seemed quite intentional and yet could not deliberately be called a lapse on the

part of his razor, Philip always remembered as one of the few, rare, lucently-forceful intellects that can vivisect the smallest nerve or joint of a subject without ever losing its place and importance in the general anatomical scheme.

In *his* classes men neither yawned, wrote surreptitious letters nor tried to bluff. He taught History—a pell-mell course from the Fall of the Roman Empire to 1815—and before this year was over he had left his own signature and the skeleton facts of the case on the logiest minds of his divisions, as a stamping-machine leaves motto and pawing buffalo on the blank of a nickel in the mint. He taught roaringly to bump sleepy intellects awake, he would break long pieces from the end of his pointer (the length of a tall man's crutch the first of the week, of a worn-down pencil at the last of it), he would smash his watch down on the desk and jar its wheels apart in the stress of the moment's question as to the "sig-nif-i-cance" of Charlemagne's imperial title or the effect of the Reformation on German trade. This was necessary vaudeville—under its cover he dug to the essential roots of things—and he insisted so forcibly on the same straining vehemence of intelligence from his men that by February they were running to keep up with him in as healthy an ardor of pursuit as if historical causes were cats and they were terriers. Only once did Philip see him genuinely out of temper. He cared little for dates as a rule, but when he happened to want a particular one he worried the class for it like a ferret. It was four days before Christmas vacation—an eight o'clock after one of the Freshman dances. He viewed the somnolent ranks before him with the amiable grin of a fed cobra.

"And now," he repeated for the ninth time, "and now, just *what* was the sig-nif-i-cance of 512 A.D.?" He paused, the name quivered and struck like an arrow, "Mis-ter *Post!*"

"Chubby" Post, an impudent cherub, cox of the second Freshman crew, was jarred into round-eyed imbecility.

"Washington at Valley Forge, sir," he said in a stupefied whisper.

302

The professor rose to his full tower of height, took his watch in his hand and threw it out of the window. "This class is dismissed," he roared. They departed on tiptoe, shivering. And after that even Chubby came to him with at least a flunking knowledge of his subject.

CHAPTER 16 · THE CURRICULUM AGAIN

It was a mistake for the advocates of the old curriculum to think that all the students required the same treatment. It is, I believe, an equal mistake for the advocates of the elective system to think that each student requires different treatment. For while there is a very large number of subjects of interest to study, and an almost infinite variety of occupations which the students are going to follow afterwards, there is a comparatively small number of types of mind with which we have to deal.

—Arthur Twining Hadley, *1909*

In the years 1908–14 the College Faculty entered upon a fresh series of experiments. This we may regard as the second phase in curriculum planning under Hadley. Strangers to academic affairs may ask why—with the elective movement arrested and a revised program of studies under construction—further experiments should have been required. But the life of a faculty is motion. In the best of times this business of tinkering with the Course of Study never stops.

With recent graduates entering the teaching ranks and adding to their remembered grievances the fresh shock of trying to lick the Freshmen into shape, it was inevitable that further improvements in the lower-class curriculum should be attempted. With the middle group rising to positions of responsibility and discovering how the upper-class programs worked out in raw practice, additional adjustments became necessary. The more so as Yale's remedies for the elective difficulties had at best been somewhat mechanical: a construction of sequences and major-minor combinations that took more account of balance and form than of incentives to study. So it happened that in the years 1905–08 there took hold the thought that the problem of student motivation—and a number of technical difficulties into the bargain—might yield to a more discriminating and intensive grouping of both students and studies.

Group programs were by no means an original idea. The segregation of courses and the separation of students had been among the more spectacular consequences of the scientific revolution. Originally the sheer increase of learning had provided the powder to explode the traditional curriculum. At the same time a psychology of individual differences, together with the new vocational-technological pressures, had undermined the inherited ideal of unity in college studies. The consequence had been subdivision, but subdivision for varied purposes or governed by conflicting interests. Wherever much specialization had been indulged, the educational authorities had had to decide who would shape the special programs—the professional faculties for professional purposes or the students for their individual enthusiasms. In the Sheffield Scientific School, at Cornell, and at Johns Hopkins, the faculties had set up series of independent but rather rigid programs—and allowed the students merely a choice between them. At Harvard under Eliot, by contrast, the theory of personal differences had been carried to its logical exaggeration in the form of individual programs constructed by each undergraduate almost at random.

Yale's Academical authorities had been reluctant to give up the unity of knowledge and positively unwilling to surrender the unity of undergraduate life. Instinctively they distrusted the extremism of the Harvard or Sheff alternatives. Yet the new forces had been well-nigh irresistible. So in their Course of Study planning the Faculty had labored to make possible some freedom and some specialization without permitting either intellectual dissipation or social splintering. Dwight's curriculum, half required and half elective, had constituted the first such accommodation. When that proved insufficient somewhat wider electives, governed by a mild system for distribution and concentration, became the answer for the average student; while the Combined Programs were introduced for the preprofessional minority. Because it was no more enthusiastic about water-tight compartments than about complete anarchy of election, the College was still holding back. Yet now that the Harvard movement toward unlicensed electives had been positively arrested, the drift toward an intermediate grouping of studies and perhaps of students was gathering momentum.

This trend of thought derived from a variety of sources. It appealed to administrative convenience. It was politically promising. The organization of alternative programs might enable the Faculty to meet the growing diversities of twentieth-century life without losing their control of academic planning.

Grouping was also suggested by undergraduate practices: by the students' own tendency to move in groups through the courses of study. It was observed that, far from distributing themselves evenly across the available areas and methods of knowledge, the undergraduates tended to follow a few well-beaten trails. Year after year a certain percentage of the courses were hardly elected at all. Instead, the more popular subjects and the more famous lecture courses were swamped, as each man followed one of a limited assortment of sequences to meet the major-minor requirements for his B.A. To a noticeable extent students were collecting professors —as "Johnny" Berdan said, "like bugs." [1] Still the lesson was unmistakable: the new psychologists must be wrong. For, whatever the preachments about individual diversity, the students by their own choices were demonstrating that they were on the whole not so very unlike.

Again it was plain that Yale's graduates were not distributing themselves evenly across all the vocations and occupations. Rather they were concentrating—a decreasing majority going into the professions, and an increasing minority aiming toward positions in business and industry. A full third of Yale's most recent B.A.'s had taken postgraduate degrees. Could not as much be done *in* College for those who were going directly into the economic occupations? With the popular callings so limited in number, it seemed by no means inconceivable that by a moderate grouping Yale might be able to offer a more appropriate preparation. The difficulty was to know just how to go about it.

A number of suggestions were canvassed.* But it was President Hadley who developed the most arresting proposals. Yale students, he pointed out in 1905, rarely wanted to study any single subject or group of subjects exclusively.[3] But they almost all had preferences "for specific kinds of teaching and specific ways of getting at the subjects." On this basis the students, with few exceptions, divided into three singularly well-defined groups, interested "in facts, in ideas, or in affairs." The first composed the scientific group: the future physicians, engineers, manufacturers, and experts in commerce. The second were the literary: the journalists, preachers, teachers, barristers. The third had the administrative bent: the merchants, financiers, legal advisers, statesmen. In his article on "Mental Types and Their Recognition in Our Schools," Hadley pointed out how men changed their professions mainly within their own groups. The preacher might become a teacher, but woe to him as a financier! The merchant might turn statesman but rarely scientist. He proposed that the three groups should not be given different subjects of instruction, but rather should be taught the same subjects in three different ways: that is, by methods that would serve the particular range of interests involved. Each man should be trained to see how all subjects enlarged his own capacities. In this way something of the breadth of the old curriculum could be restored without its dreariness and waste.

As was perhaps inevitable with such a hypothesis, Hadley proved clearer on principle than on practical application. But publicly by 1909, privately somewhat earlier, he was advocating the establishment of a series of "honor courses" comparable to those

* In 1905 T. D. Goodell, for example, called Dean Wright's attention to the fact that Chicago was working on a sort of Oxford-Cambridge plan, and that in the *Harvard Graduates' Magazine* some writers had taken up the question of how the overgrown college could be split up into groups that, for social and athletic purposes at least, corresponded to the English small college. It is interesting to note that in 1907 Lowell delivered himself of a speech in New Haven in favor of some sort of a House or College Plan. But both Universities would wait twenty years before exploring such a solution. In 1906–08 Woodrow Wilson's residential Quadrangle Plan for Princeton was decisively defeated.[2]

at the great English universities. In his estimation such programs provided a wide range of educational advantages—not least the fact that they would make possible the cultivation of the major mental types without resort to too narrow specialization.[4]

While the President theorized about mental types and his exotic Pass-Honors solution, the Faculty were at first preoccupied with subjects and courses: their location at the proper levels and their grouping with relation to each other. The need to make a clearer distinction between upper-class and lower-class kinds of work was particularly obvious. Everyone agreed that most Freshmen either did not know what they wanted to study or promptly changed their minds. Hence specialization ought not to begin too early. A man ought to complete his foundation studies and do some intelligent sampling before undertaking to choose his special field.

Theoretically, the groupings of subjects into Divisions, the A–B–C gradation of courses, and the major-minor system had assured the proper arrangement of an undergraduate's program. But it was none too easy to distinguish the two seven-hour majors for concentration from the three five-hour minors for distribution: in particular, there was nothing to require that the minors precede the majors. Taking advantage of this situation, students were too often completing their majors in Junior year, thus leaving themselves as Seniors with their neglected minors to clean up and a job lot of electives for fillers.

So experience indicated that the majors and the minors should be more emphatically distinguished from each other: the minors to be located earlier and the majors to be delayed and perhaps more fully developed. Some instructors felt that a more intensive concentration would also appeal to the better students, the scholars and prospective professional men. It might even lead on to Honors, or to special courses at the graduate level. Meanwhile, the average boy would certainly benefit from a really coordinated and positive policy of distribution in his earlier years. Accordingly, the first instinct of the Faculty was to group *studies* according to their purpose but to group *students* primarily according to their age or

Class. Lowerclassmen were amateurs; upperclassmen, potential experts.

In this movement there was much that was confident and constructive. Yet dissatisfaction also contributed its impetus. As a hang-over from the long elective revolution, and as a by-product of graduate studies, it had come about that members of the faculty were offering much inappropriate material. In 1911 Clive Day, member of an able Course of Study Committee, put his finger on this weakness:

> This danger . . . is that the instructor will teach the wrong subject, or—what amounts to the same thing—a good subject in the wrong place. *Lehrfreiheit* may be distorted in the colleges as well as *Lernfreiheit;* and if the faculty defers as readily to the personal inclination of the teacher as to that of the student, it magnifies many fold the chance that students may waste their time in the nooks and byways of the curriculum.[5]

A distinct element in the movement was therefore the continuing effort on the part of the Yale College Officers to reform their own practices.

THE REFORMS OF 1908 AND 1911

This overhauling of faculty elective offerings got under way in late 1906 with the appointment of a new Committee on the Course of Study, consisting of Professors E. S. Dana for the sciences, E. P. Morris for the languages and literatures, and Irving Fisher for studies in society. Beginning modestly and cautiously Chairman Dana and his able colleagues gradually got their mandate expanded, were asked to consider "any scheme" for the encouragement of concentration, and finally carried their ideas through an intense discussion with such address that almost within a single session the Permanent Officers heard, debated, and adopted a series of substantial alterations in the structure of the curriculum.[6]

First, the two majors of seven hours each were consolidated into a single major of twelve hours. Next, three hours of B-level work were added to the minor requirements, with the hope that these extra hours would go to that one of the three minors which was located in the same Division or field of studies as the major. Thirdly, students henceforward were to complete their minors by the end of Junior year and also to plan their courses to this end, in consultation with a member of the Freshman Tutorial Board. In the fourth place, certain "inappropriate" subjects were disestablished: the courses in music and fine arts, law and medicine were excluded from A–B–C classification and debarred from counting in either majors or minors. Finally—and this was a revolutionary vote—a new D-level was established, for work "not necessarily in course." Candidates for Honors were to take four hours of C and D work. And the exceptional student, desiring to concentrate even further, might "have his courses specially arranged for him" under the personal supervision of his instructor, be relieved from the ordinary major-minor requirements, and be likewise excused from "a part of his classroom attendance."

This reform of 1908 aimed, according to Dean Wright, at a more careful selection of studies, at more hours of connected work in all of the three main Divisions, at more concentration on the studies of one Division, and finally at better opportunities for especially qualified students.[7]

The years 1908–10 then witnessed an awkward pause. A minority of the Professors would have been glad to let well enough alone: the reformers had gone quite far enough. Once a year, at least, William Lyon Phelps would assure his colleagues that the College was in better shape than ever and they had nothing to worry about.

The new Course of Study Committee, on the other hand, felt that some promising lines of advance had only just been opened up —particularly in the treatment of upperclassmen. In private consultation Dana, Morris, Bumstead, and Day were approaching Hadley's position. "We should like to accomplish the important end of differentiating the 'pass men' from those of ability and ambition,"

Dana wrote to the President.[8] Requirements for the pass men should be made somewhat more rigid and less advanced. For those capable of taking Honors, special 24–27-hour programs should be laid out in a number of departments.* The President was naturally sympathetic but felt that it would be unfair to press too strongly for a Pass-Honors division of the College before Dean-elect Jones could take office and study the situation.

Meanwhile an influential group of able young assistant professors were as firmly persuaded that the education of the Freshmen and Sophomores could be improved. Some stressed closer personal relations between instructors and students. Some were inclined to scrutinize the individual offerings so as to eliminate inappropriate materials. And some wanted to increase the Faculty's control of elections, perhaps by grouping lower-class studies more nearly in accordance with genuine student needs.

The device of associating courses, or arranging a series of programs to fit the requirements of the commonest student types, was first applied to the foundation studies of the Yale curriculum in this same winter of 1908–09, when Herbert E. Hawkes, Assistant Professor of Mathematics, worked out a recitation schedule for the Freshmen, Class of 1912.[9] This scheme, based on some years of study of the choices and trends, grouped the Freshmen in five divisions in such a way that each division recited on the same subject to the same instructor in three out of five of their studies. The idea was to

* The date of this exploration (1908–09) is of more than passing interest. Princeton already had Honors programs in the classics and in a combination of mathematics and physics. Starting with the Class of 1908 Harvard had instituted a degree "with distinction" for concentrated work of superior quality with a thesis and oral examination. In the fall of 1910 Columbia was to begin its new Honors experiment. And at his inauguration in October 1909 Lowell would announce the principles of "Concentration and Distribution," the first of which was to lead on to the great Harvard divisional and tutorial program, starting with the Division of History, Government, and Economics in 1912 for the Class of 1917. Meanwhile both Woodrow Wilson, at the Yale Phi Beta Kappa dinner in 1908, and Lowell, in his Phi Beta Kappa address at Columbia in June 1909, urged higher respect and stimulus for undergraduate scholarship.

bring homogeneous groups of men together, to create an esprit de corps, and to give each instructor a better knowledge of his men and of the other courses that they were taking, thus recapturing an educational advantage which had once been automatically available to the tutors under the required curriculum. This principle was sound and was destined for a second revival in the curriculum of the common Freshman year in 1920, a third in the experimental program called Directed Studies in 1944.

Hawkes emphasized that these groups were "natural rather than artificial." They were not the result of any individual's opinion as to how the students ought to be obliged to select their subjects but were "simply the result of observing how they actually do choose them." It was nevertheless interesting to discover that the natural groups had a distinct intellectual or educational significance. And Hawkes wondered if a comparable system could not be worked out for upper-class electives.

At this juncture Dean Jones arrived—and at once plunged into the week-end and chapel difficulties, the dormitory and budget problems, the questions of a Student Council and of beautifying the campus. The Course of Study Committee did bring forward its Honors proposals in February 1910. But two fresh obstacles presented themselves. Quite a number of the Permanent Officers seemed to think that the general curriculum should be improved for everybody before the question of Honors programs was taken up. And the younger faculty were understood to feel that the assistant professors and instructors ought to be officially consulted about any change. In May 1910 the combination of these two sentiments carried the Honors proposals down to signal defeat. So the alternative of grouping the students on the basis of intellectual quality was at least temporarily eliminated.[10]

Implied in the vote was also a direct challenge to Dana, the Course of Study Committee, and the leadership of the Permanent Officers. Result: rather delicate behind-the-scenes negotiations. Professor Dana was perhaps the shrewdest tactician among the professors. Dean Jones, on the other hand, appeared to have no very clear-cut intellectual philosophy; he simply favored making use of the younger men. So after years of effective monopoly Dana's Committee beat a strategic retreat, and the Course of Study was turned over by the Permanent Officers to the general Faculty.[11]

But then Jones could find no better chairman for the new standing Committee than Dana. Dana said he would not serve without Clive Day, and the two of them proceeded to exercise no little influence in the selection of their new junior colleagues—Assistant Professors C. B. Tinker '99, Fred R. Fairchild, Doane College '98, and Instructor Clarence W. Mendell '04. So out of this near rebellion came the youngest and in many ways most effective Course of Study Committee that the College had seen. After a series of consultations in Dana's office in the old Peabody Museum, the Committee carried its program through some difficult debates without serious alteration, and finally by Clive Day's pen made public the most intelligible and persuasive report that the Faculty had yet issued.[12]

Clive Day had made a study of what the other colleges were doing, but he and his colleagues thought the Yale line of development as promising as any. Recognizing student types, the Committee sought to provide them with appropriate programs. Faculty advice was to be emphasized, and Faculty authority increased, yet not to the point of dictatorship. Student license was to be decreased, yet not at the expense of intelligent variation. Foundation studies were to be still further differentiated from concentration. A liberal but more useful College training was the general goal.

In deference to the younger faculty, the first attention was to Freshman and Sophomore studies. To begin with, the new curriculum attempted to answer the question as to what requirements might "properly be imposed on the average student." The reformers were not so positive as to insist that all average Freshmen should study the same things, or even that any Freshman should be required to take any single course or subject. They knew only too well what a handicap such requirements would be to the courses and teachers involved. On the other hand, it seemed reasonable to require certain types of study through the first two years, allowing each student his choice of alternative ways of gaining the

313

desired discipline and experience. Thus, as a part of his liberal education, each student was asked to gain command of at least one modern foreign language; to make himself familiar with his own cultural inheritance through either European history or English literature or both; to obtain some knowledge of modern science through mathematics, physics, chemistry, or biology; and to introduce himself to the social sciences through the medium of at least one Sophomore course in psychology, economics, or American history. Finally, Greek or Latin was required unless the student elected both mathematics and a science. Thus each man should be trained to exact work, and at the same time have his horizons enlarged, either through the classics or through additional work in the sciences.

Such requirements were constructive and positive. They corrected the tendency of many Freshmen to take too many languages in Freshman year, to the total neglect of science. Again the Faculty felt that too many marginal courses had crept into Sophomore year. Accordingly it was decided to restrict the diversity of Sophomore studies and to increase the scientific opportunities for the first-year men by bringing physics down into the Freshman courses. In general, the work of the first two years was to be confined—at least more than it had been in the preceding decade—to subjects and courses of the greatest disciplinary value.

But lower-class courses should also be taken in a proper combination. So the Committee brought forward the idea of "natural groupings" and proceeded to construct three alternative paths or curricula for lowerclassmen. The idea was not to force a great body of recalcitrant individualists through an unnatural set of paces, but to suit the requirements to the general inclination and over-all aptitude of each student. This approached the President's solution. Hadley had classified College men into the literary, the scientific, and the administrative types, and had proposed that the same subjects be taught in different ways to the three groups. Perhaps because the Committee recognized the psychological difficulty of this method, they preferred to have subjects taught in the same way but to vary the combinations. Accordingly, one curriculum was constructed for those with an aptitude for languages, a second for those interested in science, and a third for those likely to concentrate in social studies.

Some of the protagonists of the plan made capital of the argument that these three groups were neither arbitrary nor inflexible. For example, two-thirds of the Sophomores were already taking one or the other of the Sophomore groups without being aware of it, and the other third would have had to change only one course to conform. The new groupings did not even eliminate the old abuse of taking four languages in Freshman year. Could it be that the reformers had merely given the old practices and requirements a new disguise?

Critics of the plan would later make this charge—yet somewhat unfairly. For if a Freshman did take four languages, these new groups assured that his fifth course would be mathematics or science, and that in Sophomore year both social and scientific study would be a part of the training of such language and literature specialists. Vice versa, no intending scientist could any longer dodge the modern languages that would later be so necessary to his progress. Freshman and Sophomore years were once again linked together and given a positive preparatory and exploratory character. In fact, for all their apparent flexibility and variety, the new groups were so artfully put together and so carefully overlapped as to guarantee a broad foundation by the beginning of Junior year. No matter how specialized the interests of individual students might later become, all Yale B.A. students would have substantially the same sound yet diversified body of knowledge at the base of their education.

Once assured of this common denominator, the Faculty felt safe in fitting the curriculum to student types and even to particular student interests. How far they were now willing to go a study of the groupings will show.* Assuming that all Freshmen would continue to elect English but that in Sophomore year many would substitute for it their own special subject, it was plain that, under

* See Appendix, Table Q: Group Programs for Lowerclassmen, 1911–14, p. 726.

the new arrangements, a man with an aptitude for languages might in his first two years elect as many as six courses in foreign languages; or, if a student chose Group II, he might get five courses in mathematics and science; or under Group III he could get four courses in history and other social sciences. All this, while two years of advanced and elective studies still lay ahead. In short, these regulations neither strait-jacketed the student nor even prevented a considerable degree of diversity or personal concentration. As Clive Day put it, they interfered not so much with liberty as with license. And in the last two years a considerable degree of individuality was now made possible.

This *upper-class* phase of the reform of 1911 was not generally considered to be as interesting, and was not debated by the Faculty. Nonetheless it was destined to exercise a salutary influence over the Yale curriculum for more than thirty years. If the chief defect of the old curriculum, in its Freshman-Sophomore phase, had been its failure to distribute student energies over "representative parts of the field of studies," the defect in its application to Junior and Senior years, according to Clive Day, had been

> of an opposite kind, in its failure to require such concentration in some one part of the field as may properly be expected of mature students whose faculties have been trained and whose interests have been developed. Most students do not need compulsion to this end, tho of these many would certainly profit by guidance. Many others, however, possibly bewildered or attracted by the variety of subjects thrown open to their choice, possibly seeking deliberately a smattering of knowledge, lay waste their powers in unrelated lines of work. . . . The dispersion of interests, which may be a virtue at the beginning of the course, becomes a vice at its end.[13]

The decision was that Juniors and Seniors were to be required to complete a major in one subject and a minor in a related subject —presumably in the same Division—aggregating not less than 12 hours nor more than 15. Each department was to prescribe, "more or less definitely," the courses composing its major, and was also to determine the subjects and courses acceptable for the related minor. In short, upper-class studies were to be divided just about equally between absolutely free election and a more intensive and coherent specialization than had ever before been required of, or allowed to, the average student.[14]

Formerly at Yale the election of more than a course or two in any upper-class subject had been exceptional. Now, after years of searching, the principle of coordinated, concentrated work was to be the backbone of upper-class studies, even for the below-average student. The major was really to be a major, with the mastery of some one general field the goal.

The College was still far from entrusting its upper-class curriculum entirely to a single department for each student, for the minor would command six out of the thirty hours and free electives would retain fifteen. The general Faculty also felt quite unable to command that the departments should construct new courses for their major students: a better arrangement was all that could at first be insisted on. Nor had it been entirely decided how far the use of graduate or professional methods would be sanctioned in Senior year. And perhaps it had been assumed just a little too readily that student types corresponded to subject types, or that vocational diversities would be satisfied by distinguishing between language and science. So there were quite a number of problems still to be faced; and a really effective departmental major was still a long way in the future.

Nevertheless the ideal of a rational combination of upper-class studies had finally been established. Both halves of the curriculum were now to be found in group arrangements. And because the aim of the Freshman-Sophomore groupings was foundation and balanced distribution, the difference between the two ends of a college education suddenly came into focus sharp and clear. After nearly thirty years of elective confusion a new order was emerging. It was an order that was moral and intellectual and not merely mechanical. Once the division had been between the immemorial disciplines and studies for breadth. Now these had to a degree been amalgamated, and the new line lay between this amalgam and a more mature mastery of some single branch of learning. Sumner had first argued for the advance in the early eighties and now, in the hands of his disciples, this advance was finally being realized.

At Harvard, Lowell's resounding battle cry of "Concentration and Distribution" placed his education program in a wonderfully clear light. But it was also a confession that free electives under Eliot had produced neither balanced distribution nor a healthy concentration. And little did observers appreciate how little success Harvard was going to have in restoring distribution. By way of comparison, Yale had its own dissatisfactions. By some standards Yale students were much more in need of concentration than those of Harvard. But just as Yale had never allowed free electives to banish all discipline or breadth from the curriculum, so now it was not going to allow specialization in its turn to eliminate these cherished values.[15]

What the Faculty had tried to do, as Clive Day hinted, was to revive purposefulness without sacrificing balance. And the effort had educated the Faculty. The benefit "in stimulating a comprehensive view of the whole college curriculum, a critical scrutiny by each department" of its own offerings, and "a more effective cooperation between departments" seemed already unmistakable. The planners of 1911 had come too late for public acclaim: their work was evolutionary rather than revolutionary—they had no public slogan—and ultimately they would fail to carry their colleagues on certain important principles.

So they left no name in the annals of American education. Yet this Reform of 1911, all things considered, compels respect.

CHAPTER 17·HONORS AT YALE

I frankly own that I should be glad to see the English system of separating honor men from pass men introduced at Yale.
—Arthur Twining Hadley, 1909

We assume that the intention is so to stimulate, not the few only—or even specially—but the many. While opportunities for the minority who are keen for study should constantly be improved, the main purpose of Yale—as to undergraduates, at least—is to fit the majority for useful work in the world. No scheme out of line with this thought would, we are satisfied, be approved by the alumni.
—Report of the Alumni Advisory Board, 1910

THE FACULTY REFORMS of 1908 and 1911 had aimed at an improvement in the standards of education at Yale for the entire undergraduate community. The means chosen had been the elimination of inappropriate materials and the careful arrangement of the standard course within programs adapted to the age level, the known enthusiasms, and the presumed needs of the most obvious mental types—literary, political, or scientific. The stress upon grouped studies had been intended to benefit alike the slowest and the quickest minds. Yet enmeshed in the organization of these group programs was a growing concern for the problems and desires of the more gifted among the undergraduates—the ranking men. Programs thus aimed bear the generic name of Honors; and in the years 1905–17 the Honors question became an important issue at New Haven.

A stranger, glancing back through the President's Reports, might have deduced that Yale had never had any Honors program

—or at most had awarded some minor honors for the performance of extra study of the ordinary sort. Actually, two significant Honors arrangements, known as the Appointments list and as Special Honors, had long been maintained. The Appointments list had been a general honors listing designed to improve the quality of effort of all the students on the standard program—Special Honors to improve either the quantity or the type of study by the abler fraction of the students on a limited portion of the curriculum.

APPOINTMENTS AND SPECIAL HONORS

General Honors, or something of the sort, had long been awarded in most American colleges in recognition of the fact that the privilege of education was not exciting enough to induce young men to study as diligently or as intelligently as they could. Since penalties for bad performance could touch only the poorest men, systems of stimulation by organized competitions and rewards arose. At Yale these awards had taken the form not of prizes or cash benefits but of Appointments, open to the competition of all and awarded strictly on the basis of the four-year average of each student's marks. If a man did respectably, he received on graduation a Colloquy Appointment—if somewhat better, a First or Second Dispute, or even a Dissertation. Moderate scholars won the Oration and High Oration Appointments, and best of all were the small group of Philosophical Orations led by the valedictorian and salutatorian, respectively the highest stand student and the second man in the Class. The three top Appointments or Orations at Yale corresponded to the *cum laude, magna cum laude,* and *summa cum laude* in other colleges, and were listed on the Commencement program.

Originally, as the titles suggest, a duty had gone with the honor: the duty of pronouncing an oration in public, before the eyes of admiring parents and officials of state. Gradually, as student numbers increased and the prestige and art of oratory declined, this time-consuming operation had lost favor.* Still the honor of a

* Between 1868 and 1876 an average of fourteen undergraduate speeches —Orations with an occasional Dissertation or Dispute—figured on the Com-

Philosophical Oration had been great and the recognition of scholarship public and conspicuous. The Appointments list had justified the marking system, stimulated a keen competition, and lined up faculty, parents, and public behind good scholarship. To a considerable proportion of the student body it had made study seem important.

For a good many years, unfortunately, this ancient and colorful system of honorifics had been suffering a decline. Perhaps the drift from scholarship paralleled the rise of the commercial and industrial interest in Yale's constituency. The growth of intercollegiate athletics had created more strenuous competitions, more exciting spectacles, and heroes far more popular and heroic than the College grind who labored—so it came to be thought—only for himself. The introduction of electives and the progressive elimination of required studies had simultaneously undermined the faculty's interest in General Honors and shaken undergraduate belief in the fairness of the marking system. For how compare the grades in so many different courses—or two students who had hardly a single instructor in common? No doubt a four-year average still meant a good deal, but the fine distinctions first became difficult to draw and then were abandoned altogether.

At the top of the list this had been damaging. After 1886 the two leading scholars were no longer distinguished by title from the other Philosophical Appointments in the catalogue. After 1894

---

mencement program. But the going proved hard and, the graduating Class not being compelled to attend, some orators begged to be excused. The second man on the list of scholars no longer guaranteeing an adequate Latin Salutatory, this honor in 1884 began to be conferred on men ranking lower on the Philosophical list. From 1891, in an apparent effort to improve the quality of the public speaking, the DeForest Prize speakers replaced all but the valedictorian and salutatorian on the program. But the University had become too large, and Yale College could no longer monopolize Commencement. A mere speaking exhibition no longer seemed appropriate to the occasion. So after 1894 the character of Commencement was changed to one of conferring degrees: bachelor, professional, and honorary. The graduating Classes were required to attend in gowns, and the giving of brief addresses by the students was dropped.

valedictories ceased to be delivered. Meanwhile, the student prestige of these offices had declined sharply. Where once the valedictorian had been a marked man, elected to societies and respected by his Class, by the 1890's the leading scholars were no longer being elected or noticed. Partly as cause, partly as consequence, the abler students were no longer attracted to scholarship. The ancient competition was failing of its purpose. Hadley himself had been valedictorian of '76, a day when the office was a guarantee of ability, of power, and he could have listed offhand a long line of valedictorians and salutatorians who had gone before him. But now Yale's President himself thought more highly of the Chairman of the *News*.

All this gave rise to a haunting uneasiness about Yale's top scholars and, as a part of the reforms of 1899–1908, a deliberate effort was made to revitalize General Honors and to direct ambition toward scholarship early in the course.[1] From the same concern had come the efforts to reduce the more flagrant inequities in marking. But it was all too evident that no amount of care on grading and no mere redecoration of the system of Appointments would do the whole job. Whether because of elective practices or not, it was then too late to make all the studies, or a general average, important. If the abler men were to be drawn back into scholarship, perhaps it would have to be via an appeal to their special interests: by honoring advanced and concentrated study rather than all-round work.

Yet Honors, of a sort, for concentrated study had been known at Yale for a full generation. It was in the last winter of Porter's administration, 1885–86, that twenty-five men of the Class of 1886 inaugurated a new system of obtaining special one-year Honors for distinguished work in a particular field. Thereafter, these Special Honors for one year or two years of concentrated study had been regularly awarded. The purpose on the part of the Faculty had been "to promote the rational choice of elective courses." Facing an exploding curriculum, they tried to group the elective courses into subject groups or what today would be called departmental offerings. And they hoped, by Special Honors, to tempt the serious

322

student to make a reasonably coordinated selection and do work of a superior caliber in the field of his special interest.

The degree of concentration, and the standards of quality, were apparently not very high. Each candidate had to pursue courses amounting to an average of at least six hours per week in "one of the special groups." He had to do so "with distinction," and "present a meritorious thesis" by May 1 of his Senior year. How much distinction or meritoriousness was expected the College did not say. Annually for the next decade between twenty-one and fifty-two Seniors received Special Honors. The peak in popularity was in the industrious Class of 1900 when no fewer than seventy-five men achieved this form of Honors.*

Originally, Special Honors had been possible in seven fields of study, namely: Philosophy; Political Science, History, and Law; English; Ancient Languages; Modern Languages; Natural and Physical Sciences; Mathematics. One-year Special Honors could be taken in any of the seven; two-year Honors only in the last four, presumably because they alone offered adequate materials in Junior year. Gradually the opportunities increased; the elementary languages were eliminated; and the number of hours lengthened. In 1886–87, for example, two-year Special Honors began to be offered by the Political Science, History, and Law group. In 1891 Philosophy and English did likewise. Then History separated from Political Science and Law; and in 1894 Music was made a ninth group in the list. After 1891 special registration was no longer required, and all the hours taken within a group, not just the minimum required, were counted in the competition. Simultaneously for Classics, Modern Languages, and Mathematics, two extra hours were added to this minimum, to make a required total of eight. This system continued to 1901. What the theses were like and what they really amounted to, one is troubled to say. In most cases, the College records do not yield even the titles.†

* See Appendix, Table R: Special Honors Awards, 1886–1916, p. 727.

† Until 1895 at least a handful were listed each year on the Commencement programs, apparently for public delivery as orations. Essays composed for other purposes, or submitted for other prizes, could be polished up to

Two further characteristics of this Eocene period in the development of specialized study at Yale may be worth remarking. The first is the fact that as the years passed the students tended increasingly to take Special Honors in both of their upper-class years. The second is the undifferentiated nature of the subjects or groups of study. One worked in the Modern Languages rather than specifically in French, in Political Science and Law rather than in economics or politics or law. As for the History group, which had won its independence, History was willing to accept Junior courses in political science, or in Biblical history and literature, for its two-year Honors. Was this all a part of a rational plan for the promotion of "the rational choice of elective courses"? Or a matter of poverty and necessity? One suspects that the shortage of instructors and of courses was at the bottom of it.

Then in 1901 the standard program nearly swallowed Special Honors. For the regular curriculum was so reorganized as to *require* at least as much rational concentration of electives by the average student as Special Honors had hitherto been designed to *promote* among the serious scholars. Since all undergraduates were required to complete at least one major of seven hours and two minors of five hours, it resulted that every student, good or bad, would now take in no less than three different subjects approximately as many hours of connected study as would formerly have qualified him as a candidate for Special Honors. Certain differences remained. No thesis was required of the ordinary student; nor did he have to do distinguished work in his major. Yet, if he happened to do distinguished work, only the absence of a short essay would separate the Appointments man from the man who was also awarded Special Honors in a particular subject.

For this obliteration of Special Honors the faculty were not prepared and they took steps once again to differentiate their incentive arrangement from the normal undergraduate programs.

serve as theses. Thus in 1887 W. L. Phelps, winning one-year Honors in Philosophy and English, got credit for "The Didactic Methods of Aristophanes as Shown in the 'Clouds' ": an essay originally composed for Sophomore Greek.[2] See Appendix, Table S: Special Honors Theses, 1886–91, 1903–16, p. 728.

First the special groups or areas of study were reorganized and more sharply defined. Next each candidate was required to pursue with distinction no less than nine hours of advanced work in his field, or five more than were needed for a major. It followed that the programs had to begin in Junior year and might begin in Sophomore year. One-year Honors was therefore dropped. Finally, the meritorious thesis was now described as "embodying the results of individual research," and it had to be written under the direction of an instructor.

In short, as the general B.A. program moved in the direction of a major, the Special Honors program preceded it toward still further specialization, concentration, use of the library, and originality of effort. After 1901 Special Honors differed from the standard course: a little in kind because a research essay was required; a little in quality because distinction was expected; but mainly, as Hadley was to say, in quantity, because it was necessary to take more hours of the same subject. Unfortunately, this new program failed to impress. Either it looked like too much work, or it required too much concentration for undergraduate taste, or it bestowed too little honor and was not sufficiently advertised by the faculty. Whatever the explanation, the students shied away. The number of Special Honors awarded dropped from 39 in 1901 to 10 in 1905, finally to a paltry 8 in 1910.*

Under these circumstances, it was hardly extraordinary that the

---

* The chart shows that the Classes of 1906 and 1908, with 27 and 36 awards respectively, were exceptions to the trend. The reasons are not clear. A surprising number of men earned Honors in the Physical Sciences; and at irregular intervals the English instructors lured batches of promising scholars into the special effort. Not a few future faculty members appear in these dwindling lists. Samuel B. Hemingway '04, for example, first did "A Variorum Edition of *Troilus and Cressida*" his Freshman year for Robert K. Root, then as a Senior won Special Honors for "A Variorum Edition of Chaucer's *Prioresses Tale*." In the same Class of 1904 L. Mason, S. L. Mims, and C. W. Mendell earned Special Honors, the last named for his "Testimonies of Aristophanes to the Architecture of Athens." One notices also W. W. Drushel '05, W. P. McCune '06, F. A. Godley '08, S. T. Williams '11, R. J. Menner and A. Whitridge '13, F. C. Harwood and R. J. Hill Jr. '14, A. B. Darling '16.

instructors themselves should become dissatisfied. Yet the faculty felt uneasy for other reasons, as well. On the one hand, the standard course continued to move toward concentration, thus lessening the gap and diminishing the significance of Special Honors, and by 1911 the standard program actually surpassed Special Honors in the amount of concentration formally required. On the other hand, the Special Honors requirements failed to guarantee a sufficiently advanced or coordinated type of study. And the increasing distribution requirements sometimes got in the way of genuine specialization.

Accordingly the practice developed of allowing an occasional student to take special work, usually in graduate courses that were not open to his fellows. In 1908 the Faculty regularized this procedure by establishing a higher—or D grade—of College work for Special Honors. Approximately thirty-nine courses were so distinguished. The rule was changed to require, out of the nine hours of advanced courses, at least four at the C or D level. In addition the way was opened for a student to secure some compensating relief from the distribution requirements and from classroom attendance. In such Special Cases the student had to apply at a stated time, had to show exceptionally high scholarship in his earlier work, had to secure the recommendation of the department concerned, and finally had to be authorized by a special vote of the Faculty. The grim watchdogs never succeeded in being optimistic gamblers or wholly generous in their permissions. But once all these obstacles were passed a man might be relieved of a part of his classroom attendance and might have his work especially arranged for him under the personal supervision of an instructor. So once again the Faculty increased the opportunities for concentration. And once again the provisions for Special Honors were shifted ever so guardedly toward an emphasis on individual and original work.

However, the thing which seemed to deprive such gestures of much meaning was the continued indifference of the overwhelming majority of the undergraduate body. Apparently Special Honors for particular studies, like Appointments for general studies, was not destined to appeal.

326

AGITATION FOR REFORM

In this state of affairs and at this juncture harbingers of change emerged from three diverse quarters. First, President Hadley sounded the tocsin for a genuine reform. Second, the coupling of Hadley's thought of the alumni—as the greater Yale whose opinion was the most powerful of all influences on campus life—with Secretary Stokes' desire to organize the graduates for the constructive improvement of the University had a rather startling consequence. In the spring of 1909 the Alumni Advisory Board was asked to report on "ways in which the intellectual ambition of undergraduates may be stimulated." Finally and coincident with these, Dana's Course of Study Committee gave notice to the Permanent Officers that it was coming forward with a new and serious scheme for Honors courses.

So graduates and Faculty alike were confronted with a delicate problem. Yale might be doing very well socially and athletically, but intellectually the results were disappointing. Too few of the able undergraduates were taking advantage of their opportunities, and students generally were still too uninterested in study.

In coming forward with his own suggestion of a Pass-Honors division at Yale, Hadley had two thoughts in mind. First, the Faculty being stymied, so to speak, the great influential body of alumni would have to help. Second, it was his personal opinion that mere tinkering with the old Honors programs would not do. Fundamentally, the failure of students to study seemed a failure in motivation. Perhaps the substitution of a few thorough-going and coordinated programs, capped by comprehensive and searching examinations and rewarded in outstanding fashion, was the proper policy. If Yale could release its better men from the ordinary requirements, convert Special Cases into three or four English-style Honors curricula that would appeal to student types and point toward the great vocations, the College might recapture a worthwhile proportion of the student body for serious intellectual pursuits.

327

By way of preparing his constituency for an intelligent approach to the difficult problem, Yale's President undertook in 1909 to review certain of the more impressive theories of reform.[3] Some institutions, and Hadley mentioned Sheff and Princeton and the Middle States colleges, had tried to retain meaning in the curriculum by the compulsory grouping of courses around a presumed student goal. Before moving toward its own group system Yale College had enforced rules for distribution, sequence, and regular classroom attendance. Meanwhile Harvard had put restrictions on athletics and incited the able by hopes of a three-year degree. Yet none of these devices could be said to have produced the hoped-for results.

"Some authorities," by contrast, liked to think that the evil could "be met by a change in the character of the college faculties themselves, whereby more stress should be laid on ability to teach and less attention devoted to power in research as a basis for appointment and promotion." This was a sentiment to which a considerable band of Yale's younger faculty were giving audible support. But Hadley was thinking of the powerful and sometimes critical alumni. Also of Woodrow Wilson's Preceptorial Plan at Princeton. And in neither party's prescription did he fully concur. The attempt to *add* teaching "preceptors" to the professorial faculty was apparently so successful at Princeton that everyone was "watching." But it seemed inadmissibly expensive. As for the alumni idea of *substituting* teaching professors for scholar professors, Hadley was even more dubious. Broad as were his own interests, and much as he sympathized with the notion that character and human concerns were the first things a college should teach, the fact seemed to be that "teachers" who did not investigate degenerated even as teachers. It was not University promotion standards that seemed to him at fault. "It is the organization of student life rather than of faculty life which most imperatively needs our attention."

With this in mind, Hadley described two remedies of some promise. The first was the introduction of technical study, so that the students would have "a professional stimulus" to do their work well. But Hadley could no longer recommend professional study for the American undergraduate. Far more appealing were the attempts "to introduce into the framework of the American college course the English idea of intellectual competition," or Honors programs. Of all the possible remedies for student indifference, the Honors idea seemed the most promising. For the distinction between the degree with Honors and the Pass or "Poll" degree emphasized important educational objectives. The first was a gain in incentive and hence in quality of performance. The Honors programs were highly competitive. Strong men were attracted. Candidates worked harder, yet under less supervision, than the average American undergraduate. Again there was a difference in kind: the Honors programs were made tests of ability rather than of accumulated knowledge. A first-class man in an Oxford or Cambridge Honors course was recognized as a man of power. "He can *do* things."

While Yale's minimum requirement for the bachelor's degree, in both the Academic and the Scientific Departments, was well arranged and administered—better, Hadley thought, than at either Oxford or Cambridge—"we have not been so successful in meeting the needs of those who wished to do more than the minimum— chiefly, I think, because we have not seen our way clear to free them from the restrictions which were necessary for the worst." The trouble with the old Honors courses was that they had differed mainly in quantity of knowledge required, whereas they ought to have differed in kind. He argued that a real Honors program would integrate flexibly with preprofessional or technical training. Finally—and here the President came back to his concept of mental types—such Honors programs would make it possible to group ambitious undergraduates and to teach them by appropriate methods. So after exploring the intellectual problem and reviewing no inconsiderable range of academic remedies Hadley came to his bold conclusion: "I frankly own that I should be glad to see the English system of separating honor men from pass men introduced at Yale."

In June 1909 the Alumni Advisory Board heard the President

expound his Pass-Honors ideas in private session. When his Annual Report was made public all Yale's graduates could study the reasonings which had led to so unusual a proposal. There followed a winter of discussion.[4] Then in June 1910, through the Alumni Advisory Board, the graduates of Yale brought to Woodbridge Hall a most interesting Report: comprehensive, thoughtful, helpful, and diplomatic—yet altogether unmistakable in drift.

The Board approved Hadley's concept of student initiative guided by alumni influence. The Board liked cohesion in studies, and more intelligent election. Also the ideas of competition, of closer relations between instructors and students, and of making examinations true tests of power. It even volunteered approval of Lowell's suggestion of intercollegiate competitions in intellectual fields.

But the central proposal of a Pass-Honors scheme they emphatically repudiated. The minority of fine students were not so important. The main purpose of Yale College, they were sure, was to fit the majority for useful work in the world—and "no scheme out of line with this" would be approved by the men of Yale.

If such experiments were to be instituted, therefore, the Honors competitions should not be thorough-going and all-absorbing as at Oxford. Rather they should be such as to interest the poorer students too, and allow such men to qualify in Junior or even Senior year. For the same reason opportunities should be offered for competition in limited fields, so that students would not have to give all their time to competitive study. "But stimulation of interest in the intellectual life of the University depends primarily upon the character of the teachers, upon having teachers who can teach and will interest and inspire the students, not only by what they say and the learning which lies behind, but by what they are."

With this in mind the Board urged the paramount importance of increasing faculty salaries to get and maintain inspiring teachers. Also the assignment to Freshman year of teachers of the highest type, so as to prevent discouraging comparisons with the preparatory schools. Finally the longest paragraph in their Report was devoted to the thought that too much preparation was required for admission to college. "The name 'preparatory school' seems unfortunate." A schoolboy should not have his interest killed by having to spend all his time on tasks: on studies designed merely to enable him to pass the entrance examinations.*

In this fashion Hadley's scheme for more challenging programs for the competent and mature was first stretched and twisted to take care primarily of the average and below-average men, then nearly smothered with suggestions for less bookwork and more inspiring teaching for the immature. The Corporation, after gravely thanking the Board, directed Secretary Stokes to pass these recommendations along to the undergraduate faculties and to mail copies to graduates of both Schools. But already the College Faculty had subjected the Pass-Honors proposal to its own searching scrutiny.

THE FACULTY'S SOLUTION

The first Honors suggestion which emanated from Dana's committee, while it borrowed from English precedents, also leaned heavily on home experience. The gist of it was to change the Special Cases into a limited series of interdepartmental Honors programs. This "scheme for the establishment of Honors Courses" had been presented in outline and discussed at some length in the spring before Dean Jones arrived.[6] Consideration was resumed in February 1910, when the Professors heard Dana and his committee argue that a

---

* In October–November 1909 a writer in the *Alumni Weekly* had teased graduates of all ages into discussing the question: "If I Were to Go to College Again." This was also a favorite topic with reunion Classes. The result was quite a mixture of enthusiastic recommendations in favor of required studies, more sports, commercial training, but especially more English and public speaking. In 1910–11, with the publicity given to the Advisory Board Report, discussion broadened. In general the Board's recommendations were seconded. The narrowness of preparatory schooling, the conservatism of Yale's entrance standards, the inferiority of Freshman-Sophomore teaching, the desirability of closer faculty-student relations were emphasized. More training in public speaking, in writing, and in modern literature was requested. Certain faculty insiders ventured the opinion that the University itself was not giving enough honor to Phi Beta Kappa and the top stand men at Commencement.

But no one came forward to champion the Pass-Honors idea.[5]

well-organized system of Honors groups would have many advantages. It would to a certain extent solve the uneasy problems of the C courses, which had never quite fitted undergraduate needs or tastes, by allowing such courses to be especially adapted for advanced work. Thereby the "best men" would be afforded "better advantages than at present." Honors groups would develop competition and "serve to make scholarship more highly esteemed" by the entire student body. But the idea was not to promote an extreme specialization. On the contrary, each Honors group should include courses in at least two related subjects, together totaling 21 or 24 hours of work and beginning with courses in Sophomore year.

The Professors entered upon a serious consideration of the whole problem. On the whole they were favorably disposed. Nonetheless, reading between the lines of successive revisions, one detects uneasiness over the kind of line to draw between Honors candidates and the regular students. If too high a stand were required, the good "B" men would not support the scheme, and it would then fail of its effect on the intellectual standards of the College. On the other hand, if the advanced courses were diverted to the new purposes, the gain of the best men might be at the expense of the average student. As for Seniors being excused from classroom exercises, doubt was expressed that this was the proper basis for an Honors award. Listening to the comments, and noting how hard it was for their colleagues to stop thinking about the average student first, or to give up the old Yale insistence on regularity in attendance, Professor Dana's committee first set the qualifying grade at 3.00 (80%), then gave it up—first excused the regular students from C courses, then abandoned that notion—first hinted at Senior privileges, then reduced them to relief merely "from the rigid application of the usual class-room requirements."

However at this first discussion an important distinction between the two classes of students was suggested, and incorporated into the Dana plan. This idea was to require general Honors examinations at the end of Senior year. It is not clear whether the practice of the British universities, or of any rival American colleges, had given the Faculty its solution. What is clear is the Professors' indebtedness to Hadley for their interpretation of the character and purpose of such tests. What is also hinted is a growing assertion of authority by each department, or group of instructors, over their own Honors program. For the Professors finally voted that the Senior Honors work of each student should be "under the special charge of the departments concerned" and should be "tested by each department as a whole at the close of the year, preferably by examinations designed to show the degree of power and training achieved rather than the amount of information gained." That decision reached, the Professors voted their approval of "the general plan." Then Professor Dana's committee went to work on scheduling courses for specific Honors groups.

In due time seven Honors groups were constructed: one in the classics, four in the sciences, and two in the Division of social sciences. Each group included one or two Freshman requirements, two or more Sophomore courses, and three or four courses each in Junior and Senior years: a total of 27–30 hours. This meant that the normal Honors group could be expected to command about half of a student's formal study time. This was five times what it had commanded back in 1886. In addition there would be a final general examination. The Greek and Latin instructors were asking for "private reading." And Group V, the biological, premedical combination, looked as if it would have to control 34 hours, or perhaps more. In other words, exceptional concessions were being asked, and not just Senior year but the whole four-year program was now involved. The Professors looked at the proposed schedules —debated them at length—but felt unwilling to put through such a revolutionary program alone and unaided. Accordingly they voted that the younger men should be consulted and that the whole subject should be laid before the general Faculty.

Thereupon this whole Honors program went down to defeat as a result of the adverse votes of the younger members.[7] The explanation given was a simple one. Their votes were not so much against Honors as they were expressive of a desire first to improve the instruction and the arrangement of courses for Freshmen and

333

Sophomores. Yet in retrospect it would seem that departmental feeling and differences in academic philosophy had played their parts. In any event, after many months of careful nursing the whole scheme was suddenly shelved.

The postponement lasted until the spring of 1913. Then—spurred on by the knowledge that, in Yale's four-year interval of hesitation, Princeton and Columbia and Harvard had all inaugurated Honors programs of some sort—certain believers in the Honors idea brought it forward again.[8] In the new and somewhat altered proposals the concept of general examinations to test "power" was retained. So was the emphasis on publicity as a way of appealing to the students, and a word was also said about excuse from routine exercises. Otherwise, the proposals of Professor Joseph Barrell and his Honors Committee were notable for the deference paid to the standard program and for the care taken to avoid offending faculty susceptibilities.

Honors study was to be confined once more to Junior and Senior years. An Honors student should not be forced into a high degree of specialization but should "for the present" meet the major and minor requirements. He might do some of his work in another School. In part to prevent interference with the other students, in part to make possible a different and appealing program for Honors candidates, special courses and divisions were to be provided as soon and as far as possible. Meanwhile a candidate might take regular courses of a satisfactory grade, and in an arrangement satisfactory to the professors of the department of his chief interest. This meant that the idea of a few specific interdepartmental Honors groupings, organized by the general Faculty and announced in advance, was being abandoned in favor of individual departmental control.

The champions of Honors were moving with no little skill. They gave their colleagues the summer to get used to the idea, and then in October 1913 Professor Barrell adroitly got them to vote first on its underlying assumption: that "in order to encourage men to do a higher grade of work" it was "desirable" to devise an Honors plan. The Faculty preferred to approve "different" rather than "additional" examinations to determine "thinking power" and quality of work. And rather than prejudge the method in favor of segregation and special courses their vote was merely in favor of "special opportunities." There was perhaps a warning here the committee should not go too fast. The whole question was referred to a committee of fifteen to work out a more definite and satisfactory scheme. Yet by that very act the general Faculty committed itself to some sort of an Honors plan. Half the battle seemed to be won.*

Not everyone welcomed the implications. Professor Phelps thought any new Honors plan "unnecessary." Professors Beebe and Palmer feared the costs and loss of undergraduate unity. Professor Keller protested against the advance publicity, asserting there never had been a time when men wishing to do extra work were not accommodated in anthropology; and he stood out stoutly against differentiating good students from bad, or requiring his department to hire extra and incompetent instructors. Thus were marshaled for the first time the arguments and personalities against change. Professor Fairchild acted as the representative of those who were doubtful or opposed; and thanks to the word that Dean Jones would not favor the adoption of any plan that might pass the Faculty by only a small majority he was able to compel the champions of Honors to go slow. Morris, Duncan, Dana, Harrison, and others, on the other hand, gave decided encouragement. And Allen Johnson insisted that it would be "a great pity" if Yale College shrank from a wise educational policy solely because of the expense involved.

Thanks to such support the rest of the battle was gained in a series of intensive meetings early in 1914.[9] And in December 1914 the finishing touches were added for a program that was to go into

---

* The request for a vote to approve "in principle" is a parliamentary device that has come into increasing usage. In 1913 it proved its value by preventing prejudicial votes on several occasions. Professor Barrell, and his successor Professor Bumstead, also employed the strategy of giving out word of their plans and hopes to the *Yale Daily News,* and by this method enlisted support in certain influential undergraduate quarters.

operation in 1915–16 and to endure with gradual modifications clear through to 1939. Yet this victory was not won without concessions that were to affect and in some ways to limit the usefulness of the new program.

First of all, both the Honors courses and the Honors programs were to be limited by the interests of the ordinary students and to be controlled by the several departments of study. Honors candidates were not to take more hours in their major-minor subjects than the existing rules allowed. Special courses and divisions were to be provided only "so far as the department concerned shall deem it desirable." Later this vote was broadened to admit special personal instruction or direction as well; but separate instruction of any sort might be given only "when, in the judgment of the department, such separate instruction will . . . not seriously limit the opportunities of other students."

Again, the thesis requirement was abandoned except insofar as the special Honors examination assumed this form. "So far as practicable" the departments were to set one special examination in the major at the end of Junior year and another at the end of Senior year. The departments of the major were to decide whether to examine for the minor, to adjust it to their students' needs, and to certify whether their own examinations had been passed with sufficient distinction. The other quality requirements gave the Faculty no little difficulty—but finally an average of 3.00 (80%) was adjudged sufficient for entrance to or continuance in the program. It was calculated that between 60 and 75 men in each Class— or about 20%—would be eligible.

The process of negotiation also drained off much of the emphasis on *honor*, that is, the provisions for publicity and special acclaim. A proposal to group Honors candidates at the head of every class attendance list was withdrawn. All that finally remained of the proposal to substitute the Honors roll for the old Senior-Junior Appointments lists was the vote that the list of successful candidates in three graded categories should be publicly announced on Commencement week and at other suitable times. Also there was an understanding that for general excellence only the Philosophical

High Oration, and Oration Appointments would be kept and the meaningless Dissertations, Disputes, and Colloquies were to be dropped. But so strong was the force of habit, and so vague was memory on the subject, that Dean Jones' office at first failed to carry out this mandate.

One other concession to circumstance and to the ingrained institutional posture of affairs was this. In March 1914 it was voted that "the several departments shall prepare outlines of their respective plans" and "if any department finds that efficient conduct of the Honors system will require additions to its teaching force or additional appropriations, such matters may be considered with the Dean and the necessary plans made." This meant while that staff planning was mandatory staff expansion was left optional with both the Dean and the department.

So for the fall of 1915 Yale College had prepared a great new system for Honors—its third since 1885. Like its predecessors, this plan was designed to improve both the quality and the coordination of undergraduate work, including by force of example the work of the more average students. But where the original Special Honors of 1886 had asked merely for six hours within a field, and where the transitional proposals of 1910 had failed to get 30 hours, the new system took 18. Again where the original idea had been that any combination of courses within a field was good, and where the transition trend had been toward the Hadley or English idea of a few broad Honors groupings, carefully worked out by the whole Faculty and printed in advance, the new system abandoned that interdepartmental approach in favor of Honors planned and administered by single departments, each controlling within its own field.

In still another way this new Honors system of 1915 struck a note of compromise between the radical proposals of the years immediately preceding and the simplicity of the more ancient days. All three relied on publicity—on the award of *honor* at Commencement. But whereas Hadley had exhorted to competition and cited the glory and standing of a "first," and whereas Barrell's own first plan had declared the appeal to students to be "of primary impor-

337

tance," a thing to be made "as strong as possible," the final version merely contemplated a special leaflet in the Course of Study pamphlet, and the special listing of Senior Honors ahead of a shortened Appointments list. Since the College was unwilling to give up General Honors for high marks in all subjects, the new Honors listing would confer only a second honor. This was merely something additional instead of something unique.

So the special favors, the excuses from regular exercises, the personal instruction, the exclusive courses—all these had been boiled down to some promises that sounded suspiciously like extra labor rather than more fascinating and delightful work. The general Faculty had refused to deprive the ordinary student, no matter how dull or frivolous or uninterested he might be, of the slightest opportunity. Instead they had restricted the Honors man, kept him from really specializing, and had even tied him down to the schoolboy's duty of attending all of his classes.

The end result was thus a compromise program all along the line. In their consideration of Honors the Faculty had at first postponed, then curtailed, then belatedly and half-heartedly worked out a pale and bloodless substitute for the Pass-Honors idea. At first certain champions of Honors had struggled to devise broad Honors groupings. Then, in the face of considerable inertia and some downright opposition, a strategic bargain had been solemnized with certain of the more open-minded departments. One would have been tempted to dismiss the whole five-year debate with a curt summary of its all too modest results were it not that in the process the future treatment of Yale's better students was explored, and to a considerable degree prejudiced. For without some knowledge of what was rejected in the years 1909–14 it will be hard to understand and sympathize with the difficulties which were to follow in the 1920's.

In 1915 the immediate question was whether such an Honors program would stimulate intellectual ambition. While it was being developed the undergraduates had shown only the mildest interest, and some of the best and most serious men felt it offered comparatively little. This had worried Hadley, who privately advised the Chairman of the Honors Committee to consult with the leading undergraduates before taking final action. At Oxford the Honors man was ipso facto relieved of some of the burdens of the Pass man. It did not seem reasonable that there should be no relief at Yale, where the routine obligations of the Pass man were so much greater. "We must emancipate the live man from the dominion of the wooden instructor." * [10]

Then as the College was getting ready in the spring of 1915 to inaugurate the new plan, it became evident that certain departments could not be counted on. The anthropology instructors declined to make any separation between students or to offer any new instruction except outside reading. The economics professors, after first drawing up a scheme for Junior and Senior Honors courses, withdrew it, in part presumably because of a failure to secure the proper personnel. In turn the English department submitted a program calling for more work in the European languages but only the addition of outside reading in English itself. The Honors Committee did not feel that this was satisfactory; and a series of conferences failed to move Professors Beers, Lewis, Phelps, and Tinker to more positive proposals. So, starting with the Class of 1917, two of the three most popular departments of study dropped out of Honors work. As a consequence, the Honors enrollments were only 22 out of 56 eligible in the Class of 1917 and 21 out of 71 eligible for 1918.

* As Charles M. Bakewell, one of the committee supporting Honors, pointed out in his statement to the *News,*

Yale has always shown more concern than most colleges for the average and sub-average student. She has taken her democracy so seriously that she has at times almost seemed to bend over backward in her efforts to give every man an equal show. The result is that the student of good ability has sometimes been forced to slacken his pace . . . to a certain extent the brighter students have paid the price.

Bakewell thought the students, with their traditional conservatism, might be slow to enlist; yet he was optimistic enough to predict that soon all those eligible would be enrolled. What would then be needed would be a series of lectures to open the eyes of Freshmen to their intellectual opportunities.

339

The responsibility therefore descended squarely on the professors of Latin, Greek, and history, with such support as physics, chemistry, zoology, geology, French, German, philosophy, Biblical literature, and mathematics could offer. Fortunately the historians under Allen Johnson and Max Farrand were enthusiastic, and the classicists had been putting their better students into special divisions under an almost individual instruction. The historians offered four regional Honors fields, substituted Junior reading courses under personal supervision for some standard lectures, and gave their Seniors the chance really to investigate some more limited topics of special interest. The promise here lay in flexibility, added interest, and personal supervision. And the classicists proposed to develop similar schemes in Latin and in Greek.[11]

With such patronage, and with the aid of some friendly publicity in the *News*, the new Honors program got off to a modest but nevertheless auspicious start. Particularly successful were Clarence W. Mendell in the classics, and Charles Seymour in history. These two skillful young men started meeting small groups of hand-picked students two hours at a time once a week. Seymour had been listening to Woodrow Wilson, but he was particularly influenced by his experience under Goldsworthy Lowes Dickinson, who had been his tutor at King's College, Cambridge.[12] In 1915–17 he found himself facing two of the best seminar classes he would ever know. The students who were undergraduates of standing caught the spark. After one winter's experience a group of such men enrolled in various fields addressed a letter to the Chairman of the *News* to urge on lowerclassmen the splendid opportunities of Honors.*

* "To the Chairman of the *News*
"*Sir:*
"We, the undersigned, who have been engaged in Honors work in various departments during the past year, feel that the Honors Courses present splendid opportunities for the individual to carry on special study in the field in which he is most deeply interested. They provide positive intellectual stimulus through frequent conferences with inspiring advisers, through freedom from the hard and fast requirements of ordinary class-room work, and through the reading of the best works available on the particular subject.
"Therefore, we would strongly urge any Sophomore or Junior not to

The Chairman, who was himself taking Honors in history, wrote an editorial proclaiming that the new programs represented the biggest single step forward since the introduction of the elective system.[13]

Assistant Professor Edward Bliss Reed—who would have loved the opportunity of Honors instruction—made it a point to congratulate those students in his English classes whom he knew to be candidates for Honors in other subjects. A number of the undergraduates taking English majors showed they wanted Honors work. The Honors Committee publicly and privately expressed its disappointment that English—with students and instructors enthusiastic—was still not participating. But the four Permanent Officers of the department could not see their way clear to excusing men from the regular courses, or giving personal supervision and instruction, or setting an Honors examination. They insisted on exercising their departmental discretion.[14]

Then World War I descended and drew off most of the men already enrolled in classics and history. So the real development of Honors would have to wait till the 1920's.

President Hadley, while the compromise plan had been still open to amendment, had tried persuasion in his Annual Report of 1913–14. With the average student, he had argued, Yale unquestionably did rather well. Intellectual dissipation was limited, the faculty were strict, and public opinion supported the faculty. But

---

decide on his course for the coming year before considering seriously the question of electing Honors.

"Norman I. Adams, Jr.
Russell S. Bartlett
Alfred Raymond Bellinger
Henry Carter
Oliver B. Cunningham
Ellery James
Julius M. Nolte
Edward S. Pinney
Dickinson W. Richards, Jr."

a thing which we need to do, and have as yet done imperfectly, is to organize intellectual interest in things most worth while. . . . Yale has succeeded better than Harvard or Oxford in exacting certain standards of the student body as a whole. She has not succeeded as well as Oxford, and probably not as well as Harvard, in developing independent intellectual activity among groups of students . . . there are only a few class rooms, and still fewer club tables, where he gets into an intellectual atmosphere which really stimulates him to work and encourages him to do "better than his best."

But, confessed the President, perhaps it was useless to press too hard—perhaps there were too few really concerned with scholarship. "The general interest of the college community, student and graduate, appears to lie in other directions." [15] In such words Hadley had foretold his own defeat. From the first he must have recognized that it would take time to graft so intellectual a scheme as a true Pass-Honors plan on the traditional structure of an American college. *A fortiori* at Yale—where the graduates dominated but did not believe—and where student opinion determined—yet only a handful were at all keen and enthusiastic. The Faculty could legislate, it was true. But whatever slim possibilities had remained after the Alumni Advisory Board had given its opinion had quite disappeared when the Faculty divided and Dean Jones failed to lead.

The Faculty plan was better than nothing. The College had given the Honors idea verbal support. Yet no money had been provided, no men, few special courses, and no relief from routine duties. To be successful an Honors system had surely to confer honor—and give scope for student initiative. Hadley's enthusiasm had been for a real Pass-Honors division, with Honors enjoying at least equal backing. But neither graduates, students, nor instructors were yet ready—and there was no use arguing or pretending. At Yale community opinion ruled. And so, reporting to his constituency as the Faci ' 's compromise program was going into effect, Hadley failed to mention Honors at all. Instead he accepted the decision of the majority—and even defended equalitarianism at Yale against the beginnings of undergraduate criticism.

There was ground, he admitted, for such criticism of enforced uniformity, but the college democracy, like any self-governing community, did not encourage deviations from its self-imposed standards. What one could demand was a strenuous lifting of these standards, to appeal to the strong men. Meanwhile nonconformists must be prepared to strike out "at their own risk, and will almost always have to wait many years before their character as prophets procures them honor in their own country." [16]

The Faculty's *own* failure to support the prophets of a true Honors system is understandable. Theirs had been a difficult situation: between an idealistic President, who would only advise, and a graduate constituency demanding the best teaching at Yale for Freshmen and the unscholarly.

Caught between the divergent views they had then made the unpleasant discovery that fundamentally they themselves were divided in educational philosophy. On the one hand the overwhelming judgment had been that the interests of the average student should not be sacrificed. On the other, as scholars and teachers they had been anxious for intellectual improvement and quite unwilling to wait for public demand. Quite deliberately they refused to confide their hopes to the harsh mercies of the student majority, or to inspiration by the alumni, or to the pressure of parents looking forward to graduation and Honors on the Commencement program.

For they had it in mind to tap a more reliable energy, that of the faculty—or, rather, the pride and enthusiasm of each department of study and each group of teachers and specialists. To the departmental instructors were confided the duties of organizing, of controlling, of rewarding. Team play within the departmental staffs —interdepartmental competition for reputation and the best students—these would supply the stimulus that was essential. So long as the opposed departments were not required to give Honors themselves, they might be willing to allow other departments to experiment. Whatever the limitations or omissions of the new Honors compromise, there was this positive and optimistic hope about the new scheme—that it would appeal to some of the best

343

men on the faculty and by them would be carried forward to success.[17]

The risk of such a delegation and concession was great. A department might be lazy. Or it might find itself too understaffed to undertake the advisory work, advanced courses, and special examinations. Or the majority within each department might not believe in Honors, might hold with the vast majority of the student and graduate world that Yale's real duty was to the average. Who in our faculty today has not heard that battle cry of mediocrity: "the exceptional student will take care of himself"? In the 1950's, no less than in 1915, it would take a bold man to insist that the attention of the College ought to be focused on the best undergraduates.

For this state of affairs both College and country were responsible. Self-education on an informal basis seemed unreal to a nation which believed that to be educated one must "take a course." Students were repelled by the added responsibilities. The Faculty had been churlish about compensating privileges. The disciplinary ideal was still uppermost. Indeed the majority had not yet learned to see Honors programs as essentially different and individual in character. Reinforcing all this was American equalitarianism, as strong within the College as without. The Billy Phelps insistence on democratic teaching was not lightly to be challenged. As more than one instructor would discover, merely to champion the Honors idea entailed personal risks.* In 1915, at least, the climate of New Haven was such that a genuine Pass-Honors program stood not a chance in the world. And it would inevitably take years before even the compromise scheme adopted could hope to achieve standing and the hoped-for influence.

Under the circumstances the achievement of Barrell, Bumstead, Dana, Morris, Bakewell, and their colleagues is worth remarking: without injury to the established order a genuine opportunity and expectation had been created. And this opportunity and expecta-

* E. B. Reed found that Phelps was so outraged at his enthusiasm for Honors that he refused to speak to him—"Billy Phelps, who would stop and speak to every cat and dog on the street!"

tion had been put in the hands—not of the students and not of the general Faculty—but of the little teams of instructors gradually emerging within the College. In 1915 the possibilities of departmental organization and initiative were still far from realized. Perhaps in any case the departments were vehicles too narrow and specialized to have the responsibility for so important a part of general education as an Honors program. Yet they were the only vehicles available, and if they could not carry the ball, no one could.

CHAPTER 18·THE LITERARY RENAISSANCE

With Lounsbury, Beers, Chauncey Tinker and William Lyon
Phelps, Yale had outgrown its earlier indifference to let-
ters . . . The breeze that was blowing over literary Yale was
to have its effect on the new generation of writers, brilliant
groups of whom were at nurse there.
  —VAN WYCK BROOKS, *New England: Indian Summer*

COLLEGES HAVE their nightmares as well as their dreams. An old college may even be haunted by its might-have-beens, its silent shortcomings. So for generations the more thoughtful men of Yale had been disquieted. The difficulty was not something you could put your finger on or remedy by simple volition.

Yale's Presidents had always commanded attention. Yale's graduates had been lawyers, orators and statesmen, teachers and ministers, manufacturers and inventors; and in every generation a few had written distinguished books. Yale's growing band of professors had made themselves masters of the new sciences and the old languages. In its Bicentennial Publications the University had given an impressive demonstration of productive scholarship. Yet a certain uneasiness had persisted.

Once Yale had been the nursery of poets and humorists. Then in the nineteenth century Yale had become the seat of science, theology, and linguistics—but Harvard the home of letters. Then Harvard had added its scientists and philosophers without somehow losing its poets, its essayists, and historians. Secretary Stokes himself had to confess that Yale had been more *fortiter in re* than *suaviter in modo*.[1] The genius of the place had not gone toward reflection or the more delicate crafts of literary and artistic composition. The undergraduates had themselves recognized and exaggerated this contrast. In the exaltation of football victories and out of the bitterness of repeated defeats as tasted in Cambridge twin legends had been born. Yale undergraduates were either Men or mucker athletes, Harvard students either Gentlemen or parlor aesthetes.

Even as the great football machines ground out their last great seasons, however, Yale's literary philistinism was being left behind. Then in the years 1909–20, for the first time perhaps since the days of the Connecticut Wits, the College could laugh at its literary detractors. The change could be measured in a wide variety of activities. Instructors of all ages were publishing more voluminously and in better style than ever before. In 1908 the Yale University Press had been started. Three years later the *Yale Review* was reorganized as a literary quarterly. Simultaneously the new Elizabethan Club began bringing students and faculty together for companionship and discussion of their literary enthusiasms. Most gratifying and astonishing of all, the undergraduates were scribbling as never before, scribbling and play-acting and composing and reviewing and—best of all—being published. First an occasional poet, then whole shoals of poets. Where once the undergraduate had fleetingly dabbled, had heeled the *Lit.* and *Record* more for the fun of it and prestige than in the strict service of art, now these minnow authors were serious enough to grow up in their element: to plan on literature as a career.

This intellectual awakening neither began nor turned out quite as expected. The official drive had been for more scholarship, for a revival of learning. And along this line fair progress continued to be made.* No doubt it was slow and slogging work. As late as 1909

* The years 1899–1908 had seen a successful effort to raise minimum standards that were already, in Hadley's opinion, considerably above those at Harvard or at Oxford. In 1909–13 the minimum marks required for participation in certain activities or for taking extra hours were increased. The old privilege of saving up sixty cuts and converting them into a course passed (thus taking only 12 hours in Senior year, or 57 instead of 60 hours in all) was abolished. After 1913 the College began requiring "quality credits"—as well as a passing average—for promotion and graduation.[2] In effect this raised the passing average to 65. Notice has already been taken of how, over the same years, the

347

Hadley doubted whether the percentage of "really able men—men who have it in them to do something worth while afterward—is as high in the philosophical oration list as it is in the *Yale News* Board, or even in the football eleven." But he had already noted improvements in class work and the general range of undergraduate interests. By 1911 a graduating Senior would call attention to "strange bees" buzzing in undergraduate bonnets. "Today an odd belief in the value of education within the curriculum prevails. We have with us . . . a famous athlete seeking to make Phi Beta Kappa in his Senior year." Individuals were beginning to suggest that the all-round Yale man should be a good student as well as a social success. Student spokesmen were even debating philosophies of education and criticizing some of the "interesting" courses as too popular or superficial.[3] Up to the late 1880's—as Hadley pointed out, and as *News* editors echoed after him—scholars had been important, and then for fifteen years football had reigned. Since 1903 the other activities, especially the managerial or journalistic competitions, had challenged for supremacy. "In plain English," said Hadley, the editor of the *News* had now become "a bigger man" than the captain of the team or the crew. Perhaps now the pendulum would swing still further toward the intellectual.[4]

By 1913 competent witnesses in many quarters agreed that the worst days for the classroom were past. Yet the best hopes were far from realized. The valedictorian still did not count. When someone suggested raising the passing mark to 2.50 (70%), no one took the idea seriously. When Phi Beta Kappa raised its standards, there was protest. The fraternities were induced to pay a little more attention to scholarship—but only a little.[5]

In the spring of 1913 a brilliantly rebellious *News* chairman, Richard A. Douglas '14, started laying about him with biting sarcasm and abuse. What was "the Yale type"? Douglas challenged. It wore the right clothes, had faultless manners and morals, and was "offensive in being utterly inoffensive." It never had heretical

---

stimulation of intellectual interest and the development of Honors programs were carefully explored.

thoughts, because it never thought. "The dismal sands of the Desert of Sahara could not be more neglected by Yale undergraduates than the art of thinking." "Sometimes it has tremendous dumb energy. . . . And it has nearly the mental power of the original Yale Bull Dog."

Once the Yale type had been at least aggressive. Now it conformed—took down dutifully what was said in class but did only just enough work—heeled rather than wrote for the *Lit.*—loved lettered sweaters and trinkets. Why should Yale be so crowded, and with so many drifters? he asked. Why should "utterly shiftless bipeds" be treated the same as inquiring scholarly minds? Not all men ought to be "equal before the examiner." If Yale would raise its standards "the country would then receive fewer men from Yale, but it would receive no undeveloped men." Douglas admitted that "to take a book out of the Library—legitimately—no longer brings ostracism." But "of course the reading is a bore when the reader has the mental curiosity of a codfish." [6]

If such diatribes delighted not a few of Douglas' friends and teachers, the vast indifferent bulk were stirred at most to grumbling resentment—and on graduating his classmates voted Yale's greatest need a major sport championship. No successor picked up Douglas' lash. Would allurements to study work any better than goads or penalties? Allurements in the shape of new undergraduate prizes Hadley was afraid would carry too limited appeal. And only a flurry of interest would finally greet G. B. Adams' proposal to award a Y for scholarship. [7]

The situation was clearly analyzed by Assistant Professor Canby, who in *Harper's* in 1913 voiced his belief that Yale and other universities were "on the eve of a 'growing-up' of our student body. . . . One's classes 'feel' differently." Yet the response was still irregular. Though teaching had had energy poured into it, the results were still far from commensurate with the expenditure of devotion. What was wrong? The whole background was wrong, or at least unconverted. "To succeed we must intellectualize the business and scientific energy of the country (for it is just that which the undergraduate displays in his blind and immature fashion). We

349

must intellectualize it as a century ago the college intellectualized the professional and theological energy." [8]

But intellectualizing was bound to be slow. And to some of Yale's sparkling and wanton spirits it wasn't nearly as much fun as play-acting, or singing, or composing poems and writing in the established undergraduate organizations. The *Record* with its light verse and humorous skits appealed irresistibly to the playful and artistic. To its own successful heelers the *Courant* offered not only reportorial experience but a chance to publish one's essays, poems, and criticism, with theater reviews and comments on College life. The *News* was for the solid men, the campus managers, yet in its editorial columns the whole policy of the University could be reviewed and interpreted. The *Lit.*, by contrast, appealed to the few. But to the *Lit.* sooner or later looked all the real writers: the poets and dreamers and story-tellers of each class. Those interested in the theater found opportunity for play-acting in two fraternities, Alpha Delta Phi and Zeta Psi. On a larger scale the Dramat, with its Christmas trips (1908–) and its Prom and Commencement performances, provided fun, glory, and self-expression for a whole host of varied talent. For music there were the Glee, Banjo, and Mandolin Clubs.

Of course, formal, large-scale organizations had never completely satisfied the exuberant undergraduates. Rather the practice had been for each Class to found its own special clubs and groups for spontaneous entertainment. Like sparks from a great bonfire these convivial little societies would dance in the air their brief moment, then be extinguished. But now undergraduate genius was giving rise to brighter inventions, and some with the power to outlive the first graduation. In the Class of 1900, special fondness for Mory's and Louis Linder's troubles with his accounts had coalesced to produce the Hogans—who now had an annual photograph taken. At convivial Mory's again, a group of exceptional singers of the University Quartet—George Pomeroy '09, James M. Howard '09, Meade Minnigerode '10, and Carl A. Lohmann '10, with the aid of an extra roommate, Denton ("Goat") Fowler '09—all of them loving old ballads and old ale—gave birth to the Whiffenpoofs

350

with their official anthem, the Whiffenpoof song.* Drawing on his own effervescing, tuneful imagination, Cole Porter '13 wrote both words and music for no less than two new Yale football songs: "Bull-Dog" and "Bingo, That's the Lingo" to say nothing of such mirthful skits as "Annabelle Birby" who lived way out in Derby and "A Football King." [10]

No one, not even Cole Porter, quite matched the lilting metrical virtuosity and humorous satire with which Brian Hooker '02 had delighted the undergraduate world at the turn of the century. Hooker had even ventured to make fun of the faculty, and the College still treasured his *Dirty Durfee:*

> There's a place on the Campus, I weel ken its name,
> And the brawest o' views may be had frae the same—

---

* After being appropriated for commercial purposes by a later Yale troubadour, this would be shown to be an adaptation of "Gentlemen Rankers," set to a tune of doubtful authorship, with credit being disputed between the partisans of Tod Galloway, Amherst '85, and of George H. Scull, Harvard '98. The words of the anthem are about nine-tenths pure Kipling and one-tenth Minnigerode and Pomeroy.

The founders had first heard the tune sung by Tod Galloway, sometime Judge of the Probate Court of Franklin County, Ohio. They had met him after a concert in Columbus which he attended because one of his published compositions—"The Gypsy Trail"—was on the Glee Club's program. Afterwards he entertained them by singing, among other songs, a setting of Kipling's "Gentlemen Rankers." They remembered it with pleasure and, in casting about later for an anthem, found it admirably suited to their purpose. The chorus needed only the change of a word—"rankers" to "songsters." The "Louis" serenaded in the verse was, of course, Louis Linder, proprietor and later the steward of Mory's for fifteen years and the first honorary Whiffenpoof.

The founders took a name for themselves from a fish story told by Joe Cawthorn, popular comedian of the time. In a musical show called "Little Nemo," he described a fabulous creature which he had caught by boring a hole in the lake and putting cheese around the hole. The Whiffenpoof, led on by the cheese, came up the hole, squawked, and then was caught. Somehow its name seemed appropriate. One of the elders would explain it by the suggestion that they, too, could be led on by food and drinks to squawk.[9]

Gin there's onything doing ye're wishful to see,
Why, it's up wi' the windows o' dirty Durfee!

There's a braw time on Tap-Day, when down by the fence,
A' the Juniors gang buggy, and sweat most immense—
When ilka Keys heeler has jumps like a flea,
Then it's up wi' the windows o' dirty Durfee! [11]

With Hooker turned teacher and serious poet, Cole Porter was now song-smith without peer. There were also humorists and rhymesters on every hand, to say nothing of an artist or embryo art critic or two—C. C. Carstairs '13, H. E. Tuttle '14, R. M. Coates '19, Reginald Marsh '20. The College boasted musicians of such unmistakable talent as E. S. Barnes '10, Ellsworth Grumman '13, A. B. Hague '14, Douglas S. Moore '15, Bruce Simonds '17,* and Quincy Porter '19. The Pundits, who had been revived in 1903 under Billy Phelps' auspices, were full of paradox and puns.† And in 1912, when abroad on a sabbatical and following the Browning trail, Phelps founded the Fano Club. Anyone who could send a postcard postmarked Fano, proving that he also had seen a certain out-of-the-way picture in Italy, could join. [13]

However, it was through their dramatic activities that the men

* Tinker had Bruce Simonds in his Seventeenth Century Literature and, without knowing anything about his musical abilities, gave him a paper to write on Herrick. Simonds wrote so well that Tinker called him up and said, "Mr. Simonds, you should consider a career in literature." "Well, that's very nice, but of course I have my music." Simonds took Tinker back to his room and played to him.

† The Pundits, a club of the Class of 1887, had died, been briefly revived in 1899, then successfully reincarnated in 1903. The plan of its meetings— first scheduled for every third week, but so successful they had to be held weekly—called for the chosen writer "to set up an ideal as an idol," which the other members were to demolish if possible. One of their first deeds was the establishment of a prize for an essay "on some need of the College and how it may be supplied, or on some tendency of a feature contrary to the welfare of the College, and how it may best be amended." The prize was first won by F. E. Pierce '04, with an essay on how to combat the bad habit of indifference which permeated the place like malaria. [12]

352

of Yale had made their first substantial ventures into the world of art and imaginative literature. As early as 1898–1900, under the aegis of Professors Cook and Phelps, some graduate students in English together with the members of Psi Upsilon and an informal organization calling itself the Yale Dramatic Association had attracted the pleased attention of the Yale community by the public presentation of a series of early English plays. In March 1898 these graduate students had surprised the English department with a performance of *The Knight of the Burning Pestle* so successful that a public performance was given a month later. At the same time Psi Upsilon gave a serious performance in the Elizabethan style of Ben Jonson's *Silent Woman,* advised by Professor Phelps and Dr. Reed. In May 1900 the English graduate students presented *Royster Doyster,* C. B. Tinker playing Tristram Trusty. The *News* reported that Mr. Richards dominated the stage. "Of the other men, Mr. Tinker was the best and his presence on the stage was always welcome." The actor thus referred to recalls speaking the prologue and playing his part—as he says—"magnificently." The Yale Dramatic Association was formed in February 1900, and in May produced *The Second Shepherd's Play* and a dramatization of Chaucer's *Pardoner's Tale* by Harry D. Wescott '01.[14]

The literary seriousness had disarmed faculty suspicion. Success had stimulated ambition. By 1909 the Dramat was presenting the *Critic* and the *Merry Wives of Windsor,* with such future actors, coaches, and ambassadors of note as T. Lawrason Riggs '10, Edgar Montillion Woolley '11, and William C. Bullitt '12 taking leading parts. Looking back, the *Alumni Weekly* commended the ten-year record of plays produced and thought the work of the Association had become an integral part not merely of undergraduate activities but of the educational life: "almost in form, and essentially in fact, a Yale teaching department." A theater fund was started, Maude Adams gave a benefit for it, and Assistant Professor John M. Berdan came out in support. Hitherto Yale had been "teaching drama by purely theoretical methods." It was, he added, a legitimate ambition to learn to write plays. Plays paid—some of them fabulously. But the College gave no practical training; talent was going to waste. The *News* when printing these remarks thought the Dramat had done great service in knocking on the head the criticism that Yale was not intellectual. Meanwhile the *Courant* was reviewing New York productions and printing interviews with actors, producers, and playwrights—Maugham and Belasco among others.[15]

No question but that the theater was flourishing at Yale. In 1910 the Christmas play was Goldoni's *The Fan,* in a translation by Professor McKenzie of the Italian department and with a prologue by "Tom" Beer '11. Soon Shaw was on the boards, and movie scenarios were being concocted. Happily in 1913 the Dramat—that "clever pedagogical machine"—fell under the dexterous inspiration of one of its own star products, Monty Woolley '11. The next Dramat smoker witnessed "Paranoia," composed by Riggs '10 and Porter '13. The Commencement play in 1914 was *Quentin Durward* by C. A. Merz '15 and Frank W. Tuttle '15, with music and lyrics by J. C. Peet '15 and D. S. Moore '15. Whether or not this was really the first success of its kind, that spring the same C. A. Merz * won

---

* This future editor of the *New York Times,* who in College edited the *Yale Record,* also produced the following: [16]

THE FREDERICKSCHEETZ

(With apologies to Lewis Carroll)

'Twas Tinker, and the Lyon Phelps
Did Twining Hadley in the nooks;
All Mimsy were the Tutor Farrs
And the C. F. T. Brookes.

Beware the Frederickscheetz, my son!
The jaw that bites, the scowl that kills!
Beware the Gooch-Gooch bird, and shun
The Oriental Bills.

He took his Seymour sword in hand,
Long time the Deanish foe he sought—
So rested he, by the Merritt tree,
And stood awhile in thought.

And as in Mason thought he stood
The Frederickscheetz, with eyes of Flame,

354

the Pundit Prize for a "Ten-Minute Course on Modern Drama-
tists." And in 1914–15, after Yale's great football Bowl had been
inaugurated by a disastrous humiliation at the hands of Harvard,
this good-humored band of defiant intellectuals usurped the new
gladiatorial arena to sponsor Granville Barker's company in *Iphigenia in Tauris,* with students participating and music by David
Stanley Smith, before an audience of 10,000, many from out of
town. That same June the Dramat under Woolley's direction gave
what was claimed to be the world's first performance of Tennyson's
Harold—and to its Christmas-trip audiences it had presented some
one-act plays written by undergraduates. The stage could hardly
have been better set for the arrival in College of some real playwrights. And in 1914 Philip Barry, in 1917 Thornton Wilder, came
to New Haven.[17]

Of course, it wasn't just the theater. Writing of all kinds was
flourishing. Never had there been so many writers, such variety
and vigor of production, such astonishing competitions for the
editorial boards and the Cook Poetry Prize, so many young authors
of rare promise. Yale College, once Sparta to Harvard's Athens—so
lately the champion gladiator—pragmatist, activist, philistine Yale

> Came Stokesing through the Tweedy wood
> And Gruenered as he came.
>
> One two, one two! and through and through!
> The Uhler blade went snicker-snack!
> He left it dead, and with its head,
> Went Gundelfing'ring back.
>
> And hast thou slain the Frederickscheetz?
> Come to my arms, my Kreider boy!
> Oh, Parmly Day! Calloo! Callay!
> He Oerteled in his joy.
>
> 'Twas Tinker, and the Lyon Phelps
> Did Twining Hadley in their nooks;
> All Mimsy were the Tutor Farrs
> And the C. F. T. Brookes.

College had become a center for belles lettres: the home of poets and a nest of singing birds.

Looking back one sees that the sentiment for literature, like the taste for the lighter arts, had been gathering strength for a long time —perhaps since the days of Yellow-belly McLaughlin, or since Billy Phelps had first set his classes to reading modern novels and taught a joyful appreciation of contemporary plays. No doubt Charlton Lewis had set a mark, shown how a poet could teach and a teacher speak, how telling thoughts could be clothed in supple beauty. And then there was the wizardry that was "Tink." With his enthusiastic colleagues he had caught the young writers as Freshmen, entranced them, talked to them reverently about Beers. So for at least a few in every class Beers had become the literary symbol, the figure shyly worshiped. Meanwhile Sheff had been building its own tradition of criticism and letters, with Lounsbury publishing his *Shakespearan Wars,* and Cross and Canby teaching the new as well as the old and writing about pioneer novelists and living poets with power and discrimination. Both Schools had had their undergraduate poets; and writers and writing had infiltrated the faculty. In the College E. B. Reed '94 and Brian Hooker '02, in Sheff F. E. Pierce '04, had kept right on writing when they began to teach. So letters had increasingly been honored in the practice as well as in the teaching.[18]

The movement was as wide as Phelps, as deep as Tinker and Beers, and as spirited as Berdan. Billy Phelps it was who first poured in the enthusiasm, praised new books, encouraged embryo poets, and now brought writers, artists, playwrights, world travelers to lecture in New Haven: an unending stream of celebrities to be greeted and praised and introduced from the platform under the new University lectureships. Tinker, Beers, and Lewis, each in his way, provided other values: love of great literature, artistic perfection, sheer personal inspiration. But for the craft and the agonies of writing it was John M. Berdan: young Johnny Berdan with his dungeon of an office in the basement of White Hall, his strong-scented Latakia tobacco, his outrageous accusations, his way of taking your arm and turning suddenly to stare up into your face. Berdan taught the deadliest of subjects, composition—but with what flavorful exaggeration—with what irony and brutal frankness.*

> At the outset of each class in Daily Themes he approached the blackboard and, while muttering some weird and unintelligible incantations, would scratch them out in an entirely illegible scrawl. Sooner or later one went to him and asked him the why and the wherefore of these hieroglyphics. "Ah," said he, "that is precisely the idea. The more curious come down to enquire. Then they will never forget." And with that he explained his terse and forceful maxims for good writing. In the evenings those with whom and to whom he was sympathetic were wont to foregather in his little cubicle of an office or often at his home. There amid clouds of tobacco smoke we talked the moon down the sky.[19]

Perhaps the reputation of such teaching began to attract aspiring authors to New Haven. Whether or no, it is evident that the drive for good literature at Yale had behind it an effective sequence of efforts. First in the small Freshman divisions Tinker and the other instructors inspired. Then the upper-class lecture courses under the great masters gave the whole undergraduate body the chance to hear English superbly spoken as well as to read the great works of literature. In due course Beers caught the few and Phelps made it plain there was hope for the many. Finally a number of those most earnest for this craft went to John Berdan, and he laid them on the anvil of practice and beat them daily with a hammer.

Meanwhile some of Yale's graduates had begun to publish, and not just those who had majored in English. But these first brave ventures had come and gone with such fleeting notice that the outside world hardly saw the increasing coincidence. In 1912 when Professor Lounsbury's *Yale Book of American Verse* came out, a reviewer in the New York *Sun*, forgetting that there was an *Oxford Book of English Verse* and not realizing the growing interest, asked

---

* Among the dubious yet possible anecdotes that have come to hand is a story of Berdan conducting prayers in the days of compulsory chapel: "O Lord, we come before thee with unwashed faces and unwilling hearts. . . ."

"Why a Yale book of American Verse?" The very next winter, however, when B. R. C. Low '02 had *The Sailor Who Has Sailed* issued,
William Rose Benét '07S got out his *Merchants of Cathay,* and Kenneth Rand '14 while still an undergraduate published his *Dirge of
the Sea Children,* the *New York Times* could not but discover "a
Yale School" of belles lettres. Considering that this same year saw
the publication of still a fourth book of poems, Reed's *Lyra Yalensis,* to say nothing of Canby's *A Study of the Short Story,* and that
young Sinclair Lewis got out his first novel, *Our Mr. Wrenn,*
in the spring, 1913–14 did indeed seem to herald a flourishing
age.* [20]

Yet perhaps the full vigor of the literary movement should be
dated from 1910 or 1911. For just at the turn of the decade the Yale
muse passed from solo serenades and paired voices suddenly into
full chorus. In 1909 Leonard Bacon and Robert Moses had graduated. In the class of 1910 were T. Lawrason Riggs, Meade Minnigerode, H. V. O'Brien, and Robert D. French. In the next two years
Thomas Beer, Waldo Frank, S. T. Williams, E. M. Woolley,
George Van Santvoord, and Paul Rosenfeld were Seniors and
graduated. Meanwhile Cole Porter '13, Ralph Gabriel '13, Kenneth Rand '14, Frank Bergen '14, H. E. Tuttle '14, C. A. Merz '15,
and Archibald MacLeish '15 had entered and were making their
mark. Moreover it was in 1911 that the *Yale Review* was reorganized, with W. L. Cross as editor and H. S. Canby and E. B.
Reed as assistant editors. The next year Helen McAfee was added,
and almost overnight this economic journal turned into the leading literary quarterly of the nation.

In the spring of 1911 the members of the English department
had given a series of twenty readings on the Russian novel; the
English poets and Restoration drama; Synge; the speeches of C. M.
Depew and Bryant, Hadley, Eliot, and Wilson; and the works of

* "I want to say that the thing that pleases me particularly is when my
pupils, boys I have had in my class-room, publish books of their own. There
was a red-haired anarchist in the Class of 1907, Sinclair Lewis, who published
an admirable novel a year ago, and I am the advance agent for it." W. L.
Phelps to Chicago Yale Club banquet, 12 Feb. 1915.

recent Yale writers. The voluntary student audience had averaged eighty. Finally, late in this year of 1911, the Elizabethan Club opened its doors—and was a success from the start.

Hadley had been hopeful but by no means overconfident. He thought of how his own classmates in '76 would have greeted such a club, with students and professors drinking tea together and making polite conversation about books. No doubt the climate had been getting milder in New Haven. To Alexander Cochran, who donated the clubhouse and the magnificent Elizabethan collections, he wrote: "You know by experience how cranky is the sentiment even of the most cultivated members of the undergraduate body." It would be necessary to let the boys think they were doing most of the planning, or they would shy like young colts.[21]

Happily, all this was managed—and by 1913 Hadley was explaining and justifying the innovation to the graduates of the more rugged age that had gone before.[22] Another kind of recognition was accorded when Arnold Whitridge '13 sang Cole Porter's "I Am a Member of the Yale Elizabethan Club" in the Dramat's smoker play, "The Kaleidoscope." Soon Vanderbilt Webb '13 was writing back from Oxford in favor of still more tea and conversation, and in praise of the Oxford Union. C. B. Tinker found himself a member of a literary and social organization calling itself the Mince Pie Club. This had been founded one day when Bullitt and Professor Tinker were lunching together, and the Taft could produce no mince pie to Tinker's order. "See that you have it next week," said Bullitt. Thereafter, Bullitt would put a notice in the *News:* T.T.A.T.T. This meant: Twelve-thirty at the Taft. There would gather the big hunk, Chaucer Browning Tennyson, faculty member in disguise; the cheese, C. C. Carstairs; the crust, J. W. Clark; the spice, Cole Porter; the obituary writer, W. C. Bullitt. To the last meeting in the spring members invited guests, and the party ended with Berdan running like a hare down Chapel Street, with Arnold Whitridge after him.[23]

There were those who particularly appreciated the mercurial Lawrence Mason, "sartorially impeccable, flower in buttonhole, reading aloud some sonorous, ringing lines from Milton, and in-

359

toxicating himself with the music. . . . He loved the precise, the good phrase, used the language like a Cellini of words." [24] Perhaps the course was a little flowery and convivial.* Contracting friendship with the faculty—even convivial friendship—was no longer taboo. The writers and "aesthetes" were now doing what they pleased, looking their manager classmates in the eye, and ignoring the athletes. Literature had become a fashionable pursuit. As Freshmen, the Class of 1919 even decided to have no "Big Men."

The years 1912–15 were good ones for the *News*, the Dramat, the *Courant*, the *Record*, and the *Lit.* By 1914 Hadley was confident that the standards of the student body as a whole would see far more progress during the next ten years than in the last. By 1916 he even hoped that the revival of interest would extend to the field of art. In December 1915 the Brick Row Print and Book Shop opened. Writing in *The Book of the Yale Pageant*, Phelps asserted that "no first class creative writer has ever been graduated from Yale." The only author of permanent and international fame had been James Fenimore Cooper ex-1806. But "Yale's greatness as the mother of authors lies in the future." Already there were some recognized novelists, and Brian Hooker and William Rose Benét, poets. Speaking on Alumni Day, Phelps therefore told the graduates that if they wanted to worry about anything they should worry about athletics. For six years Yale had not had eight men in College

* According to J. Franklin Carter '19 "this was known as the 'hyacinth' course and was distinguished by two splendid educational innovations. If Larry didn't like you, he flunked you, so that his class was always a small and congenial group. And his semi-annual examinations—two hours was the official duration of an examination—were divided into two equal parts. The first hour was on work which you had prepared. Then there was a fifteen-minute interval, during which the entire class crossed to the bar of the Hotel Taft, had a good drink and returned to the second half which was purely inspirational and for which no preparation, other than alcohol, would equip you."

Carter, "Steve" Benét, and their roommate George Achelis used also to visit Professor Crawford's house, "drink beer and argue about dramatic literature for hours. And there was little Frank Walls, who taught in the Art School, was rather precious served excellent Bourbon whiskey and let us stage amateur-dramatics in his large living room. It was there that . . . Thornton Wilder's three-minute plays were first performed."

who could row four miles, "but in every year we have had eight good poets, in every year there have been eight good writers and speakers, and you can apply that right through. . . . The proficiency in football displayed by Yale last November compares very unfavorably with the proficiency in English literature displayed by our students in any average recitation." [25]

As the war clouds mounted in the Atlantic sky, the enthusiasm and conviviality, the brilliance of wit and the fever of writing seemed to burn with mounting intensity. Not every Class could match 1915's Archibald MacLeish. But the merest listing reveals the diversity of talent in 1916—Phelps Putnam, D. O. Hamilton, Fairfax Downey, Chard Powers Smith, H. S. Buck, C. R. Walker Jr., Donald Ogden Stewart, Danford N. Barney. The Class of 1918 had Philip Barry, playwright; Wilmarth S. Lewis, the future great Walpole editor; Pierson Underwood, poet-editor; and John C. Farrar, poet, future editor of the *Bookman,* and publisher. In 1919 there would be Stephen Vincent Benét, Robert M. Coates, and J. Franklin Carter; and in 1920 Thornton Wilder, with three exceptional editor-journalists for foils—Walter Millis, Briton Hadden, and Henry R. Luce.

The years 1919 and 1920, from the end of the war to the graduation of the Class of 1920, were destined to bring the Yale renaissance to its climax—and a triumphant transition. That last brilliant cluster—Wilder, Luce, Millis, DeVane, with Benét back for his M.A.—had a special class together under Henry Canby. Then they, too, graduated. Canby left college teaching for a career as editor and critic in New York. College was over. Writing for the nation had begun.

In 1919 was published the fourth *Yale Book of Student Verse,* followed by *The Yale Record Book of Verse, 1872–1922.* In 1919 was begun the Yale Series of Younger Poets, suggested by Clarence Day and first edited by Charlton M. Lewis. In the early contests Yale writers were unusually successful: so Howard S. Buck '16, John C. Farrar '18, D. O. Hamilton '16, A. R. Bellinger '17, and T. C. Chubb '22 each saw a volume of his poems printed. Meanwhile, R. B. Glaenzer '98, B. R. C. Low '02, Clement Wood, LL.B.

'11, and Harold C. Stearns '16 were being published regularly in the nation's magazines. W. R. Benét brought out *Perpetual Light* and reissued *Merchants of Cathay*. Danford Barney '16 got out his second book of poems, *Chords from Albireo*. And seven Yale men, five of whom had already had volumes published, issued a new magazine, *Parabalou*, which drew friendly praise from Masefield and others in England.[26]

The campus, obviously, had been alive with poets, whose broadening output could be celebrated in almost every issue of the *Alumni Weekly*. But Yale had also its prose writers, men who had come back with books from the war, and others who, as Phelps said, were putting the Eli into novELIst. In this same year, amid a flurry of novels and novel writing, in which S. V. Benét was preparing to participate, Clarence Day's *This Simian World* was published, and Sinclair Lewis' *Main Street*. "When the young alumni meet casually today," commented Phelps, "they casually discuss their latest works. During the thirty-seven years that I have been a member of the Yale Brotherhood, I have never seen anything like this." [27]

Perhaps, out of loyalty, Yale's impresario of letters was a little indiscriminate in his enthusiasm. But on the whole the College had not misjudged its sons. The word "renaissance," at first used with humorous deprecation, in time came close to being justified by production, a literary production that for virtuosity and impact had never before been approached by the men of Yale.*

In the field of the novel Thornton Wilder, out of his store of classical and Elizabethan imaginings, by discipline and exquisite workmanship created at least one minor classic: *The Bridge of San Luis Rey*. And through a succession of efforts—from *Main Street* to *Babbitt* to *Arrowsmith*—Sinclair Lewis rose to the stature of James Fenimore Cooper, a century earlier. Like Cooper Lewis could write with originality and power. Like Cooper he would be read and studied abroad for his portrait of the American character. Like the legendary Leatherstocking, again, Lewis' Babbitt would

* See Appendix, Table T: The Universities and the Pulitzer Prizes, p. 742.

perhaps caricature his age, yet take his undeniable place in the pantheon of symbolic Americans.

In the difficult fields of social history and biography, Tom Beer will be remembered for his *Mauve Decade* and *Hanna,* and Canby for his *American Memoir.* Canby's talent for criticism and literary history found effective expression, first in the *Saturday Review of Literature,* then in his studies of Thoreau and Whitman. In the genus of humor, the Yale movement would produce no Mark Twain, nor even an Oliver Wendell Holmes, but Donald Ogden Stewart '16 became known for his parodies, and Clarence Day's *Life with Father* has entertained an entire generation.

In the field of music the production comprised the serious contributions of D. S. Moore and the playing of Bruce Simonds; the collaboration of Horatio Parker with Brian Hooker on *Mona,* pioneer American opera, and on *A.D. 1919,* commemorating those who died in the War; to say nothing of the contributions of Marshall Bartholomew '07S and C. A. Lohmann to College singing, or the theatrical verve of Cole Porter's musical hits. For the stage Philip Barry would write successful comedies, and Thornton Wilder devise his ingenious and provocative techniques: *Our Town* and *The Skin of Our Teeth.* One encounters also Monty Woolley, after a brilliant but stormy career at Yale, projecting his spectacular personality on the New York stage. And a considerable group experimented with the movies and the radio.

So the Glee Club, the *Record,* and Dramat had not been sterile in their influence. Yet perhaps it was from the hard apprenticeship to the classroom, to the *News,* and to the *Lit.*—in reviewing, in journalism, and in poetry—that the sons of Eli went on to their most striking achievements. Just as in College they had heeled and helped manage more than one publication, trying their talents in varied ways, so in the 1920's and 1930's they moved with ease and from field to field. William Rose Benét wrote poetry and helped edit the *Saturday Review of Literature.* Stephen Vincent Benét edited the Yale Series of Younger Poets and produced his appealing verse novels on the American theme, *John Brown's Body* and *Western Star,* as well as such short stories as *The Devil and Daniel*

Webster which was made into an opera, with music by D. S. Moore, and into a film. Reflecting his College training and a career in journalism, Walter Millis produced a telling blend of history and political satire in *The Martial Spirit*. Most brilliantly versatile of them all was Archibald MacLeish, who passed from law and teaching into poetry, from private speech to public speech, from the musical forms in which he excelled to the organization of articles for *Fortune* on which he also left his mark; thence he moved to the Library of Congress, to experiments with poetry, the camera, and the radio, and so to the manipulation of public opinion in the grand strategy of politics, before turning again to academic teaching as Boylston Professor at Harvard. A hand in shaping public opinion attracted many. In College Henry Luce had written poetry and helped Briton Hadden run the *News*. Three years after graduating these two, by founding *Time*, set a new pattern and dialect of reporting for American journalism. The roster of their first editors and contributors reads like a Yale College catalogue.[28]

The renaissance produced, therefore, not only a cluster of Yale writers who won national reputations but a series of literary vehicles through which others, too, could gain liberty of public speech. The Yale University Press, founded by George Parmly Day '97—a brother of Clarence Day—did not confine itself to academic scholarship or to Yale authors but strove to give currency to works of serious value in varied fields and of diverse authorship. Its printer, Carl Purington Rollins (Harvard, 1897–1900), set a standard for fine printing matched by no other university press and by few of any kind.[29] In similar fashion the *Yale Review* at the outset refused to confine itself to writings by the faculty, and so won liberty to achieve an international clientele and reputation. By this means it helped draw the eyes of writers and thoughtful readers to New Haven, thereby enhancing the reputation of the University. But primarily it served the republic of letters.[30]

In the College it was the "Lizzie" Club and the *Lit.* which gave the most continuous and useful encouragement. In the lay world, on the other hand, it was probably *Time, Fortune,* and *Life* which came to exercise the most pervasive influence.* In the long run it may well be that Yale's contribution to the founding, editing, and management of publications would prove the most enduring product of her literary revival. *John Brown's Body* will be remembered. Lewis and Wilder and MacLeish will be remembered. But the truth is perhaps that the renaissance produced no giant great enough to change his world.

Why the College should have blossomed so astonishingly in literature and journalism is a hard question. Yale had the faith and drive without which no movement has the force to carry far. But earlier its energies and hopes had been rather narrowly channeled, walled in by a classical-mathematical curriculum, and directed toward social and athletic goals. What had been needed was release —release and a new inspiration. And in the 1890's and early 1900's both were provided.

The first glad release had been provided by the elective movement. With the breakdown of the required curriculum new studies had become possible, literature had won increasing popularity, and the Yale English faculty had taken glorious advantage of its opportunity. Are not the first freedoms always the most intoxicating? [31] As for intellectual inspiration, that came also from the admirable courses in history, from the emphasis on the Library and discovery of its resources, from the Rhodes Scholarships and the influence of Oxford and Cambridge ideals brought back by both students and instructors. Interest in the arts was stimulated by the new dignity of University ceremonial, by the development of the Music School and its concerts under Horatio Parker, by the Art School exhibits and courses, and not least by the nearness of New York and the excitement of Broadway. Meanwhile the cultural expectations of

* Mention should also be made of the publishing houses—Coward-McCann, Farrar and Rinehart, and successor companies, W. W. Norton and Co., Dodd, Mead and Co., Duell, Sloan and Pearce, and others—in which Yale graduates served as principal members.

the new business aristocracy had been changing. Parents, who no longer intended their sons for the ministry or teaching, were readier to pay for and encourage the theatrical and musical interests that they were themselves affecting as matters of social prestige. This helped supply a very necessary moral approval: the period saw considerable literary activity also at Harvard and at a number of other colleges, notably Princeton and Williams.

One accident or happy circumstance must also be noted: that exceptional talent found vehicles for publication at hand. With the founding of the Yale Press and the *Yale Review* the University now committed itself to the encouragement of literature as a graduate career. With the founding of the "Lizzie" Club the hopeful writers in the College were still further strengthened by being brought together. Admiration—friendship—mutual emulation followed. All these in the long run must have helped these undergraduates no little in their effort to look Yale's social system in the eye—and add a new category to Yale's definitions of success.

This suggests revolt. Indeed, other greater revivals recorded in history have always seemed to be accompanied by, even to a degree inspired by, a rebellious feeling, a desire to liberate and to make new. At Yale, however, the revolt was social, and not very destructive. One *News* editor did belabor his classmates and the Yale system with asperity. And Steve Benét and his roommate could write a "Song at which all good *News* Editors Shudder"—and make fun of Dwight Hall, the Senior societies, and all the sacred rituals of the social game: *

---

* In 1943 J. F. Carter deposited in the Memorabilia Room a sheaf of satirical poems, written by Steve Benét and himself in 1917, when they were still lowerclassmen, defiant, and not expecting to be tapped. These include the derisive "The Tapiad" and the "Uncollegiate Damned," the scornful "Sheff Monthly," and an "Ode to Dwight Hall," concluding:

> Serene, superb above the din,
>   And far from battles, plague and rumor;
> You rear, unconscious, to the skies
>   A silent monument to Humor!

> Do you want to be succcessful?
>   Form a club!
> Are your chances quite distressful?
>   Form a club!
>
> .   .   .   .
>
> Never mind the common friendships
>   that no politician has!
> Seek the really righteous rounders
>   and the athletes of the class!
> And you'll get your heart's desiring—
>   and the rest will get the raz!
>   *Form a club!*

Generally, however, these young authors found their publishing opportunities so excellent, their faculty reception so friendly, the general campus atmosphere itself so clement, that they were content to make their own place and not to destroy. They did not even rebel against their masters, the writers living and dead of the English tradition. In College most of them had written in the traditional forms. And in the early 1920's their writing was still "dominated by assimilation." One thinks of the *Class Poem* of A. MacLeish '15:

> A year or two, and grey Euripides,
> And Horace and a Lydia or so,
> And Euclid, and the brush of Angelo;
> Darwin on man, Vergilius on bees,
> The nose and dialogues of Socrates,
> Don Quixote, Hudibras, and Trinculo,
> How worlds are spawned, and how religions grow,
> All shall be shard of broken memories.
>
> And there shall linger other, magic things,—
> The fog that creeps in wanly from the sea,
> The rotten harbor smell, the mystery
> Of moonlight elms, the flash of pigeon wings,

The sunny Green, the old-world peace that clings
About the college yard where endlessly
The dead go up and down. These things shall be
Enchantment of our heart's rememberings.[32]

Waldo Frank did rebel against the mores. Sinclair Lewis lashed out at our middle-class society. And critics like Beer and Canby were not wanting. But in the later 1920's and the 1930's the most characteristic note would be one of confident Americanism. The Luce publications were revolutionary only in technique and financial success: politically they proved conservative. The poets experimented, particularly MacLeish, but within limits more modest than observed by some contemporaries. Themes from American history absorbed S. V. Benét. Fears for the nation's safety inspired much of MacLeish's later work. These writers had gone through Yale in the confident prewar period, perhaps too early to be able to accept the mood of disillusionment of the 1920's. In any case with hardly an exception the most important of them showed a faith in the country and concern for its destiny that reminded one strongly of the spirit so carefully fostered and strongly believed in at Yale.

CHAPTER 19 · COLLEGE—SHEFF—
UNIVERSITY

We have the double problem of keeping the old-fashioned social and moral life of the college community unspoiled and of giving at the same time the most modern facilities for research in literature and science. The acquisition of the Hillhouse property enables us to combine two things—to provide for 'high thinking' on the new ground, without intruding upon 'plain living' on the old.

—PRESIDENT HADLEY *to Mrs. Russell Sage,*
31 *December 1909*

THE MIDDLE YEARS under Hadley saw the resumption of University expansion and the unfolding of a new policy of unification. In 1909 the Administration proposed to establish, for the benefit of both the College and the Scientific School, an up-to-date physics laboratory.

This was to be located on an almost vacant square of land lying on the rise to Prospect ridge: to the north and a good distance beyond the confines of both the College and Sheff. Sachem's Wood the great block was called. For generations it had belonged to the Hillhouse family, descendants of "Sachem" James Hillhouse, B.A. 1773, College Treasurer and statesman. Foreseeing a land shortage for the University, Secretary Stokes with the help of some graduates had privately and quietly managed to secure the whole square. Momentarily this prize, like a millstone, threatened to pull the adventurers under. The Corporation had had to step in to rescue the Secretary and his fellow underwriters by assuming the carrying charges until a donor would be found. Happily Anson Stokes finally located a donor in the person of Mrs. Russell Sage,

369

who agreed to pay the costs of the property and present it to Yale.

Here was the opportunity to work out the University idea which the President and Secretary, with Corporation and graduate backing, had from the first been trying to develop. By the phrase University idea they meant in part that Yale's congeries of Schools and semi-independent Departments should have a new center: a University administration with its own buildings and funds, its own interests and general policy, to harmonize the desires of the several Schools and represent them before the public. More important, Yale's Schools should also work together, perhaps exchange students and instructors, in any case avoid unnecessary rivalry and duplication of effort, and whenever possible contribute to the common enterprise.

For it was the regrettable truth that the College had not always been considerate of the professional Schools. The Scientific School had struggled with the Medical School for control over certain subjects. The Scientific School had also insisted on keeping its own graduate students and master's degree in science. Most jealous of all was the relationship between the Scientific School and Yale College. The College still tended to look down on Sheff—and Sheff was proudly and bitterly resolved to become the equal of what it called Ac. Because some knowledge of science was part of a liberal education, the College wanted to give its own instruction in science. Because of the Select Course, Sheff as well as the College taught a liberal arts curriculum * and gave a bachelor's degree, but in three

---

* The official title of this course was Selected Studies in Language, Literature, History, and the Natural and Social Sciences. This three-year program for the Ph.B. degree was "intended for men who desire the essentials of a liberal education, with a leaning toward science, as a preparation for business or the study of law." In Freshman year the Selected Studies men took mathematics, physics, chemistry, and elementary biology. But in their last two years the closest they got to science was physical and commercial geography, organic evolution, and a short course in public hygiene. In addition they were given a continuous three-year course in English literature and composition, two years each in French, German, and history, and courses of a year or less in anthropology, economics, government, social evolution, and problems in business management. It was stated that "a well selected course of studies designed

years, for liberal studies. The Scientific School did have to itself a number of engineering courses and instructors. But each undergraduate School now boasted its own English and modern language professors, its historians, economists, physicists, chemists, and geologists—to say nothing of its own buildings for recitation, its own chemistry laboratory or physical apparatus.

Here was an amazing appearance of duplication and no inconsiderable duplication in sober fact. To Messrs. Hadley and Stokes it seemed not unreasonable to ask that the English professors work together and the divided chemists consider each other's wishes. It would be more efficient—and at the same time shrewd strategy— to get away from the Departmental laboratories and to substitute in each of the sciences a single University laboratory, to be used cooperatively by all the professors and by all the students of the subject, irrespective of their School or Departmental affiliation.[1]

At this juncture the happy discovery was made that Henry T. Sloane was willing to support such a venture in the field of physics; [2] and at the same time appeared an anonymous donor, apparently ready to provide the money for a University building for history.* With land, money, and policy all ready to hand, the idea of building a *University* physics laboratory, and perhaps a history building, on Yale's new Pierson-Sage Square became irresistible. In due course laboratories for zoology and the other sciences would follow and no doubt also a forestry building. Now Yale had free sites to offer, and prospective donors would no longer shy at the prospect of a rival laboratory in the same science in some other School.[3] The University had given assurances to the Hillhouses that a large part

---

to secure general training rather than specialization should include all of these subjects."

* The intimation came through the New York lawyer, John W. Sterling '64, who in the late eighties had conducted the negotiations, on behalf of Mrs. Miriam A. Osborn, which resulted in the removal of the Fence and the building of Osborn Hall. Now he was overseeing a bequest from Mrs. Osborn. In 1918 he would bequeath for Yale's use his own fortune of some fifteen million dollars, which was three times Yale's whole endowment of 1900. This bequest in turn would so increase in value that eventually almost thirty-nine millions would be realized from it.

of the property would be kept as a botanical garden; so the day after taking possession Stokes had all the trees labeled with their Latin names. But already in his mind's eye he could vision a fine stand of University laboratories replacing the dying oaks of Sachem's Wood.

At once there were difficulties. What had been Stokes' gamble now became a hornet's nest for Hadley. No sooner had the plans been taken under consideration by the Corporation than the historians strongly protested that they were professionally too dependent on the Library to be able to locate so far away. This seemed so reasonable an objection that efforts were made to see if the history building might not be located on the campus. One proposal was to transform the Art School building into a history building, and move the Art School and Gallery to the Hillhouse property. But legal difficulties and personal opposition made that impossible. So the University substituted a zoology laboratory for the proposed history building on the Hillhouse site.[4]

Meanwhile it began to look doubtful whether cooperative laboratories would be welcomed—or even accepted—by either of the undergraduate Schools. And it was still less certain that Director Chittenden would be willing to surrender his virtual domination of personnel and instruction in certain scientific fields. The President, who was apprehensive, hoped that the University's advantage in having the land and the donors at hand would prove quickly decisive. The Secretary, who was determined, was sure that in the larger interests of the University everyone would see the advantage of what was proposed. Unfortunately a trying three-cornered struggle developed.

For no sooner had the new plans become known than most of the influential College Officers showed signs of rebellion. Pierson-Sage Square was much too far away. Geographically it lay clear beyond the traditional undergraduate orbit and psychologically it was on the wrong side, beyond Grove Street. You had to go through "Shefftown" to get to it. In any case it was so far away from all the

College dormitories that the undergraduates might not be willing to make the effort. On the practical side, the scheduling Officer questioned whether there was time enough between classes to allow students to get from their campus classrooms to Hillhouse, or back again, in time for the next recitation.[5]

The problem of distance, without question, was an awkward one. Indeed this seemed to be one of the inescapable growing pains of the university movement. Woodrow Wilson at Princeton was fighting the same difficulty in his row with West over the proposed Graduate School. Hadley insisted that the new laboratories would be no farther away from the Dining Hall than was Osborn recitation hall—but this ignored the fact that Osborn was right on the campus, whereas the Dining Hall was itself on the edge of College territory. The new physics laboratory would be eight-tenths of a mile away from the classrooms for history and English.

Professor Bumstead, whom the College had recently promoted from the Sheffield faculty in order to develop its work in physics, was filled with anxiety. He had hoped to begin his work under the most favorable auspices; but it seemed as if locating the longed-for Laboratory so far out on Prospect Street would make success impossible. The College undergraduates just wouldn't elect physics; and he would have no students to work with. Or else they would shift to the Scientific School and imbibe the narrowly technical approach. Dean-elect Jones heard of the scheme from afar; and the letters reaching him from Bumstead, G. B. Adams, and others raised grave misgivings in his mind. In fact the body of Permanent Officers was so generally persuaded of the unwisdom of the scheme that in the fall of 1909 they voted unanimously in favor of University laboratories but 16 to 9 against the proposed location.[6]

Bumstead, Dana, and others argued for a laboratory nearer by, particularly for putting it on the Hopkins Grammar School lot. This is today the southeast corner of the Law School. Hadley pointed out that the University did not own this land. Dana urged that sooner or later the University would have to acquire the whole Grammar School block anyway. But Hadley could not see it. Yale did not own the land. It did own other land. And he did not propose

373

to waste Yale's capital. He referred also to the distaste of "the average millionaire" for wasteful duplications.[7]

As the Professors could hardly go out and buy in this land themselves, it seemed as if they were beaten and would have to put the best face on the matter they could.

But at this point the Scientific School proved decidedly reluctant. While the physics laboratory argument was in progress, Sheff had been quiet. But mindful of past neglect and resentful of Academic superciliousness, this stepchild of the College was in no conciliatory mood. Having been accused of different and inferior standards, its Officers had learned to make a virtue of the three-year degree. And now they were conscious of increasing power— could see that the School was growing faster than the College— could hope before long to look the proud Academic Faculty in the eye and insist on the treatment of equals. Having been appointed to safeguard the Sheffield moneys from Academic misappropriations, the Sheff Trustees were extremely jealous. And Chittenden was the most determined and independent of all. For he knew what he wanted; and he thought he could see what would happen to the School if its destiny should slip into other, less friendly hands.

Chittenden's objection was not so much to a new physics laboratory. For the truth was that the College had always played a strong role in physics, and the Sheffield facilities for instruction and experiment had not been really adequate. The proposed Sloane building would unquestionably improve the opportunities for Professor Hastings and his assistants, particularly along lines of experiment and research.[8] In any case, Stokes seemed to have the land, the money, and Corporation support all in hand.

Now, however, the Corporation indicated that a zoology laboratory would follow, then laboratories for botany, physiological chemistry, and physical chemistry. Thus, subjects which the Scientific School alone had started, developed, and fostered were also to be taken from it or turned over to joint control. The Director endorsed the principle of unified management, and of opening instruction in a given subject to students from any School in the University. But in the sciences which it had nursed, Sheff ought to do

374

the managing and the teaching. After all, he insisted, Sheff was a *Scientific* School. What would happen to its students, its funds, and its public reputation, if it no longer controlled its own subjects?

Chittenden had already had a taste of the so-called University policy. In 1906, desiring to get better teaching of biology for its general students, the College had terminated its agreement with Sheff. The University had stepped in, and Ross Granville Harrison had been called to a seat on both governing boards. For the time being the College had agreed to let its students continue to get their biological subjects from Sheffield instructors. And Harrison, at the head, made a most distinguished appointment. But Chittenden wanted to claim Harrison's loyalty and scholarship exclusively for Sheff. And the School's monopoly of biology had obviously been threatened. Now, with a new laboratory for zoology and comparative anatomy in prospect, these threats were coming true. For the College was refusing to be left out, and Harrison was insisting on being put in charge.[9]

As much concerned as Chittenden, the Sheffield Trustees at a special meeting in January 1910 resolved that while they were in sympathy with any "lawful" movement for the expansion and improvement of the University, they viewed "with apprehension" any plan depriving the School of certain subjects which it had originated and fostered. A conference with the Prudential Committee followed. And Chittenden was requested to submit a plan for the administration of the proposed laboratory—a plan which was substantially agreed to.

The words "University management" or "University control" seemed to the Director vague and wholly undefined. But on the issue of control he knew that Harrison, Dana, and Bumstead were against him. He therefore defined as sharply as he could what he meant and what the School would agree to. The laboratory was to be built by the University Corporation, but controlled by the governing boards of the two undergraduate Schools, and actually managed by a committee of the permanent professors working in the building. The Professor of Comparative Anatomy—Harrison—should continue to sit in both Faculties. But the occupants of the

375

chairs of zoology and biology, or of equivalent professorships, should exclusively be appointed by and attached to the Sheffield Scientific School. And if the College wanted to make one of the younger teachers a member of its own staff, it was suggested that one of the Sheffield assistant professors be taken. In any case the Scientific School would continue to throw its courses open to College students.

These were stiff terms: stiffer in certain details of professorial attachment than obtained in physics and the physics laboratory. Again, when a wing for botany was included in the zoology plans, Chittenden went to the mat directly with President Hadley, and in an interview obtained the promise that the laboratory and department of botany would be considered a part of the Scientific School and remain under the control of its Governing Board.[10] Having secured these concessions to the Sheffield point of view, Chittenden then agreed to go along with the Hillhouse development plans and to transfer the School's laboratories of physics, botany, zoology, and comparative anatomy to the new University buildings when they should be ready. So another great obstacle to the Hadley-Stokes plans had been successfully removed.

Unfortunately the Director and his Trustees had been put on guard and were more determined than ever to fight for the independence of the School. So a difference of view which had applied chiefly to the sciences now animated the whole policy of the School. Henceforward Chittenden would not offer to surrender his control of graduate work in engineering. He would insist on the three-year degree, continue to develop the Select Course in its fine new Leet Oliver Memorial building, increase the courses in commerce and business management, and build dormitories and social halls to rival the College. His Trustees would try to build up a Contingency Fund and his Governing Board would continue to set its own entrance standards. In these and in other ways the Scientific School would struggle to maintain its individuality and independent power.[11]

Not all of this displeased the Administration. President Hadley believed in home rule. Also he had begun with the idea that there were real advantages in the old differentiation. Men who wanted a lot of science, or who didn't want Latin or Greek, could go to Sheff. The three-year degree and the greater technical emphasis took vocational pressures off the College. But different entrance examinations in the same subjects annoyed the preparatory schools. The easier standards of admission seemed to injure the University's reputation. And the School's attitude of independence in so many routine matters made Hadley perpetually uncomfortable. One of the reasons he had been so glad to have Dean Jones consent to head the Academic Professors was that now the Dean could take on some of the burden of wrestling with Chittenden. Hadley disliked having to act as both advocate and judge.

Dean Jones was not disposed to move hastily. Yet on these larger issues his constituency plainly had made up their minds. Inheritors of long-standing prejudices, many Academic professors found it hard to be generous with Sheff. Though recognizing that it had distinguished men on its Governing Board, they disliked its vocational atmosphere, and more and more resented the competition for students now being offered by the Select Course. For a long decade the College enrollment had stood still. And Sheff had been booming. In 1907 it was noted uneasily that the Sheffield Freshmen were beginning to outnumber the College Freshmen.* How long would it be before the Scientific School, despite having but three Classes, outnumbered the College? Sheff's technical work seemed not highly respected outside of New Haven; yet most of its energies were now being applied to building up the faculty of the Select Course. Why should Yale allow another liberal arts degree, in competition with the B.A.?

Why not? retorted Chittenden. For it had been Sheff which had first established a curriculum without Greek or Latin and demonstrated how to construct a college course out of a combination of science, social science, and modern languages. Sheff had taught English literature since 1860—Lounsbury had been appointed in 1870—history and political economy also since 1860. What the Col-

* See Appendix, Table O-1: Yale College and Sheffield Scientific School Freshman Enrollments, p. 722.

lege had done was to let Sheff make the experiments and take the risks. Then, when the new subjects succeeded, the College belatedly started teaching them, too. Thus if there was duplication it was the fault of the College which now, no longer able to cling to Latin and Greek, was moving over into the natural and social sciences. One of the strong points of the Scientific School had been its insistence on literature, language, and social studies, its effort to educate as well as to train, its avoidance of purely technical programs. To deprive the School of such subjects would be unwise as well as unjust. Perhaps also illegal. The Trustees and Governing Board owed it to Joseph Sheffield and to themselves to fight any encroachments or attacks on the Select Course.[12]

Unfortunately, there was considerable historical justification for what Chittenden asserted. Also the awkward truth was that, while the Permanent Officers criticized the existence of the Select Course, they were by no means prepared to take it over. They would not consider offering a quick degree, or a compulsory program, or so much vocational content. In short, they resented the competition of the Select Course but they wouldn't drag it into Yale College with a ten-foot pole.

For their part, Hadley and the Corporation felt considerably less resolute than Chittenden and his Trustees. In 1909 this phase of the rivalry, together with the general problem of College-Sheff relations, was quietly investigated and privately discussed by the Alumni Board. But this Board itself decided discretion was the better part of valor. After Chittenden made his laboratory compromise the Board ignored the fundamental nature of the remaining problems, left the Select Course lying like an unexploded mine, and professed to believe that things were really working out.[13]

One gathers that the New Haven authorities succeeded momentarily in persuading the graduates that it would be wise to move toward a better cooperation by gradual stages: by the development of joint committees on admission, through exchange of students and credits, and through the development of common University facilities of many kinds. In this program the establishment of the new Hillhouse laboratories represented the first crucial move. This

378

move the Scientific School, whatever its apprehensions, was no longer in a position to block.

THE PROPOSAL OF A THIRD COLLEGE

On the Academic side there had been one professor who had distrusted the University laboratory idea regardless of location and had fought the Administration's policy on moral rather than financial grounds. George Burton Adams, Professor of History, had been among the original champions of Hadley and a useful supporter of his Administration. Little by little he had been growing disturbed. It seemed to him that the historic and peculiar character or unity of Yale College was being undermined by University development. First there had been the threat of professionalizing the Senior year. Hadley had caved in. Perhaps only the resistance of the Professors —the firm watchfulness of Adams himself—had prevented the Law School from seizing a larger control. This time the proposal was to break down the geographical unity and the intellectual cohesion of undergraduate life. In the hope of persuading the Corporation's committee and of enlisting support among his colleagues, Adams had drawn up an eloquent memorandum.[14]

Yale College, said Adams, unlike most university colleges and all colleges in the State universities, had spirit, cohesion, and self-government. It was a living thing and in fact the most valuable single asset of all Yale. Having come from the outside himself he called on all those who had kept in touch with developments in American higher education to bear witness to the truth of what he asserted. Colleges in other universities had become collections of students, following some designated course of studies, but generally without their own dormitories, and often without their own classrooms or instruction. Any school for the study of any subject was apt to be called a college.

Such colleges were units of convenience, not living organisms. They did not have the traditions, the solidity, and the force to seize all undergraduates and mold them through a common experience.

379

Living together, eating together, worshiping together, studying together, playing together, and competing with each other for four years, the men of Yale came to know each other and to develop loyalties such as few other places were capable of generating. Anything, therefore, which broke in upon College life, which, for example, drew alien students into College classrooms or pushed College students out into the classes and laboratories of other Schools was a threat to the moral unity of Yale College. Hence the temptation to mix and confuse the professional or graduate units with those of the undergraduates should be resisted.

Anson Stokes had replied that the College men could continue to take instruction in their *own* physics divisions, while the new policy would eliminate the duplication of laboratories, equipment, and classrooms. It would also establish the ideal of University unity in the sciences in place of competing departments. But Adams was not impressed. With some brusqueness he had taken the Administration to task for not understanding what a University was. Merely to put College and Sheff students in the same building did not make the building a University structure. The Administration's concept was horizontal and administrative, not intellectual and moral. A true University would offer different kinds of education and at different levels. But the Administration was not thinking of graduate work in physics, of unifying all the science instructors and equipment for the prosecution of cooperative research. What it wanted was to diminish the obstinate independence of the undergradute Schools. In so doing, in Adams' opinion, it was unwittingly embarking on a completely mistaken policy. What hurt him most was that Yale seemed to be throwing away its unique asset at the very moment that Harvard was trying to recapture these very values by housing its Freshmen together and breathing new life and importance into its college.[15]

As these protests and arguments grew warmer, Hadley had prudently withdrawn. But Adams knew that Stokes was the power behind the proposal, and to make the Secretary see the validity of his objection he bent the full force of his considerable energies and talents. The Secretary heard him with great patience and replied repeatedly and at great length. The unity of the College, thought Stokes, derived far more from living and playing together than from studying together. No, said Adams, studying counted. Intellectual unity was one of the essential elements. So was geographic unity.

But it was no use. The Secretary could not be persuaded that he was hurting the College any more than Hadley could be persuaded to buy the Hopkins Grammar School lot. So after Adams had had the exquisite torture of seeing President Lowell come out in his inaugural four square and impressively in favor of the "solidarity" of Harvard College—and after his own desperate anxiety had driven him to remonstrances so strong as to call for apology—the argument terminated. Thereafter, on the ground that no other feasible solution existed, the Administration had gone ahead.[16]

Having lost this battle, Adams did not despair of the larger campaign. Instead he studied to preserve the College and in particular prepared to defend its integrity against the next great attacks which he could see coming. This preoccupation led him to an unusual proposal.

When Dean-elect Jones had been in active correspondence with the Officers of the University and College, he had discovered that Adams was more exercised than most about the laboratory plans but not nearly so worried as many others over the growing power and competition of the Scientific School. Where others could see only challenge and menace in the expanding Select Course, Adams seemed strangely complacent. It developed that he thought a healthy and vigorous Scientific School, with its own social morale and pride of tradition, would help rather than hurt the College.

The explanation was simple. As Adams examined in his mind the sources of College spirit and the problem of maintaining solidarity, he became persuaded that personal intimacy and intellectual unity were essential. Next to the menace of curricular decentralization and geographic dispersion was the menace of "numbers, mere numbers, undigested and unassimilated numbers." The Scientific School ought to be encouraged precisely because it tended to keep numbers in the College down. If the Select Course were abolished

—and this would be truer still if the College took it over—the College would be flooded by students who wanted things the College was not prepared to give, and who refused to present the languages and disciplinary training that the Yale B.A. stood for. Curriculum and social unity would suffer. And Yale College would be compelled to spread its influence over so many students and so many programs of study that Class loyalty and the Yale spirit would inevitably decline.

The next step in Adams' thinking was implicit in what preceded. When he found that the high schools were throwing overboard college preparation, and when Yale's Western alumni proved unwilling to send sons thus trained to the Select Course but persisted in wanting them admitted to the College, the writing was on the wall. Adams sympathized with the Midwestern families but not with their immediate objective. For he saw that, unless some other solution could quickly be found, Yale College might be forced into accepting the high-school subjects, the high-school graduates, and the public preference for vocational training as well.

His solution was bold and original. The University should have a third undergraduate college—a college for modern subjects. The Select Course men from Sheff, with some antilanguage men from the College, could be transferred to a new organization, with its own faculty similarly accumulated, its own distinct curriculum and entrance requirements. Sheff would then concentrate on its original vocation: science and engineering. The Academic Department, no longer torn by conflicting demands, would construct a solid program in the humanities, the traditional liberal arts. And the new school would be a college for modern studies in the social sciences. No one of the three would be trying to do incompatible things or be too large for unity and morale. In the spring of 1914, in a series of articles in the *Alumni Weekly,* Adams analyzed Yale's problems and urged the third-college solution.[17]

The idea appealed to quite a number of individuals, scattered through the faculties and alumni organizations. The Midwest alumni, gathering in Cincinnati, heard Adams describe his way of meeting their entrance grievances with intense interest.[18] Obviously there were difficulties. Yale men found it hard to imagine a third college. Objection was made that the new college could not be given sufficient prestige and that, instead of eliminating duplication, it would produce triplication of classes and services, especially at the elementary levels. The obvious answers were that seventy years earlier the Sheffield Scientific School had not existed, either. Moreover, so long as the small division method of teaching was used, repetition of subjects and courses constituted no duplication, since a given number of students, divided into three colleges, would require no more instruction than if they were all in the same college. On the other hand, Adams insisted, the separation of purpose would allow the instruction to be adapted to clearly understood ends. His proposal would provide a place where the Western high-school graduates would obtain the advantages of Yale without jeopardizing the standards of either the College or Sheff. In any case the third college was the only solution which promised to take care of the menace of sheer numbers.

Studying Adams' proposal in the light of hindsight, one recognizes a great obstacle to its realization, namely, the unity of all knowledge. Dormitories and teams could be divided, recitations held separately. But how divide the faculties, or the areas of research, or even the lecture courses at upper levels? The three colleges themselves might become too large and then the problem would be to find the intellectual materials out of which to create a fourth. Adams was perhaps guilty of exaggeration in his insistence that divisions on an intellectual basis were essential. Certainly the theoretical problem was not so simple as it looked.

But Hadley would not explore Adams' suggestion quite that far. Instead he observed that it would take a long time before the new college could create the desired atmosphere and traditions.

A boy goes to college not primarily nor wholly for the sake of pursuing certain studies, but for the sake of breathing a certain atmosphere, of competing for certain traditional rewards of undergraduate life, of entering certain societies that his father had known and meeting certain men or the successors of certain men whom his father has met.*

Again the third-college plan would not solve "the present difficulty," which Hadley defined as the need for a more intellectual atmosphere. Finally, it would be excessively expensive. Far from considering that at first the third college could borrow many of the teachers and facilities it would need, he insisted on calculating the costs of a new establishment, which he estimated at two million dollars for buildings and another million for endowment. To the President of Yale—who was being made quite uncomfortable enough by the growing costs of the established Departments in the University—the proposal to raise any such sum for a third college seemed on its face irrational. So instead of inviting the Advisory Board to comment, or himself exploring the idea fully before discarding it, he gave it a rather unfair analysis in his Report for 1913–14, and dismissed it.[19]

Thus ended five years of exploration and debate over Yale's proper line of development. In retrospect it is clear that it was the sheer persistence of Anson Phelps Stokes that won the battle for a policy of University laboratories on Pierson-Sage Square. And from this the Secretary would move forward to the larger development of the University along many lines.

The expansion and improvement of laboratory facilities represented a substantial gain; but otherwise the cause of science in Yale College was distinctly prejudiced. Perhaps the thing was not to be helped. But there can be no question that subjects already unpopular enough were made even more so by the distance and extra ef-

* Hadley added that some persons thought Yale could combine the advantages of the small college with those of a large university by having the teaching under the control of the University and the colleges serve primarily as residence halls under their own social discipline. But as this was a plan totally different in principle from that "proposed by Professor Adams (or anyone else in the United States) I shall not discuss it."

fort. For a time the College science requirement, coupled with Woodruff's ability as a lecturer, gave biology a considerable vogue. But the trek to "Yale-in-Hartford," as the Hillhouse laboratories came to be called, has always been a burden to the students and a misfortune for the science instructors who have found themselves more removed than ever from the central life and councils of the College.

Twice during this period President Hadley had, on the grounds of financial difficulty, refused to give serious consideration to issues of intellectual and moral consequence. This cost him the support of certain influential professors and considerably weakened his hold on the College Faculty. At the same time the appearance of conflict within the University, the publication of irreconcilable opinions, Hadley's apparent unwillingness or inability to eliminate duplications and harmful rivalries between College and Sheff—all these advertised a weakness to the alumni, who would become more forward in pushing their own ideas or special grievances. In particular, irritation over the cavalier treatment of the Western high-school problem and impatience with the Sheff-College situation now inspired a group of Western graduates, under the determined leadership of E. J. Phelps '86 of Chicago, to try to bring these problems before the Alumni Advisory Board. So was set in motion one of the more po   ul currents of criticism which would eventually coalesce to force on the University its great Reorganization in 1918–20.[20]

Meanwhile, the idea of a third college had been rejected but no alternate solution found for handling the twin problems of diversity and numbers. So the new problems would have to be handled with the old apparatus. Inescapably the College would be subjected to increasing pressure by Yale's Midwestern clientele. In short order the issues posed by the high-school student, his certification to college, and his treatment in college would have to be fought out. Entrance and graduation standards might have to be changed. If any real accommodation were made, the College would then find on its hands the further problem of numbers.

In the 1840's and after, the practice had been to make room for new subjects and new groups of students by founding Departments or Schools. Natural history, graduate studies, and art had all been handled in this way; and the Scientific School in particular was a monument to the idea. Yale's answer to the problems of expansion had theretofore been the confederated University. But perhaps Adams was right in calling all this a blind stumble in the right direction—"an undeserved mercy of Providence" neither foreseen nor understood. At all events, out of irritation with College-Sheff rivalries, Hadley and Stokes were now breaking down the barriers within the federation, and neglecting to apply the old Yale formula for growth. That this committed Yale to the Eliot idea of the college as the *omnium gatherum* of a university's undergraduate responsibilities apparently only G. B. Adams clearly understood and foretold. But eventually the pressures upon Yale College would make everyone uncomfortable, and in the 1920's the idea of a third college was destined to be revived.

CHAPTER 20·COLLEGE AND NATION: THE ENTRANCE PROBLEM

Now I have watched the certificate system for fifteen years in the Western State universities and I am firmly convinced that it is a bad system for any institution, east or west.

So we are not going to have any certificate system, even if the Western Association of Yale Clubs tells us to. That is flat.

—Dean Jones, at the meeting of Associated Western Yale Clubs, 20 May 1911

The futility of discussion with any of the members of the Yale Faculty is as plain to me as thirty-five years ago.

—Response by Dr. I. N. Bloom '78 of Louisville

After this exchange it was "Resolved that, in the opinion of the Associated Western Yale Clubs, the requirements for admission to Yale should be brought more closely in touch with the educational conditions existing in the Western high schools and that the Corporation and Faculty should give prompt attention to this matter to the end that Yale's pre-eminence as a national University may be preserved."

So broke into the open a difference of interest and opinion that had been arousing Yale's Midwestern alumni to a pitch of agitation and criticism which irritated even a Faculty representative of so much Western experience as Dean Jones.[1] The West was losing ground at Yale, said a spokesman from Detroit. This was not strictly true, Hadley had replied, for there was not an important falling-off in Western representation at Yale. But after listening to the discussion, he remodeled his own speech a little:

387

The point is that we are not getting men from the *high schools* of the West . . . The Western boys who come to Yale are mostly going to preparatory schools in the East. That is a serious thing. It means that we are getting somewhat out of connection with the public school system of the country; not in the West alone, but in the West first, and probably in other places afterwards.

That would be a particular misfortune for a University whose motto was public service. In Hadley's view, Yale needed to get boys "from every place and from every rank" because the democratic contact with men of all kinds was an educational feature of the College quite as important as any specific curriculum. On the other hand, he did not agree that Greek and Latin were now useless. Perhaps Yale could begin to accept the history and literature the high schools wanted to teach; but no vocational training or freehand drawing could be equivalent. Yale was looking not to lower the standard but toward reconciliation on a higher plane. Acceptance of high-school certificates would not guarantee quality, for certificates were at best regional in meaning whereas examinations were national tests. Thus Yale would keep on examining its candidates. On balance, as he later said, the problem was to show the college where it is narrow and the high school where it needs discipline.[2]

But Yale's scattered alumni felt helpless against the high schools. So they concentrated on the first half of the President's equation. And because the College proved slow and reluctant, they remained restive and more than a little impatient with Yale's "aristocratic" and "antiquated" education.[3]

At first some of these spokesmen for the Yale Clubs of the Midwest must have supposed that they were making a relatively simple demand in asking the Faculty to work out means whereby more Western high-school students could be admitted to Yale. But unhappily the entrance question was neither local nor even new, and assuredly it was not so easy as it looked. In fact it was one of the most persistent and complicated problems that had ever arisen to bedevil the academic world. And its scope was now national: both geographically and in the sense that it affected the interests of all classes. So in tugging against each other Yale's Western alumni and the authorities of the College were enacting parts in a wider struggle, parts that had been played and were destined to be played in most of the independent colleges and universities of the country.

Formerly, as Yale's best informed authority—Professor Robert Nelson Corwin—pointed out, there had been no entrance problem.[4] The first high schools, succeeding to the academies and Latin grammar schools, had succeeded also to their functions as fitting schools for colleges and the learned professions. But then had come the economic and social transformation, together with the scientific enlargement of learning. The high schools became swamped by a democratic clientele. Many of these were not going on to college or the professions, most of them were no longer interested in the classics or the traditional curriculum, yet all were asking to be educated.

Quite naturally all the high schools, East or West, felt the need of adjusting their courses to the new student masses, with their technical needs or vocational interests. Quite as naturally the newer high schools of the West put the interests of the majority ahead of the desires of the minority, and the local community before the distant college. With equal inevitability representatives of the older high schools of the East asked to be allowed to substitute the sciences, social studies, and vocational subjects for the Greek and Latin that were no longer wanted. Catering to the same mass movement, the Western tax-supported State universities had been adjusting in the same way: had agreed in fact to accept high-school students on certificate.

Not so the private and church-supported colleges. These tradition-minded institutions refused to accept the very kinds of study which had made the high schools grow. Instead they insisted on so much of the older learning as to make separate college-preparatory divisions almost a necessity, or the direct preparation for life instead of for college virtually impossible. This had generated no little resentment and expostulation even in the East. As for the

Western high schools, they had thrown off the yoke entirely, and were going ahead as they pleased.

As Corwin pointed out, there was much to be said for the high-school and Western point of view. The colleges could choose either the most promising boys or those who had studied certain subjects; and the latter meant a lower average of native ability because some very able boys would be excluded from consideration. In the second place, it was difficult to justify prerequisites for college when these same subjects were not carried further in college. It was equally difficult to criticize the high-school training when high-school graduates—after being heavily conditioned on admission—so often stood near the top of their college Classes on graduation. This raised the question whether the traditional disciplines were genuinely prerequisite to success in college. Perhaps, after all, the high-school teachers were better judges of what high-school students should study. In any case the inescapable dilemma was this: even if the high schools wanted to prepare boys for college, how could they?

For the colleges did not agree. In most Eastern universities Latin was required for the arts course, but in the State universities such a requirement was practically unknown. Yale College required four years of Latin. California did not even accept Latin for the foreign language requirement. Said Corwin: "Your disagreement amongst yourselves throws your whole case for the colleges out of court."

In rebuttal the Eastern university men could ask whether the sad experiences of colleges with the elective system were to go for nothing. The colleges were convalescent from this disastrous epidemic, and now that it had been demonstrated that college men were poor judges of value in subjects and methods, were the high-school students to be encouraged to substitute liking for aptitude, easy work for discipline, vocational enthusiasms for the toilsome exercises that alone produced power? On particular subjects the high schools seemed to be discarding what was tried and proven for what was experimental and still problematical. Not only were they discarding Latin, they were slighting the modern languages of

French and German. Mathematics—the essential basis for the sciences, to say nothing of its intrinsic values—was itself being reduced to the bare everyday rudiments. Despite assertions to the contrary, one subject could not be the equivalent of another. By all tests American high-school graduates were far behind those of England or the Continent. While Yale did not want to bar able men, it could not hope to stand on a par with the best institutions of Europe unless its candidates had been well trained.[5]

This raised the question of standards. The question was whether the local high-school systems or the State universities were really capable of setting standards, or whether the best private colleges were the only reliable standard-raising agencies. The arguments waxed hot and personal. Why should the work of mediocre public schools be equated with that of the best preparatory schools in the country?[6] Up spoke the Western alumni asserting that the best preparatory schools were all in the East and only the rich could afford them. But they were better than the "womanized" public schools, trumpeted a defender. Besides, the Yale exams were not as difficult as advertised. Why, in his University School in New Haven, snorted the fiery George L. Fox, he had prepared ordinary boys for the Yale exams in a few weeks. The preparatory schools were cram schools, came back the retort. No, said Hadley, for by means of time-tested subjects these schools taught a method that would last.[7]

So the arguments of rich vs. poor, of democratic public schools vs. aristocratic private schools, were injected into a situation already complicated by the dispute over subject matter and the failure of American colleges to stand together for the same ideals of study or requirements of college entrance. The charge was that colleges like Yale wanted Western boys on Eastern terms. In other words, they wanted boys solidly prepared in the traditional subjects; but the dangerous sweets of elective practice should be reserved for colleges, not for the high schools. For their part the Western parents had the air of demanding the benefits of an Eastern college and the prestige of a Yale degree but without paying the full price paid for it in the East. Some of Yale's alumni definitely wanted a more modern and vocational education; and a few were willing to have their sons get such an education in Sheff. But many were not. Considering the matter socially, Hadley sympathized with the latter; but from the intellectual point of view there seemed to him less excuse. Immemorially the B.A. degree had been associated with the arts course and the Latin. Were not those who insisted on the B.A. without the Latin, he asked, perpetrating a kind of fraud?

> . . . nearly everybody who tries to answer this charge proves . . . he hopes to profit by it. He says that he has something else that is as good as the Latin course, and therefore he ought to be allowed to give the degree of A.B. This is the stock argument of every man who seeks to violate the law of trademarks. It may be that his wares *are* as good as the others. If so, all the more reason why he should send them out under their own label instead of a false one.[8]

One logical extreme was to insist with the classicists that only certain traditional subjects really educated a man. The other extreme was to argue as if the mere act of staying in school in company with one's fellow Americans to the age of twenty-two was warrant for awarding the Yale B.A. As there were practically no theoretical men in the Yale constituency, and only a minority of extremists, neither dogmatism was likely to be indefinitely maintained. On the other hand Yale's problem was complicated by the internal organization of the University and by a whole series of factors peculiar to the local situation.

For example, while in sentiment Yale College was inveterately national, in practice it drew a higher percentage of its students from the private preparatory schools—a lower percentage from the public schools—than any comparable institution except Princeton.[9] Hence it sympathized with the preparatory-school view and felt obligated to see that these schools and the cause of superior education were not injured by any untoward action on its part.

In similar fashion the College was torn by the sharpness of the division in its alumni ranks. For the graduates living in the Middle West, though a small minority of the alumni body, were newly organized, and a vigorous and unusually aggressive group.[10] Again, undergraduate Yale was divided against itself. For if the B.A. Latin requirement were lowered or abolished, and alternative subjects accepted for entrance, the College might very well siphon off, along with a high-school group, a substantial portion of the Select Course candidates, including some of its richer men, its society men, and athletes. That this was no idle threat to the Scientific School was now demonstrated by the conduct of its Officers.

The Scientific School had entered the twentieth century with a two-to-three-year Latin entrance requirement. Perhaps because of this, perhaps also because it insisted on teaching some cultural studies along with the technical, the School attracted a large number of private-school candidates. In any case it felt peculiarly vulnerable to any relaxation of the College requirements. In 1903, it was said, the Director had gone so far as to urge the College to keep its Greek requirement.[11] In 1909 Chittenden announced the abolition of the Latin requirement for the engineering candidates, and in 1912 the School abandoned this requirement for the Select Course candidates.[12] Meanwhile the group of subjects acceptable for entrance had been broadened. Evidently Chittenden meant to keep ahead of the College. Had the three-year Ph.B. only enjoyed a better reputation, or had Yale graduates been more willing to send their sons to Sheff, or had the Administration been content to have Sheff become Yale's vehicle of national representation, Chittenden's acceptance of the new subject demands might have come close to solving the University's problem.[13] As it was, the independent action of the Director merely intensified the New Haven rivalry, undermined the position of the conservatives in the College, and aggravated the problems of the President.

THE COLLEGE ENTRANCE EXAMINATION BOARD

Underneath all the confusion and clamor three major issues may be discerned. Each of these was general in its bearing but had particular implications for Yale. The first was: what ought college *studies* to be? The second: *who* should go to college? And the third: who should *control* the admission? Unfortunately these issues were so entangled that no one would be settled separately. In particular, the answer to the third was likely to prejudge the first two questions as well.

For the character of the entrance requirements would go far to determine not merely who might qualify but what subjects could be taught in school and college, by what methods, in what amounts, and at what levels of quality. In a word, the most important single point in the whole educational ladder had become the rung by which the student mounted from school into college. And whoever was in control at that point would in the end determine both the lower and the higher education.

This was unfortunate because to focus so many valid but competing interests at this uncertain point of transition from school to college was to make it difficult, if not impossible, to do justice to them all. In addition it was exceedingly confusing—so confusing in fact that only a few kept the whole picture clear in their minds, and many succeeded in giving only the most partial and one-sided statement of their convictions. In 1912 Hadley himself confessed that "we have not made it clear to the public schools of the country, or even to ourselves, why we were conservative on entrance requirements."

The problem was so complicated that even in retrospect it is difficult to give a clear explanation. Nevertheless, if we keep these three major issues in mind it will be possible to see how in the years 1901–11 the first gradual changes of policy were undertaken—and how then in 1911–16, through a long series of minor concessions and adjustments, Yale College moved forward to a substantial accommodation.

The first outspoken champions of a more liberal examining process had been the President and his Secretary. In his inaugural address, Hadley had given forthright expression to some rather positive views about Yale's entrance examinations:

The true policy for our university with regard to entrance requirements is to find out what our secondary schools can do for their pupils, intellectually and morally, and adapt our require-

394

ments to these conditions. Detailed questions as to what specific subjects we shall require must be subordinated to this general principle of requiring those things, and only those things, which the schools can do well. . . .

Again in his annual Report for 1904–05 he defined Yale's policy with regard to entrance requirements as "governed by two separate considerations; our duty to ourselves of not admitting boys except those who are able to do the kind of work which will be required of them, and our duty to the public of admitting all kinds of boys who can do this, on as equal terms as possible."

In this clear-cut fashion Hadley stated three educational objectives: Yale's students should be effective workers; the secondary schools should be given reasonable liberty on subject matter; Yale's constituency should be democratic and national. The implication was that if the secondary schools were encouraged to do what they did best, Yale's Freshmen would be both better trained and drawn from a wider constituency. Hadley added a warning: "It is wrong to say that whatever Yale requires the schools will furnish. . . . If the Yale requirements should get so far out of the line of the work furnished by the better kind of high schools . . . we should soon become a local institution."

So Hadley's horizon included the high schools—and in this concern Secretary Stokes emphatically concurred. At the time of the battle over Greek Stokes wrote to the College Faculty that he thought "we have been entirely too much governed by the opinion of the prominent preparatory schools of New England, which are very conservative." [14] Trying to overcome this tendency toward academic isolation, Stokes had begun the practice of visiting more of the schools which sent men to Yale. In 1903 he reported to the Faculty Committee on Scholarship and Numbers that it was not uncommon for him to be informed by a principal or headmaster that he was the first representative of Yale who had ever visited the school.

Thenceforward better relations with Yale's feeder schools were cultivated by the Faculty as well as by the Administration, especially after the Committee on Scholarship and Numbers had ana-

395

lyzed Yale's stationary enrollment and bluntly called attention to "Yale's lack of touch with the outside world." Several devices were tried. Circular letters were sent out to hundreds of school teachers explaining changes in the terms of admission and the reasons for such changes. Several conferences were called in order to bring Faculty and school men together to discuss common educational problems.

Another of Stokes' proposals for the improvement of Yale's relations with the schools was the use of advertising. In offering this suggestion he stated: "I would not like to see Yale do this in any undignified way, but I am sure we have suffered in the past through what has been over-scrupulousness on this point." Accordingly, the Corporation approved the forwarding of Yale pictures, the *Alumni Weekly*, and the University *Bulletin* to several hundred public and private schools throughout the country.

Speaking in 1901 before the Department of Superintendence of the National Education Association, Hadley summarized the college entrance problem in the following question: "How can we arrange to give to the school the necessary freedom in its methods of instruction, to give the college the assurance that its pupils will be well prepared for their work, and to give the students themselves . . . the certainty of reasonably fair treatment?" To this he gave the same answer he had already urged on the New England Association of Colleges and Preparatory Schools. Many of the defects of the existing system would be removed, he thought, by substituting a few comprehensive tests for the multitude of detailed tests employed in each subject. These comprehensive tests would have several advantages. They would encourage schools to teach subjects rather than cram for detailed tests. The candidates would not be so rushed—and the unfair advantage possessed by those who crammed would be reduced. The smaller number of examinations could be read with greater care. Finally, for the other subjects that they taught, the schools' recommendations could be accepted.[15]

In the same year Hadley was connected with still a different suggestion. This looked toward the standardization of the entrance examinations through cooperation between the institutions interested. Two possibilities along this line were opening up: on the one hand affiliation with the newly formed Middle States College Entrance Examination Board; on the other, the creation of a similar board in New England. After appointment by the New England Association of Colleges and Preparatory Schools, a committee of ten preparatory school and college educators, including Hadley of Yale, preferred the second alternative and recommended the establishment of a New England College Entrance Examination Board.[16]

So within a comparatively short time after entering office the new Yale Administration had given decisive evidence of a liberal point of view toward all the major issues. It was in favor of standardizing the subject expectations and abbreviating the examinations. It wanted boys from all regions and backgrounds. Finally, it desired closer relations with the high schools, and was apparently willing to share the control of the examining process.

Yet a liberal attitude was not quite the same thing as a liberal policy. Still less did it guarantee action. In fact for a considerable time Yale's President seemed to be helpless to swing the College and the Scientific School to his point of view. Instead there were occasions when he wobbled—or boldly embraced a conservative doctrine.

One reason was obvious. An institution which had for so long set and administered its own entrance standards was not to be persuaded overnight into sharing control. Especially as the Entrance Committee and the entrance procedures of the College were in the hands of the classicists and language men, who were slow to appreciate the menace of isolation. Incidentally, until 1904 Harvard was also opposed.

A second reason was more disconcerting. Having recommended a general line, Hadley would encounter unexpected drawbacks, discover perhaps that it jeopardized other values, or that his larger constituency could not be carried for the policy. We have already quoted his back-and-forth pronouncements about Greek, and noted how he came out first for the abolition of the requirement, then for its retention, then for equivalents at least as hard. But equivalents at least as hard were not what the high schools were looking for. So

397

the abandonment merely undermined Greek in the private schools without bringing more public school boys to Yale.

Hadley had argued that once Greek was no longer required of Freshmen it could not logically be required for entrance. But he failed to apply the same argument to Latin. Now it was becoming plain that the high schools thought they could teach other subjects better than Latin—at least they would rather drop Latin. And Hadley had every desire to accommodate them. But his Corporation and Faculty would have protested. Then he discovered in himself a great respect for Latin as a four-year study of increasing difficulty and disciplinary value.*

Hadley disliked cram schools and said so. But soon he was having to defend the private schools as preparatory in method rather than cram schools for information. He favored cooperative examining boards and standardized tests. But when Nicholas Murray Butler invited Yale to support the College Entrance Examination Board which the Middle States Association was establishing, Hadley was reluctant to withdraw from the New England situation and leave Harvard in command. He served on the committee which recommended a similar board for New England, but when this failed to win the support of Harvard and some other colleges he joined his own College Faculty in a policy of watchful waiting. He had recommended the substitution of a few comprehensive exam-

* It was a common mistake to suppose that education meant the acquiring of knowledge whereas three-quarters of it, in Hadley's opinion, consisted in learning "good *methods of acquiring* knowledge." The study of Latin taught the habits of accuracy and effort and counteracted the very dangerous tendencies in modern high schools to make "other people do our work." Hadley would appreciatively quote Dean Jones: "How can we prevent our college graduates from getting their degrees on borrowed brains?"

A generation later E. L. Woodward from experience with English public schools would echo the thought: "I have taught boys classics and history. When I was teaching them classics, they did most of the work; when I was teaching them history, I did most of the work. A Latin unseen, a difficult algebraic equation, a piece of translation into French prose give a boy much greater chances of using his brain, and developing powers of concentration and logical thought." *Short Journey* (New York, Oxford University Press, 1946), 174.

inations to the National Education Association; but inside Yale the matter was referred to the College's Committee on Entrance Examinations and nothing more was heard of it, either from the President or from the committee.

The particular factors which accounted for the Yale Faculty's reluctance to adopt uniform entrance examinations may be surmised; but two are worth notice. In the first place, many faculty members felt that Yale College would suffer by lowering its admission standards to the level of the majority of colleges. In the second place, the Yale language men seem to have persuaded their President that the *kind* of examination would also be adversely affected, inasmuch as Yale examined for grammar and for method while most schools and colleges were satisfied with information.[17]

Against the proposal to examine comprehensively in a few subjects only, many arguments were eventually developed. Some faculty members and school men feared the risk of injustice to the boys.

Many faculty members believed that fewer examinations would not test a candidate sufficiently in any subject and would let down the bars to unfit applicants. Some school men feared that the use of only three or four tests would lead to discrimination in the secondary schools against all subjects in which the candidate would not be examined, such as history and the sciences. The private preparatory schools stated that they frequently employed the Old Plan examinations as a basis for rating both their pupils and teachers.

So once again the President was touched on a vulnerable spot. In helping the high schools, he did not wish to injure the preparatory schools—any more than he wanted to substitute information for grammar or "practical" subjects for strict training in the proven disciplines. Quite aside from the opposition of classicists and conservatives, or the rivalry between College and Sheff, Hadley's way was beset with difficulties. Theoretically the issues would not stay clear, and practically he had no supporting party. For if he agreed with the Faculty about standards and method, he could not but

399

think their subject restrictions narrow. And if he agreed with the high schools' desire for new subjects, he could not accept their vocational interests and standards of teaching. So he stood alone on the middle of the seesaw, stepping now a little this way, now a little that.

Notwithstanding the confusion of values, the difficulties theoretical and practical, and the special local circumstances and personalities, Yale College in the first half of Hadley's consulship did modify its entrance procedures appreciably. When alternative studies were admitted into Freshman year the subject requirements were liberalized and, starting in 1904, equivalents in the form of more mathematics and modern languages could be substituted for the Greek requirement. In 1910–11 the College more substantially improved its reputation with the secondary schools by reducing the number of required entrance papers and permitting examinations in four new subjects: solid geometry and trigonometry, physics, chemistry, and either English history or American history and civil government.*

Meanwhile the College was also approaching the idea of cooperative examining. The first formal indication of any change in Yale's attitude toward the C.E.E.B. had come in 1904 when the Committee on Entrance Examinations proposed to include in a circular letter to all secondary schools preparing students for Yale College the statement: "Until further notice Yale College will accept the certificates of the College Entrance Examination Board, so far as these cover the Yale entrance requirements, taking for the present 65% as the passing mark.†

* In 1900 candidates had been required to take tests on twenty units of work exclusively in the classics, modern languages, English and mathematics. In 1906 these were restated as seventeen units. Starting in 1911 each candidate would have to take eleven required tests, and four more selected from a list of twelve, including the new subjects already named.

† This was not so ungenerous a gesture to the C.E.E.B. as it has been made to seem. For while the Board had deliberately made the first examinations rather difficult, it had merely suggested (not *set*) a passing grade of 60, and stated at the same time that each institution could set its own passing grade—40 if it liked—and alter the standard later. When Harvard voted to join the

This standard was severe but understandable. The C.E.E.B. tests were only beginning to win a general acceptance; and their reliability was perhaps still open to proof. But after this tentative beginning, the development of cooperative relations proved almost painless. By 1907 the acceptance of C.E.E.B. certificates, which had been granted on a somewhat informal basis as early as 1902, was made a matter of official record in the College catalogue. In 1908 it was announced that Yale would terminate the practice of having its own examiners reread the C.E.E.B. papers of Yale candidates. And in 1910 the general Faculty voted to substitute the C.E.E.B.'s official passing grade of 60% for Yale's 65% requirement.

The way for Yale's decision to become a member of the College Entrance Examination Board was paved by Dean Wright when he found by a comparison that the college work done by those admitted to the Freshman Classes in 1907 and 1908 by the Board examinations had been "of a higher grade than that done by those admitted by the Yale examinations." Then in 1909, after lengthy discussion, the general Faculty voted to "unite with the Governing Board of the Sheffield Scientific School in taking the necessary steps for the University to become a member of the College Entrance Examination Board."

For a few years the College continued to administer its own tests, as a convenience to the many schools which had become accustomed to preparing for Yale examinations. But the considerations in favor of the exclusive use of the C.E.E.B. tests were becoming strong. The number of candidates preferring these tests was growing. The C.E.E.B. now offered examinations in all Yale's required and elective entrance subjects, and the fear that its examinations would be inferior had proved unwarranted. It was clear that the board reached a much wider circle of secondary schools, and was proving itself better equipped, physically and financially, to administer large numbers of examinations in many different localities. Meanwhile many of the College faculty had begun to look

---

Board in 1904, Dean Briggs was careful to point out that the Faculty retained the right to set its grades and accept certificates that fitted its regulations.

upon their entrance examination duties as a distasteful chore. In 1909 Yale had been represented by but one man among the 45 board examiners and by no one at all among the 122 readers. As soon as the College joined, two of the 45 examiners and six of the 140 readers were chosen from Yale. Corwin became the liaison man and champion of the board. In 1914–16 he served as its Vice-Chairman, and in 1915 became Chairman.

The final action, therefore, waited only on Yale's two nearest rivals. In 1915 Professor Hollon A. Farr, Chairman of the Committee on Admissions, reported that Harvard and Princeton had agreed to join Yale in abolishing their own entrance examinations. This enabled Chairman Corwin to announce that in 1916 "Harvard, Princeton and Yale, the last of the Old Guard of examining colleges, surrendered to the College Entrance Examination Board their Old Plan examinations, thus ending, let us trust for all time, that variety in announcement, question-paper, and systems of administration, which has so long and so needlessly baffled the teachers." [18] In this fashion Yale undertook what was to prove an active and lasting and most influential role in the work of the College Entrance Examination Board.

THE PROBLEM OF THE CERTIFICATE SYSTEM

The C.E.E.B. however merely set, read, and graded the examinations required by its member colleges. And even by the new rule put into effect in 1911 Yale had still required fifteen examinations. One unit of history and two in the sciences could now be included. But Yale was not yet accepting high-school certificates for any of these subjects. Least of all was it prepared to recognize shopwork or drawing or commercial subjects. So from the point of view of the high schools and of Yale's Western alumni the College still seemed exceedingly narrow and conservative.

In November 1910—in a startling resolution suggested by Lowell of Harvard and drafted by Presidents Lowell, Hadley, and Hyde of Bowdoin—the Association of New England Colleges recommended that the New England member colleges adopt a compromise certificate-examination system, accepting certificates for the quantity of schoolwork and examining for quality in certain substantial subjects. Was Hadley prepared for this application of his theories? Some entrance requirements, he wrote to a St. Louis high-school principal, were really tests of power to go on with college work—algebra, elementary French, and the use of the English language. "On these things I would examine the candidate." But a much larger number of subjects were tests of attainment, proficiency being evidence of industry rather than of power to do other things. "On these there seems to be no reason to examine at all, and I should accept the certificates without question." * [19]

But the Yale College Faculty made no move to carry his proposal into effect. Instead it was Harvard which had created the opportunity, and now announced that for 1911 it would accept from some students a combination of certificate and examination. By this act the weight and prestige of Harvard were pulled out of the front line of the embattled Eastern colleges. Their position was breached and began to crumble. Pennsylvania had yielded to the certificate idea in 1907. Now Princeton was shaken, and Cornell readjusted its requirements. Soon Brown would admit a wide list of marginal subjects. Bowdoin would accept vocational preparation as well. Dartmouth would cease requiring examinations for entrance. And Amherst would be one of the few to hold fast. From a certain point

---

* "Indeed I should go much further than that, and say that if a boy could write proper English, do sums correctly, and understand accurately the meaning of the languages he was going to use in his advanced studies, the school authorities themselves might decide what other subjects he should be taught in his preparatory years and how he should be taught them.

"If a university is so situated that it can assume the duty of inspecting the high schools from which most of its pupils come it may properly go farther, because it can have teachers eliminated who teach their pupils a number of facts about English literature but leave them spelling badly and saying 'I done it.' . . . Where you do not have this sort of control it seems to me very doubtful whether admission based on certificates is either a wise thing for the colleges or a good thing for the schools. I am certain that a rigid system of examination requirements has tended to attract the boys who are fitted to make their way in the life of a large university."

of view, Harvard's action was entirely reasonable. From another, it was perhaps to be regretted that a common compromise could not have been jointly put forward by the more notable colleges. From the Yale standpoint, what really hurt was that the individualistic new examination arrangements at Harvard were aimed directly at the high schools and the Middle West. Very soon it became evident that Harvard was going to succeed in drawing unprecedented applications from the territory where Yale had always predominated.[20]

This brought anxiety to New Haven—and such excited pressure from the Yale Clubs of the Middle West that in the spring of 1911 Hadley and Jones were made quite uncomfortable, and Jones was moved to the flat defiance of the certificate idea that has already been quoted. Was the College going to do nothing to preserve "Yale's preeminence as a national University"? Dean Jones was admittedly disturbed that in the preceding ten years, out of three thousand Freshmen, but seventy-five had been high-school graduates from the Middle West. He likened Yale's entrance requirements to a protective tariff, and hinted at a horizontal reduction. On tour Stokes and Hadley and all other University speakers never failed to insist that the maintenance of Yale's distinctive character depended on the democracy and virility of its Western constituency. Yet wishing and flattery would not banish the difficulties.

Not only did it seem impossible to accept some of the subjects the high schools were now teaching, but the feeling was that if the traditional preparation was lacking Yale would be unable to teach some of its own subjects. The whole trend of the West was to forget about all subject requirements and insist only on so many units of credit for college entrance. The whole trend of Eastern high schools was to drop Latin and diminish the modern languages and mathematics. But without some insistence on the languages and mathematics it remained to be seen how college students could go on or what the high schools would substitute for discipline. Hadley challenged a critic of the Yale position to give him a single instance of a class in sociology where the students' work was as good as that of a ten-year-old boy in a good common-school class in geography.

Yale had to insist on training, as on quality. Yale wanted men from the high schools—but not just for the sake of numbers. "The most fundamental principle of democracy is that every career should be open to ability." But that did not mean that ability in one line qualified for advancement in another. In short, Yale's President was for accommodation but not for surrender. Could not Yale adopt the Harvard solution?

> If we were still first in the field, I should be ready to try this experiment now, but when we are second in the field and have an alternative plan equally promising I would rather try a new plan than repeat Harvard's experiment. If we trail on after Harvard and the plan is successful, Harvard will get most of the credit. If it is unsuccessful, we shall share the discredit in equal measure. I would rather, in our interests and in the interests of education as a whole, make an experiment of our own.[21]

So began a fresh series of investigations, conferences, adjustments. The College Admissions Committee mailed a questionnaire to all public schools which had sent boys to Yale since 1901, asking why more Western high-school graduates did not apply for Yale. "Although 'distance' was the most frequent response, 'entrance requirements' was a close second, well ahead of 'expense' in third place and 'lack of advertising' in fourth position." [22]

A tempting solution was to permit exceptions to the customary entrance requirements. In the past an occasional candidate—personally known to the authorities—had been admitted under special terms, but the practice had not been officially endorsed. In May 1911 the Faculty for the first time considered admitting for exceptional scholarship without examination in special cases. But this startling recommendation was finally withdrawn to await the creation of a joint College-Sheff committee.

Next the Associated Western Yale Clubs appointed a Committee to examine the high schools of their districts. In 1912 the Grand Rapids Alumni Association set an example soon followed by others of encouraging local high-school boys to try for Yale by making the Yale examinations available locally and without charge.

In the winters of 1911–12 and 1912–13 four positive steps were taken in New Haven. First the Scientific School moved toward the high schools by widening its science alternatives, abandoning its requirement of two years of Latin for the Select Course candidates, and allowing the latter to substitute a science or modern language for the fourth year of mathematics. Secondly the Corporation, having set up University laboratories, set up a University Committee on Admissions, too. This committee was composed of two men representing the College and two men representing Sheff, rather than of four representing a common interest. Under the influence of Chairman Corwin and the C.E.E.B. the two Schools agreed in 1913 to issue the same definition of requirements, to set the same tests in identical subjects, and to use the same schedules and blanks. The third step was to consult with the Connecticut Association of Classical and High School Teachers, and then to write representative school men asking them to suggest revisions in the forthcoming examinations.[23]

The fourth and most striking step was taken when it was agreed for 1914 to make the Yale examinations more general, so as to test and give credit for the whole subject rather than stress failure in some particular part. In addition, the school record was to be given "careful consideration," and school principals were allowed to recommend a student of unusual ability who had followed a course of study differing from the Yale requirements. At the same time the College voted to add medieval and modern history, and physical geography, to the list of alternatives, and to allow a candidate to elect two units of history for entrance.[24]

The wider electives and more general examinations were impressive. But when Yale College so far abandoned its principles as to give consideration to school records and to candidates who had not met the Yale requirements, the public announcement made a tremendous impression in the East. The Boston *Transcript* proclaimed that "the last stronghold of the narrow and highly specialized college examination system in New England has fallen. . . . The university is now for the first time in its history open to the great mass of American boys of college age." The *Harvard Alumni*

Bulletin said that the adoption by Princeton and "now probably by Yale" of the essential features of the Harvard plan ensured "that the strong and ancient traditions of these three colleges shall remain a part of the opportunities of boys from good schools all over the country." The *New Haven Register* employed a provocative metaphor:

> It has long been the belief of the orthodox that those who live as they ought to live here will find open gates when they reach the celestial land, instead of having to storm the barriers and scale the walls. After past [*sic*] two centuries of deliberation, some such conception of the position of Yale . . . seems to have dawned upon its faculty.[25]

But there were those who were still sure that the gates had not been opened wide enough. The fact that Yale was still examining in fifteen units, whereas Harvard and Princeton had come down to four, was not lost on the Western contingent. Harry A. Peters '02, head of the University School of Cleveland, wrote in to say that Yale would continue to lose his students to Harvard. George L. Fox, of the University School of New Haven, replied that this simply confirmed the "effeminate and demoralizing tendency" which was so strong in the West. Earlier he had used the word "pusillanimous." [26]

To the high schools generally, Latin remained another stumbling block. Latin, thought the *Alumni Weekly,* would have to follow Greek. Harvard got around its Latin problem by letting non-Latinists in but giving them instead the B.S. degree. Since these men were not otherwise handicapped, and could obtain all the honors and advantages of Harvard College, the dodge seemed to work. But Yale College had only one degree to offer, and for the B.A. it felt the Latin was essential.*

---

* Harvard had by far the easier problem. In 1906–10 the unsuccessful Lawrence Scientific School was merged with Harvard College, thus making the B.S. available. In the second place Harvard had long since lost a feeling for the organic unity of the curriculum or the superior merit of certain liberal disciplines. By contrast, at Yale both the Scientific School and the College were

It was at this point in the argument that G. B. Adams came forward in 1914 with his plan for a third college for the modern humanities. At the invitation of the Associated Western Yale Clubs he journeyed to Cincinnati and spoke with considerable frankness about Yale's problems. Yale must meet the high schools and get Western boys. But the College could not digest too many. The solution was to enlarge the Select Course, widen its entrance standards, and perhaps make of it a third college. The champions of the West, upon hearing Adams with intense interest, offered motions to endorse his views and to support a reorganization of the curriculum that would bring College and high schools closer together, presumably by dropping Latin. But ex-President Taft and William Lyon Phelps succeeded in blocking such endorsement and such intermeddling. And back in New Haven Adams' third-college plan was rejected.

Meanwhile it could have been argued that it would at least be safe to admit the very top-stand high-school students from the West. Dean Jones had thrown out a veiled suggestion looking in this direction at the same stormy meeting of the Associated Yale Clubs in 1911. But no one seemed prepared to expand the exception in favor of occasional promising men of irregular preparation into a regular policy of admitting the very ablest Western students without examinations.* So the issues of certification and of Latin had still to be fought out.

Yale's Latin requirement, argued Corwin, was now almost unique. But a defender demonstrated that at least fourteen leading colleges still stood by the four-year requirement.[27] Corwin an-

---

strong and self-conscious. Hence Sheff required four years of mathematics of its engineering candidates and three (now) of the Select Course men. And the College insisted on its characteristic languages.

* As for the Western alumni, one gathers that they were not really interested in sending only the brightest. What they wanted was reasonable terms for boys of average scholarship but promising character. So in the 1920's it would be Harvard which would once again get ahead of Yale by adopting a device proposed earlier but rejected at Yale. In the light of after events one cannot but feel that in passing up the proposals of Adams and Jones Yale had missed two golden opportunities.

swered that Latin had become symbolic and that what mattered now was the attitude and general reputation of Yale in the West. Could not the College accept men with less Latin and give the remaining years of instruction in Latin in College? Latin had lost its utilitarian justification, so what the colleges should insist on was not the Latin but the degree of preparedness which had always been associated with it. In turn the high school should "devise means of making the pursuit of the sciences and vocational studies develop powers and qualities equal to those found in the study of the older disciplines which they replace." College requirements ought "to coincide as closely as possible with the normal high school course." And the high-school subjects, in turn, should be graded into three or four categories, according to the degree of discipline or information possessed by each.

But the College was not ready to teach prep-school Latin. And the New England High School Superintendents, after hearing Corwin, launched into a general attack on colleges for not giving them a larger voice and accepting vocational studies. So Corwin concentrated on getting a reduction in the number of entrance examinations, with school recommendations to be accepted for the rest of the desired preparatory studies. And by 1915 Dean Jones had come around to support this Harvard-style compromise.[28]

On the issue of straight certification the Faculty remained adamant. For, aside from Yale's peculiar situation in the West, the College was no longer suffering for lack of applicants, and the arguments against the certificate system seemed much stronger than those in favor. In 1915 it was decisively voted that "this Faculty sees no practical way to admit students to College entirely without examination." Nevertheless, with Harvard drawing ever more successfully from the Middle West, and with the graduates beginning to clamor against Latin as well as examinations, it was plain that some further accommodations would have to be made. The upshot was that, following the lead of Corwin, Hadley, and Jones, the College authorities decided to strike a bargain that would give the schools more credit and more liberty yet would preserve the subjects and disciplinary values in which the College was most interested. And for 1916, at the same time that they gave up their own Yale examinations to the C.E.E.B., the College Faculty agreed "without a dissenting vote" to adopt an alternative plan for admission.[29]

This New Plan made the following provisions. In order to qualify a candidate had to submit a satisfactory school record. He was then required to take comprehensive examinations in not more than four subjects. The College would then admit those candidates who were accepted without "conditions," * while allowing those who were rejected to try to enter under the Old Plan of fifteen specific tests.

In practical terms this meant that in school a candidate would have to pursue a satisfactory four-year course including languages, mathematics, science, and history. Then for entrance to Yale College he would be examined in Latin, mathematics, French or German, English. For entrance to Sheff he would be examined in one subject from each of four groups: (1) English; (2) mathematics; (3) Latin, French, German, or Spanish; (4) physics or chemistry or botany and biology or mechanical drawing or history. The College's plan was therefore similar to Princeton's requirement of four fixed subjects, whereas Sheff's plan was similar to the Harvard system of allowing alternative choices. Both schemes recognized the problems of the public schools and allowed them considerable freedom in determination of methods and curriculum, and both there-

---

* In the Yale practice this device had been made to serve two ends. On the one hand it had been used *in terrorem* against the schools, and to discourage candidates from divagation. Thus C. W. Mendell, trained at Roxbury Latin School, had taken examinations which qualified him for the Sophomore Class in Harvard. When he then presented himself at New Haven in 1900, Dean Wright sternly assigned him to the Freshman Class, "in the conditional division." In the normal course of events if the students did well such "conditions" were forgotten and nothing more was said. But Dean Jones, who had also been conditioned in his day, still harbored resentment at the treatment.

On the other hand, the same device allowed the College to admit quite a group of men annually who had failed in one or two subjects or had obviously been handicapped by inferior school preparation. The College, however, had not received public credit for this latitude—and by 1916 the usefulness of conditions was probably past.[30]

410

fore applied the certificate idea in a modified and reasonable form. On this point Yale's Western critics were at last mollified.

WORKING YOUR WAY THROUGH COLLEGE

The problem of the cost of a Yale education had been receiving increased attention. This problem was not of Yale's making. In 1888 tuition charges had been set at $155, and these were not changed until 1914, when they were raised only to $160 for incoming students. Meanwhile the price of ordinary necessities had been rising somewhat, and the opportunities for luxury expenditures had increased remarkably. But what really made such variable costs an issue was the rise of tax-supported and free-tuition colleges nearer home. The spread of this low-cost higher education, especially through the Middle West, was adding a financial barrier to those of subject matter and distance. The private seaboard colleges were in danger of being regarded as plutocratic.

Yale had always been a place where a poor boy could go and make his way, financially as well as socially and athletically. To foster the democratic traditions of the College was one of the first objects of the Hadley Administration. There followed a whole series of efforts to hold down student expenses, increase student earnings, and help out deserving individuals by gift scholarships or loans. To keep down the costs of studying, eating, and sleeping, the University not only refused to raise tuition charges but struggled valiantly to run a reasonable Commons without too great complaints or deficits; and the College developed a dormitory policy to give adequate accommodation to all. As we have seen, this was connected with the drive against the Sophomore societies and against the Hutchinson—and hence represented also the policy of keeping Yale's social opportunities opened to boys of modest means.*

* A statistical investigation by Secretary Stokes in 1915 proved that Yale had been relatively successful in the matter of costs. One quarter of the College undergraduates spent less than $800 a year, another quarter between $1,000 and $1,100, and only 10 per cent spent over $1,600. In Sheff there seemed to be more men at the two extremes. The median expenditure was

The opportunities for loans, scholarships, and paying jobs were at once brought together to be administered and developed by a single office. This was first called the Bureau of Self-Help (1900–03), then the Bureau of Self-Help and Appointments (1903–08), then the Bureau of Appointments (1908–). Established under the Reverend C. L. Kitchel '62, the Bureau of Self-Help was first asked to administer beneficiary aid in the College, to organize opportunities for self-support, and to help find positions for graduates: functions which had previously been carried informally by the President and Deans, the Cooperative Association, and Dwight Hall. In 1902–03 Director Kitchel was associated with the Bursar and Professor Goodell in order to administer the private emergency loan funds formerly in Goodell's charge. In 1910 the Corporation placed the scholarships connected with alumni associations, schools, and localities in its charge. And in 1914 the bureau was made a bureau of the Secretary's Office, with an advisory committee reorganized to include the Secretary, the Deans of the College, Scientific School, and Graduate School, and the Chairmen of the two Student Councils.[32]

At the beginning the bureau announced that there had never been more chances for a student to earn his way. In 1900, to advertise and improve this situation, the bureau issued a pamphlet, *Self-Help at Yale,* and thereafter this was regularly reprinted and revised for circulation among candidates for entrance and assistance. In 1902–03 the bureau reported known earnings of $38,116, with unreported earnings raising the total to perhaps $50,000–60,000. By 1915–16 the known student earnings would be $221,870, of which $37,146 had been secured directly through the bureau. And

---

about $1,000 for everything except vacations. Altogether Stokes thought that the costs of a Yale education had risen just about 10 per cent in twenty-five years.

Hadley thought an allowance of $500 made College quite possible; an allowance of $800–$1,000 avoided any risk to health through unwise economies; and for full enjoyment of college $1,200 could safely be entrusted to a boy of steady habits. But anything above that, he warned Yale parents, was of doubtful advantage or an invitation to dissipation.[31]

the bureau confidently asserted that no student properly prepared and sufficiently in earnest need forego a college education at Yale. For the best enjoyment of college benefits the possession of a small reserve fund, equivalent to the cost of tuition, was of course desirable. In any case the potential candidate of limited resources could now determine quite accurately, either in cash or in effort, what it would cost to come to Yale. If he cared to investigate, he would discover at least that he was not barred.

Yale's policy on scholarships and student loans was as clearly defined and effectively developed. On such matters Hadley was positive—and of a Spartan temper. No poor boy should be barred. But equally no aid should be given that was not earned. Boys should therefore repay any University help, either by exceptional scholarship and performance in the community or by cash repayment after graduation. Hadley therefore favored new loan scholarships and the conversion of some of the older scholarships into this type of grant. And, beginning in 1908, the Administration began to accumulate and set up such funds.[33]

Meanwhile, starting in 1903 with the Yale Club in Chicago, a movement had got under way among the scattered alumni associations to establish scholarships or to pay the expenses of boys from their own localities. In 1911 the Corporation voted to offer fifteen freshman-tuition scholarships to the graduates of Connecticut public secondary schools, and two more to graduates of New Haven public schools, "in order to strengthen our connection with the high schools of Connecticut." Already there were a number of high-school scholarships and endowed scholarships open to everyone. By 1916 twenty-eight students, many from the West and South, were reaching Yale via the alumni association scholarships; and there were about forty graduates of New Haven and other Connecticut high schools holding additional scholarships. In the same year Secretary Embree of the Bureau of Appointments reported that Yale was annually granting scholarships, fellowships, and loans totaling more than $96,000. He indicated also that a considerable portion of this sum was being allocated to Freshmen, since they were unacquainted with the facilities for self-help.

413

The results of this fifteen-year argument under Hadley's gentle urging were therefore a substantial compromise. Yale College had not abolished the old style examinations, for many preparatory schools were geared to and might continue to prefer them. On the other hand it had agreed to uniform examinations, widely and impartially administered by the C.E.E.B. Next, it had opened an alternative channel of admission by four comprehensive examinations on the most valuable academic subjects. This New Plan transferred emphasis from detailed knowledge to general scholarship, gave to the schools some of the latitude they asked, and at the same time gave to the best high-school boys the hope that they would not be barred by irregularity of preparation. Finally the University had taken steps to keep open a wide gate in the barrier created by the relatively forbidding costs of an education at Yale.

Whether Yale had delayed too long in making these gestures was a question. The great mass of the high-school students probably did not realize or feel equal to the financial opportunities at Yale. Some of the high-school heads were openly resentful that the certificate system pure and simple had not been adopted. The College still insisted on Latin but was perhaps impotent to save it. There was a further question whether the Eastern colleges would stick together to arrest the drift from the modern languages and mathematics. In any case, if the New Plan proved at all attractive, what was Yale going to do with its increased numbers? Would the College be able to preserve either its social unity or its solidity of curriculum under the changed conditions? The new compromise raised these doubts at the very moment that it laid to rest some old and trying disagreements. But by and large the arrangements for 1916 were hailed by the vast majority with satisfaction and relief.

CHAPTER 21 · THE RETURN TO REQUIRED STUDIES

The courses of action open to Yale College seem to reduce themselves to three: We may turn more positively toward the practical, or we may turn away from the practical, or we may refuse for the present to make a choice.
—Report "On the Policy of Yale College," 22 April 1915

In the years 1914 and 1915 the Permanent Officers of Yale College held some discussions, and in 1917 they embarked on a policy that had much of the appearance of a reaction. For they were committing the College once again to prescription. And the subjects that they first prescribed were the classics, modern languages, mathematics, and the elementary sciences. Vocationalism was taboo. Even the promising Reform of 1911—that deft grouping of Freshman and Sophomore subjects to match the major interests of undergraduates: linguistic, scientific, or social—was cavalierly abandoned.

The pendulum, one is tempted to say, had swung. The liberals must have been out and the reactionaries in control. From 1876 to 1900 had been the first great swing: a swing toward freedom of choice, diversity, specialization, and preprofessional courses. In 1901–03 had come the pause, and then the pendulum had started perceptibly to swing back. Not in all things at once, or equally, yet on the whole back. Now it was gathering speed and rushing toward the traditional extreme.

Yet it is to be doubted that academic motion is really so repetitious and futile as the years slip by. Indeed, after considered observation, I incline instead to liken the faculty to a ship's crew, sailing their vessel through all weathers toward an invisible mark. Now shaken by a sudden storm, again set far off course by the irresistible

415

sweep of some great popular tide, the College yet plows on. Ever and again, as the helmsman is relieved, the ship shows a different motion. Always when the wind is adverse she must tack. Then, like a pendulum, she does seem to swing: back and forth across the desired course. Remember that education is prevailingly up-wind work. At least it seemed so at Yale under Captain Hadley.

Suddenly, about 1913–15, the weather thickened, and the College found itself pitching in a boisterous and uncertain sea. Sharp gusts of criticism had begun to lash the vessel. Abroad the black cloud of war was blotting out an entire horizon. After hesitating almost a year the College came sharply about and began to drive into the rising wind. Momentarily a few men on deck could be seen lashing things down and making all secure. Then the heavens opened, and the deluge of war blotted Yale College from sight.

The precise date the Faculty as a whole first showed signs of uneasiness—of dissatisfaction with the way things had been going —is hard to ascertain. From the point of view of such questions, the session of the full Professors on 23 April 1914 was unusually significant. On this occasion

> On invitation of the Dean, Prof. Morris presented some considerations on general questions of College policy emphasizing particularly the need of determining what are the peculiar advantages and limitations of Yale College. Prof. Adams called attention to the influence on Yale of its geographical situation, and to the undergraduate life of the College as its most distinctive element of strength. After a general discussion, in which a large proportion of those present participated, adjourned.[1]

So G. B. Adams had spoken once again of the value to the University of Yale College, and E. P. Morris had emphasized the value to the College of knowing its own character and mind. Yet what had aroused these two Professors to speak so earnestly about the place and duty of Yale College in the nation? And what accounted for the evident concern of "a large proportion" of their fellow Officers? Apparently it was a growing uneasiness stemming from many

416

sources. With Adams it was the conviction that modification of the entrance standards would bring in so many students, of such disparate interests and preparation, as to threaten the social and intellectual solidarity of the College. What concerned Morris was the particular menace to the style of liberal and linguistic education for which Yale had always stood. What worried Dean Jones, in his turn, was the administrative consequences of increased numbers, for ever since his arrival in 1909 the Freshman Classes had been growing. The Chapel had become overcrowded, and transfer students had had to be excused from attending. Already there was a serious dormitory shortage for Freshmen and Sophomores. The classroom divisions were getting too big. New men would have to be hired for the faculty. As for the other Permanent Officers, they also had their reservations about the state of undergraduate affairs. But chiefly they were moved to concern by the shafts of criticism that were increasingly being loosed against the College.

A number of these criticisms have already been encountered, for they had to do with entrance examinations, the requirement of Latin, and the refusal to admit vocational studies into the old-fashioned curriculum. Still other criticisms now stressed the poor quality of Freshman-Sophomore teaching, the lack of adequate guidance by the faculty, and the lack of objective in the College course. In January 1914, addressing the Northwestern Yale Alumni Association, the railroad builder James J. Hill had branded the American common-school system "a dismal failure."

> The education a boy or girl needs is something that will help him to make a living in the lot in which his or her life is cast. . . . Our public school education must be more practical. . . . Your college education should be followed up by your taking up in a serious way the problems of your communities and your nation. . . . If I were running an institution of learning I would simplify the curriculum and get all the facts classified into those that are true and those that are not.

Hill had never attended college and the last sentence alone ought to have revealed his educational innocence. But as a railroad statesman he had been given an honorary LL.D. by Yale in 1910.

And in the popular view a man so successful in business automatically qualified as an expert on things educational. Hence an immense furor in the public press and—what must have been discouraging to the Yale faculty—not a few signs locally that he had made an impression. "So much of what he is quoted as saying is the opinion of many other less qualified judges," observed the *Alumni Weekly*, that the university man "will not lightly lay it aside." [2]

The second alumnus to trouble the academic waters was Dr. John Rogers '87, who in a communication to the *Alumni Weekly* asked: "Can I Send My Son to Yale?" In this article the vigorous doctor first reviewed the program that "Tom," an average boy, might take—then criticized the ideal of "mental discipline"—finally came out against the Latin requirement and concluded: "Yale needs a new educational ideal." [3]

A Senior and a recent graduate promptly tore Dr. Rogers' article to pieces. They pointed out that Tom was lazy and unambitious and his program was bad only because he had carefully avoided all the hard and worth-while courses in order to take all the elementary courses and "guts." Yale did not need a new educational ideal so much as some of the alumni "may need a new idea about education." But to no avail. Graduate after graduate took up the cause of poor Tom, adding his own criticisms, assigning his own pet remedies. Tom should have been given better advice. Tom should have been better taught. Tom ought to have taken the Select Course instead—this, naturally, from a Sheff graduate. Anyhow, it wasn't Tom's fault. "Yale simply failed to help and direct wisely a fine, good boy, and gave him a hodge-podge education based on Heaven-knows-what kind of a pedagogical theory." [4]

Two demands that cropped up sooner or later in every educational discussion, and that were part of the theme song of the preparatory-school men, were for better teaching and faculty guidance. The Faculty had already taken cognizance of dissatisfaction with lower-class studies, and meant now to improve the personnel as well as the content of the Freshman-Sophomore courses. As for guidance, many of the graduates seemed to be thinking in terms of vocational preparation. One asked for a course in character building, another for a course in public affairs. Still a third view was that the College should advise or even force lowerclassmen to choose their upper-class programs more coherently and wisely.[5]

One thing had always stood between a Freshman and wise selection of his upper-class courses—or so it seemed to certain individuals in the Faculty. This was the fact that the limitations on his choices as a Freshman prevented his getting any experience of certain upper-class fields of study in advance of having to elect. So Professor Bakewell, head of the philosophy department, proposed to Dean Jones that the College give an encyclopedic lecture course on the sciences and the social sciences, each subject to be presented by an expert and all Freshmen to be required to attend. On request Bakewell nominated the subjects and some lecturers. The Course of Study Committee sympathized with the objective but questioned the method. The language people perhaps objected to being left out. In any case, the Freshman Faculty and the Committee turned it down decisively.[6]

The result was that, instead of instituting a sort of Freshman survey course, the College let the University experiment with two other devices. On the one hand Joseph B. Thomas '03 came forward with a gift of $10,000 to subsidize lectures each autumn on the "real purpose" of a college course, on the "opportunities open" to each student, and on the "responsibilities" of every student taking such a course. The addresses did not need to exceed twenty minutes in length; they were to be given by "men of public distinction and personal charm"; and were to be open to all but required of Freshmen. In the second place, Hadley encouraged the development of the Bureau of Appointments; and by 1915 Edwin R. Embree '06, Executive Assistant to the Secretary, was advising Seniors on their choice of profession with sufficient success so that a good many lowerclassmen were attending his talks and getting some incidental advice on their choice of electives, too.[7]

While such forms of guidance were being tried, the Professors took hold of the underlying problem: What ought the ideal college education to be? And what did Yale College propose to stand for? On this the President's pronouncements and the Thomas Lectures cast only a fitful light. If the principles at stake were not to go by default, together with the Faculty's authority over the curriculum, it was quite evidently up to them to make up their own minds and prepare to stand by the consequences.

An immediate consequence was an intensification of discussion about Honors and the development of the Honors compromise that has already been described. But a much larger number were concerned over the lower-class offerings and resolved to restate the requirements in such a way that the purpose of college would be brought home to all the undergraduates—the average students as well as the superior. Yale College should make its curriculum so definite, and its advice to students so positive, that not even strangers would have room to doubt. Then the entrance requirements themselves would emerge as a logical necessity rather than an arbitrary imposition. Aroused to such possibilities the Professors appointed a special committee of five, with Professor Morris as chairman, to investigate and report.[8]

These Permanent Officers appreciated the difficulties. In particular they realized that the Faculty was divided. There were those who had accepted the 1911 reform with enthusiasm and now looked forward to developing upper-class opportunities for the able. Dana was still Chairman of the Course of Study Committee, and in 1913 his Committee had been empowered to exempt students from the strict application of the major and minor requirements. The Freshman opportunities had been enlarged by the admission of Spanish as a possible alternative. And to the Sophomore alternatives the history of philosophy had been added, with biology and geology to follow. Under Dana, evidently, the trend would be toward wider opportunities.

On the other hand, many of the younger men, and some of the full professors, had thought of the Dana-Day group arrangements as merely temporizing with vocationalism and so were impatient to proceed to a more positive order of things. The more conservative believed in a strict, disciplined, required course, especially for

Freshmen and Sophomores—and with this view the Morris committee sympathized. But caution would be necessary. An influential element were persuaded that the two philosophies of education might be combined. Mendell held to that opinion. As the able and persuasive young Charles Seymour put it:

> Our admissions test should be democratic in the sense that it should give equal opportunity to all candidates to demonstrate their qualities, whether they come from a Western high school or an Eastern preparatory school. The first year or two years of our undergraduate curriculum should be democratic, in that it should prescribe for all the same or similar training. Those who have then proved themselves the actual or potential intellectual aristocrats, have the right to ask that they receive the attention and inspiration that their qualities merit.[9]

Given such diversity of views, Professor Morris' report "On the Policy of Yale College" made no attempt to dictate that policy or to set up a specific curriculum.[10] Rather it presented two alternative philosophies in the form of a very positive dilemma. For it was Morris' plan that the Professors, when confronted with the committee's dilemma, would find it so clearly described and so cogently argued that they would be made uncomfortable—and feel compelled to choose. The choice, he said, was between the vocational and the nonvocational.

On the one hand, Yale College might so select, and so arrange, the subjects of instruction as to "make them contribute directly toward vocational success." Morris did not caricature the idea. Such an aim did not necessarily imply straight technical training. Rather the reasonable method would be to give a student the chance to take those studies which, without being in themselves distinctly professional, would lay the foundation for his professional training. With this in view the College might establish closer relations with the public school system, and introduce more semiprofessional studies, to be given by its own instructors or selected from the courses offered in the professional Schools. The occupational and social advantages were evident, but the policy would tend to subordinate the College to the technical and professional Schools "as the Arts course is subordinated in a state university." That last touch must have come from G. B. Adams: it was a favorite comparison.

On the other hand, Morris observed, Yale College might so shape its work as "to make it contribute primarily to a richer intellectual and emotional life, without immediate reference to the particular career which the student may expect to follow." And Morris suggested reviving—with necessary changes—an ideal which he had found described in the Yale catalogue for the year 1846–47:

> The object of the system of instruction to the undergraduates in the College, is not to give a *partial* education, consisting of a few branches only; nor on the other hand, to give a *superficial* education, containing a little of almost everything; nor to *finish* the details of either a professional or a practical education; but to *commence* a *thorough* course . . . [containing] those subjects only which ought to be understood by every one who aims at a thorough education. The principles of science and literature are a common foundation of all high intellectual attainments. They give that furniture, and discipline, and elevation to the mind, which are the best preparation for the study of a profession or of the operations which are peculiar to the higher mercantile, manufacturing, or agricultural establishments.[11]

To carry through this conception, Morris pointed out, would give Yale College a distinctive function in the University and a very high rank among American colleges, but at the cost of some narrowing of influence and loss of numbers. Indeed his committee wished to emphasize that the rejection or adoption of either ideal would entail losses and limitations. By choosing a definite field Yale College would narrow its range and scope. Nevertheless a clearly defined policy would be worth all it cost.

Morris reminded his colleagues that the Faculty would soon have to make up its mind about entrance requirements and the Combined Programs: decisions which could hardly be made intelligently "until we decide what the work here is to be." He called attention to the inconsistency of including in the traditional program practical music, or courses for those expecting to teach Latin, or courses in accounting and insurance, or methods of religious education. No doubt the professional or nonprofessional character of such offerings depended upon the spirit and aim of the instructor. But how was the instructor to know which method to adopt, without the help of some guiding principle? Taking all such matters into consideration, on behalf of his committee Morris wished to lay before his colleagues three resolutions:

1. Resolved that Yale College shall direct its policy more distinctly than at present toward vocational training.

2. Resolved that it shall be the policy of Yale College to give a nonvocational education.

3. Resolved that the time is not ripe for the adoption of a distinct policy for Yale College.

The third of these resolutions was a shrewd inspiration, and its proposal a trifle unfair. For it hit Hadley's weakest point; it struck the very note that the alumni were starting to pound so hard that all Yale was beginning to wince. Surely the committee could not mean the Faculty or the Administration to concede that it couldn't make up its own mind.

That seemed to leave just two possible policies. And between the two the scales could hardly be level. For even a champion of preprofessional preparation could scarcely claim that the combined law and medical programs were working to satisfaction. And what was to be done, under such a philosophy, with the future businessmen or with the undecided? It took the Professors just two meetings to reach the decision that Morris had planned they should. They did not adopt the committee's second resolution verbatim. Instead, "On motion of the President, Voted, that the subjects of instruction should be chosen with reference to their intellectual stimulus to the students, rather than with reference to the prospective utility of the knowledge acquired." [12] Note the Hadleian touch. Given his adherence, the Professors were apparently content to allow the President to phrase their policy. But at once Professor Morris introduced the specific recommendations that he had been holding back for the occasion.

His specific recommendations were three. To begin with, each department was to revise its course offerings so as to make sure that all of them were suitable "to the ideal and purpose of the college." Secondly, each department was to simplify and improve its work by the establishment, or by the strengthening, of an introductory course to be taught by instructors specially chosen for such work. As for Freshman and Sophomore years, it was recommended that the Committee on the Course of Study "be requested to propose a plan for the *positive* recommendation of courses, specifying certain introductory courses or certain alternatives, to be required of all students or of all candidates for Honors."

This left the specific requirements for debate and negotiation. In due course Morris' committee named its own medicine, the Professors discussed and amended the proposals, the Course of Study Committee reduced them, and on 15 December 1915 the general Faculty adopted a surprisingly innocuous plan.[13]

This plan canceled the group arrangements that had governed lower-class choice since 1911, and substituted in their place the straight requirement that all Freshmen should take a modern language and mathematics or a science, and all Sophomores should take a modern or ancient language and a science. Yet the old group alternatives of the 1911 Reform had been so organized that all of the Freshman-Sophomore groups included these studies, plus English or history for all Freshmen and a social science for all Sophomores. So the net product of all this complication was merely a pair of requirements in each year, where before there had been three. And a year and a half of effort, directed toward making the College return to first principles, had apparently wound up in more liberty and less principle than ever—especially as the old "natural" grouping of subjects had been jettisoned.[14]

Yet before we allow ourselves to dismiss this affair as much ado about nothing, certain facts merit attention. The first is political: Morris and his supporters had been trespassing on the prerogatives of the Course of Study Committee and had been constrained to put their ideas in a form acceptable to Dana and the general Faculty. Next it would be well to notice that the abolition of the natural groupings represented a defeat for vocationalism. The vocationalism involved in trying to group studies by way of foundation and preparation for three broad types of career had been a diluted form of vocationalism indeed. Yet the theory of the Reform of 1911 had looked toward student interests and utility. Now that *utility* was expressly repudiated. In its place the Professors had voted for subjects chosen with reference to their "intellectual stimulus" to the student. They had returned to a preference for liberating and stimulating *disciplines,* as against courses more immediately practical. "The principles of science and literature are the common foundation of all high intellectual attainments"—Morris had quoted the catalogue of 1846–47. And he had been applauded.*

Finally, where the natural groupings had tended to conceal a triple requirement in each of the lower-class years, the Faculty were now more blunt. What had been disguised was to become a "must." And what had been justified in the interest of student types and student aptitudes was henceforward to be defended on no such specious or dangerous grounds. Instead, it was to be required because a liberal education demanded it, and the Faculty, not the student, knew what such an education should contain.

In short, this apparent simplification in lower-class requirements concealed an ideological revolution. What had really changed or been clarified was the Faculty attitude toward what they were *trying* to do. If for the moment the means of doing it remained almost unaltered, that was diplomatic and deceptive and could hardly last. In fact, it was already in the process of change. For while the Professors had been discussing the Freshman-Sophomore groups of subjects, they had realized that their theory was still less compatible with the premedical and prelegal courses. Accordingly they had authorized their committee on the B.A. to go into this question, and the elimination of Combined Programs had at

---

* As Billy Phelps somewhat less elegantly put it: "I thank God I learned nothing useful in Yale College."

last been started.[15] Simultaneously a strong defense against the invasion of the curriculum by military or premilitary subjects was begun. And the Professors, following up the improvement of lower-class instruction, voted to ask the departments to outline to Dean Jones "plans by which they could, with additional sums of money, improve the quality of instruction in Freshman and Sophomore years." [16]

The Faculty did not revolutionize the curriculum in December 1915. But they assumed a far firmer control of it. They said they knew how to improve it. And they were preparing, apparently, to spend money on Freshmen and Sophomores that it had not occurred to them to spend on Honors men. A further modification in actual requirements could hardly be very far off.

The new proposals came after a year of confusion, anxiety, and disintegration, as the European war first shadowed, then invaded the campus. For a while the Faculty had stood off the mounting demands for military training, and had then been forced to concede academic credit for such training. For a time the Dean had refused to let students enlist or join the Allied Services, but the students took to leaving without permission. Faculty members were beginning to receive calls, or to consider what they might do. It was hardly the moment for so theoretical and remote a business as discussing the B.A. curriculum.

Yet there were factors favoring such an undertaking. Whatever the momentary exigencies of war, the philosophy of the curriculum had been pretty well settled. Already the Faculty had taken some steps to improve the quality of Freshman and Sophomore instruction by moving against the tutoring schools, by exploring for able instructors, and by considering giving more weight to distinction in teaching in certain lower-class appointments.[17]

The decisive action, however, had been the reorganization of the Course of Study Committee, with the retirement of Dana as its chairman. For years the hand of Eddie Dana had guided the Faculty in much of its most important work. Chairman of the Committee on Ways and Means, as well as of the Committee on the Course of Study, he had been the single most influential professor in Academic councils, Dean Jones not excepted. Coatless on the coldest days yet sensitive to the mood and needs of the times—busy, executive, persistent—from his old office in Peabody Museum Dana had "managed" many of the College's affairs. Now he was about to retire. For his last year he kept his chairmanship of Ways and Means but relinquished the Course of Study to younger hands.[18]

The new chairman was not E. P. Morris of the special committee, who was himself to retire from teaching in 1919, but the brilliant and sensitive young English Professor, Chauncey Brewster Tinker. Those who have heard the man will recall the intense inner feeling, the white fire of the poet, beneath an outward austerity. They will remember too his eighteenth-century courtesy, and his insistence on conduct becoming a gentleman. Under the charm there was the touch of authority, and he believed in order and due form. Later he would become recognized as an accomplished parliamentarian.

In 1914–15 Tinker had served on Morris' original committee of five on the future policy of the College. Likewise he had served under Dana, as well as under Professor Gustav Gruener on the committee on the B.A. to which the revision of the Combined Programs had been entrusted. Now his assumption of the chairmanship vacated by Dana, coupled with other changes in the membership, meant that the new committee was composed of three language-literature men and two from the biological sciences, with the language men carrying the greater personal weight. What was most important was the fact that Tinker was a humanist, a student of Johnson, and an ardent believer in the classics—also a devout and humble Christian, a lover of France, and a follower of the arts.* [19]

* Among the new courses recommended that winter by Tinker's committee and accepted by the Faculty were English and Continental Philosophy, Medieval Architecture, Renaissance Painting, the French Novel after 1850, and New Testament Greek. In November 1917 the Art School courses would also, for the first time at Yale, be admitted into the scheme for upper-class majors and minors.

In 1917 the first action of the Tinker committee, once the military training question had been settled, was to get control of its own procedures by securing from the Faculty specific rules to govern the introduction of new courses. Then after months of considering what kind of an education Yale College ought to give all of its students, and therefore what courses ought to be required of all its students, Professor Tinker on behalf of his committee next brought before the Faculty the following "Proposed Required Courses in College":

1. Greek or Latin—Greek A3 or Latin A1
2. French or German—including A5
3. English—A1
4. European History—A1
5. American History—B2
6. Economics—A1
7. Philosophy or Psychology—A2 or A4
8. & 9. Two of the following:
   Mathematics—A1
   Physics—A1
   Biology—A1
10. Either:
   Chemistry—A1
   Geology A1 and B3 including Descriptive Astronomy [20]

Evidently the new requirements were to be in terms of specific and rather elementary courses as well as of subjects. This disregarded Clive Day's warning about the inevitable unpopularity of required courses in an otherwise elective curriculum. Certain new regulations were also suggested. Freshmen had to study either Greek or Latin; they had to take either mathematics or a science; and the study of modern languages was required to be consecutive.

The Tinker proposals demanded a tremendous amount of required work: greater than had been asked at any time since President Hadley had come into office. This new ten-course program would require thirty hours in addition to, and generally prior to, the continuing twelve-hour major-minor. In 1911 the Faculty had ventured to arrange the whole of the first two years, allowing in each year a choice between three alternative groupings, and within each of these groups still further choices. Now Yale College would be demanding not merely a reasonable coordination of the appropriate subjects but *ten specific subjects*. In each subject everyone would take the identical course, and everyone would have to take either Greek or Latin. In defiance of alumni criticism, the Faculty would insist on Latin. Since the famous Corporation ruling of 1903 some three-quarters of the Freshmen annually had taken Latin. But that was because they were required to continue three school subjects and did not wish to take mathematics. Now, if mathematics ceased to be an alternative and were added to the sciences, the result would be that every undergraduate would have to take not only Latin but mathematics and two sciences, or three sciences, as well. Again, almost all Freshmen had elected English, and more than half had taken European history, but now these majority practices were to be made universal.[21]

Insofar as this ten-course program represented the basic subjects and the indispensable disciplines—the experience that could *not* be spared from any liberal education—it would be as good and necessary for one man as for another. Yet the fact remained that some of the better prepared would already have been taught the materials in one or more of the ten requirements. Logic and prudence suggested that such advanced men be given the opportunity to anticipate by examination. Five courses were accordingly so marked: both histories, physics, chemistry, and mathematics. Still a sixth requirement—French or German—could be in part so fulfilled. Having defined what a B.A. education should contain, Professor Tinker's committee was willing that its contents be acquired outside of Yale.

Yet one wonders about that willingness. The modern language concession was a little disingenuous. For passing the examination did not remove the obligation to continue with French or German: all that was gained was admission to a more advanced course. Again, one wonders how many schools taught history, or the sciences, near enough to the way Yale Freshmen were taught to make their anticipation really feasible. None evidently taught Latin or Greek or English or economics in more than a remotely acceptable way. Were these subjects so *necessary* they had to be required, yet so *feeble in themselves* that only the teachers at Yale could give them power? Five subjects could be anticipated: a year's work. Yet nowhere was there any suggestion of a three-year B.A. for the able.

One draws the conclusion that two things were regarded as essential for the B.A. The first was four years in New Haven, and the second a proper curriculum, properly weighted along broad, old-fashioned, and elementary lines. The ten suggested courses were not all as ancient as Latin or as elementary as second-year French or as unpleasant as first-year economics. But they were hardly light entertainment. Such charm as they would have for the helpless victims would have to come from intrinsic merit, and from the superlative ability of some teachers to rise above the unpleasant fact of compulsion, and their own distaste for teaching the same matter over and over again.

One further comment is in order. In the fall of 1916 the first handful of students had entered under the new alternative admissions arrangements. Thus the Tinker proposals were brought forward just after the College had felt compelled to compromise the entrance requirement issue. If the New Plan really attracted high-school candidates, it seemed certain that many of these men would be of limited backgrounds and irregularly prepared. Presumably their vocational enthusiasms would also be marked. One obvious solution would have been to go along with the popular tide in College studies, too.

But just because the conservative interest had been forced to compromise on the entrance issue did not mean that Yale College had to surrender its ideal of a liberal education. Challenged in its beliefs, Yale College ought to reassert those beliefs in the domain where it still controlled—in its own curriculum. As Morris had observed, perhaps this would repel applicants, reduce numbers. So be it. Whether it would prove possible to reimpose homogeneity in this way was a question. And whether it would be safe to adopt such a policy of exclusiveness without providing a third college for modern studies was still worth asking. In any case, would the alumni allow the Officers of Yale College to turn the clock back?

The Faculty heard the Tinker report, discussed it once, amended it by requiring Sophomores as well as Freshmen to take mathematics or a science, and then voted it through.[22] In less than two full meetings, and apparently without serious debate, they adopted a program of the most far-reaching implications. The principles behind it were idealistic but their application was drastic indeed. Now for *required studies* exactly one half of the entire four years had been commandeered. Yale College had not even contemplated so definite a curriculum since the middle of the 1890's.

Even given the entrance situation, the speed of the Faculty seems incredible. Incredible, that is, until one looks at the date. The program was presented on 27 April 1917 and voted through on 10 May. On 6 April the country had declared war on Germany.

PART FIVE:
WAR AND
REORGANIZATION

CHAPTER 22 · AMERICAN HIGHER EDUCATION AND WAR

Be it enacted . . . *That all male persons from sixteen years of age to fifty, shall bear arms and duly attend all musters and military exercises . . . except . . . church officers, the rector, tutors and students at the collegiate school, master of art . . .*

— An Act for Regulating the Militia, May 1741

We rejoice that the motive which led so many to the war, was not the love of reputation nor the love of adventure, nor any lower motive; but mingled with and rising above all, a pure, disinterested patriotism. And we rejoice to believe that this patriotism was kindled under the influence and within the walls of their Alma Mater.

— THEODORE DWIGHT WOOLSEY, 26 July 1865

THE ROLE OF OUR COLLEGES in the first World War has been rather taken for granted. The service record of students and graduates is the measure accepted and commemorated by each college constituency. As for the period of neutrality and mobilization, that is remembered for its excitement and confusion. Those who lived through it in New Haven recall that in June 1914 hardly a handful dreamt of war. In 1916–17 the nation and the campus were still enmeshed in uncertainties and a chaos of half-formed plans. Yet by 1918 the graduates, students, professors, and administrators of Yale were in uniform everywhere. Behind closed doors the University's laboratories worked for the Government. Secretary Stokes and Director Chittenden, among others, were abroad. An Army major and a retired rear admiral were in residence. The campus was an

435

armed camp, with strangers in command and stranger-students coming in. Dean Jones had to write out his own pass to get by the sentries. In the emergency the whole place had been converted to war.

Whatever the confusion and derangement, the tangible results were astonishing. By Armistice Day it was already clear that so well had Yale trained its students, so capable were its graduates and so expert its professors, that even in a short year and a half they had compiled a stupendous record of service. In the Army and the Navy and the Marines—in signal work, gas warfare, war surgery, and mobile hospitals—in ambulance work, the Red Cross, and the Y.M.C.A.—in intelligence and war administration and diplomacy —most significantly of all in the training of officers for the artillery and in the preparation of materials for the drafting of the peace Yale, mother of men and scholars, had contributed magnificently. Happily the main lines of the war effort have been described by the participants and Yale's effective achievements made part of a permanent record. So those who would imbibe a little of the patriotic consecration—and those who would get some faint inkling of what Yale men in that inspiration accomplished—may read again in *Yale in the World War*.

Suffice it here to set down that, however doubtful and slow the beginnings, or harassing the passage from neutrality to participation, the ultimate record of the men of Yale was such that its sons would never thereafter have cause to feel ashamed.

As for the University's corporate contribution, or work as an organized American institution, that too was outstanding.

But how are we to understand such a corporate war service? Colleges had seldom—voluntarily—been put to such use before Colleges had been companies of youth selected for other ends, clusters of scholar-teachers, nurseries of learning and the quiet way of life. Today we forget, but historically their beginnings and their early purposes had been religious. And since time immemorial the soldier and the priest have been enemies. Champions of antipathetic values, seldom through the long centuries have the military and clerical elements in society been able to understand each other. Wars, in particular, have proved scant respecters of learning. *Inter arma silent leges,* the lawyers say. Yet education has fared no better. In times of trouble the recurring story has been of scholars scattered; of books trampled and lost; of colleges burned, or occupied for barracks. Even where the occupying army chanced to be friendly, it has often required long generations to replace the university's riches or restore to intellectual vigor schools thus overrun. Steeped in their tragic past, instructed by repeated and bitter experience, continental Europeans had come to know and expect such things.

Not so with Americans. They recognized neither the risks nor the incompatibilities. Instead an innocent confidence prevailed: in public opinion, in alumni circles, within the colleges themselves. In 1914, when the Germans burned the great library of Louvain, it seemed to the average educated American an act of needless destruction, a wanton atrocity. Education and learning should be apart, should be spared. Yet in 1917–18, when the American people plunged into the great conflict, it did not seem to occur to them to exempt their own colleges from participation and military derangement. Still less did it occur to deans and other academic officers to lock up the cloisters and hide. Instead there occurred the unprecedented spectacle of eager and even sacrificial participation—by colleges, professors and students alike—in the great war effort.

It would be tempting to account for this paradox on the grounds of circumstance, especially the circumstance that modern war allows of no noncombatants. Yet this would be a misapprehension. For total war was a nightmare reserved for a later generation. What Americans did come to understand at that time was at best a partial totality, i.e., a citizen's responsibilities: with manhood suffrage the manhood draft, and with democratic danger a general social obligation. Thus participation would be inevitable, and military service universal within the limits of age, sex, and fitness. But the legal obligation would still be distinctly personal. To explain how institutions also got involved, how campuses became parade grounds, how laboratories were militarized and the quiet men of learning turned to teaching the arts of defense and destruction becomes, therefore, an important and by no means easy problem.

Perhaps our national character and a peculiarly fortunate past were in part accountable. For example, it is to be noted that American society had always been organized for peace. Free from the menace of invasion, like old England the United States had elected to depend on the militia and a volunteer standing army. For historical reasons this professional army had always remained small in numbers, inferior in prestige. Wars, when they came, had always been fought by amateurs. Naturally, among the amateurs had always been college volunteers, students eager and enthusiastic, now and again also a patriot teacher or minister, like Nathan Hale the spy, or old Naphtali Daggett riding out by himself to defend New Haven.

So within our oldest colleges, even in their early, ministerial days and despite antimilitary regulations, a patriotic tradition had been created. At both Harvard and Yale the College Laws had forbidden students indulging in military training. The Yale Laws of 1759 and 1787, in addition to the standing prohibition of firearms or gunpowder or firing the same, had added a penalty for tumultuous action by three or more students and "likewise all military exercises, fighting with Swords, Files [Foils], or Canes." [1]

On the other hand war had not been so complicated as to stand in the way of leadership by graduate amateurs. So to the French and Indian wars, out of 550 living graduates many of whom were ministers, Yale had furnished some 60 officers and men. In the Revolution, out of about 900 living graduates, 234 had served in the Continental Army—with 4 major generals, 8 brigadier generals, and 2 lieutenant colonels who were aides-de-camp to Washington himself. In the War of 1812, 65 graduates had served, among them 3 major generals, 5 brigadier generals, and 8 colonels or lieutenant colonels. The incomplete records of the Mexican War reveal that Yale offered a captain, a colonel, and the son of Zachary Taylor to the struggle. Of the 4,500 living graduates and former students at the outbreak of the Civil War, 837 from the College and 207 from

438

the other Schools wore the blue. These included 3 major generals, 21 brigadier generals, and among the youngest a sergeant, Henry Parks Wright, who was later to graduate from the College and become Yale's beloved Dean. In the same conflict 6 general officers and more than 200 men wore the Confederate gray. Finally the Spanish War had drawn 300 men, including 2 brigadier generals and 96 commissioned officers.

Hence at Yale, as at other noted colleges, there had been perpetuated a tradition of volunteering in the country's service and a proud record of lives given in the nation's wars.[2] This spirit could be counted on, and, now that the manhood draft had come, the conflicts of the twentieth century would necessarily take more graduates than ever. But it was hardly anticipated that the draft age would be lowered to eighteen, and so for the first time draw off as well practically all the undergraduates who kept the colleges going.

In other ways, too, the risks to the colleges were hardly appreciated. The ravages wrought by the Revolutionary War had long since been forgotten. In that struggle, for eight months in 1775–76, Harvard's buildings had been taken over by the Revolutionary Army and the college moved to Concord. Princeton's Nassau Hall, after being used by the British forces, had also been occupied by Continental troops for five months, and then turned into a military hospital for over a year. For a time the Yale Classes had had to be dispersed to Wethersfield, Glastonbury, and Farmington in search of food. Other colleges had been occupied or temporarily abandoned. College undergraduates had also organized for drill, at Harvard in the Marti-Mercurian Band in 1769 or 1770 and at Yale in 1775. Both groups had appealed to the civil authorities for arms to be placed at their disposal and at Yale these arms were lodged in the library. But such devastation and derangements had gradually faded from memory, as physically the colleges found themselves safe from invasion and not seriously interfered with in our national conflicts. Neither the War of 1812 nor the later wars against Mexico and Spain had seriously shaken them. Even the Civil War had left the older and Northern establishments intact. What that grim struggle *had* done was to introduce the requirement of military

439

training into the land grant institutions: the colleges for agriculture and mechanic arts, so many of which were now expanding into great State universities.

In short, the American experience had been peculiarly fortunate. Neither by fears inherited from times of disaster, nor by political rivalry with the military, nor even by any theory of specialization or separation of function had any impassable gulf been fixed. Instead, American education had been growing into a public industry, and within that industry the moral barriers had been crumbling. Even colleges had been gradually so secularized as to lose their distinctive character.

One way of change was by expansion and diversification. Since the Civil War our institutions of higher learning—the universities, colleges, professional schools, and institutes of technology—had grown so numerous, so diverse, and of such varying standards that it was no longer possible to think of a liberal arts college as distinct or privileged or in any way untouchable. The very word college had come to be used for so many things which were not collegiate, or even literary. Some quite small colleges now called themselves universities. And many a real university boasted of schools of law and of medicine, a college of commerce or of agriculture, perhaps a department of physical training or an institute of applied science, most of these competing with its liberal arts college for students, and several drawing superior numbers. Were these vigorous younger branches really so different, or in any way less important, than the old-fashioned college with its languages, its mathematics, and its medieval degree?

Traditionally the college had come first, and in the older private foundations it still exercised a superior hold on the affection of the graduates and the attention of the governing boards. But even locally this sentimental priority was beginning to be challenged. And if the trustees found it steadily more difficult to distinguish among their trusts in time of peace, what they were going to do in a world war could be safely predicted. If science could be applied to war as well as to agriculture, and if engineering schools were to be placed at the disposal of the Army or Navy, it would be

440

hard indeed to say why the arts colleges should not be turned from the general cultural training of future business leaders to the general all-round training of officers—especially when the officers were so badly needed.

Theoretically, of course, there had been special religious and humanistic obligations. And these two peculiarities of character ought still to have distinguished the colleges and served to protect them from conversion to military use. But if almost all of our colonial foundations, and many of the nineteenth-century colleges of the South and Middle West, had been denominational establishments, this special dedication had now for the most part been lost. Their students were no longer studying for the ministry, their teachers had long since become laymen. In conservative Yale the President was a layman, and among the trustees lawyers, bankers, and industrialists were replacing Congregational ministers.

As for the other distinctive ideal, of a liberal education by means of the humanistic disciplines, this faith had survived somewhat better. But Yale's recent history by itself makes plain why the liberal arts were no longer an obstacle to militarization. No doubt the more conservative church colleges, with Yale and Princeton among the universities, still tried to practice a general and disinterested learning. But more and more were they expected to be accessible to any high-school graduate, and usable for the most miscellaneous purposes of democratic improvement. With this new mass patronage, exclusiveness had become unpopular. The term ivory tower was now coming into usage, as an epithet of reproach. Classical education, in particular, had lost favor. Instead, more practical studies were in vogue. And it will bear repeating that practical utility was hardly likely to provide arguments against the conversion of these institutions to war training.

Finally, it is worth noting that what made these changes of character and educational ideals decisive was the uncertainty and lack of cohesion within the older leadership. The private colleges of the Atlantic seaboard had remained independent units, each still going it alone. In no two colleges, even in New England, were the requirements for a liberal education the same. That the Faculty at

Yale was able to legislate a stiff set of requirements into the B.A. course of study at the very moment of our entrance into the war would be a tribute to exceptional organization and spirit. But this was no guarantee that the antivocational and nonmilitary standards would either succeed at Yale or be insisted on elsewhere.

In short, among the nation's colleges one group were no longer disqualified from war service by religious scruples or by intellectual dedication. They had become secular, all-purpose institutions, as usable for war as any other industry. And as for those colleges which retained some of the older idealism, they were isolated from each other and unorganized.

All of this implies that there might have existed, on the part of the private colleges still devoted to the old-fashioned arts, a conviction hostile to participation, or at least a subconscious wish to stay out of the business of military training. Actually—if the examples of Princeton and Williams and Dartmouth and Harvard and Yale are at all representative—nothing of the sort was the case. After the emergency had been recognized a few men still clung to moral scruples and many, no doubt, regretted the need. But the situation soon admitted of no choice. Indeed the actions of these colleges and universities, before as well as after the declaration of war, showed them as eager as most public institutions and far more eager than many to place their entire facilities at the service of the government. Realizing the loss, they were still so sacrificially eager that their conduct can only be interpreted as a self-conscious and determined identification with the purposes and welfare of the nation.

As for society itself, whether from these causes or from ignorance and carelessness, whether because of a democratic reluctance to distinguish or perhaps also because of anti-intellectualism—of a growing hostility to the past and to books, to the things of the spirit and of the mind—society was apparently ready to accept the sacrifice without misgiving.

These things being so, it needed only the involvement and the discovery that the colleges could be of real use. Such having become the prevailing attitudes, it did not surprise men then and it ought not to surprise them now that the people of the United States proceeded to use their colleges and universities, their institutions for the preservation of the highest learning and the broadest leadership, in a more direct, military, and thoroughgoing fashion than ever before in the experience of the western world. So what would once have been impossible was fashioned into a pattern for all future wars.

Let us not suppose, however, that this utilization was instantaneous or that it developed in an effective and orderly fashion. On the contrary, the mobilization of our complex, industrial nation proved so difficult, the government services were so understaffed and unprepared, the fortunes of the European conflict changed so swiftly, and the armed services were so slow to understand the capacities of our colleges that confusion and inefficiency long obtained. Those tax-supported State or city institutions which made a policy of following public demand were therefore slow to get going. Those which were ahead of the public, on the other hand, discovered that the exploitation of the war potentials of American higher education had at first to be approached privately and locally, by the colleges themselves, and through a forest of difficulties and delays. In the neutrality period, accordingly, those colleges and universities which saw what was coming and wished to get ready secured such informal advices as they could from Washington. Yet for a considerable time they had to carry forward without adequate supplies and under the handicap of heartbreaking reversals of policy. Only after our entrance into the war did official policy really take hold. Then, however, the movement went so far and so fast that in the last few months of the war the forward and the following colleges alike found themselves almost entirely taken over.

This is another way of saying that Governmental policy exhibited a progression from initial neglect, through the use of youthful manpower and specialist university services, to a final utilization of the collegiate institutions themselves. The steps—and the changes of attitude involved—are worth noting. Not that they were always clearly or evenly applied. For example, the need for collegiate manpower and leadership, beyond the cadet corps of the land grant colleges, was early foreseen by a number of military and po-

443

litical figures. The classic instance had been Leonard Wood's effort to get college men to train themselves for war in summer encampments (Gettysburg and Monterey in 1913; Burlington, Asheville, Ludington, and Monterey in 1914; and Plattsburg and others in 1915). The first of those encampments even antedated the outbreak of war in Europe. But they aimed at a National Reserve, did not give specifically an officer's training, accommodated only limited numbers, and were conducted on a volunteer basis.

The early neutrality period, from August 1914 to June 1916, then witnessed an intensification of effort along these lines, the first calling of scientists and qualified experts to Washington to aid in the organization of preparedness, and the rather grudging issuance of permission, to a few selected and demanding institutions, to set up training plans within the colleges themselves.

The third phase opened with the Mexican crisis in June 1916, when the Army was enlarged and the National Guard units were federalized and mobilized for action. National legislation also authorized the establishment of Reserve Officers' Training Corps in a number of universities. Thus, after an irregular number of student militiamen had seen active service, arrangements were made for regular winter training and for the entrance of the military into university laboratories and buildings. In the process it was recognized that, in this world-wide and highly technical warfare of the twentieth century, scientific experts and facilities would also be needed. It followed that the whole duty of these universities could no longer be fulfilled entirely by their graduates or even by student volunteers.

Owing to the passing of the Mexican crisis and dissatisfaction with the inefficiency of the militia, the implementation of this phase came only gradually, and the new R.O.T.C. units in particular were organized but slowly.* Then, with the breaking of relations with Germany, things began to move faster, and on the actual dec-

---

* There was a considerable opposition to the R.O.T.C. idea on equalitarian grounds. Only sons of the wealthy, it was charged, could afford to go to college. Hence to restrict officer commissions to the colleges seemed to certain elements in the public essentially undemocratic.

444

laration of war in April 1917 mobilization became the pressing concern. Yet at first it was contemplated that American participation was to be directed primarily toward supplying the Allies with goods and weapons. Only gradually did the sending of a large army become important, as the news from Europe pointed toward an urgent need for men.

This phase, from April 1917 to the spring of 1918, meant a deteriorating campus situation and an uneasy and exasperatingly limited role for college men. The 1917 Selective Service Act set the draft age at twenty-one and so affected only the older students. Alerted, impatient, increasingly doubtful of the utility of peacetime studies, the younger undergraduates began to seek some quicker way into the services than a four-year R.O.T.C. course. Some got their parents' permission, left college, and enlisted. Others simply faked their ages and joined up.

Finally, in the spring and summer of 1918 came the great German offensives, the desperate pleas of the Allies, the decision to lower the draft age to eighteen, and a great effort to register, train, and forward all eligible males. Arbitrarily applied, this emergency program might have emptied American colleges and universities of half their faculties and all but a handful of handicapped or underage students. This might have meant financial collapse and perhaps a permanent closing for a number of institutions. Fortunately, these same colleges happened to be well supplied with dormitories and the other physical accommodations needed by army encampments. Also, they commanded the services of usable instructors and were eager to be given a chance. It was arranged, therefore—and with somewhat less struggle, one gathers, than the same dilemma was to occasion in World War II—to leave the young students at the colleges and train them there in Students' Army Training Corps. Army officers were sent, uniforms issued, discipline begun, and in the fall of 1918 at least four hundred academic campuses sprouted suddenly into armed camps. In forehanded institutions the half-and-half instruction of 1917–18 became wholly military. In others the change was even more abrupt. Extracurricular activities and the humanities were out.

445

In this step-by-step fashion it came about that the liberal arts colleges throughout the country were separated from their traditional functions. Pre-eminently designed for the cultivation of a general humanity and the disinterested pursuit of truth, after a year and a half of war they stood almost wholly converted to studies in the use of force and the newer arts of killing. In sober afterthought such a conversion seems no small matter. At the time it happened to be so necessary, and it promised to yield so much, that greater sacrifices still might cheerfully have been undertaken. There was no holding back. Rather, in company with the schools of science and engineering and technical institutions of all kinds, the arts colleges in the main asked only for further duties. Afire for the cause of freedom and justice for mankind, not a few had been in advance of the public authorities. Now, patriotic and detesting militarism, they encouraged the Government and helped the military to take over.

Almost overnight there ensued the sudden victory in Europe and demobilization for the S.A.T.C. and the Army. So in December 1918 the colleges changed back. In no time at all the war was left behind, and what might have been an academic devastation soon came to be remembered less for its social tensions than as a confused, exciting, and invigorating interlude. The colleges were sure they had made important contributions to the war. And they had survived.

446

CHAPTER 23·YALE AND THE GUNS

*The United States has plenty of guns, but very few men who
know how to manage them.*
—ARTHUR TWINING HADLEY, *August 1915*

*The action of Yale University in this crisis offers the most
notable example in her history of the intelligent adaptation
of means to a great patriotic end.*
—HENRY L. STIMSON, *1920*

YALE WAS far from rising as one man to the support of Belgium
and the Triple Entente. In August 1914 the University had been
on vacation. The sudden deterioration in Europe, the swift series of
declarations of war, the horrible slithering into violence as half the
civilized world was engulfed: all this made a stupefying spectacle.
Obviously the United States could do nothing save stand clear and
hope, and perhaps work, for the return of peace. The strict neutrality which President Wilson at once proclaimed was therefore easily
accepted.

Yet almost from the outbreak of fighting, students and officers
found themselves personally involved. Trying to be neutral in
thought as well as in deed proved particularly difficult for the members of the faculty. Professor William Howard Taft echoed Wilson's
counsel of impartiality in strong terms. University men, he urged,
ought to be especially careful in their expressions of sympathy or
disapproval because such declarations were taken seriously abroad.
But the war outraged too much that was part of the fiber of academic idealism. To the older professors thinking of their student
years, to the younger men dreaming of summers in Europe, each
ship, each cable, enlarged the horror. The names of places shelled,

447

the plight of invaded countries, the stories brought back by colleagues who had been caught and almost failed to get away, the letters from friends abroad added sorrow and pity and presently anger. Some had not known an instant's hesitation. Neutral in thought? Not from the first gun. Before August 1914 had even passed away, sensitive Edward Bliss Reed had poured out his anguish in searing stanzas:

> They who take the sword . . .
> . . . With the sword they shall be slain.[1]

Just back with his family from overseas, Professor Frank C. Porter of the Divinity School confessed that "the feeling of neutrality appropriate in a neutral land is not easily cultivated . . . by those who were in England when the war began." G. B. Adams, historian and elder statesman, did not even make such an attempt. "Germany must be defeated in this war," he sent word from England. "If it comes to a point where it is necessary for the United States to aid the allies to the end that they should win, then I hope it will be done. She is opposed to everything for which we stand, and our turn would be next if Germany were successful." * [2]

NEUTRALITY AND PREPAREDNESS

Officially, the University scrupulously refrained from adopting a policy. Individual speech and opinion should be free. But Yale was also an educational institution and could hardly escape interpreting the disaster for its students. Sunday, 4 October 1914, was the day set apart for the offering of prayers for peace in all the churches. Delivering his Matriculation Sermon to the future war Class of

* The Dean of the Graduate School was not coming back. Caught while on his sabbatical, Hanns Oertel, philologist and scholar, was staying in Munich to engage in relief work for his fatherland. His letters, friendly and dispassionate, hoped for American neutrality. Less discreet was the glorification of the German cause by a College undergraduate, who had at first preferred service in the German army to returning to finish his course. The *Alumni Weekly* impartially printed letters from Yale men on both sides, while cautioning the students not to get excited.

1918, President Hadley chose his text from Romans (14:19): "Let us therefore follow after the things which make for peace." Prayer, he insisted, was not enough. International treaties and peace machinery were not enough. What was necessary was understanding, fairness, courtesy, and consideration on the part of the people themselves: internationally toward other peoples and individually toward each other. "This is not a time for thanking God that we are not as other men are," but for self-improvement.

The College listened—and went on about its business. Football and the fall competitions were getting under way. Classes had resumed. The Faculty set to work on the Honors compromise, and the Morris committee went forward with its moves against vocationalism.

Yet even the coolest and most hopeful found it increasingly hard to ignore what was taking place across the water. For the war persisted in touching the University, directly, injuriously—and not just in its emotions. Out on Prospect Hill, as the autumn evenings lengthened, Yale astronomers went back to their lonely vigil of the stars—only to find the sky often obscured by smoke from Winchester's, working overtime on munitions for England. Victor Michels, who had been invited as Professor of German Literature, was unable to leave Germany. To the Library the paralysis of the second-hand book markets and the drying up of institutional publication abroad brought immediate loss. The News began to note the progress of the war on maps. Two historians and an economist organized a committee to collect materials for the history of the war.[3] And one of these men, Charles Seymour, at this point began those studies on the diplomatic background of the war which were to influence American opinion, earn him a role in the drafting of the peace, and lead to great preferment in his University.

As for the undergraduate community, there was some talk about an eventual international socialism, much curiosity about American foreign policy, but practically no advocacy of United States participation in the conflict. Hardly anyone seemed to favor the Central Powers. Most apparently agreed with President Eliot's position: they were not against the German people so much as against

449

the government and the militarist elements who were making war. In the same way the attitude toward the Allies was one of sympathy for their cause but of even stronger sympathy for the Belgian and French people, and for the Serbians as the first and chief victims.

These feelings carried quickly into war relief and the desire to play the Good Samaritan. Toward the end of October 1914 a great mass meeting was held to raise funds for the Red Cross. Taft presided; Hadley, Mabel Boardman, Surgeon-Major Lyster, and Waterloo Wheeler spoke. From additional collections at football games eventually $9,000 was raised and twelve ambulances were furnished: three each to Germany, Austria, Belgium, and France. In November and early December came the news of what Yale men were doing in Red Cross work in Belgium, or in a Paris hospital; also the first list of Yale participants in the war, and a call for volunteer ambulance drivers in France.

Suddenly on 3 December appeared the first brief notice on Student Military Camps. It was written for the *News* by an Assistant Secretary of War, described plans for training camps in the summer of 1915, and referred to President Hadley as a member of the Advisory Board of University Presidents. A few days later the *News* reprinted an item from the *Daily Princetonian* advocating sane preparedness by military service. And on 5 January 1915 the *News* reprinted a long article by President Hibben upholding the students who wanted organized military work at Princeton.[4]

So within three months there opened a new debate and a different campaign: the campaign for preparedness. Yale alumni were actively supporting the summer camps; President Hadley was obviously interested; and influential undergraduates had been won over. Almost automatically many others reacted in favor of pacifism, or at least complete separation from the war. Already William Lyon Phelps had called out in agony: "From the standpoint of Christianity, there is no such thing as a foreign war. Every war is a civil war. . . . War means murder and destruction on the largest possible scale. There is nothing beautiful about it; nothing fine; nothing admirable; nothing noble." [5]

The undergraduates reacted to the preparedness idea partly for sport, partly in enthusiastic earnestness. A Yale graduate student became Treasurer of the Collegiate Anti-Militarism League. In February, when Germany declared the waters around the British Isles a war zone and Wilson threatened to hold the Imperial Government "to a strict accountability," the *News* got out an issue of special war articles. By March 1915 preparedness opinions had become so positive that representatives of the rival views were invited to New Haven under the auspices of the Debating Association. First Oswald Garrison Villard spoke on "The Folly of an Increase in the Army and Navy of the United States." Then a second mass meeting in Woolsey Hall listened intently to Congressman A. P. Gardner plead "The Need of a Larger Army and Navy for the United States." In April President Hadley was quoted as urging national preparedness; and influential alumni were beginning to think about military training in College, with credit granted toward the degree.

Officially, Yale continued neutral. Even after the sinking of the *Lusitania,* in which four well-known Yale men lost their lives, appeal to international law and an effort at pacific settlement with the German Reich seemed on the whole preferable to war. The *Alumni Weekly* could still print a somewhat hysterical letter from a former Sheff instructor in the German artillery, a milder letter from a Sheff graduate in the French ranks, and a plea for neutrality from Dean Oertel, side by side. But when about a thousand undergraduates were rumored to have joined some Columbia students in a strong and rather injudiciously worded petition for peace to President Wilson, some tempers flared.

Remote as the fighting had at first appeared, these few months had brought anguish, restriction of educational opportunity, and general uneasiness. Now as the year of 1914–15 drew to a close, there was more than a hint that Christian ideals and academic standards might be seriously compromised. But that the country as a whole was slipping, helplessly, down the road to war few had both the foresight and the courage to say. Summer came and scattered the students. And even into the winter of 1915–16 the bifocal campus mood would persist. Alluding to his own undergraduate experience, Stephen Vincent Benét was later to write:

The war came, watched by Philip and most of his class with the fascinated interest of spectators before a burning house, but its cloud was as yet no bigger than one's personal convictions. Men took sides, ally or German, some from reason but more from the fun of taking sides, a fun comparable to that of backing the Cubs against the Giants. A handful left for ambulance service, two or three to join various armies—to the others no warning came at all that each casual step taken was on earthquake-ground.[6]

HADLEY AND THE ARTILLERY BATTERIES

In August 1915, in perhaps the boldest Report Hadley ever wrote, he declared his belief that military training had a place in college education. Simultaneously he began quiet negotiations for the establishment of an artillery battalion on the campus. Later, upon occasion after occasion, the Yale constituency would acknowledge the foresight and resolution with which their sparkling President had anticipated the rising storm.

This whole question of the character and proper place of military training had been actively discussed during the spring of 1915. Indeed so many inquiries and suggestions had come in from graduates and friends of Yale, and such differences of opinion still persisted within the Corporation and the several Faculties, that some statement was unavoidable yet a flat declaration of policy exceedingly difficult.

R. R. McCormick '03 had pressed strongly for compulsory campus drilling. But members of the faculty who had witnessed peacetime training at Cornell or Minnesota, or learned of the failures elsewhere, were decidedly opposed. General Leonard Wood kept suggesting winter lectures, to be given a definite place in the curriculum and counted toward the degree. But it had been necessary to remind the General that only West Point, Annapolis, or the Jesuit colleges any longer had an absolute curriculum. Again, at Commencement, the Alumni Advisory Board had urged voluntary military training for academic credit. But even if the training officers could be found it was becoming evident that at least three or four members of the Corporation would be wholly opposed to taking funds and facilities which had been given to Yale for other purposes and applying them to military ends.

All these issues interested Hadley intensely, and he knew his own mind. For the country he believed in preparedness. For the boys he believed in the moral value of training for the nation's service. And as for military strategy, it fascinated him.

War was a game. Like whist or tennis it called for brains and the shrewd application of force. Mere marching wasn't exciting—tactically it was much more important that boys should learn to get across open fields without getting caught in bunches. Morally, uniforms were not what would improve them. Rather they should be taught to command themselves and learn to command others. Further,

> It seems to me that there are two ways to invite war: one by having so strong an army that it tempts you to attack somebody else, and the other by having so weak an army that it tempts somebody else to attack you. The United States appears to me to be clearly in the latter position.[7]

But the public was apathetic. In Washington Woodrow Wilson's policy ruled and the War Department itself seemed only half aroused. In New Haven the special difficulty was Yale's federal structure, particularly the tradition of autonomy and participation in policy on the part of the Officers of Yale College. What was a President, so unsupported abroad and so diffident of dictation at home, to do? The answer, clearly, was to try persuasion. So in his first neutrality-period Report he marshaled the full brilliance of his powers for the advocacy of military education.

Hadley began his great argument on a historical note. Yale had never had an effective system of military instruction. Prior to the

Civil War there had been none at all. Then, off and on for about thirty years, the Sheffield Scientific School—as the land grant college of Connecticut—offered some courses. But people were tired of war, and the actual teaching of either military science or practice amounted to very little. There had been no compulsory drill and, until the nineties, no real interest in developing it on a voluntary basis. Then in 1893 the Scientific School lost the land grant to Storrs Agricultural College, and with it had gone the right to demand the detail of officers from the Army. For a time the War Department generously supplied some able and enthusiastic younger men. But the Spanish War and colonial responsibilities promptly claimed them and afterward but a single detail had been made. Since 1906 Yale had found itself back in pre-Civil War conditions.[8]

Starting in 1913, however, the War Department had organized five-week summer encampments, for college students and college graduates, to prepare a reserve of partly trained officers. The camps at which Yale had been chiefly represented were Gettysburg in 1913, Burlington in 1914, and Plattsburg that very summer—1915.

> To those who are interested in the Yale tradition of public service it is a gratifying fact that Yale has had a larger aggregate enrollment in the different United States student camps than any other institution in the country. . . . we have had considerable opportunity to watch the educational effect of this system; and I have no hesitation in saying that . . . the camps have an educational value that much more than justifies their organization and their maintenance.

They would fill half the vacation with mental and physical training of an extremely exacting type. And Hadley enlarged on the theme of too long summers with attendant habits of idleness. Four other characteristics made the summer camp valuable. It would train the intelligence. It would familiarize students with a line of life and work which, whether they approved it or not, was still playing a supremely important role in world history. It would give them a sense of patriotic obligation. Finally, it would teach them moderation in the discussion of public affairs.

454

Having thus bowed in turn to professors, patriots, Yale men, and pacifists, President Hadley swept grandly into a discussion of *winter* training. There were, he said, three proposals. The War Department was prepared to furnish officers to give students who attended summer camps winter instruction in military science by "a system of lectures and of tactical walks." Secondly, many officers and students wished the summer camps plus such winter courses to count toward the degree. Finally, many Yale graduates wished to see military drill "made part of the course itself," that is, required in the curriculum, so that every Yale graduate would be prepared to serve his country as a soldier unless disqualified on grounds of health. With the first two of these proposals he sympathized, with the third, not. Militarism no less than pacifism could lead to disaster; whereas a reasonable preparedness, through cooperation with the summer camps, "will lay the basis for a foreign policy, to which, in Webster's words, we may owe 'safety at home, dignity and consideration abroad.' "

But there were educational conservatives who still felt that "proficiency in military affairs is not a thing to be taken into account in estimating a boy's fitness to receive a bachelor's degree." In the old days of Latin, Greek, mathematics, and metaphysics, he acknowledged, this objection would have been valid. But the bachelor's degree no longer connoted proficiency "in this narrow group"; in fact it no longer indicated any particular subjects or studies. The modern criteria were rather more general. Though these criteria debarred manual training and such subjects as art appreciation, serious military instruction, winter and summer, qualified easily. It was, first of all, "an intellectual course," the routine drill being limited and bearing "about the same relation to the study of tactics as the routine of laboratory manipulation bears to the study of physics." He cited the map problems. Again, the requirement of good teaching was fully met, "for the Army itself is a great training school, and every good officer is to a greater or less extent a professional educator." As for the desideratum of competition, the work called out both emulation and esprit de corps. Finally, military training met the special test for the Academic de-

455

gree of B.A. because it required sacrifice, and "represents training in the duty of a citizen." Very few men were likely to make the Army a career. Therefore "it is not professional study."

Quod erat demonstrandum. The whole argument had the deft, the brilliant, the Hadleian touch. It appealed to national issues against the narrowly professorial, to practical men against the theoretical, to the cool-minded and reasonable against the extremists. It was illuminating, it was ethical. It was conclusive. In categorical, systematic logic he had demolished the objections to military education. Few men reading the case, fewer still hearing it presented, would be able at once to pose rebuttal. They might feel uncomfortable, persuaded there must be a flaw somewhere. But where?

The fact was Hadley had reconciled military training with liberal study, in small part by making all good army officers into professors, in the main, however, by redefining the criteria for the B.A. degree. In the last analysis his criteria boiled down to good, hard intellectual work plus public duty. The hard work test applied to any bachelor's curriculum. But Hadley was thinking of the College: he wanted the Academic man to take training. So the words liberal arts, or humanities and natural and social sciences, never appeared in his argument. Instead the distinctive purpose of the B.A. curriculum was to make the candidate "a profounder thinker and a better citizen." The gain should be public rather than personal. In this fashion "liberal" was subtly metamorphosed into "patriotic." And in 1915 it was the duty of patriotic citizens to prepare for war.

The President even had a specific program in mind. He hoped and intended that a student artillery battery would be established at Yale. "It is in the artillery that the need of trained officers is greatest." Artillery was less showy than the cavalry, and more demanding of intellectual ability. The usage of Connecticut was favorable to the enlistment of a student company in the militia. And the United States Government was ready to place battery material at the disposal of any such student company whenever it could be maintained and housed. Yale had looked into the housing, and would supply the land, if an armory costing $30,000 could be given.

In this fashion Yale's President stepped forward as an advocate of *voluntary* military training, practical as well as theoretical. Some credit—how much he did not venture—should be given for military science; much private extracurricular energy and money should be put into learning to handle the guns. That was his recommendation. Sensing what was coming, Hadley had made his decision, and so put together the most appealing and rallying arguments for what he was sure imperatively needed to be done.

On his own responsibility Yale's President next did something considerably more positive. He entered upon practical arrangements. Hardly had College opened in the fall of 1915 when plans were announced for the organization of a Field Artillery Battery.* Until a promised armory could be built, the baseball cage was to be used. The *News* quoted Hadley, Dean Jones, and General Wood as favorable to the project. It was hoped that 138 applications, the number required for the Connecticut Militia, would be received from graduates and undergraduates of Yale.

With a rush nearly a thousand undergraduates tried to sign up. The State could not accept so many. Eventually 486 men were recruited, and four batteries constituting a whole battalion were mustered into the Connecticut Tenth Field Artillery of the National Guard. In one battery the President's son, Morris Hadley '16,

---

* Who was really responsible? Hadley was too modest to claim all the personal credit. But his correspondence files leave no reasonable doubt. Hoping to be able to set up training for infantry officers, he had visited Plattsburg at the beginning of August 1915 and had consulted with Leonard Wood. Then he got Wood to meet with a committee of men from the large Yale delegation, and they had asked Wood how Yale could best serve the armed forces. The answer was: by specializing in Field Artillery.

The strategic intelligence of the assignment appealed to him strongly. He verified the opportunity, made arrangements with the Connecticut Militia, and—when three Corporation members developed strong conscientious scruples against using Yale's endowment for military training—persuaded the Corporation to allow the use of vacant land and personally wrote to ask for financial help from interested Yale graduates. Reading between the lines it is easy to see that he also had not a little to do with enlisting responsible undergraduate support.[9]

served as lieutenant. A student mass meeting had already been held to debate whether or not academic credit could be given for regular work in such a connection. But this was going considerably too fast for the Academic authorities, who thought of the one night per week of gunnery work as interfering neither with the curriculum nor even with extracurricular activities. It was further miles ahead of the military. In fact the rush to volunteer went so far beyond the calculations and capacities of the one available officer that it was not until November 22 that the first assembly and inspection could be held.

Meanwhile President Hadley had been engaged in a herculean struggle to extract from the War Department a suitable instructor. On December 10 he emerged with Lieut. Robert M. Danford of the Fifth Field Artillery. If the ingenious and persistent President had done nothing else, this appointment alone would have brought satisfaction and credit to Yale. Danford was young, able, friendly, and effective. In short order he won the unswerving loyalty of the students and the confidence and respect of their elders.[10] It was well that this was so. For nothing else went according to plan. Drilling began at once on Danford's arrival. Despite undergraduate readiness, however, it was not until 1 March 1916 that the guns, caissons, sights, fuse setters, and other necessary equipment arrived, or that a lieutenant and four noncommissioned officers were detailed for a month from West Point, so that thoroughgoing technical training could also be carried on. Horses were still in short supply, and more were promised for October. Training was far behind schedule, but College enthusiasm was counted on. That, and a ten-days encampment for each battery at Camp Summerall, Tobyhanna, Pennsylvania. Said Major C. P. Summerall, "It is significant that while the country is talking preparedness, Yale is acting preparedness."

But preparedness for what? In May 1916 Congress cut off appropriations for the Tobyhanna encampments. All but the Seniors went home. Suddenly in mid-June, with the troubles with Mexico getting worse, President Wilson mobilized the Army and called out the National Guard. This meant barracks on the campus, all the scattered battery members recalled to New Haven, and desperate efforts to recruit to war strength. The Federal inspection rejected some battery members for defective eyesight. Others were under age. All hands turned into recruiting agents. Cooks, horseshoers, and a band had to be found. Then followed three weeks of feverish organizing and marking time—and off went the batteries to Tobyhanna, after all. But not for any ten days; nor indeed for service on the Mexican border.

That was longed for by some, and would have been exciting to many. But they were almost without fire training, officers, or equipment, and the sanitary provisions were totally inadequate. When they were called out the first idea had been to send them direct to the border—and for some time severe political pressure was brought on General Wood. Hadley was appalled at such suicidal folly. For two weeks after Commencement he and others exerted their utmost influence: first, to prevent the boys being sent direct to the border; second, to get proper medical service organized; third, to get enough good officers assigned for their training. For the rest of that summer much of Hadley's time had to be given to vigilance and negotiation, trying to reconcile the demands of the War Department with sound public policy, trying to head off any Leagues of Indignant Parents, trying to forward preparedness by an intelligent treatment of the student trainees. The National Defense Act of June 3 provided for R.O.T.C. units in colleges having a four-year course of study. This was followed by two General Orders disqualifying for membership in the R.O.T.C. any member of the National Guard. Accordingly one of Hadley's concerns was that, as soon as the Mexican crisis was past, the Yale guardsmen should be released from the Army and the Militia and returned to college for further training.

All summer long the Yale batterymen fought "the battle of Tobyhanna." It was grueling work and an experience that would later prove invaluable. They learned how to bury horses and picked up a shocking proficiency at swearing. Finally on September 18–22, after much War Department backing and filling, the Yale batteries were mustered out of Federal service at Niantic. But, in spite of

459

promises, it was not until December 1916 that they were discharged also from the State Service. With a year of odd experiences behind them, and a sulphurous contempt for the whole militia system inside them, Yale's student volunteers found themselves back where they had started. The troubles with Mexico were over, and the European War appeared hardly much closer than before. It seemed almost as if the University and Leonard Wood had got them off on the wrong trail. Unless, of course, a successful R.O.T.C. unit could be set up at Yale.

MILITARY INSTRUCTION, 1916–17

Formal military instruction, in the classroom and for credit, had been in the minds of many preparedness men from the beginning. Yet Hadley had stated his own preference as personal rather than official, knowing that Leonard Wood's lectures and tactical walks would be hard to organize and that it would be difficult to get proper instructors from the Army. Moreover he recognized that graduate opinion was far ahead of general public sentiment, and he perceived more clearly than the organized alumni the human obstacles: the disinclination of the College Professors, the reluctance within his own Administration,* the scruples of the clerical members of the Corporation. While in his capacity as President he felt free to make practical arrangements for the *extracurricular* batteries, in the summer of 1915 he did not seek to establish classroom instruction for academic credits. Instead, in the fall he laid the Alumni Board's recommendation before the College Professors. Then the Professors, after prolonged deliberation, in December 1915 made the smallest of concessions. For 1916–17 Danford would offer a single course in American military history or policy.[12]

* Secretary Stokes did not believe that the United States was in real danger of attack, or that military training was the best training for manliness or self-sacrifice, or that armaments were guarantors of peace. The military propaganda drove him to public protest: "In preparedness there is only good; in Preparedness both good and bad." He quoted Sumner: "What we prepare for is what we shall get."[11]

460

Yale's President himself kept holding back. He realized, as many did not, that military instruction would be a novel form of public service for Yale to be sponsoring. It was not the immemorial service in either church or *civil* state. "But the spirit of the charter is more important than its letter. If Yale and colleges like her should fail to take their share in providing for the defense of the nation's integrity and honor . . . they would fail miserably in their duty." Hadley thought the dangers were real. International arbitration would only work, he assured an alumni gathering at Albany, if backed by force. Nor would a strong Navy be sufficient preparedness unless it could be got out of the hands of politicians and into the hands of "intelligent fighters."

Facing the excited alumni of Cleveland, Hadley had hit the same note of keeping the peace by preparing for war. The boys who had gone into the batteries were not militaristic in spirit. "Yale believes heartily in preparedness, but she spells it with a small 'p' and not with a large one." The more vociferous alumni were not satisfied. In March 1916, and repeatedly thereafter, pressure was brought to make military instruction a part of the required curriculum for credit. To them the College was still spelling preparedness with entirely too small a "p." [13]

The early summer of 1916 brought decision. With the National Defense Act opening opportunities for the training of Reserve Officers at volunteer colleges, Hadley and Danford made up their minds to get a regular R.O.T.C. unit established at Yale in place of the militia batteries. This meant securing War Department approval and essential Army aid for the training of officers for the Reserve. Fifteen other universities proposed to take advantage of the new opportunity—but Yale was the first and in the end the only civilian college to attempt artillery training. Such specialization was bound to be difficult, technical, and expensive. But a new armory was in sight; Yale had had valuable experience in this branch of instruction; and the batterymen could be given advanced standing in the new Corps. However, it was not until the end of January 1917 that the War Department was able to supply the necessary officers of instruction.

Meanwhile the general Faculty, back from the summer of the Mexican crisis, heard Hadley present "a suggestion that a course of practical and theoretical military training be established in the College." With Woodrow Wilson just re-elected, in part on a platform of having kept the country out of war, it was some weeks before the College awoke to the full seriousness of Hadley's "suggestion." Finally, on 7 December 1916, the President got Captain Danford invited to meet with the Professors, and announced that the Corporation, not feeling the question could be deferred to the opening of College, had already entered into a provisional arrangement with the War Department. The question before the Faculty was therefore not whether but how much credit was to be given for this elective work. Captain Danford stated that one hundred men from the entire University would have to elect the work in order to have the War Department supply the instruction. "The War Department determines the amount of time, but the Faculty determines the academic credit."

The Permanent Officers, thus reminded that their power had been limited, referred the subject to the Committee on the Course of Study, and to the general Faculty the following week. After further discussion, the general Faculty decided that a student electing R.O.T.C. for credit had to take the whole course, and might not drop any portion of his major or minor work. On 21 December Captain Danford appeared before the general Faculty, and both he and President Hadley gave assurances that the arrangement with the War Department could be terminated by due notice from the President. In other words, military study should be at the expense of electives, not of distribution or concentration, and it need not continue forever. Thus reassured, the Faculty came out of the Committee of the Whole and voted to grant seven hours of credit toward the B.A. degree. This work would be spread through four years, with three summer encampments in addition. The vote was 38 to 0; but it was recorded that Professor Phelps was excused, that Professor Morris was opposed to the whole plan, and that 24 were present and not voting. The Faculty also attached to their vote a preamble, reciting the fact that President and Prudential Committee had been responsible for the policy, the Faculty merely recommending certain asked-for regulations.

On behalf of the Faculty, it should be said that they were no doubt more opposed to giving Academic credit than to military training, per se. Students and parents, however, wanted both the training and the B.A. degree, and they did not want the degree postponed. Moreover the law contemplated R.O.T.C.'s for college credit. Thus the issue of preparedness vs. nonpreparedness hinged rather arbitrarily on the transference of military training from an extracurricular to a curricular status. What the Faculty had tried to do was to allow such a transfer without jeopardizing hard-won academic values.

The obstacles having been cleared, the undergraduates returned from Christmas vacation to attend a well-advertised meeting explaining the new R.O.T.C. course. Danford pointed out that the delays had been due to the Government, not the Faculty. Only 200 or 220 were to be allowed to join. And with the opening of the second term, on 8 February 1917, the Yale R.O.T.C. under Captains Danford, Potter, Moretti, and four noncommissioned officers would finally get going for the prospective four-year pull.

Meanwhile relations with Germany had once again started to deteriorate—and the tense question of a manhood draft was being debated in Washington. Hadley had hoped that order and intelligence could govern the process. He was for increasing the regular Army first, then training officers to train citizens, and finally training the great body of citizens, at encampments, under a compulsory service system. Hearing that the Senate Military Affairs Committee suspected Yale and other college men of desiring exemption, the students reacted in no uncertain fashion. *News* Board and Student Council came out unanimously for the draft. And in a straw ballot the student body voted 1,112 for universal military training to only 288 against, with 50 for further discussion: a ratio of almost four to one in favor.[14]

In February 1917, the Germans having resumed unrestricted submarine warfare, there loomed the immediate possibility of war. At its first opportunity the Corporation voted support for Presi-

dent Wilson, and Faculty members had already stated their sentiments in strong terms. Professor Taft said war couldn't be avoided,
and compulsory training was necessary. Charles Seymour urged
conscription for war, and total mobilization. A mass meeting under
the auspices of the National Security League heard Henry L. Stimson argue for military training and Rear Admiral Fiske for a two-
ocean Navy. Alumni University Day gave emphasis to speeches on
student training. On 21 March 190 University officers sent a memorial to Wilson urging greater national preparedness, and on 2
April still further petitions were circulated by Faculty and New
Haven members of the Security League.

Needless to say, the R.O.T.C. had started work in intense earnest. Seniors, having only a year, had not been allowed to enroll. But
they were admitted into military history, and given intensive coaching for the Reserve Officers' examinations. The other old batterymen had been given advanced standing. It was thought that the
Corps would go to Fort Sill for summer training. By the end of a
month Hadley and the officers were sure that Yale was at least a
year ahead of other colleges, and was giving artillery training by
no means inferior to that given at West Point.

In addition enthusiastic students, faculty, and graduates had
been anticipating the Government's needs by organizing training
for other branches of the service. One branch in which the country
was obviously unprepared was aviation. As early as the summer of
1916 F. Trubee Davison '18 and some friends and classmates had
formed a Volunteer Coast Patrol unit, hired their own seaplane,
instructor, and equipment, and begun training at Port Washington. In the fall they had taken part in naval maneuvers off Sandy
Hook, and as the Aero Club continued work with donated planes
at the submarine base at New London. When winter weather
stopped flying they went on with study of theory and took in more
members. Already interested, in March the Navy would carry forward from this informal beginning, enlist the Yale men as its Aerial
Coast Patrol Unit No. 1, and thus create for the first time a Naval
Air Service. Again, just as the R.O.T.C. was being set up, the

464

United States Government sent a request for a Reserve Aero Corps, to give training at Mineola to some fifty men for the Signal Officers' Reserve. And early in March 130 volunteers applied.

Toward the end of February, at the suggestion of Secretary Stokes and others, and with the active cooperation of Professor Mather A. Abbott, the *Yale News,* and interested graduates, a Yale Naval Training Unit had also been organized. First called the Motor Boat Patrol, this large and enthusiastic group was to be disciplined and instructed by faculty and graduates; and in May it would be offered to the Secretary of the Navy with merely the request for a commanding officer.

Before March was out the College and University had announced their own plans in the event of war. On 3 April Walter Camp proposed a Senior Service Corps for overage men. Record crowds turned out for patriotic meetings. And the excitement was so intense that Hadley had to caution the students on impromptu parade that "Brain, not Brag, Wins Wars of Today." On 28 March the first of three units of the Aerial Coast Patrol left for southern training. Then the College found itself suddenly—on vacation.

At the very height of the war fever David Starr Jordan had visited New Haven to plead for peace. The views of the retired President of Stanford were hardly those of Hadley. He had been refused permission to speak at Princeton and unsympathetically used by some of his audiences elsewhere. So when his inquiry came, accompanied by a request from Professor Phelps that he be allowed to speak in a Yale hall, the President was profoundly distressed. Secretary Stokes, it appears, favored granting the request—and finally the President was won to promise support. The provisions were that Stokes find a hall, talk to the Student Council and persuade them to give Jordan a hearing on the ground that Yale should stand for freedom of speech.

Secretary Stokes met the Student Council and told them they could raise Cain afterward but they ought to give the man a fair hearing. Jordan was threatened with physical harm in a letter in the *News*. Billy Phelps himself received threatening communications. But he told his class in American literature that day—it was just a week before the declaration of war—that he believed in the fairness of the undergraduates and he thought the honor of Yale was involved. The meeting was called for the same big lecture hall in Lampson that night. As the affair opened, with Jordan and Phelps on the platform, the first two rows were still empty. This must have been by prearrangement, for Benjamin Strickler Adams '18 and a crowd of undergraduates, every one in uniform, marched down and filled up the first two rows. Phelps was equal to the occasion. One of his students recalls:

> He stepped to the lectern and
> raised his hand. Then he intoned:
> *Nos morituri te salutamus.*
> It went over. The crowd gave him
> a hell of a hand. Then he introduced
> Jordan and the meeting was on.

After a few minutes it had to be adjourned to Woolsey Hall because of the crowd outside, still clamoring to get in. Jordan and Phelps made the passage between the two buildings not only without physical harm but almost unnoticed—so anxious was the audience to get to new seats. In Woolsey Jordan spoke again, and at length. The students behaved "magnificently"—and afterward swung out to parade behind the band, as it marched away playing patriotic airs. Phelps wrote a letter to the *News* in which he said:

> Although they did not agree with the speaker before, or during, or after his address, they gave him full opportunity to speak and thus a great victory for free thought was won, a victory that left no bitterness in anybody's mind. As for the subsequent parade, I think it was the best possible way for the students to show the majority sentiment. Every time I think of last Thursday night, I am proud of Yale.[15]

THE COLLEGE AT WAR

War was declared during vacation, and the students came back to a different academic world. Intercollegiate athletics were out. The Adee Boat-House had been turned over to the Navy for its reserve training and rendezvous. The laboratories had been put at the disposal of the government. Two faculty batteries were beginning to drill under (Assistant Professor) Captain E. B. Reed, and the University Emergency Council was organizing training for everyone who desired it and was physically fit. It was recommended that everyone in the College should do early morning calisthenics on the campus. Those who now wished to be candidates for admission to the R.O.T.C. should drill daily from four to six, and take evening instruction in drill regulations, gunnery, military law, and hygiene from seven to eight. The instruction was to be given by faculty members who either had had experience or were being trained in normal classes under Captains Danford, Potter, and Moretti. Four hours of credit would be allowed, and simple service uniforms would be required.

Not counting the established R.O.T.C., some 1,300 students signed up and almost the whole College found itself in khaki or blue: *a volunteer military school.* Yet they were not entirely satisfied. For the training took too much time and promised too little result. Those members of the R.O.T.C. who helped in drilling their classmates felt particularly overburdened and had to be relieved of some course work. Some harassed participants wanted to abolish chapel. It was abbreviated. Some wanted to cut down regular classes in favor of more military training. Classes were decidedly speeded up.* Many fondly hoped the Faculty would

---

* Morris Hadley tells a story of his father passing outside a lecture building and hearing the voice of Professor "Eddie" Reed. Eddie Reed was known not exactly as a disciplinarian but as one who expected hard, thorough work. "Now take this down. It is important for the examination. We come now to Edmund Spenser, spelled with an s. Be careful about that. He wrote the *Faerie Queene*, spelled F-a-e-r-i-e Q-u-e-e-n-e. Got that? It will be necessary. Now we come to Christopher Marlowe."

omit the dreaded but somehow irrelevant June examinations.

Some boys had enlisted during vacation and more now began going off. Hadley instructed Dean Jones to keep them in College if possible and give leaves only in case of government call. Thus the thirty-six men who had enlisted in the Coast Defense Reserve had to be allowed to drop classes, but the rest of the volunteer Naval Unit were kept in College under training. The Emergency Council had promised that Seniors in good standing, who applied for commissions and were called by the Government, would be given their degrees. The American Ambulance Service enlisted two units. The second Aerial Coast Patrol was ordered out by the Navy. The Canadian Air Force lured others. Some graduates began raising money for a balloon observation unit. Tap Day was held a month early, and simultaneously at New Haven and for the aviators at Palm Beach. But what was a patriotic student's duty?

Taft urged underage men to enlist in the Field Artillery—perhaps in a body so as to form a Yale regiment, which could then be trained as a unit at Yale. Captain Danford and the University authorities strongly deprecated this advice; they urged underage men to stay and prepare themselves to be officers. College men should set a national example by enlisting, urged some. College men should use and train their brains, insisted Hadley. But many undergraduates found it hard to discipline themselves to such patience. They were afraid the war would be over before they could lend a hand. In the turmoil Congress had not yet made up its mind to universal military training; but within a very few days the War Department announced two critical decisions. First, a large number of Reserve Officers' Training Camps would be opened. Second, the Army could spare no regular officers for instruction in the Yale R.O.T.C. in 1917–18.

The camps, giving opportunity for quick qualification as officers, provided the students with a much-needed safety valve. Danford and the Faculty were deluged with requests for recommendation. In May more than five hundred students, generously certified for the first series of camps, began leaving College. To their consternation, the Yale authorities had heard that there were no special artillery camps, and that in only two were there provisions for artillery elements. Moreover, these camps had been planned for untrained civilians. So it looked at first as if all the training and experience of the Yale men was once again in danger of being thrown away. Finding that certain high artillery officers were equally troubled, Hadley protested to the War Department against this disregard of prior training and artillery skill. Certain influential alumni went further, and urged the enlistment of a Yale regiment, to be trained separately. Unfortunately the impression got about that Yale was asking for special privileges. So Hadley drew back and, once artillery opportunities at the camps had been improved, refrained from further pressure. Eventually a gratifying number of undergraduates managed to get their commissions that summer, and in the Artillery.

The future of the College R.O.T.C., however, was much less reassuring. First Congress had failed to appropriate adequately, and Yale had to call on its alumni to help meet expenses. Now by its camp policy the War Department was offering a quicker road to commissions. In fact commissions were to be obtainable only at these camps; and this seemed to remove official recognition from the R.O.T.C. Presumably it was still useful for colleges to train their underage students to be more efficient officers as well as educated leaders; but the Army could no longer spare its skilled personnel. In late May Captain Danford and his fellow instructors were ordered away, and Yale was notified that the Army could not provide a summer camp for the Yale R.O.T.C. The University at once proposed to hold its own camp, but the Army could not spare guns or equipment. For similar reasons the Navy could not supply a vessel for the promised summer cruise. Eventually the Naval Unit managed to get in a cruise on a borrowed yacht. Almost a hundred Army candidates accepted the generous invitation of the Harvard summer camp for underage infantry candidates. Still other men attended the Yale farm camp at Choate School in Wallingford. But already in June the drift from College was setting in again. It was

469

by no means certain that Yale could keep its R.O.T.C. alive—or make it serious enough to bring the students back to College in the fall.

Yale was still interested in training officers. Having sacrificed and spent considerably, having just dedicated what was said to be the finest artillery armory outside of Fort Sill, and having already achieved an unmatched record in artillery training, the University was not disposed to give up. Rather the President, the alumni, and the Faculty were resolved if need be to run the whole thing themselves. So Professor Reed prepared himself by taking summer training at Fort Sill. After some delay a retired rear admiral was obtained to head the Naval Unit. And for the R.O.T.C. the University secured the services of a retired artillery captain, to be assisted by Captain Adolphe Dupont of the French Military Mission to Harvard, and Captains A. G. Bland and Raymond Massey, disabled veterans of the Canadian Field Artillery. But what about guns?

Without guns, said Hadley, an artillery school would be like *Hamlet* without Hamlet. Happily André Tardieu, of the French High Commission, was at Yale to receive an LL.D. Hadley talked with him and explained the whole problem. Almost instantly upon Tardieu's return to France, Yale got word that it would receive a battery of four 75-millimeter guns. So the embarrassing problem of matériel was solved. Finally, to meet the newly voted draft age of twenty-one, Yale revised its R.O.T.C. and Y.N.T.U. programs into more intensive, three-year programs, with allowance of nine hours of academic credit, and only twelve hours of academic work required each year.

In the fall of 1917 the University reopened with more than thirty members of the faculty absent in Government service and with student enrollment reduced from 3,262 to 2,122. The enrollment in the new R.O.T.C. was 674, in the Y.N.T.U. 278. Eight members of the faculty began giving the naval instruction and another group filled out the R.O.T.C. staff. Some fifty-four would ultimately be engaged. In early October the French 75's arrived.

And so began a hectic winter. At first the French guns were a great attraction. Captain Dupont was on hand and delegations of artillery officers began arriving at Yale to study the guns. But soon Captain Dupont had to leave. The retired artillery captain at the head of the R.O.T.C. proved unable to handle his job and the War Department was too busy to see about acceptable substitutes. Major Reed and the Canadian officers had to run the whole unit. Undergraduates found it hard to study with friends already in service abroad. Morale began to sag. Rumors started that the draft age might be lowered to eighteen. But what was most disquieting was the lack of assurance that the Army would recognize the training being given by the Yale R.O.T.C. If a man got no credit, what was the use of staying and taking training? The trickle of departures began flowing again more rapidly.

So in January 1918 a fresh drive had to be made to give some stability to affairs. A message was secured from Secretary Baker urging underage students to stay in College. A new Government order promised to give the R.O.T.C. men at least a fair chance to gain commissions. The *News* made a drive to get everyone left in College into the R.O.T.C. The alumni presented the R.O.T.C. with six more horses. Then the Faculty, on recommendation of a committee under Major Reed, took the most drastic action of all.

This action was to revise the R.O.T.C. and Y.N.T.U. study programs, substitute more technical courses, and make them compulsory for all enlisted members. Yale had already gone farther than most private colleges to make its R.O.T.C. electives serve the interest of military instruction. Now for 1918–19 a fifteen-hour, three-year required program was announced that would be a straight military course of instruction: that is, a separate military curriculum which yet would qualify toward a Yale degree.*

The response was decidedly mixed. Some parents and students were much comforted by the intensified purposefulness. Others criticized the abolition of electives and the choice of required subjects. Dean Jones defended the plan and said it had not been imposed by the military. The *Alumni Weekly* hoped that the military curriculum and degree would make it possible for Yale to solve its

* See Appendix, Table U: Proposed R.O.T.C. Course in Field Artillery, 1918, p. 743.

entrance and high-school problem. Some students didn't want Yale a second West Point. At least one graduate thought it an excellent idea.

In April 1918 the Yale R.O.T.C. men began being called to training camps again and had to be excused from their classes. It was ruled they could be given their June examinations two months early. The Corporation voted to award degrees *honoris causa* to those prevented from graduating by war service.* A move to organize the physically disqualified into a third group for war training was taken up and abandoned. A group of Sheff trainees got into a riot with the New Haven police. Somehow the dwindling University staggered through the rest of the spring.

In May the Army, moving inexorably under the compulsion of its enormous necessities, announced a radical change and expansion in its college programs. For 1918–19 it would establish by voluntary enlistment in the colleges a great many military training units, rather than a few officer training units, and would coordinate the existing R.O.T.C.'s to these units. Each institution enrolling a hundred able-bodied underage students would have such a unit. Yale naturally agreed to become one of the cooperating colleges.

Almost up to the end of the summer of 1918 it was not supposed that the draft age would be lowered to eighteen. When this change came it meant that the great majority of undergraduates everywhere would be drafted, and assigned by the Army to the new college units of the Students' Army Training Corps. At once Hadley accepted the implications, agreed to let the Army use the College as a training camp, and moved to make Yale's participation in the S.A.T.C. an intelligent and useful affair. In view of Yale's experience and facilities, the War Department made an exception and allowed the S.A.T.C. to train for artillery rather than for infantry. Hadley saw to it also that the artillery curriculum was not diluted but was maintained at a theoretical level at least equal to that at West Point.

---

* This was a difficult and much disputed issue. Harvard and a number of other colleges refused to award academic degrees for nonacademic work. Columbia awarded regular degrees for satisfactory war service. Yale chose the middle ground of awarding the B.A. and Ph.B. *honoris causa*.

Every effort was made to get Yale's students and entrance candidates to return to New Haven to be inducted. Meanwhile additional scientific staffs and facilities were made available to the Government for the training of non-Yale officer candidates.

So in September 1918, at the beginning of its second war winter, Yale was made over from a volunteer military school into an armed camp. In all there remained only about 200 civilian students, underage or physically unfit, as against some 2,400 in khaki or blue.[16] Of the University faculty, 75 were now absent in war service and 125 assisted in the instruction of the S.A.T.C. and Naval and other units. Under Hadley's leadership the University had already expended more than $400,000.

Obviously it was no longer service for *civil* state. Perhaps it was no longer for church or learning. The authorities insisted that there was not an Army student at Yale who could not be enrolled as a candidate for a Yale degree. But when the first batch went off, the second batch would be men sent by the Army rather than selected as students by Yale. Meanwhile the Laboratory and Signal Corps schools had absorbed so many facilities that there was no room for a Marine Corps unit—or for accelerated secondary-school seniors. Characteristically, having decided to do a thing, Yale had gone all out. Hadley tried to reassure his constituency by stating that the only difference between the new S.A.T.C. and the old R.O.T.C. programs would be that the students had to be trained more quickly, under discipline at all times, and with draft age men having their expenses paid by the Government. But there was an inevitable decline in the quality and thoroughness of the work, to say nothing of the difference in spirit between an Army camp and a volunteer college.

Certainly there were differences in comfort, convenience, and diversion. Major Welldon proved an excellent commander. But the S.A.T.C. men found themselves packed in, four and six together in a two-man suite. They had to stand in line for hours for equipment and multiple inoculations. In mid-October the influenza epidemic took its toll. The undergraduate papers, after a vain effort, suspended publication. Camp entertainments began to be

473

needed. Relations between students and faculty changed. Hadley wrote to the faculty asking them to take in good part the personal inconvenience of obeying orders from students in uniform.

One evening, leaving the campus, Dean Jones was stopped by a stranger at the gate who poked a gun in his stomach and asked him to show his pass. The Dean explained he was a member of the faculty. This had no weight with the guard, who seemed unimpressed by the word Dean. Finally Jones explained that he was the man who wrote out the passes for everyone else. In the end he wrote out one for himself and went out. Some of the professors proved absent-minded—especially Billy Phelps, who kept forgetting to bring a pass or learn the password. It is said they finally got so used to him that the order of the day, handed on from sentry to sentry, always wound up: "and pass Professor Phelps." * [17]

On that incongruous note we may end this incongruous story. The complete militarization of the College lasted only about two months. But two months was quite long enough to give everyone a distaste for the S.A.T.C. It was a crude, unsatisfactory, quantity-production enterprise—to be discarded with relief. In 1917 Hadley had hoped that after the war a system of compulsory military instruction might be retained for all able-bodied students. But when the S.A.T.C. was being mustered out he was glad enough to settle for a volunteer R.O.T.C. At that, it was unquestionably a compliment to the University that Harvard and Princeton, and a score of colleges in all, should be asked like Yale to carry on Field Artillery units for the postwar R.O.T.C.

The war cannot be said to have benefited Yale's academic interests. Nearly everything that was advanced or theoretical or critical suffered; the study of German very nearly ceased.[18] Yet in one particular the emergency had served the University well, and the Administration had been quick to take advantage of its opportunity.

* When I first heard this story, at a Fellows' dinner in Jonathan Edwards, "Baldy" Crawford said it seemed only fair to pass Professor Phelps as he had in his day passed many men.

474

With increasing faculty shortages, interdepartmental planning and inter-School cooperation had become not merely an ideal but an imperative. Sheff students as well as Academic had wanted the R.O.T.C. training, and the two Schools had cooperated in planning the new three-year course. In department after department the needs of instruction required a redistributon of labor. Finally in March 1918 the Corporation went so far as to direct that the professors in the same department of study but in different Schools should meet together to arrange the instruction and the hours of the different members of the staff in a way most advantageous to the University as a whole—if necessary without waiting for action by the separate Faculties or Governing Boards.

Thus were initiated two policies—the diminution of School autonomy and the organization of the faculties into university-wide Departments of Study—that would play a striking role in Yale's postwar history. But the most immediate example of this new spirit and practice of cooperation was the spectacular S.A.T.C. War Aims Course, organized by the historians but taught by volunteers from a wide range of hitherto self-contained departments.[19]

Because of the sudden collapse of Germany the S.A.T.C. itself perhaps never had a chance to show what it could accomplish. In any case Yale's major contributions to the training of soldiers had been made in the neutrality and early war periods, or before the Army was ready to make full use of the colleges. By volunteer effort, and on its own initiative, the University had helped supply a competent officer personnel for the A.E.F. By Armistice Day the *Alumni Weekly* could point proudly to the fact that, of about 8,000 Yale men in service, some 3,500 had already earned commissions and at least 130 had lost their lives. "These are facts which . . . may well afford Yale men generally a quiet satisfaction in the University's redemption of its ancient pledge of service to public state."

The achievement had been no accident. It had been made possible by active support of the summer encampments of 1913, 1914, 1915; by choosing the difficult and much-needed service of artillery for its main effort; by enlisting and training the Yale militia batteries, 1915–16; by establishing and twice intensifying R.O.T.C. and Naval Training programs, 1916–18; by furnishing a self-trained faculty competent to carry the military instruction when service personnel failed; by building an armory, and an artillery hall, and by raising funds for other needed facilities; and by bringing in the first French 75's, which served as models for the making of American 75's, as well as training pieces.

Perhaps the greatest contribution of all was made by President Hadley. He had believed in preparedness, yet stood firm for an intelligent rather than an emotional patriotism: that is, for a sensible, forehanded, and disciplined use of brains, character, teaching power, and technical facilities. His forehandedness had netted Yale such a long series of disappointments that one is impressed rather forcibly with the disadvantages of anticipating popular reactions in a democracy. But few Yale men, in retrospect, would have had it otherwise.

All this makes no mention of the work of Yale graduates, or student or faculty volunteers, in almost innumerable fields; from Military Intelligence to the National Research Council to the scholar-diplomats of the Inquiry and the masters of gas warfare and military medicine. Secretary Stokes had gone abroad to plan the Army's educational work, Professor Nettleton to start the American University Union, Professor Mendell and others to head the Yale Bureau in Paris, while Professor Bumstead had become the scientific liaison officer for the government in London. Many others could be mentioned. But here we are mainly concerned with what the College and the undergraduates accomplished in Hadley's chosen line—artillery.

In this single line, when the figures had been finally added up, it turned out that Yale by a persistent disregard of the innumerable obstacles had contributed some two thousand men. And out of all the American officers commissioned in that branch before the end of the war at least one in every twenty had come from Yale.

CHAPTER 24·THE GREAT REORGANIZATION

We are through for good . . . with the old aimless college course.
                    —*Yale Alumni Weekly, 14 June 1918*

I want him to work. I also want him to get under the influence of some inspirational "teachers." I want his studies to be tied up with the times. . . . I want the broadest "results."
                    —*Pater Studentis, 22 November 1918*

. . . the structure of the University needs changing to meet the new problems . . .
                    —*Report of the Alumni Committee on a Plan for University Development, February 1919*

THE SUDDEN ARMISTICE brought to the campus, as to all corners of the land, an exuberant haste to revive the activities and usages of peace. In this feverish conversion the faculty, the students, the Army itself seemed to share. Instantly demobilization set in. Uniforms came off the boys, war courses stopped. Within six weeks the S.A.T.C. was disbanded and the military left town.

First in a trickle, but soon in a mounting torrent, the volunteers and the draftees came surging back. Familiar figures reappeared behind familiar desks and the famous prewar lectures began again. By mid-January 1919 an abbreviated civilian term was in full swing. Apparently Yale could look forward to salvaging the major part of a winter thought altogether lost to military instruction. No doubt an R.O.T.C. program would have to be allowed, and the matter of credit for war service, with degrees *honoris causa,* would

477

have to be handled generously. But happily the fine ten-course requirement for the B.A.—so forlornly and defiantly voted in the fatal month of the declaration of war—was all ready to be put into operation for the underclassmen. So the Faculty could count on an exceptionally solid foundation and were free at last to give attention to developing the upper-class work. The upper-class major could be strengthened, and the interrupted Honors programs made more exciting and important.

With the undergraduates already reviving intercollegiate athletics and the publications resuming, with the social system getting back into full swing and the baseball men clamoring for an Easter vacation trip, in no time Yale would certainly be giving a true old-fashioned education. Only it would be an even better education than before. For the College now knew, and all the better for having passed through fire, what work it ought to be doing. The day of achievement had come.

In the light of after events, it is hard to believe that anyone could have been so sanguine. As early as the spring of 1917, and even while the University was being converted to war, disquieting rumors had begun to circulate. Now, with the Armistice, these rumors suddenly multiplied and one by one exploded into ugly facts. It seemed the alumni were on a rampage. The University must be reformed. Yale must be made over. And there was no time to lose.

By Thanksgiving there was uneasy excitement. By mid-December a powerful alumni committee was in full cry, the Corporation was being stampeded into action, and consternation ruled the Faculties. By January 1919 the Administration in Woodbridge Hall would be badly worried, and individual professors either advocating their pet ideas or getting angry. In February, when the Corporation in turn was to show signs of relaxing, with the job half done, the well-organized alumni would put on fresh pressure. The result was that in March 1919, when Reorganization was pushed through to a vote, the Faculty of Yale College would come ominously close to rebellion.

To those experienced in the ways of Yale the whole thing was as incredible as it was unexpected. Indeed this movement affected so many Schools and gave the whole place such a thorough shaking-up that it can only with difficulty be described apart from the history of the entire University. Yet Reorganization was to a considerable degree inspired by feelings about Sheff and the College; and in its course the purposes, clientele, and authority of both Schools were drastically affected. In fact the educational debates and difficulties of the 1920's will scarcely be comprehensible without some knowledge of this mysterious, unprecedented, alumnidominated crusade for reform, which came down on old Yale like a thousand of brick at the end of the war.

From unpublished documents it would appear that Reorganization was a promising but very complex movement, which derived its official authority from the Corporation but its management increasingly from some influential graduates and its ideas and emotional drive from the widest variety of sources.

The most general sanction was supplied by the war and by the feeling that the good old days were gone forever. New and serious responsibilities confronted the University. Nineteenth-century solutions would no longer do for twentieth-century problems. It was up to Yale to seize "the chance for intellectual and moral leadership" in a "forward movement of educational reform."

A modest stimulus was supplied by President Hadley, who saw in the reconversion a longed-for opportunity to advance the University idea. In particular, he hoped it might be possible to replace certain of the traditional duplications and jealousies by a more rational distribution of functions and a more cooperative sharing of responsibilities. By a happy accident the wartime emergencies had broken down the barriers between the undergraduate Faculties and reduced the financial power and perennial isolation of Sheff. Now perhaps was the time to do something about the Select Course, define more clearly "the *objects* if not the *subjects*" of the two undergraduate Schools, and assign the rival professors of the same studies to common University-wide departments serving the common cause. Now also was the time to transfer the graduate degrees in

479

science from Sheff to the Graduate School and make the latter a strong and progressive institution.

The movement to build up the Graduate School, started by the appointment of Dean Oertel in 1911, had been slowed up by his absence, resumed in 1916 by Dean Cross, then checked again by the war. But Cross had succeeded in setting up a very loyal and effective Executive Board. And the detachment of the Graduate School from Yale College had been forwarded by the transfer of the M.A. degree in 1912. Now it remained to get control of the advanced degrees in science and to set up the Graduate School's own Board of Permanent Officers. "Uncle Toby" Cross thought the University ought to be constructed the way the deacon built the one-horse shay: equally sound in all its parts.* [1]

A most important stimulus, and indeed the original push, had been supplied by two other members of the Administration, the Secretary and the Treasurer. Anson Phelps Stokes and George Parmly Day had long entertained ambitious plans. Stokes, in particular, had been impatient of Chittenden's intransigence, more interested than Hadley in building up the Medical School, more bold in looking toward growth along many lines. One of his pet schemes was the establishment of an active and forward-looking Department or School of Education. Another was an aggressive drive to increase the University's endowment and improve faculty salaries. Between them, in 1916–17, Stokes and Day had persuaded the Corporation to recognize the necessity of long-range planning for the future needs and expansion of the University. At their suggestion the Corporation had created an Alumni Committee on a Plan for University Development and asked a number of prominent graduates—men of influence and large affairs—to look into the situation and help advise. [3]

Meanwhile in alumni circles generally an ever-widening dis-

* Two other incitements to planning should perhaps also be mentioned. In August 1918 the Sterling bequest was announced. And in the months of October–December 1918 a visiting British Education Mission, interested in the international exchange of professors and students, roused Dean Cross and the Yale University Council to an active discussion of British, German, and American educational ideals. [2]

480

content had been making itself felt. The graduates of the Middle West had not forgotten Yale's entrance barriers. Influential alumni East and West insisted on better teaching for lowerclassmen and criticized the indefiniteness and impracticality of the College curriculum. The Western alumni wanted better representation on the Corporation and in Yale's councils. Certain supporters of the Alumni Advisory Board were dissatisfied with the minor and ineffective role permitted the board. Increasingly, Yale's constituency had become critical of the College-Sheff situation, impatient of the Select Course, and sensitive to the failure of the Scientific School— with its three-year rule—to keep pace with the reputation of other scientific and engineering institutions. Inevitably many of these graduates, removed as they were from the local scene and daily exposure to the inherited attitudes, had grown disgusted with academic gradualism and isolationism. It didn't seem to them that President Hadley was handling the situation with sufficient force and courage. They feared the College was falling behind the times.

The Corporation's appointment of the representative Alumni Committee early in 1917 therefore provided an unlooked-for channel and released into the University situation a flood of pent-up dissatisfaction. In effect this committee, which had been thought of as a way of securing the interest and cooperation of influential graduates in working out broad University plans to be presented to the Corporation, found itself pressed by elements in its constituency to proceed instead toward reform. When its members then began joint interviews with the Deans and Administrative Officers and discovered for themselves the attitudes of the undergraduate Schools and the President's apparent timidity, they turned quite naturally from "Development" to an investigation of the internal duplications, rivalries of authority, and needless inefficiencies that seemed to have been allowed to grow ever more damaging under Hadley's leadership.

Two final factors must be reckoned in. The war had heightened the emotional tensions, decreased the patience and willingness to compromise, and convinced many a graduate that what was practical and efficient was what was desirable. With other universities announcing their plans for meeting the requirements of the new age, there seemed not a moment to lose. Again the war had intensified the interest of the alumni in Yale, raised the *Alumni Weekly* subscription list to 8,000 and given to its editor, Edwin Oviatt, a strong and pressing sense of responsibility.

So by Armistice Day the authorized representatives of Yale's graduate constituency had acquired not only a decidedly critical attitude—and a heightened sense of urgency—but a powerful ally and spokesman, on the spot and able to make their sentiments heard. Oviatt's impatience with Latin and with the old entrance restrictions has already been noted. As early as 1915 he had suggested that the College might "come into its mission as a military school for the development of captains of industry." In January 1918 he had proclaimed that the old days had "gone forever . . . we don't want to know how cultivated a given youth in college is; we want to know how well equipped he is going to be to do his share in the Army or Navy. . . . We refuse to talk 'Business as Usual.' *We want results.* [Moreover] we are going to 'want results' in the new education immediately after the war ends and from then on." By November 1918 Oviatt saw Yale standing "on the threshold," but Hadley tired from the war effort and hesitating. It would take some "tall hustling," he warned. "Are we to fall back into the old and to-day discredited order of things or are we to come out of them into a new and practical order?" A more promising organization of the University was imperatively demanded.[4]

In this fashion the Stokes-Day plan for a bigger and better University had become transformed, in alumni hands, into a demand for reform first, then growth perhaps afterward—and as Armistice Day freed busy College Officers for the resumption of educational activities, this graduate group prepared to come to New Haven, to urge on President and Corporation their own rather different ideas. The alumni, as well as the College Faculty, had great expectations.

With the Faculty hoping to improve, the Administration to revise, but the alumni to reorganize, the curious fact is that no one

482

with the possible exception of Anson Stokes quite realized how serious the dissatisfaction of the graduates had become. It was known to a few in authority that the Alumni Committee on a Plan for University Development, with headquarters in New York, had been doing some investigating. An inactive subcommittee of the Corporation had sat down once or twice with some surprisingly aggressive Yale Club officers and graduates. Here and there a dean, or a critical planner like Robert Nelson Corwin, had been asked about the entrance problem, or the Sheff-College jealousies, or the reasons for complaints about Freshman teaching. Also the editor of the *Alumni Weekly* had taken to publishing in a proprietary manner some rather startling recommendations.

Yet the Faculties of the undergraduate Schools had never been called together or systematically consulted. They knew that Hadley was not one to dictate. Also they were still rather disorganized. Director Chittenden, the Napoleon of Sheff, was just getting back from England. In the College the most influential leaders had stepped down, while the rising chiefs were absent on war duty. E. S. Dana and G. B. Adams had joined B. Perrin in retirement. E. P. Morris was in his last year; C. B. Tinker was in Washington; Clive Day, Charles Seymour, and Clarence W. Mendell were all abroad. As for the men on the spot, they were without question distracted and busy.

Suddenly, and with no more warning than some additional alarums in the *Alumni Weekly* about Yale's "educational unpreparedness," the first blow fell. On 23 November 1918 this Alumni Committee on a Plan for University Development visited New Haven, interviewed the Treasurer, the Secretary, and one professor. Then it voted six recommendations.[5] The first four proved extraordinary:

1. That steps be immediately taken to provide that all undergraduate instruction shall be under a common control while the teaching force may be subdivided into such separate departments of instruction as may be deemed necessary.

2. That a definite course of instruction, or that a curriculum

consisting of a consistent and largely prescribed character be provided in such undergraduate school leading to each of the several professional schools, or towards the life work of various students.

3. That emphasis among the instructors in such undergraduate school be laid on teaching rather than on research work.

4. That steps be taken as soon as practicable to consolidate, if possible, the Corporation known as the Trustees of the Sheffield Scientific School with Yale University . . .

Still wilder rumors began to circulate and on 6 December the second blow fell when the *Alumni Weekly* published some reorganization schemes that suggested setting up a Junior College.

Was the President going to take such startling suggestions seriously? What soon became clear was that the impetus of the alumni was stiffening Mr. Hadley's resolution, and perhaps enlarging his own concepts of what could usefully be attempted under the head of postwar reconstruction. Secretary Stokes was fertile with suggestions. Dean Cross was aggressive. And the Prudential Committee showed determination.

The first great pressures were directed against the Scientific School; and in three weeks this opening engagement had been won. Director Chittenden did not cave in, but finding the authorities so resolute, and his own alumni and Governing Board divided, he signed a limited capitulation and dug in to hold what was left. So by 16 December the Corporation abolished the Select Course and accepted the Scientific School's offer to lengthen its three-year courses in science and engineering to four. Whereupon, looking both ways, the Corporation ordered Yale College and the Scientific School to appoint conference committees to make it possible for qualified students in either School to take courses in the other. The entrance examinations were also to be overhauled and jointly administered; and it was hinted in broad language that any division between the College and Sheff in Freshman year might have to be abandoned.

How far were Yale's governors proposing to go? From his Washington desk Chauncey Brewster Tinker wrote up in consternation to ask if matters could not be delayed a little till the leading professors and the men of influence in old Yale College got back and could be consulted. Characteristically, Professor Morris replied he thought the old College would weather the storm.[6] Despite the growing uneasiness of many professors, and regardless of the resolute conservatism of the conference committee under the gruff leadership of Dean Jones,[7] the Reorganization movement went on gathering momentum. When Hadley hesitated the Corporation replaced their President with Alfred Ripley on its Reorganization committee. When Anson Stokes undertook to ride the storm, alumni excitement mounted and the powerful Alumni Committee asked the Corporation not to reach any final decisions before they could submit their own report. In December–January came another series of precedent-shattering votes, with the Corporation giving the Graduate School control of all graduate work, degrees, and policy, and taking steps toward a uniform nomenclature and organization for all the Departments and Schools.

Still the graduate reformers were not satisfied. They were determined that reform should be introduced into the College as well, and the more the Administration hesitated, and the more the Professors resisted, the more drastic and punitive their attitude became.[8] In February the pressures became fierce. The Alumni Committee hurried in their own tremendous report. Alumni Day saw graduates swarming into New Haven. And what had started as a confused, four-cornered struggle between Alumni, Corporation, Administration, and Faculty now turned into a headlong rush. By mid-March the Corporation had voted most of what the reformers wanted.[9] The Professors were licked.

That is, the Select Course, instead of being dropped entirely, was now to be transferred to the College. Among other changes it was ordered that a Common Freshman Year for all undergraduates should be set up. Also a common entrance examination was to be administered by a University committee. Thenceforward all men teaching a given subject were to be organized into University Departments, with budgetary and personnel functions. These Depart-

485

ments were in turn to be allocated to University Divisions, which likewise crossed school boundaries. Finally representatives of these Divisions were to sit on a University Council under the chairmanship of a Provost.

For Yale College these changes meant added duties and many subtracted powers. Never before had the College been asked to handle two classes of students, coming from different backgrounds with different preparation, and candidates for different degrees. Socially, this threatened the addition of indigestible numbers to a College already so large that Class loyalties and the Yale spirit were breaking down. On the educational side, it threatened curricular confusion. The more so as Yale College would no longer control admissions policy. Indeed if the Corporation really went through with their order and set up a Common Freshman Year, Yale College might not even be able to say what its Freshmen should study. The College Faculty, perhaps more painstakingly than any other in America, had for twenty years been trying to pump meaning and order into the elective course for the Bachelor of Arts degree. Now it suddenly found its curricular authority cut in half.

The organization of University Departments, the policy of University laboratories, the invigoration of the Graduate School, even the somewhat artificial creation of grand alliances or Divisions of teaching personnel had a great deal to be said for them, and they drew decided and increasing support. Nevertheless, under one light, even these improvements were so many ill-concealed flank attacks on the old College. Henceforward an instructor's loyalty would be divided and diffused. For promotions, for permission to give new courses, even for that confidence and esprit de corps that comes with joint endeavor, he would now have to look first to his Department and only afterward, apparently, to his College.

Certainly, the Dean and the Committee on Ways and Means knew themselves shorn of that grand monetary semi-independence whose growth for a generation they had been nursing so carefully. In matters financial and political, as well as curricular, the College's own graduates had surely cut it down to size. The Age of the

486

Barons was over. From now on Yale was to be organized like a good business, with uniform departments, symmetrically connected, and all alike overseen by a new educational factotum called the Provost, to the end of efficient production. How were the mighty fallen.

Yet the worst beating was in morale. For apart from the virtues or demerits of particular provisions there was no blinking the unpleasant fact that Reorganization had been initiated, shaped, and finally put through without adequate consultation, and in some matters in almost casual or scornful defiance of Faculty wishes. More accurately, it had been rushed through, largely by outsiders, in disregard alike of their constitutional powers, their experience, and their most cherished beliefs. They had asked for time, they had protested, and to a degree they had fought. Dean Jones had urged the alumni not to take away the educational authority of the Faculty. Tinker had come back from the wars raging against the measures taken and contemplated. Clive Day, Seymour, and Mendell had been shocked by what they had found on their return from Paris, and promptly set to work. But it was already too late. The thing was driven through. The Faculty felt they had never been given a hearing.[10]

This charge the Alumni spokesmen, and Secretary Stokes as well, repelled.[11] It was pointed out that the votes of the December Corporation meeting, and the recommendations of the Alumni Committee, had been circulated to all the Permanent Officers, and that each had been invited to express his views, in person or in writing, to the special Corporation Committee on Educational Policy. The Alumni Committee had interviewed a number of professors; and, as Samuel H. Fisher said, there was hardly a reform but had originated outside the committee and with some member of the University faculty. Then, after the Armistice, at least a dozen professors had been consulted. A number of School Faculties had submitted their official views, and Dean Jones' Conference Committee had been heard. The opposition arose out of narrow-minded stubbornness. Apparently the Yale College Professors could see only Yale College. After the original votes the Faculty had neither suggested their own ways of reform nor been willing to go along. Hence somebody had to seize the opportunity for improvement presented by the end of the war.

Without question there appeared some selfishness and some narrowness, and a good deal of home pride in the attitude of Yale College. The Professors were also incoherent; they had been taken by surprise and they lacked leadership. As for consultation, the established usage had been to do nothing important without first bringing it to the floor of the Faculty, for open debate and approval. Yet, in spite of positive assurances,[12] not once had they been called together by the Administration to discuss or to vote on the main issue. Instead there appeared to have been a deliberate effort by the Corporation to divide and rule—in any case to deal with no larger units than conference committees. When, at the last minute, a large number of the Faculty had met in secret conclave and sent up a protest, they had been reproved for their pains.* Now they were being asked to help make a success of measures whose wisdom many honestly doubted.

They would try. But one could hardly expect them to be cheerful and constructive. For in two further ways their confidence and morale were being undermined. On the one hand, the steep postwar inflation was rapidly impoverishing them; on the other, their liberty of self-government and their very security of tenure were under attack.

The salary crisis was acute. How on earth was an instructor to live on $1,000 a year, asked the younger men. "The pleasure of work in a place like Yale and of association with its traditions will

---

* As for the charge of obstruction, hear one of the accused: "It is hard to let the charge of professional stubbornness pass unchallenged. There is certainly much of that as there is of 'corporation stubbornness,' 'human stubbornness.' But the charge does not come with the best grace from the body with the ultimate power. It then smacks of impatience. The corporation in 1920 had been hustled by the alumni and having decided what to do wished to do it at once. Their position is indicated (a) by the fact that none of the reorganization was adequately presented *for action or revision* to the faculties and (b) that the most effective parts of reorganization were aimed at the reduction of faculty power. Subsequent history has confirmed this."[13]

make our Faculty content with half the pay they have elsewhere," Hadley told his Alumni Day audience. But, as an instructor in physics had already protested, "families cannot be supported, nor children educated, on these abstractions. With the possible exception of those who enjoy independent incomes, *Yale's teachers are not content.*" [14]

A committee of the Corporation was working on the problem, but by mid-February no action had been taken. What complicated the situation was the prospect of having to budget for a lot of new administration—a Provost, a Dean of Men, a special Dean and staff for Freshmen—on funds already insufficient. With the deficit more and more on his mind the harassed President was appalled at the thought of a series of salary increases and felt driven to suggest a sensational expedient. Yale should select instructors able to supplement their salaries by outside work, especially in the summer. "An Assistant Professor who is getting two thousand five hundred dollars ought to have his schedules so arranged that . . . he could earn from a thousand to fifteen hundred dollars additional in outside work. That is largely what our vacation is for." [15]

When the Alumni Day audience understood the President to suggest not only vacation drudgery for Yale's instructors but postponement of the rest of Reorganization for similar reasons of finance, the reaction was phenomenal. This time alumni, deans, and faculty all together came down on their leader in indignant protest. So Mr. Hadley "came around" and Reorganization was pushed forward again, regardless of its inevitable cost.[16] Then on 17 March, after the important issues had all been decided and voted, the Corporation gave the salaries of instructors and assistant professors a modest boost.*

---

* Salary raises for professors were postponed until the fall, in part to give the University time to see which men taught large courses or took on extra work. The Alumni Report had recommended that increases be accompanied by improved methods of teaching "and better division of work" among the teachers—and that "no tradition or rule limit the number of hours of teaching of the members of the Faculty." This came close to deliberate intimidation, as well as threatening the privileges of seniority.

The powers and status of the Professors were the next target of attack. For the Report of the Alumni Committee proposed the entire abolition of the Yale College Board of Permanent Officers and the substitution of an elective board of nine members, composed in part of assistant and associate professors. The Report had also recommended that permanent tenure be abolished, that all professors be put on term appointments, and that their nominating and promoting powers be shared with other bodies and with the Educational Policy Committee. To leading members of the Alumni Committee it seemed unreasonable that the University could not discipline its full professors—if recalcitrant or mediocre. Moreover they thought that the exclusive authority to nominate and promote— subject only to rejection by the Corporation—put in the hands of the Yale Faculties too great a power of self-perpetuation, especially as most university faculties did not appear to enjoy such rights.

The implications for professorial freedom and security were plain. Fortunately the President was not so weak, nor the Corporation so reactionary, as to countenance anything so drastic. But the Corporation did seem to be taking away the Professors' privilege of selecting their Departmental chairmen.[17] And it hardly went down well to have the alumni still hinting that if the faculty would only show a better spirit and get behind Reorganization, they, the alumni, would feel much more disposed to dip into their pockets in order to raise salaries. Hadley had made Yale's graduates into "stockholders" and now the stockholders seemed bent on reducing the College Officers to the status of factory employees.[18]

On top of all this was the uncertainty and impatience for results. Before either the men or the endowment had been supplied, the Alumni Committee seemed to expect the new organization to spring into the air. In the turmoil after the storm it was hardly surprising that the local interests should try to consolidate themselves —or that the centralizing reformers should in their turn show irritation. The spring of 1919 in New Haven was anything but serene. Nor did the following year see peace and good feelings entirely restored.

Perhaps only Chittenden and a few others fully understood that

Sheff as an undergraduate Scientific School had been dealt a blow from which it must eventually bleed to death. But everyone had his mind on the new School that was just being organized. Without comparison the most disputed and regretted feature of the whole Reorganization, from the point of view of many College Officers, was the proposed Common Freshman Year. This led Samuel H. Fisher, one of the most ardent champions of the venture, to accuse some of the professors of playing Achilles and sulking in their tents. To which Charles Seymour gave answer: [19]

> Now the enthusiastic co-operation of the faculty has been hindered by the very spirit shown in your letter, namely the tendency to regard honest opinions not in accord with the opinions of the corporation as evidence of a desire to "block." The faculty is responsible for the active application of the education given at Yale. The welfare of Yale demands that they should feel that responsibility as theirs. If you discourage it by hinting that honest thought and honest expression of that thought are undesirable, you aim a deadly blow at one of the great traditions of Yale. Her greatness has largely resulted not merely from the calibre of the men on her faculties, but also from the fact that they regarded themselves as responsible for the welfare of Yale.
>
> That feeling of responsibility has been weakened. Do not weaken it further. Above all do not question the honesty and loyalty of the Yale graduates on the Faculty. Yale is their vocation and their life. It probably means more to them than to anyone else.

Obviously there is more to be said in favor of Reorganization than has been alluded to here. It cauterized the festering feuds of the undergraduate Schools. It brought together the separated scholars. It gave the professional Schools new status and the Graduate School true vigor and independence. It strengthened the central Administration, promoted the University idea, and converted Yale into a better-balanced institution. To notice exclusively the plaints of the Academic conservatives is therefore to underestimate the benefits of Reorganization to Yale as a whole.

491

Nevertheless, looking back at the war and this great Reorganization, it becomes plain that the years 1917–21 did mark an unhappy turning in the career of the College Faculty. To Yale men on the outside the war had been a glorious crusade, and Reorganization a magnificent redirection of energy and idealism toward a consolidated and forward-looking University. To many of those inside the war had been a most unpleasant experience, and the peace had never even come close to giving back all that the war had taken. In ways only dimly understood the war had brought the whole value of a liberal education into question. Then, in ways only too obvious, this imposed Reorganization had reduced the independence of the College and shaken the Faculty's morale. Authority and confidence itself were undermined.

President Angell was therefore to find the Professors of Yale College sometimes suspicious and hypercritical, sometimes indifferent to the point of stupor: in any case hardly the confident and constructive, self-administering company of captains that had ruled the Academic roost back say in 1914. All this, of course, would have seemed a shocking nightmare in 1914. Even in 1921 it was only beginning to be appreciated.

CHAPTER 25 · RECONSTRUCTION

. . . it became necessary for Yale to choose between its character as a national institution and its position as an upholder of the old classical traditions. It chose the former; and it chose wisely. I . . . think that the value of classical study is underrated, and that of some forms of science overrated by the American public today. But in determining the subjects on which to base its requirements . . . a university must meet the public demand.

—ARTHUR TWINING HADLEY, *1921*

GRADUALLY THE tide of graduate anxiety receded. Whatever their feelings about individual professorial attitudes, the organized alumni did not degenerate into snipers. On the contrary they accepted their own defeats, supported the raising of salaries, and helped find funds and candidates for the new administrative offices. After one more winter of intermittent activity, in the spring of 1920 the Alumni Committee on a Plan for University Development retired from the field and let the Administration and the several Faculties work out the Reorganization in the light of local conditions.

From the viewpoint of the College Officers the trouble therefore became not the continuance of outside interference but the tremendous influx of new students into an institution that had been badly shaken. Administratively Yale College would have to handle far greater numbers, with more diversified interests, in less time, with less authority, and above all with a very greatly diminished sense of corporate responsibility. From the curricular point of view the problem was to find new bearings. The subjects, the standards, the sequence, and the distribution of study, all these once familiar buoys and markers of a College course had come loose from their moorings and were drifting on storm-tossed waters. As a consequence the old collegiate ferry service between school and career, momentarily interrupted by the war, continued for some years afterward to operate erratically. Hardly a Class completed its bachelor's voyage in the exact wake of its predecessor.

No doubt such irregularities reflected the disturbed state of faculty feelings. But primarily the curricular confusion resulted from the alumni effort to impose certain preconceived ideas upon an unstable, highly complicated, and imperfectly appreciated situation. Inevitably it took time for Yale College to realize those ideas —or to discard them.

The first or strongest wish of the alumni was said to be for better teaching. What they meant by teaching, what kinds of teachers they had in mind, or how they proposed to get teachers was not made clear. Except that research was singled out as a danger. Academic emphasis on research was said to be the usurper of time and of promotions and hence the enemy of teacher and student alike.[1] By inference the ideal teacher would not be the explorer, not even primarily the inspiring lecturer. He would be the instructor, the effective inculcator of facts. If so, Yale College was meant to become less like a university and more like a school—an effective training school.

This deduction was debatable, yet not without warrant. For a second compelling notion of many alumni was that College studies should not be at such loose ends. They should be better organized. There should be much less elective choice or foolishness; the studies should be more compactly grouped and the students should be compelled to take such courses as were good for them.

This, of course, raised the question of who was to decide as to the goodness and who was to do the choosing. By degrees the Alumni Committee had become aware that here they were poaching on time-honored Faculty prerogatives. Yet for two years they persisted. In some ways they felt better judges of the graduate, or product, than any cloistered pedagogue.[2] At least they were competent to say what should be the *ends* of schooling. The means they were

494

willing to leave in College hands—provided President Hadley and the Faculty showed energy enough.

The ends or objectives of a College education—no more on this than on the other points of their program did the Alumni Committee pause to formulate a philosophic thesis. But the bundle of impulses that served to guide their reform was tolerably clear. They wanted the gates more widely opened and, within, a more practical instruction. There had been much criticism of duplication and unbusinesslike inefficiency. In addition and in particular the members of the committee wanted to do something about the Select Course.

Translated into standards, this meant that they wanted admissions still more generously handled. At the Freshman level the alumni were after a single curriculum that would be general yet largely compulsory: general enough to serve as a common foundation and allow the student to postpone his choice of concentration; compulsory yet so well taught that no student could escape a substantial and varied body of knowledge. Then, for upper-class years they sought a more direct preparation for future career. Studies should be grouped into preprofessional or prevocational programs: for law as for medicine, for business and public life even as for law. This was sensible and it was efficient. It would invigorate the students and economize resources.

Whether this three-level program was consistent, or in any case humanly realizable, seems not to have been questioned. It just seemed natural, in fact statesmanlike, not to pause with criticism but to offer a constructive plan. Yet in passing from correction to suggestion the Alumni Committee had step by step pushed into a field whose pitfalls and deceptions they were a long way from guessing. That educational administration could be a thorny business they were beginning to appreciate. But that there was anything mysterious about educating the young, that the educational process itself had been the bafflement and despair of the wisest since time immemorial, such thoughts hardly shadowed their path. Yale's troubles, after all, had arisen from internal mismanagement. The Alumni Committee prescribed accordingly.

495

At once these governing ideas of the reconstruction collided with the facts of an awkward and tangled situation. For the procedures of the College were so intertwined that no single substantial policy could be altered without affecting standards all along the line.

For example, if more boys were desired from the Middle West and South, that meant that Latin could no longer be required of distant candidates, and perhaps other requirements would have to be lowered or broadened as well. This in turn would mean either a lower general standard, for both admissions and college work; or a schooling so diversified, and college studies so split up, as to diminish the common basis of American education; or the adoption of a double standard by Yale College at the very moment that the Sheff and the College entrance committees were being told in no uncertain tones to eliminate their distinctions of quality and subject matter.

Again, the surrender of the Latin entrance requirement for some or all of the candidates would almost irresistibly lead to the surrender of college Latin as a prerequisite for the degree for some or all of the students. But perhaps it would lead to other surrenders as well. For bound up with the language was the principle of required studies, a disciplinary system of instruction, and a humanist insistence on the great classical-Christian tradition.

Vice versa, the establishment of prevocational programs would introduce a series of alien elements. No doubt a selected program of modern studies, lengthened to four years, did seem a logical program for the Western high-school boys. And in the interest of efficiency and common sense the alumni had been keen to have the Administration transfer the Select Course itself from Sheff to the College. But this meant Yale College would be offering two curricula and two degrees, or at best two different pathways to the same degree. So once again the old College-Sheff rivalries were perhaps merely to be transplanted into the College and not exorcised for good.

Even plainer than such difficulties as these were the problems of personnel: the scorn in certain quarters for the Select Course, the loyalty to bygone standards, departmental jealousies, and the ineviable struggle for survival into which the classicists would be plunged. Finally, the all-important drift of popular opinion was divergently interpreted. By the reformers it was presumed that the times would demand more pragmatic studies, whereas certain of the Faculty thought that a wider appreciation of the arts was dawning. If we remember, with all this, that Reorganization was a reform imposed in haste, then the vacillations and the frustrations of these postwar years are easy enough to understand.

That the confusion was not even greater Yale owed in no small part to the essential modesty and good will of the Alumni Committee.[3] More yet was owed to habit and tradition: to the established curriculum, to the fact that there were still sound old ways of doing things while new ways were being debated or tried out. This institutional momentum was even strong enough to disguise the theoretical inconsistencies into which the Faculty had been plunged. As we shall see, after the first rout, they were able to take up their problems piecemeal, debating the application of their orders, point to point.

THE PROBLEM OF LATIN

The educational struggle set going within the walls of Yale College by the alumni mandates was a four-cornered one. It involved Latin, the Ph.B. degree, admissions, and the Freshman year. The opening gun had gone off as early as 19 December 1918, when President Hadley secured from the reluctant Permanent Officers appointment of a committee to confer with the Scientific School on the interdepartmental problems foreshadowed by the proposed changes in the reorganization of these undergraduate departments. As the Professors' minutes record, President Hadley and the Dean took the position that the crux of coordination between the two departments "lay in the possible admission of superior students without examination in Latin." [4] The nose of the camel, pushing under the tent flap, had been draped in the words "possible" and "superior."

Dean Jones was persuaded to appoint a tough committee, which deliberated with obstinate resistance through a critical six

497

PART FIVE : WAR AND REORGANIZATION

weeks. Then in February the committee endorsed "the principle of interchange" of courses and facilities, and a joint entrance committee to recommend (*sic*) such measures as would ensure a uniform administration of entrance requirements and correlate the requirements of admission with the work of the secondary schools. The Professors so voted, but they also agreed that the routine work of admission should be handled by separate committees as before. And a motion that Latin be transferred from the list of required entrance subjects to the elective group was laid on the table.

On 11 February Dean Jones quoted the Corporation Committee on Educational Policy. They were asking for an *informal* expression of opinion, first as to whether the Faculty expected to continue to require Latin for the B.A.; second, whether the Faculty would be willing "to confer the B.A. degree upon men of high standing in certain groups of study without Latin"; and finally whether the Faculty would be ready to provide "a special degree, such as the B.Litt., for men taking the four years' course in the College without Latin." Evidently the admission of superior non-Latin men was no longer "possible" or even debatable. It was taken decidedly for granted. To this the Professors gave guarded answer that, provided no course in business administration or commercial science were set up in either School, they would enable well-qualified students entering without Latin or Greek and studying in College an approved group of courses "to qualify for a [*sic*] degree without taking courses in the Classics." [5]

Whether offended by this haggling or because their hand was being forced, the Corporation Committee brusquely recommended, and the Corporation in Committee of the Whole endorsed, the transfer of Latin to the elective group of entrance requirements. Provision was also to be made for a degree—and the Faculty was to choose which one—for "well-qualified students in College without Latin." At the same time the Corporation determined to set up a Common Freshman Year—and about this neither of the undergraduate boards had even *informally* been consulted or asked to vote.[6]

Secretary Stokes got out a voluminous announcement of what

the Corporation was planning on 11 March. This left just six days before the Corporation itself would ratify the whole. As Professor Hendrickson remarked to Professor Mendell, "Our speed is positively vertiginous." In a desperate final effort to stave off the Common Freshman Year and to recapture control as to Latin and the B.A. degree, the general Faculty of Yale College came together in a special meeting on the afternoon of 15 March. President Hadley had not been notified and even Dean Jones was absent. The meeting was called together by Secretary pro tem Gruener, and Professor Morris, who had been the moving spirit, was elected Chairman pro tem. Professor Phelps read such sections of the Corporation Report as were called for. Then the offering of motions began.[7]

Suffice it to record that after entertaining a motion to ask the Corporation to refer both the matter of a Common Freshman Year and the entrance requirement in Latin to the Board of Permanent Officers "for previous action," the Yale College Faculty apparently persuaded itself that it was too late to ask for a fresh start on these matters. It was therefore:

> Voted: that the General Faculty of Yale College does not approve of a common Freshman year.
>
> Voted: to respectfully request . . . That the Faculty of Yale College be requested to consider the question whether Latin be continued as a requirement of candidates for the B.A. degree, and whether, if so, provision should be made for another degree for well qualified students who wish to take a college course without Latin.
>
> Voted: to transmit the above vote to the Corporation.
>
> Upon motion of Professor Lewis the following vote was passed, to be transmitted to the Corporation; Resolved: that the General Faculty of Yale College learns with concern of the intention of the Corporation to establish a common Freshman year for the College and the Scientific School, and hopes that the Corporation will cooperate with the Faculty to prevent the change from exerting any deleterious influence upon the life of the institution.

499

If understandable under the circumstances, this was nevertheless strong language. The Corporation can hardly have relished the
hint that their own actions might be as deleterious to the institution as the alumni and the *Alumni Weekly* had more than once
accused the Faculty of being. They did not like the exclusion of
President Hadley from the meeting, and in any case they were
unanimous for trying a Common Freshman Year, being only too
aware of alumni sentiment on that subject. On 17 March the Corporation therefore declined to regard the Faculty action as official
or as more than "an expression of opinion of those present"; they
authorized Stokes to reprove the Faculty for the "accident" of
Hadley's lack of notification; and they stuck by their own resolve
to go ahead with a Common Freshman Year, consulting Faculty
representatives only on what its organization and studies should be.[8]

As to Latin, however, the feelings of the Fellows were mixed.
Though provoked at Faculty obstinacy, the Corporation members
were themselves interested in maintaining Latin and uncertain of
the best course to pursue.[9] They therefore postponed the whole degree question pending further recommendations. To this limited
extent had the Faculty revolt been effective. The Officers of Yale
College could not prevent the admission of men without Latin or
their arrival in Yale College or their getting a degree. But they
could say what degree these men should get; and whether the Latin
requirement, before College or in College, should be maintained
for the B.A.

The die having been cast, the Academic Professors did exactly
that. First they voted to continue to require Latin for the B.A. Next
they voted to recommend the Ph.B. degree rather than the Litt.B
for candidates without the Latin. In order that the barrier between
these two classes of students might not be impassable, the Professors expressed their willingness to accept two or more years of Latin
for entrance from Ph.B. candidates—who might then, in College
qualify for the B.A. degree by passing the B.A. Latin entrance ex
amination and fulfilling the other requirements. This was no:
going to be too easy, for it was voted also "that no provision be now
made for the teaching of the Latin of the entrance requirement:
in the curriculum of Yale College."

These distinctions being recommended, the Corporation accepted and promulgated them [10]—to the immense relief of Secretary Stokes, whose mail the long delays had made increasingly embarrassing. By no means was everyone pleased. The dominant element in the College Faculty, and members of the Corporation also, could not but regret that for the first time in Yale's whole two hundred and twenty years' history, it would now be possible to get into the College without Latin. On the other hand, the *Alumni Weekly* deplored the maintenance of Latin for the B.A., predicted that the distinctions between the B.A. and the Ph.B. would not last, and pointed out that Oxford itself was dropping Greek for Responsions, or entrance examinations. There was unquestionably an element of the inconclusive about these Corporation decisions of 1919, especially as the content of the Ph.B. curriculum was still to be determined.

THE PH.B. DEGREE

In designing the new Yale College course of study for the Ph.B., the Faculty had for guidance the old three-year Select Course— the last of whose students would not graduate until the spring of 1922—plus the known wishes of the alumni and the explicit instructions of the Corporation. The gist of both was to convert the Ph.B. into a four-year program but to retain the emphasis on a *required* selection or *grouping* of courses. Also the single Sheff program was to be expanded into a number of alternative groups of courses leading toward different careers. After a Freshman year training which would enable a student to discover his interests or aptitudes, Sophomore and Junior years would be given over to a series of broad group programs prescribed by the Faculty, and in Senior year the student would specialize intensively in studies leading to professional training, with some degree of election. The old major and minor plan had secured both breadth and concentration, but there had been too much latitude. As the *Alumni Weekly* expressed it:

The divergence from this plan of the new proposals is not only to put *more* prescribed work into the curriculum, but also to restudy these groups with a more *practical* end in view. . . . under the new plan a student will not be able to make as many mistakes as previously . . . No college student is able to decide for himself what he ought to have, though he can choose his main group. It is the graduate hope that the College Faculty will restudy the whole problem in the light of *careers* . . .* [11]

For what careers were the Faculty to make it possible to study? Perhaps because it was manifestly impossible to prepare students directly for all possible callings, only one main line was explicitly marked out by the Corporation mandate. Among the various new groups to be formulated after interfaculty consultation, there should be provided "a course of study in Political and Social Science which shall concentrate attention upon those problems which are of chief contemporary importance and which may serve as an introduction to Law, Journalism, Business or Public Life."

The Select Course had itself been advertised as "adapted to the needs of men who expect to engage in business, manufacturing and banking, to enter professions like law and journalism, or to seek administrative positions with corporations or in the public service." So no doubt the Corporation had been paraphrasing: making sure that the Select Course kind of opportunity would not be murdered in Yale College. Yet the implications of this mandate were nonetheless extraordinary.

Three things in particular were and still remain remarkable about this seemingly broad and moderate suggestion. The first was the attention to problems of "chief contemporary importance." This was an emphasis which might have revealed Yale's most suc-

---

* Apparently the alumni reformers had only a vague conception of what had been going on in the College curriculum—and so not only slighted the fact that the Faculty had already voted perhaps as much prescription as could be absorbed but failed to realize that the vocational idea had itself been pretty thoroughly discussed, experimented with, and rejected. In effect, under the plea of a hopeful novelty, they were asking the College to repudiate the Morris-Tinker humanist policy (1914–17) and go back to develop the unsatisfactory Combined Programs for upperclassmen (1904–) and the discarded Dana-Day group programs for lowerclassmen (1911–15).

cessful alumni cheerfully getting into the same inviting ideological bed with John Dewey and the Progressive school of reformers. Unfortunately, it did not occur to anyone to draw that damaging cartoon. It is questionable whether these alumni had the slightest suspicion that the vocational objectives for which they were campaigning had been one of the great aims of the very elective system that they now condemned.

What Yale's graduates did assume was that contemporary problems were important and that they would remain contemporary and important. They forgot that the Freshmen in the Class of 1922 could hardly hope to reach positions of responsibility and power before 1930–50; and the possibility that the future Classes of say 1929–33 would graduate not into a calling but into a Great Depression and then a second World War the reformers of 1919 never contemplated. What they apparently did pay attention to was their own vocational enthusiasms, the changed occupational distribution of Yale's graduates as a whole, and, for students then in College, the years immediately after graduation. Without their quite realizing it theirs was a short-range program. The long-range value of a more liberal education they distinctly repudiated.

A second feature of their reform was the final distribution of emphasis. The Alumni Committee had listed a wide range of professions, but in the process of consideration the Corporation had let many of them drop. The failure to require a Group Program preparatory to theology was hardly surprising—the B.A. course was supposed to serve well enough, and Yale College had ceased to be a nursery of theologians and missionaries. But journalism was evidently more important than literature. Ostensibly the Corporation was saying that just as in undergraduate life the *Yale Daily News* had conquered the *Lit.*, so in the brave postwar world Henry Luce and Briton Hadden would have more to say than Thornton Wilder and the two Benéts. If so, they were in the drift of the day. Archibald MacLeish himself would begin with the law and give hostages to *Fortune.*

But what about teachers—the very teachers the alumni were so hotly demanding? Apparently teachers were born and not made. To

503

this the Professors of the College agreed. No pedagogy or educationalists for them. It mattered not that old Yale, which had once been mother of colleges and schoolmasters, had lately been sending out only candidates for research Ph.D.'s, or green and untrained young graduates into the private schools. It made no difference that the vast field of American public education was being lightly abandoned to the more forehanded universities. Secretary Stokes, of course, disagreed. In fact one of his great hopes in Reorganization had been that Yale would at last establish a really strong School of Education—and with the appointment of Frank E. Spaulding, George S. Counts, and others, a promising new start was made. But the Secretary had only partly persuaded the Corporation, and the most he now could get admitted into the College Course of Study was a minor in education allowed in connection with a major in Biblical literature.[12] So Yale College was not going to make teachers for America any more than pastors or philosophers. Other professions, too, had been forgotten. One notices the omission of the foreign service or colonial administration, as well as preparation for welfare work or careers in the arts.

A third conclusion arises. Obviously the Corporation was more interested in placating the aggressive alumni than in staffing certain quasi-professions or driving the Faculty into preprofessional specialization. This same broad program in political and social science was evidently meant to serve as foundation for journalism, banking, politics, corporation law, manufacturing, transportation, and all sorts and varieties of business. If successful, such a program might attract the majority of the undergraduates. But that would make variation necessary, at least in Senior year. At which point reflection ought to have revealed almost as many possible variations as there were students. Thus the groups could remain neither fixed nor required. Apparently it was thought that the Select Course device could be multiplied into a series of distinct programs. But Chittenden himself would never have created even two Select Courses, to overlap, and poach each other's materials, and break down requirements by competition. In a well-worked-out prepro-

504

fessional grouping the reformers had hold of an alluring idea. The difficulty was that it had not been thought through.

Thus admonished, the College Faculty got to work on a long-range program with a deliberation that exasperated the *Alumni Weekly*. In the spring of 1919 they reached several decisions: Ph.B. candidates were to be held to the same required breadth, or ten-course foundation program, as the B.A. men except for the substitution of mathematics or a third science for the B.A. Latin. In the remaining half of the program neither class of student was to be allowed to specialize so far as to take more than one half of his electives in the field of his concentration. Thirdly, the College would accept and offer a detailed program in social and political science, covering Sophomore through Senior years. The remaining Ph.B. candidates, however, would be restricted in their choice of majors to certain Departments of Study and certain preprofessional or combination courses.

The Group Program in Social and Political Science had been carefully worked out by Professor Fred R. Fairchild and the newly formed Department of Social and Political Science. This was to occupy almost all of a student's entire time from entrance to graduation. It was made up from the materials at hand, that is, the course offerings developed and left behind by Sumner—a mixture of economics with anthropology, sociology, a little political science and history. A kind of School of Economics was the inevitable result. For there was not enough of political science, or even of Keller's social science, to allow of Senior specialization. Even in economics, two sophomore term courses—in economic resources and evolution of American industry—had to be invented and assumed. These would require, presumably, a part of the time of one man. Yet so pinched was the University for money that by 1921 not only was the development of a faculty in political science indefinitely shelved but even these two little term courses had to be dropped. So the first obstacle facing a new Group Program—

even when as here the professors were keen on the idea—was turning out to be cost. Unless Yale was to be content with a patchwork
of elective specialties, both time and money would be needed.

The second discovery issuing from this process of reconstruction
was that if the Group Program was any good—and even, perhaps,
if it was not—B.A. men would demand the right of admission. By
saving out one elective in each of the first two years, Professor Fairchild's committee had made this just possible. Clearly, if the able
sons from the better Latin-teaching schools were excluded, the
alumni would howl. So all candidates, for whichever degree they
were enrolled, could look forward to preparing for business or
public service through this refurbished program. This permission
was reasonable enough, except for one awkwardness. It made this
new Select Course no longer selective of students. In fine the only
difference between the educational experiences of Ph.B.'s and many
B.A. men might thereby be reduced to one or more years of Latin.

Elements in Yale College were resolved, however, that the
fusion should not go too far. If some B.A. sheep could not be prevented from joining the goats, at least the goats could be kept out
of the more sacred humanistic pastures. So it was decreed that, for
their upper-class work, Ph.B.'s could not major or take Honors in
the classics, or in any of the modern languages, or in English, history,
or philosophy. There would remain open to them majors in the
Division of Mathematics and the Natural and Physical Sciences, in
anthropology and economics, in the old combined law course, and
in the new combined architecture major. But no other majors
unless, as Dean Jones announced, the list might be increased "on
further consultation with omitted departments." So the Ph.B.'s
would be taken into Yale College, but hardly on the basis of complete equality.

For many instructors there were persuasive arguments in justification. It wasn't simply that the conservatives had not wanted the
Select Course idea and that they were now going to take out on the
students some of the distaste and animosity aroused by outside
dictatorship. While resentment must have figured, the decision was
also a genuine judgment as to quality. The Select Course men had

506

always seemed less well prepared, less serious, less able, more anxious to get educated quick and in a vocational way. According to Professor Hendrickson "quite a few of us objected to dissolving the Select Course." It ought to have been maintained at three years and left where it was, so that sons of good Yale fathers could "get to New York for a little lower price." [13] In any case boys without Latin genuinely lacked a certain background, a certain sympathy with the humanities; hence, it seemed reasonable to let them take basic courses but exclude them from the major.

Yet the injustice of the exclusion, and the stiff Departmental competition for student elections, were alike too obvious to allow the College Faculty to rest with the acts of that first spring. All through 1919–20, therefore, the Course of Study Committee labored to create additional opportunities or Group Courses for the Ph.B. men to come. History offered an obvious field, and combinations in the sciences were for the first time exploited. The result was that no fewer than thirteen Group Programs were finally made available as the exclusive property and opportunity of candidates for the Ph.B.* At the same time a strong effort had been made to save about two-fifths of a man's upper-class time for free electives. The effort of the second winter of deliberation was to make the Ph.B. curriculum a richer and a less confining experience.

Yet numerous dissatisfactions continued to beset the venture. For one thing, the balance was still not even. The B.A. men were henceforth technically restricted to their majors and minors, just as Ph.B. candidates were to be limited to the Group Courses. But the major-minor programs left more free electives, and by a judicious use of these the B.A. men could take a Group Course.

---

* If he were interested in the social sciences, a non-Latin man could take a prescribed group of courses in Sophomore and Junior years, then specialize either in economics, or in history and politics, or in law. Again, as a Sophomore he could begin the architecture group or a program in military science, or a provocative group in psychology, social science, and biology with later emphasis on either the social or the biological aspects of psychology. Finally, he could, if he were so gifted, make various combinations of mathematics with physics and chemistry, of geology with biology and chemistry, or of chemistry with biology.

Whereas the Ph.B.'s were not allowed to reduce their Group Courses to a major-minor. Also if they had gained history and military science and architecture, they still could not major in the very popular subject of English. It seemed that students from the Middle and Far West, by the very accident of their origins and preparation, were to be restricted in their educational opportunities.

Another difficulty was internal. Since a Common Freshman Year was to be inaugurated, the Group Courses could not hope to control Freshman studies or begin an effective differentiation before Sophomore year. At the other end, in Senior year, the only courses available as yet were the advanced Departmental or specialty courses. There were no courses essentially interdepartmental in character—either in the shape of broad introductory surveys or in the form of comprehensive, integrating Senior year reviews. Nor had the Faculty been built up or trained to such correlating work. Nor was money for new appointments in sight. Moreover, now that the power of the general Faculty had been reduced, one could feel the rising menace of Departmental independence. The Acting Provost urged the development of comprehensive courses as an antidote to narrowness. But until that happened even the shrewdest planning could not conceal the somewhat fragmentary and disjointed character of many of the courses and combinations within each group.

Meanwhile the moral and technical obstacles in the way of popularity had only partly been cleared. The obvious lack of enthusiasm on the part of Yale College, the fact that the Ph.B. shift had been announced before either courses or programs were ready, the haziness about Reorganization in the public and private schools, and the year's delay in applying its spirit to the admissions standards—all these had contributed to an apparent falling off in the number of Ph.B. candidates enrolling at Yale in the summers of 1919 and 1920.* There was a not inconceivable risk that by the

* Corwin reported to Fisher a statement by a Princeton Dean that seventy five men who had originally intended to enter the Select Course at Yale had come to Princeton.[14]

508

time the College finally developed its Ph.B. program there would be no candidates to take it.

On the other hand, by no means was everything serene within the B.A. sphere. For the humanities Departments faced the same loss of Freshman control, a slowly dwindling supply of Latin-equipped students, and the sober fact that they had not yet made a real success of their majors—while only the History Department had been at all effective in developing Honors. The new Ph.B. arrangements threw this difficulty about upper-class concentration into sharp relief. For the motive of preparing for profession or career lent obvious interest and stimulus to the Group Programs, whereas the comparative aimlessness of the B.A. majors might tend to repel the ambitious and attract only the indecisive. It was this want of unity and purpose that led Acting Provost Brown to make a second recommendation, namely, that Schools of Literature, History, or Political Science be set up in the Graduate School. To these the undergraduate major would serve as introduction, and thus all the work done by teachers and pupils at all levels would be recognized as being "parts of a single and rounded whole." [15]

It was this same disturbing indefiniteness that had begun to make even the humanities professors wonder whether they themselves might not profit by converting their majors and minors into Group Programs. The Course of Study Committee—which included Tinker, Mendell, Bumstead, and Seymour—was reported to be leaning toward the giving of a single degree. That degree of course would be the B.A., but the course of studies would be modeled on the Group Programs. Instead of going under, therefore, it might turn out that the Ph.B. idea would swallow the whole of Yale College. In short, on the eve of their inauguration, these Ph.B. Group Programs threatened both to fail and to be entirely too successful. And if neither thing happened, their legitimate domain in subject matter, method, and student body was still to be ascertained.

Out of the silence of retirement G. B. Adams lifted up his prophetic voice. To transfer the Select Course would introduce into Yale College an element alien in training and difficult to assimilate.

509

To establish a separate curriculum and a second degree would widen this split. If it meant increased numbers as well it would still further destroy the solidarity of the institution, for the Classes had already reached about their limit of assimilation. Adams also thought that increasing the technical character of the Sheff courses would end in that School's ceasing to be the undergraduate College which it had been. He could only pray for Faculty wisdom—and no increase of numbers.[16] It would not have surprised him to know that in 1931 both the Latin requirement and the Ph.B. would be dropped, and that in 1946 the Sheffield Scientific School would have to give up its undergraduate work.

THE PROBLEM OF ADMISSIONS

The third major problem of curricular reconstruction was more successfully handled. To irritated alumni this problem of the admissions requirements seemed an open-and-shut proposition. Yale College should make it easier for Western high-school students to enter. If that meant sacrificing Latin, or examining in new subjects, or even accepting students on certificate, let the changes be made. The 1919 decision to keep Latin as a requirement for the B.A. candidates but to allow Ph.B. candidates to offer substitutes had been a strategic compromise. In this wise the College had hoped to preserve its standards and its influence on the Eastern preparatory schools, while at the same time it opened the way by an alternate door to the high-school men from the West.

Two further milestones in this progress toward abdication and accommodation were now quickly reached and passed. In 1920, after a mighty struggle, the Corporation succeeded in setting up a single, unitary Board of Admissions. It was to govern as well as administer the admissions to the Freshman Year, Yale College, and the Sheffield Scientific School. The President and the Provost were members, ex officio, and the Chairman was Professor Robert Nelson Corwin, Professor of German in the Sheffield Scientific School, long head of its admissions committee, and Yale's champion and defender of the College Entrance Examination Board. Henceforward the Academic Department would have its representation on the Admissions Board and a considerable influence, but the days of dictation or of autocratic refusals were past. Admissions would be a University affair.[17]

In its very first year the new Board instituted what is known as the Plan B method of admission. This was an innovation at New Haven which was destined to be adopted by most other examining colleges and to have a far-reaching influence on the theory and practice of examining. Under this Plan B the comprehensive examinations, which had been the feature of the New Plan of 1916, were changed to examinations on the four subjects most nearly corresponding to the senior year's work in the regular school curriculum.

Practically, this meant easier examinations and a wider choice. The comprehensive examinations, which had been intended as a concession to the high schools, had in fact covered so much ground that the schools had been forced to do a good deal of review and of cramming. And little or no credit had been given to school records or recommendations. Now under Plan B the latter were to count, and a candidate for Yale College would be examined only in English and in three of the following at his choice: Greek, history, Latin, mathematics, modern languages, and science. Theoretically, the shift was even greater. As Corwin himself was later to recall, the plan represented for Yale

> . . . the first serious break in the long tradition of reliance wholly upon written examinations for determining fitness for college work. It instituted a new attitude as well as a new method of admission. The change was neither abrupt nor spectacular. It was primarily and progressively one of emphasis and point of view. Under the new dispensation the problem of preparation was approached from the standpoint of the school and the applicant rather than from that of his later college instructor. The requirements were construed as far as possible in the interests of the applicant as interpreted by the school. Prescription as to subjects of study was relaxed to give ample scope to the aptitudes, needs and desires of the individual pupil. Less concern was shown and felt as to prescribed quantities of certain specific subjects of study and the details of preparation

and more as to general excellence of scholarship and character. The activity of the college examiner thus became in large measure advisory rather than inquisitional.[18]

In the three years of reconstruction Yale had taken the semi-final steps. It had not given up Latin for some of its students. And it was still trying to keep Latin, mathematics, and modern languages taught in the schools. But it had reached the point of realizing and acknowledging that what Yale wanted it could no longer absolutely insist upon. As President Hadley himself put the matter, in his valedictory on the curriculum, Yale would "render greater service by insisting on good methods of study in things that the nation wants to know than by teaching things it does not want and refusing to teach others." [19]

By 1921, accordingly, the probabilities were that the disintegration of the tight little College would continue. With increased enrollment the Faculty would have to be expanded. With the reassignment of the staff into University Departments of Study, these new groups would grow in power as the College Faculty's authority declined. With the intrusion of Ph.B. students it would be a question whether Latin could be preserved or whether all students would have to be channeled through a single curriculum. In either case, the classics would yield authority to English and the social sciences. And the purely cultural would have a hard struggle against increasing vocationalism. Add to these probabilities the decision to establish a Common Freshman Year and it could almost be foreseen that the effort of the invigorated Departments, cut off as they were from the planning of basic studies, would gravitate toward the upperclass years, and in that area emphasize the development of the major.

So from the curricular point of view Reorganization had broken the problem into three parts. The first was the question of what the Freshman studies should be. The second was the question of whether the B.A. could any longer be kept tied to the older, time-honored academic studies. And finally it remained to be seen how far and how successfully Departmental specialization could be developed as the raison d'être for a university college.

CHAPTER 26 · THE COMMON FRESHMAN YEAR

The opportunity to weld together the men as they enter Yale . . . and the great possibility educationally in offering these men an opportunity to find themselves under University teaching before deciding on their particular lines of work, are advantages clearly outweighing any risk.

—SAMUEL H. FISHER, *1919*

THE INSTITUTION of a Common Freshman Year was something of an accident.* In the beginning a distinct undergraduate School for Freshmen had been far from the minds of the University authorities. The alumni chiefs themselves had started with simpler wishes. When accumulated dissatisfactions led them on to really drastic changes, their first recommendation in November 1918 had been the complete consolidation of the Scientific School with Yale College.

The elimination of the Sheff problem by the elimination of Sheff proved legally and socially unrealizable. So in December the possibilities of partial consolidation began to be considered. A two-year or a one-year Junior College was proposed. For various reasons the more limited consolidation in a joint Freshman Year seemed preferable. Indeed Samuel H. Fisher and the *Alumni Weekly* had already discovered in this scheme some unsuspected advantages. And as the Alumni Committee began to appreciate the sweeping changes

* See Note on the Origins of the Common Freshman Year at head of Reference Notes for this chapter.

After the first year of planning, reasons of foreign policy made it expedient for Yale to drop the word "Common" from the title, and to refer simply to the "Freshman Year." To retain the word "Common" would have advertised the old rift between the undergraduate Schools, and Yale's difficulty in closing it.

that might be instituted through it, they poured in so many ideas of all kinds that the Common Freshman Year became one of the really pregnant recommendations of their far-reaching Report, the vehicle for reforms to which they continued to attach the most emphatic importance.

Thus an unlooked-for institution, which owed its invention to the legal durability of Sheff and its character to a belated merger of alumni dissatisfactions, would in the end emerge as one of the most logical and significant products of the whole Reorganization movement.

Originally, the reformers had had no idea of depriving Yale College of its Freshmen. So far as the College was concerned, the first and indispensable reform had been simply much better Freshman teaching and a better social morale: better living conditions, better supervision, and a more satisfactory introduction to the traditions of Yale life. The charge against the College was that its lowerclassmen had been getting too little attention, and that such attention as they had been receiving had too often been of inferior quality. The results were a tendency of the weak to dissipate or flunk out, a tendency of the abler to complain to their parents or school heads, and an embarrassing tendency of the latter to remonstrate with the Corporation. More dynamic and competent instructors would have to be assigned to Freshman classes. Teaching would have to be better paid and the hiring and promotion policies would have to be revised.

In the experience of colleges the complaints of schoolmasters are perennial. So some of the Corporation were skeptical. But key men like Fisher of the Alumni Committee and Ripley, who was a trustee of Andover and intimate of Alfred E. Stearns, were persuaded that Yale's drawing power might be seriously affected if the heads of the great Eastern preparatory schools were to be disappointed on teaching and social life as well as by Yale's retreat from Latin. Hence strong official sanction for action. Here was placation not of Western parents or high schools but of the strongest private schools. If these schools kept a close watch on their boys, then it might be that Yale should not set them too suddenly at liberty. And if the private school faculties believed in teaching in small sections by the recitation and discussion method, then it was altogether probable that Yale's better teaching, to be satisfactory, would have to build on like classroom units and methods. The school-to-College transition, intellectual as well as social, would have to be made less abrupt, and more time would have to be given to supervision and advisory work. Whether the Corporation fully realized it or not, the simple idea of better treatment of Freshmen thus contained the germs of a special study program— closer supervision—and a Freshman faculty unusually numerous, highly skilled in personal relations, and especially devoted to elementary teaching by methods akin to those used in the better schools.

The most decisive force which sparked the proposal of a Common Freshman Year, however, had been the desire to do something drastic about the Scientific School: about its degrees, programs of study, and the unsatisfactory morale and morals of its Freshmen. When it turned out that Sheff could neither be abolished nor absorbed, the Alumni Committee were nevertheless resolved to bring it up to par and get rid of the poisonous College-Sheff rivalry. In addition to the transfer of the Select Course, this required a fourth year in the Science and Engineering programs. Yet prominent Yale industrialists, and men like G. G. Mason of the Alumni Committee, preferred educated engineers to engineers. They persisted in the old Yale doctrine that a scientist or mining man would be a better prospect if he graduated with a general knowledge of the world in addition to his specialty. The obvious place to put this liberal training was at the beginning. Furthermore, a dormitory union of the Sheff Freshmen with the College Freshmen would improve the dubious living conditions of the former as well as do worlds to destroy prejudices and antipathies. Hence the positive insistence of the reformers on a Common Freshman Year. Intellectually, no insuperable barriers would stand in the way because the Alumni Committee were also resolved to get rid of the

515

exclusive sets of entrance requirements in favor of a broader list
of tests. Thus the candidates for the B.S., the Ph.B., and the B.A.
would all qualify via common University examinations and begin
not as Sheff Freshmen or as College Freshmen but as *Yale* Freshmen, living together, eating together, playing together, and—
naturally—studying together.

The nature of their common studies can almost be inferred
from what has been noted. If future chemists, journalists, lawyers,
and engineers were to study *together* for a single year, just after
graduating from a wide variety of schools, then the instruction
would have to be general, somewhat elementary, broad, not deep,
exploratory rather than preparatory. The Alumni Committee believed that Sophomores in both College and Scientific School should
go into prescribed Group Programs of a preprofessional character.
While some preliminary divergence perhaps could be permitted
in their second term, all Freshmen should be required to take at
least a minimum number of fundamental courses. In these not too
much attention should be paid to the later degrees, or to any sort of
Freshman specialization. This was particularly important because
the Alumni Committee and the Administration were falling under
the charm of an afterthought: the thought that it would be nice if
a man could switch his destination, a Ph.B. change to the studies for
the B.A. or a B.S. candidate decide for the Ph.B. Freshman Year
should be good for all study sequences, the year for a man to "find
himself" and make intelligent choice.*

Needless to say, no such broad and neutral program could be
entrusted to the tightly organized governing boards of the rival
upper-class Schools. Nor would it be safe to rely for teachers on the
new University Departments, with their research proclivities and
demands for publication. The Freshman Year should have its own

---

* Samuel H. Fisher had become so keen on this kind of Freshman Year
that he was almost impervious to attacks on that most sensitive point: Yale
spirit. Rumors that the number would be too large, or that the association
of Academic with Scientific Freshmen would lessen Class spirit, seemed to him
entirely unwarranted. "After all, all of us are Yale men first and representatives of our particular Schools afterwards."

Faculty and its own governing board. "The dignity of a separate Faculty and the encouragement of teaching should attract men of real inspiration." [1]

What in the end made complete home rule indispensable was of course the human equation. Professor Roswell P. Angier, when invited to be Dean, insisted on "coequal autonomy" with the other Schools: the same organization, powers, and representation in University councils. Moreover, he thought educational matters important, wanted scope in shaping the Freshman curriculum, and feared the cramping effect of rigid upper-class requirements. Even more strongly than the alumni he believed in encouraging Freshmen to defer their choice of degree. And his ambitious young faculty were at once intrigued. They could hardly be expected to take the required interest in teaching, or to give so much effort to "personal contact, personal supervision, personal guidance, personal care," yet remain indifferent to what they themselves taught or to what combination of studies their counselees were taking.

So by the logic of their interests and situation, alumni reformers and the prospective Freshman Officers alike came to insist not merely on a common classroom and dormitory life but on a full-fledged Junior College. Yet all hands were more concerned with local problems than with Western parallels. They were talking about only one year. And the members of the faculty opposition, however apprehensive, were not versed in such epithets of American educational vituperation. So the term Junior College was hardly used in all the heat of the controversy. Instead Common Freshman Year was the phrase—a phrase which partially protected insiders, even as it almost completely cushioned outsiders, from realizing the full implications of what was afoot.

What was realized in New Haven from the start was the break with tradition, the extreme reluctance or antipathy of large numbers of the faculty, and the difficulties and complications sure to arise in setting up any new educational or administrative division. Despite the impatience of the alumni, therefore, the University Administration felt impelled to go slowly, to consult with the Faculties as far and as long as possible, and to proceed to the organization of the new Freshman venture with sensible caution—finding a Dean before naming a Faculty, and organizing a governing board before settling on the final details of the curriculum.

This process of finding friends and defining the scope of the new undergraduate School took a full year. But when Dean Angier was finally appointed he was given the powers he wanted. The Freshmen should be enrolled under the jurisdiction of a self-perpetuating Faculty, with its own Board of Permanent Officers. In the first instance the Dean was to recommend the necessary assignments of professors and instructors to his board and to the general Faculty. In the enabling legislation of December 1919 the Corporation added that

> the establishment of the foregoing Faculty shall involve, in addition to a common administration of all other Freshman affairs, such degree of common Freshman curriculum as is consistent with the requirements for the Bachelor's degrees offered by Yale College and the Sheffield Scientific School, and permits deferment until the end of the first term of Freshman year, or later if necessary, of the decision on the part of each Freshman as to the undergraduate degree for which he will be a candidate.

Meanwhile, pending the completion of his organization, the Dean of Freshmen was to take the necessary steps to secure "a suitable curriculum" for the year 1920–21.

Backed by the Administration, and supported by a small but increasingly enthusiastic nucleus of professors and assistant professors who were enlisting for the crusade on behalf of better Freshman teaching, Dean Angier took the midwinter plunge. From December 1919 to June 1920 was given over to intensive planning, and 1920–21 became the first exciting year of operations. In this crucial period Angier's objectives were precisely the ones that had been developed by alumni criticism, but his methods of realization had to a considerable extent to be invented and tried out.

The Dean had been asked to devise a suitable curriculum. Since a degree of commonness and a deferment of choice had been strongly emphasized, the first objective was a single Course of Study to replace the four distinct programs of the past—for the B.A. in the College and for the engineers, natural science men, and Select Course candidates in Sheff. Yet this new curriculum would have to take account of inequalities of preparation and differences of ultimate aim. At the same time it would have to be sound educationally, that is, allow for differences of personality and aptitude. As Angier modestly put it, these aims proved "so persistent in trying to trip one another up" that the work on the curriculum at once began to take more time and effort than anything else during that hectic winter. As Hadley so lucidly explained to the alumni, the trouble was that the demands in Freshman Year conflicted.

> The faculties of the College and the Scientific School which were to receive students at the end of their Freshman year, wanted the boys prepared for advanced work in the subjects in which they were specially interested. . . . On the other hand, the graduates wanted the Freshman year to be as far as possible a general course common to all students. . . . But when we came to speak of the common groundwork of education we faced another difficulty, for students from different schools had presented different studies. Instruction that was much needed by one boy was almost superfluous for another.[2]

Latin and mechanical drawing illustrated one difficulty. The College Faculty required Latin for the B.A. and argued, altogether convincingly, that the year of College Latin ought immediately to follow the years of Latin in school. On the other hand, not everyone would be taking Latin. In the same way, the engineering professors insisted that boys would not be prepared to go into Sophomore engineering work unless they had had an introductory course which included mechanical drawing. To meet such specialized and conflicting demands in a way to satisfy all parties was obviously impossible.

The first and fundamental compromise of the spring of 1920 came in the abandonment therefore of the ideal of a single, uniform curriculum in favor of similar and overlapping programs of study. Considering the strength of the established Faculties and the legitimacy of many of their demands, something of the sort was unavoidable. Accordingly there was substituted for the impossible ideal a triad of programs. Group I looked toward the B.A.; Group II prepared for either the Ph.B. in the College or the natural science B.S. in Sheff; while Group III pointed for the engineering B.S. Yet these programs retained enough work in common to make a deferment of decision possible.

The common ground was that all Freshmen should be required to take five courses of which two would be English and European history. The third study for all would be either chemistry or physics, unless a B.A. candidate should prefer to substitute mathematics. In other words, for two out of his five courses each student would presumably read the same books and attend the same classes as all the other Freshmen, and for the third all Freshmen would take either a science or mathematics. Then, for their remaining two courses, the three programs parted company. Looking toward the different degrees, they required respectively a classical and a modern language, or a modern language and mathematics, or mathematics and Introduction to Engineering plus mechanical drawing. Within a compact and intelligible framework both community and diversity of study had apparently been achieved.[3]

After this scheme was tried for the first year, it was modified in two significant ways. Biology was introduced as an elective, thus encouraging premedical study in both upper-class Schools. And Groups II and III were telescoped into a single program preparatory for the Ph.B., the natural science B.S., and the engineering B.S. In this new second curriculum drawing was now made a full year course, to include freehand as well as mechanical drawing—"a much more adequate course from either a general educational point of view or as a direct preparation for later professional studies."[4]

Officially it was stated that the latitude of choice had been increased by these changes and deferment of decision made less bothersome. Actually what had happened was that the engineering Departments were dissatisfied with the limited character of the engineering preparation and alarmed by the drift of Freshmen away from engineering. On entering, in the fall of 1920, the 681 Freshmen had enrolled as follows: Group I, 223; Group II, 211; Group III, 247: a distribution that was very even but that favored engineering. During the winter 102 men (about 15%) had left the Class. The final choices in April 1921 then showed: B.A., 240; Ph.B., 94; natural science B.S., 123; engineering B.S., 122. In other words, where a loss of 15% might have been anticipated in each group, both the B.A. and the Ph.B.–natural science groups had actually gained, and 50% of the engineering prospects had disappeared.* Strong pressures were therefore brought to bear which succeeded, in the very first year, in somewhat breaking down the uniformity of Freshman studies. In such subtle but unmistakable fashion were the corrosive acids of upper-class requirements already at work.

A comparable attack from below the Freshman Faculty parried easily. If men came underprepared, they could be given intensive or longer courses; if well prepared, then shorter courses in the same subject. This expedient was adopted in mathematics, in physics, and in chemistry, thus bringing all Freshmen to the same point of achievement by the end of the year. Since Greek and the modern languages were already being taught at three levels, from elementary to advanced, and since new courses were presumably to be offered for men who had entered with only three or even two years of Latin, the problem posed by diversity in school preparation seemed to be solved.

Yet hidden in the solution were two uneasy decisions. The first was the decision to aim at equality of achievement in the sciences at the end of the Freshman Year, rather than at encouraging the

---

* In the nature of things, the general education of a Common Freshman Year, with its compulsory English and history, was bound to expose the Freshmen to more courses, more instructors, and more influences from the College than would reach them from Sheff. Whether because of such influences, or because of decisions reached earlier, in school or at home, the Freshmen were drifting toward the College. Soon the natural sciences would notice an ebbing in their own popularity, and would join the engineering Departments in pressure for a better deal. So far as Sheff was concerned, its shotgun wedding with the Common Freshman Year was to be solaced by no honeymoon.

able and the well prepared to forge still farther ahead. Such equalitarianism had good American foundations, and was characteristic of Yale democracy in certain of its intellectual aspects. Yet the inevitable consequence was to emphasize the average and the handicapped men at the expense of the most promising. It might be a question whether a university college ought to aim at a standard product, even for a single year. It was certain to be a question whether boys from the best schools would remain content when herded in the same subjects with those a year or two behind them in preparation and whether the abler men would gladly make a common pace with dullards.

In the languages, the matter of pace was handled by advanced divisions; and presumably this device could be extended to the other subjects in due course. Yet how much commonness of study was there, actually, between elementary Spanish and advanced work in French literature? Here lay concealed the second uneasy assumption. It was assumed by the Freshman planners—it had to be assumed—that the curriculum was still general, uniform, and of the Freshman caliber, even though *some* subjects were taken in different quantities or at different levels. Already in its second year a common curriculum, which in its ideal form might have contained just five subjects taught at the same level to all, was offering thirteen subjects taught in no fewer than twenty-six divisions, each differing in content or difficulty. While this Freshman curriculum retained its identity, already the fragility of its intellectual structure was showing through.

Suitable materials and methods of instruction were a second objective. The Freshman Year was to improve not only the grouping of studies but the character of the individual offerings. Here, once again, its political position was equivocal. Nominally it determined studies and selected its own instructors, yet it was powerless either to control the conditions of entrance or to moderate standards for the bachelor's degrees already frozen by the higher Faculties. For instructors and methods of instruction the dependence proved hardly less. But here the higher authorities to be placated were the rising Departments of Study, in charge of the teaching of specific subjects throughout the University, across all the Schools, and from Freshman Year into graduate work. It became necessary for Dean Angier and his Governing Board to persuade these Depart-mental professors and chairmen to delegate good young teachers, to release in part the more inspiring older men, and above all to en-courage the experiments and the expenditures of effort and time without which the teaching of the first-year men could not be raised to the hoped-for excellence.

The difficulties of instruction and the resourcefulness of the Freshman Year planning were illustrated particularly in the field of the modern languages. Here the differences of prior preparation were serious, with students from the Middle West showing a tend-ency to be almost as ill-prepared in the modern languages as in Latin. This offered a double challenge. Yale would not only have to compensate for deficiencies but also if possible so rejuvenate the teaching as to arrest the flight from the languages in American schools. Professor Luquiens' solution was to borrow the device of teaching the spoken as well as the written language, intensively and in sections of twenty men or less, so that every student could be given personal attention and practice. Dean Angier liked the idea, and Hadley authorized the additional instructional costs. In the elemen-tary Spanish courses Luquiens began teaching in the foreign tongue, constructed a syllabus, trained his young instructors to insist on the use of the language for recitation, and persuaded the French Department to increase the use of oral French. In this fashion he emphasized some of the methods to be used by the Army in World War II. In modern language instruction the Freshman Faculty felt that it was among the pioneers.[5]

Other traditional subjects were scrutinized for breadth of ap-proach and method of handling, and such improvements as com-mended themselves or could be wrung from a conservative Depart-ment were instituted. Not always were Angier and his lieutenants successful. They were keen to get a general course introductory to science, with illustrations from chemistry, but the scientific Depart-ments, perhaps shortsightedly, declined the venture.[6] In Latin the course required for the B.A. degree was revised so as to avoid repetition and to use three of the greatest branches of the literature with which the Freshmen were as yet unacquainted—the comedy, the essay, and the lyric—as "the medium for an introduction into the literature and life of the Romans." Similar changes were initiated in Greek.

The crucial negotiations were over English and history, in which subjects the Scientific School and the College had been requiring quite dissimilar courses. In English the chairman of the Department and all the undergraduate professors save one were unsympathetic to a consolidated course. Dean Angier, however, realized that if separate courses were continued in this nontechnical subject, it would probably be impossible to insist on common instruction for Sheff and College candidates in any field. So he tried to persuade Professor Tinker, who had built up the old College course for Freshmen in the classics of English literature, to take charge of a new Freshman course, combining his ideas with the composition and modern reading of the equally traditional Sheffield course. Rather than destroy his work, however, Tinker withdrew altogether. It made a delicate situation in a College Department which had just been invaded by the English teachers from the old Select Course. Happily Assistant Professor Hemingway proved available and was put in charge. For a year or two a compromise between the rival Freshman courses was taught. Then the program reverted to Shakespeare and selected classics. And soon Tinker would be happily back again, sharing in a Freshman course which in spite of being required was stimulating and popular enough to be carried back and imitated in the preparatory schools.[7]

In history the difficulty was that the Scientific School had specified American history for its single history requirement, and the Corporation, under the influence of wartime feeling, had requested both undergraduate Schools to require courses in American history and government for all students without adequate knowledge of those subjects. On the other hand, the History Department, the College Course of Study Committee, and Dean Angier himself all felt that general European history gave a broader and more fundamental education, and this latter view prevailed. The old College course for Freshmen was revised and developed into a course in civilization, not just politics: a general survey of European development and expansion "from antiquity to the present." It was conducted in small sections of about thirty students each, by means of reading in the best historical literature and by informal lectures, discussions, and ten-minute papers. Sydney K. Mitchell, the grizzled Visigoth now filling the shoes of the first great Visigoth, G. B. Adams, ran things with a free hand and a gay heart. And well he could, with Assistant Professors Allison, Newhall, Woodbine, and George as his lieutenants. Each instructor found that so long as he conformed to the general aim and methods of the course, as decided at periodic meetings of all participants, he was left to his own devices. The course began to hum.[8]

Rarely did they try the spectacular or the daring. The Common Freshman Year attempted no encyclopedic introduction to life. The popular furor for orientation courses—which obviously presented temptations of simplicity and coverage to harassed planners —failed to sweep away the solid time-tested materials or the old thoroughness of instruction.[9] Rather the effort was to organize still more closely the instructional work within the subjects taught, by placing responsibility on teams of enthusiastic instructors, each guided by a Professor or course head. Once a week the heads met with the Dean to concert general policy. In general the aim in all subjects was to humanize instruction, to abolish formalism, and to make the introductory courses valuable for the amateur and nonspecialist as well as for the minority intending to go on to advanced work in the field. Specific teaching problems encountered by the instructors were to be taken up with the heads. Angier encouraged the latter to make the rounds of the classrooms, and he himself visited a number to see how the teaching was going and to make suggestions. The teachers' conferences were exceedingly valuable in generating esprit de corps: according to Angier it was not easy "to conceive of a better school of education for the young instructors, or of a more suitable device for keeping the older ones young and flexible." [10]

The greatest reliance and the most resolute emphasis were

placed on securing good teachers and on having the teaching done in small sections. From personal experience lecturing to large classes was known to be above the heads of some Freshmen and too impersonal a method for others. From the start therefore a cornerstone of policy was the limitation of the numbers in any one division. In English and the modern languages the sections were rigidly kept down to twenty men or fewer, in other subjects to twenty-five, occasionally rising to thirty or thirty-five. Never were the sections allowed to become too big for recitation and general discussion—practices which, with occasional informal lectures interrupted for questioning, were thus established as the proper modes of instruction. Daily assignments, ten-minute papers, term examinations, and mid-term warning marks were also the rule. It followed that each instructor early made the acquaintance of every man in his class and was encouraged to an unremitting watch against slacking. Since each instructor was also likely to be a counselor, with twenty men from his own sections as his counselees, acquaintance often ripened into friendship and lasting intimacy. Schoolmasters and alumni had complained that the gap between the drill of school and the larger freedom of University lecture courses had been too great. The new Freshman Year made a specialty of a more gradual transition.[11]

It remained to make sure of teaching that would be inspiring as well as thorough. Dean Angier was a psychologist and fond of formulas. But he knew that the sure recipe for inspiration did not exist, nor any talisman for recognizing the great teacher on sight. He therefore took advice from his Governing Board. The first year he appointed from the existing faculties several men of recognized teaching ability, and if thereafter his administration developed any yardstick, it was that of teaching experience. The Freshman Year made it a policy not to employ graduate students working for their Ph.D.'s nor to staff any large course exclusively with instructors.

Most of all reliance was placed on the enthusiasm and crusading spirit that seemed to generate spontaneously among the able young instructors and assistant professors who flocked to the dangerous new venture. To join the Freshman Faculty was certainly dangerous, for many a senior professor was not yet reconciled, an inordinate amount of time and energy would go into teaching, and publication would be correspondingly difficult. Young men were told that they risked their personal standing at home and their scholarly standing abroad.* Yet the alumni and the Corporation had called for and had promised to reward fine teaching. In any event the scorn and the half-sensed persecution under which the new venture opened only gained it supporters. Reform called for sacrifice. Youth called to youth. In no time a shining galaxy of teachers had been brought together. At the head were the big four, the suns of the new system—Longley, Luquiens, Mitchell, and Walden—all now professors and all devoted teachers, the first in mathematics, the second in Spanish, the third in history, and the last-named in chemistry. The second year Woodruff, from biology, made it five.

Then there were the assistant professors and the instructors— the stars and planets of the new Freshman firmament. Some sparkled frosty and clear. Some, like cloudy nebulae, filled work-a-day classrooms with a depth and mystery. A few fierce comets, blazing across the sky, drew romantic youngsters headlong in their shining train. Inescapably there was also some inert matter. But who that had the fortune to enter Yale in the years 1920–24 will not recall his first teachers with wonder and with gratitude?

In history there was John Allison. Tall, slim, almost patrician in his reserve, this thirty-year-old Princetonian was just coming into his great powers for lecturing and for friendship with young men. No less appealing were "Bob" Greenfield, a playful and friendly counselor, and Richard Ager Newhall, sarcastic and incisive, his

* Professor Gustav Gruener, kindly and deliberate German teacher— vintage of the 1880's—had little sympathy for the Freshman Year; he acquiesced but never approved. So the Head of Freshman German, blue-eyed, ruddy Carl Schreiber, homespun philosopher and guide to youth, found himself in a difficult spot. He was only an assistant professor, and the department had lost students and standing since 1917. Gruener used to warn Schreiber that he would never be promoted and would question him about the Freshman work very sharply.[12]

shrewd eye on the student as he cut away at the disguises of the past.

In Freshman English there were "Sam" Hemingway, "Bob" French, and Stanley Williams—a trio destined to make Freshman and College history. Among the instructors was also TenEyck Perry, a smiling bean pole of a dreamer and inspirer of dreams. To drift after his lilting voice and shambling figure into the office of his friend George H. Van Santvoord was to step out of a warm and rosy mist into a clear, chill brook where the intellectual footing seemed suddenly and unaccountably sharp. In English there were others destined to make names for themselves at Yale and elsewhere: "Ned" Noyes, later Chairman of Admissions; "Bob" Menner, the scholar; "Ros" Ham, later President of Mount Holyoke; and stout John Archer Gee, football fan and lover of sea stories. In the classics, under Assistant Professor Hubbell stood Alfred Bellinger and Floyd Harwood; in mathematics there were Tracey and Miles; in chemistry "Stu" Brinkley; in French, Seronde and later Jackson, and in German, Carl Schreiber.

On the Freshman masthead in its second year there were fifty-three names—to take no account of many a noted upper-class professor giving a part of his services and devotion to the brave undertaking. Professor Walden, second Dean of the Freshman Year, would later quote Tinker as saying: "I just cannot stay out of Freshman Teaching. Freshman Teaching is the only teaching worth while. I would give up all my graduate teaching for that." Example was infectious; the thing was beginning to go. This enthusiastic teaching band were youthfully sure they were not far from the best Freshman faculty in the country. And years later President Angell, who inherited the headaches of Reorganization as well as its noble experiment, was willing to testify to the success of this feature of the Freshman Year.

Another aspect that attracted much favorable notice was the principle of individual supervision and in particular the counselor system. The Freshman Year was interested in the health of its students, moral, physical, and social as well as intellectual. And it cultivated that health through close contacts and friendly guidance by the faculty. Whereas for many years the College had maintained the so-called Freshman Faculty—a mere corporal's guard under Tute Farr to keep track of the marks, cuts, illness, and misdeeds of the entire Class—now Van Santvoord commanded the help of some thirty enthusiastic volunteers. Each of these faculty members was assigned but twenty students, all of whom he taught. He was given an allowance with which to entertain them and was expected to act more as a friendly adviser than as an inquisitor-disciplinarian. Of course this was a difficult relationship to define. It added four hours of conference work to the normal teaching load of four sections per junior instructor; and many of the Freshmen were not at all sure they wanted or needed such advice. But the counselor system was invaluable in helping the Freshman Office to keep in touch with the Class. And it did so much to make the Freshman Year a human and personal institution that Van Santvoord and his volunteers were credited with an outstanding job.

Angier was sure that his organization should be more than a mere administrative device for the realization of Reorganization reforms. The Freshman Year should be a live institution, with its own character and peculiarities, generating its own loyalties and commanding its own facilities. For symbolic and practical reasons he wanted a new Freshman building: to house the Dean's office, a Faculty chamber, a great meeting hall, and a library or reading room for the improved Freshman courses. But he had to content himself with the two small frame houses on College Street—Nos. 100 and 120—where so many of us began our Yale careers. I remember, as if it were yesterday, walking in and being referred by Miss Allen to the Registrar, Joseph R. Ellis, in the front room. This approachable gentleman, who was also the guide, philosopher, and sponsor of the University band, sat in his shirt sleeves tip-tilted in his chair. Afterward, for some special permission, I had also to go to the room at the back of the house. Here the august Dean turned out to be a short man with dark eyes, an enormous dome of a head, and a clear, matter-of-fact and reasonable way of decision. Another warm smile from Miss Allen—and one more Freshman felt inducted.

Esprit de corps among his Faculty Dean Angier cultivated with outstanding success. He did not think it wise for all his instructors to give their entire time to Freshman teaching, but he did try to secure a nucleus of men who would devote themselves completely to the enterprise—and the men on his Governing Board were expected to teach at least two Freshman sections. As for the students, they were to be loyal to each other and to the University: members of a single Class and men of Yale. Ceremonies were organized and a requirement was instituted that Freshmen eat together in Commons, attend their own chapel services, and live in their own dormitories, as well as maintain their own athletic teams and social life.

Here some difficulties were encountered, and compromise had to be accepted. The University had no new dormitories to offer. The Freshman Year therefore had to make out with such dormitories as the undergraduate Schools were willing to turn over, plus assorted rooming houses. By the terms of the gift the Vanderbilt dormitories could be used only for Sheff students, so the intending engineers and scientists had to be located there. This left the Berkeley Oval largely for B.A. candidates.

Another threat to unity came from the proselyting by the upper-class fraternities and societies. The Sheffield societies, in particular, were worried about finding enough good men to man their halls and hence anxious to learn as soon as they could which School each Freshman was choosing. A pressure of this sort would go directly against the principle of deferment of choice and would also lead the Freshmen to determine their education on social rather than academic grounds. So Angier refused to furnish preliminary lists of choices. Freshman Year, he said, should not be "a hunting ground"; and at the cost of some bitterness among the society alumni he stuck by his guns.[13]

When the Common Freshman Year opened in the fall of 1920 the entering Class numbered some 681 students: a decline from the combined Sheff and College Freshman enrollments of the year before. This had perhaps been caused by the lateness of Yale's announcements and the abolition of the three-year degree, but it was disturbing nonetheless. Also Dean Angier had not been in office long before he learned at first hand of disaffection among the headmasters. From an important Connecticut school there came complaints of lack of personal attention to its boys; and from St. Paul's a request that its boys be allowed to anticipate some Freshman subjects, since the reduction in entrance requirements left them with comparatively little to do in their sixth-form year.

Angier suggested that the counselors might write to the schools, and perhaps even let parents know that their boys were not "loose in this big and wicked institution." He then went on a tour of schools. The complaint of overpreparation was more of a poser. But Corwin and Angier agreed on the answer. On the one hand the better schools should broaden out and teach subjects not required for entrance, and on the other the Freshman Faculty should stiffen up their courses and standards of marking. The results were spectacular. The headmasters were enthusiastic over what Angier told them. The very next year the applications for admission increased enormously, and almost immediately, it seemed, Freshman scholarship began to go up.

Yet this improvement of scholarship was not won without a struggle. The smaller sections, the closer supervision, the hour of personal conference work undertaken by the instructors for each section taught, the whole drive for more satisfactory teaching all led inescapably toward an insistence on sound and steady work, toward the raising of average and minimum standards if not so strongly toward brilliant individualism. The wells of learning having been cleaned out, and the Freshmen led to the trough, it was only natural for the Faculty, laboring to pump the living water under the critters' noses, to insist that each one drink. But it was also human, or at least characteristic of Freshmen, for many to be obstinate and decline. They hadn't come to College to be schoolboys. College was freedom. They weren't going to spoil the shortest, gladdest years of life by a lot of studying.

What happened in 1920 was that a new idea at Yale, as to what Freshman Year might become, collided with the romantic legend of what College had always been. These Freshmen were saturated with the attitudes long current at their schools and keyed up by fascinating, distorted glimpses of College life passed on by elder

531

brothers and schoolmates. Having been encouraged also by parents whose memories were rosy and social expectations premature, these young men descended on New Haven eager for other pleasures than sober study. Many were not cut out to be Spartans, or even noble Romans on the old Yale pattern. They were gay and restless adventurers, cynics and rebels.

This first year—in fact the first several years—were tough for all concerned. Between the seriousness of the faculty and the equally determined frivolity of the first common Freshman Class a pitched battle was soon raging. Under the influence of Prohibition this last year of Hadley's consulship was no era of sober conduct, and in the Freshman arena produced no atmosphere of truce. Challenged, the Faculty stuck to their minimum standards and to their disciplinary rules. The result was that the Class of 1924, before the winter was done, heroically lost 21% of their membership, 16% for scholarship. The big Class of 1925, unwarned and unlicked, were to lose 18% of theirs, including 14% for scholarship.

After the first midyear slaughter Professor Allen Johnson congratulated the Dean on having done a courageous and wise thing. He wrote, "If you don't look out you will make this dear old college a real educational institution." In the summer of 1922, Dean Angier had the courage to send out a letter to parents of prospective Freshmen stating bluntly:

> The main purpose of a college is intellectual. . . . All else is secondary. Character, vital as it is, is a by-product, to be secured largely through doing the tasks for which a boy is primarily at college. Other things than study have great value certainly. . . . But the chief job is study. . . . More boys fail in Freshman year because the attitude with which they enter is awry than from any other cause.

In the second year of President Angell's administration the mammoth Class of 1926 would stage the greatest riots of all. But already the persistence and good teaching of the faculty were telling. For all their disorderliness and wild originality, these individualists of 1926 were to part with only 17% of their boon companions and send others on to the Graduate School and places on the faculty. The next fall, 1923, Yale would be forced to place a limit on the numbers admitted and the percentage of loss would again drop. By 1928 an intellectual renaissance, general through the student body, would be under way.*

If prospects were promising, and the Freshman Faculty hopeful of some such success from the very start, there was, nevertheless, no disguising the wear and tear, and various early failures. Soon there were too many students to handle and too few men to handle them. It was particularly hard in the modern languages, in mathematics and the sciences to get teachers of the caliber desired, and harder still to hold such men, whatever their subject. For able men inevitably wanted to teach older students as well, and to do original work. Moreover they still had to look out for reappointment and for promotion. Would 100% teachers be rewarded like publishing scholars? The question was crucial. A handful of stimulating personalities had been promoted to professorships in order to start the venture. But in the first year this issue had not met a decisive test. That would be for the future, under Angell's administration.

So also would be the question of curricular control. If Departments insisted on prerequisite courses and declined to furnish suffi-

* I am not at all sure how much of the later renaissance may be credited to the Freshman Year. There were other important causes. The phenomenal increase in the numbers of those seeking admission was part of a tide swamping colleges everywhere, and would have come to Yale no matter how shabbily the Freshmen were treated. Again, the more careful selection, first made possible by this increase and thereafter forced on the Admissions Office, was bound to be reflected in improved undergraduate scholarship. Yet the reports that had quickly come in from the schools, the changed attitudes of certain headmasters, the inquiries from other colleges, the pleased reactions from parents all testified to what the Faculty already knew was happening. Fewer students were slacking; more students were working hard; classes were doing better work; standards were rising. The improvement was hard to measure exactly but it was impossible to ignore. What may be more significant is that the national academic revival, which did not appear in most colleges before the Great Depression, was discernible at Yale at least as early as 1927 or 1928.

cient instructors, both the content and the small-section method of Freshman instruction might be affected. A coalition of hostile Departments might conceivably wreck the whole undertaking. It all depended on the senior professors, the Chairmen, and the Deans.

Yet in a way it didn't. For the able younger men counted for something. Indeed in the Yale Faculties, with their traditions of consultation and team responsibility, the sentiment of the younger men had been growing steadily more important. By 1921 these younger men were enthusiastic over their hardships and opportunities. To them the organization of the Freshman Year had been a challenge, not a defeat. Idealistically, they were sold on teaching. The novel problems, the intensive methods, the changed courses exercised their imaginations. In the new organization causes beckoned, reputations were to be made. For they were working in no lost or neglected corner of the University. The Reorganization fight had been too bitter, and already the success and power of the Freshman Year were plain.

Yale's new Junior College experiment had not solved everything or originated much. No new types of courses or methods of teaching or combinations of subject matter had been invented. The continuity of higher education had been interrupted. The natural flow of talents had been walled in and perhaps slowed up. The solidity of the new curriculum was doubtful, and the Faculty's own character for scholarship might suffer. Yet since one of the first functions of a university is to teach, and since a part of good teaching is the inculcation of the habit and desire of study, the creation of an autonomous Freshman Year had served a constructive purpose. It had refreshed the calling of teaching. It had made Yale Freshman-conscious.

534

CHAPTER 27 · THE LAST YEARS
UNDER HADLEY

Under President Hadley, Yale has emerged from a provincial College . . .

—*Yale Alumni Weekly, 1921*

FOR YALE COLLEGE these postwar years were a time of unsettlement yet recognizable recovery. On the one hand the old familiar routines ran smoothly in their channels once again. On the other, authority was redistributed and purposes were confused. Change was in everything.

Unquestionably the restoration of confidence, restaffing of the faculty, and closer integration of the College with the University were impeded by difficult conditions. Four particular circumstances retarded the hoped-for recovery. The first of these was a serious financial stringency. The second was the unrealized promise of the great Sterling bequest. The third was the need of finding competent administrators to regularize procedures and to staff the new posts created by the Reorganization. And finally there was the disconcerting conduct of the students returning from camps and trenches or sent up to college by the jangled and aggressive postwar world.

The steep inflation, the financial plight of the faculty, the unwillingness to increase tuition too fast, and the inability to raise such charges in the needed proportion—all these coming on top of wartime deficits created a distressing situation. In February–March 1919, in the midst of Reorganization debates, the emergency was already such that the Corporation felt compelled to act. Instructors' salaries were raised from a starting figure of $1,000 to a minimum of $1,250, with additions of $250 per year up to $2,000. Assistant professors' salaries were to be raised $500 per grade to

$2,500, $3,000, and $3,500—all this provided the individual's work was "positively good." Then the minimum salary for full-time professors was set at $4,000. But all real raises at the upper levels were postponed until the costs of Reorganization should become clear or ways could be figured out of rewarding the deserving. Meanwhile the Corporation emphasized its conviction that the "primary object" of professors as well as instructors in the undergraduate Schools was "the education of their students." The Corporation further went on record as being "anxious that Yale should take the lead among the colleges of the country in placing the teaching profession on a basis of compensation that is more adequate and dignified." These several raises were to be regarded as only the first step in a program that would emphasize the reward of inspiring teaching.

In the fall of 1919 Secretary Stokes insisted on the need for immediate relief to the upper ranks yet argued that salaries should not be raised until certain principles were established. He recommended that instead of reverting to private and irregular arrangements the *normal scale* should be continued; that professors' salaries should be substantially increased; that a new grade to be known as Associate Professor should be recognized "as a help in limiting full professorships to men of real power and distinction"; and that the Corporation should establish certain criteria for salary advances. He further proposed that in order to meet these and other salary costs the University should undertake a ten million dollar endowment drive.

The influential alumni on the Corporation considered this last proposal ill timed. But they agreed to the rest, voting to establish the associate professorship at $4,500 and $5,000, and to raise professorships to $5,000, $6,000, $7,000, and in cases of exceptional merit to $8,000. As criteria for these salary advances they approved:

Usefulness as a teacher
Productivity and standing in world of
    science, letters or art

536

Public service, including service to
the University
Executive responsibility and efficiency

The Secretary's release said: "It is believed that this action . . . places the average salary scale for Professors at Yale University above that of any other university in America." The total cost of all the new salaries and wages would be about $500,000 annually. "It is confidently believed that this amount can be raised through the alumni fund." [1] Rallying to this appeal, Yale's graduates proceeded to contribute magnificently to the annual Alumni Fund drive. But it was evidently unwise to mortgage that fund in advance to what had already become routine costs. So the Harkness family pledged three millions to endowment, if two more millions could be found. And the indefatigable and imaginative Treasurer, George Parmly Day, set out on his own "A.E.F." (After Endowment Force) expedition through the Atlantic States and the Middle West, appealing to the self-sacrificing cooperation of many a loyal graduate, to secure the vital pledges. [2]

Meanwhile, under Stokes' resolute statesmanship, salaries had been raised in advance of funds in hand. Unfortunately, one important thing had proved impossible. *Additions* to the staff for teaching and research had to be postponed. This was particularly hard on the chairmen of the newly invigorated Departments of Study who, with a fresh sense of responsibility and visions for the future, ran headlong into frank impossibilities.*

Paradoxically, Yale appeared to have the Sterling millions in its grasp. But the amount of this enormous bequest was still unknown,

---

* So the hoped-for development of political science had to be postponed. An Honors instructor in English could not be provided. Psychology, chemistry, economics, and geography all experienced disappointment. It was also hard on Hadley, who found that the Departmental chairmen—with their new budgetary authority—lacked the motives of restraint which had formerly enlisted Deans and Directors on the side of economy. In effect, Reorganization had made it a good deal harder to say No. Unintentionally, the division between President and Faculty had been sharpened.

537

the trustees were not ready to begin disbursement, and in any case the terms of the will seemed to destine most of the funds to building. Fearful of the burden of upkeep, Secretary Stokes launched into a vigorous and successful effort to persuade the executors that maintenance funds should be provided with every building. It was gratifying that a great University Library was apparently acceptable to the trustees as the central Sterling Memorial, and further encouraging that a University chemistry laboratory and a new Medical School building should also seem possible. Hadley and the Corporation now bent every effort to get as much as possible of the rest of the bequest earmarked for the endowment of professorships and fellowships. It looked therefore as if the strengthening of scholarly personnel was only being postponed.[3]

Reorganization had called for the establishment of three new offices. Yet the finding of a Provost, a Dean of Freshmen, and a Dean of Students and the definition of their proper functions proved more difficult than had been anticipated. In the case of the Freshman Year, once Angier had been drafted he showed a happy firmness in establishing his own powers in forthright fashion. The provostship, on the other hand, was an educational office without any Yale antecedents. When the logical man could not be found William Adams Brown, educational policy leader in the Corporation, agreed to act as Provost for a year. With generous enthusiasm, from his post in Union Theological Seminary, Professor Brown then commuted each week to New Haven to apply his friendly personality and broad ideas to the better integration of the Schools. Yet not everything could be done in so short a time, and when Professor Williston Walker was chosen to succeed him, many of the educational functions of the office still remained to be worked out.[4]

By all odds the most tantalizing problem was the Dean of Students. Candidates shied away from so vague an office. Originally the Alumni Committee had recommended a Student Counselor, to take over the specific disciplinary and advisory work of the existing Deans and Directors. But the Corporation had voted that "The Dean of Students shall be concerned primarily with morale and with student relations. He shall assist the President in matters affecting University student organizations." So whether the serious work of undergraduate discipline would be transferred remained undecided. When Burton P. Twichell 'o1 finally arrived, he discovered that the existing authorities were unwilling to abdicate their powers—which left him with the vague and impossible job of looking after the general morale by supervising the plays, dances, and other minor activities. Conscientiously, and without complaint, Twichell was to fill the office for one three-year term and then quietly withdraw.[5]

These matters of student entertainment, activities, and discipline were of unusual importance because the students had come back from the war in a strange mood. They were restless, rowdy, and dissatisfied. Disturbances occurred. On the occasion of a military parade in the spring of 1919, undergraduate remarks addressed to classmates in the ranks so incensed other veterans that rioting followed. Undergraduates were attacked on the streets, sailors were brought up from Bridgeport to give Yale students a lesson, and for two days the College campus was under virtual siege.[6]

Under prohibition, drinking and drunkenness seemed to be increasing. Sex standards had obviously changed, in some ways very much for the worse. There were rumors of goings-on at undergraduate society dances. Orderliness and courtesy were on the decline. Dean Jones, gruff, bossy, and kind, found the students strangely hard to get hold of. To his Faculty, in turn, it was not clear how well the literary interests would survive, and a good deal of scholarly momentum seemed to have been lost.

So Yale College discovered that more than classes had been interrupted by the war. The gentlemanly atmosphere of undergraduate life, the fair play and the loyalties, in particular the spiritual idealism that Hadley had worked so hard to foster, were threatened.

Troubled as he was and harassed by financial anxieties, Hadley must himself have known moments of discouragement and regret. In certain respects it would have made a more dramatic conclusion if he could have gone out of office in the flush of victory and patriotic achievement on Armistice Day, before Yale's alumni stepped in to reform their University. Then at least he would have been spared the humiliation and the disorganization, the quarrels and the feeling of unrest.

Yet Hadley was not one to complain. For so brilliant an intellect he was extraordinarily modest and patient. "The great achievements of history are those which have been worked out with others and for others. This cooperation can only be obtained at the price of patient waiting. Real leadership belongs to the man who can patiently feel the needs and limitations of other men, and who has that power of self-renunciation which will enable him to compass this result." [7]

Such patience and self-renunciation President Hadley now exhibited in magnificent fashion, together with undaunted courage and good will. For whatever the temporary checks and difficulties, he remained devoted to his University and full of confidence in its future. Just because the Alumni Committee and the Corporation had overridden his views of economy and given Yale some elaborate administrative machinery was no excuse for recrimination or holding back. Instead it was up to all the men of Yale to pitch in and make the new system work.

This was bound to take time. But unmistakably the results of the Administration's persistently cheerful and patient efforts were beginning to show. Their momentary impatience forgotten, Yale's graduates once again listened to their President with that delight and sense of togetherness which made the old bonds so strong. By 1921 Hadley was confident that the institution was in much better shape than in 1918–19 and that he could retire with the reconstruction job well started. What was chiefly needed was to find a man with the patience and vision to make use of the new tools. He wrote a member of the Corporation that the three essential things to look for in the new President were "courage, the habit of getting things done, and the power to inspire loyalty."

Originally Hadley had thought of his own Secretary for the job. Anson Stokes had earned the place; he knew the job; he had outstanding faith, courage, and executive ability. But when the Corporation decided otherwise and finally went outside the Yale family for his successor, Hadley supported their venture with characteristic devotion.

No sooner had James Rowland Angell been invited by the Corporation than Hadley personally called on him in New York to urge his acceptance and show him the opportunities. The next day he then wrote to reassure Mr. Angell on some points about which the latter had seemed doubtful. Yale's financial difficulties, Hadley was sure, were transient. The alumni would support the new President loyally. "The difficulties about professorial nomination and other matters of faculty authority" would prove nothing like as great as Mr. Angell supposed. Under any system whatever, success would depend on the tact and alertness of the President coupled with the support of the strongest men in the faculties, to bring the rest into line. "You would have that advantage. Cross and Chittenden and Angier are for you and back of you."

As for equipment, in the new Memorial Quadrangle Yale College possessed the greatest of assets: the intangible influence of beautiful buildings. Like Newman, Hadley believed that such things constituted "a large element in what makes our ideals take hold on the students." For his own part, he told Angell, the two monuments of his twenty-two-years administration in which he took the greatest satisfaction were the Yale University Press and the Harkness Memorial Quadrangle.

I think you will find people wide awake intellectually. The success of the Yale University Press and of the Yale Review is no mere accident, but represents, I am sure, an actual development of the things which make a university worth while. This growth of interest is not confined to the professors. It shows itself in the success of the Yale Law Journal. . . . It shows itself in undergraduate developments like the Dramatic Association or the Elizabethan Club, and in the general level of writing of undergraduate students themselves. It shows itself in . . . so many of our undergraduate classes in modern language . . . In fact, I think you will find everywhere the material ready for the hand of the man who knows how to build for the future.[8]

541

It was characteristic of Hadley to hand on his office with these words, "build for the future." It was equally characteristic for the world at large, in reviewing his administration, to take note of Yale's physical growth: the increase of endowment and the Sterling Fund, the Memorial Quadrangle and the Hillhouse laboratories, the Reorganization of 1919 and the rise of the professional Schools. Against such an inspiring panorama the College was hardly what caught the public eye.

Nevertheless, as we look back it would appear that Hadley's administration had been an extremely important period for Yale College. For in the twenty-two years of his presidency a series of vital decisions had been taken and carried through—decisions so fundamental as to shape the character and outline the purposes of the College for years to come.

First of all Yale's academic opportunities and liberties had been substantially increased. Timothy Dwight's half-and-half curriculum of two years' required studies and two years' elective had been abandoned. All the old privileged subjects save Latin had been disestablished. In turn, variety and choice had been carefully brought down into Sophomore year, into Freshman year, and into the entrance requirements.

At the same time, the ideal of the humanistic disciplines had been painstakingly reasserted. Fundamental studies should be hard, exact, literary, and examinable. In College not all new fields of knowledge could be assimilated, for some studies belonged there and some did not. Yale College still believed in the languages, mathematics, the natural and the social sciences both as the best mental training and as the soundest preparation for citizenship. After the first years of Hadley's administration it had therefore been decided that the College should resist the growing pressures from above, from below, and from the material world. Yale should not give up lower-class work to the schools. It should not reduce the four-year curriculum to three. It should admit preprofessional programs only for the learned professions and then only after much careful reservation. In general, it should not sacrifice the liberal arts to technical courses or straight vocational training.

542

Instead the liberal arts college, creating its own order and rationale of study, should reassert the ideal of academic unity. The licensed chaos of the elective system should give way to a planned and guided sequence, with first the preparatory languages and sciences, next a broad sampling of the major fields of knowledge, and finally a more advanced mastery of some one department of learning. This implied a program from foundation to distribution to concentration; and the most important of these, for College men, was distribution.

Another inescapable duty of the liberal arts college was to provide good teaching, moral standards, and ethical ideals. Good teaching was something that the upperclassmen had always had and that now the Freshmen would be guaranteed. As for moral standards and ethical ideals, it is doubtful if any university college of the period had worked harder to realize those commands. Dean Wright and Dean Jones had both cared most of all for character; and certainly no college had been able to put forward a President more sparkling in precept, more winsome in personality, more appealing in his practical idealism than Arthur Twining Hadley.[9]

Socially the ideal had been a responsible Americanism, and under his leadership Yale College had reaffirmed its ambitions to be national in its constituency and feelings and democratic in its accessibility to boys from all walks of life or kinds of school. Democratic also in its dormitories, campus activities, and social opportunities. The impress of a common Yale inheritance and loyalty should mold them all. Indeed, the community had been so permeated by this conviction that even in its intellectual life there could be no privileges or distinctions: no real Pass-Honors division.

Yale College, therefore, retained its idealism and its distinctive integrity. Yet little by little it had been moved to recognize its wider opportunities and responsibilities. In particular it had begun to enlarge its useful relations with the other Schools. And now the common Admissions Board, a common Freshman Year, common laboratories and Departments of Study, and the potential coordination of all educational activities through that single educational officer, the Provost, had laid the foundation for a wider and more balanced development. In this the whole University might share. In the process some of the strong points of the federal principle and of local autonomy had been brushed aside. Yet in the 1920's, for the first time, there would be the chance to develop Yale University, without conflict with Yale College.

To be sure, not all of the College's desires or duties had been fully realized. It was obvious, for example, that not all the outside pressures had been completely resisted or all the intellectual issues clearly decided. The theory or core of upper-class studies was still undeveloped. Instead, first the Combined Programs had been allowed to capture some Seniors. Then various ways of grouping studies and students in the interest of aptitude or career had been tried and discarded. Now the idea of vocational majors was again being thrust into the College by Reorganization and the transfer of the Ph.B.

It was true also that Yale's decisions had not always been cheerfully taken—nor were they always received with uniform approbation. The reluctance to compromise had been widely noted. To champions of vocational education, or of the public schools, Yale's entrance standards seemed still aristocratic. Many educational theorists were convinced that Yale College had been an obstacle to the realization of hopeful new experiments. While Hadley's brilliant common sense and generous open-mindedness were widely recognized, so were his insistence on hard discipline and his apparent indecisiveness. He had said what he wanted but he had not seemed to control.

In other universities the scientists and research men noted Yale's emphasis on undergraduate teaching, at the expense, so it seemed to them, of scholarship and investigation. The power of the alumni and the insistence of the Reorganization on this point of teaching did not sound to American scholars exactly like progress. By reputation Yale's athletics had of old been too good, its professional Schools too neglected; and the improvements in professional scholarship, like the passing of the football juggernauts, had not yet made their impression. That the Law School was on the way to the top and the Divinity School stood second only to the Union Theological Seminary, that the School of Forestry was without compare and the Medical School in the opinion of Abraham Flexner had just been transformed into the most promising institution of its kind in the country—these facts were known to a few but were not widely appreciated. What was remarked rather were Yale's difficulties with engineering and the Scientific School, and its delay in creating a great Graduate Faculty in the arts and sciences. To a considerable portion of the educational world it still seemed that Yale College was too powerful, and pretty obdurately conservative.[10]

Conservative the College certainly was. Obdurate it may also have shown itself. But equally we must recognize that Yale College had a character to preserve, and values to hand on. This character and these values had not always been perfectly realized. Confusion and indecision had marked the course. Yet whatever the human failings of the Faculty, our study of their educational debates makes clear that the College policy had been far from the purely negative. Rather was it instinctively organic and constructive. It had stood for academic experiences of proven excellence. It had sought to adjust those practices to twentieth-century conditions. And it had succeeded, on the whole, far better than was conceded by its critics.

Everywhere in the first two decades of the century the disruptive forces in American life had been at work on the old liberal arts colleges, filling them with new desires, pulling them in every direction, wrenching them apart. Some colleges were being torn in two, between junior college and university. Others were becoming technical or vocational schools. Still others were now trying to satisfy the most diverse and inharmonious demands. Obviously Yale College had not come through unscarred.

But this could be said for Yale College. In Hadley's administration and with his aid, it had changed its curriculum but not its aims. It had improved its relations to the public schools and its connections with the University without turning itself into either a preparatory or a graduate institution. It had survived a dangerous period without loss of character.

And so it had helped preserve for future Americans the ideal in practice of a liberal education.

545

APPENDIXES

ACKNOWLEDGMENTS

THE TIME has now passed, I believe, for the history of a great University to be written single-handed. No account of recent developments, on the scale here attempted, can be carried forward without much research and technical assistance, without personal guidance and help from many individual Officers, indeed without the good will and co-operation of the University community. In all these things I have been fortunate.

This book owes its inception to President Charles Seymour, who in 1938 proposed a long-range history of Yale—for the two hundred and fiftieth anniversary—and made it possible for me to undertake it. There came war interruptions and other difficulties. Investigation of twentieth-century developments turned out to be a stupendous undertaking, and the educational problems of Yale College proved more absorbing than had been anticipated. Finally, for reasons both personal and technical, my project limited itself to a history of Yale since the Civil War. Throughout, President Seymour has continued to give me not only the benefit of his intimate knowledge of the University but his unfailing encouragement and support. To stand in this relationship is to experience personally the qualities of understanding and magnanimity for which he will be remembered.

Under President Seymour I am indebted to the Committee on the Yale History: Secretary Carl A. Lohmann and former Secretary the Reverend Dr. Anson Phelps Stokes; Clarence W. Mendell, Sterling Professor of the Latin Language and Literature and formerly Dean of Yale College and Master of Branford; Frederick A. Pottle, Sterling Professor of English; and John S. Nicholas, Sterling Professor of Biology, Director of the Osborn Zoological Laboratory, and Master of Trumbull College. Theirs has been the role of suggestion, not dictation. They have guided, criticized, read, and patiently reviewed. Without being responsible for either the content or approach of this volume, they have added much that is illuminating while saving me from many errors and misconceptions. In particular I am under obligations, both professional and personal, to the loyal graduate and Secretary who did

549

so much to make President Hadley's Administration a success, and who has never ceased to show his concern for Yale's welfare.

In revising, cutting, and compacting my manuscript—and in improving the style of the presentation—I have had the help of Dudley C. Lunt '18, whose tact and craftsmanship in this difficult art I cannot enough commend.

As fellow laborers in the finding and preparation of materials I have had one indispensable research assistant, a succession of part-time secretaries, and a procession of bursary students. As my research assistant since 1943—latterly with the rank of Instructor and Assistant Professor of History—Helen C. Boatfield has proved herself a scholar, a reference librarian, and a living encyclopedia. It is her knowledge, gained from working in the sources, that has made possible the bibliography, the reference materials, and the interpretation of many a difficult point. But for her devotion and learning this book could hardly have been written. My secretaries, to all of whom I am much beholden, have been Ruth P. Gray, G. Katherine Grimm (now Mrs. Charles F. Stafford Jr.), Georgialee B. Furniss, Miriam P. Roens (now Mrs. Geoffrey Torney), Donet M. Roelofs, Eleanore Doban, and Vera M. Ferguson.

At the start of this enterprise I had the help of two able and enterprising undergraduates, assigned to the office as bursary students, Shepard F. Palitz '42 of Davenport College and Bernard N. Millner '42 of Calhoun. Their successors have been many, some of outstanding talent, and all of them useful. James L. Bryan '50 was tragically killed returning by plane from Seattle. I send thanks and greetings to:

Joseph W. Neubert '45	Daniel P. Weinig '47N
Edzard S. Hermberg '45	Daniel A. Austin Jr. '48
Lee B. Kasson, Jr. '45	Robert M. Northrop '49
Martin J. Aronstein '45S	Paul A. Rinden '49
Homer D. Babbidge '46	Orville H. Bathe '49
Gerard Mandelbaum '46M	Paul E. Klebe Jr. '50F
Richard J. Selcoe '47M	John J. Schurdak '50
John G. G. Finley '47	Rushton H. Little '50
John D. Diehl '47	George F. Dole '52
George L. Thurlow Jr. '47M	Henry H. Seward '53

Bernhard Knollenberg and James T. Babb, Librarians of Yale University, have given me office space and every consideration. To them and to the other Officers of the Library—to the curators and reference librarians—to the photographic department, to those in charge of library supplies, the bindery, and the shipping departments—this enterprise is indebted. In particular the author and his assistants have been guided and advised by Anne S. Pratt, Mary C. Withington, the late Emily H. Hall, Zara Jones Powers, Jane W. Hill, and their associates, to know whom is better than a catalogue. As a former pupil I have many times presumed upon the friendly helpfulness of Hollon A. Farr, Curator of Yale Memorabilia, as I did also with the late N. Burton Paradise, Class Officer and Associate Curator of Manuscripts in the University Library.

For aid of miscellaneous kinds, especially in the gathering or processing of materials, I am indebted to Dean Richard C. Carroll and Registrar Ronald C. Marsh and their staffs in the Office of Yale College; to Director Albert B. Crawford and Ruth M. Rowe of the Bureau of Appointments; to Nellie P. Elliott of the Admissions Office and A. Louise Allen and the office staff of the Freshman Year; to Marion L. Phillips and Marjory L. Jones of the Alumni Records Office and members of the Clerical Bureau. In the beginning Cornelia Reese and more recently the late R. Carter Nyman and George H. Griswold of the Personnel Office have been most helpful in securing secretarial assistance.

I particularly wish to express my appreciation to Dean William C. DeVane, and to my friends and colleagues in the History Department, for their willingness to reduce my teaching duties and for the generosity with which they have taken off my shoulders many of the obligations normally incumbent on a professor. To John H. McDill '27 of Woodstock, Vermont, my friend and former associate in Davenport, I am indebted for heartwarming encouragement. Finally there has been the host of my colleagues and teachers and friends who have given of their time and knowledge and faith to further this work. If I name here only the late President Angell; my mentor in History, John M. S. Allison; and Emerson Tuttle, first Master of Davenport, I trust I shall not be misunderstood. My thanks go to all. What I owe to Laetitia V. Pierson, my wife, I cannot begin to express.

BIBLIOGRAPHY

THE MODERN university is as broad and deep as the society whose highest interests it struggles to serve. Its activities have become so complex, and leave records so voluminous, that the inquirer is overwhelmed. Trying to dig into such materials puts me in mind of one of my father's clients, the late Colonel E. H. R. Green, who sported a wooden leg. The story is told that once at a bar in Texas a sympathetic stranger wanted to know how he lost his leg. He hadn't lost it, the Colonel morosely replied, he knew just where it was. Such must be the word with librarians and students of Yale history. The University having been given very little money for such purposes, its records have been laid down and cared for by many Officers as well as they could, with the consequence that these documents have never been gathered all into one place, or sorted, or adequately catalogued.

I. ARCHIVES—COLLECTIONS

GUIDES. There is no satisfactory guide to the published and unpublished materials for the history of Yale. The pamphlet *Publications of Yale University to 1840,* reprinted from Joseph Sabin, *A Dictionary of Books Relating to America,* 29:196–202, edited by R. W. G. Vail (Portland, Me., 1936), furnishes the indispensable list of College, Departmental, and miscellaneous publications, 1701 to 1840, and makes unnecessary any catalogue of early imprints here. Guidance to eighteenth-century Yale materials in the Connecticut State Library is provided by a photostat negative copy of "Connecticut State Archives. Colleges and Schools, 1657–1789. Index" (Hartford 1913).

For the modern period a useful list of official and unofficial publications, issued by or relating to the University, appeared in the *Report of the Librarian of Yale University, July 1, 1909–June 30, 1910* (New Haven 1910), 42–52. The student may find brief notes on the Corporation records and official publications in the *Report of the President and Secretary of Yale University and of the Deans and Directors . . . 1909–1910,* 41, 52–56. A short list of the early histories is in F. B. Dexter,

Sketch of the History of Yale University (New York 1897), 102–04. W. S. Lewis, *The Yale Collections* (New Haven 1946), is a general introduction to the Library, the Art Gallery, and Peabody Museum—to be supplemented by the forthcoming *Survey of the Resources of the Yale Libraries* by H. W. Liebert, and by Josephine Setze and Anna Wells Rutledge, *Yale University Portrait Index* (New Haven 1951) in the anniversary publications. For biographical information *A Catalogue, with descriptive notices, of the Portraits, Busts, etc. belonging to Yale University 1892,* compiled by F. B. Dexter (New Haven 1892) is still useful. The Librarian's Office has a list of University Archives. The General Manuscript Catalogue is being built up into a comprehensive file on the Library's unpublished resources; while the Yale University cards in the Union Catalogue make possible an organized employment of the materials in print. But incomparably the best approach to Yale documents of all kinds is through the individual card catalogues of the major collections in the Sterling Memorial Library.

YALE LIBRARY COLLECTIONS. The most important historical archives are the Yale Memorabilia. The Yale Memorabilia Room, established in 1918 and adequately housed in the Sterling Memorial Library in 1930, has become the grand repository for official and semi-official publications of the University and of its Schools and Departments; student publications; books and pamphlets by and about the University and its Officers and graduates; portraits, relics, scrapbooks, society insignia, models of buildings, and pieces of the true Fence; to say nothing of an important and growing collection of manuscripts, personal and official papers, statistical records, reports, prints, photographs, and other documents. Of considerable interest for the colonial period is the "Yale Library in 1742," containing those books which have survived since that faraway day, now again shelved in the intellectual sequence given them by President Clap. Most of the eighteenth-century manuscript materials are in the Rare Book Room, together with Corporation and College Faculty Records and some groups of personal and official papers coming down past the Civil War. Still other collections of manuscripts of importance and Yale interest are in the custody of the Historical Manuscripts Room; while papers of figures belonging to the literary history of the country are in the Yale Collection of American Literature.

office archives. Outside of the Library in the University Offices may be found a wide variety of documentary collections, both official and personal. In 1939 the Corporation voted that all archival material no longer in active use should be sent to the Library for preservation. But this directive has been unevenly observed, and since the death of N. Burton Paradise '18 there has been no one to stimulate and oversee the transfer. For the student interested in the modern history of Yale College, the most important collections outstanding are the Corporation and Administrative records, in the Office of the University Secretary, and the Faculty and other records still in use by the Dean of the College. Other important archives are in the Office of the University Treasurer; in the Alumni Records Office; in the Offices of the other undergraduate Schools, the professional Schools, and the Board of Admissions; in the files of Departmental and Committee chairmen; in the University's Museums, Institutes, and special Bureaus.

other collections. For materials on the founding and early history of the College the student must also go outside the University collections: to the archives of Harvard University, the Colonial Society of Massachusetts, the Massachusetts Historical Society, and the American Antiquarian Society; to the Connecticut State Library, the Connecticut Historical Society, and the New Haven Colony Historical Society. The important Samuel Johnson papers in the Columbia University Library and in the New York Public Library should not be overlooked; and significant materials will be found in the New York Historical Society, as probably in most of the famous libraries of the Atlantic seaboard. On Yale in the nineteenth century the Yale Club of New York has materials of interest; and the Senior societies in their "tombs" all have accumulated substantial memorabilia collections. Hardly more accessible, but of outstanding significance for the scientific development of the University in the twentieth century, are the Yale files in the records of the Rockefeller, Carnegie, Commonwealth, and other great foundations.

II. Unpublished Source Materials

corporation papers. For the historian the fundamental documents are those of Yale's government and administration. The early records of the Corporation, with some exceptions, are in the Rare Book Room of the Library. Certain proceedings of the Trustees are to be found in the Archives of the General Assembly in the State Library. The proceedings of the Corporation from 1858, and of its Prudential Committee from 1800, are in the Secretary's Office in Woodbridge Hall. Here also are a typed copy of the early Records for ready reference, and the proceedings of the Committee on Educational Policy since its establishment in 1919, with important committee reports appended. The Records of the meetings of the Finance Committee are in the Treasurer's Office. The following members of the Corporation have deposited their Yale files in the Library or lent them to the author: Alfred L. Ripley (Fellow, 1899–1933), Henry B. Sargent (1902–20), John V. Farwell (1911–31), Samuel H. Fisher (1920–35), George Grant Mason (1922–36), and Francis Parsons (1925–37). Of these the Ripley file is illuminating on finance and general policy, the Farwell file on building developments, the Mason file on the Alumni Committee on a Plan for University Development (in which connection the papers made available by the committee's secretary, P. Lyndon Dodge, should also be consulted); finally the Fisher file is invaluable for the whole Reorganization movement, for the election of President Angell, and for many of the most important developments of the Angell administration. Valuable historical materials on the property interests, legal problems, and public relations of the University Corporation since the turn of the century are in the files of University counsel, Wiggin and Dana.

PRESIDENTIAL PAPERS. Of Presidential papers there is either a famine or a surfeit. Without attempting a complete listing for the first 150 years, it may be mentioned that the Rare Book Room possesses important papers of Rector Elisha Williams, Presidents Clap and Daggett, the incomparable literary remains of Ezra Stiles, and very considerable letter files for Jeremiah Day. A large body of Jeremiah Day papers is also in the Historical Manuscripts Room. Some Theodore Dwight Woolsey papers are in private hands. Apparently no body of official and personal papers survives for either Noah Porter or the second Timothy Dwight: only some scattered pieces or small clusters in other groups. Of inestimable value is the correspondence of Arthur Twining Hadley, consisting of 37 well-arranged Letter Books of copies of letters sent 1899–1921 (Hadley Letters), with about 150 boxes of letters received (Hadley Correspondence), in the Memorabilia Room. So extensive is this collection that it was only possible to use the outgoing letters for this volume. Use has also been made of a small exchange of correspond-ence between President Hadley and Secretary Stokes in the Historical Manuscripts Room. The letter files of James Rowland Angell and Charles Seymour are in Woodbridge Hall; and President Angell's rather general and unfinished manuscript sketch of his years at Yale is in the hands of members of his family.

SECRETARY—TREASURER—PROVOST. The files of the chief adminis-trative officers, under the President, have not been tapped for this vol-ume on Yale College, but for the operation of the University they are in-dispensable. The earliest Secretaries to the Corporation were chosen for each meeting, and until 1815 were themselves Reverend Fellows. In 1770 the Secretary became a Permanent Officer, but it was not until Franklin Bowditch Dexter, 1869–99, that the office acquired University-wide functions sufficient to differentiate the Secretary's records from the general records of the Corporation. Some files left by Dexter are in the Secretary's Office in Woodbridge Hall, and a considerable collection of Dexter's papers is in the Memorabilia Room. The very extensive files of Anson Phelps Stokes, 1899–1921, with those of Thomas Wells Farnam, 1921–23, Robert Maynard Hutchins, 1923–27, and Carl Albert Lohmann, 1927–, are in Woodbridge Hall. Here, too, are the Minutes of the University Council, and of various University committees, such as the Bicentennial Committee, the Committee on the Protection of the Yale Name, the Council's Committee on Publications, etc. The personal papers of Anson Phelps Stokes during the period of his secretaryship, involving much correspondence on unofficial Yale matters and on civic and public questions, have been deposited in the Library.

"The Accounts of Yale College . . . 1740–83," with Corporation ac-counts, treasury books, and most of the eighteenth-century financial papers, are in the Rare Book Room of the Library. In a series of deposits since 1930 the unexploited and voluminous Treasurer's papers, from 1795 to 1920, have been transferred from the Treasurer's Office to the Memorabilia vaults, leaving the recent files of the University Treasurer in Alumni Hall. Apparently the first four Provosts came and went, 1919–27, without handing down their papers or creating a distinct archive for the office; but the Provost's files of Charles Seymour, 1928–37, and of Edgar Stephenson Furniss, 1927–, are today in the Hall of Graduate Studies.

COLLEGE RECORDS. Of first consequence for the history of the College, and indispensable for its educational development, are the Faculty records. The Judgments of the President and Tutors, 1751–68, in three volumes—some scattered judgments in individual cases, 1771–94—and the regularly continued Records of the Faculty, 1807–83, in four bound volumes which are likewise more concerned with student conduct and discipline than with the curriculum—are in the Rare Book Room. The manuscript of the famous Faculty Report of 1828, in the hands of Jeremiah Day and James Luce Kingsley, is in the Historical Manuscripts Room. For the rest of the nineteenth century no systematic collection of committee Reports survives; but the important Reports for 1875 and 1884–85 are in a collection of miscellaneous papers on the "Academic Department under President Porter" in the Rare Book Room. The two bound volumes of minutes of the Permanent Academical Officers of Yale College, cited as Record of the Academical Professors 1871–1923, Record of the Permanent Officers 1923–50, are in the office of the Dean of Yale College. So also is the Yale College Faculty Record 1883–1950. With these are six volumes or scrapbooks of Committee Reports and Papers filed by the Permanent Officers and the general Faculty, 1904–50; the Minutes of the Executive Committee and a number of separate Reports; and the Reports of the Freshman Committee and Faculty, 1906–18. Separate and duplicate copies of committee Reports are also to be found scattered through the official and personal papers in the Library. Surviving from the office records of H. P. Wright and F. S. Jones, 1884–1927, are the old marking-books for 1884–93 and an enormous collection of Deans' and Registrars' papers of an administrative nature: in all more than four hundred volumes or boxes of attendance records, matriculation and admissions records, transfer and room location files, election statistics, and batches of correspondence—all in the Memorabilia Room. Here, too, are the Records of the Freshman Office, 1920–38, of special value for the organization of the (Common) Freshman Year and its relations to the College.

For the ten residential colleges, in addition to the Presidential and Corporation papers, there are the files of the Committee on Undergraduate Reorganization, deposited in the Library by President Seymour, and a considerable selection transferred there from his Provost's records. Bound copies of the Minutes of the Council of Masters (1932–) are in the Office of the University Secretary, together with the unpublished reports of the Masters of the residential colleges (1934–). Extensive files and scrapbooks are maintained also in the several Masters' Offices.

FACULTY PAPERS. The Library's collections of personal correspondence and papers—Presidents, professors, prominent graduates, and families associated with Yale—are perhaps richer for the earlier years of the College and University, or for the scholarly work of the authors, than for recent College affairs. Of interest for the Faculties since the Civil War are the papers of William Dwight Whitney, James Dwight Dana, Josiah Willard Gibbs, Thomas R. Lounsbury, William H. Brewer, John Hays Hammond, and the Schwab family, and six boxes of Russell H. Chittenden papers. The voluminous papers of Simeon E. Baldwin and of Henry W. Farnam contain materials not only on Yale but on relations with New Haven and the State, and on Yale participation in national movements. The George J. Brush correspondence, given by Miss Eliza Brush Pirsson, is useful for College history as well as for the Sheffield Scientific School.

Bearing more directly on the College, the papers of Henry Parks Wright, primarily of letters to Wright with some papers and copies of his own letters, are useful, though limited by Wright's indifference to the modern passion for record keeping. The papers of Professor Clive Day '92, from his student days to his retirement in 1936, are especially important for his services as Secretary to the Permanent Officers, on the Course of Study Committee, and on committees for the election of Deans. In addition to this collection in the Memorabilia Room, he has also lent some letters and papers relating to committee activities. Professor George Burton Adams, one of the most active leaders of Faculty and College affairs under Hadley, has left in the Historical Manuscripts Room a large collection of drafts of his own letters, letters to him, committee papers, and other College documents, as important for his academic service as for his work as historian. The letters and diaries of Edward Gaylord Bourne, 1879–1908, covering both his student days and experience on the Faculty, were lent to the author by his sons. Professor Kan-Ichi Asakawa's personal diary was examined by permission of his executor. Of value for the curriculum of the eighteenth and early nineteenth century are the notes and studies left in manuscript by E. P. Morris and put in my hands by Mrs. Morris.

558

STUDENT LIFE. On student life between the Revolution and the Civil War there are occasional diaries and groups of letters; the interesting records of the Linonia, Brothers in Unity, and Calliopean literary and debating societies; records of the College Church, College Missionary Society, and Moral Society; the papers of the Beethoven Society, 1825-46, and of the Boat Club, etc. For the period since the Civil War diary material is conspicuously wanting; letters are scarce; there are records or minutes of quite a variety of student clubs and associations; and photographs, banners, insignia, and mementos keep descending on the Memorabilia Room like showers of hail. But these generations expressed themselves as never before in print, and it is in their Class Books and periodicals that their life is most fully recorded.

INTERVIEWS. Mention must finally be made of the files gathered by the author, and in particular of the records of interviews and correspondence with Yale Officers, active or now departed. A considerable effort was made to get in touch with many of the most influential professors and administrative Officers of the University from the days of Porter through the administration of Angell. This proved an absorbing pursuit, appealing in itself and invaluable for the light it shed on personalities, motives, and the atmosphere and attitudes of earlier times. The results are recorded in almost two hundred typed interviews, to say nothing of countless anecdotes and scraps of incidental talk: a collection that has served as background for this history and should be of interest to future historians in their turn. Notable are a series of twenty systematic conversations with President Angell after his retirement; another series of eight interviews with President Seymour; repeated communications and advices from former Secretary Anson Phelps Stokes; conversations with Deans Jones, Mendell, and Nettleton of Yale College; with Director Chittenden and Dean Warren of the Sheffield Scientific School; with Secretary Lohmann and Treasurers George Parmly Day and Laurence G. Tighe; with Samuel H. Fisher and Henry Sloane Coffin of the Corporation; with Wilbur Lucius Cross and Edgar Stephenson Furniss, each Provost and Dean of the Graduate School; with Librarian Andrew Keogh, Dean Charles E. Clark of the Law School and Dean Milton C. Winternitz of the Medical School; with Edwin Oviatt of the *Yale Alumni Weekly* and James Gamble Rogers, University Architect; and with Professors Robert Nelson Corwin and Robert Dudley French, among many in the Faculties. The author was also fortunate in being able to use some interview materials collected in the early 1920's and turned over to him through the Alumni Records Office. All these materials will eventually be deposited in the Library.

III. PRINTED SOURCE MATERIALS

The basic sources in print are the charters, laws, and by-laws; the annual reports of officers; the annual catalogues, registers, directories, and obituary records; the student and alumni periodicals, annuals, and class books; and regular and miscellaneous issues of bulletins, Commencement programs, inaugural exercises, memorial addresses, anniversary celebrations, and the like.

CHARTER AND LAWS. For the early order of authority, and the structure of Yale government in all its branches from Corporation to student body, one must refer to the Charters and the long series of College Laws. The originals of the "Act for Liberty to Erect a Collegiate School" of 1701 and the Charter of Yale College of 1745 are now in the Rare Book Room. First published in President Clap's *The Annals or History of Yale-College* (1766), they are most conveniently printed with additional acts in *The Yale Corporation. Charter and Legislation* (1938).

The Rules and Laws enacted by the Trustees, for their own procedure as well as the government of faculty and students, from 1701 to 1745, are printed in F. B. Dexter, ed., *Documentary History of Yale University* (see below). The Yale Memorabilia Room has several of the early manuscript copies—1718, 1720, 1721, 1726—of the "Orders and Appointments" transcribed by students at their admission; that of 1726 appears in Dexter, *Yale Biographies and Annals* (see below), 1:347–51. Out of these materials President Clap compiled "The Laws of Yale College . . . 1745," printed in Dexter, *Yale Biographies and Annals,* 2:2–18; a manuscript copy, by Ezra Stiles, is in the Memorabilia Room. A revised Latin edition, *Collegii Yalensis . . . Statuta, a Præside et Sociis Sancita. In Usum Juventutis Academicæ* (New London 1748, revised New Haven 1755, 1759, 1764) begins the series of printed Laws, continued through many revisions as *The Laws of Yale College . . .* (New Haven 1774 to 1868).

For the modern period the legal basis and the frame of government are set forth in the *Acts of the General Assembly of the State of Con-*

necticut, with Other Permanent Documents Respecting Yale College (1871, 1878, 1889, 1901); *The Yale Corporation. Charter, Legislative Acts, By-laws and Rules of Procedure* (1907); *The Yale Corporation. Charter, Legislative Acts, By-laws, and Other Official Documents* (1915, 1923, 1928, 1932); *The Yale Corporation. Charter and Legislation* (1938); *The Yale Corporation. University Agreements and Boards Organized for the Benefit of the University* (1939); and *The Yale Corporation. By-laws and Regulations* (1943, 1945, 1948, 1950). The working code for student conduct and discipline is embodied in *The Laws of Yale College . . .* (1870 to 1892); the overlapping and succeeding *Regulations* (from c. 1840); *Yale College. Rules* (1885 to 1926); *Yale College. Regulations* (1927 to 1948); and *Yale University. Dormitory Rules* (from 1935).

OFFICIAL REPORTS. For over a century the College issued no regular Reports. Some statements of official or quasi-official rank were published when defense or appeal seemed necessary, e.g., Clap, *The Religious Constitution of Colleges, Especially of Yale-College . . .* (New London 1754), and Clap, *The Annals or History of Yale-College* (see below). President Dwight's account of his College, in his *Travels in New-England and New York* (New Haven 1821–22), 1:199–213, was a kind of President's Report; and Professor J. L. Kingsley's *Remarks on the Present Situation of Yale College; for the Consideration of Its Friends and Patrons* (New Haven? 1818?, 1823), and the Faculty Report of 1828 (see below) may be regarded as the forerunners of Officers' Reports.

The annual Reports on the state of Yale begin with *Yale College in 1868: Some Statements Respecting the Late Progress and Present Condition of the Various Departments of the University, for the Information of Its Graduates, Friends and Benefactors* (New Haven, 1868), issued by the Executive Committee of the Society of the Alumni (in fact, by alumni who were College Officers), and continued annually to 1886. These were succeeded in 1887 by the *Report of the President of Yale University,* from 1889 to 1899 covering the calendar, not the academic, year. With President Hadley, this became the *Report of the President of Yale University and of the Deans and Directors . . . 1899–1900,* and so continued, with some variation in title, through 1923–24. From 1914 the *Report of the President* was also issued as a separate pamphlet. In 1922, and from 1925 through 1934, the *Reports Made to the President and Fellows, by the Deans and Directors of the Several Schools and Departments* were issued independently. Since 1935 the Reports of the Deans and Directors have not been published; instead the collected typescript Reports are held in the Secretary's Office, with copies deposited each year in the Yale Memorabilia Room. Certain School and Library Reports, however, have appeared as separate bulletins.

From 1830 to 1875 a series of short annual statements of expenditures, receipts, and funds was printed for the alumni, and from 1876 the *Report of the Treasurer of Yale College (University* since 1887) has been published annually. An account of endowments is included in *Acts of the General Assembly . . . Respecting Yale College* (1871–1901); in 1917 A. P. Stokes prepared *Yale Endowments. A Description of the Various Gifts and Bequests Establishing Permanent University Funds;* and briefer summaries, itemized and classified, have been included annually in the *Report of the Treasurer.* An excellent summary of the many Library funds and bequests is in the *Report of the Librarian . . . 1944–45,* 39–96. Besides the statements of the Trustees of the Sheffield Scientific School in the *Report of the Treasurer,* the parallel *Treasurer's Report. Board of Trustees of the Sheffield Scientific School* (from 1904) should be consulted. The *Annual* (later *Biennial) Report of the Visitors of the Sheffield Scientific School of Yale College to the General Assembly of the State of Connecticut,* 1866–93, offers pertinent information. The semi-official activities of the Alumni Advisory Board are covered by *An Account of the Alumni Advisory Board of Yale University* (1911), practically an abstract of its records from 1906 to 1911, and by its *Summary* or *Report* of the year's work, issued annually from 1913.

CATALOGUES. For the operating rules and procedures, the best authority has long been the annual *Catalogue.* From a simple broadside listing only the Seniors, the *Catalogus Recentium* (1771–) was expanded in 1796 into the *Catalogue of the Members of Yale College,* to include all four Classes; in 1803 this became the *Catalogue of the Officers and Students of Yale College,* and in 1813 was issued in pamphlet form. Between 1815 and 1826 it was again enlarged to include the Faculty and Students of the Medical Institution, the Theological Department, and the Law School, and to present statements on terms of admission, Courses of Instruction, public worship, expenses, and awards of degrees and prizes. Thereafter it pretty well kept pace with institutional growth and, as the *Catalogue of Yale University,* from 1886 it has become the indispensable reference volume on personnel, buildings, history, policy, degrees, honors, and statistics, as well as School requirements and courses. Since 1875 it has been supplemented by the prospectuses of optional or elective courses, now the *Course of Study* pamphlets; and since 1883 the Academical Department and other Schools have also issued their separate Bulletins.

As the annual *Catalogue* of the College developed, so, even earlier, did the catalogue of graduates. Carrying on from the first broadside of 1714, the *Catalogue of the Officers and Graduates* of Yale University appeared, in Latin through 1892, regularly as a triennial from 1724 to 1904, and as a quinquennial in 1910 and 1916. The last of these *Catalogues* (1924) includes all graduates from 1701 to 1924 and is an indispensable biographical guide. A new edition is much needed. A similar compilation was made for Faculty and Officers, the *Historical Register of Yale University, 1701–1937* (New Haven 1939), and is about to be supplemented. The *Alumni Directory of Yale University* has appeared at irregular intervals from 1872 to 1950; since 1920 it has incorporated the *Directory of Living Non-Graduates* which appeared in 1910 and 1914.

BIOGRAPHICAL SERIES. The outstanding biographical series is the noble collection of memoirs of early graduates, from 1701 to 1815, compiled by F. B. Dexter, *Biographical Sketches of the Graduates of Yale College with Annals of the College History* (6 vols., New York and New Haven 1885–1912). Continuing this monumental work are Dexter's *Biographical Notices of Graduates of Yale College,* for the years 1816–84 (New Haven 1913), and the fuller series, *Obituary Record of Graduates of Yale College Deceased . . . ,* published each year since 1860, and continuing Professor Kingsley's manuscript Reports prepared for the alumni meetings from 1842, now in the Yale Memorabilia Room. The Alumni Records Office has a file for every graduate since the 1850's, with scattered materials for earlier Classes, in which have been systematically collected returns from Class questionnaires, letters from the files of Class secretaries, alumni notes from the *Yale Alumni Weekly* and the *Yale Alumni Magazine,* and clippings from the public press. Supplementing this archive is an alphabetical file of graduates, nongraduates and Yale families, 1701–1860, in the care of Lottie G. Bishop. Such files are expensive to collect and maintain, but in combination with the biographical series and the Class histories (see below) they give Yale what is believed to be the most complete documentation on its graduates of any American university. For the members of the faculty who did not happen to be graduates of the College the records are less complete; but an annual bibliography of their writings used to be published in the *Report of the President and Secretary,* and is now regularly deposited in the Memorabilia Collection.

PERIODICALS. For the intimate life of the College the most lively and important materials are provided by that mixed flood of semi-official and unofficial periodicals issued more or less under Yale sponsorship by students, alumni, and Officers. Valuable not only as mirrors of campus life and outlets for self-expression but as forums for student discussion and as historical repositories are the *Yale Literary Magazine,* founded in 1836 and proud of its claim to be the oldest "monthly" magazine in America; the *Yale Daily News,* 1878–, the O[ldest] C[ollege] D[aily]; their rival the *Yale Courant,* 1865–1918; and the *Yale Record,* 1872–, in its early years a journal of general college doings, later dedicating itself to humor. In the years 1871–1937 at least fifty campus periodicals were born, and no fewer than thirty failed to survive into their second year. But among these ephemeral outpourings were a few of more than passing interest, notably the explosively critical *Harkness Hoot,* 1930–34. A useful table of the principal Yale publications, with comments on their character and lengths of run, was published by the *Harkness Hoot,* June 1932, 2:62–63.

Meanwhile Yale's graduates found their outlet in the *New Englander* which, if never a Yale organ, devoted so much attention to Yale policies from 1843 to 1892 that it justifiably added *Yale Review* to its title in 1885. In 1892, under Henry W. Farnam, the *New Englander and Yale Review* was reorganized as the *Yale Review,* a quarterly "for the scientific discussion of economic, political and social questions." In 1911 it was again reorganized, and under the editorship of W. L. Cross made into a distinguished quarterly of literature and public opinion. As early as 1818 Yale's scholars also took advantage of "Silliman's Journal" or the *American Journal of Science* which, under the editorship of Benjamin Silliman, his son B. Silliman Jr., and son-in-law James Dwight Dana, became recognized as the leading scientific periodical of the country, and was continued under the editorship of his grandson, E. S. Dana, until 1935, since when it has been continued under boards of editors headed by Yale professors. With a less ambitious program, but useful as a local vehicle of education, has been the *Yale Scientific Magazine*, 1927–, published by the students of the Sheffield Scientific School. Mention should perhaps also be made of the *Yale Scientific Monthly*, 1894–1913, changed to *Yale Sheffield Monthly*, 1913–18, which was the general literary outlet for Shefftown. Beyond compare, however, for a historian of the modern University is the *Yale Alumni Weekly*, 1891–1937, which was much more than a record of alumni meetings, Class reunions, football enthusiasm, photographs, and obituaries, though these were its stock-in-trade; it served also as the expositor of graduate sentiment, voice of the University policy-makers, and sounding board for undergraduate opinion. Its successor, the monthly *Yale Alumni Magazine*, 1937–, attempted a coverage much less full and satisfactory, but now bids fair to become once again the University's indispensable organ.

CLASS BOOKS. The College has been prolific in annuals and Class books. Social comparisons across the generations can be drawn from those registers of the undergraduate world, the annual *Yale Banner* (1841–1907) and *Pot-Pourri* (1865–1907), combined as *Yale Banner and Pot Pourri*, 1908 *et seq*. The individual Classes have also kept and published their own records, both before and after graduating. For their postgraduate careers the graduates of 1821 apparently started the series of Class Records with a ten-years-out retrospect in 1831. Succeeding Classes, and some earlier ones, followed suit at irregular intervals until by the end of the 1840's the three-year, ten-year, fifteen-year, twenty- or twenty-five-year Records had become established convention. These Records or Class Books or Memoirs or Histories or Statistics (the titles were ambiguous and interchangeable) were primarily reports of reunions, obituaries of deceased members, Class rolls and statistics; but the materials sometimes ranged from the purely personal and local to contributions of lively current interest or fine retrospective analysis of the ways of Yale.

In the early 1800's it had become customary for Seniors to form Class Albums, with autographs of their classmates (to which pictures would sometimes be added much later). By the 1840's these personal mementos were embellished by lines of sentiment, with lithographs of the Faculty and views of the College buildings, too; and through the rest of the century the Albums grew like dinosaurs, ever larger and more elaborate, until in the 1890's they could no longer meet the competition of the printed annuals or the Class Books, and so disappeared from the scene. Meanwhile the Seniors of 1858–69 had begun publishing Class statistics in the *Yale Literary Magazine;* the Class of 1870 brought this material out as a separate pamphlet of *Statistics of the Class* . . . which grew into the *Class Book* (1884–1904). In 1905 the undergraduate Class Book and postgraduate Records were brought into one, *The History of the Class of* . . . , with the Senior production as Volume I, to be followed with such anniversary numbers as the Class Secretary (later aided by a Class Secretaries Bureau under the competent direction of Marion L. Phillips) could achieve. From 1910 to 1921 *Freshman Blue Books,* from 1922 to 1934 *Freshman Year Books,* were published, followed by the Freshman edition of the *Banner and Pot-Pourri,* 1934–39, and *The Old Campus,* 1940–. These give data not available in later publications of the same Class. Numerous Class Albums and complete sets of the Class Books are available in the Memorabilia Room, with representative sets of the latter also in the Secretary's Office and in the Yale Club of New York.

PUBLIC PRESS. The New Haven newspapers, from the *Connecticut Gazette* and the *Connecticut Journal and New-Haven Post-Boy* of the eighteenth century to the *New Haven Evening Register* and *Journal-Courier* of the twentieth, are useful sources for College events and, particularly before 1900, for critical discussion of policies. Also very useful for the period between 1865 and 1885 are the New York *Evening Post* and the *Nation,* to which Yale alumni and the faculty contributed much. The Memorabilia Room has a file of the University's news releases from 1918, and since 1940 a complete and carefully indexed file has been kept by the Yale News Bureau.

IV. SECONDARY WORKS

UNIVERSITY HISTORIES. One cannot write the history of Yale College within the greater University without gratitude and indebtedness to those historians who have chronicled the College's earlier and simpler days. On the eighteenth-century beginnings the authorities are Thomas Clap, *The Annals or History of Yale College* . . . (New Haven 1766); J. L. Kingsley, *A Sketch of the History of Yale College in Connecticut* (Boston 1835) reprinted from the *American Quarterly Register,* August 1835, February 1836, Vol. 8; Ebenezer Baldwin, *Annals of Yale College from Its Foundation to the Year 1831* (New Haven 1831; 2d ed. 1838; 3d ed., *History of Yale College,* 1841); E. P. Belden, *Sketches of Yale College* (New York 1843); T. D. Woolsey, *An Historical Address Pronounced before the Graduates of Yale College, August 14, 1850* (New Haven 1850); F. B. Dexter, *Biographical Sketches of the Graduates of Yale with Annals of the College History;* Dexter, ed., *The Literary Diary of Ezra Stiles* (3 vols., New York 1901); Anson Phelps Stokes, *Memorials of Eminent Yale Men* (2 vols., New Haven 1914); Dexter, ed., *Extracts from the Itineraries and Other Miscellanies of Ezra Stiles . . . with a Selection from His Correspondence* (New Haven 1916); Dexter, ed., *Documentary History of Yale University* (New Haven 1916); Edwin Oviatt, *The Beginnings of Yale (1701–1726)* (New Haven 1916); Dexter, *A Selection from the Miscellaneous Historical Papers of Fifty Years* (New Haven 1918); and Robert Dudley French, *The Memorial Quadrangle: A Book about Yale* (New Haven 1929).

For the nineteenth century, in addition to some of the foregoing, there are a number of useful histories. Bringing the story down into Porter's administration are the monumental volumes of W. L. Kingsley and his collaborators, *Yale College: A Sketch of Its History with Notices of Its Several Departments, Instructors, and Benefactors, Together with Some Account of Student Life and Amusements* (2 vols., New York 1879), familiarly known as the "Yale Book." A very useful but all too brief guide is F. B. Dexter, *Sketch of the History of Yale University* (New York 1887). B. C. Steiner, *The History of Education in Connecticut,* Bureau of Education Circular of Information No. 2, 1893, Contributions to American Educational History No. 14 (Washington 1893), is three-fifths a history of Yale, drawing heavily upon Kingsley but useful for later developments under Porter and Dwight. Professor C. H. Smith brought the account to the end of the century in his contribution to J. L. Chamberlain, ed., *Universities and Their Sons* (New York 1898), Vol. I, reprinted with a supplementary chapter and the Yale biographical articles as *Yale University* (New York 1900). There is also material of interest in the historical addresses by William Henry Welch, Cyrus Northrop, Daniel Coit Gilman, and others in *The Record of the Celebration of the Two Hundredth Anniversary of the Founding of Yale College, Held at Yale University in New Haven Connecticut, October the Twentieth to October the Twenty-third, A. D. Nineteen Hundred and One* (New Haven 1902).

Yale has no general history carrying beyond the threshold of the

567

twentieth century, but varied materials on the last fifty years, together with glimpses of earlier times, are to be found in Stokes, *Memorials of Eminent Yale Men;* G. H. Nettleton, ed., *The Book of the Yale Pageant* (New Haven 1916); French, *The Memorial Quadrangle;* The Bicentennial issue of the *Yale Alumni Weekly,* Jan. 1902; *Fifty Years of Yale News: A Symposium on Yale Development* . . . (New Haven, 28 Jan. 1928), which is especially useful for articles on the developments of the 1920's; and the Centennial Number of the *Yale Literary Magazine,* Feb. 1936. A vast collection of materials, from a copy of President Clap's *Annals* to press reports of the twentieth century, has been gathered into "Yale Old and New," more than seventy scrapbooks compiled by Arnold Dana, chronologically and topically arranged, in the Yale Memorabilia Room.

SCHOOLS AND DEPARTMENTS. Materials are not yet at hand for complete bibliographies of the several University Schools, but among the Departmental histories the student will find Russell H. Chittenden, *History of the Sheffield Scientific School of Yale University, 1846–1922* (2 vols., New Haven 1928) irreplaceable. For the Law School the series of historical essays by Frederick C. Hicks in the Yale Law Library Publications, *Yale Law School: The Founders and the Founders' Collection,* No. 1 (1935), *Yale Law School: From the Founders to Dutton, 1845–1869,* No. 3 (1936), *Yale Law School: 1869–1894, Including the County Court House Period,* No. 4 (1937), *Yale Law School: 1895–1915, Twenty Years of Hendrie Hall,* No. 7 (1938), is most useful.

W. H. Welch, "Yale in Its Relation to Medicine," in *The Record of the Celebration of the Two Hundredth Anniversary* is decidedly useful. For the founding and early years of the Medical School there is W. R. Steiner's account in *Memorial of the Centennial of the Yale Medical School* (New Haven 1915); while modern developments may be followed in *The Past, Present and Future of the Yale University School of Medicine* (New Haven 1922) and C.-E. A. Winslow, *Dean Winternitz & the Yale School of Medicine* (New Haven 1935). Good historical addresses by Henry B. Wright and others are in *The Centennial Anniversary of the Yale Divinity School, October 23–25, 1922* (n.p., n.d.). There is also a series of unpublished Ph.D. theses: J. T. Wayland, "The Theological Department in Yale College, 1822–1858" (1933), G. E. Knoff, "The Yale Divinity School, 1858–1899" (1936), J. G. Johnson, "The Yale Divinity School, 1899–1928" (1936); and for the two hundred and fiftieth anniversary of the University Professor Roland H. Bainton delivered a series of historical addresses, on the Nathaniel W. Taylor Lectureship, for expansion later into a history.

For the Art School there is a general survey by J. F. Weir, *Fiftieth Anniversary of the School of Fine Arts in Yale University* (New Haven 1916). The development of Peabody Museum is traced in Charles Schuchert and C. M. LeVene, *O. C. Marsh, Pioneer in Paleontology* (New Haven 1940). On the School of Forestry the student should consult Henry S. Graves, "The Evolution of a Forest School," in *The First Thirty Years of the Yale School of Forestry* (New Haven 1930), and the very informative *The First Half-Century of the Yale School of Forestry, in Commemoration of The Semicentennial Reunion at New Haven, Connecticut, 11–12 December 1950,* a collaborative work edited by S. N. Spring. For most of the Schools, Departments, or special Institutes there are also biographical studies or memorials and addresses of some value. In general, however, their histories still remain to be written; and on the Departments of Study within the Faculty of the Arts and Sciences very little work has been done.

The Yale University Council (established in 1948 and not to be confused with the earlier University Council) has been sponsoring a series of reports by special committees on the several Divisions or Schools. Most of these are in mimeographed form, a few have been quoted in the *Alumni Weekly,* and two have been printed: *Report of the Committee on the Division of the Humanities* (New Haven 1949), and *A Further Interim Report of the Committee on the Law School* (1 Aug. 1950). These are analytical rather than historical treatments, but historians of the future will find them revealing on mid-century conditions.

COLLEGE LIFE. The materials for a picture of College life in the earlier days are scattered thick through all the histories and early biographies. Of special value for the eighteenth and early nineteenth century are H. W. and Carol Schneider, eds., *Samuel Johnson, President of King's College: His Career and Writings* (4 vols., New York 1929); President Stiles' *Literary Diary* and *Itineraries;* Leon Howard's thorough study of *The Connecticut Wits* (Chicago 1943); Alexander Cowie's brief *Educational Problems at Yale College in the Eighteenth Century,* Publications of the Tercentenary Commission of the State of Connecticut, No. 55 (New Haven 1936); and Dexter's papers on student life under Clap and the first Dwight and in his own College years, 1857–61, in his *Historical Papers.* For the intellectual and moral temper of the College,

President Dwight's Decisions of Questions Discussed by the Senior Class in Yale College in 1813 and 1814, edited by Theodore Dwight Jr. (New York 1833), is of the first importance. Charles Cuningham, *Timothy Dwight, 1752–1817: A Biography* (New York 1942) is excellent for its picture of College life and its bibliography. The second Timothy Dwight in *Memories of Yale Life and Men* (see below) has left a vivid picture of the mid-century.

On the life of the College community in the last seventy-five years, in addition to the periodicals already listed, there are several noteworthy books and articles. Henry A. Beers, *The Ways of Yale in the Consulship of Plancus* (New York 1895) stands at the beginning of the modern period, with his "Yale College," in *Scribner's Monthly Magazine,* Apr. 1876, 11:761–84. "A Graduate of '69," Lyman H. Bagg, gathered an almost fantastic treasure of campus and classroom lore in *Four Years at Yale* (New Haven 1871), and Lewis S. Welch and Walter Camp created a lively and sympathetic picture of the last thirty years of the century in *Yale: Her Campus, Class-Rooms, and Athletics* (Boston 1899). For student life in the eighties, see also C. H. Patton and W. T. Field, *Eight O'Clock Chapel* (see below). In the nineties Arthur Twining Hadley contributed a thoughtful analysis, "Yale University," to *Harper's Magazine,* Apr. 1894, 88:764–72, republished in *Four American Universities* (New York 1895); while Henry E. Howland covered a wide and humorous range in "Undergraduate Life at Yale," *Scribner's Magazine,* July 1897, 22:1–22. Of the many descriptions by visitors to Yale, one may mention as particularly illuminating George Santayana, "A Glimpse of Yale," *Harvard Monthly,* Dec. 1892, 15:89–97; E. E. Slosson, *Great American Universities* (New York 1910), and Edmund Wilson, "Harvard, Princeton, and Yale," *Forum,* Sept. 1923, 70:1870–79.

For the information of prospective students and possible benefactors, the Alumni Advisory Board issued *Life at Yale* (New Haven 1912, 1914, 1920), and *An Introduction to Yale* (1935, 1938, 1939, 1945); while the Endowment Fund Committee printed *For a* Finer, *not a Bigger Yale* (1926), and *Campus and Classroom at Yale* (1927); and the *Yale Alumni Weekly* issued a special number, *The Yale Residential Colleges,* 22 Dec. 1933. The most recent statement and appeal is that issued by the Office of University Development, *Yale Plans for the Future* (New Haven 1950).

BIOGRAPHIES. It would require a Dexter to marshal the full biographical resources for the first century and a half of Yale's history. In addition to the Yale biographical collections and Stokes' *Memorials* already described, much may be gathered from the *Dictionary of American Biography* (1928–44); from J. L. Sibley, *Biographical Sketches of Graduates of Harvard University,* continued by C. K. Shipton (Cambridge 1873–); and from the *National Academy of Sciences. Biographical Memoirs* (1877–), each with excellent bibliographical apparatus. The following works, published more recently, may suggest how the wealth of biographical materials is yearly being augmented: Hiram Bingham, *Elihu Yale, the American Nabob of Queen Square* (New York 1939); O. E. Winslow, *Jonathan Edwards, 1703–1758: A Biography* (New York 1940), and Perry Miller, *Jonathan Edwards* (New York 1949); Leon Howard, *The Connecticut Wits;* T. A. Zunder, *The Early Days of Joel Barlow* (New Haven 1934); Alexander Cowie, *John Trumbull, Connecticut Wit* (Chapel Hill 1936); Charles Cuningham, *Timothy Dwight;* George Dudley Seymour, *Captain Nathan Hale . . . Major John Palsgrave Wyllys . . .* (New Haven 1933); H. N. Warfel, *Noah Webster, Schoolmaster to America* (New York 1936); J. F. Fulton and E. H. Thomson, *Benjamin Silliman, 1779–1864* (New York 1947); Carleton Mabee, *The American Leonardo: A Life of Samuel F. B. Morse* (New York 1943); Francis Parsons, *Six Men of Yale* (New Haven 1939); S. E. Mead, *Nathaniel William Taylor, 1786–1858, a Connecticut Liberal* (Chicago 1942).

For the biographies of the Yale Presidents of the modern era, there is first G. S. Merriam, ed., *Noah Porter: A Memorial by Friends* (New York 1893). Timothy Dwight, *Memories of Yale Life and Men* (New York 1903) covers his years as student, professor, and chief executive with wise reflections on policy and detailed if circumspect comment on personalities. There is a sketch of Dwight in Francis Parsons, *Six Men of Yale.* About his father Morris Hadley has recently written an able and discriminating biography, *Arthur Twining Hadley* (New Haven 1948); and there are numerous colorful appreciations (cf. Reference Notes, Chapter 6). On President Angell there is as yet no adequate study; a considerable number of biographical articles appeared on the occasion of his election, retirement, and death, and there is autobiographical material in Carl Murchison, ed., *A History of Psychology in Autobiography* (Worcester, Mass., 1936) 3:1–38. Sketches of Porter and Dwight by H. E. Starr, and of Hadley by R. D. French appear in the *Dictionary of American Biography,* and one of Hadley by Max Lerner in the *Encyclopedia of the Social Sciences.*

PRESIDENTIAL WRITINGS. Besides their reports and addresses in the University publications, the following collected papers on educational problems are important: Porter, *The American Colleges and the American Public* (New Haven 1870; 2d ed. enlarged, New York 1878); Dwight, *Yale College: Some Thoughts Respecting Its Future* (New Haven 1870); Hadley, *The Education of the American Citizen* (New York 1901), *Baccalaureate Addresses* (New York 1907), *The Moral Basis of Democracy* (New Haven 1919), *Education and Government* (New Haven 1934); Angell, *American Education: Addresses and Articles* (New Haven 1937). The addresses delivered at their inaugurations are fundamental: *Addresses at the Inauguration of Professor Noah Porter, D.D., LL.D., as President of Yale College, Wednesday, October 11, 1871* (New York 1871); *Addresses at the Induction of Professor Timothy Dwight, as President of Yale College, Thursday, July 1, 1886* (New Haven 1886); *Inauguration of Arthur Twining Hadley, LL.D. as President of Yale University, October Eighteenth A.D. Eighteen Hundred and Ninety-nine* (New Haven n.d.); *Inauguration of James Rowland Angell, LL.D. as Fourteenth President of Yale University, June Twenty-second Anno Domini Nineteen Hundred and Twenty-one* (New Haven 1921).

THE FACULTY. Among the biographies, autobiographies, and reminiscences of faculty members who had also been Yale undergraduates, the following have proved particularly useful: O. W. Firkins, *Cyrus Northrop: A Memoir* (Minneapolis 1925); H. E. Starr, *William Graham Sumner* (New York 1925) and A. G. Keller, *Reminiscences (Mainly Personal) of William Graham Sumner* (New Haven 1933); W. L. Phelps, *Autobiography with Letters* (New York 1939); W. L. Cross, *Connecticut Yankee: An Autobiography* (New Haven 1943); R. N. Corwin, *The Plain Unpolished Tale of the Workaday Doings of Modest Folk* (privately printed, New Haven 1946), and his fuller manuscript "Reminiscences"; H. S. Canby, *Alma Mater: The Gothic Age of the American College* (New York 1936), which was "heavily cut and revised, though not rewritten" as Part Two of *American Memoir* (Boston 1947); C. P. Sherman, *Academic Adventures* (New Haven 1944); and George Stewart, *The Life of Henry B. Wright* (New York 1925).

Certain biographies in science and other fields should not be overlooked: Daniel C. Gilman, *The Life of James Dwight Dana* . . . (New York 1899); Muriel Rukeyser, *Willard Gibbs* (New York 1942); Schuchert and LeVene, *O. C. Marsh*. Among the publications to mark the two hundred and fiftieth anniversary are *Josiah Willard Gibbs, the History of a Great Mind* by Lynde P. Wheeler (New Haven 1951); *Diary, 1843–1852, of James Hadley, Tutor and Professor of Greek, in Yale College, 1845–1872* (New Haven 1951), edited by Laura Hadley Moseley; and Francis Steegmuller, *The Two Lives of James Jackson Jarves* (New Haven 1951).

Some vivid portraits of the faculty, by students who did not become teachers at Yale, are drawn in H. C. M. Thomson, ed., *In the Early Eighties and Since with Yale '83* (1923); in *Father of Radio. The Autobiography of Lee de Forest* (Chicago 1950); in *Semi-Centennial: Some of the Life and Part of the Opinions of Leonard Bacon* (New York 1939); in Thomas Beer, *The Mauve Decade* (New York 1926); in S. V. Benét, *The Beginning of Wisdom* (New York 1921); and in J. F. Carter, *The Rectory Family* (New York 1937). Not to be overlooked also are the biographies of three distinguished graduates of the College, who came to be associated respectively with the Corporation and the Law School, the Corporation and the Provost's office, the Medical School and the Library: H. F. Pringle, *The Life and Times of William H. Taft* (2 vols., New York 1939); W. A. Brown, *A Teacher and His Times* (New York 1940); J. F. Fulton, *Harvey Cushing: A Biography* (Springfield, Ill., 1946).

SPECIAL STUDIES. Certain accounts of particular aspects of Yale development have been of considerable value. On the curriculum, early or late, there is, unfortunately, nothing adequate; but the manuscripts of E. P. Morris are suggestive; there are materials in Howard, *The Connecticut Wits;* J. C. Schwab made two studies, "The Yale College Curriculum, 1701–1901," *Educational Review,* June 1901, 1:1–17, and a broadside, *A Partial List of the Textbooks Read in Yale College in the Eighteenth Century* (n.p., n.d.); and there is the incomparable Faculty Report of 1828, *Reports on the Course of Instruction in Yale College by a Committee of the Corporation, and the Academical Faculty* (New Haven 1828). The collection of *Papers in Honor of Andrew Keogh, Librarian of Yale University, by the Staff of the Library, 30 June 1938* (New Haven 1938) offers much on the early Library and its growth. We are beginning to understand the development of colonial science through the publications of S. E. Morison and I. B. Cohen of Harvard; Theodore Hornberger, *Scientific Thought in the American Colleges, 1638–1800* (Austin, Tex., 1945); and L. W. McKeehan, *Yale Science:*

The First Hundred Years, 1701–1801 (New Haven 1947). On modern entrance problems there is H. P. Rodes, "Educational Factors Affecting the Entrance Requirements of Yale College" (unpublished doctoral dissertation 1948, in Sterling Memorial Library); while A. B. Crawford in *Incentives to Study* (New Haven 1929) and other books and articles deals with the problems of aptitudes and tests.

G. P. Fisher, *A Discourse, Commemorative of the History of the Church of Christ in Yale College . . .* (New Haven 1858), is useful for the early College church; and Walter D. Wagoner is completing a doctoral thesis on "Three Yale Chapels." The history of religious activity, long and intimately associated with the curriculum as well as with the moral and social life of the community, has been substantially developed in J. B. Reynolds, S. H. Fisher, H. B. Wright, *Two Centuries of Christian Activity at Yale* (New York 1901); more recent materials are given in *Some Annals of the Yale Christian Association,* edited by George Stewart (New Haven 1937). The role of Yale's graduates in the nation's wars is recorded in Henry P. Johnston, *Yale and Her Honor-Roll in the American Revolution, 1775–1783 . . .* (New York 1888); Ellsworth Eliot Jr., *Yale in the Civil War* (New Haven 1932), G. H. Nettleton, ed., *Yale in the World War* (2 vols., New Haven 1925), and Eugene H. Kone, *Yale Men Who Died in the Second World War* (New Haven 1951).

No student should ignore the influence that Yale and Yale men have exercised over the imagination of American youth through the creation of a fictional image of the College. The most prolific contributor to this unofficial legend was "Burt L. Standish" or Gilbert Patten, who created the hero-athlete Frank Merriwell of Yale, and in a series of more than eight hundred installments in the *Tip Top Weekly* (1896–1914—revived over the radio in the 1930's), made his Courage, Daring, Loyalty, Ginger, Power, Dilemma, Generosity, Baseball Victories, Set Back, Auto, Iron Nerve and other qualities nationally famous. (See J. L. Cutler in *The Maine Bulletin,* Mar. 1934.) Drawing from personal experiences, and with greater artistry and restraint, Owen Johnson '00 made *Stover at Yale* (New York 1910) a classic of American student life.

For present-day Yale a fine collection of views has just been published in Samuel Chamberlain and R. D. French, *The Yale Scene* (New Haven 1950). There are also many earlier collections of pictures, of which *Yale University Illustrated,* edited by J. O. Moré and O. M. Clark (New Haven? 1897) is useful. A. P. Stokes, *Historical Prints of New Haven, Connecticut, with Special Reference to Yale College and the Green*

(New Haven 1910) will lead to the older materials. C. A. Lohmann has published *The Arms of Yale University and Its Colleges at New Haven* (New Haven 1948).

For Yale in colonial Connecticut, Benjamin Trumbull, *A Complete History of Connecticut, Civil and Ecclesiastical* (Vol. I, Hartford 1797; reprinted with Vol. II, New Haven 1818), is still useful. For the period from Stiles to Woolsey there are two excellent studies: Richard J. Purcell, *Connecticut in Transition, 1775–1818* (Washington 1918) and Charles R. Keller, *The Second Great Awakening in Connecticut* (New Haven 1942). On Yale and New Haven H. T. Blake, *Chronicles of the New Haven Green from 1638 to 1862* (New Haven 1898) has considerable interest; and there are materials in E. E. Atwater, *History of the City of New Haven* (New York 1887); but the best general treatment will be Rollin G. Osterweis' forthcoming *Three Centuries of New Haven, 1638–1938*. On one side of the economic relations between the University and City are M. F. Tyler, *The University as a Business Institution in New Haven* (New Haven 1900); A. P. Stokes, *What Yale Does for New Haven* (New Haven 1911); and *Yale and New Haven* (New Haven 1937), issued by the University. Arnold Dana has presented the other side in *New Haven's Problems. Whither the City? All Cities?* (New Haven 1937), 56–66.

AMERICAN HIGHER EDUCATION. Of the vast stream of works on college and university education in America, the following general and comparative surveys have been of particular use: C. F. Thwing, *The American College in American Life* (New York 1897); E. E. Slosson, *Great American Universities* (New York 1910); R. L. Duffus, *Democracy Enters College: A Study of the Rise and Decline of the Academic Lockstep* (New York 1936); and J. E. Kirkpatrick, *Academic Organization and Control* (Yellow Springs, Ohio, 1931). C. H. Patton and W. T. Field, *Eight O'Clock Chapel: A Study of New England College Life in the Eighties* (Boston 1927) gives a broader picture of the college milieu and a more particular view of Yale than its title indicates. For a comparative or international point of view, there are cogent passages in James Bryce, *The American Commonwealth* (2 vols., New York 1888; rev. ed. 1909); Abraham Flexner, *Universities: American, English, German* (New York 1930); and the essays of Paul Farmer, C. C. Gillispie, and G. W. Pierson in Margaret Clapp, ed. *The Modern University* (Ithaca, N.Y., 1950).

On the earlier stages in the evolution of the curriculum, L. F. Snow,

The College Curriculum in the United States (New York 1907), W. T. Foster, *Administration of the College Curriculum* (Boston 1911), and M. L. Smallwood, *An Historical Study of Examinations and Grading Systems in Early American Universities* (Cambridge 1935) are the best available. Comprehensive studies of college curriculum problems, interesting for recent developments, are Mowat G. Fraser, *The College of the Future* (New York 1937); R. F. Butts, *The College Charts Its Course* (New York 1939), and J. S. Brubacher, *A History of the Problems of Education* (New York 1947). Brubacher and Butts have useful bibliographies, but the latter's strong "progressive" bias distorts his historical analysis.

Among the many stimulating studies of liberal education from a more humanistic point of view, the following may be mentioned: L. B. Richardson, *A Study of the Liberal College* (Hanover, N.H., 1924); H. M. Wriston, *The Nature of a Liberal College* (Appleton, Wis., 1936); T. M. Greene and others, *Liberal Education Re-examined: Its Role in a Democracy* (New York 1943); Mark Van Doren, *Liberal Education* (New York 1943); *General Education in a Free Society: Report of the Harvard Committee* (Cambridge 1945); *Amherst College. Report of the Faculty Committee on Long Range Policy* (Amherst, Mass., 1945); Sidney Hook, *Education for Modern Man* (New York 1946); Emanuel Cohn, *Minerva's Progress* (New York 1946); Jacques Barzun, *Teacher in America* (Boston 1946); and *The Idea and Practice of General Education: An Account of the College of the University of Chicago, by Present and Former Members of the Faculty* (Chicago 1950).

Among Yale's own recent contributions to the theory of a liberal education have been: W. C. DeVane, "American Education after the War," *Yale Review,* Summer 1943, n.s. 33:34–46; *Report of the Committee on the Course of Study* (Yale College, 20 Jan. 1945, mimeographed); W. C. DeVane, "Plan of Study for the Bachelor of Arts Degree at Yale," *Higher Education,* 1 Nov. 1945, 2: No. 5, 1–3; W. C. DeVane, "The New Program in Yale College," *Journal of Higher Education,* Apr. 1947, 18:189–93; Maynard Mack, "Directed Studies," *Yale Alumni Magazine,* May 1949; and the *Report of the Committee on the Division of the Humanities* by Frank D. Ashburn and his associates for the Yale University Council.

Throughout its history Yale has maintained its independence of character. Yet since as College and University it has been an observer and borrower as well as competitor, no history can be written without indebtedness to the parent institution in Cambridge. I cite with profound respect the books of Samuel Eliot Morison on Harvard, in particular *The Founding of Harvard College* (Cambridge 1935), *Harvard College in the Seventeenth Century* (2 vols., Cambridge 1936), and *Three Centuries of Harvard* (Cambridge 1936). S. E. Morison, ed., *The Development of Harvard University since the Inauguration of President Eliot* (Cambridge 1930) collects the indispensable materials for the modern period; and Henry James, *Charles W. Eliot, President of Harvard University* (2 vols., Boston 1930), and Henry Aaron Yeomans, *Abbott Lawrence Lowell, 1856–1943* (Cambridge 1948) have illuminated the contrasting development of Yale at many points. Under the same head should be mentioned the impressive Merle Curti and Vernon Carstensen, *The University of Wisconsin: A History* (2 vols., Madison, Wis., 1949); the delightful but all too brief *Princeton, 1746–1896* (Princeton 1946) by T. J. Wertenbaker; and C. G. Osgood and others, *The Modern Princeton* (Princeton, N.J., 1947).

Directly pertinent and useful are also the writings and the biographies of the graduates of Yale who went out as educational leaders. Foremost among these are D. C. Gilman, *The Launching of a University* (New York 1906); Fabian Franklin, *The Life of Daniel Coit Gilman* (New York 1910); *Autobiography of Andrew D. White* (2 vols., New York 1905); Carl Becker, *Cornell University: Founders and Founding* (Ithaca, N.Y., 1944); and Walter P. Rogers, *Andrew D. White and the Modern University* (Ithaca 1942); T. W. Goodspeed, *William Rainey Harper, First President of the University of Chicago* (Chicago 1928), and *History of the University of Chicago: The First Quarter Century* (Chicago 1916); R. M. Hutchins, *The Higher Learning in America* (New Haven 1936). James Gray, *The University of Minnesota, 1851–1951* (Minneapolis 1951), with brilliant pen portraits of many Yale figures, appeared too late for citation in this volume.

Since it is impossible in a general bibliography to list all the departmental materials or articles and special studies on particular aspects of modern collegiate development, additional brief bibliographies, appropriate to the topics treated, are given at the head of the Reference notes for each chapter.

REFERENCE NOTES FOR
CHAPTER 1 · YALE COLLEGE IN THE NINETIES

Indispensable for the study of Yale in the era from the Civil War to the Spanish-American War are the general histories by W. L. Kingsley, B. C. Steiner, and C. H. Smith which are cited in the Bibliography. Written much more from the students' view of the things that really mattered are those two storehouses of College lore: Bagg, *Four Years at Yale* (1871), and Welch and Camp, *Yale: Her Campus, Class-Rooms and Athletics* (1899). Among personal recollections, Beers' classic, *The Ways of Yale,* comes first, followed at a distance by Howland's "Undergraduate Life at Yale," *Scribner's Magazine,* July 1897. Two useful collections of articles from college and other papers are J. A. Porter, *Sketches of Yale Life* (Washington 1878), and Clarence Deming, *Yale Yesterdays* (New Haven 1915). Autobiographies and biographies rich in personal recollections are President Dwight, *Memories of Yale Life and Men,* O. W. Firkins, *Cyrus Northrop,* W. L. Cross, *Connecticut Yankee,* W. L. Phelps, *Autobiography with Letters,* J. F. Fulton, *Harvey Cushing,* and H. S. Canby, *Alma Mater,* revised in *American Memoir.* Some entertaining sidelights appear in the diary of James Donnelly, "Record of Twenty Years as a Campus Policeman," typescript copy in the Yale Memorabilia Room.

These descriptions and interpretations are at best selective from the rising stream of official and unofficial records. Yale became articulate as never before in the era after the Civil War. The first Annual Statements for the Alumni—*Yale College in 1868* and its succeeding issues—became in 1887 the annual *Report of the President of Yale University.* The *Yale Literary Magazine,* with its "Memorabilia and Notabilia," was supplemented and supplanted as a chronicler by the *Yale Courant* (1865–1918), the *Yale Record* (1872–), the *Yale Daily News* (1878–), and the *Yale Alumni Weekly* (1891–). With the Class of 1870 the Class statistics began to appear as separate pamphlets. The Class of 1876 introduced a year-by-year history of the Class, and their successors expanded their records in bulk and variety, covering all kinds of curricular and extracurricular activities. With the new century the anniversary and reunion histories began to include articles of reminiscence, of comparison, and critical comment. Among the more notable may be listed: *History of the Class of 1868 . . . 1864–1914* (1914); *Quarter-Centenary Record of the Class of 1878* (1904); *A History of the Class of Seventy-Nine . . . 1875–1905* (1906); *A History of the Class of 'Eighty-One . . . 1877–1907* (1909); *Yale 1883 . . . after Its Quartercentenary Reunion* (1910), and H. C. M. Thomson, *In the Early Eighties and Since with Yale '83* (1923); *Quarter Century Record of the Class of Eighteen Eighty-Seven* (1912); *Thirty Year Record. Class of 1890* (1922); the *Quindecennial Record* of 1895, the *Sexennial* and *Decennial Record* of 1896, the *Decennial* and *Half Century Record* of 1897, and the *Decennial Record* of 1898.

I have quoted with great freedom from George Santayana's "A Glimpse of Yale," which appeared in the *Harvard Monthly,* Dec. 1892, 15:89–97, and which may be rated as the most perceptive study of Yale ever penned by a stranger. Santayana wrote of this visit again, with greater freedom as to personalities, in *The Middle Span* (New York 1945). His host, W. L. Phelps, responded with "The Average Harvard Undergraduate," in the *Yale Courant,* 10 June 1893, 29:213–15. The game of comparative analysis was later extended by Edmund Wilson, "Harvard, Princeton, and Yale," in the *Forum,* Sept. 1923, 70:1871–79. Three very useful surveys of American colleges and universities are C. H. Patton and W. T. Field, *Eight O'Clock Chapel,* C. F. Thwing, *The American College in American Life,* and E. E. Slosson, *Great American Universities.*

The quotations at the head of this chapter are from the *Yale Alumni Weekly,* 1 Mar. 1892, C. F. Thwing, 177, and Edmund Wilson, 1872.

1. "[Yale] students are not very sophisticated, but they are extremely enthusiastic. They love their college customs; they are proud of their classes; they are frantically loyal to Yale itself. They think nothing else so great and glorious; and they have a magnificently barbarian contempt for anything outside their own university." Harry Thurston Peck, "Life at Harvard," *Bookman,* Apr. 1898, 7:146.
2. Slosson, 59–60, quotes the Harvard alumnus who sent his son to Yale, because he found that "all the Harvard men are working for Yale men."

3. Santayana, "A Glimpse of Yale."
4. "Nothing could show a greater contrast than the comparative stillness of the Yale Campus and the Harvard Yard. No games are ever seen in front of the Harvard buildings; no one yells 'Fire' or blows a horn . . . men do not even shout for a friend under his room. A Harvard man would not be able to understand the Yale fondness for pure noise." Phelps, "The Average Harvard Undergraduate," 214–15. On the "fire" calls, see Howland, 25.
5. Slosson, 34–37.
6. *Yale College: Some Thoughts Respecting Its Future,* 13, and *What a Yale Student Ought to Be,* 23.
7. Conversation of W. L. Phelps with G.W.P., 17 Nov. 1939, and "The Average Harvard Undergraduate," 215.
8. Thwing, 156. He did, indeed, add that the Congregational was the least denominational of all colleges. But President Hadley would later have to spend a good deal of time protesting against Yale being classed as a "Congregational" institution.
9. Welch and Camp, 24; A. P. Stokes, *Memorials of Eminent Yale Men,* 2:375.
10. Welch and Camp, 44–49. On bowing out the President, see also C. H. Smith, 248. I am indebted to President Seymour for the story of President Dwight's magic touch. For typical criticism of the chapel service see F. A. Lord, "Some Things and Others," *Yale Literary Magazine,* Dec. 1897, 63:93, and Professor Perrin's caustic description quoted by Welch and Camp, 221.
11. Slosson, 59. For the Dwight Hall "Oligarchy," the O.D.P., and the attack led by the "Holy Pokers," see Welch and Camp, 61, and J. B. Reynolds, S. H. Fisher and H. B. Wright, eds., *Two Hundred Years of Christian Activity,* 203–06.
12. Thwing, 160; H. S. Canby, *American Memoir* (Boston, Houghton Mifflin, 1947), 144, 142.
13. Welch and Camp, 146–47.
14. Canby, 149.
15. *Yale Daily News,* 10, 12 Mar. 1897; *Yale Alumni Weekly,* 11, 18 Mar. 1897; *The Yale Class Book '98,* 125–26.
16. Julius S. Mason, *A Yale Footnote to Kipling* (New Haven 1928), and Phelps, *Autobiography with Letters,* 312–13.
17. *Yale Alumni Weekly,* 1, 8 Oct. 1896; Canby 144–45; and Mason.

18. Dwight, *What a Yale Student Ought to Be,* 15; Wendell in the *Harvard Monthly,* Dec. 1901, 33:101.

19. Welch and Camp, 36; Thwing, 169.

20. The debating revival saw graduate athletes, unintellectual but loyal, coming up from New York to lend a hand. Anson Phelps Stokes, a member of the first team to defeat Harvard, probably owed the fact that he later became Secretary of the University largely to his contact with Professor Hadley as the effective coach of the team. Stokes to G.W.P., 3 Apr. 1946.

21. Quoted by Welch and Camp, 161.

22. "Harvard, Princeton, and Yale," 1874.

23. For feeling on the war, especially among the faculty, see Professor A. M. Wheeler's speech against intervention in the *Yale Daily News,* 5 Apr. 1898, and comments in the *Yale Alumni Weekly,* 5, 26 May 1898. Sumner's famous speech, "The Conquest of the United States by Spain," was delivered in Jan. 1899, after hostilities were over.

24. Donnelly, "Record of Twenty Years as a Campus Policeman," 28. In a Sophomore outburst, the marching song was "Cuba, Cuba, Cuba libre [three times repeated], To H——, to H—— with Spain," sung to the tune of "John Brown's Body." The fad spread to the high-school students, who shouted the forbidden swearwords with great glee. *Yale Class Book 1900,* 141. Conversation of Charles Seymour with G.W.P.

25. Welch and Camp, 161–63.

26. The *Lit.* boards of 1896 and 1897 tried hard to shatter complacency, and the campus query changed from "Is the *Lit.* out?" to "What's the *Lit.* into?" General Daniel H. Chamberlain '62 delivered a stronger attack to (and on) his fellow alumni: "If I were to name today what I deem the least commendable trait of Yale sentiment . . . I should call it the present, all-pervading Yale spirit of self-satisfaction; and if I were to go farther and indulge in a more specifically critical word, I should say the great exemplar of this spirit is our worthy and much-beloved president, Timothy Dwight." The *Alumni Weekly,* 24 Feb. 1898, confessed there was too much truth in this.

27. John Lord O'Brian, *Yale Alumni Magazine,* July 1948.

REFERENCE NOTES FOR
CHAPTER 2 · THE YALE SYSTEM

Students of the Yale system should consult the sources listed for Chapter 1. On the theory and custom of campus life the chapters by Lewis S. Welch in Welch and Camp are particularly full and sympathetic; while Hadley, Canby, and Santayana give penetrating analyses. For the physical growth of the College, President Dwight, *Yale College: Some Thoughts Respecting Its Future,* and his *Reports,* notably that for 1896, are excellent. Maps were printed in the annual *Catalogue;* and a vivid, three-dimensional view of the Yale scene is given by the large-scale model of the old campus prepared by Francis T. Gilling for the Yale exhibit at the St. Louis Exposition of 1904, now in the Yale Memorabilia Room. The transformation of South Middle into Connecticut Hall is well told by Dean Wright in *Report of the President and Deans, 1904–05,* 77–82, but for full flavor the columns of the *News* and the *Alumni Weekly* from Nov. 1902 to June 1903 should be scanned. Extracurricular activities are treated more or less fully in all the general sources and have an abundant literature of their own. Particularly useful on football are Harford Powel Jr., *Walter Camp, the Father of American Football* (Boston, Little, Brown, 1926), 112–13, 199; and *Touchdown!* as told by Coach Amos Alonzo Stagg to Wesley Winans Stout (New York 1927). *The Yale Football Story* by Tim Cohane (New York 1951) appeared after this was written. W. L. Kingsley deliberately omitted any discussion of the societies, on the ground that their secrecy made adequate description impossible; but Bagg is detailed on their origins and early development, and C. H. Smith and Steiner give fairly competent accounts. The periodical literature of criticism, defense, exposure, and speculation is voluminous.

1. *Yale College: Some Thoughts Respecting Its Future,* 82–83.
2. Slosson, 35.
3. Bagg, 701, quoting "an unknown genius." There are many versions.

4. "We are here to prepare for the future, and many honestly think it is more beneficial to spend less time with books and more with men. It is a fair question as to which plan is the better." E. B. Reed '94, *Yale Literary Magazine,* Feb. 1894, 59:221.

5. Canby, 142, 155, and cf. 173, 183–84 on student-faculty relations. President Seymour, who knew the campus intimately from childhood, has remarked that the picture of the faculty-student gulf, or of the faculty retreat from life, can easily be overdrawn.

6. *What a Yale Student Ought to Be,* 22; Welch and Camp, xviii.

7. Howland, 25–26. The quotations that follow are drawn from this passage.

8. So Harvey Cushing '91 wrote to his father, adding "It is the only place one ever sees any of the 'Sheff' boys and connects them more to the College proper than anything else." J. F. Fulton, *Harvey Cushing: A Biography* (Springfield, Ill., Charles C. Thomas, 1946), 41–42.

9. *Yale Banner* (1895–1900), for titles and membership. There is a lively account of the earlier eating clubs and Commons in Bagg, 237–49.

10. The petition was printed in the *Yale Literary Magazine,* May 1888, 53:375–76. Welch and Camp, 28–34, gives a stirring account of "The Fight to Save the Fence." President Seymour recalls that President Dwight hated to lose the Fence. But he felt compelled to accept Osborn Hall, with its architect, because it was the first important gift in his administration and because he looked to future aid from the same source: a hope that was justified.

11. A. N. Lewis '52, in the *News,* 29 Nov. 1902; Slosson, 72. President Hadley first inclined to save the ancient building, then faltered as he learned the cost of "preserving it as a mummy." See Hadley Letters, especially Hadley to Otto T. Bannard, 15 Apr. 1903.

12. Canby, 152.

13. Welch and Camp, 451–52.

14. Powel, 112–13, 199.

15. Professor Wallace Notestein has told me of the great influence the Yale code of sportsmanship had in the West, and President Seymour has contributed the Rockne anecdote. See Curti and Carstensen, *The University of Wisconsin,* 1:696, quoting Parke Davis, *Football: The American Collegiate Game* (New York

1911), 93; O. L. Elliott, *Stanford University: The First Twenty-five Years* (Stanford University, Calif., 1937), 225, 227; Stagg, *Touchdown!* and the tribute to Stagg in T. W. Goodspeed, *A History of the University of Chicago* (Chicago 1916), 381–82.

16. Hadley, in *Four American Universities*, 767, 770, 772.

17. The history of the athletic system and the development of gymnastics, physical education, and hygiene will be treated in the second volume of this work.

18. Graduate members of the societies had incorporated as trust associations: Russell Trust Association (Skull and Bones), 1856; Kingsley Trust Association (Scroll and Key), 1860; Phelps Trust Association (Wolf's Head), 1886; Trumbull Trust Association (Psi Upsilon), 1862; Winthrop Trust Association (Delta Kappa Epsilon), 1865.

19. Welch and Camp, 454–55.

20. *Ibid.,* 37.

21. *Ibid.,* 13.

22. For typical discussion of the values of the societies, see W. L. Phelps in the *Yale Courant,* 10 June 1893; E. S. Oviatt, "On Shams," G. H. Nettleton, "On Realities," and Nathan A. Smyth's Junior Exhibition oration, "The Democratic Idea in College Life," in the *Yale Literary Magazine,* Jan., Feb., Apr. 1896, 61: 131–36, 177–80, 271–76. This last made a strong impression on the College.

REFERENCE NOTES FOR
CHAPTER 3 · COLLEGE OR UNIVERSITY

The bibliography on the elective system, and on the growth of particular universities, is enormous; but nowhere is there a study which sums up university development as a whole and places the elective issue in its college-university setting. I have quoted and borrowed from my brief reconnaissance of this problem, "American Universities in the Nineteenth Century: The Formative Period," in Margaret Clapp, ed., *The Modern University* (Ithaca, Cornell University Press, 1950), 59–94. For the pronouncements of the three Presidents who spoke for the old and new trends, one may refer to their inaugural addresses: *Inauguration of James McCosh, D.D., LL.D., as President of the College of New Jersey, Princeton, October 27, 1868* (New York 1869), 70–74; *Addresses at the Inauguration of Professor Noah Porter, D.D., LL.D. as President of Yale College, Wednesday, October 11, 1871* (New York 1871), 44–47; and *Addresses at the Inauguration of Charles William Eliot as President of Harvard College, Tuesday, October 19, 1869* (Cambridge, Mass., 1869), 38–42, reprinted in S. E. Morison, ed., *The Development of Harvard University . . . 1869–1929* (Cambridge, Mass., 1930), lxiv–lxvi.

For President Eliot's achievements and influence at Harvard and in the field of American education, particularly in regard to the elective system, see the discriminating discussion in Henry James' biography, *Charles W. Eliot;* S. E. Morison, *Three Centuries of Harvard,* 341–47, 384–90, and *The Development of Harvard University,* xli–xliv. For some of the rising doubts and dissatisfactions, see H. A. Yeomans, *Abbott Lawrence Lowell,* 65–70. President McCosh's regime at Princeton is described in W. M. Sloane, *The Life of James McCosh: A Record Chiefly Autobiographical* (New York 1896), and T. J. Wertenbaker, *Princeton, 1746–1896.*

Besides G. S. Merriam, ed., *Noah Porter,* and the other biographical articles, there are excellent appreciations of President Porter's personality and educational philosophy in A. P. Stokes, *Memorials of Emi-*

nent Yale Men, 1:329–35, and Timothy Dwight, *Memories of Yale Life and Men,* 157–66, 342–52. There are interesting passages in H. E. Starr, *Sumner,* and, from a typically modern point of view, in H. W. Schneider, *A History of American Philosophy* (New York 1946), 456–57. The most important source is the collection of Porter's essays in *The American Colleges and the American Public* (New Haven 1870). These papers appeared originally in the *New Englander,* Jan.–Oct. 1869. A new edition of this widely noticed book, with several additional papers, was published in New York in 1878. The citations in this chapter are to this second edition.

The Faculty programs were effectively set forth in several articles and pamphlets. First J. D. Dana published *The Yale University Scheme: The Academic College and the Scientific College at New Haven, in Their Relationship to the University* (New Haven 1870). This pamphlet, a reprint of an article in the *College Courant,* 4 June 1870, was an enlargement of an earlier letter in the *Courant,* 4 May 1870. He followed up with *The New Haven University: What It Is and What It Requires* (New Haven 1871), a reprint from the *College Courant,* 17 June 1871. Dana also dealt fully and trenchantly with the needs of the Academic Department in the *Nation,* 1 June 1871, 12:279–80; and in the *Courant* of 24 June he sketched the character to be desired in "Our Next President." Timothy Dwight contributed *Yale College: Some Thoughts Respecting Its Future* (New Haven 1871), reprinting articles which had appeared in the *New Englander,* July 1870–Oct. 1871. Young William Graham Sumner, not yet called to his professorship, hammered grimly on "The 'Ways and Means' for Our Colleges," *Nation,* 8 Sept. 1870, and a representative body of professors presented *Yale College. The Needs of the University, Suggested by the Faculties to the Corporation, the Graduates, and the Benefactors and Friends of the Institution. July 10, 1871.* The Young Yale movement among the alumni is well treated in H. E. Starr, *Sumner,* 80–95; of the numerous articles called out, those in the *College Courant,* 23 July 1870, and the *Nation,* 15 Dec. 1870, are valuable.

The beginnings of the University Departments are traced in all the general histories and in the special articles cited in the Bibliography. President Stiles' "Plan of a University" is printed in part in *The Book of the Yale Pageant,* 131–32, and there is some interesting material on the first Timothy Dwight's ambitions in Charles Cuningham, *Timothy Dwight, 1752–1817: A Biography* (New York 1942). R. H. Chittenden,

History of the Sheffield Scientific School (New Haven, Yale University Press, 1928) is indispensable not only for Sheff but the beginnings of the Graduate School. Fabian Franklin, *Life of D. C. Gilman,* is useful. For a judicious summary of what President Dwight had succeeded in doing and had had to leave undone, see President Hadley, *Report of the President and Deans, 1920–21,* 17–25.

The quotations at the head of the chapter are from J. C. French, *A History of the University Founded by Johns Hopkins* (Baltimore, Johns Hopkins University Press, 1946), 65, and *Yale College in 1884,* 9.

1. *Yale Literary Magazine,* March 1883, 34:211. Cf. Porter, *The American Colleges and the American Public,* 117.
2. The charge that Eliot tried to make over Harvard into a German university has been warmly refuted. And with reason. For Eliot himself insisted that a university was a matter of growth. "It cannot be transplanted from England or Germany in full leaf and bearing. It cannot be run up, like a cotton-mill, in six months, to meet a quick demand. Neither can it be created by an energetic use of the inspired editorial, the advertising circular, and the frequent telegram. Numbers do not constitute it, and no money can make it before its time." The American university when it appeared, therefore, would be distinctively American. "The New Education," *Atlantic Monthly,* Feb. 1869, 23:216.

   Nevertheless the fact cannot be escaped that, instead of simply adding new growth to Harvard College, Eliot was deliberately eliminating certain characteristic features and substituting a series of ideas and practices borrowed pretty directly from German sources.
3. The extracts quoted from the Corporation Records, 19 Aug. 1846, 17 Aug. 1847, 24 July 1860, are given in *Historical Register of Yale University,* 20, 21.
4. W. L. Kingsley, quoting T. R. Lounsbury, 2:106.
5. *College Courant,* 2 Oct. 1869.
6. C. P. Taft, *The German University and the American College* (Cincinnati 1871).
7. *Yale College: Some Thoughts Respecting Its Future,* 92.
8. *The Needs of the University,* 3–5.
9. Dexter, *Sketch of Yale University,* 81.
10. See Merriam, 149–50, for Porter's protest against the change of

name, and Porter's own comments on universities in *The American Colleges and the American Public,* 98–99, 275–80, 381–96.

11. "You will see first of all that we have a theory. We are not the blind followers of tradition or custom, but have a definite system which we intelligently hold." *Inauguration of President Porter,* 56.

12. "Greek and a Liberal Education," *Princeton Review,* Sept. 1884, 60(2):213, perhaps his most succinct expression of a sentiment developed in most of his writings on education.

13. Porter, *Professor Thomas A. Thacher. In Memoriam* (n.p., 1886), 10; *The American Colleges and the American Public,* 40–52, 333.

14. *The American Colleges and the American Public,* 326, 330, 129–30, 153–56; *Inauguration of President Porter,* 33–34. See also Merriam, ed., *Noah Porter,* 65–66, 80–83.

15. In *The American Colleges and the American Public* Porter commented incisively on the program of the "sanguine" and "adventurous" President, and the "new, and newer, and newest departures" of Harvard; and the course of fifteen years only strengthened his distrust of Eliot's New Education. When, in the mid-eighties, Harvard was debating the abolition of Greek and Yale hesitating on electives, Porter set forth his last defense of Greek and the liberal education as hitherto recognized by the "organized commonwealth of scholars" in "Greek and a Liberal Education," cited above, and "A Criticism from Yale of the Last Harvard Educational Move—Greek and the Bachelor's Degree," *New Englander,* May 1885, 44:424–35. This last article, in fact, was his ex post facto contribution to the debate between President Eliot and President McCosh. See W. M. Sloane, *James McCosh,* 199–201, and Eliot's "Liberty in Education" in his *Educational Reform* (New York 1898). For the college presidents' protest to the Harvard Overseers, see Morison, *Three Centuries of Harvard,* 359.

16. Address at the inauguration of President Gilman of Johns Hopkins in 1876, in *Educational Reform,* 43.

17. The Gymnasium Fund had brought in over $200,000 in less than three years; the Alumni University Fund had in eight years realized $78,346.60. *Report of the President, 1892,* 23–24; *1898,* 10. For the information in the footnote, see *Addresses at the*

Inauguration of Daniel C. Gilman . . . (Baltimore 1876), 20–21. I am indebted to Mr. Stokes for his reply to Mr. Rockefeller.

18. Corporation Records, 13 Mar. 1872, quoted in *Historical Register of Yale University*, 23.

19. *Yale College: Some Thoughts Respecting Its Future,* 7, 16–17.

20. Chittenden, *History of the Sheffield Scientific School,* 1:166–67, 215–17. For something of the feeling aroused, see Hadley's alumni luncheon speech, in the *Alumni Weekly,* 8 July 1910, and R. N. Corwin's recollections, in *Fiftieth Year Record of the Class of Eighty-seven, Yale College,* 16.

REFERENCE NOTES FOR

CHAPTER 4 · THE ELECTIVE STRUGGLE

The chief unpublished sources for the curriculum are the Record of the Academical Professors, the Faculty Record, and the Faculty memorials and memoranda in the collection, Academic Department under President Porter. The organization of the Course of Instruction and the operation of curricular changes may be studied in the annual *Catalogues*, the series of Annual Statements, *Yale College in 1876—Yale College in 1886*, and the *Report of the President* (1887–99).

An invaluable current record of student sentiment on instructors and studies is preserved in the undergraduate periodicals and the Senior Class Books. The recollections of W. L. Cross and W. L. Phelps, who were students and instructors through this period of transition, are particularly illuminating. Starr's biography of Sumner is essential for the outstanding leader in the reform movement and his share in the struggle of 1884. Sumner's significant "Our Colleges before the Country," *Princeton Review*, March 1884, 60(1):127–40, and the conservative exposition of George Trumbull Ladd, "The Recent Changes in the Academic Curriculum at Yale" in the *New Englander*, January 1885, 44:114–21, are important contemporary articles. E. S. Dana drew on his recollections in "The Changes in Yale's Curriculum," *Yale Alumni Weekly*, 28 Apr. 1911, and "Yale, Past, Present, and Future," *ibid.*, 20 May 1927. J. C. Schwab, "The Yale College Curriculum, 1701–1901," is useful for the old curriculum; and brief summaries may be found in the *Report of the President, 1895*, 28–35; *Report of the President and Deans, 1902–03*, 40–45; and Welch and Camp, 224–46.

The first quotation is from *Reports on the Course of Instruction in Yale College, by a Committee of the Corporation, and of the Academical Faculty* (New Haven 1828), 7. This famous Faculty Report, in defense of classical and disciplinary education, has been described as "the third great contribution that the colleges of the United States have made to literature dealing with the history of their curriculum." Snow, *The College Curriculum in the United States*, 143.

The Sumner quotation is from "Our Colleges before the Country," 132.

1. Dwight, *Yale College: Some Thoughts Respecting Its Future*, 8–10, 21. For President Porter's increasing conservatism, compare his praise of the Scientific School and wide liberal studies in the Academic College (1871) with his attack on too much history, political economy, and physics in 1884. *Addresses at the Inauguration of Noah Porter*, 57, and "Greek and a Liberal Education," *Princeton Review*, Sept. 1884, 60(2):205–07.

2. *Yale Courant*, 8 Mar. 1871. The program seems to have varied slightly from year to year. The *Catalogue* described the Course of Instruction as "a scheme of studies, or, more correctly, of equivalents which will be accepted from candidates for advanced standing."

3. The system ran on three classes a day, each an hour long, coming after prayers, at 11:30 in the morning, and (except on Wednesday and Saturday) at 5:00 in the afternoon. One gathers that Cyrus ("Gutsy") Northrop met the Freshmen in rhetoric on Saturday mornings, and that the lectures on hygiene were given at the Medical Institution at irregular hours. In any case the daily grind went to Greek, Latin, and mathematics, often in the same authors studied for entrance. Despite these facts, Freshmen covered only four books of Homer and half a book of Herodotus. Bagg says that in the last part of each Freshman term the advanced work stopped and the whole time was given to review for examinations. *Four Years at Yale*, 551–68.

4. Yale also maintained a chapel choir; and the musical activities of the Beethoven and Cecilia societies, the Class and Yale glee clubs should not be dismissed without mention. As for the formal teaching of music, in 1854 Joseph Battell had made a gift to provide for scientific instruction in music, for such as might wish it, and the next year Gustave Jacob Stoeckel had been appointed Instructor in Vocal Music with the prospect of a two-year course emphasizing church music. It was as College organist and choirmaster, however, that Stoeckel had found his services in institutional demand. The projected musical instruction came to no more than a private and voluntary study, somewhat below the status of an optional or elective, and not counted for the degree.

In the same way, before his appointment as Battell Professor of Music in 1890, Stoeckel's position was that of a faculty member not quite in full standing, his name being listed after the tutors, and among the foreign language instructors. For light on a neglected subject see the forthcoming history of music at Yale by Marshall Bartholomew.

5. *Yale Record,* 14 June 1876.

6. According to Poultney Bigelow '79, "In Freshman year I attempted to read history, and asked my instructor on the subject. He gave me this reply: 'Young man, if you think you came to Yale with the idea of reading, you will find out your mistake very soon.' And I did!" "Personal Notes," *Independent,* 20 Mar. 1902, 54:673. How strong the disciplinary force was appears in the admiring account of Professor Sumner's advanced course in 1874: twenty-five pages are assigned for each lesson and recited paragraph for paragraph—but questions may be asked, bringing up new topics, and extra reading is "almost a necessity" for doing well in the classroom. *Yale Courant,* 7 Feb. 1874, and *Yale Record,* 18 Feb. 1874.

As for the originality of prize essays, A. T. Hadley's classic formula deserves to be remembered: "Take four parts of Poole's Index, well mixed and triturated; dissolve in two parts of a liquid composed of equal proportions of extracts from Buckle's History of civilization and Benton's Thirty years' view of the American government; flavor to suit the taste." In the seventies, Hadley admitted, the particular solvents prescribed were clearly somewhat antiquated, but the picture was substantially a true one. A. T. Hadley, "The Library in the University," *Public Libraries,* Apr. 1909, 14:115–16.

7. The Committee—J. D. Dana, H. A. Newton, and W. G. Sumner —was appointed 1 Mar. 1876. In May the Corporation accepted the scheme with the warning that, if it called for encroachment on the permanent funds, it would have to be modified. Rec. Acad. Profs., 1 Mar. to 17 May 1876; Corporation Records, 1875–1900, May 1876; *Yale College in 1876,* 4–6.

8. The student reception of the change showed a rather reluctant gratitude that, at last, *some* freedom was gained, though only "a dry crust rather than a nutritious loaf." *Yale Courant,* 13 May 1876.

9. Starr, *Sumner,* chap. 15 gives a full account of this contro-

versy. President Porter's unpublished statement to the Corporation is in the Rare Book Room collection, Academic Department under President Porter.

10. Gibbs had been teaching, without salary, in the Graduate School, and the College felt that it "had reason to congratulate itself that his attachment" had caused him to refuse a flattering offer from another college [The Johns Hopkins University] to remain in connection with the College and take on optional classes. *Yale College in 1880*, 3. The want of "the place, the apparatus, and the requisite instruction" for the sciences was being met in part by the appointment of E. S. Dana as Assistant Professor of Natural Philosophy, 1879, the building of the Sloane Physical Laboratory, 1881–83, and the promise of the Kent Chemical Laboratory in 1883. *Yale College in 1881*, 6; *Yale College in 1883*, 4–5.

11. Daggett records from the Registrar's Office. *The Statistics of the Class of 'Eighty-Four, Yale College* (New Haven 1884), and *A History of the Class of Eighty-Four, Yale College, 1880–1914* (n.p. 1914); *'85 Class Book, Yale College* (New Haven 1885) and *The Yale '86 Class Book* (New Haven 1886).

12. For their characteristically individual reactions to mathematics, the classical curriculum, and Lord Coleridge, see Cross, *Connecticut Yankee*, 63–65, and Phelps, *Autobiography with Letters*, 140, 147–48. The *Lit.* editorialized on the contrast between Coleridge's view and the actual classical reading of students, Nov. 1883, 49:47–51.

13. "Alumnus" [D. C. Eaton], *Yale College in 1881* (n.p., n.d., four articles reprinted from the *New Haven Evening Register*, not to be confused with the Annual Statement of the same title), 20, 24–31. For a slashing personal attack on the teachers and the teaching of the early eighties, see Harlow Gale, "A Yale Education versus Culture," *Pedagogical Seminary*, Mar. 1902, 9:3–17. The unhappy tutor's remark, quoted below in the text, is from the *Yale Record*, No. 25, Mar. 1876.

14. Tutors were regularly used as stopgaps, and even professors on occasion had to bend to the rule. Professor Thacher once remarked to his division: "Young gentlemen, the Faculty has ordered me, Professor of Latin, to *hear* your political economy. I ask your charity." *Yale Alumni Weekly*, 22 Apr. 1910.

593

15. *Connecticut Yankee,* 64. For characteristic stories of Northrop and others, see Phelps, *Autobiography,* H. C. M. Thomson, *In the Early Eighties and Since with Yale '83,* and O. W. Firkins, *Cyrus Northrop.*

16. Phelps, 136–37; Cross, 77.

17. *Yale Literary Magazine,* Nov. 1883, 49:47; Apr. 1885, 50:253; Oct. 1885, 51:1–4; Jan. 1887, 52:153; *Yale Record,* 17 Jan. 1885. See also *History of the Class of 1884 . . . 1880–1914.*

18. *Yale College in 1881,* 3; *Yale College in 1882,* 4.

19. For the series of committees and their proposals, see the Faculty Record, 27 Feb. to 10 May 1884. For the sequel see H. E. Starr, *William Graham Sumner* (New York, Henry Holt, 1925), 334–42.

20. Faculty Record, 14 May, 21 June 1884; Corporation Records, 16 May, 23 June 1884. See also Faculty drafts and memoranda, including the full manuscript of the memorial of 14 May, and a recapitulation, apparently prepared for the conference committee, in the papers on the Academic Department under President Porter. Dana's account is in Starr, *Sumner,* 342.

21. Faculty Record, 2, 20 May, 24 Oct. 1885. Corporation Records, May, Oct. 1885.

22. "Our Colleges before the Country," 132. There is a draft for the proposed "Schools" in Academic Department under President Porter. See also Dana, "The Changes in Yale's Curriculum."

23. *Extracts from the Memorial of the Academical Faculty, Presented to the Corporation of Yale College, May 16, 1884.* See also *Yale College in 1884,* 9; *Yale College in 1885,* 8. For the conservatives, Ladd dwelt on the defenses against "caprice" and "self-indulgent ease," in "The Recent Changes in the Academic Curriculum at Yale," 115.

24. *Catalogue of Yale University, 1886–87,* 31–32; 55. Special Honors were established in 1885. *Yale College in 1885,* 9–10.

25. Gale, "A Yale Education versus Culture," 12. See also the tributes in Cross, 71–72, and Phelps, 140–43, and the outbursts of the Class of 1885 and 1886, *Triennial Report . . . 1885,* 14–15; *Triennial Record . . . 1886,* 7. For the Greek cheer, see the account of the setting up of the tablet in Durfee Hall, *Yale Alumni Magazine,* 5 May, 2 June 1939; also the sketch of Tarbell by Robert Herrick in the *Dictionary of American Biography.*

26. The first year of electives ended with unbounded enthusiasm of students for "Utopia almost realized," and almost unanimous approval from the Faculty. Even Ladd conceded "unexpected wisdom and manliness" in student choices. Some had taken twenty or twenty-five exercises. *Yale College in 1885*, 6–7; *Yale Courant*, 5 Mar., 17 June 1885.

27. The demand for chemistry and biology was apparently pressing as hard on natural philosophy (astronomy and geology) as psychology on theism and evidences of Christianity. The formidable Elias Loomis, Munson Professor of Natural Philosophy and Astronomy, died in 1889, at the time when Porter was letting philosophy pass into younger hands. Physics had been in the curriculum since the days of Rector Pierson and his "manuscript of Physicks." Dexter, *Biographies and Annals*, 2:115.

28. *Report of the President, 1891*, 29–30. See also his welcome to Freshman English and the fine arts optionals, *ibid.*, 32–33, and his pleasure in the new studies, *Memories of Yale Life and Men*, 468.

29. Rec. Acad. Profs. 23 Apr. 1894, 12 Mar., 15 May 1895.

30. President Dwight's comparison of the electives in 1885–86 and 1895–96 is enlightening. *Report of the President, 1895*, 28–35.

31. There is an excellent account of the growth of the English Department in Welch and Camp, 342–49. Phelps' *Autobiography with Letters*, 279–303, has a lively account of his early years as a teacher. A still livelier one was contributed by one of his first students, G. H. Nettleton '96, "Revolution in the Nineties," to the Centennial Number of the *Yale Literary Magazine*, Feb. 1936, 101:34–39. Conversations of G.W.P. with W. L. Phelps, 17 Nov., 18 Dec. 1939. For McLaughlin, see S. D. Thacher, *Edward Tompkins McLaughlin* (privately printed, n.p., n.d.), and Welch and Camp, 344: ". . . in recent times no other . . . has moved on the mind and spirit of those who came under him with quite the same power of personal inspiration."

32. *Yale '90 Class Book*, 22.

33. A. W. Colton '90, Vicennial Ode quoted in *Thirty Year Record. Class of 1890*, 182.

34. "In the majority of the senior elective courses the mingled *seminar* and lecture system of the German universities" was giving more satisfactory results. *Yale Courant*, 4 Oct. 1890.

595

35. Phelps, *Autobiography with Letters*, 297–302. Phelps introduced most of the American novels he wanted into his American literature course in 1897–98. During these same years W. L. Cross introduced a course on the English novel into the Graduate School, and thanks to Professor Lounsbury's intervention was able to get the ban removed. Cross, *Connecticut Yankee*, 116–17.

36. Quoted in Welch and Camp, 220–23.

President Dwight's *Memories of Yale Life and Men* is an invaluable source for his educational opinions and reflections, to be supplemented by his early *Yale College: Some Thoughts Respecting Its Future,* and by his annual *Reports* from 1887 to 1899 for the discussion of current and recurrent problems. Besides the biographical articles by H. E. Starr and Francis Parsons, also listed in the Bibliography, one should consult his own autobiographical sketch, "Formative Influences," *Forum,* Jan. 1891, 10:497–507; *Timothy Dwight, President of Yale University 1886–1899: Memorial Addresses* (n.p., n.d.), by B. W. Bacon, Francis Parsons, S. C. Bushnell, and A. T. Hadley; President Hadley's résumé in *Report of the President and Deans, 1920–21,* 16–25; and Patton and Field, *Eight O'Clock Chapel,* 103–08. Professor R. N. Corwin's "Reminiscences," and conversations with him and A. P. Stokes have given much useful information.

The quotation at the head of the chapter is from the *Yale Alumni Weekly,* 7 June 1899.

1. Corwin, "Reminiscences," 3–4.
2. W. L. Phelps, *Autobiography with Letters,* 161.
3. *Memories of Yale Life and Men,* 459–71.
4. Corwin, "Reminiscences," 3–5, and conversation with G.W.P., Dec. 1941; Innis Young to G.W.P., 25 Feb. 1944.
5. See, for instance, his references in 1871 to the "distinguished teacher whom the Divine Will called to the Presidency" at the beginning of the century, and in 1899 to his own completion of the work "begun so grandly by his ancestor." *Yale College: Some Thoughts Respecting Its Future,* 106, and *Report of the President, 1898–99,* 108.
6. *Memories of Yale Life and Men,* 497.
7. *Ibid.,* 479–86, and *Report of the President, 1898–99,* 136–38.

8. *Ibid., 1898–99,* 104–06. He had always intended to retire at seventy, he told the Corporation, and he had stated, unofficially, that he "proposed to resign while he still knew enough to know that he ought to." *Timothy Dwight . . . Memorial Addresses,* 25. For the visit to the newspaper office: conversation of G.W.P. with E. S. Oviatt, 27 Feb. 1942; and A. P. Stokes to G.W.P., 3 Apr. 1950.

9. C. F. Thwing, *The American College in American Life,* 283–84; Canby, *American Memoir,* 139.

10. Thwing, 190, 288–91.

11. *Report of the President, 1898–99,* 31; *Memories of Yale Life and Men,* 94–95.

12. *Report of the President, 1898–99,* 14–15.

13. *Memories of Yale Life and Men,* 471–76. This philosophy always characterized the later speeches of Dwight to alumni coming out to his home on Hillhouse Avenue after the Commencement game. President Seymour recalls his saying: "On the whole the world is better and better and I have to tell you that I am happier and happier as I get older."

14. "Formative Influences," 505–06, and *Yale College: Some Thoughts Respecting Its Future,* 106.

15. A. P. Stokes to G.W.P., 29 Apr. 1950.

16. Welch and Camp, 38.

17. Santayana, "A Glimpse of Yale," 97; A. T. Hadley, in *Four American Universities,* 51.

18. For Dwight's anxieties and recommendations, see the last chapter, "Questions of the Future," of *Memories of Yale Life and Men,* and *Report of the President, 1898–99,* 22, 28–29, 32–47.

19. *Ibid., 1898–99,* 136–37.

REFERENCE NOTES FOR

CHAPTER 6 · THE FIRST LAY PRESIDENT

On President Hadley and his Administration the most important materials in print are the addresses at his inauguration, his collected addresses and annual *Reports*, the biography by Morris Hadley, the biographical articles by French in the *Dictionary of American Biography* and by Lerner in the *Encyclopedia of the Social Sciences,* and the periodical articles and appreciations by others, listed in the Bibliography. Excellent appreciations are Charles Johnston, "Arthur Twining Hadley," *Harper's Weekly,* 23 June 1906, 50:889; P. C. Macfarlane, "The President of Yale," *Munsey's Magazine,* June 1914, 52:29–35; B. J. Hendrick, "President Hadley, of Yale," *World's Work,* June 1914, 28:141–48; and the memorial by Charles Seymour, *Arthur Twining Hadley, April 23, 1856–March 6, 1930* (privately printed, New Haven 1931). The most valuable of the unpublished sources are of two kinds: the rich files of Hadley letters and correspondence in the Library; and the vast store of lore and legend that enlivens the reminiscences of all who knew him and still for so many gives warmth and sparkle to the very atmosphere of New Haven. By letters and conversations I have benefited particularly from the knowledge gained through long and devoted personal association with Hadley by Anson Phelps Stokes, from the reminiscences of Charles Seymour, C. B. Tinker, Robert N. Corwin, W. L. Cross, and other members of Hadley's faculty.

The opening quotation is from the memorial by Charles Seymour.

1. Memorial by Seymour; "The Inauguration of President Hadley," *Harper's Weekly,* 28 Oct. 1899, 43:1102; C. H. Smith, *Yale University,* 264.
2. Macfarlane, 29–30; Hendrick, 143.
3. Conversations of G.W.P. with C. B. Tinker and C. W. Mendell, 24 Jan. 1939.
4. Hendrick, 143; *The Record of the Class of 1876, Yale College, 1876–1892* (New York 1893), 98.

5. Memorial by Seymour; *Report of the President and Deans, 1908–09*, 13, 12; *Yale Alumni Weekly*, 1 Apr. 1908.

6. This memorial has not been preserved in the Corporation files. The two men deputed to draft a respectful letter in favor of Hadley were G. B. Adams (history) and E. P. Morris (Latin) of Yale College. At the first meeting of 22 Mar. 1899 it was reported that 28 permanent professors were favorable, 14 noncommittal, 8 against, and 40 others unknown. T. S. Woolsey of the Law School took a hand in the drafting and the negotiating through F. J. Kingsbury of the Corporation. Others present at one or more of the group meetings were: Bacon (Divinity); Mixter, Penfield, and Hastings (Sheff); Schwab, Bourne, Pierpont, and Beebe (Yale College). Ultimately at least fifty full professors were understood to favor Hadley's election. Memoranda and drafts of letters, Mar. 1899, and Woolsey to Adams, 30 Mar. 1899, with copy of Kingsbury to Woolsey, 29 Mar., George Burton Adams Collection, Correspondence and Papers, Box 14–21, File 17. See also *Yale Alumni Weekly*, 7 June 1899, quoted in M. Hadley, *A. T. Hadley* (New Haven, Yale University Press, 1948), 105–06.

7. Keller, *Reminiscences of Sumner*, 61.

8. A favorite New Haven legend had it that when Arthur Hadley first came into the world he did not emit the usual preliminary cry; instead "he joyfully uttered *erchomai*, meaning 'I have arrived.' The elder Hadley, indignant that the precocious boy had made a mistake in the tense, caught him up, gave him a spanking, and corrected: 'You should have said *elthon*.'" See also Hendrick, 141, and the delightful family story of Hadley counting out in Greek, M. Hadley, *A. T. Hadley*, 9.

9. E. P. Parker to A. T. Hadley, 11 May 1899, quoted, with Hadley's draft of a reply, in M. Hadley, 106–08.

10. The inaugural address is given in *Inauguration of President Hadley*, 21–49, from which the following quotations are made.

11. *Yale Alumni Weekly*, 15 Nov. 1899, 10 Jan. 1900, 13 Dec. 1899; *Report of the President and Deans, 1900–01*, 5; *Yale Alumni Weekly*, 1 Apr. 1908.

12. The best insight into Hadley's moral idealism may be gained from his talks in chapel as collected in *Baccalaureate Addresses* and *The Moral Basis of Democracy*. For some private advice on

routing the devil, see Hadley's conversation with his seven-year-old son, M. Hadley, *A. T. Hadley*, 71–72. The quotations in the analysis that follows are taken from *The Moral Basis of Democracy*, 174, 36, 179, 43, 136, 54, 45–46, 161–62; and *Baccalaureate Addresses*, 90, 158, 141, 80, 149.

13. For the social ostracism speech before the Candlelight Club in Denver, see the *Yale Alumni Weekly*, 31 Jan. 1900, and M. Hadley, *A. T. Hadley*, 182–83. It was the duty of the universities, as he saw it, "to stand as a protest against exclusive devotion to this ideal of money-making." Johnston, 889. See the illuminating analysis of Hadley's moralizing of social controls by Lerner; also Seymour on "morality enlarged."

14. Hendrick, 144. Hadley's list of qualifications for a college preacher is in Hadley to Howell Cheney, South Manchester, Conn., 4 Mar. 1918, Hadley Letters.

15. *The Moral Basis of Democracy*, 84; M. Hadley, *A. T. Hadley*, 199.

16. A. P. Stokes to G.W.P., 20 Oct. 1944.

17. Mrs. Hadley is gratefully remembered by many persons, in and out of New Haven. M. Hadley, *A. T. Hadley*, 68–69; Corporation Records, 11 June 1921; *Yale Alumni Weekly*, 5 July 1935; A. P. Stokes to M. Hadley, 24 Nov. 1948 (copy); conversations of G.W.P. with A. P. Stokes, 19 June 1939, with C. B. Tinker, 24 Jan. 1939, and with others.

18. I am indebted to the late Robert N. Corwin for the use of his unpublished "Reminiscences," and to Anson Phelps Stokes for a copy of his letter to Morris Hadley, 24 Nov. 1948.

19. Macfarlane, 34; Johnston, 889. On his openness of mind, see Corwin, "Reminiscences"; Cross, *Connecticut Yankee*, 142–43; and Hendrick, 148.

20. *Report of the President and Deans, 1906–07*, 3–4.

21. *Ibid., 1904–05*, 12–17.

22. *Ibid., 1908–09*, 14–15. See also Johnston, 889.

23. *Report of the President and Deans, 1901–02*, 25–26. See also *ibid., 1902–03*, 12–14; and Hadley's letters to President H. S. Pritchett of the Carnegie Foundation for the Advancement of Teaching, 13, 27 Aug. 1907, for a discussion of the growth and relation of American universities to colleges. Hadley Letters.

24. R. D. French, in *Dictionary of American Biography*, Allen

Johnson and Dumas Malone, eds. (New York, Charles Scribner's Sons, 1928–44), 8:79.

25. *Report of the President and Deans, 1902–03,* 20–21.

26. A. P. Stokes to Dr. W. A. Brown, 16 May 1939 (copy), and to Dean G. Acheson, 28 May 1937 (copy).

The best accounts of the Yale government are President T. D. Woolsey, "Relations between the Trustees and Faculties of Colleges," *Congregationalist*, 18 May 1871, 32:153; F. B. Dexter, *An Historical Study of the Powers and Duties of the Presidency in Yale College* (Worcester 1898), reprinted from American Antiquarian Society, *Proceedings*, n.s. 12 (1899):27–42; President Hadley's *Report* of 1910–11, the two articles by him condensed in M. Hadley, *A. T. Hadley*, 122–32, and his numerous letters of explanation; and the very valuable memorandum for the President, "Faculty Control in Tradition and Statute," 2 Jan. 1930, by Carl A. Lohmann, Secretary of the University. For an outsider's view, J. E. Kirkpatrick, *Academic Organization and Control*, is useful. The editions of the Charter and the Corporation By-laws, listed in the Bibliography, contain the essential documents. In the operation of the system custom and spirit have been as important as formal structure and are to be traced in the innumerable records and recollections of daily experience. I have drawn particularly from conversations with G. L. Hendrickson, Clive Day, and R. N. Corwin. This chapter analyzes the Yale system at its height (c. 1899–1909). Since then, for many reasons, there has been a gradual decline.

The opening quotations are from James Bryce, *The American Commonwealth* (New York 1910), 2:718, 748, and Timothy Dwight, *Memories of Yale Life and Men*, 489.

1. Kirkpatrick, 79.
2. Conversation of G.W.P. with G. L. Hendrickson, 10 Dec. 1943.
3. *Report of the President and Deans, 1910–11*, 16–18, 20–21. The Corporation statute, quoted by Hadley from *The Yale Corporation. Charter . . . By-laws . . .* of 1907, had originally been passed in 1885.
4. Kirkpatrick, 59–73.

5. *Addresses at the Inauguration of President Porter,* 12. See also "Relations between the Trustees and Faculties of Colleges."

6. See especially "The Congratulatory Address" of George Park Fisher, *Inauguration of Arthur Twining Hadley,* 17–18.

7. Corporation Records, Mar. 1913.

8. Hadley to E. P. Parker, 24 Jan. 1906; to M. Carey Thomas, Bryn Mawr, 6 Feb. 1916; to W. S. Sutton, University of Texas, Austin, Texas, 6 Feb. 1918, Hadley Letters. Corporation Records, Sept. 1913.

9. In 1911 Hadley stated that it was the custom, nevertheless, to refer such changes as (1) creation of a new degree; (2) marked change in residence requirements; (3) radical change in conditions of admission; (4) legislation making a group of required studies optional; (5) changes involving considerable expense, including curriculum changes affecting the budget. Hadley to President James M. Taylor, Vassar College, Poughkeepsie, N.Y., 12 May 1911. On the President's financial responsibilities, Hadley to C. H. Ferry, Chicago, 7 Jan. 1904.

10. The reference to "any right-minded President" takes added interest from the fact this letter was written to Dean Andrew West, Princeton University, 2 May 1906.

    In 1907 the Yale Corporation statutes were changed to allow emergency vacancies, in vacation or at other times when a governing board could not be consulted, to be filled by Dean and President alone. Also a limited number of University professors or other Officers might, after proper consultation, be appointed by the Corporation without previous nomination; but their salaries should not be charged to any School without its consent. Lohmann, "Faculty Control in Tradition and Statute," 5; *The Yale Corporation* (1907), 28.

11. On Hadley and the so-called veto see Hadley to President E. B. Craighead, Tulane University, New Orleans, La., 4 May 1907; Hadley to Governor E. L. Philipp, Madison, Wis., 19 Apr. 1915; Hadley to President Thomas, 8 Apr. 1916; Kirkpatrick, 68.

12. Cross, 143. Conversation of G.W.P. with A. G. Keller, 14 May 1942; Keller, *Reminiscences of W. G. Sumner,* 61; and Starr, *W. G. Sumner,* 527.

13. To a correspondent troubled by his use of the word, he cited

with some pleasure the *Century Dictionary* illustration: "an *educational opportunist,* which means a man who does the best he can under the circumstances." Hadley to Miss Annie B. Jennings, New York, 15 Feb. 1918.

REFERENCE NOTES FOR
CHAPTER 8 · THE AGE OF THE BARONS

There is no satisfactory account of the development of the Yale College Faculty in recent times. The changes in its structure, the refinement of its functions, and the development of esprit de corps through the exercise of great powers and responsibilities must all be traced through the various Faculty Records, the Corporation Records, the annual *Catalogues*, the Letters of Hadley, and such personal papers as are available. Some recognition of accomplished changes may be gained from comparison of the Corporation laws as printed in the 4th edition of 1901 and the revised by-laws printed in 1907. Some light on Faculty evolution is cast by the résumés of President Dwight in the *Report of the President, 1897*, 26–36, and of Dean Wright in *Report of the President and Deans, 1906–07*, 66–68.

The quotation at the head of the chapter is from Keller, *Reminiscences of W. G. Sumner*, 48.

1. *Report of the President and Deans, 1903–04*, 77–79.
2. There are many scattered references to the unsatisfactory status of the tutor. See Starr, *W. G. Sumner*, 77–79; Cross, *Connecticut Yankee*, 66; Horace D. Taft, *Memories and Opinions* (New York 1942), 63–64; and, notably, M. Hadley, *A. T. Hadley*, 39–47. For a defense of the tutorship, see President Dwight, *Report, 1897*, 35–36. For Keller's experience, see his *Reminiscences of W. G. Sumner*, 43.
3. Policy on leaves and retirements, insurance and salaries, was also being regularized. In 1897 a pension plan had gone into effect, permitting retirement at sixty-five after twenty-five years of service. In May 1903 the Corporation voted that Officers on leave should receive only half salary, and that, starting three years later, professors who had reached sixty-eight should automatically be retired at the close of the fiscal year, unless by special

vote the Corporation should determine otherwise. This retirement rule disturbed the elders among the Academical Professors, and Seymour, Adams, and others protested strongly to Secretary Stokes on the ground of impairment of morale. In 1905 the first application of the Yale rule was moderated for "Waterloo" Wheeler and "Buffalo" Wright. The same year the Carnegie Pension plan superseded the Yale Pension system. A. P. Stokes to G.W.P., 6 Jan. 1950; and Corporation Records, May 1903, Nov. 1905.

For the evolution of the intermediate ranks in the faculty see Hadley to Dr. R. D. Harlan, George Washington University, Washington, D.C., 21 Dec. 1908; to Prof. G. W. Kirchwey, Columbia University, 3 Apr. 1909; to Prof. G. H. Marx, Stanford University, 22 Nov. 1909; to Payson Merrill, 25 June 1910, Hadley Letters. Also Corporation Records, May 1915.

4. *Report of the President, 1897*, 31; Hadley to Howard C. Sherwood, New York, 24 Dec. 1906, Hadley Letters; conversation of G.W.P. with Charles Seymour, Nov. 1950.

"Administrative Officers" was first set off as a category, following "Corporation" and "Corporation Committees" and preceding "University Council" and "Faculty and Instructors," in the *Catalogue* for 1901–02; but this list was limited to University and Departmental (School) Officers. Chairmen came in with the Reorganization, being listed as Heads of Departments in the *Catalogue* of 1920–21 and as Chairmen in 1921–22.

5. Originally the Academical Professors had been distinguished from the Faculty only informally if at all. In 1871 the "Permanent Academical Officers of Yale College" began keeping a separate record of their meetings, though assistant professors were for some years invited to attend except when appointments were discussed. In 1885 the differentiation was made positive by the Corporation, which authorized separate sessions of the Academical Professors on permanent policy and appointments. Meeting on different days, the general Faculty maintained its own minute book, continued to enforce discipline, took a greater part in organizing courses, and somewhat irregularly shared in the appointment of tutors.

6. In 1902 the Corporation voted that the minimum teaching obligation of a full professor was eight hours a week. In 1904

Hadley stated that full-time instruction (for the rest?) was ten hours of lecturing or fifteen hours of recitation in repetitious sections. He also estimated that the average faculty member spent four hours per week in Faculty and committee meetings; and that perhaps two hours a week had to be given by full professors to meetings with departmental colleagues. Prudential Committee Records, Mar. 1902; Hadley to G. M. Lane, Boston, 7 Dec. 1904, Hadley Letters.

7. The troubles of the department of philosophy and psychology fill much space in the Records of the Academical Professors, of the Corporation, and of the Prudential Committee, 1902–04. President Hadley's letters and copies of letters from some of the participants in the laboratory controversy are in the Hadley Papers, and Professor Ladd's long and bitter résumé of Jan. 1905 is in the Henry P. Wright Collection, Letters and Papers, 1898–1911. On the consequences for philosophy and psychology —nationally as well as locally—see the comments by C. E. Seashore, C. H. Judd, and E. W. Scripture, in Carl Murchison, ed., *A History of Psychology in Autobiography* (Worcester, Mass., 1930–31), 1:250–51, 2:224, 3:234–41.

8. The quotation is from Phelps, *Autobiography with Letters*, 197. See also Keller, 57, 60–61, and E. G. Bourne, Diaries, 30 Mar. 1905, Bourne Papers.

9. Rec. Acad. Profs., 1 June, 5 Oct.–21 Dec. 1905; 8, 15 Feb. 1906; 17 Jan. 1907; 14 Jan. 1909.

10. E. G. Bourne, Diaries, 9 Jan. 1891, Bourne Papers.

11. Prudential Committee Records, Nov. 1904; Rec. Acad. Profs., 2 Feb., 2 Mar. 1905.

12. See the tribute of the Faculty, transmitted through its Secretary, A. W. Phillips, to Dean Wright (copy), 21 Nov. 1907, H. P. Wright Collection, Correspondence, Folder 1865–1908.

13. R. H. Chittenden, *History of Sheffield Scientific School*, 1:224–25. Hadley to President N. M. Butler, Columbia University, 20 May 1904; to E. P. Parker, Hartford, 24 Mar. 1906; to J. A. Leighton, Ohio State University, Columbus, Ohio, 8 Oct. 1915, Hadley Letters. On Jones' election the Corporation revised the statute to allow election for indefinite periods.

14. This committee must have been virtually self-appointed, as the same men had begun meeting on the subject the preceding

spring. In due course they recommended and the Professors elected George E. Vincent, who declined. Then, on the last day of the year, Professor Seymour died. With the work all to do over, Morris was added to the committee and Dana named chairman. Hadley to Prof. T. D. Seymour, 5 Oct. 1907; to Prof. Frederick S. Jones, Seabreeze, Fla., 27 Mar. 1908, Hadley Letters; conversation of G.W.P. with Charles Seymour, Dec. 1950.

For the later explorations and negotiations see the interesting letters in the Clive Day Papers, Correspondence, 1907–25, notably the copies of Day to William Kent, Chicago, 20 Oct. 1907; to E. S. Dana, 21 Dec. 1907, 19 Jan. 1908; to Louis S. Haslam, St. Louis, 21 Dec. 1907; to John Crosby, Minneapolis, 30 Dec. 1907, 20 Jan., 2 Mar. 1908; to C. W. Pierson, New York, 11 Jan. 1908; to J. E. F. Woodbridge, Columbia University, 4 Mar. 1908; Day's notes on the qualifications of the Dean, and possible candidates for "Jr. Dean"; C. K. Bancroft to Day, 14 Nov. 1907; E. S. Dana to Day, 20 Jan. 1908. See also E. S. Dana to Hadley, 20 Jan. 1908, Hadley Correspondence; and Hadley to Governor P. B. Stewart, Colorado Springs, Colo., 2 Apr. 1917, Hadley Letters. For the official records, see Rec. Acad. Profs., 4 Oct., 21, 27 Nov. 1907, 26 Mar. 1908; and Corporation Records, May 1908.

REFERENCE NOTES FOR
CHAPTER 9 · TYRANNOSAURUS SUPERBUS

Besides the official President's and Deans' Reports, the Corporation and Faculty Records, and correspondence in the Hadley and Clive Day Papers, much material for this chapter has come from conversations of G.W.P. with Dean Jones, 21 Nov. 1938, 21 Mar. 1939, and with faculty colleagues, notably G. L. Hendrickson, 10, 22 Dec. 1943, Clive Day, 25 Nov., 12 Dec. 1941, H. A. Farr, 6 Jan. 1944, C. W. Mendell, 30 June 1941, 5 Jan., 30 Mar. 1948, S. B. Hemingway, 14 Dec. 1945, Emerson Tuttle, and C. F. Stoddard. On the daily routine of the Dean's Office there is the enormous accumulation of clerical records in the Memorabilia Room. For brief biographical sketches see *A History of the Class of Eighty-four, Yale College 1880–1914*, 213–15, and *Obituary Records of Graduates . . . July 1, 1944*, 25–26. Much anecdote and comment is scattered through Class histories and other student and alumni publications.

The first quotation at the head of the chapter is from Hadley to President A. L. Lowell, Harvard University, 18 May 1916, Hadley Letters. The origin of the lines that made Dean Jones a "one-poem man" is told in a broadside prepared and circulated by the Reverend Samuel C. Bushnell '74. Bushnell sent a version of Dr. John C. Bossidy's quatrain on Boston, the Lowells, and the Cabots, to Dean Jones, who replied (under the injunction, "Tear this up") with "A Toast on New Haven: Lux et Veritas." The following month, Feb. 1915, Bushnell recited the lines at the dinner of the Naugatuck Valley Yale Alumni Association, and they were widely quoted and printed. See S. C. Bushnell's broadside, "To Whom it May Concern:—." (n.d., n.p.); interview with Dean Jones in the *Yale Daily News*, 20 Apr. 1937; the letter from Joseph Hollister in the *New York Times*, 20 Jan. 1944; and the entry and notes in John Bartlett's *Familiar Quotations* (12th ed. rev. and enlarged, Boston 1948), 752.

1. A. P. Stokes to G.W.P., 20 Oct. 1944. Conversation of G.W.P. with G. L. Hendrickson, 10 Dec. 1943; *History of the Class of 1905, Yale College*, 2(1908):86. See also, in *Twenty-five Years After with Yale 1902*, 2:54, Brian Hooker's tribute to "the Judge whose humor turned Blue Laws to gold."

2. W. F. Kaynor to President Charles Seymour, 12 Aug. 1942; *History of the Class of 1906, Yale College*, 2(1911):40.

3. S. V. Benét, *The Beginning of Wisdom* (New York, Henry Holt; copyright, 1921, by Stephen Vincent Benét), 55–56.

4. *Twenty Years with Nineteen-twenty*, 21.

5. Hadley to Jones, 27 Mar. 1908, and compare Hadley to President Lowell, Harvard University, 22 Oct. 1909, Hadley Letters.

6. *History of the Class of 1906, Yale College*, 2(1911):41; *Report of the President and Deans, 1909–10*, 106–07.

7. For the budgetary problems and improvements, see E. S. Dana to Hadley, 26 Apr. 1909, Hadley Correspondence; Hadley to Dean Jones, 5 May 1909, Hadley Letters; *Report of the President and Deans, 1909–10*, 105–06. For the successive steps in administrative reform, see Rec. Acad. Profs., 13 Jan. 1910, 23 Oct. 1913, 22 Jan., 12, 26 Mar. 1914; Faculty Record, 8 Dec. 1910, 23 Feb. 1911; Corporation Records, Sept. 1913, Nov. 1914; conversation of G.W.P. with H. A. Farr.

8. Conversation with Dean Jones, 21 Nov. 1938.

9. *Report of the President and Deans, 1909–10*, 43, 105–06; *1916–17*, 39–40.

10. Conversation of G.W.P. with G. L. Hendrickson, 10 Dec. 1943. *Report of the President and Deans, 1909–10*, 106–07; *1911–12*, 129; *1912–13*, 121–22.

11. See the heart-warming minute in the Corporation Records, Apr. 1917. Wright Hall was completed in 1912.

12. Conversations of G.W.P. with Dean Jones, 21 Nov. 1938; with C. A. Lohmann, 8 Dec. 1943. *Report of the President and Deans, 1910–11*, 25–26; *1915–16*, 35–36; *1916–17*, 55–59, 132–35, 336–37.

REFERENCE NOTES FOR
CHAPTER 10 · A NEW AND PROMISING LINE

There is no adequate account of the turning reached by the Yale College authorities in the years 1899 to 1905. On the first revisions in the curriculum the only article published was John C. Schwab's curiously neutral and unimaginative "The Yale College Curriculum, 1701–1901," *Educational Review,* June 1901, 22:1–17. This chapter is based chiefly on the Record of the Academical Professors; the diaries and letters of E. G. Bourne, Bourne Papers; the annual *Report of the President and Deans;* and the columns of the *Yale Alumni Weekly.* There is also the "Memorandum Suggested by a Study of Opinions Expressed at the Meeting of the Academical Professors on Tuesday November 28th," H. P. Wright Collection, College Affairs.

The head quotation is from *Report of the President and Deans, 1900–01,* 3–4.

1. Rec. Acad. Profs., 17 Nov. 1899. For the following discussion and Hadley's suggestion, see *ibid.,* 28 Nov. 1899.
2. "Memorandum Suggested by a Study of Opinions . . ."
3. Rec. Acad. Profs., 7 Dec. 1899, with Schwab's "A Proposed College Curriculum" (misplaced at 6 Dec. 1900 and labeled "A").
4. Rec. Acad. Profs., 1 Feb. 1900.
5. Bourne, Diaries, 3, 8 Feb. 1900; B. Perrin to Bourne, 11 Feb. 1900, Bourne Papers; Rec. Acad. Profs., 1, 8, 22 Feb. 1900.
6. Rec. Acad. Profs., 13 Dec. 1900; and 17 Jan. to 7 Feb. 1901 for the sequel.
7. For this discussion see *Report of the President and Deans, 1900–01,* 4–7, 33–35, 92. An opinion by the *Harvard Crimson* is quoted in the *Yale Alumni Weekly,* 27 Mar. 1901. More widely noticed, and more significant as indicating that influential men in the Harvard faculty were thinking along parallel lines, was

LeBaron R. Briggs, "Some Old-Fashioned Doubts about New-Fashioned Education," *Atlantic Monthly,* Oct. 1900, 86:463–70.

8. The cancellation of the philosophy requirements and Ladd's transfer to graduate work were to set off ructions within the philosophy department and inaugurate a series of guerrilla struggles between its members and the Administration that would come close to producing an academic scandal. Ladd's public repudiation of current educational trends was a trenchant statement of the old-line point of view, embittered by defeat. As an exposure of the weaknesses and failures of the elective movement, and as an appeal for studies that should be liberal rather than professional, these *Forum* articles still pack punch: "The True Functions of a Great University," Mar. 1902, 33:33–45; "The Disintegration and Reconstruction of the Curriculum," Apr. 1902, 33:165–78; "The Degradation of the Professorial Office," May 1902, 33:270–82; "Shall the College Curriculum Be Reconstructed?" July 1903, 35:130–45.

9. Speech to Boston alumni, quoted, *Yale Alumni Weekly,* 25 Feb. 1903.

10. Rec. Acad. Profs., 8 Feb. 1900. E. G. Bourne, Diaries, 8 Feb. 1900, Bourne Papers.

11. By a curious fatality, the Course of Study reorganization of 1899–1901 and the Bicentennial observances of October 1901 were followed by the publication of a series of sharp thrusts at Yale's perennial conservatism. In Mar. 1902 Poultney Bigelow '79 condemned the Yale educational system of the 1870's; Harlow Gale '85 subjected the courses and Faculty of the 1880's to scorching review; and finally an undergraduate Ten Eyck Prize speaker, H. H. Clark '03, confessed that Yale was still culturally narrow and artistically indifferent: the home of manliness rather than liberal education. Poultney Bigelow, "Personal Notes among Our Universities," *Independent,* 20 Mar. 1902, 54:672–76; Harlow Gale, "A Yale Education versus Culture," *Pedagogical Seminary,* Mar. 1902, 9:3–17; H. H. Clark, "The Yale Type of Man," *Yale Alumni Weekly,* 26 Mar. 1902.

REFERENCE NOTES FOR
CHAPTER 11 · FAREWELL TO GREEK

While this chapter records one of the strategic battles over the place of the classics in American education, no attempt can be made here to review the polemical literature of the Greek wars. Perhaps the most striking presentation for both sides is still Charles Francis Adams, *Three Phi Beta Kappa Addresses* (Boston 1907). For the end of required Greek at Harvard and its effects, see S. E. Morison, ed., *The Development of Harvard University*, 33–37, 55–63, and Morison, *Three Centuries of Harvard*, 359–60, 389–90; and for the Princeton and Yale recoil consult T. J. Wertenbaker, *Princeton, 1746–1896*, 304–06, and Noah Porter, "Greek and a Liberal Education," *Princeton Review*, Sept. 1884, 60(2): 195–218, and "A Criticism from Yale of the Last Harvard Educational Move—Greek and the Bachelor's Degree," *New Englander*, May 1885, 44:424–35. The most important materials for the Yale developments of 1900–14 have been drawn from the Record of the Academical Professors with attached Reports; Yale College, Faculty Record; Hadley Letters; G. B. Adams Collection; E. G. Bourne Collection; H. P. Wright Collection; T. D. Goodell Papers; and *Reports of the President and Deans*.

The head quotations are taken from Matthew Arnold, *Discourses in America* (1885), 131; and from a conversation with Bernard N. Schilling, Ph.D. '36. It is well known that Yale Seniors, applying for admission to the Graduate School, would be asked by Professor Young not whether they had done brilliantly in English in College but whether they had had Latin and Greek. If not, they were flatly told they were illiterate.

1. Rec. Acad. Profs., 19, 20 Jan. 1901; Report of the Committee Appointed to Suggest a Possible Alternative for the Entrance Requirement in Greek, attached to Rec. Acad. Profs., 6 May 1901; 13 June 1901. From documents in the G. B. Adams Collec-

tion, Correspondence and Papers, 14–21, File 17, it appears that schedules were drawn up showing the proportion of study time given to various subjects by the German and French classical schools and by the German and French modern schools as compared with the time given by a Yale Freshman who had also had an Andover or a Taft or a Hillhouse High School preparation.

Analysis then showed that among twelve colleges (Harvard, Chicago, Columbia, California, Michigan, Cornell, Amherst, Dartmouth, Williams, Pennsylvania, Princeton, Yale) there was prescribed for the classical course:

Mathematics in 11	English in 11
Latin in 7	History (not ancient) in 5
Greek in 6	Science in 3
Latin and Greek in 1	French or German in 2

Of the six colleges requiring Greek, all but Princeton offered an alternative course, leading to the Ph.B. or B.L. degrees. Such courses tended to be literary rather than scientific and were inferior neither in quantity nor quality of study, except for the substitution of modern languages, history, or science for the entrance Greek.

By contrast the Select Course Ph.B. in the Yale Scientific School seemed to require a lesser total of work and to be literary only for two years instead of for four. "Yale differs from those eleven Colleges in that it requires its students to choose between a course where Greek is required and one which is neither literary in quality nor equivalent in quantity." Insofar as the Professors were prepared to accept this view of Sheff, it was hard to see how Yale College could escape the duty of itself offering alternatives to Greek.

The committee then discussed a series of possible substitutes for three years of Greek, with emphasis on the modern languages, perhaps in combination with history or some other subject taught in both school and College. Eventually all but the German equivalent for Greek were rejected on the grounds that the secondary schools could not give adequate preparation, so much diversity would destroy Class unity in the very first year, and the easing of preparatory work would "lay too great emphasis on the possibility of shortening the college course to three years."

2. Rec. Acad. Profs., 31 Oct., 21 Nov., 5 Dec. 1901, with Dana's scheme, "Possible Choices to Be Offered to Each Candidate," 12 Dec. 1901.

3. *Report of the President and Deans, 1901–02,* 7–8. See also Rec. Acad. Profs., 30 Jan. 1902, and Hadley's letters of 13–16 Jan. 1902 in Hadley Papers.

4. "With the schoolmen, the Corporation, and several other interests opposed to the change, the requirement of Greek cannot be abolished without a far greater degree of unanimity on the part of the faculty than has been indicated hitherto." Hadley to Prof. William Beebe, 9 June 1902, Hadley Letters.

5. *Report of the President and Deans, 1901–02,* 21. Cf. Hadley to J. C. Hendrix, New York City, 23 July 1902, Hadley Letters.

6. Rec. Acad. Profs., 15, 22 Jan. 1903; E. G. Bourne, Diaries, 23 Jan. 1903; "Proposed Requirements of the Freshman and Sophomore Years," H. P. Wright Collection, Letters and Papers of Yale Interest; Hadley to the Rev. D. H. Chase, Middletown, Conn., 3 Nov. 1902, and to Arthur Marvin, Union Classical Institute, Schenectady, N. Y., 20 Jan. 1903, Hadley Letters.

7. The vote was

> *For* the proposition: Professors Duncan, Fisher, Wheeler, Sumner, Gooch, Phelps, Emery, Sneath, Bourne, Williams, Schwab, Adams, Lang, Gruener, Lewis = 15
>
> *Against:* Professors Peck, A. W. Wright, Reynolds, Goodell, Oertel, Gibbs, Seymour, Smith, Kent, Phillips = 10
>
> *Not Voting:* Professor Warren = 1
>
> *Absent:* Professors Richards, Beers, Perrin, Dana, H. P. Wright, Cook, Beebe, Morris, Pierpont, Palmer, Torrey = 11

The formal ratification in Rec. Acad. Profs., 7 Mar. 1903, shows that Oertel, Smith, A. W. Wright, and Kent swung over to the majority and that, from the previous absentees, Torrey, Beers, Pierpont, and Dean Wright all supported the abolition of the Greek requirement. So all the available professors of history, political economy, science, and philosophy, with all (but Cook?) in English, finally stood together for the change.

8. Corporation Records, 9 Mar. 1903, and Rec. Acad. Profs., 12 Mar. 1903. It was rumored about the campus that the College

had never before waited upon the Corporation. G.W.P. conversation with Samuel H. Fisher, 19 Oct. 1945.

9. Rec. Acad. Profs., 19 Mar. 1903.

10. *Ibid.*, 23, 30 Apr., 7 May 1903.

11. *Report of the President and Deans, 1902–03,* 6–8. This same year the Governing Board of the Sheffield Scientific School rejected a proposal to allow modern languages to be substituted for its requirement of Vergil or Cicero as an entrance requirement. Chittenden, *History of the Sheffield Scientific School,* 2:478.

12. New York *Evening Post,* 12 May 1903; *Nation,* 16 July 1903, 77:47; New York *Sun,* 13 May 1903; *New Haven Register,* 11 May 1903; the Indianapolis *News,* quoted in the *New Haven Register,* 1 July 1903. The beginnings of a reaction were evident in A. F. West, "The Present Peril to Liberal Education," in C. W. Eliot, A. F. West, W. R. Harper, and N. M. Butler, *Present College Questions* (New York 1903), 29–44; J. H. Canfield in *National Education Association. Journal of Proceedings and Addresses . . . 1905* (Winona, Minn., 1905), 484–501. See also Chapters 12 and 14.

13. *Yale Alumni Weekly,* 20 May 1903.

14. *Yale Literary Magazine,* Mar. 1908, 73:242.

15. *Report of the President and Deans, 1903–04,* 38; *1904–05,* 22, 39–40, 56–62; *1905–06,* 42–45; *1906–07,* 44–46.

16. Hadley to A. P. Butler, Morristown, N.J., 8 Mar. 1904, and to C. W. A. Veditz, George Washington University, Washington, D.C., 4 Feb. 1907, Hadley Letters.

17. Yale College, Faculty Record, 20 Oct. 1904; *Report of the President and Deans, 1904–05,* 61. The *Nation,* 27 Dec. 1900, 71: 504–05, had already spoken out against the whole notion of equivalents.

18. *Yale Alumni Weekly,* 15, 22, 29 Apr., 13 May, 9 Dec. 1908.

19. *Report of the President and Deans, 1908–09,* 9, 18.

REFERENCE NOTES FOR

CHAPTER 12 · CLAIMANTS TO THE CURRICULUM

For an understanding of the forces competing for attention in the College curriculum one must refer to the whole literature on American higher education. The problem of the length and character of the B.A. course calls forth all the basic disagreements over the liberal arts—or general education. In addition the character and proper location of training programs for the professions and for the economic vocations are involved. This raises the question of the function of the professional schools and their place in a university. Should a university be a horizontal federation of specializing schools, or a vertical sequence of programs proceeding from what is general and liberal toward studies ever more technical and advanced? But this last depends in part on the preparation of the students and on the intelligence and tolerance of the lay public. Every university has felt the tug and strain of antagonistic interests, and none has compromised to entire satisfaction.

How complex and difficult the problem is the experience of Yale College shows. This chapter is based primarily on the Records and *Catalogues* of the College, the *Reports of the President and Deans,* and President Hadley's Letters. Before final conclusions are drawn, the records of the professional Schools should also be consulted.

The head quotations are from the *Reports on the Course of Instruction,* 14, and from the *Report of the President and Deans, 1906–07,* 18.

1. S. E. Morison, *Harvard College in the Seventeenth Century,* 1:66, 300–02, 328, and "President Dunster's Quadrennium Memoir, 1654," translated and edited by Professor Morison, *Publications of the Colonial Society of Massachusetts,* 31(1935): 277–89.

2. R. H. Chittenden, *History of the Sheffield Scientific School,* 2: 486–87. In 1887 Eliot had suggested to Director Brush that Sheff should "go mighty slow towards that four years' course." For

President Eliot's advocacy of the three-year course at Harvard, see his Reports of 1901–02 and 1907–08, and Henry James, *Charles W. Eliot*, 2:145–48; S. E. Morison, ed., *The Development of Harvard University*, xliv-xlvi; and H. A. Yeomans, *Abbott Lawrence Lowell, 1856–1943*, 72–76. For President Conant's revival of the three-year idea for emergency use, see his *President's Report, 1949–50*, 5–6.

3. These arguments on "The Length of the Baccalaureate Course" were presented at the National Educational Association meeting in 1903, and were reprinted (with Eliot's presidential address and Dean West's "The Present Peril to Liberal Education") as *Present College Questions* (New York 1903). For the original papers and the discussion following, see *National Educational Association. Journal of Proceedings and Addresses of the Forty-Second Annual Meeting . . . 1903* (Winona, Minn., 1903), 489–516.

4. On receiving advance sheets of President Butler's Report, Hadley observed that "the next year some enterprising man may recommend a one year college course"—Hadley to Butler, 7 Oct. 1902, Hadley Letters. See also Hadley to Edwin D. Worcester, 8 Oct. 1902 (also printed in M. Hadley, *A. T. Hadley*, 151); and *Report of the President and Deans, 1902–03*, 4.

5. *Yale Alumni Weekly*, 1 Apr. 1903. Hadley often used the existence of the Select Course to justify inaction. In the eighties, under Lounsbury's leadership, a strong but unsuccessful effort had been made by the Sheff Professors to lengthen their program to four years (Chittenden, 2:487; *Yale College in 1886*, 11), but Hadley thought that Director Brush had been "wise in resisting the change until we could see further into the future." To a member of an investigating committee of Harvard alumni he stated that, with both alternatives available at Yale, and with each Department having its own social organization, there was no need for change or even deciding which system was superior. Hadley to Rome G. Brown, Minneapolis, 11 Mar. 1905, Hadley Letters.

6. *Report of the President and Deans, 1901–02*, 50–51; *1903–04*, 39; *1904–05*, 41–42; Rec. Acad. Profs., 1, 15 Mar. 1906; Yale College Faculty Record, 7 Oct. 1915.

7. *National Educational Association. Journal of Proceedings and*

Addresses . . . *1903*, 516; Henry James, *Charles W. Eliot*, 2:147, 181.

8. This course, which had its roots in the old Aristotelian Senior-year introduction to political science, and which was developed into an independent elective in 1882, at first served two purposes. On the one hand it was intended for amateurs, or for all who might be interested in law "as a branch of general education," the aim being to educate Yale Seniors to their civic rights and responsibilities as citizens and servants of the nation. So the course dealt rather generally with jurisprudence and the history and philosophy of law, both international and constitutional. These subjects were handled with such mastery and breadth by the Kent Professor of Law, E. J. Phelps, that amateur law was recognized as one of the most interesting and rewarding of electives in the 1880's, and so continued under Phelps and W. C. Robinson, and Phelps and Edward G. Buckland, to the turn of the century.

   On the other hand students passing the Yale examinations were at first in many States entitled to a certificate counting as a year of study for admission to the bar; and the College added readings and a special examination in Blackstone for those with professional ambitions. As State standards were raised, professional law-school training became more and more necessary. Hence pressure for courses which should teach not jurisprudence and international law but contracts, torts, property, wills, conveyances, etc. So with the development of the Combined Programs the College found itself providing one kind of law for amateurs, another for the preprofessionals. With the death of E. J. Phelps the difficulty was to find law teachers cultivated enough to continue the amateur course. In 1913 Hadley got William Howard Taft to accept the Kent Professorship, in the hope that his character and prestige would restore the old vitality. Taft, however, was preoccupied with outside lectures and public affairs. He also had no conception of the progress in teaching, and conducted the course as an old-fashioned, mechanical recitation, as he remembered things had been done in the 1870's. The undergraduates who had crowded in to hear him, began to stay away in droves; and a bold group of Seniors had to go to the ex-President and tell him he couldn't teach that way any more. Then came the war; and afterward sporadic efforts to revive amateur law unfortunately failed. *Yale College in 1882,* 3; Dwight, *Memories,* 424–26; C. P. Sherman, *Academic Adventures. A Law School Professor's Recollections and Observations* (New Haven 1944), 79–82; F. C. Hicks, *William Howard Taft, Yale Professor of Law and New Haven Citizen* (New Haven 1945).

9. Hadley's preoccupation with the professional training problem and his back-and-forth pronouncements may be traced through his speeches, his correspondence, and almost every one of his first ten annual Reports, especially the *Report of the President and Deans, 1901–02,* 13–29. See also Hadley to President Butler, 7 Oct. 1902, and to Edwin D. Worcester, 8 Oct. 1902, Hadley Letters. These letters were written on receiving the advance sheets of Butler's report; in his own annual Report for 1902–03 Hadley referred to the "very distinct check" to the three-year movement administered by President Butler's last report.

10. Hadley, "Alleged Luxury among College Students," *Century Magazine,* Nov. 1901, 63:314; "Educational Methods and Principles of the Nineteenth Century," *Educational Review,* Nov. 1904, 28:332. In this paper Hadley expressed concern over the tendency of professional schools to become too exclusively professional at the expense of their ethical standards. "It is a bad thing to encourage the individual to think that his success and his happiness are the ultimate ends for which he is to work."

11. For the College-Law School negotiations, see Rec. Acad. Profs., 7 Mar. 1903, 3, 10 Dec. 1903, 28 Jan. 1904; Prudential Committee Records, Nov. 1903; *Statement Submitted to the Prudential Committee of Yale University in Support of the Request of the Law Faculty for an Extension of the Right of Election of Juniors and Seniors of Yale College as to the Study of Law,* 23 Nov. 1903. At the request of Secretary Phillips, Professor Adams wrote out for the Record an abstract of what he had said, that "we regarded the proposed courses as Academic courses which we asked the Law Faculty for the present to give for us; that we reserved the right to resume charge of them if we should ever be able to give them ourselves . . . that we wished them to be given as nearly under Academic conditions as possible and reserved the right to object to incompetent or unsatisfactory instructors." Dean

621

Rogers assented—but the next day by letter indicated that the Law Faculty would have been "somewhat better pleased to have had our plan accepted in toto."

12. Hadley, speech to New York alumni, 11 Dec. 1903, *Yale Alumni Weekly,* 16 Dec. 1903; Hadley to E. R. A. Seligman, Columbia University, New York, 5 Mar. 1904, Hadley Letters.

13. *Yale Alumni Weekly,* 15 July 1903.

14. For the elevation of the Law School to postgraduate status, see particularly the Prudential Committee Records, 2, 16 May 1904; Corporation Records, June 1904; *Report of the President and Deans, 1903–04,* 10; *1910–11,* 220–22; *1918–19,* 272–73; F. C. Hicks, *Yale Law School: 1895–1915, Twenty Years of Hendrie Hall,* 42–47.

15. The College objected that its law students were not held to the same frequent tests and rigorous standards of attendance as in the rest of their academic work. The Law School felt only mildly interested in the courses with cultural connotations, like constitutional and international law, and wished to substitute or add more technical instruction.

16. It had followed the Harvard Law School by about the same space of time, the steps taken at Yale in 1919–20 and 1929–30 having been put into effect at Harvard in 1895 and 1897. See Morison, ed., *The Development of Harvard University,* 498.

17. For the development of the Combined Program in medicine see *Report of the President and Deans, 1905–06,* 79–81; *1906–07,* 8–9, 165–66; *1908–09,* 196–97; and "Statistics of Students in Combined Medical and College Courses," 27 Jan. 1916, in Reports, Permanent Officers of Yale College, 1910–21. For difficulties with the New York State Board of Regents, which controlled the licensing of the important metropolitan field, see Hadley to C. F. Wheelock, Albany, N.Y., 3 Sept., 13 Nov.; to A. S. Draper, New York State Commissioner of Education, 19, 21 Nov.; to Dean H. E. Smith, 9, 13 Nov.; to Prof. J. W. D. Ingersoll, 23 Nov. 1908, Hadley Letters. See also *State of New York. Sixth Annual Report of the Education Department for the School Year Ending July 31, 1909* (Albany 1910), 349–50, 590–91, 635, and compare the University *Catalogues, 1907–08,* 458 and *1908–09,* 469.

18. For the background and problems peculiar to the Divinity School, see B. W. Bacon, *The Yale School of Religion,* and *Reports to the President, 1928–29,* 107–10.

19. *Ibid., 1902–03,* 38–39; *Yale Alumni Weekly,* 3 Feb. 1909.

20. For College–Art School relations, see Hadley to Dean J. F. Weir, 10 Dec. 1909, Hadley Letters; Rec. Acad. Profs., 27 Jan. 1910; *Report of the President and Deans, 1908–09,* 21, 222. In 1916 an interesting struggle developed when Professor A. Kingsley Porter proposed to endow the teaching of the history of art in his will, and Dean Kendall made a strong drive to get art electives admitted into Sophomore year. At first Hadley cited again the snap courses at Harvard. Then he got Dean Jones to promise exceptional treatment for especially qualified students. By Nov. 1916 he was acceding to Porter's request for a course in Italian Renaissance painting under the auspices of the history department, provided the history department thought it could utilize such a course as "part of the hard work of men who are studying history and not playing with it." Nevertheless, he still had doubts about the mere "taking" of courses in art—and wanted the equivalent of hard laboratory work attached.

> The use of the word "take" in this connection is based on the idea that college education is like the administration of a series of drugs. You take a course as you would take a pill. The old theory of college education, like the old theory of medicine, was that the contents of the pills should be as disagreeable as possible. The later theory, which was made popular by President Eliot, was that the contents of the pills should be made agreeable, and if necessary the pills should be sugar coated. Both theories had a common defect: the idea that the introduction of information into the student was education.
>
> We now see that education is teaching a boy to *do* things . . . for getting him to work we have available two motives: the professional motive and the competitive motive. President Eliot thought that we had available a third motive: the inherent pleasure which a boy would take in listening to a course of lectures. Experience seems to have proved pretty clearly that he was wrong.

623

Hadley to R. C. Sturgis, Boston, Mass., 6 Feb. 1917. See also Hadley to A. Kingsley Porter, 29 Jan., 7 Feb. 1916; to Dean W. S. Kendall, 7 Mar., 17 Nov. 1916; to Dean Jones, 7 Mar. 1916, Hadley Letters.

21. Everett V. Meeks, "The Place of Art in Higher Education," *American Magazine of Art*, Oct. 1928, 19:544.

22. The Drama Department laid considerable emphasis on the bachelor's degree; but until 1931 only a certificate was awarded, and from one-half to one-third of its students were admitted simply on satisfying the Chairman of their qualifications for further study. Later the M.F.A. was awarded to students who had acquired a bachelor's degree before, during, or after their three years of dramatic study.

23. *Report of the President and Deans, 1899–1900,* 16; *1905–06,* 25–26; Hadley to A. P. Stokes, 8 Feb. 1906, Hadley Family Collection, 1900–35; Hadley to A. W. Burnham, Chicago, 1 Feb. 1909, Hadley Letters.

24. Hadley to J. W. Dodsworth, Managing Editor of the *Journal of Commerce,* New York, 25 Nov. 1908; Hadley to W. C. Malin, Editor, *Cleveland Leader,* Cleveland, Ohio, 8 Feb. 1919, Hadley Letters.

REFERENCE NOTES FOR
CHAPTER 13 · DISCONTENT,
INVESTIGATION, AND REFORM

In 1888 Bryce had written: "Diligence is the tradition of the American college." On the decline of diligence and scholarship in the next two decades a good deal was written in serious criticism and often ill-considered attack, but little comprehensive study has been given to the active efforts of college authorities to remedy the evils. The tenor of the criticisms is well summed up in two contemporary studies: Abraham Flexner, *The American College: A Criticism* (New York 1908), and the broader but often inaccurate *Individual Training in Our Colleges* (New York 1907) by C. F. Birdseye. At Princeton the fundamental reorganization of the curriculum came at the hands of the faculty in 1903–04, but made no such sensational headlines as Woodrow Wilson's attack on the Club system, 1906–08, or his charge that the side shows "have swallowed up the circus": "What Is a College For?" *Scribner's Magazine*, Nov. 1909, 46:570–77. The complicated Princeton story may be traced in A. S. Link, *Wilson: The Road to the White House* (Princeton 1947), 39–54. For the Harvard investigation of 1902–03, the "Report of the Committee on Improving Instruction in Harvard College," *Harvard Graduates' Magazine*, June 1904, 12:611–20, and H. A. Yeomans, *Abbott Lawrence Lowell, 1856–1943*, 67–82, are the best accounts. On the conditions and reforms at Yale there are scattered materials in the *Reports of the President and Deans*, in the *Class Books* from 1900 to 1905, and in the papers of Hadley, Bourne, and Dean Wright. The indispensable sources, however, are the Faculty Record, and three special Reports compiled by members of the general Faculty and submitted for its consideration: Report of the Committee on Numbers and Scholarship, 16 Apr. 1903; Report of the Committee on Improving Instruction, 21 Apr. 1904; Report of the Committee on Weekend Absences, May 1908. The first two of these documents are handbooks of information on conditions, practices, and points of view just after the turn of the century.

The head quotations are from the *Yale Class Book, 1901,* 104; the Report of the Committee on Numbers and Scholarship, 68; and the Report of the Committee on Improving Instruction, 50.

1. The most sensational attacks on drinking at Yale in the nineties had come from the wife of a local clergyman and a New York temperance journal. Mrs. Poteat's exclamation that she would "as soon send a boy to hell as to send him to Yale" had considerable notoriety for a week or two. The New York *Voice* two years later attempted something of a national campaign, attacking football game orgies and supine authorities, comparing wide-open New Haven with no-license Cambridge, and urging a boycott by temperance families. Much vivid language was called out, and some notable defenses, including D. L. Moody's statement:

   > I have been pretty well acquainted with Yale for twenty years, and I have never seen the University in as good a condition religiously as it is now. My oldest son graduated here, and if my other son, who is now in the Freshman Class, gets as much good out of Yale as his brother did, I shall have reason to thank God through time and eternity.

   After these episodes, Carry Nation's two visits to the campus were purely gala occasions. See the *Yale Alumni Weekly,* 20, 27 Nov. 1895; 16 Dec. 1897, 10, 17 Feb., 3 Mar. 1898; the New York *Voice,* from Nov. 1897 to Apr. 1898, particularly the Extra Number of Feb. 1898; the *New Haven Register,* especially 3 Jan., 13, 15 Feb. 1898; D. L. Moody, quoted in Welch and Camp, 65. For Carry Nation's visits, the *Alumni Weekly,* 30 Sept. 1902, 17 Feb. 1904.

2. Conversation of G.W.P. with Prof. S. B. Hemingway '04, 14 Sept. 1945.

3. Hadley to William F. McDowell, 13 Nov. 1899, Hadley Letters; Dean Wright to Joseph F. Daniels, Fort Collins, Colo., 7 Dec. 1904 (copy), H. P. Wright Collection, Letters and Papers, 1898–1911.

4. Yale College, Faculty Record, 18 Oct. 1900; 22 May, 5, 14 June 1902; 6 Dec. 1900.

5. Information from Hollon A. Farr. For Omega Lambda Chi and Thermopylae, see Welch and Camp, 183.

6. *New Haven Morning Journal and Courier,* 2 May 1900. Hadley to Dean Wright, 9 May 1900, H. P. Wright Collection, Correspondence, 1865–1908; Faculty Record, 10, 21 May 1900; *Yale Daily News,* 15, 21 May, and *Yale Alumni Weekly,* 16 May 1900.

7. *Report of the President and Deans, 1899–1900,* 5–7.

8. For the rise of the Sophomore societies and the growing criticism, see Welch and Camp, 111–14, the summary in the *Yale Alumni Weekly,* 19 Dec. 1900, and the influential Ten Eyck Prize oration of Nathan A. Smyth '97, "The Democratic Idea in College Life," *Yale Literary Magazine,* Apr. 1896, 61:271–76. The schemes of reform and Faculty action may be traced in the *Yale Alumni Weekly,* 21, 28 Feb., 2, 16 May, 10, 31 Oct., 7 Nov., 12 Dec. 1900, and the Faculty Record, 21 May, 18 Oct., 6 Dec. 1900. What the Faculty actually voted was that the termination of the societies was inevitable, and that prompt action on their own part would best pave the way for a prompt reorganization of the whole society system. An account of the final scene is given in M. Hadley, *A. T. Hadley,* 115–16. On the connection between the Sophomore societies and the Hutchinson, see the passages in the Report on Numbers and Scholarship, 64–65, with the letter quoted there, and *Report of the President and Deans, 1903–04,* 87–90; *1904–05,* 86–88. For the verse on Professor Beebe I am indebted to an old graduate's recollection.

9. Faculty Record, 18 Dec. 1902.

10. The Report of the Committee on Numbers and Scholarship, with its 21 diagrams, 42 tables, and copious quotations from witnesses within the College and without, is the source for the account here given.

11. *The Yale Class Book 1900,* 110, 102, 214; *The Yale Class Book 1901,* 108; *History of the Class of 1905 Yale College,* 25; *Yale Courant,* Dec. 1906, 43:129–30.

12. Faculty Record, 16 Apr. 1903; Rec. Acad. Profs., 7 May 1903; Prudential Committee Records, May 1903; Corporation Records, May 1903.

13. Rec. Acad. Profs., 10 Mar., 2 June 1904; *Report of the President and Deans, 1903–04,* 5.

14. The Report of the Committee on Improving Instruction, presented to the Faculty, 21 Apr. 1904, describes its work. Some additional light is cast by Professor Reed's Notebook, Secretary of Committee on Courses, May 1903–Mar. 1904, and papers in the H. P. Wright Collection, Letters and Papers, 1898–1911.

15. Faculty Record, 21 Apr. 1904.

16. Conversation of G.W.P. with C. W. Mendell, 29 May 1950.

17. *Report of the President and Deans, 1907–08,* 7–8. See also Dean Wright in *Report, 1908–09,* 92–98, and the comments on the "pause" in the elective system, and the "monitory" relation to cost, *Yale Alumni Weekly,* 28 Dec. 1904, 27 Jan. 1909.

18. The tortuous history of rhetoric and its adjunct public speaking can be traced through the Record of the Academical Professors and the University *Catalogue* from 1902 to 1911. The differing attitudes of the English professors and the rhetoric teachers are well indicated in the *Report of the President and Deans, 1907–08,* 88, and *1908–09,* 107.

19. *Report of the President and Deans, 1914–15,* 17–19.

20. *Ibid., 1911–12,* 117–18; *1912–13,* 118; *1913–14,* 120.

21. *Ibid., 1906–07,* 14.

22. *Ibid., 1908–09,* 10–11. For the charge against Eliot, see Hadley to President Lowell, 6 Aug. 1909: "My impression was that President Eliot's influence had rather been to reduce the minimum and that the efforts of the Faculty to maintain the standards had not had the success in the last ten years that they will have in the next ten, because they had not been encouraged by the central authority." Hadley Letters.

23. Report of the Committee on Weekend Absences, May 1908; Faculty Record, 5 Mar., 14, 21 May 1908; *Report of the President and Deans, 1908–09,* 99–113.

24. *Ibid., 1904–05,* 81–89; *1908–09,* 108–11. Conversation of G.W.P. with President Seymour, Dec. 1950.

25. President Hadley himself thought the Faculty were going too fast. And in Faculty meeting he quoted Mrs. Hadley about acting in haste and repenting at leisure: the only mistakes the Faculty had made were from acting too hastily. But the shock of this unprecedented citation and criticism from their President only

stiffened the Faculty's determination and left a rather unfortunate impression. E. G. Bourne, Diaries, 23 June 1905, Bourne Papers. Faculty Record, 23 June 1905. Hadley to Miss E. S. Reed, 27 June 1905, with a number of similar letters, Hadley Letters. See also considerable correspondence in the H. P. Wright Collection, Letters and Papers, 1898–1911, and Correspondence, 1865–1908. For efforts to deal with cheating: *History of the Class of 1905, Yale College*, 1(1905):28–29; 2(1908):22. Conversation of G.W.P. with A. P. Stokes, 18 June 1941.

26. See the *Report of the President and Deans, 1905–06*, 18–19, for a pacific statement of the laissez-faire victory. The intensity of the reform drive appears in the Faculty Record, 13, 20 Jan., 22 Feb. 1906, and the letters and draft of Dec. 1905–Jan. 1906 in the G. B. Adams Collection, Correspondence and Papers, 35–42, File 35.

27. *Report of the President and Deans, 1904–05*, 75–77; *Yale Daily News*, 14 Feb., 8 Apr. 1905; *Yale Alumni Weekly*, 21 Feb., 14 Mar., 4 Apr. 1906, and 26 Mar. 1909.

28. *Report of the President and Deans, 1904–05*, 74–75; *1905–06*, 47; *1908–09*, 83–85. Hadley to Dean Wright, 8 July 1902, Hadley Letters..Dean Wright to C. K. Bancroft, 23 July 1902, and T. D. Goodell to Wright, 24 Aug. 1905, Correspondence, 1865–1908, and C. K. Bancroft to Wright, 8 Jan. 1906, Dean Wright Papers, in H. P. Wright Collection.

29. *Report of the President and Deans, 1904–05*, 71, 72, and *1908–09*, 86.

30. The Class of 1904 was quite willing to believe that it had "more gentlemen and fewer scholars than any other class in the memory of man." *Yale College Class Book 1904*, 180. Not many years ago Dean Clarence W. Mendell, acting as a toastmaster at a dinner, is said to have described the Class of 1904 as undoubtedly the poorest in scholarship that ever went through Yale. "Gentlemen, it gives me great pleasure to introduce as the next speaker my friend and classmate, Thomas D. Thacher of the Class of 1904." On behalf of the claim of 1904 to the low record, see the table of Class standings from 1899 to 1910, *Report of the President and Deans, 1910–11*, 86.

A judicious history of the rise and decline of the elective movement has not yet been written. The issue has been too controversial. The facts themselves are still in dispute. In part because promises were sometimes taken for performance, enthusiasts for reform in the age of Eliot exaggerated the victories of the system, even as in the age of Hutchins the champions of general education are now perhaps a little too confidently dancing on its grave. I have described some of the problems involved in "The Elective System and the Difficulties of College Planning, 1870–1940," in *Journal of General Education,* Apr. 1950, 4:165–74. In the same issue of the *Journal,* 175–77, President Conant summed up the achievements of his two immediate predecessors, and the revolution in the college that curtailed the free elective system: "Some Aspects of Modern Harvard." Surveys from Midwestern longitudes tend to date the turn away from the elective system somewhat later, as in O. C. Carmichael, *The Changing Role of Higher Education* (New York 1949), and *The Idea and Practice of General Education* (Chicago 1950).

From the point of view of certain parties, Yale played the heavy villain of this drama. For example, an anthology of statements on Yale's blind obduracy against the elective system may be compiled from R. Freeman Butts, *The College Charts Its Course* (New York, McGraw-Hill, 1939)—the most extensive and able but nonetheless extremely partisan application of the Dewey-inspired progressive philosophy of education to the historical development of American colleges. To quote a few excerpts for flavor: as early as the eighteenth century Butts finds "another difference that tended to prevent the ultimate acceptance by Yale of the elective system." In Porter's day "as Harvard was the leading light in reform, so was Yale the leading opponent of the elective system." "Dwight also showed himself fearful." "Between the extreme of theoretical free election as maintained by Harvard and the extreme of prescription as maintained by Yale and Princeton, all varieties of inter-mediate positions were devised." "By the end of the century" Yale and Princeton are credited with a half-prescribed, half-elective curriculum; but small indication is given that this actually placed them in the middle group of colleges, and no hint at all that Yale was in the act of opening its Sophomore and Freshman years. After celebrating the victorious progress of the elective system, Butts concedes that evils arose largely for lack of a guiding educational philosophy. But the efforts of Yale and other colleges to blend older values with newer interests, through majors and minors and distribution programs, are dismissed as "ad-ministrative shuffling." The turn in the elective tide is located by the Harvard reversal, and so in 1910 rather than in 1900–06. So likewise the redevelopment of prescription and integration are treated almost as if Yale and other liberal arts colleges had not participated in the movement.

The best brief statement of the Harvard point of view, quoted in the text, is from S. E. Morison, *Three Centuries of Harvard*, 384. For the public recantation of Charles Francis Adams, see his "Some Modern College Tendencies," first published in the *Columbia University Quarterly*, Sept. 1906, 8:347–71, and reprinted with a supplementary note in *Three Phi Beta Kappa Addresses* (Boston and New York 1907). Adams reaffirmed his opinion of Harvard and President Eliot's elective system, with more brevity and equal vigor, in *Charles Francis Adams, 1873–1915. An Autobiography* (Boston and New York 1916), 35–36, 200–01. For the change of view in the Harvard presidential office, see A. L. Lowell, "Competition in College," *Atlantic Monthly*, June 1909, 103:822–31, reprinted in the *Columbia University Quarterly* for Sept. 1909. The *Quarterly* acknowledged no one in late years had told so many home truths in so pleasant a way. Lowell had safeguarded his flank by saying, "No sane man would propose to restore anything resembling a fixed curriculum in any of our larger colleges."

Some educators were disillusioned with both Yale and Harvard, as witness Abraham Flexner, *The American College* (New York 1908). For comparative developments at other leading universities, consult *Princeton University Bulletin*, Sept. 1904, 15:201–08; O. L. Elliott, *Stanford University: The First Twenty-five Years* (Stanford University Press 1937), 509–16, 576; *Report of the President of the Johns Hopkins University* (Johns Hopkins University Press 1906), 90–92; *Columbia University Quarterly*, June 1905, 7:267–69, 389–98; *Cornell University*.

Fourteenth Annual Report of President Schurman, 1905–1906 (Ithaca, N.Y., 1906), xxxi–xxxvi. For an illuminating intercollegiate survey, see D. E. Phillips, "The Elective System in American Education," *Pedagogical Seminary,* June 1901, 8:206–30.

The Abraham Flexner quotations are from his *The American College,* 45–46; the H. C. Emery quotations from the *Yale Alumni Weekly,* 7 Feb. 1906.

1. *Yale Alumni Weekly,* 20 Jan. 1909, 20 Dec. 1905, 5 Dec. 1906, 1 Apr. 1908. Hadley to Prof. Marshall B. Snow, Washington University, St. Louis, Mo., 18 Jan. 1904, Hadley Letters.
2. D. E. Phillips, *op. cit.*
3. For Yale reactions, see *Yale Alumni Weekly,* 20 June 1906; Hadley to C. F. Adams, Boston, Mass., 25 Apr. 1907, Hadley Letters. For restrained comment elsewhere see the *Columbia University Quarterly,* 8:425–26, and the *Harvard Graduates' Magazine,* June 1907, 15:745.
4. In Apr. 1907 a writer in *Scribner's Magazine* (41:506) did allow that the growing suspicion of the elective system had been "authoritatively expressed by the president of Yale, where in truth 'election' has never been so free and untrammelled as in some other institutions. . . . But now it is to be expected that President Hadley's outspokenness will embolden other sceptics."

REFERENCE NOTES FOR
CHAPTER 15 · TEACHERS AND TEACHING

In assessing the personality of this faculty before the wars, I am particularly indebted to the noted editor and literary critic Henry Seidel Canby, whose portrait of the community at the turn of the century, issued as *Alma Mater: The Gothic Age of the American College* (New York 1936), has been revised and republished as Part II of *American Memoir* (Boston 1947). This latter version is quoted, unless the earlier is specifically cited. Canby began as an undergraduate in the Select Course, Class of 1899. After taking his Ph.D. in 1905, he served in the Scientific School for seventeen years as Instructor, Assistant Professor, and Adviser in Literary Composition with professorial rank, teaching class after class of Select Course students, under Thomas R. Lounsbury and Wilbur L. Cross. Gifted with a sharp eye and a reflective temperament, he has recalled not only what it was like to sit under the faculty of the 1890's but also his view of the student world of the 1900's from the other side of the desk.

The contention that Canby knew only Sheff seems unwarranted. It is true that in the effort to re-create a type he so generalized and fused his impressions that the unwary reader may never realize Yale boasted two undergraduate colleges, each with traditions and attitudes peculiar to itself. Perhaps it was primarily in the Scientific School that the factualism of the teaching was remarkable, and that the sense of loneliness and expatriation was strong. But that the College faculty were altogether different—none of them feeling the doubts and depreciation, most of them serene, and the best of them as confident and sure of their world as Billy Phelps—I am not able to believe. In *American Memoir* will be found diagnosis as well as description: the atmosphere of the campus plus a glimpse into the shadowy places of Yale's soul. I have borrowed Canby's chapter title, and ventured to repeat a number of his major judgments.

In this chapter I am also under particular obligations: to C. Seymour,

633

C. W. Mendell, A. P. Stokes, C. B. Tinker, S. B. Hemingway, W. Notestein, F. A. Pottle, R. J. Menner, and other senior colleagues for reminiscences or corrections; to R. N. Corwin's *Plain Unpolished Tale* and to the autobiographies of W. L. Phelps and W. L. Cross for miscellaneous impressions; to Harris E. Starr and Albert Galloway Keller for their studies of William Graham Sumner; to Thomas Beer's *The Mauve Decade* (New York, Alfred A. Knopf, 1926), Leonard Bacon's *Semi-Centennial* (New York, Harper, 1939), and S. V. Benét's *The Beginning of Wisdom* for brilliant pen portraits of various celebrated professors. The Class histories also contain much lively comment by those who were taught and those who returned to teach. Particularly interesting are the observations of outstanding faculty members from the Class of 1896 as given in the *Decennial Record of 1896,* edited by Clarence Day, and *The '96 Half-way Book* (1915).

It is to be noted that most of the evidence is by and about literary figures. This is perhaps due to the paucity of scientists in the faculty or their failure to leave behind their autobiographies. Yet it would seem to testify also to the weakness of undergraduate interest in the sciences, and to the further fact that it was in the English department particularly that the new and enthusiastic voices were teaching. For the new faculty, in addition to the sources above listed, the annual *Catalogue,* the papers of Hadley and G. B. Adams, and *The Quarter-Century Chronicle. Class of 1921, Yale College* (1946) are of use.

The head quotation is from Canby, *American Memoir,* 171.

1. E. B. Reed, "To a Senior," *Lyra Levis* (New Haven 1922), 64–65. For corroboration, cf. R. E. Danielson '07, applying Canby's analysis to the forty-year record of his own Class, *History of the Class of 1907, Yale College,* 9(1947):39–42.
2. These quotations are from Canby, 163–65, 246, 248.
3. Conversation of G.W.P. with Dean Jones, 31 Oct. 1939.
4. For testimony to the satisfactions that faculty life offered to its members, see the contributions by and about the faculty members of 1896 in *The '96 Half-way Book* by J. C. Adams, J. M. Berdan, E. L. Durfee, H. A. Farr, H. E. Gregory, H. E. Hawkes, A. G. Keller, G. H. Nettleton (in Sheff), and C. P. Sherman (in the Law School). Nettleton confessed that Yale life "absolutely fascinates me."

It is worth noting that the "unscholarly" Class of 1904 now

contributed more men to the junior ranks of the faculty than any of its predecessors since '96. Among them were C. W. Mendell, R. T. Hill, S. B. Hemingway, W. H. Durham (in S.S.S.), G. E. Nichols, F. E. Pierce (S.S.S.), Lawrence Mason, W. B. Kirkham. *Sexennial Record of the Class of 1904, Yale College* (1911), 25–27.

5. For this analysis, see Canby 176–83, 193–97, 208–09.

6. See Bacon, 31, and Canby's caustic reference, *Alma Mater*, 82, to the later use of Gibbs' name "to persuade the world that we were an institution primarily devoted to learning." Cf. Welch and Camp, 370, on Gibbs "so widely and favorably known abroad." In 1906 one man out of 150 thought "the scholar pure and simple is the greatest need" at Yale. *Decennial Record of 1896*, 101.

7. For analysis of the shift in Sumner's thinking and its relation to the changing climate of opinion, see R. H. Gabriel's chapter on Sumner in *The Course of American Democratic Thought* (New York 1940). For the quotations and comments on Sumner, see Starr, *W. G. Sumner*, 544–48; Keller, *Reminiscences of W. G. Sumner*, 22–23; Van Wyck Brooks, *New England: Indian Summer* (New York, E. P. Dutton, 1940), 477; Canby, 246–47; Beer, 174–76, 207–08.

8. See *Yale Alumni Weekly*, 27 Sept. 1912; *Obituary Record of Graduates . . . June 1, 1913*, 392–95; W. L. Phelps, 369; conversation of G.W.P. with Professor Richards' daughter, Mrs. J. Locke, 5 June 1939.

9. This sketch draws from J. W. White, *Thomas Day Seymour, 1848–1907: Memorial Address . . . February 12, 1908* (n.d., n.p.); from *Yale Alumni Weekly*, 8 Jan. 1908; and from conversations with S. B. Hemingway, W. Notestein, and others. The quotations are from White, 16–17, and Bacon, 28–29.

10. Beer, 184. All Classes agreed that academic education was incomplete without Sumner's and Wheeler's courses, and even as the listeners became conscious of changing demands in historical study, they cherished the tradition. Bacon, 39; *Yale College Class Book 1903*, 185; *History of the Class of 1905*, 2(1908):83–84; and Danielson, *History of the Class of 1907*, 41.

11. On Perrin, Professor E. P. Morris has written an appreciation that reveals the dignity and sheer quality of Morris at the same

time that it illuminates the life and scholarly art of his subject: *Bernadotte Perrin,* printed by the Classical Club for private distribution, 1922. The quotation is taken from the appreciation by Wright in *The Recovery of a Lost Roman Tragedy* (New Haven 1910), 13–14. Wright also gives a magnificent description of Perrin's graduate teaching. Among other testimonials on my desk is a letter from a "gentleman scholar" of the Class of 1907 who, after forty years, is "still reading the New Testament in Greek."

12. See the tributes to Bourne in the *Yale Alumni Weekly,* 25 Mar. 1908, by Albert Bushnell Hart and A. G. Keller, and Keller in *The '96 Half-way Book,* 203.

13. See C. W. Mendell, *An Address: Edward P. Morris, Scholar and Teacher* (New Haven 1941). E. P. Morris, *The Fore-and-Aft Rig in America: A Sketch* (Yale University Press 1927). I am indebted to Mrs. Morris for the comprehensive notes and unpublished manuscripts on the colonial and classical curriculum.

14. Conversation of G.W.P. with Emerson Tuttle, 2 Nov. 1944; Phelps, 137; *Yale Alumni Weekly,* 18 Oct. 1929; *History of the Class of 1905,* 2:77.

15. "Nunc Dimittis," *Poems* (New Haven 1921), 75.

16. On Beers I have had the advantage of conversations with Miss Helen MacAfee, Nov. 1938, and Miss Elizabeth C. Beers, Feb. 1945, and the guidance of his colleagues. Among the tributes to him, see Bacon, *Semi-Centennial,* 37–39, and *Guinea Fowl and Other Poetry* (New York 1927), 87; also Canby, 209–13.

17. On Cook New Haven opinions seem still almost as divided and downright as they were in the days when Yale's graduate students in English almost automatically divided into two camps. For appreciations of his scholarship and teaching, see the sketches by Canby, 213–15, and Bacon, 34–35, and the tributes by Lane Cooper in *Speculum,* Oct. 1927, 2:498–50; C. G. Osgood in the *Journal of English and Germanic Philology,* 27(1928):289–92; and C. H. Whitman in the *Rutgers Alumni Weekly,* Nov. 1927, 7, No. 2. For the best statements of his creed by Cook himself, see *The Artistic Ordering of Life,* Rutgers College Publications, No. 6 (1898) and *The Higher Study of English* (Boston 1906). I am indebted to F. A. Pottle, R. J. Menner, and René Wellek for guidance and criticism; to Professor Sanford B. Meech of

Syracuse University for a copy of his unpublished paper, "The Traditional Program of Graduate Studies in English," for the College English Association, Rochester, N.Y., 1928; and to Miss Beers and Miss Mary Withington for additional information.

18. *Yale Alumni Weekly*, 16 May, 21 Feb. 1913.

19. He tried in vain to interest Mr. Rockefeller in subsidizing what he said would be an efficient redistribution of Yale's talents and energies. Hadley to J. D. Rockefeller Jr., New York, 29 Apr. 1902, and to Starr Murphy, New York, 7 Feb. 1903, Hadley Letters.

20. *Yale Alumni Weekly*, 14 Feb. 1913; and *Report of the President and Deans, 1912–13*, 29, on the reception of the appointment.

21. Hadley to A. L. Ripley, Boston, 23 Jan. 1913, and to A. P. Stokes, 8 Feb. 1906, Hadley Letters. The "dose of bumble bees" seems to have come from President Dwight, who picked it up from Dr. Leonard Bacon and was much impressed by this addition to the academic *materia medica. Memories of Yale Life and Men*, 307.

22. Hadley to E. M. Haggerty, Indiana University, Bloomington, Ind., 13 Jan. 1914, and to Dean J. R. Angell, University of Chicago, 16 Dec. 1912, Hadley Letters.

23. Canby, 196. For contemporaneous comment, see the editorial and the letter from E. D. Fite, "The Finances of an Assistant Professor," in *Yale Alumni Weekly*, 20 May 1910, and H. E. Gregory on freshman professors who should be given posts in the administration or the Graduate School, "where their expense to Yale College will be less . . . and their usefulness to the University still retained." *Decennial Record of the Class of 1896*, 124–25.

24. *Yale Alumni Weekly*, 4 Mar. 1908.

25. Conversation of G.W.P. with President W. E. Weld of Wells College, assistant to Dean Hawkes at Columbia, 1922–29. Also *The '96 Half-way Book*, 166. For other cases, see the Hadley and G. B. Adams Papers.

26. For the normal salary scale, see *Report of the President and Deans, 1909–10*, 22–28; *1910–11*, 10–14; *1914–15*, 44–47.

27. See Hadley's hopeful letter to Hiram Bingham, 7 Nov. 1906, and his hint to Elihu Root on Yale's interest in plans for the teaching of South American geography, history, and literature,

as expressed in his invitation to Elihu Root to deliver the Dodge Lectures, 12 Nov. 1906, Hadley Letters. Also, Isaiah Bowman, "Geography at Yale," *Journal of Geography,* Nov. 1908, 7:60–61.

Missionary motives also figured in the pursuit and teaching of Asiatic history. Witness Professors Williams, Beach, and Archer. See also K. S. Latourette to G. B. Adams (undated, probably 1909): "When I began my graduate work my aim, I am afraid, was merely to get enough training to satisfy the requirements of the New Yale Mission Committee, and then to pursue my work no further. I have come to be more and more interested in history, and hope to do some little work at it all my life." G. B. Adams Collection, Letterfile 22, File 48.

28. *Semi-Centennial,* 32–33.

29. *The '96 Half-way Book,* 153.

30. For suggestive comment on the history department's feeling on these courses, see Hadley to Dean Jones, 28 Feb. 1910; and to Dean Oertel, 8 Oct. 1912, 7 Jan. 1913, Hadley Letters. Adams did not regard Bingham as a historian, and his high appreciation of Asakawa's work was based on its value for the study of feudalism, not apparently on the possibility of developing an interest in modern Asia among undergraduates. See his protest when dropping Asakawa was proposed in 1921: Adams to Provost Walker, 2 Dec. 1920, 10 Jan. 1921, G. B. Adams Collection, Letters, Yale and Others, File 211.

31. Hadley to Allen Johnson, 17 Nov. 1911, Hadley Letters. See also *Yale Alumni Weekly,* 21 Feb. 1913.

32. *History of the Class of 1905,* 2:76; conversation of G.W.P. with Emerson Tuttle, 2 Nov. 1944.

33. Appreciations of Billy Phelps are too numerous to list. See Bacon, 33–34; *History of the Class of 1905,* 2:76; and R. E. Danielson in the *History of the Class of 1907,* 9:39, for the quotation in the text. See also Gilbert Highet, *The Art of Teaching* (New York 1950), 248–49.

34. Besides earlier appreciations see "But Yesterday—" in *The Quarter-Century Chronicle. Class of 1921, Yale College* (1946), for the feeling of one Class at the close of the period. See also Van Wyck Brooks on how a "noble Yankee humanism" was maintained by Lounsbury and Beers, "despite the militant philistinism of the formidable Sumner," and was then carried on

by Tinker and Phelps and Cross and their students. *New England: Indian Summer,* 506–07. For a caustic comment on the general drift to English literature and the overemphasis on fiction, see Beer, 185.

35. *History of the Class of 1906,* 2(1911):35.
36. W. L. Cross, *Connecticut Yankee* (New Haven, Yale University Press, 1943), 155–59; *Report of the President and Deans, 1912–13,* 14–23, 110; and *1916–17,* 251–52, 254–55. Cf. Hadley to William Lyon Phelps, London, 16 Feb. 1912, Hadley Letters.
37. *Semi-Centennial,* 32; *History of the Class of 1905,* 2:72.
38. *The Beginning of Wisdom,* 57–58.

There is no adequate study of the vigorous and continued efforts of American colleges—by means of group programs, majors and minors, concentration-distribution requirements, or Pass-Honors courses—to construct a Course of Study intermediate between the wholly pre-scribed curriculum and absolutely free electives. Butts, *The College Charts Its Course,* especially 239–48, summarizes the factors involved, and W. T. Foster, *Administration of the College Curriculum,* brings to-gether a considerable body of statistics on the variety of programs about 1910. The most valuable sources for the Yale changes are the Clive Day Papers; a group of Day's letters to C. M. Lewis, copies of which he has kindly lent; Day's indispensable article, "A New Course of Study in Yale College," *Educational Review,* Apr. 1911, 41:371–81; the Hadley Letters and Correspondence; the G. B. Adams Collection; and the Records of the Academical Professors and the general Faculty. I am also indebted to Mr. Day and Mr. Mendell for reminiscence about their work on the Course of Study Committee.

The head quotation is from the *Report of the President and Deans, 1908–09,* 22.

1. *History of the Class of 1906, Yale College,* 2(1911):37.
2. T. D. Goodell to Dean Wright, 24 Aug. 1905, H. P. Wright Col-lection, Correspondence, 1865–1908. Goodell thought the Shef-field groups offered the best solution. The Chicago plan was a division of the Junior College into eight colleges (four for men, four for women) classified by curriculum, each with its faculty and dean. A year's trial proved the scheme impracticable for the curriculum, highly successful for social activities. University of Chicago, *The President's Report, July 1905–July 1906* (Chicago 1907), 8, 42. For the Harvard discussion of the possi-bilities of the "English collegiate hall system," see the *Harvard*

Graduates' Magazine, June 1905, 13:585–92. Lowell's address as Harvard lecturer at Yale is quoted in Yeomans, *Abbott Lawrence Lowell, 1856–1943,* 182–83. Lowell favored subdivision only for social life, not instruction. The *Alumni Weekly,* 1 May 1907, recalled that Yale leaders some twelve years earlier had discussed and decried this type of federated-college plan. But the problem of securing intellectual and social coherence remained. For Wilson's attack on the Eating Clubs, and his Quadrangle Plan, see A. S. Link, *Wilson,* 46–57.

3. "Mental Types and Their Recognition in Our Colleges," *Harper's Magazine,* June 1905, 111:123–29.

4. *Report of the President and Deans, 1908–09,* 22.

5. "A New Course of Study in Yale College," 371–372.

6. Rec. Acad. Profs., 15 Nov. 1906, 24 Jan. 1907, 21 Nov., 10 Dec. 1907, 9, 16 Jan. 1908. Clive Day to H. C. Emery, 21 Dec. 1907, Clive Day Papers, Correspondence, 1907–25. E. S. Dana to Hadley, 20 Jan. 1908, Hadley Correspondence.

7. *Report of the President and Deans, 1907–08,* 77–80. In 1908–09 the elective pamphlet offered approximately 29 A courses, 100 B courses, 95 C courses and 39 D courses—with 40 more courses unlettered. Latin, for example, now offered one A, two B, five C, and five D courses; English literature one A, fourteen B, thirteen C, and four D; economics and law one A, six B, eight C, five D, and ten unclassified.

8. E. S. Dana to Hadley, 20 May 1909, Hadley Correspondence; Hadley to E. S. Oviatt, 15 Mar. 1909, and to Dana, 24 May 1909, Hadley Letters. A scheme for "honor courses" was presented to the Academical Professors, 27 May 1909.

9. *Report of the President and Deans, 1908–09,* 45–47.

10. Rec. Acad. Profs., 24 Feb., 7 Apr. 1910; Faculty Record, 20 May 1910; statement of the Course of Study Committee in the *Alumni Weekly,* 10 June 1910.

11. Clive Day to C. M. Lewis, 23 Sept., 9, 13, 21 Oct. 1910. Conversations of G.W.P. with Clive Day, 25 Nov. 1941, and with C. W. Mendell, 5 Jan. 1948.

12. Day to Lewis, 21 Nov., 11, 24 Dec. 1910, for an intimate account of the committee at work, and his article, "A New Course of Study in Yale College," for exposition of the new arrangements.

13. "A New Course of Study in Yale College," 375.

14. The gain in coherence, and in a more conscientious departmental planning, was notable. The English department for the first time divided its offerings into four great periods of English literature, plus a group in composition, and required of its majors at least one course in each of four groups, plus a minor in either Greek, Latin, Italian, French, or German. The history department organized three alternative majors (ancient, European, or American). If such faculty planning proved successful the Yale Course of Study would become "a vertebrate course" for every undergraduate. Day to C. M. Lewis, 21 Nov. 1910.

15. "Fifty complete programs of study taken at random, alphabetically, from the Class of 1909 at Harvard, and an equal number from the Class of 1909 at Yale, reveal the following facts. At Harvard 22 per cent, at Yale 68 per cent, did not take one-third of their work in one subject." Foster, 180. G. B. Adams particularly was concerned that Day should make it clear that Yale had never gone over to wide-open electives; at least Yale ought to get credit for that, as the reaction set in. Adams to Day (draft), 29 Jan. 1911, G. B. Adams Collection, Correspondence and Papers, 35–42, File 36.

Summary accounts of the traditional speaking Appointments, their place on the Commencement program, and their transformation into honor lists for general scholarship may be found in Kingsley, *Yale College*, 1:373–74, and C. H. Smith, *Yale University*, 103–04. See also Dwight, *Report, 1894*, 22–26; *1895*, 3–6. The later devolution of the Appointments system, and the rise and decline of Special Honors, have to be studied through the *Catalogues* and Commencement programs, with the Faculty Record shedding some light on objectives.

Since the dissatisfactions with Appointments and with Special Honors were beneath the surface, and since the succession of proposals for a real Honors reform (1905–17) never captured public attention, the story of this three-cornered debate must be pieced together from the publications and records of the interested parties. Hadley's proposal for Oxford-style Honors groups was clearly brought forward in an address at Johns Hopkins University, abstract in *Yale Alumni Weekly*, 24 Feb. 1909, and repeated in *Report of the President and Deans, 1908–09*, 18–23. On 18 Feb. 1909 the Corporation voted to ask the Alumni Advisory Board to report on "ways in which the intellectual ambition of undergraduates may be stimulated"; Secretary Stokes' letter to the Board was printed in the *Yale Alumni Weekly* of 5 Mar. 1909; and the deliberations and final Report of the Board were recorded in the same forum: 16 July 1909, 20 May and 16 July 1910. The Board's Report was also printed in *An Account of the Alumni Advisory Board, Yale University* (1911), 19–22.

For the Faculty, from May 1909 through May 1910 the Permanent Officers of Yale College held jurisdiction over the Honors question; and the succession of schemes put forward by Dana's Course of Study Committee or thrashed out in Committee of the Whole may be found in Rec. Acad. Profs. and in the Reports of the Permanent Officers, with copies in the Honors Committee papers and in the G. B. Adams Collec-

tion. After the general Faculty assumed jurisdiction further proposals and votes were entered in the Faculty Record, especially 19, 20 May 1910, May 1913 to Feb. 1914, with committee reports and minutes of the Committee of the Whole being filed in the volumes of Faculty Reports, 1904–21. Copies of the Honors Committee's reports, correspondence, and miscellaneous papers are in Honors Committee, Box I and Box II, in the Yale Memorabilia Room; and a statement of the "Revised Honors Plan," voted 5 Mar. 1914, is in *Report of the President and Deans, 1913–14*, 148–50.

The head quotations are from *Report of the President and Deans, 1908–09*, 19; *An Account of the Alumni Advisory Board*, 19.

1. See Chapter 13 for the Fisher committee's findings, and the consequent efforts at reform. Before 1894 there had been also a Junior Appointments list, organized on the basis of average grades for the first three years. In 1894 these Junior Appointments were made two-year honors, on the (required) studies of Freshman and Sophomore years. In 1903 the practice of awarding Freshman Appointments was started; and in 1905 a fourth list, to honor the work of Junior year, was published. It seemed to many that Colloquies and Disputes made the whole Honors idea ridiculous. So Junior and Freshman Honors were limited to three Oration groups or an average of 80. But it was not until 1919 that the Senior Appointments list was similarly restricted to men of some real pretensions to knowledge.

2. W. L. Phelps, 146–47, and the Commencement program of 1887. In Dec. 1885 the Faculty Honors Committee saw no objection to the use at Commencement of such Honors theses as the Professor of Rhetoric deemed suitable. Cobden Club Medal essays and Townsend Premium essays were also acceptable. In this way some winners of Special Honors and an occasional winner of some particular prize joined the Appointments scholars on the Commencement Program.

3. *Report of the President and Deans, 1908–09*, 13–23.

4. See *Yale Alumni Weekly*, 16 July 1909, 20 May and 16 July 1910; Hadley to E. J. Phelps, 29 Mar. 1910, Hadley Letters.

5. *Yale Alumni Weekly*, 14, 21 Oct. 1910, 3 Nov., 22, 29 Dec. 1911.

6. Rec. Acad. Profs., 27 May 1909; E. S. Dana to Hadley, 20 May 1909, and Hadley's reply, 24 May 1909, Hadley Correspondence

and Letters. In the G. B. Adams Collection, "Letters—Yale etc." File 162, are memoranda of the last term of 1908–09, and for 1909–10, on possible schemes for Honors work in history. For the labors of the Dana committee in 1910 see the Report of the Course of Study Committee, 24 Feb. 1910, with "Revised Suggestions as to Honors Groups," 10 Mar., 21, 28 Apr. 1910, in Permanent Officers, Reports and Papers, 1910–21.

7. Rec. Acad. Profs., 7 Apr., 12, 26 May 1910; Faculty Record, 19, 20 May 1910. See also the statement of the Course of Study Committee in the *Yale Alumni Weekly,* 10 June 1910.

8. "Plan of a System of Honors Courses in Yale College," May 1913. Faculty, Reports and Papers, 1904–21, and Honors Committee, Box II, File Barrell and Angier.

9. Faculty Record, 15, 20 Jan., 5 Mar. 1914. Minutes of the Committee of the Whole, of the same dates, Faculty, Reports and Papers, 1904–21. Minutes of the Honors Committee, 30 Jan., 24 Feb. 1914, with Fairchild's revised plan of 13 Feb. 1914, Honors Committee, Box II, File Barrell and Angier.

10. Hadley to H. A. Bumstead, 26 Oct. 1914, Hadley Letters. For Bakewell's statement, see *Yale Daily News,* 24 Mar. 1915.

11. The proposals and explanations of the departments are in Honors Committee, Box I, File Honors Replies from Departments, Oct. 1914. See also the statements of Honors courses arranged by the departments in the Course of Study pamphlet for 1915–16.

12. Conversations of G.W.P. with Charles Seymour, 26 Nov. 1943, 26 Nov. 1950. Seymour was invited to join the Honors Committee, as there were so many candidates for history Honors. Honors Committee, Box II, File Honors Correspondence, etc.

13. *Yale Daily News,* 13 Apr., 1916.

14. E. B. Reed to H. A. Bumstead, 4 June 1915; Joseph Barrell to Bumstead, 7 July 1916; Bumstead to W. L. Phelps, 24 Nov. 1916; C. M. Lewis to Bumstead, 10 Dec. 1916—a full explanation of the English professors' position, all in Honors Committee, Box II, File Honors Correspondence, etc.; Professor Bumstead's statement in the *News,* 9 Nov. 1916.

15. *Report of the President and Deans, 1913–14,* 19–20.

16. *Ibid., 1914–15,* 26–27.

17. See "Memorandum of conversation with H. Bumstead on the

Honors System," 29 Oct. 1924, Hadley Letters. Apparently Bumstead consulted H. E. Hawkes about the system at Columbia, for on 17 Nov. 1914 Hawkes wrote him that the most serious difficulty was that of interesting the Faculty. Like Professors Day and Fairchild he warned that unless at least one or two men in each department were seriously interested no Honors system could succeed without a large increase in the budget. Honors Committee, Box I, File Princeton and Harvard Honors.

The literary renaissance did not produce a Yale school to take its place in American literary history, and the time has not yet come to fix the rank of individuals. This chapter, in any case, is not concerned with the history and criticism of American letters but with the *milieu* and the *moment:* the academic training and the socio-literary excitement which inspired the men of Yale to dramatize and to write. The files of the *Lit.,* the *News,* the *Record,* the *Courant,* and the *Alumni Weekly* are packed with their contributions and comment, as are their Class histories. The Centennial Number of the *Lit.,* Feb. 1936, is especially rich. Of all books of reminiscence, the *Autobiography with Letters* of William Lyon Phelps, whose faculty status carried him through the changing student generations, and who was one of the presiding geniuses of the new era, catches most of the life of the time. See also the chapter "A Group of Yale Poets" in Phelps' *The Advance of English Poetry in the Twentieth Century* (New York 1918). H. S. Canby, "The Undergraduate," *Harper's Magazine,* Mar. 1913, 126: 592–98, is a more temperate analysis of the movement, and *American Memoir* has scattered comment on his friends and pupils. Leonard Bacon's *Semi-Centennial* and J. F. Carter's *The Rectory Family* (New York 1937) give vivid sketches of the young littérateurs of their days. I have learned much from conversations with W. L. Phelps, 18 Dec. 1939, with C. B. Tinker, Maynard Mack, and F. A. Pottle, 23 Feb. 1949, with Thornton Wilder, 9 Mar. 1949, and J. C. Peet '15, Apr. 1949.

The dating of this Yale renaissance is elusive. Phelps, perhaps, would find its origins in the Class of '96. By 1906 Hadley could recognize a wider range and better direction of student effort. Wayland Williams '10 declared that his College years marked the passing of "the blood and iron period" into a new civilization, *History of the Class of Nineteen Hundred and Ten,* 2(1917):46; and by 1915 various witnesses acclaimed the changes of the last decade: the students had established their own university, in art, in music, and in literature, said W. C. Abbott in the *Alumni Weekly,* 5 Mar. 1915. Still a later generation saw the development as a postwar outburst. Yet Thornton Wilder would be sure that the giants had all gone before.

The head quotation is from Van Wyck Brooks, 506–07.

1. A. P. Stokes, *Memorials of Eminent Yale Men,* 1:109.
2. Faculty Record, 17 Feb. 1910, 16 Nov. 1911, 8 May, 23 Oct. 1913. See comment in *Yale Alumni Weekly,* 7 Feb., 31 Oct. 1913.
3. See G. F. Ingersoll '11, addressing the fifth reunion of the Class of 1906, in *History of the Class of 1906, Yale College,* 2(1911):42, and his "In Defense of the Grind," *Yale Alumni Weekly,* 28 Feb. 1911. Also the editorials and articles in the *Yale Courant* in 1911–12, by E. N. Hickman, R. H. Gabriel, F. L. Daily, G. H. Day, and G. E. Hamilton.
4. Hadley to the Cleveland alumni, *Yale Alumni Weekly,* 7 Feb. 1906; Hadley to E. S. Oviatt, 11 Mar. 1909; to Prof. O. M. Johnston, Stanford University, 14 Feb. 1912, and to Owen Johnson, New York, 29 Mar. 1912, Hadley Letters. Also his addresses to alumni and Phi Beta Kappa, *Yale Alumni Weekly,* 13 Feb. 1913, 13 Mar. 1914, 16 Apr. 1915; and R. H. Macdonald '15 at the *News* banquet, *Yale Daily News,* 4 Mar. 1915.
5. For typical and contradictory complaints see the *Courant,* Feb. 1912, on the "ridiculously low" passing grade, and Apr. 1915 on a Phi Beta Kappa standard too high for the "normal Yale man" even to try to meet. Professor Reed described the changes in *Catalogue of Members, Yale Chapter of Phi Beta Kappa, Alpha of Connecticut* (n.p. 1915), 3–4. When the prize award of the Class of 1913 went to R. J. Menner '13 for an essay on "Common Sense in Pronunciation," the *News,* 22 May 1913, blasted the chapter for neglecting real scholarship to reward "dogged pertinacity." Menner's essay was nevertheless published in the *Atlantic Monthly,* Aug. 1913.
6. Quotations from Douglas' editorials in the *News,* 24 Feb., 5 Mar., 5 Apr., 10 Mar., 7 Mar., 15 Feb. 1913. The *Alumni Weekly,* 11 Apr. 1913, praised Douglas for conducting "perhaps the most brilliant editorial page in the history of the *News,*" and Prof. G. H. Nettleton paid tribute to the "high devotion and invincible courage" of the 1914 chairman, *ibid.,* 3 Apr. 1914. The majority

of the Class of 1914 voted Yale's greatest need was a major championship, and the most valuable gain from College was friendship rather than education; but their *History* reprinted a selection from Douglas' editorials, daily themes, and Kenneth Rand's poems, and the dominant note of its advice to Freshman was "don't forget why you came to college." *History of the Class of Nineteen Hundred and Fourteen*, 1(1914):462–64.

7. Adams made the suggestion to the Yale Phi Beta Chapter in 1917; the proposal fell through because of war absences, and in spite of Dean Jones' encouragement was not taken up again. D. E. Bronson '18 to Adams, 16 Dec. 1917; Adams to Bronson 7, 13, 19 Jan. 1918 (drafts), to Jones, 25 Dec. 1917, 26 Apr. 1923 (draft); Jones to Adams, 22 Dec. 1917, 30 Apr. 1923, G. B. Adams Collection, "Letters—Yale etc." File 183.

8. Canby, "The Undergraduate," 595, 597–98.

9. The origins of College lore and undergraduate customs are difficult indeed to ascertain. I have taken this account from "The Origins of Mory's," *Yale Alumni Magazine*, June 1948, and *A Brief History of the Whiffenpoofs . . . Prepared for the 40th Anniversary Celebration, 15 January 1949* (n.p., n.d.); also the *Yale Alumni Magazine*, Oct. 1950, quoting Sigmund Spaeth, *The History of Popular Music in America* (New York 1948), 579.

10. "A Football King" and "Bull-Dog" were included in *The New Yale Song Book* (1918) and, with the later ones, in *Songs of Yale* (1934), these collections carrying on the collections which, with various titles and revisions, had appeared since 1855.

11. This, with more of Hooker's, is to be found in *Achievements of the Class of 1902, Yale College, from Birth to the Year 1912* (1913), 106.

12. *Yale Alumni Weekly*, 22 Feb. 1899, 6 May 1903, and Pierce's essay in *Yale Literary Magazine*, May 1903.

13. Phelps, 542–49.

14. For the beginnings of organized dramatic activities, see the program of the Psi Upsilon play, 5 Apr. 1898; *Yale Daily News*, 29 Mar., 30 Apr. 1898, and *Yale Alumni Weekly*, 31 Mar., 5 May 1898; *News*, 3 May 1900, and *Alumni Weekly*, 28 Mar., 16, 30 May 1900; *Report of the President and Deans, 1899–1900*, 19; conversation of G.W.P. with Professor C. B. Tinker, 22 Feb. 1949; *Fifty Years of Yale News*, 28 Jan. 1928, 44.

The Dramat then covered the historical course of drama in English to Pinero, and in 1907 advanced to the first production in English of Ibsen's *The Pretenders*. T. Achelis '08, T. L. Riggs '10, and C. R. Hopkins '07 took parts. Hopkins became a professional actor, 1908–19, and a manager and producer. Phelps gave an account of the early years of the Dramatic Association in his introduction to *The Pretenders by Henrik Ibsen. Acting Version of the Yale Dramatic Association* (New Haven 1907). See also G. S. Haight, "Yale Dramatic Association Celebrates 50th Anniversary," *Yale Daily News*, 10 May 1949.

15. *Yale Alumni Weekly*, 4 June 1909; *Yale Daily News*, 18 Mar. 1910. As early as 1904 Harry D. Wescott '01, one of the founders, had suggested the need for a theater to President Hadley, who expressed much sympathy but saw difficulties of finance and control. Hadley to Harry D. Wescott, Philadelphia, Pa., 18 May 1904, 21 Aug. 1911; also Hadley's memorandum for Prof. J. M. Berdan, 30 Nov. 1909, Hadley Letters. Maude Adams, at her own expense, brought her company to New Haven for a special benefit for the fund. *News*, 20, 21 Apr. 1909. For the Maugham interview, see the *Courant*, Jan. 1911. Belasco was interviewed in May. In July appeared the play by A. J. Jenks '14, which had won the Dramat's prize.

16. *Yale Alumni Magazine*, 25 Apr. 1941.

17. For some of these high lights in Dramat history see the *Alumni Weekly*, 20 Dec. 1910, 7 Oct. 1913 on Woolley's return from Harvard, and 22 May 1914 on the all-student production of *Quentin Durward*. For the strong public interest in *Iphigenia in Tauris* in the Yale Bowl and other university stadia, see the *Yale Daily News*, 17 May 1915, the *New Republic*, 22 May, and the *Literary Digest*, 29 May 1915.

18. Sheff had also graduated Lee Wilson Dodd, poet and playwright, in 1899 and William Rose Benét in 1907, and in E. E. Paramore '17 discovered a parodist whose *Ballad of Yukon Jake* contributed "hardboiled as a picnic egg" to the American vocabulary.

19. Dudley C. Lunt '18 to G.W.P., 29 Oct. 1950. The tributes sent to the *Yale Alumni Magazine*, 21 Mar. 1941, on Berdan's retirement are a partial roster of the Yale writers he had trained.

20. *Yale Alumni Weekly*, 13 Dec. 1912, 12 Dec. 1913, 5 Mar. 1915. Conversation of G.W.P. with W. L. Phelps, 18 Dec. 1939.

21. Hadley to Alexander S. Cochran, 21 Mar. 1911, Hadley Letters. An account of the Club is in the *Alumni Weekly,* 8 Dec. 1911. See also *Report of the President and Deans, 1911–12,* 29–30; Phelps, *Autobiography,* 292–93.

22. Speech in Louisville, *Yale Alumni Weekly,* 16 May 1913.

23. *Yale Alumni Weekly,* 29 Nov. 1912. Conversation of G.W.P. with C. B. Tinker, 23 Feb. 1949.

24. *The Quarter-Century Chronicle. Class of 1921* (New Haven 1946), 19; see also J. F. Carter, *The Rectory Family* (New York, Coward-McCann; copyright, 1937, by John F. Carter), 261–62. Reprinted by permission of Coward-McCann, Inc.

25. Phelps, "Literature at Yale," *The Book of the Yale Pageant,* 172–73; *Yale Alumni Weekly,* 5 Mar. 1915. See also Faculty Record, 30 Oct. 1913.

26. Only three numbers of *Parabalou* appeared, 1920–21. See the account in the *Alumni Weekly,* 18 June, 30 Dec. 1920.

27. *Yale Alumni Weekly,* 5 Nov. 1920, and also "The Glorious Year A.D. Nineteen Twenty," *ibid.,* 17 Dec. 1920, for another résumé.

28. Phelps wrote on this new journalistic enterprise, pointing out the representation from the *News,* the *Courant,* the *Lit.,* and the *Sheff Monthly.* The circulation manager was a Harvard man. *Yale Alumni Weekly,* 16 Feb. 1923.

29. See G. P. Day's statement on the aims and work of the Press in *The Book of the Yale Pageant,* 182–85, and in the *Alumni Weekly,* 18 June 1920, 3 Mar. 1922, and Clarence Day's *The Story of the Yale University Press Told by a Friend* (New Haven 1920). Also Carl P. Rollins, "Fifty Years of Work and Play with Type," *Yale University Library Gazette,* July 1948, 23:19–24. I have also had the privilege of using Mr. Rollins' manuscript "A Quarter-Century of Printing at Yale."

30. Besides the formal statement in the *Yale Review,* Feb. 1911, see Cross, *Connecticut Yankee,* Chapter XI, "The Yale Review," and Canby, *American Memoir,* 252–53.

31. It is interesting to find that quite early a Ten Eyck Prize speaker, H. H. Clark '03, had called attention to these possibilities. "With the advance of the elective system into Sophomore year under the present administration, a growing number of men dare champion the aesthetic. . . . Thanks to the personality of our ex-President and to the introduction of clubs where professors

and students may meet in an atmosphere freer than that of the classroom, teacher and taught have become reconciled. . . . After ninety-seven years, Yale seems ready for her second great renaissance." *Yale Alumni Weekly,* 26 Mar. 1902.

32. *The Yale Book of Student Verse, 1910–19* (New Haven 1919), 50.

The proposal to advance the University and coordinate its undergraduate Schools by building University laboratories at some distance from
the old campus initiated a drama of deep complexities and emotions.
In the interest of brevity one aspect of this struggle—the relations of
Secretary Stokes with the Hillhouse heirs, the misunderstanding over
the use of the square, and the consequent litigation and building difficulties—has had to be omitted. By direction of the deceased the beautiful
Hillhouse mansion, which would have made an admirable and dramatically situated President's house, was pitilessly torn down; while
Peabody Museum and Osborn Zoological Laboratory took over the two
lower corners of the great block and other laboratories crept their
massive way up Prospect Hill. Yet the physical remains of the Hillhouse
square are still impressive: the little park at the head of Hillhouse
avenue, the two great oaks over the hillside garden, the long open slopes
looking down on the intruding colony of quonset huts, the paths winding
north to Whitney and Edwards. These are testimonials to a rurality and
seclusion which the Hillhouses valued, which the Yale Administration
perhaps underestimated, and which even today has not quite been
shattered. The problem of distance remains; and as a new physics
laboratory is planned, to replace the Sloane laboratory which caused
so much commotion, there are signs that the authorities would be happy
if the new facilities could be located somewhat nearer the center of the
University.

For the official attitudes and actions one must go to the Corporation
Records, the files of Secretary Stokes, and the letters and Reports of
President Hadley. The Corporation papers of Alfred L. Ripley are useful, as are the columns of the *Yale Alumni Weekly* for public repercussions. The materials for an understanding of the deeper implications,
however, are the letters and memoranda in the G. B. Adams Collection,
together with Adams' articles: "The College in the University," *Edu-*

cational Review, Feb. 1907, 33:121–44; and "The Need of an Internal Reorganization in Yale," *Yale Alumni Weekly,* 27 Mar., 17, 26 Apr. 1914. On the policies and attitudes of the Scientific School the second volume of Chittenden's *History of the Sheffield Scientific School* should be consulted, especially 314–22, 435–50, 511–19; also Chittenden's Reports and his articles in the *Yale Alumni Weekly,* 5 Jan. 1912, 4 Dec. 1914. For the interests and activities of the alumni, see *An Account of the Work of the Alumni Advisory Board* (1911), *The Year's Work of the Alumni Advisory Board,* 1912–13 and 1913–14, and *Eleventh Annual Meeting of the Associated Western Yale Clubs . . . May 22 and 23, 1914* (n.p., n.d.). The head quotation is taken from the Hadley Letters.

1. This was not entirely a new idea. When the Kent Chemical Laboratory was given and Gooch appointed Professor of Chemistry in 1885, it was hoped that friends of the College would give a laboratory for physiology and biology, to be open to students from all Departments. *Yale College in 1886,* 5.

2. The Sloane Physical Laboratory, just off the old campus, had been given to the College by Henry T. Sloane '66 and Thomas C. Sloane '68. A bequest from the latter, with aid from Henry T. Sloane, was used for the improvement of the building and apparatus in 1906–07.

3. *Report of the President and Deans, 1909–10,* 18–19, describing the possibilities for development. The discussion of the Hillhouse site was begun at the Corporation meeting of Apr. 1909, and a committee appointed on location, but the formal decision on policy was not reached until Nov. Corporation Records, Nov. 1909, and "The Beginning of a University Plan at Yale," *Yale Alumni Weekly,* 26 Nov. 1909.

4. A. L. Ripley to President Hadley, 25 Mar. 1909, A. L. Ripley Papers; G. B. Adams to Dean-elect Jones (draft), 30 Apr. 1909, and A. P. Stokes to G. B. Adams, 7 Aug. 1909, G. B. Adams Collection, Letterfile 22, File 51.

5. J. W. D. Ingersoll to Dean Wright (copy) and G. B. Adams, 15 May 1909, "plunging in where angels might fear to tread." Secretary Stokes thought this the most serious objection. A. P. Stokes to G. B. Adams, 30 Apr. 1909, G. B. Adams Collection, Letterfile 22, File 51.

6. Rec. Acad. Profs., 2 Oct. 1909; Corporation Records, Apr., May,

Oct. 1909. Bumstead's letter to the Corporation committee on the location of buildings, 5 June 1909, is in H. B. Sargent Papers, Box 2, File Yale Corporation. Hadley also explained Bumstead's position to Dean Jones at some length, 5 May 1909, and to Henry T. Sloane, 30 Sept. 1909, Hadley Letters; Dean Jones to G. B. Adams, 4, 10 May 1909, G. B. Adams Collection, Letterfile 22, File 51; E. S. Dana to A. L. Ripley, 14 May 1909, Ripley Papers. Another anxiety was created for Hadley by the possibility that B. B. Boltwood, then studying in London with Rutherford, might not return or might prefer an appointment in chemistry. To assure him of a foothold in the new physics laboratory, without risk of complications with Director Chittenden and the chemists, Hadley suggested the title of radiochemistry. Hadley to Boltwood, 6, 31 Dec. 1909, and to H. A. Bumstead, 21 Dec. 1909, Hadley Letters.

7. The arguments are stated particularly by Hadley to Dean Jones, 5 May 1909, Hadley Letters. E. S. Dana to A. L. Ripley, 14 May 1909, Ripley Papers, and to G. B. Adams, 18 May 1909, G. B. Adams Collection; Bumstead to the Corporation Committee, 5 June 1909, Sargent Papers; and A. P. Stokes to G. B. Adams 18 Oct. 1909, G. B. Adams Collection, Letterfile 22, File 51.

8. Corporation Records, Nov. 1909. In 1911 Chittenden moved to create a department of electrical engineering through the appointment of Professor C. F. Scott.

9. Rec. Acad. Profs., 26 Oct. 1905, 26 Jan., 1, 15 Feb., 1906, 24, 31 Jan. 1907. E. S. Dana to Ripley, 10 Jan. 1910, Ripley Papers. President Hadley, memorandum, 11 Jan., and to R. G. Harrison, 14 Feb. 1910, Hadley Letters. Conversation of G.W.P. with R. G. Harrison, 23 Nov. 1939.

10. Chittenden, *History of the Sheffield Scientific School*, 2:444–50; Corporation Records, Jan., Feb. 1910. In Feb. 1911 the Corporation voted that a botanical laboratory if possible should be included in the plans.

11. See Chittenden's discussion of the five-year engineering courses, *Report of the President and Deans, 1909–10*, 124–26. "Many times during the past twelve years the question has been put to the writer, when does the Scientific School intend to lengthen its undergraduate course to four years? The answer invariably has been 'never.'" Chittenden, "The Growth of the Scientific

School," *Yale Alumni Weekly,* 20 Sept. 1912; the article was prepared for the Record of the Class of '75S.

The Leet Oliver Memorial Hall was built in 1907. The following year W. C. Abbott was appointed to the School's first professorship of history; C. C. Clarke was promoted to the first professorship of French; Canby became Assistant Professor of English, and the work in English and Spanish was enlarged. At the same time a course of lectures on problems of business management was instituted for Seniors, carrying further the attention shown by the establishment of the Page Lectures on business ethics the year before. Social sciences were set apart from history in 1909. Political economy had been taught by Gilman, Professor of Physical and Political Geography, from 1860 to 1872; then by F. A. Walker, as Professor of Political Economy and History. Anthropology and social evolution, and commercial geography, had since their introduction in 1901 been given by Keller and later Fairchild from Yale College; but in 1909 the School's own Assistant Professor of Geography took the last subject over, in 1911 A. L. Bishop transferred from the College to teach geography and commerce, and in 1913 Loomis Havemeyer was appointed instructor in geography and anthropology. In 1914 a large gift enabled the School to establish its Graduate Course in Business Administration (offered in 1915). See Chittenden, *History of the Sheffield Scientific School,* 2:314–22, 478–79, 511–18, 543; also his annual Reports, particularly that of 1910–11 on the aim of the social sciences courses to "ally themselves . . . with the natural sciences, rather than to cling to the old-time relations with the so-called mental and moral sciences." *Report of the President and Deans, 1910–11,* 176.

12. Chittenden gave a statement on the Select Course to the *Yale Alumni Weekly,* 5 Jan. 1912. The *Weekly's* editorial comment was that the historical justification for its institution was not perhaps sufficient for its continuance under modern circumstances. On 4 Dec. 1914, after the third-college proposal had intensified alumni interest in the relation of the two Schools, Chittenden developed his theme still more fully.

13. The Alumni Advisory Board in June 1909 asked the Corporation for information as to "legal and other obstacles which interfere with a closer correlation of Yale College and Sheffield Scientific

School." A special committee reported on the legal status and referred to the early "lack of cordiality . . . remnants of which have continued to the present day," though with evidence of growing cooperation, as in the laboratory policy. On receiving this report the Board, in June 1910, voted that no further action was necessary or desirable. *An Account of the Work of the Alumni Advisory Board,* 33–36. Payson Merrill to H. B. Sargent, 30 Nov. 1909, and A. P. Stokes to H. B. Sargent, 23 Feb. 1910, Sargent Papers, Box 4, Yale Scientific School.

14. This question had apparently begun to preoccupy Adams as early as 1906 when in a draft on the development of the University and its Graduate School he had noted Yale's advantage in having preserved its academic department. "It means atmosphere, life, influence." Correspondence and Papers, 34–42, File 35. In Feb. 1907 he published "The College in the University," *Educational Review,* 33:121–44. His argument was most carefully given in this "Memorandum Not Published" prepared in May for the Corporation committee on locating the laboratory, and distributed among the faculty. G. B. Adams Collection, College and University, Memoranda on College Affairs. In October, after the Professors' vote and President Lowell's inaugural address, Adams renewed the discussion, first in a letter to President Hadley intended for Secretary Stokes' eye, 8 Oct. 1909, and then directly with the Secretary. Adams to Stokes, 25 Oct., 2, 5, Nov. 1909, and Stokes to Adams, 18, 27 Oct., 3 Nov. 1909, G. B. Adams Collection, Letterfile 22, File 51.

15. "The executive authorities of the University seem to me to be taking now relatively the same position to the chief movement now beginning in the American university world, that Pres. Porter took in regard to the chief movement of his day." Adams to Hadley, 8 Oct. 1909. To his colleague in history, Max Farrand, he wrote of "the peculiarly cruel blow of fate" that Yale should lose the opportunity "which ought especially to belong to it" while "Pres. Lowell has put himself and Harvard . . . squarely in the lead." Adams to Farrand, 8 Oct. 1909, and to President Lowell, 14 Oct., in much the same terms. G. B. Adams Collection, Letterfile 22, File 51. His last desperate efforts to persuade Stokes, 2, 5, 11 Nov. 1909, are in the same file.

16. The announcement of the Corporation action, in the *Alumni*

Weekly, 26 Nov. 1909, was followed by many letters of protest, concluded by Professor Bumstead's reluctant adherence, and Stokes' statement, 24 Dec. 1909. After the announcement of Mrs. Sage's gift, when the newspapers were telling of the Faculty struggle against the Corporation, some statements had to be made to show that the decision had been made *before* the gift, and that the Faculty was loyal and grateful. *New York Times,* 2, 4 Jan. 1910; E. S. Dana in the *Alumni Weekly,* 6 Jan. 1910; and see also Hadley to Newell Knight, Chicago, 6 Jan. 1910, Hadley Letters.

17. "The Need of an Internal Reorganization in Yale," *Yale Alumni Weekly,* 27 Mar., 17, 26 Apr. 1914. The immediate occasion for Adams' articles was Professor Corwin's attack on the Latin requirement: "Is Yale's Democracy in Danger?" *Yale Alumni Weekly,* 20 Mar. 1914, which pointed out the complications of two undergraduate Colleges and degrees.

18. In 1914 the Executive Committee called a special February meeting to discuss the potential usefulness of alumni associations. The committee from the Central West—L. S. Haslam and I. N. Bloom—gave two-thirds of its report to the Western high-school problem: *The Year's Work of the Alumni Advisory Board,* 1912–13 and 1913–14 (see also Chapter 20, below).

    For the Cincinnati meeting of the Midwest alumni, L. S. Haslam suggested a list of topics, from which Adams chose "Better Educational Team-Work at New Haven" rather than "Does Yale Need Another Undergraduate College?" Adams was in some doubt as to treatment and proposed a public speech in general terms, to be followed by free questioning and discussion. After a lively discussion of the third college, curriculum, and entrance requirements, three resolutions were presented, expressing "endorsement" of Adams' views and noting with "satisfaction" and pledging "support" to such readjustment of the curriculum as would, without lowering entrance standards, bring entrance and courses into closer relation with high schools. Taft and Phelps led an attack that changed "endorsement" to "interest" and tabled "satisfaction" and "support" of any change in the curriculum. *Eleventh Annual Meeting of the Associated Western Yale Clubs,* and the letters of Haslam to Adams, 28 Apr., 1 June, Adams to Haslam, 3, (?) May, Bloom to Adams,

25 June 1914, G. B. Adams Collection, "Letters—Yale etc.," File 178.

19. *Report of the President and Deans, 1913–14*, 25–27. See also *Yale Alumni Weekly*, 5 July 1914. Adams commented that he had never expected the third college to be taken as a solution for creating a more intellectual atmosphere: that was an exceedingly important but entirely different question. For the problem he had been discussing, he could only repeat "that a university which prides itself upon being a national institution ought to be ashamed to let such a situation go on from year to year with no serious attempt to change it." Draft of a letter "not used" in comment on part of the President's report in the *Alumni Weekly*, Dec. 18, 1914, G. B. Adams Collection, "Letters—Yale etc.," File 178.

20. E. J. Phelps to G. B. Adams, 2 June 1914. G. B. Adams Collection, *loc. cit.* See also *The Year's Work of the Alumni Advisory Board, 1914–15*, 13–14; and Chapter 24 below.

REFERENCE NOTES FOR
CHAPTER 20 · COLLEGE AND NATION: THE
ENTRANCE PROBLEM

The amorphous literature on the admissions problem is unmanageable. For this chapter of Yale's relations with other colleges, with the secondary schools, with the high-school movement, the College Entrance Examination Board, and its own Western alumni I have relied to a considerable extent on the speeches and reports of Robert Nelson Corwin. Corwin not only served as Chairman of the Sheffield Scientific School Committee on Admission, 1900–19, and as Chairman of the Joint Committee on Admissions established by the Corporation in 1912 and reorganized as the Board of Admissions, 1919–33, but was Yale's representative on the College Entrance Examination Board from 1910 to 1934 and its Chairman from 1916 to 1919. His numerous contributions to the *Yale Alumni Weekly* and his "Comprehensive Examinations of the College Entrance Examination Board," *Education,* Jan. 1917, 37:302–11 are indispensable; but perhaps his best survey of the high-school and Latin problem is "The Western High School and the Eastern University," printed in the *Yale Alumni Weekly,* 16 May 1913, and in *Tenth Annual Meeting of the Associated Western Yale Clubs . . . May 2 and 3, 1913.*

The only comprehensive historical analysis of Yale's admissions policies is the unpublished doctoral thesis (Yale 1948) "Educational Factors Affecting the Entrance Requirements of Yale College," by Harold Potter Rodes, Ph.D. '48. I am indebted to Dr. Rodes for allowing me to make free use of the summaries and quotations in his lively study. Among the primary sources, in addition to the records of the College Faculty, the Letters, annual Reports, and other pronouncements of President Hadley are of first interest, especially the inaugural address and his article on "The Use and Control of Examinations," both printed in *The Education of the American Citizen,* 191–217, and "Con-

660

flicting Views Regarding Entrance Examinations," in *Official Report of the Fifteenth Annual Meeting of the New England Association of Colleges and Preparatory Schools . . . 1900* (Chicago 1900).

For the determined agitation among Yale's Western alumni the student should consult the columns of the *Yale Alumni Weekly,* the successive Reports of the Alumni Advisory Board, 1911–14, and the printed proceedings of the Associated Western Yale Clubs for 1913 and 1914. Of particular value for the regional and national dimensions of the problem are the *Official Reports* of the Annual Meetings of the New England Association of Colleges and Preparatory Schools, the *Annual Report* of the College Entrance Examination Board, and the *Journal of the Proceedings and Addresses* of the thirty-fifth and fifty-third annual meetings of the National Education Association (1896, 1905).

The head quotations are from the partial report of Dean Jones' speech to Associated Western Yale Clubs, in the *Yale Alumni Weekly,* 26 May 1911, and the fuller report of the discussions, with President Hadley's address, in the issue of 2 June.

1. Several developments had been bringing dissatisfaction to a head. Dean Jones' first report, like the penultimate reports of Dean Wright, had found high-school boys, in spite of a poorer entrance showing, doing better work in College. In particular, the Chicago Yale Club was impressed by the standing of its scholarship boys. The *Annual Reports* of the Carnegie Association for the Advancement of Teaching had received much attention; the section of the Fourth Report on the provenance of college students had been analyzed in the *Alumni Weekly.* Also the Harvard New Plan produced much discussion in the spring of 1911. *Report of the President and Deans, 1906–07,* 88–98; *1907–08,* 42; *1909–10,* 88; *Yale Alumni Weekly,* 25 Mar., 1 Apr. 1910, 27 Jan., 17, 24, 31 Mar., 7, 14 Apr., and 12 May 1911.

2. For repeated expressions of Hadley's views, see *Yale Alumni Weekly,* 9 Mar. 1904, 2 June 1911, 19 Jan., 1 Mar. 1912; *Report of the President and Deans, 1904–05,* 19–20; *1911–12,* 10–11.

3. Typical expressions of alumni sentiment may be found in *Yale Alumni Weekly,* 7 June 1912, 2 May 1913, 10 Apr. 1914, 5 Feb., 28 May 1915. Dean Jones denied that the alumni conception of Yale as "aristocratic," "a rich man's college," was justified: Yale had "no fear of being overrun by a horde of the 'criminal rich,' "

but she was not getting enough high-school and Western boys. *Ibid.,* 19 Jan. 1912.

4. "The Western High School and the Eastern University."

5. On the international comparison Corwin and others made much of the report on American Rhodes Scholars published in the *Fifth Annual Report of the Carnegie Foundation for the Advancement of Teaching . . . October 1910,* 56–63.

6. Hadley had discussed the matter of standards and examinations in *The Education of the American Citizen,* 199–200. The *Alumni Weekly* commended this paper of 1901 as a "Yale view of the matter," 17 Mar. 1911. Speakers at the Associated Western meeting of 1913, and Corwin and G. H. Nettleton, conceded the consideration had weight, *ibid.,* 20 Mar. 1914, 15 Mar. 1912.

7. See particularly N. Glicksman of Milwaukee, *ibid.,* 2 June 1911, I. N. Bloom of Louisville, 7 June 1912, and Corwin's forthright attack, 20 Mar. 1914. Fox '74, Rector of the Hopkins Grammar School 1885–1901, was now conducting the University School in New Haven. He had been irritated by descriptions of the coaching school as a combination of highway robbery and deceitful promise, an excrescence. See the letters in the *Alumni Weekly* of 24 Mar., 7, 14 Apr. 1911, 5 May 1911; also Hadley to G. J. Pierce, Stanford University, 5 Apr. 1907, Hadley Letters.

8. Hadley to H. W. Wright, Lake Forest College, Ill., 14 Sept. 1908, Hadley Letters.

9. The Carnegie Foundation gave the percentages, for the fall of 1909, of students admitted from private schools to leading colleges:

Admission only by Examination	%	Admission by Certificate	%
Columbia University	23	Cornell University	33
Harvard University	47	University of Michigan	9
Massachusetts Institute of		University of Minnesota	5
Technology	29	University of Missouri	10
Princeton University	78	Western Reserve	6
Radcliffe College	24	University of Wisconsin	8
Stevens Institute of Technology	63		
Yale University	65		

Fourth Annual Report of the Carnegie Foundation for the Advancement of Teaching . . . October 1909 (1910), 148.

10. The Associated Western Yale Clubs, organized in 1904, had

been a main force in launching the Alumni Advisory Board, to bring Western influence to bear as it could not be done in the Corporation. *Yale Alumni Weekly*, 1 Mar. 1905. In 1911 it resolved to make its meetings occasions of serious discussion as well as joyful reunion. At this same time its members were carrying on a successful campaign to elect a Western member to the Corporation—John V. Farwell of Chicago—and planning to organize the Yale Bureau. For their interest in the third college, see Chapter 19.

11. Corwin, unpublished "Reminiscences." The Governing Board at the same time was voting against giving up its Latin requirement. Chittenden, *History of the Sheffield Scientific School*, 2:478.

12. In 1895 the Scientific School had dropped arithmetic and geography but increased the Latin and mathematics slightly, and added English literature, English history, elementary French or German, and botany. In 1899 ancient history, and the science alternatives of chemistry and physics had been added. In 1911 mechanical drawing, medieval and modern European history, and advanced French or German (for the engineers) were added to the optionals. The abandonment of Latin for the engineering candidates went into effect in 1911, but simultaneously the Latin requirement for the Select Course was slightly *increased* to meet the usual secondary-school course. When Latin became optional for all in 1912 the change was based flatly on the desire to keep in touch with the schools, not on dissatisfaction with the requirement. *Report of the President and Deans, 1911–12,* 150.

13. Actually, it could not have solved the problem entirely, for the needs of its scientific and engineering students required a substantial amount of mathematics for entrance—whereas the high schools were beginning to abandon their mathematics along with their Latin. In 1915–16 Select Course candidates would be allowed to substitute additional language or science for part of the mathematics requirement.

14. This quotation, and much of the account which follows, are taken directly, and often nearly word for word, from the excellent passages on Yale's school relations in H. P. Rodes' thesis, 123, 107–08, 111–12.

15. "The Use and Control of Examinations," 196, and cf. "Conflicting Views Regarding Entrance Examinations."

16. *Report of the Committee on Admission Examinations by a Joint Examining Board Presented to the New England Association of College and Preparatory Schools . . . 1900* (Cambridge 1901). Owing to doubts and opposition on the part of a number of colleges, this plan for an examining board was not adopted by the New England Association—which left the New England colleges the choice of forming their own certificating board or accepting the Middle States examinations. This division had been brought about not only by social and intellectual differences of long standing but by the politics of intercollegiate rivalry. General accounts are *The Work of the College Entrance Examination Board 1901–1925* (New York 1926); C. M. Fuess, *The College Board. Its First Fifty Years* (New York 1950).

    For Yale Hadley felt that it was essential to keep in touch with Harvard and the other New England colleges; but failing agreement there he was inclined to use his influence for the Middle States examinations. For the Yale College Entrance Committee, Professor Morris expressed a "considerable expectation" that the plan would be adopted when the Association had put it into form for the colleges to act. *Official Report . . . of the New England Association . . .* (1901), 35–37. Meanwhile Yale was one of the universities willing to accept the C.E.E.B. examination certificates, and in fact did so in 1901.

17. See particularly Hadley's discussion in *Report of the President and Deans, 1904–05*, 18–23, and the opinions from the schools, 62. Also Hadley's letter to Wilson Farrand, Newark, N.J., 23 Nov. 1905, Hadley Letters. Cf. W. L. Cross, *Connecticut Yankee*, 132–34; Rodes, *op. cit.*, 95–96. The following passage on arguments against comprehensives is from Rodes, 105.

18. Corwin, "Comprehensive Examinations of the College Entrance Examination Board."

19. Hadley to W. M. Butler, St. Louis, Mo., 7 Dec. 1911, Hadley Letters. The recommendation of the New England Association was reported in *Yale Alumni Weekly*, 27 Jan. 1911, and *Harvard Alumni Bulletin*, 8 Feb. 1911, with Harvard insisting that this was not a combination of certificate and examinations. Hadley's willingness at this point to let Harvard steal the ball and do all the scoring is hard to explain, unless on the grounds that he was himself too busy as Chairman of the Railroad Securities Commission and was trusting to Dean Jones for energetic leadership.

20. *Yale Alumni Weekly*, 6, 27 Oct. 1911, 28 Feb. 1913, citing President Lowell's Report. See also Hadley to Lowell, 6 Nov. 1911, Hadley Letters.

21. *Yale Alumni Weekly*, 7 June 1912. Hadley could not refrain from remarking, in this address to the Western alumni and in his Report for 1910–11, that he had suggested the idea ten years before. It might be well to let Harvard experiment with the practical difficulties of combining certificate and examination, while Yale tried to reframe examinations in a comprehensive direction. For the preceding quotations in text see Hadley to Clarence D. Kingsley, Brooklyn, N. Y., 27 Nov. 1911, Hadley Letters; *Yale Alumni Weekly*, 1 Mar. 1912.

22. Rodes, 18, citing Faculty Record and Reports of 16 May 1911.

23. *Report of the President and Deans, 1911–12*, 95; *1912–13*, 105–06.

24. Faculty Record, 2, 16 May 1912, 27 Feb. 1913, and the accompanying committee Reports. The *Yale Alumni Weekly*, 7 Mar. 1913, simultaneously with the appearance of the new *Catalogue*, gave a full exposition of the changes and a history of the movement for reform.

25. Quotations from the *Yale Alumni Weekly*, 14 Mar. 1913.

26. *Ibid.*, 14 Apr. 1911, 5, 21, 28 Nov. 1913.

27. *Ibid.*, 3 Apr. 1914. Eight years later a study of 300-odd colleges granting over 500 degrees would produce these revealing statistics:

Sections	% Degrees Requiring Latin		% Latin Degrees Requiring 2 Units		% Latin Degrees Requiring 3 Units		% Latin Degrees Requiring 4 Units	
	1913	1922	1913	1922	1913	1922	1913	1922
Middle	82	54	12	9	8	24	80	68
Southern	76	51	9	14	40	41	51	45
New England	75	62	0	0	23	40	77	60
North Central	37	20	23	43	10	11	66	46
Western	33	6	43	0	14	0	43	100

H. C. McKown, *The Trend of College Entrance Requirements, 1913–1922*, United States Bureau of Education, Bulletin, 1924, No. 35 (Washington 1925), 140–51.

665

28. *Yale Alumni Weekly,* 22 May 1914; speeches of Professor Corwin and Dean Jones at the Kentucky alumni meeting, *ibid.,* 22 Jan. 1915.

29. Faculty Record, 7 Jan., 8 Apr. 1915, and *Yale Alumni Weekly,* 16 Apr. 1915.

30. For the history, theory, and practice of conditions, at Yale and in general, see Dean Wright's account in the *Report of the President and Deans, 1908–09,* 61–67; *Third Annual Report of . . . the Carnegie Foundation for the Advancement of Teaching . . . October 1909* (New York 1909), 107–12; Hadley to H. S. Pritchett, New York, 10 Nov. 1909, Hadley Letters; McKown, 127–33. Conversation of G.W.P. with C. W. Mendell, 5 Jan. 1948.

31. *Report of the President and Deans, 1914–15,* 27–31, 128–31.

32. The Bureau at first was administered by the Rev. C. L. Kitchel, who became Secretary in 1904. He was succeeded by W. H. Sallmon '94, 1909–14, and E. R. Embree '06, 1914–17. The annual reports of the Bureau are published in the *Report of the President and Deans,* from 1900. For student costs see *1902–03,* 164–66; *1907–08,* 242–43; *1915–16,* 79, 85. Also *Student Self-Support,* 1919.

33. *The Education of the American Citizen,* 221–22. *Report of the President and Deans, 1907–08,* 246–47. *An Account of the Alumni Advisory Board,* 30–33. *Report of the Treasurer of Yale University, 1907–08,* 5–6.

The return to required studies, in years overshadowed by the approaching cloud of war, has to be worked out from local materials: the Record of the Academical Professors, the Faculty Record, the *Report of the President and Deans*, the Hadley Letters, and the *Yale Alumni Weekly*.

The head quotation is from the Morris Committee Report in Permanent Officers Reports, 1910–21.

1. Rec. Acad. Profs., 23 Apr. 1914. See Professor Adams in *Yale Alumni Weekly*, 5 June 1914.
2. *Yale Alumni Weekly*, 23 Jan. 1914.
3. *Ibid.*, 16 Oct. 1914. He continued his attack on the entrance requirements and the curriculum in the issues of 4 Dec. 1914, 28 May 1915, 31 Mar. 1916. The curriculum of the future should lead to the degree of Bachelor of Sociology instead of Arts.
4. *Ibid.*, 23 Oct., 6, 13, 27 Nov., 4 Dec. 1914. Yandell Henderson '95, Professor of Physiology, later suggested that colleges give the B.A. degree for two years' work, accepting whatever the professional schools desired, with a nonvocational C.G.L.—Cultivated Gentleman of Leisure—for other students. *Science*, 18 Feb. 1916, n.s. 43:241–42.
5. *Yale Alumni Weekly*, 3 July, 23 Oct., 27 Nov., 18 Dec. 1914.
6. C. M. Bakewell to Dean Jones, 1, 4 Dec. 1914; E. S. Dana to Bakewell, 24 Dec. 1914; Bakewell to Dana, 14 Jan. 1915; Dana to Bakewell, 15 Mar. 1915, copies in Samuel H. Fisher Papers, Yale Miscellaneous Correspondence and Papers, 1920–30.
7. Corporation Records, Feb. 1915; *Yale Alumni Weekly*, 18 June 1915; *Report of the President and Deans, 1914–15*, 164–65. The lecturers on the Ralph Hill Thomas Foundation were President Lowell of Harvard and President Vincent of the University of

Minnesota in 1915; President Hyde of Bowdoin and President Meiklejohn of Amherst in 1916; President Alderman of the University of Virginia and Dean Briggs of Harvard in 1917. On the Bureau of Appointments, see Hadley to C. D. Reid, Springfield, Mass., 4 Nov. 1911, 22 Nov. 1915, Hadley Letters.

One other experiment pushed through the University Council was the device of a short summer "reading term." The College dormitories were to be opened early in the fall to all those who wished to do extra work, compete for prizes, study for Honors theses, anticipate courses (or get ahead on business in connection with University organizations). The Corporation vote on the reading term was announced in the *Yale Daily News,* 18 May 1915 and the *Alumni Weekly,* 21 May. Faculty members were expected to cooperate by suggesting reading but they were not required to be present in September. One student gathered lists of reading from the departments for publication in the June *Courant* but queried the *News* in vain for some really definite information about procedure. *Yale Daily News,* 10 June.

8. Rec. Acad. Profs., 30 Apr. 1914. The other members were Adams (replaced by C. B. Tinker in the fall), A. Johnson, H. E. Gregory, and H. C. Emery. The committee presented a preliminary report at the end of May, for study during the summer. *Ibid.,* 28 May 1914, and editorial comment in the *Yale Alumni Weekly,* 12 June 1914.

9. *Ibid.,* 16 Apr. 1915.

10. Rec. Acad. Profs., 22 Apr. 1915, and Permanent Officers Reports, 1910–21, 45–48. The quotations that follow are from this report.

11. *Catalogue of the Officers and Students of Yale College, 1846–7* (New Haven 1846), 35. "For a more particular view of the plan of education in Yale College" the *Catalogue* referred readers to the famous Report of 1828.

12. Rec. Acad. Profs., 13 May 1915. Cf. Hadley's speech to the Western Alumni, 22 May, in praise of the things so often despised as unpractical. *Yale Alumni Weekly,* 28 May 1915.

13. Rec. Acad. Profs., 7, 14 Oct., 4, 11 Nov., 2 Dec. 1915, and Faculty Record, 15 Dec. 1915. The requirements adopted are in the *Report of the President and Deans, 1915–16,* 130–31.

14. Originally, Morris' committee had recommended a third require-

668

ment in each year. Sophomores were to be required to take a course from the third Division of studies (that is, from philosophy, education, history, anthropology, economics, or law). Freshmen were to take either English or history. Moreover, mathematics would not have been acceptable as a substitute for science in the second Freshman requirement. On consideration, Dana's Course of Study Committee struck these out, and the Faculty sustained Dana.

15. Paradoxically, the first result of negotiation with the professional Schools was to increase the law hours from eight to ten, and to concede fifteen hours for premedical study. But all of these hours would henceforth have to be confined to Senior year. And the Yale College Faculty reserved the right to review the whole matter in 1919—and decide what combined courses "if any" were wise thereafter. *Report of the President and Deans, 1915–16,* 131–32, and Rec. Acad. Profs., 7 Oct. 1914, 27 Jan., 3 Feb. 1916.

16. Rec. Acad. Profs., 2 Dec. 1915.

17. *Report of the President and Deans, 1915–16,* 18, 132–33; *1916–17,* 24; *Yale Alumni Weekly,* 26 Mar. 1915.

18. Dana voluntarily retired from the Faculty in June 1917. See the appreciation of his service in *Report of the President and Deans, 1916–17,* 125–26.

19. There isn't anything on Tinker the educational statesman as good as is the characterization of Tinker the teacher by W. S. Lewis in his introduction to *The Age of Johnson,* edited by F. W. Hilles (New Haven 1949).

20. Faculty Reports, 27 Apr. 1917.

21. One should notice that these requirements were stated not in terms of fields or even of departments or subjects, but in terms of specific courses, some of which Freshmen could not take. The courses had to have many divisions and many instructors; the modern languages would also be offered at several levels. But—with this exception—the same assignments would be covered, at the same pace presumably, in all.

22. Faculty Record, 27 Apr., 10 May 1917. *Report of the President and Deans, 1916–17,* 159–60. The new plan was to go into effect in the fall for Freshmen, if legal counsel saw no objection. For

a pungent attack on allowing the College to become a mere feeder for the professional Schools—and defense of a required course of study to be laid down by men of experience acquainted with students and the society in which they were to live—see A. G. Keller, "The B.A. Degree in America," *Scientific Monthly*, Feb. 1918, 6:142–56.

REFERENCE NOTES FOR
CHAPTER 22 · AMERICAN HIGHER
EDUCATION AND WAR

The development and organization of the new system of national defense in its general relation to the political background is given in F. L. Paxson, *American Democracy and the World War*, I, *Pre-War Years, 1913–17*, and II, *America at War, 1917–18* (Boston 1936, 1939). But Paxson succinctly remarks that the colleges and universities were eager and much better organized than the agencies of the Council of National Defense, then omits to tell their story. Military training before 1914 is described in detail in I. L. Reeves, *Military Education in the United States* (Burlington, Vt., 1914). The beginnings of the preparedness movement are dealt with in R. B. Perry, *The Plattsburg Movement* (New York 1921). Two very useful surveys are P. R. Kolbe, *The Colleges in War Time and After* (New York 1919) and C. F. Thwing, *The American Colleges and Universities in the Great War, 1914–1919* (New York 1920). The discussion at the meeting of the Association of American Universities in 1919 brought forth opinions of university presidents fresh from the Students' Army Training Corps ordeal. Association of American Universities, *Journal of Proceedings and Addresses . . . 1918* (Chicago, n.d.).

The experiences of American colleges in past wars must be put together from individual college histories: cf. S. E. Morison, *Three Centuries of Harvard*, 28, 133–63, 214, 302–04, 413, 450–61; T. J. Wertenbaker, *Princeton, 1746–1896*, 55–62, 111, 134–35, 265–71. For Yale consult H. P. Johnston, *Yale and Her Honor-Roll in the American Revolution* (New York 1888); Ellsworth Eliot Jr., *Yale in the Civil War* (New Haven 1932); W. H. Taft, "Yale's Contribution to the Spanish-American War," in *The Book of the Yale Pageant*, 122–26; the chapters on the Revolution and the Civil War in Kingsley, 2:198–273, and the chapter "Patriots and Soldiers" in Stokes, *Memorials of Eminent Yale Men*, 2:284–97. These are, for reasons this chapter will make clear,

671

records rather of men *from* Yale in war than of military activities by or in the College.

The head quotations are from *The Public Records of the Colony of Connecticut*, 8:379, and *Addresses and Proceedings . . . at the Commemorative Celebration, Held July 26th, 1865, in Honor of the Alumni of Yale College Who Were in the Military or Naval Service of the United States during the Recent War; Together with the Names Comprised in the Roll of Honor* (New Haven 1866), 51.

1. Besides these rules of college discipline Connecticut, following the Massachusetts and Harvard precedents, in 1703 exempted scholars of the Collegiate School from watching and warding, etc. And the militia law of 1741 exempted the rector, tutors, students, and M.A.'s—along with the holders of government posts, justices of the peace, physicians, surgeons, schoolmasters, attorneys, one miller to a mill, mariners and ferrymen, herdsmen, sheriffs, the lame and disabled, Negroes and Indians—a clear summary of the socially indispensable and the militarily undesirable. In Dec. 1776 a special alarm list of males aged 16–60 also specifically exempted the President, tutors, and students. See H. P. Johnston, 13–14; *Collegii Yalensis Statuta* (1759, 1764) and *The Laws of Yale College* (1774, 1787); C. J. Hoadley, ed., *The Public Records of the Colony of Connecticut*, 4:440, 8:379, and *The Public Records of the State of Connecticut*, 1:92.

2. At the great commemorative celebration at the close of the Civil War, President Woolsey said: "When I think of such things, I rejoice that these high principles have animated our young men. They furnish a more substantial foundation of honor, than all the scholarships and all the science in this country."

REFERENCE NOTES FOR
CHAPTER 23 · YALE AND THE GUNS

The years 1914–19 are among the most chaotic and most generously documented of Yale's entire history. Stirred by the mounting excitement the *Yale Alumni Weekly* poured out reports, orders, and addresses, letters from abroad with running commentaries, special issues and special articles, all as rousing and bewildering as the times. In the files of the *Yale Daily News* are many details on the gradual mobilization; and on official policy the *Reports of the President and Deans* are of the first importance. The most revealing and indispensable documents, however, are the thousand-odd letters of the President who almost singlehandedly conducted Yale to war.

On the early neutrality period, see the *News* and the *Alumni Weekly*. There is an interesting group of letters from Hadley to friends in Germany. "I am making every effort to have the students here look at the problems of the war seriously and dispassionately; and I think I have had some success. Certainly the atmosphere here at New Haven is fairer and less emotional than in most other places to which I go." But, he told them frankly, it was difficult to accept the German invasion of Belgium and almost impossible to accept the German justification of it. To an English friend he described the difference in political ethics as appalling. Hadley to Herr Friedrich Schmidt, Kultusministerium, Berlin, 28 Nov. 1914; to Professor F. von der Leyen, Munich, 9 Nov., 21 Jan., 17 Mar. 1915; to William Acworth, London, 19 Oct. 1914, Hadley Letters.

The beginnings of the preparedness debate are given in the *News* of Dec. 1914. Hadley's position became unmistakable on 15 Apr. 1915 when President H. S. Drinker of Lehigh appealed in the *News* for summer training camps and quoted Hadley's letter in *The National Reserve Corps,* published by the Society of the Reserve Corps. This Society had been formed in Aug. 1914, and in Nov. an Advisory Board of University Presidents had been created with Hadley a member and

President J. G. Hibben of Princeton as chairman. The development of Hadley's ideas, in considerable detail, was given in private letters to Major General Wood, 30 Mar. 1914, 11 Jan. 1915; to Hon. Carroll S. Page, U.S. Senate, Washington, D.C., 21 Oct. 1914; and to R. R. McCormick, Chicago, Ill., 14 Dec. 1914. I am indebted also to a conversation with Dean Jones, 14 Mar. 1941. The most important document of the prebattery period remains Hadley's Report for 1914–15, *Report of the President and Deans*, 3–26, which is summarized and quoted in this chapter.

For the story of the Yale batteries, "The Organization of the Yale Undergraduate Batteries," *Yale Alumni Weekly*, 10 Mar. 1916, and Colonel Robert M. Danford's account in *Yale in the World War*, 1: 427–31, should be consulted; also *History of the Class of MCMXVII* (New Haven 1917), 54–55, 401–10, and *History of the Class of Nineteen Hundred and Eighteen* (New Haven 1918), 377–80. Through the summer of 1916 Hadley carried on a lively correspondence, punctuated by telegrams, with Brigadier General Cole, Major General Wood, A. C. Goodyear, Vance McCormick, Henry L. Stimson, Charles Evans Hughes, and others, Hadley Letters.

The change-over from the militia batteries to an R.O.T.C. system was a complicated negotiation. The relevant sections of the National Defense Act and General Orders No. 49 are printed in P. R. Kolbe, *The Colleges in War Time and After*. See also John Dickinson, *The Building of an Army* (New York 1922). General summaries of the Yale units were given by Hadley in *Report of the President and Deans, 1916–17*, 7–12, and in the speeches by him, Colonel Danford, and Captain Potter, in the *Alumni Weekly*, 8 June 1916. But the detailed and exasperating story has to be traced in Hadley's letters, notably those to A. C. Goodyear, Buffalo, N.Y., 5 June, 19 Oct. 1916; to Colonel Danford, 4, 10, 18 Aug., 3 Oct. 1916; to Major C. P. Summerall, War Department, 18, 25 Aug., 8 Sept. 1916; to General A. L. Mills, War Department, 18 Aug., 5 Sept. 1916; to Major General Leonard Wood, Governors Island, N.Y., 31 Aug. 1916; to Major General H. L. Scott, Chief of Staff, War Department, 30, 31 Oct., 1916, 29 Jan. 1917. For the Faculty action, see Faculty Record 3 Oct., 2 Nov., 14, 21 Dec. 1916; Rec. Acad. Profs., 7, 14 Dec. 1916; *Report of the President and Deans, 1916–17*, 157.

The preparation for war, Jan.–Apr. 1917, is graphically portrayed in the *News* and the *Alumni Weekly*, especially in the latter's issues of

9 Mar. and 8 June. For the Aero Club and the Naval Unit, see the *Alumni Weekly* for 20 Oct. 1916, 26 Jan., 30 Mar., and 4 May 1917. A "Memorandum on the Attitude of the University in the Present Crisis," drafted by the Secretary, was issued on 28 Mar., signed by the President, Secretary, and Treasurer of the University, the Dean of the College and the Director of the Scientific School, and the Professor of Military Science. This group was formally constituted an Emergency War Council by the Prudential Committee in April. This and later memoranda are given in *Yale in the World War*, 1:366–73. See also Dean Jones' statement in the *News*, 21 Mar. 1917. For the Jordan episode, see *Yale Daily News*, 29, 30, 31 Mar., 2 Apr. 1917; *Yale Alumni Weekly*, 6 Apr. 1917, and Hadley in *Report of the President and Deans, 1916–17*, 21. Phelps describes the incident vividly and at length in his *Autobiography*, 639–43. Conversation of G.W.P. with the Reverend A. P. Stokes, 13 Feb. 1940. For the account of the beginning of the lecture, and Phelps' riposte, I am indebted to Dudley C. Lunt '18.

The official acts of the University during the war are compiled in *Yale in the World War*, 1:374–86. The *Report of the President and Deans* for 1916–17 and 1917–18 give general accounts. But the files of the *News* and the *Alumni Weekly* are the great source for the shifting current of events, plans, and sentiment, with Hadley's letters invaluable for the multitudinous problems. See also *Yale and the Guns* (published by the New York Yale Club, 1917).

For the origins, organization, and problems of the Students' Army Training Corps, see Kolbe, especially 69–73; Thwing; and the address by Brigadier General R. L. Rees and the following discussion at the December meeting of the Association of American Universities, in *Journal of Proceedings and Addresses . . . 1918*, 106–28. Also Hadley's letters, and his statement at the opening of College in the *Alumni Weekly*, 20 Sept. 1918, with the fuller explanation in the issue of 27 Sept., and the article "A Militarized Yale," 11 Oct. 1918.

The head quotations are from *Report of the President and Deans, 1914–15*, 25; and *Yale in the World War*, 1:10.

1. *Independent*, 24 Aug. 1914, 79:271.
2. *Yale Alumni Weekly*, 23 Oct. 1914; *New York Times*, 3 Nov. 1914.
3. Professors W. C. Abbott, Charles Seymour, and H. C. Emery. Henry W. Farnam, whose appointment as Roosevelt exchange

professor at Berlin was canceled by the war, contributed "Political Theory and the War" to the *Alumni Weekly*, 16 Oct. 1914, and Hadley wrote on "The Political Theories of Treitschke" for the *Yale Review*, Jan. 1915, 4:235–46. The check he received he sent to the relief of refugees from Louvain, thus making Treitschke "contribute to Belgian relief in spite of himself." Hadley to Lady Osler, Oxford, England, 23 Dec. 1914, Hadley Letters.

4. On 14 Dec. the National Security League had a letter in the *News* entitled: "Striving for Peace; but Ready for War." The *News* editors came out in favor of summer camps but opposed military drill in College, 12 Jan., 19 Apr. 1915.

5. W. L. Phelps, "War," *North American Review*, Nov. 1914, 200: 673–77. In Apr. 1916 Phelps delivered a pacifist address before the Connecticut Peace Society which was misquoted in the press and brought down on him a torrent of criticism. *Yale Alumni Weekly*, 19 Apr. 1916.

6. S. V. Benét, *The Beginning of Wisdom*, 97.

7. Hadley to G. H. Myers, Stafford Springs, Conn., 19 Aug. 1915.

8. A rather more favorable account is given by Director Chittenden in his *History of the Sheffield Scientific School*, 2:503–05.

9. For Hadley's negotiations with Wood, the State Militia, and his own Corporation, and for the procuring of an armory, see Hadley to Brigadier General G. M. Cole, Adjutant General, Hartford, Conn., 19 Aug. 1915; to A. C. Goodyear, Buffalo, N.Y., 19 Aug., 17, 24 Sept., 11 Oct., 17, 18 Dec., 1915; 18 Feb., 13, 18, 29 May, 5 June, 4 Dec. 1916. In Apr.–June 1917, from funds raised by A. Conger Goodyear '99, the armory was completed. See account of the armory dedication, *Yale Alumni Weekly*, 6 July 1917.

10. There are many references and tributes to Danford in the Hadley Letters. See also the addresses at the dinner given him at the New York Yale Club, *Yale Alumni Weekly*, 8 June 1917. After the war he was Yale's first choice for Dean of Students and would probably have accepted had he not been appointed Commandant at West Point.

11. A. P. Stokes, "The Question of Preparedness," *Yale Review*, Jan. 1916, 5:241–66. It has been suggested to me that Stokes' stand in

this matter helped kill his chance to succeed Hadley in the presidency.

12. This course was to be taken in addition to the normal 60 hours, and was to be open only to summer-camp Juniors or Seniors who were three hours ahead in their work. One hour of advance credit was voted to the Yale batterymen. Rec. Acad. Profs., 7 Oct., 2 Dec. 1915, 6 Jan. 1916.

13. *Yale Alumni Weekly,* 21 Jan., 4 Feb., 1916. On 10 Apr. the Washington alumni bluntly recommended "that credit be given toward bachelor degrees at Yale University for work in military history, science, and training." And at Commencement Henry T. Rogers '66, reviewing the grudging concessions by the Faculty, insisted that there should be a course of military instruction counting toward the degree and open to all students, whether they had advanced credits or not. *Ibid.,* 21 Apr., 2 June, 7 July 1916.

14. *Yale Daily News,* 19 Jan. 1917.

15. *Yale Daily News,* 2 Apr. 1917. For the next six months, as Phelps would later recall, "I received (not once from Yale, but from many places all over the country) insulting letters, some signed, some unsigned. . . . President Hadley and the Corporation were daily besought to expel me from my professorship, being told that instead of being on the Faculty, I ought to be in prison. I shall always be grateful to President Hadley for standing by me, especially because he did not agree with me at all. He was subjected to tremendous pressure but he insisted that I had a right to do exactly what I had done." Phelps, *Autobiography,* 642–43.

16. The men in training under the S.A.T.C. were distributed approximately as follows: Artillery unit, 558; Engineer, Chemical, and Signal units, 236; Medical and Premedical units, 123—a total of 917. The Naval Training Unit numbered 556. The Yale Army Laboratory School, to which the Army sent all its men to be trained for base and mobile hospitals, etc., numbered 600; and the Signal Corps Training School for officer candidates enrolled another 350.

17. Conversations of G.W.P. with Dean Jones, 14 Mar. 1941; with Professor Robert D. French, 29 Oct. 1942.

18. Editorials in the *Alumni Weekly*, 19 Apr., 3 May 1918, and many letters in the Hadley Papers, e.g., to G. B. Richards, Kansas City, Mo., 26 Apr.; to E. J. Phelps, Chicago, 13 May 1918. See also *Report of the President and Deans, 1917–18,* 105–06; *1918–19,* 141.
19. Cf. H. S. Canby, *American Memoir,* 261.

A full and fair history of the great Reorganization is next to impossible
to write. The movement had too many causes and participants. No one
predicted it; no single party dictated or controlled it; no one completely understood its implications; and few remained calm. Indeed
several important elements felt deeply disappointed and hurt, and the
memories are still alive. The consequences for good or ill, for the University as a whole, I postpone for later treatment. The present chapter
deals primarily with its origins and with its immediate effects for Yale
College. It is based on the following sources: *Report of the Committee
on Educational Policy to the Yale Corporation, March 17, 1919* (New
Haven 1919); *Report of the Alumni Committee of Yale University on
a Plan for University Development,* 14 Feb., 1919; A. P. Stokes, "University Reorganization Problems and Policies," *Yale Alumni Weekly,*
17 Jan. 1919; the Minutes and Papers of the Alumni Committee on a
Plan for University Development; the extensive and valuable files on
the Alumni Committee in the Samuel H. Fisher Papers; the Alfred
L. Ripley Papers; the Henry B. Sargent Papers; conversations of G.W.P.
with alumni leaders George Grant Mason, 13 May 1940, and Samuel
H. Fisher, 22 Dec. 1938, 15 July 1940, 14 Oct., 4 Dec. 1942; communications from Secretary Stokes, 21 Nov., 5 Dec. 1947, 2 Feb. 1950; and conversations with C. B. Tinker, G. L. Hendrickson, F. S. Jones, Clive Day,
C. W. Mendell, and others of the faculty.

The columns of the *Yale Alumni Weekly,* from Nov. 1918 through
1920, are full of recommendations, arguments, and reports on Reorganization, with the alumni point of view receiving the fullest exposition.
For official acts and attitudes, the Corporation and Prudential Committee Records, the *Reports of the President and Deans,* Hadley's
Alumni Day speech as reported in the *Yale Alumni Weekly,* 28 Feb.
1919, and the files of A. P. Stokes should be consulted. Rev. Dr. William
Adams Brown, Chairman of the new Corporation Committee on Edu-

cational Policy and later Acting Provost, ultimately published a brief
account of Reorganization in *A Teacher and His Times,* 273–91.

The second of the head quotations is from the *Yale Alumni Weekly,*
22 Nov. 1918 and evidently from the hand of its editor, Edwin Oviatt.

1. W. L. Cross, *Connecticut Yankee,* 155–58.
2. *Yale Alumni Weekly,* 25 Oct., 8 Nov. 1918, 26 Sept. 1919; and
   Report of the President and Deans, 1918–19, 67–68. For Hadley's
   remarks in the general discussion of Anglo-American exchange
   at the meeting of the Association of American Universities, see
   Journal of Proceedings and Addresses . . . 1918. See also his
   address to Freshmen in the *Alumni Weekly,* 10 Jan. 1919.
3. *Report of the President and Deans, 1916–17,* 53–54, 60–61; and
   Report of the Committee on Educational Policy, 6. A. P. Stokes
   to G.W.P., 2 Feb. 1950.
4. *Yale Alumni Weekly,* 24 Sept. 1915, 25 Jan., 8 Mar., 14 June,
   22 Nov. 1918. Edwin Oviatt to Hadley, 5 Nov., 21 Nov. 1918,
   Hadley Correspondence.
5. Minutes of the Alumni Committee, 23 Nov. 1918, published in
   the *Alumni Weekly,* 20 Dec. 1918.
6. Conversation of G.W.P. with C. B. Tinker, 24 Jan. 1939. See
   the protest by "College" in the *Alumni Weekly,* 6 Dec. 1918.
7. The role played by Dean Jones in those troubled negotiations
   is far from clear. The faculty had the impression that Jones had
   rather "scuttled the Ac. cause." It wasn't that he believed in
   Reorganization. But he had not insisted on delay until the
   "Peers" of Yale College could give their official judgment. Probably the true picture would reveal a loyal Officer of the College
   who was better at dealing with boys than with plans—who was
   anxious to do what was best for all but found himself caught in
   an embittered broil that was none of his making or liking. At
   times Dean Jones seems to have listened to the graduates, at
   times to his own embattled faculty. At no time does he seem to
   have exhibited decisive leadership.
8. Both Oviatt and Fisher were disappointed with Hadley, and the
   Corporation votes of 16 Dec. E. Oviatt to S. H. Fisher, 24 Dec.
   1918, S. H. Fisher Papers, Yale Pub. Assoc. See also Fisher's address to the New Haven alumni, *Yale Alumni Weekly,* 14 Feb.
   1919.

9. The Alumni Committee Report was presented to the Corporation at the meeting of 17 Feb., referred to the Educational Policy Committee for report at a special meeting on 8 Mar. The Committee then brought in its amended report, which was formally adopted by the Corporation on 17 Mar. See *Yale Alumni Weekly* for 28 Feb., 7, 14, 21 Mar. 1919.

10. Conversation of G.W.P. with G. L. Hendrickson, 10 Dec. 1943. On their constitutional powers, cf. Hadley in *Report of the President and Deans, 1910–11*, 16–20; also Chapter 7 above. See Dean Jones in *Yale Alumni Weekly*, 21, 28 Feb. 1919. See also E. Oviatt to S. H. Fisher, 5 May 1919, and C. Seymour to Fisher, 19 Mar. 1920, S. H. Fisher Papers, Alumni Committee Nos. 2 and 4.

11. A. P. Stokes to S. H. Fisher, 30 Dec. 1918, S. H. Fisher to L. S. Welch, 29 Jan. 1920, S. H. Fisher Papers, Alumni Committee Nos. 1 and 4.

12. See the implied promise of 12 Dec., recorded in the minutes of the Yale College Faculty:

> The matter of University reorganization was brought before the Faculty and discussed informally.
>
> Professor Mims offered the following motion. Moved: that it be expressed as the opinion of this body that the cause of wise reform will best be served, if, prior to the final vote by the Corporation on any and all important measures affecting the organization, administration, regulations, course of study of Yale College, or concerning the relation of Yale to any other department or departments of the University, ample opportunity be given to this body in its corporate capacity for a thorough examination and thorough discussion of said measure or measures.
>
> After general discussion of this motion and upon the assurance of the President that it was the intention of the Corporation to take no important steps that would contravene the sentiment expressed in the motion offered, it was
> Voted: to lay the motion on the table.
>
> Faculty Record, 12 Dec. 1918.

13. C. W. Mendell to G.W.P., 15 Mar. 1941.
14. *Yale Alumni Weekly*, 31 Jan., 28 Feb. 1919.

15. *Ibid.,* 28 Feb.

16. Dean Jones, in the following afternoon session, rejected the "summer vacation fallacy," and Oviatt confessed "an entire inability to understand or accept" the idea. *Ibid.* See Oviatt to Hadley, 27 Feb., 3 Mar. 1919; W. A. Brown to Hadley, 21 Mar. 1919, Hadley Correspondence. Also Hadley to E. B. Wilson, Massachusetts Institute of Technology, 24 Mar. 1919, Hadley Letters; Hadley's open letter is in the *Alumni Weekly,* 7 Mar. 1919. See M. Hadley, *A. T. Hadley,* 212–14, for Hadley's distress at the reaction to his speech.

17. Departmental chairmen were henceforward to be appointed "on nomination of the President, after consultation with the Professors of all grades." In Apr. 1919 the Departments of History, Mathematics, and the Social Sciences vainly sent up resolutions asking for a restoration of their former powers of election. In the following fall Mr. Fisher discovered that the President was in almost all instances nominating on the recommendation of the Departments concerned.

18. For a blunt use of the figure see S. H. Fisher's speech: "The engraved parchments presented at graduation may be considered certificates entitling the holders to shares of the stock of knowledge dispensed at Yale. The graduates moreover have a pecuniary interest. [They invest.] They are the products of this great plant." In the same issue of the *Alumni Weekly,* 14 Feb. 1919, "Pater Studentis" (Oviatt) referred to "getting the most out of your help." For an outsider's view, see J. McKeen Cattell on the "Chart of Reorganization": "The most perplexing aspect . . . is to find out . . . whether the Faculties, professors, and students have any place in Yale University." *Yale Alumni Weekly,* 11 Apr. 1919.

19. S. H. Fisher to L. S. Welch, 29 Jan. 1920, and to Charles Seymour, 18 Mar. 1920; Seymour to Fisher, 19 Mar. 1920, S. H. Fisher Papers, Alumni Committee No. 4.

REFERENCE NOTES FOR
CHAPTER 25 · RECONSTRUCTION

This chapter is based on the sources listed for Chapter 24, on the *Catalogues,* and on the Record of the Permanent Officers and the Faculty Record.

The head quotation is from *Report of the President and Deans, 1920–21,* 26.

1. To the charges of research and Ph.D. domination that "choked down the interpretive genius" of promising young teachers, Professor C. M. Andrews replied that the causes of poor teaching were more likely to be found in the economic policy that hired inexperienced and inexpensive instructors and crushed them with large classes, long hours, inadequate equipment, and finances. See his letter and the skeptical editorial in the *Yale Alumni Weekly,* 28 Mar. 1919.

2. "We do not, of course, pretend to understand the problems of Yale as well as those on the ground, but I am inclined to think that a committee of graduates can understand the product to be evolved from the University education better than the teachers themselves." S. H. Fisher to A. P. Stokes, 24 Dec. 1918, S. H. Fisher Papers, Alumni Committee No. 1.

3. Following a suggestion of Hadley's the Alumni Committee appointed S. H. Fisher, F. W. Allen '00, and J. H. Hammond '92S to sit with the Committee on Educational Policy.

4. Rec. Acad. Profs., 19 Dec. 1918. The committee was Morris, Phelps, Farrand, Gregory, and Fairchild. For their report, see *ibid.,* 6, 11 Feb. 1919.

5. This was *informally* voted, 13 to 2, with three or four not voting. At this point the Professors themselves removed the disguise of *superiority,* and faced the brutal prospect of *ordinary* students without Latin. But they did not concede the B.A. And they were

683

apparently determined to prevent the alumni from setting up a business course which—if in Sheff—might be too much like the Select Course or—if in the College—too vocational. No College of Commerce or School of Business Administration was wanted.

6. *Report of the Committee on Educational Policy*, 10, 25–26. The recommendations were then sent as a courtesy to the Permanent Officers, the Alumni Committee, and other alumni officers, and published in the *Alumni Weekly*, 21 Mar. 1919.

7. Faculty Record, 15 Mar. 1919.

8. A. P. Stokes to Gustav Gruener, 20 Mar. 1919, Faculty Reports; copies also in the S. H. Fisher Papers, Alumni Committee No. 2, and the A. L. Ripley Papers.

9. A. E. Stearns of Andover was one of the headmasters who wrote to Secretary Stokes expressing strong disapproval of giving *any* Yale College degree without Latin. Stokes replied as tactfully as he could that the headmasters were divided, that the Yale Corporation with one possible exception were deeply interested in maintaining Latin as a disciplinary and cultural study, but to insist on Latin for all would be unfair to the Select Course constituency and would keep out candidates from the South and West. A. P. Stokes to A. E. Stearns, 21 Mar. 1919, A. L. Ripley Papers.

10. Rec. Acad. Profs., 17 Apr. 1919; Prudential Committee Records, 3 May; Corporation Records, May; *Yale Alumni Weekly*, 11 Apr., 23 May, 6 June 1919.

11. *Yale Alumni Weekly*, 9 May 1919. The Alumni Committee had recommended twelve courses preparatory to careers: law, theology, education, mercantile business, manufacturing, language and literature, government service, social service, journalism, transportation, art, music. After the Corporation accepted "the principle of group courses" the *Alumni Weekly* talked of "half a dozen" courses, e.g., business, law, teaching, civil administration, literature, and the arts. *Ibid.*, 25 Apr. 1919.

12. The new Department of Education was placed in the Graduate School. It was allowed to open three courses to qualified undergraduates. *Report of the President and Deans, 1920–21*, 155–59.

13. Conversation of G.W.P. with G. L. Hendrickson, 22 Dec. 1943.

14. R. N. Corwin to S. H. Fisher, 20 Oct. 1920, S. H. Fisher Papers, Yale Corporation, A–E.

15. *Report of the President and Deans, 1919–20,* 59–61, 73. He also suggested a University Course of Study Committee to be established by the University Council.

16. Anson Stokes cheerfully foresaw Sheff devoting itself to science and engineering, the Common Freshman Year developing a moral unity, and the Ph.B. attracting a new College clientele—all at less cost in complication and money than such a *tertium quid* as a third college. G. B. Adams to A. P. Stokes, 27 Oct. 1919 (draft) and Stokes to Adams, 28 Oct. 1919, G. B. Adams Collection, Letterfile 26.

17. The Board of Admissions was created 10 Jan. 1920, to become active at once. The decision was "contested rigorously" by the College Faculty, which in Apr. 1921 came close to passing a motion to set conditions for entrance from Freshman into Sophomore year. But the day for such independence was past, and finally—as Corwin later stated in his "Reminiscences"—all but a few were persuaded that bars, "even Latin bars, are not an infallible means of sorting out and selecting those best fitted for college work." Cf. Corporation Records, Jan. 1920; Records, Committee on Educational Policy, 12 Nov., 10 Dec. 1920; Faculty Record, 14 Apr. 1921; Corwin to Provost Walker, 23 Oct. 1920 (copy), S. H. Fisher Papers, Yale Corporation, A–E; and Corwin in *Report of the President and Deans, 1920–21,* 233–34.

18. *Reports to the President, 1932–33,* 11.

19. *Report of the President and Deans, 1920–21,* 26.

A Note on Origins. Credit for the invention of the Common Freshman Year is not easy to assign. In the Minutes of the Alumni Committee on a Plan for University Development, under date of 8 Dec. 1917, one finds that "the possible advantages of a consolidation of the lower years, at least, of Sheff and the College were discussed." Dean Jones, who was present, expressed the opinion however that the undergraduate units were already "as large as could be conveniently handled," and the arrangement would involve further administrative difficulties.

The first direct allusion to the possibility of a "Third College" seems to be in a letter from Oviatt to Hadley of 21 Nov. 1918. At that moment Oviatt believed in a series of four-year prescribed courses, starting with a year of common Freshman instruction and diverging afterward. But "this arrangement would not create a Junior or a Third College." Within a few days, Oviatt's thinking had progressed so far that on 6 Dec. he printed three alternative plans for reorganization, and in two of these the term Junior College was used. In one it was proposed to replace the vertical Sheff-College alignment by a horizontal division. All Freshmen and Sophomores would be together in a Junior College for general studies; all Juniors and Seniors in an upper-class College for preprofessional studies. The other plan postulated a less drastic realignment on a three-college basis. It was this latter proposal with its Junior College for Freshmen only that was taken seriously.

The next day the Prudential Committee, meeting to discuss plans for Reorganization, heard Dean Jones bring forward the scheme of a common year for Freshmen, to be followed by separation to College and Scientific School. Secretary Stokes spoke in support, and he and the President were appointed a committee to outline alternative plans and make specific recommendations.

For the special meeting of the Corporation on 16 Dec. Secretary

Stokes outlined a series of possibilities. The simplest was Chittenden's proposal to lengthen the Sheff course to four years and transfer the Master of Science degree, but not the higher engineering degrees, to the Graduate School. More radical was a proposal to consolidate all undergraduate work in a single college but divide the work for graduate degrees between the Graduate and Scientific Schools. A third plan simply reversed this idea, consolidating all graduate work in a single Graduate School, but leaving the College and Sheff as four-year undergraduate Schools. Still another way of rearranging jurisdictions was to make Yale College into a two-year College for all undergraduates, then give the Graduate and Scientific Schools control over the last two years of work for the B.A. and the Ph.B. In effect this would have created a Junior College, topped by a series of University Departments: an arrangement akin to this was being developed at the University of Chicago. However, the chief emphasis was apparently given to still a fifth or compromise proposal to create a one-year Junior College for all Freshmen, preserve the College and Scientific Schools as separate Schools for Sophomores, Juniors, and Seniors, and then reunite all divisions of study in a single Graduate School.

Some members of the Corporation proved far from enthusiastic about this idea of a joint Freshman year. Vance McCormick was afraid that Yale might be moving to set up a glorified preparatory school. Howell Cheney thought it a mistake to deprive Freshmen of upper-class contacts. Others agreed in fearing the creation of one more vested interest. After much discussion at the Corporation meeting of 16 Dec., therefore, the most that the Corporation was willing to vote was that by its silence it did "not thereby commit itself to maintaining as a permanent policy the present division between the College and the Sheffield Scientific School in Freshman Year."

By now the Alumni Committee were clear in their intention, but the Administration and Corporation were by no means so quick to set up a new Division as they had been to destroy the old Select Course. As for the faculty, opinions differed; but by and large the Academic Professors did not like the idea at all. All around them people were talking about the gains for unity and good teaching—but no one was considering the losses. From Dec. 1918 to Mar. 1919 consideration and negotiation continued, while faculty opposition smoldered without effective outlet until Morris got together his vain protest meeting. On 17 Mar. the Corporation made its decision in principle but instructed Hadley to appoint a representative committee "to report to the Corporation on the organization and studies" of a "Common Undergraduate Freshman Year."

In May Hadley appointed his committee, with the following members:

> For the Corporation: W. A. Brown and O. T. Bannard
> For the Alumni Committee: G. G. Mason and S. H. Fisher
> For the College: Dean Jones, Professor Farr (Chairman of the old Freshman Faculty), Professors Tinker and Mendell
> For the Scientific School: Director Chittenden, Professor Smith (Scientific School Freshman Class Officer), Professors Breckenridge and Corwin.

Had not the Corporation delivered its mandate, even the firmness of Fisher and Mason, the enthusiasm of Brown, and the weight of Bannard might not have carried the project any further. All four of the College men were more or less opposed. Tinker felt so strongly that he was going to withdraw from Freshman teaching. Mendell would refuse to head the new School. Dean Jones had not fought, but he knew his jurisdiction was being invaded; and Farr saw his administrative functions entirely done away. As for Chittenden, what he felt about the whole Reorganization can only be described in terms of a broken heart. His own professors Smith and Breckenridge, perhaps, saw some good in it; and Corwin had been one of the inspirers and advisers in reform. But Corwin himself was doubtful of the wisdom of delaying the choice of studies, and more than doubtful of the wisdom of trying to reduce two independent fortresses by the expedient of creating a third. Under the circumstances, these Faculty representatives were reduced to "going along"; but there was no concealing the difficulty they were having in reconciling themselves to this Junior College experiment in disguise.

What really held up planning, however, was the inability at first to find a man to be Dean. First, Hawkes of Columbia declined politely. Next the Permanent Officers in a body declined, and not so politely, to support Hadley's selection of the dynamic but unstable Mather A. Abbott. When Clarence W. Mendell was urged by the Provost and the Secretary to take the post, he refused. Finally, when a Harvard-educated but otherwise innocent member of the Psychology Department was picked for the job, he was looked upon in certain quarters with something less than enthusiasm. In Dec. 1919, however, as soon as Roswell

688

P. Angier had stated his terms and been appointed, things really began to move.

The foregoing is based on the Minutes of the Alumni Committee; the *Yale Alumni Weekly* of 6 Dec. 1918; the mimeographed material prepared by Secretary Stokes for the special Corporation meeting of 16 Dec.; the Records of the Corporation for Dec. 1918; conversations of G.W.P. with Howell Cheney, 27 Oct. 1939, with Vance McCormick, 18 Apr. 1940, with C. W. Mendell, and others. A. P. Stokes has assured me that he did not suggest or know who suggested the Freshman Year idea. The first time he heard it advocated was by Dean Jones at a University Council meeting. A. P. Stokes to G.W.P., 2 Feb. 1950.

The work of organizing the Freshman Year, and its first year of operations, may be followed through the *Report of the President and Deans, 1919–20*, 3–7, 264–68; *1920–21*, 2–3, 246–64; *1922–23*, 11–12, 180–95; *Reports to the President, 1921–22*, 158–74; and through the columns of the *Yale Alumni Weekly*. The S. H. Fisher Papers and the G. G. Mason Papers are useful; but the most valuable collection of documents is contained in the four Boxes of Freshman Office Records, 1920–21. I have benefited also from the "Reminiscences" of R. N. Corwin; a recorded interview with Dean Walden, 3 Dec. 1925; and from personal conversations with S. B. Hemingway, C..B. Tinker, C. F. Schreiber, and W. A. Brown.

The head quotation and the second footnote are from S. H. Fisher to G. G. Mason, 17 May 1919, G. G. Mason Papers.

1. *Report of the Alumni Committee, 12.*
2. *Report of the President and Deans, 1919–20, 5;* for Angier, *ibid., 1920–21, 250.*
3. Minutes and Report of Committee on Plans and Policies, 2 Mar.–27 Apr. 1920, Freshman Office Records, Box 1, Files A3.41 and A3.70; Dean Angier to Dean Jones, 6 Apr. 1921, Jones to Angier, 8, 11 Apr. 1921, and Angier to R. R. Shrewsbury, Phillips Exeter Academy, 20 Apr. 1921, Box 4, File D20.09; Corporation Records, June 1920. A one-hour course in military science, preparatory to more intensive upper-class R.O.T.C. work, could be elected as an optional or sixth course—but, despite some pressure, the art of war was not made a common denominator or indispensable factor in a Yale education.

4. *Report of the President and Deans, 1920–21*, 252–53. Professor Tracy tried to persuade the Academic Faculty that drawing was a universal language, fit to be included in all programs; but this proved too much for the Academic men to swallow. Conversation of G.W.P. with S. B. Hemingway, 17 June 1944.

5. *Report of the President and Deans, 1920–21*, 216–18; *Reports to the President, 1921–22*, 136–38.

6. Conversation of G.W.P. with Dr. W. A. Brown, 13 May 1939. See also Dean Angier's suggestion on science teaching in the *Alumni Weekly*, 27 Feb. 1920.

7. Conversations of G.W.P. with C. B. Tinker, 27 Jan. 1939, and with S. B. Hemingway, 17 June 1944. See also Hemingway's account of the Freshman English course in the *Alumni Weekly*, 1 Apr. 1921. The lively negotiations over the beginning of the course can be traced in the letters of the participants. Deans Angier and Jones, Professors G. H. Nettleton, C. M. Lewis, C. B. Tinker, Director Chittenden, Provost Walker, and Dr. W. A. Brown in Freshman Office Records, 1920–21, Box 1, File A3.70 and Box 3, File B5.50. See also Angier to S. H. Fisher, New York, 5 Mar. 1920, S. H. Fisher Papers, Alumni Committee No. 4.

8. Letters of Dean Angier, Provost Walker, Director Chittenden, Professor Allen Johnson, and Dr. Brown, Freshman Office Records, Box 1, File A3.70, Box 3, File B8.20. See also *Report of the President and Deans, 1920–21*, 184–85; *Reports to the President, 1921–22*, 109, 161–63; and the *Alumni Weekly*, 28 Jan. 1921.

9. In the spring of 1919 Professor Bakewell had revived his suggestion for encyclopedic lectures on the main Departments of Study, but had been turned down. In the spring of 1920 the Freshman Curriculum Committee seriously considered a general orienting course, hoped that such a course might be arranged later, but did not consider it feasible at the moment because of the radical adjustments that would have to be made in the degree requirements and in the teaching personnel. For the later experimental Introduction to the Social Sciences, see the history of the College under President Angell. Faculty Record, 8, 22 May 1919. Proposed Report of the Freshman Curriculum Com-

mittee, 23 Mar., 21 May 1920, Freshman Office Records, 1920–21, Box 1, File A3.70.

10. Angier's statement, 22 Nov. 1920, Freshman Office Records, 1920–21, Box 1, File A1.20. The class visitation policy worked less well. The Dean knew too little about certain subjects to make useful suggestions, while the visit of a Senior professor could be paralyzing to a young instructor. I have found no evidence that inspection by outsiders, in the line of boards of visitors or overseers, was ever seriously considered.

11. Dean P. T. Walden, interview, 3 Dec. 1925. Not everyone thought it was wise to make this transition smooth and unnoticeable. "My own poor psychology tells me that it were better for him to get something of a reawakening intellectual jolt." R. N. Corwin, "Reminiscences."

12. Conversation of G.W.P. with C. F. Schreiber, 7 Feb. 1944.

13. Dean Angier to S. H. Fisher, 24 Nov. 1920, and Fisher to Angier, 13 Dec. 1920, Freshman Office Records, 1920–21, Box 4, File D6.10.

REFERENCE NOTES FOR
CHAPTER 27 · THE LAST YEARS UNDER HADLEY

This résumé is based on the Reorganization reports, the *Report of the President and Deans,* the *Yale Alumni Weekly,* the Hadley and Fisher Papers, and personal communications from A. P. Stokes, J. R. Angell and others.

The head quotation is from the *Alumni Weekly* review of President Hadley's administration, 10 June 1921.

1. Corporation Records, Oct., Nov. 1919 and the *Alumni Weekly* 20 Nov. 1919. For Stokes' proposal of an endowment drive, and alumni doubts, see A. P. Stokes to President Hadley, 11 Sept 1919, copies in A. L. Ripley Papers and the S. H. Fisher Papers Alumni Committee No. 3; and Fisher to Stokes, 19 Sept., 7 Oct 1919, *ibid.*

2. There is a humorous group of G. P. Day letters, written on the road, in the S. H. Fisher Papers, Yale University—Endowment Fund—G. P. Day. See also *Yale Alumni Weekly,* 9 July 1920, and *Report of the Treasurer, 1919–20,* 6–9, 34–36.

3. Sterling Estate—Yale Papers, Vol. I, and A. P. Stokes to W. A. Brown, 16 May 1939. See also Corporation Records, Apr. 1919, and the extracts in the *Report of the President and Deans, 1918–19,* 44–46.

4. W. A. Brown, *A Teacher and His Times,* 284–91, and Brown's and Walker's discussion of the post in their Reports, 1919–20 and 1920–21.

5. *Report of the Alumni Committee,* 6, and *Report of the Committee on Educational Policy,* 16–17. For some of the uncertainties involved, see Hadley's letters to A. P. Stokes, 3 Dec. 1919; to Ray Morris, New York, 29 Jan. 1920; to B. P. Twichell, 20 Apr. 1920, Hadley Letters. See also the *Alumni Weekly,* 25 Mar. 1921 and *Report of the President and Deans, 1922-23,* 12.

692

6. *New Haven Evening Register,* 25–31 May, *New York Times,* 28, 29 May 1919, and the editorials in the *Yale Daily News,* 28 May and the *Yale Alumni Weekly,* 6 June 1919; *Report of the President and Deans, 1918–19,* 148–49.

7. Hadley, *Baccalaureate Addresses,* 18.

8. Hadley to J. R. Angell, New York, 16 Feb. 1921, Hadley Letters. See also Hadley to A. L. Ripley, 12 Jan. 1921, *ibid.*

9. "His leadership showed itself more in his public addresses and lay preachments than anything else. Here was the field where Mr. Hadley was *facile princeps.* . . . I must have heard him speak hundreds of times, and never heard him say anything that was not worth saying or that was not brief and to the point." A. P. Stokes to G.W.P., 27 June 1941.

10. There has been wide difference of opinion as to the University's standing at the end of the Hadley Administration. Impressions difficult to harmonize have been given me by J. R. Angell, 9 Dec. 1946; Wallace Notestein to G. B. Adams, 23 Feb. 1921, G. B. Adams Collection, Box "Letters—Yale and Others," File 265; and A. P. Stokes to G.W.P., 21 Nov., 5 Dec. 1947, 2 Feb. 1950. My own inclination is to think that the lay public was slow to recognize the great improvements in the Law and Medical Schools, while the world of scholars noted the apparent preoccupation with undergraduate problems.

TABLES

Table A: Rectors and Presidents

The "Act for Liberty to Erect a Collegiate School," 9 October 1701, gave authority to the "Trustees Partners or undertakers" to delegate the direction of the institution to a Rector or Master. A supplementary act, passed in October 1723, provided that the Rector should be ex officio a Trustee. The title Rector was used until the passage of "An Act for the more full and compleat Establishment of Yale College in New-Haven and for enlarging the Powers and Previleges thereof" on 9 May 1745, which designated the legal title of the corporation as the "President and Fellows of Yale College in New-Haven." The name Yale University was approved by act of the General Assembly of Connecticut in 1887.

Rectors

1701, 11 November	*Abraham Pierson* †	*5 March 1707
1707	*Samuel Andrew (pro tempore)*	24 March 1719
1719, 24 March	*Timothy Cutler*	17 October 1722
1726, 13 September	*Elisha Williams*	31 October 1739
1740, 2 April	*Thomas Clap*	1 June 1745

Presidents

1745, 1 June	*Thomas Clap*	10 September 1766
1766, 22 October	*Naphtali Daggett (pro tempore)*	25 March 1777
1778, 23 June	*Ezra Stiles*	*12 May 1795
1795, 8 September	*Timothy Dwight*	*11 January 1817
1817, 23 July	*Jeremiah Day*	21 October 1846
1846, 21 October	*Theodore Dwight Woolsey*	11 October 1871
1871, 11 October	*Noah Porter*	1 July 1886
1886, 1 July	Timothy Dwight	28 June 1899
1899, 29 June	Arthur Twining Hadley	22 June 1921
1921, 22 June	James Rowland Angell	30 June 1937
1937, 1 July	Charles Seymour	30 June 1950
1950, 1 July	Alfred Whitney Griswold	

* Died in office.

† *Italics* designate ordained ministers.

This table is based on the work of the notable Secretaries Franklin Bowditch Dexter, Anson Phelps Stokes, and Carl Albert Lohmann, and on Welch and Camp, *Yale, Her Campus, Class-Rooms and Athletics.*

The Founding

1701 "Proposalls for Erecting an UNIVERSITY in the Renowned Colony of *Connecticut.*" Meeting of Ministers in Branford.
Oct. 9. Meeting of the General Court of the Colony in New Haven.
Oct. 16 (probably). General Court or Assembly authorizes a "Collegiate" School and votes annual subsidy of "£120 in country pay."
Nov. 11. Trustees vote to locate the School in Saybrook under Rev. Mr. Pierson as Rector.

1701—*Rector Pierson*—1707

1702 *March.* First student, Jacob Heminway, received at Rector's house in Killingworth.
Sept. 16. The first Commencement held, in Saybrook. Eight students.
Sept. 30. Daniel Hooker, Harvard 1700, elected Tutor to assist the Rector.
1703 *Sept.* 15. John Hart awarded first B.A., for work in course, and elected Tutor.
1707 Death of Rector Pierson. Seniors sent to Trustee, Rev. Samuel Andrew, in Milford. Eighteen students graduated B.A., 1702–07.

1707—*Rector Andrew (pro tempore)*—1719

1707–16 Students under Tutors at Saybrook. Rector Andrew in Milford.
1708 Synod composed of eight Trustees, four other ministers, and four laymen draws up the Saybrook Platform establishing Congregational order and doctrine in Connecticut.
1714 Publication of "*Theses & A Catalogue,* as in other Schoolse." (No copy known.) Receipt of books collected in England by the Colony Agent, Jeremiah Dummer, from Sir Isaac Newton, Elihu Yale, and others. During the following years Dummer's efforts, particularly with Governor Yale, proved of inestimable value to the struggling Collegiate School.
1715 Assembly votes five hundred pounds for "a College house."
1716 Trustees vote to remove Collegiate School to New Haven.
1716–18 Hartford Trustees continue struggle to have it located up river. A number of students enrolled at Wethersfield under Tutor Elisha Williams.
1717 *Sept.* 11. First Commencement in New Haven.
Oct. 8. The first building raised. Completed, 1718. Partially removed in Nov. 1775, kitchen and dining rooms retained until 1782.
Student enrollment: 13 in New Haven, 14 in Wethersfield, 4 at Saybrook.

1718 Rev. Cotton Mather writes to Elihu Yale that "if what is forming at New Haven might wear the name of YALE COLLEGE, it would be better than *a name of sons and daughters*. And . . . much better than an Egyptian pyramid."

1718–21 Gifts to the value of £562.12s received from Governor Yale, with 417 books and a portrait and arms of King George I.

1718 *Sept.* 10. The Collegiate School named Yale College at first public Commencement in New Haven.

Dec. Removal of books by oxcart from Saybrook to New Haven.

1719 *Mar.* Rev. Timothy Cutler chosen Rector for the remainder of the year.

1719—*Rector Cutler*—1722

1719 Wethersfield School adjourns to New Haven in June. At Commencement Rector Cutler's service approved and he is desired to continue in office.

The First Society (Center Church) admits students to sit in gallery.

1721 Impost on rum appropriated by Assembly to build a Rector's house. Completed 1722, near southwest corner of College and Chapel Streets. Occupied by Rector Williams, Presidents Clap, Stiles, and Dwight.

1722 A "Common Seal" granted to Trustees by the General Assembly. Rector and Tutor declare for Episcopacy, and are excused further service. Subscription to Saybrook Platform required of College Officers

1722—*Trustees and Tutors*—1726

1722–26 College continues under Tutors, with occasional supervision by Trustees and with Rev. Samuel Andrew acting at Commencements. After the office is several times declined, Trustees elect Rev. Elisha Williams and induct him into Rectorship, 1726.

1724–26 Jonathan Edwards '20, Tutor.

1726 Trustees create office of Scholar of the House and appoint a Senior student; "his Work to observe & note down all Detriment the College receives in its Windows Doors Studies Tables Locks & Salary to be three pounds & to give an account Quarterly."

1726—*Rector Williams*—1739

1732–33 Dean Berkeley conveys his farm in Rhode Island to encourage graduate study by providing support for Scholars of the House residing at the College between their first and second degrees. Surplus to be laid out in Greek and Latin books—Berkeley Premiums—for Latin compositions by undergraduates.

1733 Dean Berkeley ships a valuable collection of books to the College.

1739 Elisha Williams resigns and Rev. Thomas Clap elected Rector.

1740—*Clap, Rector and President*—1766

1740–41 The revivalist George Whitefield visits New Haven. First great religious awakening. David Brainerd expelled for his persistence in New Light tendencies and for saying that Tutor Whittelsey had "no more grace than the chair I am leaning upon."

1743 Classified catalogue of the Library published.

Colony grant increased and a third tutor engaged.

1745 Declaration of the Rector and Tutors against George Whitefield. Revised Charter. The Trustees become the President and Fellows of Yale College.

Laws of the College compiled by Clap (first published 1748).

"Scholastical Exercises" to include Rhetoric, Geometry, and Geography for Sophomores; Natural Philosophy, Astronomy, and "Other Parts of the Mathematicks" for Juniors.

1746 First professorship (Divinity) established with funds given in 1745 by Colonel Philip Livingston "as a small acknowledgement of the sence I have for the favour and Education my sons have had there."

College of New Jersey, later Princeton, founded by six sons of Yale and one of Harvard, and Rev. Jonathan Dickinson, Yale '06, elected President. The first of many colleges to be founded or first presided over by Yale graduates.

1747–53 General Assembly authorizes a lottery, 15 per cent of proceeds to go for building a new College. In 1749 proceeds of sale of French vessel, taken by Colony frigate, voted; and in 1751 additional funds. Foundation of the new College laid in 1751; exterior completed in 1752; partially occupied in 1753. Ordered to be named Connecticut Hall. Repaired and fourth story added 1797, and called South Middle. Restored to original shape and name, 1905.

1748 Jared Eliot '06, *An Essay upon Field Husbandry in New-England* (1748–59).

1753 *Sept.* 12. Reputed date of founding of Linonia, literary and debating society.

President directed to hold Sunday services in the College Hall.

1754 Rev. Jonathan Edwards, *A Careful and Strict Enquiry into . . . Freedom of Will.*

1755 General Assembly ceases granting £100 annually. Beginning of pamphlet war on Clap's policy.

Rev. Naphtali Daggett elected Livingston Professor. Becomes College pastor.

1757 College Church founded. Today the Church of Christ in Yale University. Brick Chapel and Library built 1761–63. Remodeled in 1824 and designated Athenaeum. In 1893 torn down to make way for Vanderbilt Hall.

1760–66   Student disorders. Opposition to Clap increases.

1763   Clap defeats attempt to subject the management of the College to the Assembly.

Algebra first introduced into curriculum by the Tutors.

1766   Clap publishes his *Annals* . . . , the first history of Yale College. Student disorders. Clap resigns. Management of the College confided to one of its own sons, Professor Naphtali Daggett '48.

1766—*President Daggett (pro tempore)*—1777

1767   Students listed alphabetically, instead of by the President and Tutors.

Tutors give instruction in English grammar, language, and composition.

1768   Literary and debating society of Brothers in Unity founded.

1770   Second professorship, in Mathematics and Natural Philosophy, established.

1772–73   Tutor John Trumbull '67 publishes *The Progress of Dulness*, a satire on College studies.

1773   Honorary degrees of D.D. and LL.D. first conferred.

1775–80   Unrest after Lexington forces suspension of classes. Student military company drills for General Washington and escorts him through town. Commencement of 1775, and next five Commencements, private. Recurring interruptions from camp distemper and want of food. In 1777–78 Classes scattered to Farmington, Glastonbury, and Wethersfield. In July 1779 the British under General Tryon invade New Haven. Professor Daggett captured and maltreated but College buildings spared. Altogether about 74 weeks out of 280 lost from classes in seven years.

1776   Seniors instructed in history and belles lettres by Tutor Dwight '69. Dr. Daggett resigns the presidency.

1777   Third professorship, in Ecclesiastical History, established.

Rev. Dr. Ezra Stiles '46 submits his PLAN OF A UNIVERSITY, proposing the teaching of Law and Medicine, with the addition of four professorships. In July 1778 Stiles inaugurated, the first Yale graduate regularly elected President.

1778—*President Stiles*—1795

1780   Connecticut Alpha chapter of Phi Beta Kappa founded.

1782   Bequest of £500 from Daniel Lathrop '33—the first substantial gift from a graduate.

New dining hall built.

1783–85   *A Grammatical Institute of the English Language*, by Noah Webster '78.

1785   Seventy students graduated: the largest Class in the first century.

1787   College Laws list "History and Civil Policy" as a Senior study. Stiles had been using Locke for Seniors. In 1789 Montesquieu introduced.

1789   Noah Webster '78, *The American Spelling Book.*
Jedidiah Morse '83, *The American Universal Geography.*
1792   President and Fellows accept financial assistance, and amendment to Charter adding to Corporation "the Governor, Lieutenant Governor and six senior assistants in the Council of this State."
1793   Union Hall, later called South College, built. Demolished 1893.
1795   Ezra Stiles dies in office. Rev. Timothy Dwight elected to succeed him.

1795—*President Dwight*—1817

1795   Government vested in President, Professors, and Tutors—later styled the Faculty.
1797   Moral Society founded.
1799   Connecticut Academy of Arts and Sciences chartered.
1798–1801   Almshouse and jail removed. Ownership of College Street front of old campus completed. New President's house built where Farnam Hall now stands. Lyceum and Berkeley Hall (North Middle) erected, extending the Brick Row.
1801   In one hundred years the B.A. had been conferred on 2,333 students.
Jeremiah Day '95 appointed Professor of Mathematics and Natural Philosophy. Professorship of Law instituted.
1802   A revival of religion experienced in the College.
Benjamin Silliman '96 appointed Professor of Chemistry and Natural History; in 1803 Lyceum Laboratory completed; his first lecture delivered in 1804.
1804   Fagging abolished.
1805   James L. Kingsley '99 appointed Professor of Hebrew, Greek, and Latin Languages and Ecclesiastical History and Librarian.
1807–10   Mineralogical Cabinet begun with the purchase of the Perkins Collection, 1807, and the deposit of the Gibbs Collection, 1810, purchased in 1825.
1810   Charter granted for the Medical Institution of Yale College, to be conducted jointly with the Connecticut State Medical Society Building acquired 1812; Institution organized in 1813; first M.D. in course conferred 1813.
1812   Musical Society formed—later the Beethoven Society.
1813   *A Hebrew Grammar* . . . , the first in English, by Moses Stuart '99
1817   Timothy Dwight dies in office. Professor Jeremiah Day ordained to the ministry and inaugurated President.

1817—*President Day*—1846

1817   Institution of professorship of Rhetoric and Oratory; in 1839 changed to Rhetoric and English Language, in 1863 to Rhetoric and English Literature. The first professorship in a modern language.

1818 Society for Inquiry Regarding Missions founded.

First issue of the *American Journal of Science* (Silliman's Journal).

Constitution of Connecticut confirms Yale College Charter. In 1819 six senior Senators substituted for six senior Assistants on Corporation.

1818–19 Timothy Dwight, *Theology; Explained and Defended.*

1819 Calliopean Literary Society organized.

1819–21 New Dining Hall erected. Old Dining Hall fitted up as Chemical Laboratory. Cabinet Building erected. North College added to Brick Row.

1821 Chi Delta Theta founded by Professor Kingsley.

1822 Theological Department organized. Rev. Nathaniel W. Taylor '07 called to the Dwight Professorship of Didactic Theology.

1823 Requirement of assent to Saybrook Platform by members of Faculty abrogated.

1824 Second Chapel built, next to North College.

Private law school conducted in New Haven, first by Seth P. Staples '97, then by Judge David Daggett '83 and Samuel J. Hitchcock '09, affiliated with Yale College and names of students included in the *Catalogue.* In 1826 Daggett made Professor of Law in the College. In 1833 his chair named the Kent Professorship in honor of Chancellor James Kent '81, whose *Commentaries on American Law* had appeared 1826–30.

1825 Optional instruction in modern languages (French) begun.

1826 Apparatus purchased for an outdoor gymnasium, set up behind Chapel.

The graduating Class number 101. Largest previous Class numbered 82.

1827 The Society of the Alumni formed, to support the College.

1828 *Reports of the Corporation and Faculty on the Course of Instruction.*

Bread and Butter Rebellion.

The Illinois Association formed in the Theological Department, for home missions.

Noah Webster, *An American Dictionary of the English Language.* "The three great books of Yale and New Haven are Dwight's *Theology,* Webster's *Dictionary,* and Silliman's *Journal of Science.*"

1830 Conic Sections Rebellion.

Tutors allowed to teach a single subject, instead of hearing a Class in Greek, Latin, and Mathematics.

1831 The "Great Revival."

Return of Theodore Dwight Woolsey '20 from Germany and appointment as Professor of the Greek Language and Literature.

1831–36 The Centum Millia Fund, the first movement for raising a large amount for general endowment, secures just over $100,000 from graduates and other friends.

1832 Opening of the Trumbull Gallery, the first art museum connected with a college or university to be built in the United States. Designed by Colonel John Trumbull and erected by the College, with funds appropriated by the Connecticut General Assembly, to house his collection of paintings acquired by Yale in 1831.

Skull and Bones, first Senior society, founded. Scroll and Key founded 1842.

1834 Yale Natural History Society organized.

The Corporation accepts an Act of the General Assembly which provides exemption of College funds with the exception of real estate having an annual income of more than $6,000. The faculty lose their exemption from taxation.

1835 Library increased to 10,000 volumes.

1836 The *Yale Literary Magazine* founded.

First Greek letter fraternity, Alpha Delta Phi. Followed by Psi Upsilon in 1838.

Old Brick Row completed by erection of Divinity College.

Professorship of Mathematics and Natural Philosophy divided.

1837 Publication by James Dwight Dana '33 of *A System of Mineralogy*, perhaps the most famous of Yale texts. After having gone through a series of revisions and enlargements at the hands of J. D. Dana and E. S. Dana '70, it reached a seventh edition in 1944.

1840 Office of Class Bully abolished. No election of a permanent Class leader allowed.

1841 Graduate instruction, outside medicine, divinity, and law, begun. Edward E. Salisbury '32 appointed Professor of Arabic and Sanskrit Languages and Literature.

Student football game on Green interferes with annual firemen's hose-playing demonstration. Firemen escort students before justice. Students attack firehouse. First numbers of *Yale Banner* issued to present students' case.

1842 Commons abandoned.

1843 First number of the *New Englander* published.

Five Townsend Premiums for Seniors established for the best original composition in English.

School of Law placed under Corporation. LL.B. first conferred. The number of students, 1824–42, was 410.

Edward Claudius Herrick appointed first full-time Librarian. In 1845 Professor Kingsley abroad to buy books. New Library designed by Henry Austin begun in 1842, partly occupied in 1844, completed 1846. Known as the Old Library, 1889–1931, it is now Dwight Hall and Dwight Memorial Chapel.

1846 John P. Norton and Benjamin Silliman Jr. '37 appointed Professors of Agricultural Chemistry and Applied Chemistry, and set up Chemical Laboratory in old President's house.

Jeremiah Day resigns and is elected to the Corporation. Professor Theodore Dwight Woolsey ordained and inaugurated President.

1846—President Woolsey—1871

1847   Noah Porter '31 becomes Professor of Moral Philosophy and Metaphysics on Clark's foundation. President Woolsey freed for teaching History, Politics, and International Law. Senior work stiffened. Written biennial examinations added at end of Sophomore and Senior years.

Department of Philosophy and the Arts established, later to develop into the Scientific School and the Graduate School. The School of Applied Chemistry included. Eight students enrolled.

Horace Bushnell '27 (Tutor 1829–31) publishes *Views of Christian Nurture*. Enlarged in 1861, *Christian Nurture* is still being republished.

1850   James Dwight Dana made Silliman Professor of Natural History. Title changed to Geology and Mineralogy in 1864.

Total endowment reaches $180,489.59.

1851   Graduates of Yale College, 1701–1851, number 6,093.

1852   Degree of Ph.B. authorized in Department of Philosophy and the Arts, and awarded to six men. John P. Norton dies and John A. Porter '42 is appointed to his chair. William A. Norton made Professor of Civil Engineering, thus establishing a School of Engineering.

First award of the DeForest Prize for the Senior who "shall write and pronounce an English oration in the best manner."

1853   Alumni Hall completed. Here for generations the candidates for admission would be examined.

Organization of the Yale Navy, later known as the Yale Boat Club. First race against Harvard, 1852, won by Harvard.

1854   William Dwight Whitney appointed Professor of Sanskrit Language and Literature.

Riot in theater, man killed. Firemen called out. South College threatened.

1854–61   The name Yale Scientific School given to the School of Applied Chemistry and the School of Engineering. In 1855 George Jarvis Brush, Ph.B. '52, appointed Professor of Metallurgy. In 1856 fundraising pamphlets issued, and Samuel W. Johnson made Professor of Analytical Chemistry. In 1859 Rev. Chester Smith Lyman '37 appointed Professor of Industrial Mechanics and Physics. In 1858–60 the old Medical School building bought, renovated, and given for the School by Joseph E. Sheffield, Esq., whose gifts and bequests ultimately exceeded $1,000,000. In 1861 the School renamed the Sheffield Scientific School. Select Course established, 1860.

1855   Gustave Jacob Stoeckel appointed Instructor in Vocal Music.

1857   Football on the New Haven Green abolished by city ordinance.

A course of Art Lectures given.

1858   Junior Crocodile Club, returning singing, gets into altercation at firehouse on High Street. Fireman killed. Enginehouse shortly bought by Faculty.

1859 Daily evening prayers abolished, and morning prayers placed after breakfast.

1860 Completion of the first indoor Gymnasium. In 1892 converted into University Dining Hall and in 1901 into Laboratory for Psychology. Torn down in 1917 to make way for Calliope Court of Harkness Memorial Quadrangle.

Corporation establishes the degree of Doctor of Philosophy, as recommended by the Faculty of the Scientific School "to enable us to retain in this country many young men, and especially students of Science who now resort to German Universities for advantages of study no greater than we are able to afford."

The Ph.D. awarded for the first time in the United States at Yale in 1861.

1861 *Jan.* Palmetto flag of South Carolina placed on west tower of Alumni Hall during chapel service. Attack on Sumter comes in spring vacation. Before studies resume all Southern students leave except one who waits to say goodbye. Drill companies organized by Classes. Eventually 1,044 students and graduates serve in the Union forces and 206 or more in the Confederate Army.

1863 Josiah Willard Gibbs '58 awarded Ph.D. and appointed tutor in Latin. In 1871 appointed to a chair in Mathematical Physics without remuneration.

Yale Glee Club established, and makes a trip to the White Mountains.

1863–64 Sheffield Scientific School designated to receive the Land Grant Fund of the State. The College Librarian Daniel Coit Gilman '52 elected Professor of Physical and Political Geography in the School, and Secretary of its Board. Brush made Treasurer. In 1864 William H. Brewer, Ph.B. '52, elected Professor of Agriculture; Daniel Cady Eaton '57, Professor of Botany; and Addison E. Verrill, Professor of Zoology.

Professorship of Divinity for the Pastor established in the College, 1863. Also Street Professorship of Modern Languages, 1864. Professorship of Sacred Literature, changed in 1886 to New Testament Criticism and Interpretation, founded in Divinity School.

1865 Corporation adopts plan for the School of the Fine Arts. Art School completed 1866.

Professorship of History established, and Arthur M. Wheeler '57 elected. Addison VanName '58 appointed Librarian.

Publication of *Yale Courant* and *Yale Pot-Pourri*.

First baseball game with another college, Wesleyan. Score, Yale 39–Wesleyan 13.

1866 Peabody gift for a Museum of Natural History. O. C. Marsh '60 appointed Professor of Paleontology—the first in America and second in the world.

"Public Lectures to Mechanics." As the Sheffield Lectures, this course to be given for forty-four years. School announces course in Mining and Metallurgy.

William Graham Sumner '63 appointed Tutor, 1866–69. In 1872 he returned as Professor of Political and Social Science.

1867 Degree of Bachelor of Divinity first conferred. From 1822 to 1866 the number of students was 883. East Divinity, Marquand Chapel, and West Divinity Hall built 1870–74, where Calhoun College now stands. Rev. Dr. Samuel Harris elected Professor of Systematic Theology 1871. James Jackson Jarves deposits in the School of the Fine Arts 119 paintings from his collection of Italian primitives. They were purchased by the University in 1871.

1869 Law Department placed in charge of Simeon E. Baldwin '61, William C. Robinson, and Johnston T. Platt.

School of the Fine Arts opened to students, the earliest professional training school in the fine arts connected with an American institution of the higher learning. John Ferguson Weir appointed Director and Professor of Painting and Design, and D. Cady Eaton '60 appointed Professor of the History of Art. In 1871 John H. Niemeyer added as Professor of Drawing.

1870 Erection of Farnam Hall, first dormitory in new campus quadrangle. Followed by Durfee 1871, Battell Chapel completed in 1876, Dwight Hall and Lawrance Hall in 1886, Osborn Hall 1889, Chittenden Library 1890, Welch Hall 1891, Vanderbilt Hall 1894, and Phelps Hall 1895.

Thomas Raynesford Lounsbury '59 appointed Instructor in English in the Scientific School, Professor in 1871. Henry Augustin Beers '69 appointed Tutor in English in the College, 1871.

First Yale scientific expedition to the Far West organized by Professor Marsh.

In 1870–71 Yale had an endowment of one and a half million, a Faculty of 64, and 755 students. On its rolls were 3,760 living alumni of the College, and for all the Departments a total of 10,501 graduates and former students, living and dead, with 828 others holding honorary or *ad eundem* degrees.

1869–71 Young Yale movement among the graduates. Agitation among the Faculty to develop the University. Publications by W. G. Sumner, J. D. Dana, T. Dwight, and a statement of the *Needs of the University* by the Faculty.

1871 *Feb.* 8. Articles of Incorporation of the Board of Trustees of the Sheffield Scientific School.

July 6. General Assembly provides for the election of six graduates as Fellows of Yale College instead of the six senior Senators of the State.

Theodore Dwight Woolsey resigns and is elected to the Corporation. Election and inauguration of the Rev. Dr. Noah Porter, eleventh President.

TABLE C: THE OLD COURSE OF INSTRUCTION, 1875–76

	Term	Full-time Studies				Part-time Studies	
Freshman Year	Fall	GREEK	LATIN		MATHEMATICS	Hygiene	
	Winter	GREEK	LATIN		MATHEMATICS	Roman History	
	Spring	GREEK	LATIN		MATHEMATICS	Rhetoric (Comp.—one hour)	
Sophomore Year	Fall	GREEK	LATIN		MATHEMATICS	Rhetoric (Declam. and Comp.)	
	Winter	GREEK	LATIN		MATHEMATICS	Rhetoric (Declam. and Comp.)	
	Spring	GREEK	LATIN		MATHEMATICS	Rhetoric (Declam. and Comp.)	
		Upper-class Studies					
Junior Year	Fall	Greek	Logic		Physics	Rhetoric (Disput. & Eng. Lit.)	
	Winter	Latin (or)	Math.	Ger. or Fr. *	Physics	Rhetoric (Disput.)	
	Spring	Greek	Astron.	Ger. or Fr.	Physics		
Senior Year	Fall	Mental Philos.	Chemistry			Pol. & Soc. Sci. (Econ.)	History (Europe)
	Winter	Moral Philos. and Evid. of Christianity	Astron. or Ger.	Geology		Pol. & Soc. Sci. (Polit.)	History (England)
							Rhetoric (Comp. & Disput.)
	Spring	History of Philos.	Anat. & Physiol. & Jurisprudence & Law			Pol. & Soc. Sci. (Int'l Law)	History (Amer. Constit'n)
						Study of Languages	Rhetoric (Comp. & Disput.)

* After the year had started, the schedule of the winter term was altered by allowing Juniors to take two out of three languages: Latin, French, German. In the third term Juniors were allowed to take a new course in Anglo-Saxon, as well as either French or German.

Year	Full-time Studies			Part-time Studies				
	GREEK	LATIN	MATHEMATICS					
Freshman Year First Term	GREEK	LATIN (w. Hist.)	MATHEMATICS	Hygiene				
Second Term {First Half	GREEK	LATIN	MATHEMATICS	Rhetoric				
Second Half	GREEK	LATIN	MATHEMATICS	Rhetoric				
Sophomore Year First Term	GREEK	LATIN	MATHEMATICS	Rhetoric				
Second Term {First Half	GREEK	LATIN	MATHEMATICS	Rhetoric				
Second Half	GREEK	LATIN	MATHEMATICS	Rhetoric				

	Required Studies				Optional Studies		
							4 hours
Junior Year First Term	Physics	Chemistry	English Lit. & Disput.	German	Greek 10 (Latin) Hist. 7	Math. 28	French 91
Second Term First Half	Physics	Zoology	English Lit. & Disput.	German	Greek 13 Latin 17	Math. 14	French 85
Second Term Second Half	Physics	Astronomy	Logic	German	Greek 11 Latin 13 Physiology 40	Math. 8 French 54	Anglo-Saxon 6
							4 hours
Senior Year First Term	Mental Philosophy	Geology	Political Economy	Rhetoric	Greek 6 (Latin) German 52 History, U.S., 48	Math. 3 Astronomy 11 (French) (Mineralogy)	
Second Term First Half	Moral Philosophy & Evidences of Christianity	Evolution & Cosmogony	Political Science	Rhetoric History (England)	Greek 5 (Latin) German 30 Polit. Econ. 60	Math. 4 Physics 6 (French) (Meteorology)	English 16 Geol. & Paleont. 5
Second Term Second Half	History of Philosophy	International Law	Political Science	Jurisprudence & Law	Greek 4 (Latin) German 21 Polit. Econ. 60	Math. 4 Physics 6 (French) (Meteorology)	English 18 Geol. & Paleont. 3 Linguistics 6

Note: Figures indicate number of students who elected each optional in 1876–77. Parentheses indicate course planned but either not given or not elected. In 1877–78 the Junior enrollment in French was curtailed (in favor of Latin) by requiring a previous knowledge of the elements; and the Seniors elected Political Science particularly, then German and English.

TABLE E: COURSE OF INSTRUCTION WITH ELECTIVES, 1885–86

	GREEK	LATIN	MATHEMATICS	MODERN LANGUAGES German (or adv. French or German)	ENGLISH Literature
Freshman Year	GREEK	LATIN	MATHEMATICS	MODERN LANGUAGES German (or adv. French or German)	ENGLISH Literature
Sophomore Year	GREEK	LATIN	MATHEMATICS w. Mechanics	MODERN LANGUAGES French or German	Rhetoric & Elocution

Junior Year

Required: 7 year-hours

LOGIC
PSYCHOLOGY
PHYSICS
ASTRONOMY
GEOLOGY

Electives: 8 year-hours to be chosen from:

Group of Subjects	Courses	Term Hours
Ancient Languages & Linguistics	16	32
Modern Languages	14	57
Natura & Physical Science	2	6
Mathematics	8	19
History	6	10
—Totals—	46	124

Senior Year

Required: 3 year-hours

PSYCHOLOGY
ETHICS & NATURAL THEOL.
EVID. of CHRISTIANITY

Electives: 12 year-hours to be chosen from

Group of Subjects	Courses	Term Hours
Ancient Languages & Linguistics	19	44
Modern Languages	13	70
Natural & Physical Science	8	24
Mathematics	13	31
Mental & Moral Science	4	12
Political Science	5	12
History	6	18
—Totals—	68	211

Notes: A number of the Senior electives were the same courses as were open to Juniors. In all 79 electives were offered. Four themes annually in English Composition were required of Juniors and Seniors.

TABLE F: THE COURSE OF INSTRUCTION UNDER DWIGHT, 1894–99

Year	Year-Hours Required	Elective	Choice	Subject	
Freshman Year	15		All Required	GREEK, LATIN, MATHEMATICS (with Mechanics): 11 hours FRENCH or GERMAN: 3 hours ENGLISH: 1 hour	
Sophomore Year	12	3	Single Option	5 out of 6: GREEK, LATIN, MATHEMATICS, FRENCH or GERMAN, ENGLISH, PHYSICS: all 3 hours	
Junior Year	3	12 or 15	Single Requirement	LOGIC—PSYCHOLOGY—ETHICS	Free Electives
Senior Year	2	13 or 10	Single Requirement	PHILOSOPHY: 1 course	Free Electives
	32	28			
	60				

TABLE G: INCREASE OF UPPER-CLASS ELECTIVE OFFERINGS

Term-Hours Offered

Subject	1876–77	1883–84
I. PHILOLOGY OR LANGUAGES		
Ancient Languages	67	117
Greek	41	57
Latin	16	16 ⎫
Sanskrit & Linguistics	16	16 ⎬ 16
	9	9
Modern Languages & Lit.	26	60
French	16	16
German	8	8
Spanish	0	8
Italian	0	16
English	2	12
II. MENTAL AND MORAL PHILOSOPHY		2
III. HISTORY AND POLITICAL SCIENCE	8	13
IV. MATHEMATICS AND ASTRONOMY	20	20
V. MOLECULAR & TERRESTRIAL PHYSICS	8	10
VI. NATURAL SCIENCE & GEOLOGY	10	10
VII. FINE ARTS	0	4
Total Term-Hours:	113	176

1898–99

Subject	Courses Offered*	Courses Starred†	Year-Hours Offered
I. ANCIENT LANGUAGES & LINGUISTICS	21	8	37
Greek	7	3	13
Latin	12	3	20
Sanskrit & Linguistics	2	2	4
II. BIBLICAL LITERATURE	11		17
III. MODERN EUROPEAN LANGUAGES & LIT.	21	15	50
French	6	6	14
German	9	5	21
Spanish	2	1	5
Italian	2	2	5
Scandinavian	2	1	5
IV. ENGLISH	14		25
V. PSYCHOLOGY, ETHICS, PHILOSOPHY	22	5	37
VI. POLITICAL SCIENCE & LAW	11	2	25
VII. HISTORY	11		22
VIII. MATHEMATICS	10	2	22
IX. PHYSICAL & NATURAL SCIENCES	15	6	36
Physics	3	1	7
Chemistry	4	2	11
Geology & Mineralogy	3	2	6
Physical Geography & Botany	2	1	5
Biology	3		7
X. FINE ARTS	4		8
XI. MUSIC	6		11
XII. PHYSICAL EDUCATION	1		2
XIII. MILITARY SCIENCE	1		1
Totals:	148	38	293

For convenience in comparison the groups in all three tables have been renumbered and reorganized. Because of the uneven length of the terms in 1876–77 and 1883–84, it is not possible to make an exact comparison with the total year-hours offered in 1898–99.

* Figures include starred courses, but not courses listed though not given.

† Starred courses required that permission be obtained from the instructor.

TABLE H: "CLASSIFIED" ELECTIVES, 1901–03

Year	Year-Hours	Choice	Courses
Freshman Year	15	None (Fr.-Ger.)	*All 3-hour courses:* 1. Greek 4. English 2. Latin 5. Mathematics 3. French or German (elem. or 2d yr.)
Sophomore Year	15 or 18	Limited Option	*All 3-hour courses:* 1. Greek 6. Mathematics (3 courses) 2. Latin 7. Physics 3. French (3 levels) 8. Chemistry 4. German (3 levels) 9. History 5. English 10. Psychology and Ethics 11. Philosophy
Junior Year	15 to 18	Electives	(Distribution—Concentration) *One Major and Two Minors* Each student required to complete connected courses of levels A-B-C totaling at least seven year-hours in one of the following Divisions of Study, and connected courses of levels A-B totaling at least five year-hours in each of the other two Divisions: I. LANGUAGE & LITERATURE: Latin, Greek, Classical Archaeology, Sanskrit, Linguistics, & Comp. Philology, Semitic Langs. & Biblical Lit., French, Spanish, Ital., German, Scandinavian, English II. MATH. & NATURAL & PHYSICAL SCIENCES: Math. & Astronomy, Physics, Chemistry, Geology, Phys. Geog., & Mineralogy, Biology, Anat. & Histology, Botany & Forestry III. PHILOSOPHY, HIST., & SOCIAL SCIENCES: Psychology, Ethics, Logic, Philosophy, Pedagogics, Ancient, Medieval, & Modern History, Economics, Politics & the Science of Society
Senior Year	12 to 15	Electives	

TABLE J: ELECTIONS UNDER THE NEW SYSTEM, 1901–02

Division	Subject	Juniors		Sophomores
		Major Choices	*Course Choices*	*Course Choices*
	Latin	21	36	132
	Greek	5	21	107
	Classical Archaeology		5	
Language	*Biblical Literature*		10	
and	French	13	97	155
Literature	German	18	117	162
	Italian		3	
	Spanish		65	
	Rhetoric		49	
	English	93	374	258
	Mathematics	17	47	125
Mathematics	Physics	3	29	201
and	Chemistry	20	85	48
Natural Science	Geology		112	
	Physiology		23	
	Forestry		5	
	Philosophy	2	336	73
Mental, Historical,	History	94	390	216
and	Social Sciences			
Social Sciences	(incl. *Law*)		323	
	Fine Arts		17	
	Music	1	8	

(*Italics* indicate subjects with marked professional connections.)

TABLE K: REGULATED ELECTIVES: THE SECOND PHASE, 1903–08

Year	Year-Hours	Choice	I. Language & Lit.	II. Math. & Sciences	III. Philos., Hist., Soc. Sciences
Freshman Year	15	Limited Option 3 of 5 courses to continue subjects offered for entrance	1. Greek (3 courses) 2. Latin 3. French (3 levels) or German (2–3 levels) 4. English	5. Mathematics 6. Chemistry	7. History
Sophomore Year	15 or 18	Wide Option*	1. Greek 2. Latin 3. French (3 levels) 4. German (3 levels) 5. Spanish (elementary) 1905– 6. Biblical Lit. 7. English	8. Math. (2 courses) 9. Physics (1–2 courses) 10. Chemistry (1–3 courses) 11. Physical & Commercial Geography 12. Biology 1907–	13. Psychology with Logic or Ethics 14. History of Philosophy 15. History 16. Economics
Junior Year	15 to 18	Electives	(Distribution—Concentration) *Two Majors*† of at least 7 hours each		
Senior Year	12 to 15	Electives	*Three Minors* of at least 5 hours each		

* Physiology, and Mineralogy and Crystallography, could be elected, but not within the fifteen hours.

† In 1908 the two majors were consolidated into a single major of 12 hours; and the minors were increased to 18 hours, to be completed before Senior year.

TABLE L: PRESENTATION OF GREEK FOR ENTRANCE

Class	Entered with Greek	Entered without Greek	Year
1907	98 %	2 %	1903
1908	89 %	11 %	1904
1909	83 %	17 %	1905
1910	77 %	23 %	1906
1911	63 %	37 %	1907
1912	60 % (approx.)	40 % (approx.)	1908
1913	57 %	43 %	1909
1914	Minority	Majority	1910

The figures for the Classes of 1907 and 1908 show the percentage of accepted candidates; the rest show the percentage of each Freshman Class.

Source: Dean's Reports.

Table M: Subject Choices by Freshmen, 1903–19
Percentage of Classes Electing Each Subject

Class	Greek	Latin	French	German	Spanish	English	Math.	Chem.	Physics	History
1907	60	83	58	49	—	98	78	25	—	47
1908	55	77	59	54	—	97	75	30	—	51
1909	50	73	60	55	—	99	73	31	—	60
1910	46	76	62	59	—	95	64	33	—	63
1911	44	73	67	60	—	96	65	33	—	61
1912	41	73	66	62	—	95	60	36	—	68
1913	38	73	69	61	—	95	52	42	—	65
1914	29	75	71	61	—	96	48	47	—	66
1915	25	78	64	57	—	98	54	44	24	58
1916	26	75	68	56	—	95	49	45	28	57
1917	21	74	71	52	—	96	47	43	40	59
1918	21	72	68	49	2	96	45	41	36	67
1919	17	77	70	46	6	97	42	45	32	63
1920	17	71	57	36	6	98	45	47	35	80
1921*	8	65	67	29	4	95	42	45	27	53
1922†	9	56	84	21	4	97	49	39	24	86
1923	7	62	80	21	5	95	63	46	22	69

Military Science: 1921*—72%; 1922†—18%; 1923—23%.

Fraction of percentage .5 or over considered as 1; less than .5 not recorded.

* Final choices of Freshmen after first week of semester.

† Choices of Freshmen as of January 1919.

Source: Dean's Reports.

School Year Ending	Total Number of Students	Total Number of College Graduates	Yale Graduates	Graduates of Other Colleges	Percentage of College Graduates
1871	23	5	4	1	22
1876	75	26	18	6	35
	Spec. Stud. 1				
1881	58	31	27	4	53
	Grad. Studs. 6	3	1	2	
1886	52	20	14	6	38
	Grad. Studs. 8	3	1	2	
	Spec. Studs. 2	0	0	0	
1891	111	47	30	17	42
	Grad. Studs. 5	0	0	0	
1896	186	74	48	26	40
	Grad. Studs. 24	5	3	2	
	Spec. Studs. 14	1	0	1	
1901	194	67	40	27	34
	Grad. Studs. 12	2	1	1	
	Spec. Studs. 7	0	0	0	
1906	240	57	37	20	25
	Grad. Studs. 13	1	0	1	
	Spec. Studs. 25	3	1	2	
	*203				
1911	219	79	31	48	36
	Grad. Studs. 19	6	1	5	
	Spec. Studs. 47	0	1	3	
	*218				
1916	101	101	54	47	100
	Grad. Studs. 9	1	0	1	
	Spec. Studs. 9	1	0	1	
	*75				

* Students from other Schools, not listed before 1903.

TABLE N-2: PRIOR EDUCATION OF YALE MEDICAL SCHOOL
STUDENTS

School Year Ending	Total Number of Students	Total Number of College Graduates	Yale Graduates	Graduates of Other Colleges	Percentage of College Graduates
1871	33	6	5	1	18
1876	42	12	9	3	29
1881	25	6	5	1	24
1886	25	10	8	2	40
	Grad. Studs. 2	1	1		
	Spec. Stud. 1	1		1	
1891	62	22	18	4	35
	Spec. Stud. 1				
1896	119	31	21	10	26
	Spec. Studs. 6	1		1	
1901	131	25	19	6	19
	Spec. Studs. 2	1		1	
1906	133	17	9	8	13
	Spec. Studs. 4				
1911	81	19	14	5	23
	Spec. Stud. 1				
1916	58	38	25	13	66

School Year Ending	Total Number of Students		Total Number of College Graduates	Yale Graduates	Graduates of Other Colleges	Percentage of College Graduates
1871		53	40	21	19	76
	Licentiates	2	2	1	1	
1876		97	84	17	67	87
	Licentiates	2	1	1	0	
1881		86	65	10	55	76
	Licentiates	2	1	0	1	
	Grad. Studs.	5	5	1	4	
1886		98	78	13	65	80
	Licentiates	2	2	1	1	
	Grad. Studs.	10	10	2	8	
1891		119	107	13	94	89
	Licentiates	4	1	0	1	
	Grad. Studs.	16	16	4	12	
1896		87	73	10	63	84
	Licentiate	1	0	0	0	
	Grad. Studs.	17	13	3	10	
1901		67	57	8	49	85
	Licentiates	12	10	2	8	
	Grad. Studs.	10	9	2	7	
1906		52	49	4	45	94
	Grad. Studs.	19	19	3	16	
	Spec. Studs.	11	6	2	4	
		*4	3	1	2	
1911		71	58	2	56	82
	Grad. Studs.	18	18	3	15	
	Spec. Studs.	4	1	0	1	
		*17				
1916		78	60	3	57	77
	Grad. Studs.	16	16	1	15	
	Spec. Studs.	12	6	2	4	
		*13				

* Students from other Schools, not listed before 1906.

Yale Class of:	Yale Law School	Harvard Law School	Columbia Law School	New York Law School	Other Law Schools	Totals	Percentage Taking LL.B. Outside Yale Law School
1871							
B.A.	4	0	12	0	4	20	80
Ph.B.	0	0	0	0	0	0	—
Total	4	0	12	0	4	20	80
1876							
B.A.	8	0	23	0	13	44	82
Ph.B.	0	0	2	0	2	4	100
Total	8	0	25	0	15	48	83
1881							
B.A.	17	1	9	0	5	32	47
Ph.B.	4	0	0	0	1	5	20
Total	21	1	9	0	6	37	43
1886							
B.A.	6	0	8	1	7	22	73
Ph.B.	1	0	1	1	2	5	80
Total	7	0	9	2	9	27	74
1891							
B.A.	11	6	4	13	12	46	76
Ph.B.	2	0	0	1	3	6	66
Total	13	6	4	14	15	52	75
1896							
B.A.	21	8	4	21	25	79	73
Ph.B.	1	1	1	2	1	6	83
Total	22	9	5	23	26	85	74
1901							
B.A.	9	14	5	9	10	47	81
Ph.B.	1	1	1	0	0	3	66
Total	10	15	6	9	10	50	80
1906							
B.A.	11	12	7	11	14	55	80
Ph.B.	1	1	3	2	0	7	86
Total	12	13	10	13	14	62	81
1911							
B.A.	12	26	10	1	10	59	80
Ph.B.	1	1	0	1	4	7	86
Total	13	27	10	2	14	66	80
1916							
B.A.	11	20	3	1	6	41	73
Ph.B.	3	0	1	0	1	5	40
Total	14	20	4	1	7	46	70

TABLE N-5: WHERE YALE UNDERGRADUATES TOOK THEIR MEDICAL DEGREES

Yale Class of:	Yale Medical School	Harvard Medical School	Columbia Medical School	Johns Hopkins Medical School	Other Medical Schools	Totals	Percentage Taking Medical Degrees Outside Yale Medical School
1871							
B.A.	0	0	5	0	4	9	100
Ph.B.	0	0	0	0	0	0	—
Total	0	0	5	0	4	9	100
1876							
B.A.	4	2	7	0	7	20	80
Ph.B.	2	0	1	0	1	4	50
Total	6	2	8	0	8	24	75
1881							
B.A.	1	3	4	0	1	9	89
Ph.B.	1	0	4	0	2	7	86
Total	2	3	8	0	3	16	88
1886							
B.A.	1	6	6	0	1	14	93
Ph.B.	1	0	3	0	2	6	83
Total	2	6	9	0	3	20	90
1891							
B.A.	1	2	5	0	2	10	90
Ph.B.	0	0	5	0	1	6	100
Total	1	2	10	0	3	16	93
1896							
B.A.	7	0	5	2	4	18	61
Ph.B.	0	0	2	2	4	8	100
Total	7	0	7	4	8	26	73
1901							
B.A.	1	2	4	1	8	16	94
Ph.B.	0	2	1	0	4	7	100
Total	1	4	5	1	12	23	96
1906							
B.A.	0	0	2	4	0	6	100
Ph.B.	2	0	0	0	2	4	50
Total	2	0	2	4	2	10	80
1911							
B.A.	5	2	6	0	0	13	62
Ph.B.	2	0	1	3	0	6	67
Total	7	2	7	3	0	19	63
1916							
B.A.	5	5	4	1	5	20	75
Ph.B.	4	0	1	4	0	9	56
Total	9	5	5	5	5	29	69

TABLE N-6: ADVANCED DEGREES TAKEN BY YALE B.A.'s

Yale Class of:	M.A.		Ph.D.		LL.B.		B.D.		M.D.		M.F.		Engineers Degrees		Other Degrees		No. Receiving Higher Degrees	No. Graduating in Class	Total No. of Higher Degrees	Percentage of Graduates Receiv'g Higher Degrees
	Yale	Elsewhere	Yale	Elsewhere	Yale	Elsewhere	Yale	Elsewhere	Yale	Elsewhere	Yale	Elsewhere	Yale	Elsewhere	Yale	Elsewhere				
1871	31	7	3	0	4	16	5	0	0	9	0	0	0	7	3	0	61	105	73	58
1876	1	0	2	7	8	36	4	0	4	16	0	0	0	0	1	2	70	127	75	55
1881	7	4	3	3	17	15	4	0	1	8	0	0	0	0	1	7	58	130	64	45
1886	13	4	11	2	6	16	4	0	1	13	0	0	0	7	1	2	63	139	74	45
1891	16	11	9	3	11	35	1	6	1	9	0	0	0	7	2	7	83	186	106	45
1896	14	6	17	4	20	58	1	6	7	11	1	0	0	2	2	8	137	278	157	49
1901	25	5	3	2	9	38	3	7	1	15	2	0	0	7	2	6	101	254	113	40
1906	29	10	11	3	11	44	1	4	0	6	4	0	0	4	3	3	108	297	133	36
1911	16	13	4	3	12	47	0	3	5	8	2	0	1	2	1	8	118	297	125	40
1916	6	8	4	2	11	30	3	2	5	15	0	0	0	2	1	7	81	318	90	25
Sub-totals	158	62	67	23	109	335	26	22	25	110	9	0	1	14	17	32	880	2131	1010	41
Totals	220		90		444		48		135		9		15		49		88.2*	213.1*	101	

* Average per year.

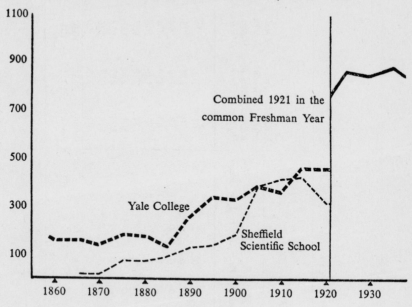

TABLE O-1: YALE COLLEGE AND SHEFFIELD SCIENTIFIC
SCHOOL FRESHMAN ENROLLMENTS, 1859–1937

Combined 1921 in the
common Freshman Year

Yale College

Sheffield
Scientific School

TABLE O-2: YALE COLLEGE AND HARVARD FRESHMAN ENROLL-
MENTS, 1859–1937, WITH YALE'S COMMON FRESHMAN YEAR

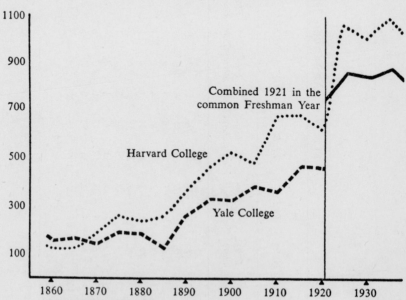

Combined 1921 in the
common Freshman Year

Harvard College

Yale College

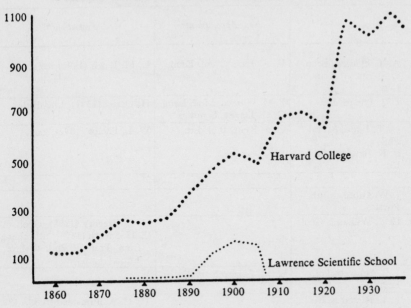

TABLE O-3: HARVARD COLLEGE AND LAWRENCE SCIENTIFIC
SCHOOL FRESHMAN ENROLLMENTS, 1859–1937

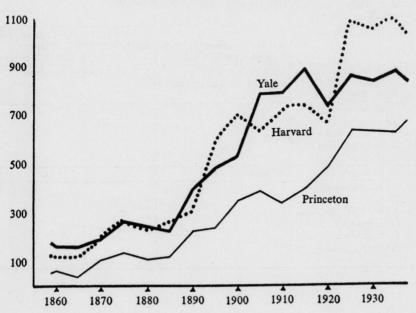

TABLE O-4: YALE, HARVARD, AND PRINCETON FRESHMAN
ENROLLMENTS, 1859–1937

Losses, New Appointments, and Promotions

	Losses	New Appointments	Promotions*
1899	Tr. A. T. Hadley, Econ. D. J. Luquiens, Rom. Lang.	H. C. Emery, Pol. Econ.	C. M. Lewis (1895), Eng.
1900	D. E. J. Phelps, Law	F. M. Warren, Mod. Lang. C. C. Torrey, Semitics	H. Oertel (1891), Linguistics
1901	Tr. G. T. Ladd, Moral Phil. Tr. F. K. Sanders, Bibl. Lit.	C. F. Kent, Bibl. Lit.	W. L. Phelps (1892), Eng.
1902			
1903	D. J. W. Gibbs, Math. Physics		
1904	Res. H. S. Williams, Geol.		H. E. Gregory (1898), Geol. [E. H. Sneath (1898), title changed from Prof. of Phil. to Prof. of Educ.]
1905	Tr. J. C. Schwab, Pol. Econ.	C. M. Bakewell, Phil.	
1906	Ret. E. L. Richards, Math. Ret. A. M. Wheeler, Hist. (Lecturer to 1911) Ret. A. W. Wright, Physics Tr. C. C. Torrey, Semitics (To Grad. School)		Tr. H. A. Bumstead (S.S.S. 1893), Physics
1907	Res. E. H. Sneath, Educ.	E. W. Brown, Math. R. G. Harrison, Comp. Anat. (also in S.S.S.)	C. Day (1894, 1899), Econ. Hist. C. H. Judd (1901), Psych. A. G. Keller (1900), Sci. of Soc.
1908	D. E. G. Bourne, Hist. D. T. D. Seymour, Greek Ret. Tracy Peck, Latin	M. Farrand, Hist. G. L. Hendrickson, Lat.	J. Barrell (1903), Str. Geol.
1909	Ret. W. G. Sumner, Pol. & Soc. Science Ret. H. P. Wright, Latin Ret. B. Perrin, Greek Res. C. H. Judd, Psych.		C. S. Baldwin (1895), Rhetoric
1910	Ret. C. H. Smith, Hist.	A. Johnson, Hist.	
1911	Ret. A. M. Wheeler, Lect. Hist. Ret. A. W. Phillips, Math. (also Grad.) Res. C. S. Baldwin, Rhetoric		

	Losses	New Appointments	Promotions*
1912			
1913		W. H. Taft, Law	F. R. Fairchild (1904), Pol. Econ. W. E. Hocking (1907), Phil. C. B. Tinker (1903), Eng.
1914	Res. W. E. Hocking, Phil.	A. K. Rogers, Phil.	Prof. rank, H. A. Farr (1898) Prof. rank, J. C. Adams (1900)
1915	Res. H. C. Emery, Pol. Econ.	E. F. Nichols, Physics	L. L. Woodruff (S.S.S. 1907, Tr. to Y.C. 1913), Biol.
1916	Ret. H. A. Beers, Eng.	A. M. Harmon, Greek & Latin	
1917	D. Wm. Beebe, Math. Ret. G. B. Adams, Hist. Ret. E. S. Dana, Physics		R. P. Angier (1906), Psych.
1918	D. A. H. Palmer, German Ret. F. A. Gooch, Chem.		M. A. Abbott (1916), Latin C. Seymour (1911), Hist.
1919	D. J. Barrell, Str. Geol. Ret. E. P. Morris, Latin Res. M. A. Abbott, Latin Res. S. L. Mims, Hist. (appted 1919)	J. Johnston, Chem.	C. W. Mendell (1907), Latin S. L. Mims (1908 S.S.S., 1910 Y.C.), Hist. Res. 1919
1920	D. T. D. Goodell, Greek Res. E. F. Nichols, Physics Res. A. K. Rogers, Phil.	W. H. Sheldon, Phil. Vis. Prof. N. W. Stephenson, Hist.	F.Y., S. K. Mitchell (1907), Hist. F.Y., P. T. Walden (1894), S.S.S. Chem. F.Y., W. R. Longley (1906), S.S.S. Math.
1921	D. H. A. Bumstead, Physics (d. Dec. 31, 1920)		

* Dates of first appointment at a rank of instructor or above are given in parentheses.

TABLE Q: GROUP PROGRAMS FOR LOWERCLASSMEN, 1911–14

The Dana-Day Course of Study Committee designed these lower-class curricula for those interested primarily in languages, in science, or in social studies. At the same time upper-class specialization was encouraged by converting the distributional major-minors into a related major-minor of 12–15 hours in a single Division of Study.

Freshman Groups

Group I
1. Latin or Greek
2. French or German
3. Mathematics or Physics or Chemistry
4. The alternative ancient or modern language
5. English or History

Group II
1. French or German
2. Mathematics
3. Physics or Chemistry
4. } English and History, or, in place of one of these,
5. } either Latin or Greek or the alternative modern language

Group III
1. Latin or Greek
2. French or German
3. Mathematics or Physics or Chemistry
4. English
5. History

Sophomore Groups

Group I
1. } Two of the following: Latin, Greek, French,
2. } German (or Italian or Spanish)
3. Mathematics or Physics or Chemistry or Biology
4. Psychology (with Logic) or History or Economics
5. English or any other Sophomore subject

Group II
1. French or German (or Italian or Spanish)
2. } Two of the following subjects: Mathematics,
3. } Physics, Chemistry, Biology
4. Psychology (with Logic) or History or Economics
5. English or any other Sophomore subject

Group III
1. Latin or Greek or French or German (or Italian or Spanish)
2. Mathematics or Physics or Chemistry or Biology
3. } Two of the following: Psychology (with Logic),
4. } History, Economics
5. English or any other Sophomore subject

TABLE R: SPECIAL HONORS AWARDS, 1886–1916

SPECIAL HONORS "to promote the Rational Choice of Elective Courses"

Transition Experiments

Subjects	Totals
Ancient Lang.	60
Classics	27
Modern Lang.	40
French	10
German	12
English	127
Music	4
Natural and Phys. Sciences	49
Natural Science	81
Physical Science	41
Mathematics	28
Philosophy*	60
History, Pol. Sci., Soc. Sci., and Law	66
History	112
Pol. Sci. & Law	116
Social Science	47
Totals	880

* In 1886 called Mental and Moral Science.

† Romance Languages.

‡ One-year and two-year Honors discontinued in 1903. Greater concentration required thereafter.

YALE COLLEGE COMMENCEMENT ORATIONS AND
SPECIAL HONORS

1886

W. Hunt, Latin Salutatory (Salutatorian, Philosophical Oration, Honors Classics)

G. E. Eliot Jr., Renaissance Italy in the Elizabethan Drama (Oration, Honors English)

W. E. Nichols, Goethe's *Sorrows of Werther* (Oration, Honors Modern Languages)

W. Lee Cannon, Horace Mann as an Educator (Oration, Honors History, Political Science)

J. S. Dutcher, The Alexandrian University in Mathematics (Philosophical Oration, no Honors)

B. J. Davis, Socialism (Oration, no Honors)

C. A. Moore, The Early Greek Humanists (Oration, no Honors)

A. Goebel, Wordsworth's View of Nature and of Man (Oration, Honors English)

A. L. Shipman, The Eastern Question (Oration, no Honors)

W. A. Brown, Lucretius as a Moral Teacher (Philosophical Oration, Honors Classics)

J. C. Schwab, Life Philosophy of Schopenhauer and Hartmann (Oration, Honors Mental and Moral Science)

C. W. Pierson, Modern Progress and the Stationary State Doctrine (Valedictorian, Philosophical Oration, Honors History, Political Science, & Law)

1887

Two-year Honors

T. H. Curtis, The Blessing and Curse of Machinery (Valedictorian, Honors Ancient Languages)

One-year Honors

G. H. Beard, The Reality of Mind (Honors Philosophy, English)
W. L. Phelps, The Didactic Methods of Aristophanes as Shown in the *Clouds* (Honors Philosophy, English)
J. C. Diehl, Some Similarities of Stoicism and Christianity (Honors Philosophy)
C. T. Morse, The Development of the Arthurian Legends (Honors English)

G. C. Rosenzweig, Historic Attitude of the Democratic Party toward the Tariff (Honors Political Science, History & Law)

Y. P. Lee, The Other Side of the Chinese Question (Honors Political Science, History, Law, and English)

C. L. Brownson, Latin Salutatory (Salutatorian, Honors English)

1888

Two-year Honors

I. Fisher, Conservatism, as Presented by the Comparative Study of Man (Valedictorian, Honors Mathematics, One-year Philosophy)

B. C. Steiner, Latin Salutatory (Salutatorian, Honors Ancient Languages)

H. G. Platt, Simon de Montfort (Honors Political Science, History & Law)

H. C. Tolman, Philosophy of the Hindus (Honors Ancient Languages)

One-year Honors

E. W. Harter, Marlow and Shakespeare (Honors English)

H. L. Stimson, John Hale and the Latitudinarians (Honors English)

D. B. Hardenbergh, The Intellectual Worth of Abraham Lincoln (Honors English)

1889

Two-year Honors

W. A. McQuaid, The Mission of Labor Organizations in American Politics (Valedictorian, Honors Political Science, History & Law)

One-year Honors

H. F. Walker, Latin Salutatory (Salutatorian, Honors Modern Languages)

J. H. Daniels, Herbert Spencer's Unknowable (Honors Philosophy)

F. W. Ellis, The Historic Attitude of the Church toward the Drama (Honors English)

1890

Two-year Honors

G. L. Amerman, Latin Salutatory (Salutatorian, Honors Ancient Languages)

S. H. Rowe, The Military Policy of the United States (Honors Ancient Languages)

W. C. Lusk, Peter Waldo and the Poor Men of Lyons (Honors Ancient Languages)

E. P. Joslin, The Retirement of Prince Bismarck (Honors Natural & Physical Sciences)

One-year Honors

G. L. AMERMAN, Latin Salutatory (Salutatorian, Honors Natural & Physical Sciences)

1891

Two-year Honors

L. B. MENDEL, American Navigation Laws, 1789–1839 (Honors Political Science, History, & Law)

N. GLICKSMAN, Valedictory (no title) (Valedictorian, Honors Political Science, History, & Law)

W. N. THATCHER, The Causes of the Failure of the Reformation in France (Honors Political Science, History, & Law)

*H. W. GRUENER, The Volumetric Determination of Antimony and Its Degree of Oxidation (Honors Natural and Physical Sciences)

*J. BOWDEN JR., Curves and Cones of the Third Degree

One-year Honors

WM. T. BARTLEY, Salutatory (Salutatorian, Honors Modern Languages)

YALE COLLEGE SPECIAL HONORS

1903

Classical Languages and Literature

HERBERT C. KELLY, Theocritus and Tennyson

English

CHARLES R. ALDRICH, Introduction to Deloney's *Pleasante History of Thomas of Reading*

L. A. HOWARD, John Bunyan

L. S. KIRTLAND, Notes to Deloney's *Pleasante History of Thomas of Reading*

Mathematics

R. G. D. RICHARDSON, Application of the Theory of Curvature of Gear Teeth

Physical Sciences

E. R. CLARK, The Spleen and Pancreas of the California Limbless Lizard Anniella

A. C. LANG, A Study of the Reaction between Silver Oxalate to an Alkali Chloride in Solution

* Theses of exceptional distinction but not proper for delivery.

Philosophy

E. H. CAMERON, Experiments Dealing with the Effects of Practice on Certain Geometrical Illusions

W. M. STEELE (Same title as above)

History

H. M. SAWYER, The Primitive Jury in England

Social Science

J. H. BENTON, Low Grade Gold Ores

A. L. BISHOP, Relative Prices and Wages, 1890–1901

H. H. CLARK, Our Merchant Marine in the Foreign Trade

H. RANKIN, Federal Regulation of Trusts in the United States

J. J. REILLY, The Nickel Industry

M. B. TERRILL, The Culture of Corn

W. B. WALKER, The Erie Railroad from 1865 to 1872

W. G. WING, The Wabash Injunction

1904

Classical Languages and Literature

C. W. MENDELL, Testimonies of Aristophanes to the Architecture of Athens

Germanic Languages and Literature

H. W. CHURCH, Goethe's Political Opinions

Romance Languages and Literature

O. M. BIGELOW JR., The Castigat Ridendo Mores in Molière's Plays

English

S. B. HEMINGWAY, A Variorum Edition of Chaucer's *Prioresses Tale*

L. MASON, The Lyrics of Ben Jonson

E. L. POND JR., Social Life in English Lyric Poetry, from Henry VIII to Queen Anne

Mathematics

S. W. BALDWIN, Solution of the Cubic Equation by Infinite Series

Physical and Natural Sciences

J. A. BANCROFT, The Geological Structure of Saltonstall Ridge

G. B. MORRISON, Ganglion Cells in the Human Heart Ventricle

D. L. RANDALL, The Oxidizing Action of Silver Sulphate on Reduction Products of Molybdic Acid

History

S. H. Evans, The Secession of Virginia
C. W. Lawrance, The Genesis of the Movement for Negro Suffrage
A. P. Lovejoy Jr., The Secession of Virginia
S. L. Mims, The Genesis, Development, and Adoption of Negro Suffrage as an Essential Part of Reconstruction
B. E. Smith, The Beginnings of Japanese Diplomacy

1905

Classical Languages and Literature

I. N. Countryman, Gaius Gracchus
R. H. White, The Oratory of Gaius Gracchus

English

B. Cowell, The Puritan Attitude toward the Graces of Life and of Anglican Worship
G. B. Hotchkiss, Thomas Carew
C. W. Nichols, Nature in the Poetry of Vaughan
C. F. Wicker, Dante's Conception of Monarchy, and Its Relation to Our Own Political System

Mathematics

W. A. Drushel, Applications of Projective Geometry to Perspective and Bas-Relief

Social Sciences

W. E. Lagerquist, Trans-continental Railroads
H. J. McLatchey, Dorchester (New Brunswick) Copper Mine
C. F. Wicker, The Relation of the Trust Companies to the Banks

1906

Classical Languages and Literature

I. H. Hughes, The Caesuras in Book VI of Vergil's *Aeneid*

English

C. E. Andrews, The Work of Stephen Phillips
H. Beal, The Return of Romanticism to the English Stage in the XVIII Century
W. P. McCune, The Plays of Maurice Maeterlinck
F. H. Markoe Jr., Symbolism in Ten of the Plays of Maurice Maeterlinck
W. G. Robinson, A Theory of Poetry
J. H. Wallis, A Theory of Poetry

History

L. O. BERGH, The Recognition by the United States of the Republic of Panama

W. P. HALL, The Rise of Canal Building in the United States.

E. G. HOWE, The Campaigns of the Democratic Party since 1860

S. F. REED, The History of the Federalist Party in the South

Mathematics

E. G. BILL, Graphical Solution of the Cubic and Biquadratic Equations

H. T. BURGESS, The Coefficient of Accuracy in Geometrical Constructions

J. C. RAYWORTH, On the Measurement of the Perimeter of the Circle

Natural Sciences

C. M. MORSE, The Geology of Pine Rock

Physical Sciences

R. W. OSBORNE, The Hydrolysis of Aluminium Sulphate

E. W. TILLOTSON, An End-product in the Reaction between Dinitrotartaric Acid and Urea

H. L. WARD, On a Urea Derivative of Dinitrotartaric Acid

Social Sciences

H. B. JAMISON, Historical Analysis of the 1903–04 Labor Situation in Colorado

C. T. TILESTON, American Communistic Societies

E. L. WARREN, Recent Tendencies in International Migration

1907

Classical Languages and Literature

T. A. TULLY, The Grammatical System of Varro

Germanic Languages and Literature

E. R. SMITH, Grimmelshausen and His *Simplicissimus*

English

H. S. LOVEJOY, The Works of Thomas Middleton

C. P. OTIS, The Parsons on the Stage

S. R. STRONG, Rabbi Ben Ezra and Omar Khayyam

C. F. TODD, A Biographical Sketch of A. C. Swinburne

Mathematics

E. W. SHELDON, The Variation of Latitude

J. A. WHITE, A Mathematical Discussion of the Determination of *g* by Atwood's Machine

B. D. YORK, The Graphical Solution of the Quintic Equation

Physical Sciences

J. L. HUBBARD, The Preparation of Ethyl Succinic Ester

H. E. PALMER, A Method for the Qualitative Separation of Ferro-cyanides, Ferricyanides and Sulphocyanides

History

H. S. LOVEJOY, Seward's Career in President Johnson's Cabinet

M. T. RILEY, The Drift Toward America in Hawaii

C. W. SEYMOUR, Centralization of Power in the United States

1908

Classical Languages and Literature

H. M. BURROWES, The Homeric Legend in Plautus

H. T. F. HUSTED, The Homeric Simile

H. H. JACKSON, Vergil's *Georgics* I done into English Verse

A. H. WESTON, A Translation of *Aen.* II into Blank Verse

Germanic Languages and Literature

J. C. BARRY, Wieland and his *Agathon*

F. N. STEVENS, Gottfried Keller and his *Der grüne Heinrich*

English Language and Literature

H. M. BRUSH, Recent Collections of Oral Ballads

T. J. CAMP, Examination of Burton's *Anatomy of Melancholy*

O. H. COOPER, The Future of Drama in Poetry

W. M. CRUNDEN, Sources of the Saga of the Volsungs

L. C. EVERARD, The Poetry of Herbert, Donne, and Carew

F. A. GODLEY, A Study in the Origins of Poetry

Mathematics

W. S. BISSELL, The Discriminant Configuration of the Cubic Equation

Physical Sciences

S. ALPERT, The Estimation of Manganese by Potassium Ferricyanide

F. BEYER, The Electrolytic Determination of Lead and Manganese by the Use of the Filtering Crucible

R. S. BOSWORTH, The Determination of Silver, Gravimetrically and Idometrically by Means of Precipitation as the Chromate

E. A. EDDY, Some Catalytic Effects of Zinc Bromide and Hydrobromic Acid in Comparison with those of Zinc Chloride and Hydrochloric

Acid in Ester Formation

C. R. Housum, The Action of Dry Ammonia on Ethyl Oxalate

H. B. Lewis, The Esterification of Lactic Acid

O. C. Pickhardt, A Study of the Action of Hydrochloric Acid and Other Chlorides upon Tartaric Acid and Its Ester

C. M. Smith, Telephone Circuits

H. V. S. Taylor, Field Tests of an Electro-Magnet

L. H. Weed, Certain Organic Acids and Acid Anhydrides as Standards in Alkalimetry, Acidimetry, and Iodimetry

Natural Sciences

D. Hooker, A Study of the Habits and Instinctive Reactions of the Loggerhead Turtle

H. A. Riley, The Anatomy of an Undescribed Species of Nemertean

Philosophy

A. E. Avey, Various Conceptions of Being in the Philosophy of Aristotle

E. H. Reisner, Kant and the Notion of Truth

History

J. C. Barry, The Developments of the French Policy towards the American Colonies from 1763 to 1778

Social Sciences

L. B. Clark, Economic Development of Litchfield County

W. S. Culbertson, Socialism in the United States

L. H. DeBaun, Causes of the Rise of Prices since 1898

W. W. Naman, Basic Theory of Labor Unions

I. D. Whitestone, Adam Smith and Alexander Hamilton

W. W. Wynkoop, An Inquiry into the Causes of the Present Financial Crisis

1909

Classical Languages and Literature

D. H. Fenton, Internal Structure of the Plays of Sophocles

Romance Languages and Literature

H. B. Richardson, Anatole France

Germanic Languages and Literature

R. L. Walkley, The Historical Dramas of Ernst von Wildenbruch

C. V. Graham, Hermann Sudermann as a Dramatist

English Language and Literature

R. M. MERONEY, A Theory of Poetry
F. J. SCRIBNER, English Religious Lyrics

Physical Sciences

F. L. GATES, The Phenomena of the Electrolytic Decomposition of Hydrochloric Acid
H. L. READ, The Electrolytic Determination of Chlorine in Chlorides by the Use of the Silver Anode
R. SMILLIE, The Effect of Sulphuric Acid and Acid Sulphates on the Esterification of Succinic Acid

Natural Sciences

C. H. DAVIS, The Taconic Question

Philosophy

J. P. KAUFMAN, Plato's Theory of Ideas

Social Sciences

P. H. M. CONVERSE, Organized Labor and Politics in the United States
R. N. GRISWOLD, A Study of the Growth of Business in the United States
M. C. TERRILL, United States Currency Reform

1910

Germanic Languages and Literature

R. JENTE, The Dramas of Ludwig Fulda

Mathematics

T. H. BROWN, Some Phases of the Vortex Atom Theory

History

L. L. BARBER, President Johnson and Congress
D. BELLAMY, The Presidential Election of 1876
R. B. CRISPELL, The Speaker of the House of Representatives
A. B. GILBERT, The Public Life of Henry Clay
T. L. MARSHALL, The Economic Condition of the South during the Civil War
A. VAN BRUNT, United States' Legal Tenders

1911

English Language and Literature

S. E. BROWN, A History of the Rondeau Verse Form in English Literature

R. MITCHELTREE, The Optimism of Henrik Ibsen
C. I. STIX, Brieux's Place in Modern Drama
S. T. WILLIAMS, Some Relations of the Elizabethan to the Restoration Drama

Physical Sciences

F. C. RECKERT, The Dehydration of Silica in Analysis
E. O. WATERS, The Mathematical Theory of Alternating Currents

Natural Sciences

W. B. EMERY, Post-Glacial Deposits of the Quinnipiac Valley
J. E. FISHER JR., The Conglomerates of the Connecticut Triassic
J. H. REISNER, Physiography of McConnell's Cave

History

H. T. FOULKES, History of the Cistercian Order in England

1912

Classical Languages and Literature

R. C. NEMIAH, The Greeks' Knowledge of Geography before the Age of Pericles

Germanic Languages and Literature

W. M. CLAFLIN, A Study of Selected Dramas of Joseph Viktor Widmann

English Language and Literature

E. P. DAWSON, The Tendencies of Modern Poetry
R. W. FROHMAN, A Study of Fielding's *Tom Jones*
T. M. PETERS, The Tristram and Iseult Stories

Physical Sciences

C. G. HILL, Hertzian Waves
W. A. PETERS JR., The Gyroscope
T. R. WAUGH JR., The Presence of Acetone in Expired Air under Normal and Pathological Conditions

Natural Sciences

L. W. GARDNER, Comparison of the Pigments Produced by Certain Bacteria upon Sugar Agar Media when Grown Aërobically and Anaërobically
H. D. HOOKER JR., The Development of the Peristome in Ceratodon

Philosophy

D. H. WILTSIE, The Ethics of Thomas Hill Green

History

A. H. ARMSTRONG, England and the Near East

E. J. KILDUFF, The Constitutional Aspects of the Acquisition of Louisiana

L. B. LILES (Same title as above)

E. H. MEAD, The Napoleonic Navy

O. MORNING, The Historical Significance of the Fronde

Social Sciences

J. K. BURRELL, The Finances of the City of New Haven

E. T. CONNOLLY, The Influences of the London Stock Exchange on the Economic Development of England

1913

Classical Languages and Literature

J. B. McNELLIS, A Comparison of the Spirit of Satire in Horace and Juvenal

Romance Languages and Literature

W. G. DICKEY, The Plays of Brieux

Germanic Languages and Literature

W. N. MAGUIRE, The Novels of Gustav Frenssen

English Language and Literature

W. E. BUCKLEY, A Study of the Plot of *Measure for Measure*

J. F. COOPER JR., Some Correspondence of James Fenimore Cooper

G. H. DAY JR., The Character of Robert Herrick: A Biographical Study of the *Hesperides*

R. J. MENNER, The Staging of Marlowe's Plays

G. E. SeBOYAR, Two Satires of John Skelton, with Introduction and Notes

A. N. SHERIFF, A Study of *Hero and Leander*

A. WHITRIDGE, Contemporaneous Criticism of Chesterfield, with Bibliography

Physical Sciences

L. BULL, The Adjustment of a Quartz Spectrograph and the Arc and Spark Spectra of Certain Elements

Natural Sciences

H. BERMAN, Induced Variation in the Staphylococcus Pyogenes Aureus and Bacillus Prodigeosus

L. CURTIS, The Separation of Iron from Aluminum by Amyl-Alcohol

L. W. MASON, The Separation of Iron from Zirconium by Amyl-Alcohol

P. G. RUSSELL, The Borders of the Triassic at Bethany, Connecticut

History

M. B. LANE, The Struggle for Suez: the Purchase of the Khedive's Shares

Social Sciences

W. I. BADGER JR., Protected Industries vs. "Free" Labor

F. E. BRIGHAM, The International Harvester Company, 1902–1913

P. B. CAMP, The Swedish Factor in the American Population

F. L. KLINGBEIL, Is State Life Insurance Expedient?

H. T. NEARING, What the United States Has to Learn from the Canadian Banking System

E. RANDALL JR., National Insurance in Great Britain

R. C. TAYLOR, An Investigation into the Expenses of Industrial Insurance in the United States

1914

Classical Languages and Literature

A. H. T. BACON, Repetitions in Homer

K. D. BURROUGH, An Edition of Selected Letters of Cicero

F. C. HARWOOD (Same Title as above)

O. P. KILBOURN, L. Annaeus Seneca

Romance Languages and Literature

R. J. HILL JR., Le Théâtre de Maeterlinck

E. W. WILLIAMS, Le Comique de Molière

English Language and Literature

A. E. CASE, The Plays of Otway

B. CLIFFORD, Nashe's Legend of the Earl of Surrey

T. L. DANIELS, Realism in Modern English Poetry

R. J. HILL JR., The Horatian Influence in Tottel's Miscellany

F. B. KUGELMAN [KAYE], Study of Contemporary Short Story Writers

Physical Sciences

M. M. BRANDEGEE, A Method of the Estimation of Certain Forms of Organic Nitrogen by Means of Hydrochloric Acid

E. M. HAYDEN JR., A Comparison of the Use of Chlorine to Bromine in the Separation of Cerium from the Cerium Earth Oxides other than Cerium . . .

W. J. HUFF, Some Phenolic Color Tests

H. MENDELSOHN, The Action of Chromic Acid on the Cerium Earths
V. N. VERPLANCK, The Preparation of Metallic Calcium by the
Electrolysis of the Fused Chloride

Philosophy

H. H. DUBS, The Value of the Study of Individual Differences for
Education
J. R. SIMONDS, The Psychology of Belief

History

P. M. ATKINS, Special Legislation: Its Evils and Some Remedies
D. M. PARKER, The Conditions leading to the Judicature Acts of 1873
H. D. SAYLOR, The Socialistic Theories of Louis Blanc
B. E. SHOVE, The Treaty of Ghent

Social Sciences

P. M. ATKINS, A Discussion of the Taylor System of Scientific Man-
agement
R. W. BUCK, Non-Federal Income Taxation in the United States
Noticing Especially the Present Wisconsin Activity
J. H. JOHNSON, Scientific Management
E. GLICK, Syndicalism: Industrial Workers of the World and Social
ism

1915

Classical Languages and Literature

R. T. ARVIDSON, Character Presentation in the *Annals* of Tacitus
J. J. CAMERON, The Influence of Seneca's Ghost Scenes on Eliza-
bethan Tragedy
O. McKEE JR., Sophokles' Treatment of His Plots
DuB. MURPHY, Beowulf and the *Iliad*

Romance Languages and Literature

C. A. MERZ, Un Nouveau Troisième Acte pour *Le Duel* par Lavedan

Germanic Languages and Literature

T. M. HEQUEMBOURG, The Three Novels of Wilhelm von Polenz
Dealing with Modern Social Problems
F. W. MEYER, Theodor Fontane als Romanverfasser

English Language and Literature

R. F. EVANS, An Interpretation of *Mother Hubberd's Tale* by Edmund
Spenser
C. A. MERZ, Thomas Love Peacock as Satirist
S. MORRISON, Beowulf and Grettir

J. A. Moseley Jr., Dorothy Wordsworth
L. Smith, A Study of *Hero and Leander* by Marlowe and Chapman

Physical Sciences

W. H. T. Holden, The Preparation and Properties of Hydrocrylic Esters
D. R. Knapp, Investigations on Glycocoll and Diethyl Carbonate
F. H. Randolph, The Preparation of Metallic Strontium by Electrolysis

Philosophy

A. Ohlson, The Philosophy of Christopher Jacob Bostrum

History

R. E. Mathews, Kossuth in New Haven
R. M. Naylor, The Early Diplomatic Career of John Quincy Adams
C. Y. Offutt, Beaumarchais' Services to the American Revolution
G. F. Train, Germany's Responsibility for the European War

Social Sciences

M. P. Bloch, The System of John Law
M. R. Davie, Acclimatization
R. M. Gifford, The Ford Plan of Profit Sharing
L. Gluick, Recent American Socialism
J. R. Howard, Maintenance of Resale Prices

1916

English Language and Literature

W. K. E. Abel, Coverdale's Adaptations of the Lutheran Hymns
D. N. Beach Jr., The Poetry of Poe
G. R. Cutler, Cross Currents in Contemporary English Fiction
M. L. Firuski, A Critical Study of Three Russian Novels
E. Longstreth II, A Comparison of the Diary of Mme. D'Arblay with the Memoirs of Dr. Burney
L. S. Morris, The Art of Joseph Conrad

Physical Sciences

C. M. Elston, The Estimation of Sulphide Sulphur
A. R. Felty, The Ionization of some Organic Acids
L. E. Porter, On the Qualitative Separation and Detection of I, Tellurium and Arsenic, II, Iron, Thallium, Zirconium, and Titanium

History

G. R. Blodgett, Proportional Representation
A. B. Darling, A Comparison of the Foreign Policy of Bismarck and William the Second

TABLE T: THE UNIVERSITIES AND THE PULITZER PRIZES, 1917–50

The Pulitzer Prizes will not be accepted as the ultimate measure of creative art, but the division of awards between the major universities and the undergraduate and professional schools provides an interesting commentary on the strengths and weaknesses of the Yale renaissance.

	Harvard					Yale					Princeton					Other Leader Universities in Each Field			
	College Degrees	Higher Degrees	Studied At	No. of Individuals	No. of Awards	College Degrees	Higher Degrees	Studied At	No. of Individuals	No. of Awards	College Degrees	Higher Degrees	Studied At	No. of Individuals	No. of Awards	No. of Individuals	No. of Awards		
History	8	10	—	14	14	—	1	—	1	1	1	1	—	2	2	3	3	Chic/Col	History
Biog.	4	5	1	9	9	2	—	—	2	3	1	—	—	1	1	4	4	Columbia	Biog.
Plays	—	—	4	4	8*	1*	—	—	1	2	2	—	1	3	5*	2	2	Columbia	Plays
Novels	2	—	2	4	4	3	—	—	3	3	1	—	1	2	3	2	2	Stanf/Chic/Col	Novels
Poetry	3	1	4	7	12*	4	—	—	4	5	—	—	—	—	—	1	4*	Dartmouth	Poetry
Totals	17	15†	10†	37	47	9†	1	—	11†	14	5	1	2	8	11				

* R. E. Sherwood (3 awards for plays, 1 for biography) studied at Harvard 1914–17. Eugene O'Neill (3 play awards) studied at Princeton 1906–07, at Harvard under G. P. Baker 1914–15. E. A. Robinson (3 poetry awards) studied at Harvard but did not graduate. Robert Frost (4 poetry awards) studied at Harvard and Dartmouth but did not take a degree.

† Winners in more than one category were Sherwood, S. F. Bemis (history and biography), and Thornton Wilder (2 awards for plays and 1 for a novel).

Table U: Proposed R.O.T.C. Course in Field Artillery, 1918

Year	Term	"A" 3 hrs. + 1 hr. evening lecture	"B" 3 hrs. each subject	"C" Drill three afternoons
First Year	First Term	Military Science Customs and Courtesies of the Service Drill Regulations Elementary Gunnery and Matériel Review	English History Modern Language (French) Science (Trigonometry)	Physical Training Dismounted Instruction General Rules The Soldier Dismounted The Squad The Manual of the Pistol
	Second Term	Military Science Meteorology Military Geology Mapping	English History Modern Language (French) Science (Firing Data)	Physical Training Dismounted Instruction The Squad Manual of Pistol Drill of Gun Squad Gunners' Instruction
Second Year	First Term	6 hrs. + 1 hr. evening lecture Military Science Communication Drill Regulations Engineering Fire Control Hippology	Military History and Diplomacy Modern Language (French) Science (Physics)	Physical Training Mounted Instruction The Soldier Mounted Firing Instruction Use of Instruments Signalling
	Second Term	Military Science Drill Regulations Duties as Cadet Officers Field Service Regulations Hygiene Motors and Ordnance	Military History and Diplomacy Modern Language (French) Science (Physics)	Physical Training Mounted Instruction Equitation School of Driver Battery Mounted Firing Instruction Signalling
Third Year	First Term	6 hrs. + 1 hr. evening lecture Military Science Battery Administration Military Law Tactics and Coördination of Arms of Service	Governments Modern Language (French) Science (Chemistry)	Physical Training Duties as Cadet Officers School of Battery Duties of Special Details Subcaliber Practice
	Second Term	Military Science Machine Gun Trench Mortars War Pamphlets Review of all Work	Governments Modern Language (French) Science (Chemistry)	First Term Continued

INDEX

Abbreviations

C.E.E.B. College Entrance Examination Board
C.F.Y.   common Freshman Year
S.S.S.   Sheffield Scientific School
Y.C.   Yale College
Y.U.   Yale University

ABBOTT, MATHER ALMON, 465, 688
Abbott, Wilbur Cortez, 656, 675
Academic freedom, Jones on, 155
Academical Department (Y.C.), name, 53 n.
Academical Professors (Permanent Officers of Y.C.), 144 ff., 168 ff.
educational policies and procedures, 168 ff., 177–178, 214, 219. See also Curriculum; Educational ideals of Y.C. Faculty powers: given title, Board of Permanent Officers, 144 n.; power over appointments, 147 ff.; procedure on appointments, 149–150. See also Faculty of Yale College; Government of the Faculty
Accounting, 423
Achelis, George Theodore, B.A. 1919, 360 n.
Achelis, Thomas, B.A. 1908, 650
Adams, Benjamin Strickler, B.A. 1918, 466
Adams, Charles Francis, on college subdivision, 265; recants on elective system, 264–265
Adams, George Burton ("Visigoth"), B.D. 1877, 89, 91, 149, 188, 253, 281, 300, 422, 483, 525, 600, 607, 616; on Greek for admissions, 188–189, 195; on Hillhouse laboratories, 373 ff., 380; law to be taught liberally, 219, 621; menace of numbers, 381–383; on Midwestern demands, 382, 658; proposal of third college for modern humanities, 379 ff., 382–383, 658–659; threats to Y.C. solidarity, 380–382, 416–417; on unique values of Y.C., 379, 657; warning on transfer of Select Course,

509; on World War I, 448; "Y for scholarship" proposal, 349; Yale surrendering to centralization, 386, 657
Adams, John Chester, B.A. 1896, M.A. 1898, Ph.D. 1904, 90 n., 160, 299
Adams, Maude, 353, 650
Adams, Norman I., Jr., B.A. 1917, 341 n.
Adee Boat House, 467
Admissions, 104, 393, 511–512, 544, 660
general history under Hadley, 387–414; Hadley views, 391 ff.; Faculty on, 399 ff., 406–410, 664, 685. See also Hadley, A. T.; Corwin
Greek for entrance, 187; equivalents for Greek, 188 ff., 194, 196, 397–398
Latin, problem of, 389, 390, 404, 408 ff., 414, 496–501, 665
stages in Yale policy, 187 ff., 394 ff., 400–402, 406, 409, 410, 414, 485, 495–501, 510–512; certificate problem, 387 ff., 402 ff.; "conditions," 410; New Plan, 410, 414, 511; Old Plan, 410; Plan B, 511; University Board of, 510, 543
subjects required, 391 ff., 400, 404, 414, 511–512. See also particular subjects: Greek; Latin; Mathematics; Modern languages; etc.
Alderman, Edwin A., President of the University of Virginia, 668
Allen, A. Louise, 529
Allison, John M. S., 298, 525, 527, 551
Alpha Delta Phi, 36; plays 350. See also Junior fraternities
Alumni:
activities and role, 3–5, 38, 39–40, 55–57,

745

Gardner, Congressman Augustus Peabody (Mass.), 451

Gee, John Archer, B.A. 1916, M.A. 1921, 528

General education, Preface, 630

Geography, 51, 252, 537 n., 656; Hadley's efforts to build up, 294–296; physical and commercial, physical and political, in S.S.S., 295, 656; Y.C. not interested, 295

Geology, 70, 85, 86, 173, 180, 252, 420, 507 n., 595

Geometry, descriptive, 180; solid, for admission, 400

George, Henry, 78

George, Robert Hudson, 525

German, 55, 70, 74, 75, 86, 88, 92, 173, 175, 188, 189, 192, 194, 198, 428–429, 615; scholarship divisions in, 248; in World War I, 474; Germanic languages, 149

German, Department of, 135

Germany, influence, 92, 595; German methodology and scientific scholarship, 284, 286–287; Hadley on, 286; tragic results, 287

Gibbs, Josiah Willard, B.A. 1858, Ph.D. 1863, 52, 75, 127, 192, 273–274, 290, 292, 593, 616, 635

Gill, Charles Otis, B.A. 1889, and football coaching on West Coast, 34

Gilman, Daniel Coit, B.A. 1852, 44, 51, 52, 61, 62 n., 656

Glaenzer, Richard Butler, B.A. 1898, 361

Glee Club, 350, 363

Godley, Frederick Augustus, B.A. 1908, 325 n.

Golf, 34

Gooch, Frank Austin, 149, 191, 616

Goodell, Thomas Dwight, B.A. 1877, Ph.D. 1884, 149, 175, 194, 243 n., 256, 284, 287, 412, 616; on residential colleges, 307 n., 640

Government studies, Hadley's skepticism, 296–297. See also Political science

Government of the Faculty, 129–154
comparisons with other faculties, 129; Bryce and Dwight on American college presidents, 129; Hadley on Western university corporations and Eastern university guilds, 130–131, 133
the Yale system: Hadley on, 130–135; beginnings, 133–134; Board of Permanent

Officers, 130; Corporation and, 131, 133, 135; powers of the President, 131–133, 135, 136–138; President's veto, 132, 137; results, good and bad, 132–133

later developments: the Age of the Barons, 140–154; Academical Professors give in to Corporation on Greek, 191–194. See also Faculty of Y.C.; Jones, F. S.; Reorganization

Graduate School, 54, 63, 65, 68, 96, 98, 113, 212–213, 227, 289, 292, 296, 300 n., 545, 687; first formal instruction, in arts and sciences, 49–50; Ph.D. first offered and awarded, 50; more instruction needed, 54–56; women first admitted, 113; Combined Programs, 227; rise and expansion, 227, 300 n.; strengthened by Reorganization, 480, 485

Graves, Henry Solon, B.A. 1892, 176

Greek, 56, 58–59, 68, 70, 75, 84, 86, 99, 149, 172, 174, 175, 183, 242, 314, 427 n., 428–430, 498–501, 511, 524, 588, 591; for B.A., 615; alumni on, 190, 196; Yale finally gives up Greek requirement, in College and for entrance, 186–200; scholarship divisions in Greek, 248. See also Admissions; Classics; Curriculum; Discipline

Greek cheer, 84

Greenfield, Kent Roberts, 527

Gregory, Herbert Ernest, B.A. 1896, Ph.D. 1899, 90 n., 149, 290, 294–296

Groton School, 190

Gruener, Gustav, B.A. 1884, Ph.D. 1896, 75, 149, 427, 499, 527 n., 616

Grumman, Samuel Ellsworth, B.A. 1913, M.A. 1918, 352

Guizot, *History of European Civilization*, 70

Gymnastic Association, 34

Gymnasium, 35, 62, 588

HADDEN, BRITON, B.A. 1920, 361, 364, 503

Hadley, Arthur Twining, B.A. 1876, President of Yale 1899–1921, 25, 35, 62, 69, 83, 89, 91, 95, 96, 102, 103, 119, 128, 150, 151, 152–153, 155, 168–169, 182, 183–184, 213, 214, 233, 236, 237, 252, 260, 275, 276, 291, 310–311, 325, 333, 339, 359, 360, 371, 383, 416, 419, 423, 428, 540, 581, 583, 608, 647

759